Asbestos Medical Research

Volume 4 of the

Sourcebook on Asbestos Diseases:

Medical, Legal, and Engineering Aspects

Edited by

GEORGE A. PETERS, J.D., C.S.P., P.E.
Registered Professional Engineer (California; Safety and Quality)
Licensed Psychologist (California Medical Quality Assurance Board)
Counselor at Law (California and U.S. Supreme Courts)
Fellow, American Association for the Advancement of Science
Los Angeles, California

BARBARA J. PETERS, J.D.
Attorney at Law
Peters & Peters
Los Angeles, California

Garland Law Publishing
New York & London

15 14 13 12 11 10 9 8 7 6 5 4 3 2 1

Library of Congress Cataloging-in-Publication Data
(Revised for vol. 4)

Peters, George A.
Sourcebook on asbestos diseases.

(Garland safety management series)
Barbara J. Peters' name appears first on v. 2.
Vol. 2, 4 published by: Garland Law Pub.
Vol. 1 lacks numbering.
Vol. 2 accompanied by supplement entitled: Asbestos review and update (vi, 150 p. : ill. ; 23 cm.), 1987.
Vol. 4 edited by: George A. Peters and Barbara J. Peters.
Vols. lack series statement.
Includes bibliographies.
1. Asbestos industry—Health aspects. 2. Asbestosis. 3. Asbestos—Toxicology. I. Peters, Barbara J., 1950– II. Title. III. Series.
RC965.A7P47 1986 363.17'91 86–1980
ISBN 0-8240-7175-1 (v. 1)

Published by Garland Law Publishing
136 Madison Avenue, New York, New York 10016

Printed in the United States of America

Contents

Preface

OBJECTIVES

There are some very good reasons for the publication of this Asbestos Medical Research volume. First, a comprehensive review of new discoveries, improved practices, and useful information is needed if there is to be early resolution or effective minimization of the asbestos public health problem. There have been significant advances worthy of publication. Second, the usefulness of the previously published volumes of the *Sourcebook on Asbestos Diseases* can only be maintained and enhanced by supplemental volumes that reflect significant advances in the field. The utility of the prior volumes as a basic reference book series will be improved by the addition of this new knowledge. Third, each independent discipline can benefit by a better understanding and perspective of what is happening in the other disciplines involved in the asbestos disease problem. This Asbestos Medical Research volume emphasizes the need for an overall understanding of the total context in which decisions and actions are occurring. Thus, it continues the multi-disciplinary approach that was unique to the earlier volumes. Fourth, there is good reason why the prior authors have now become editors and commentators. The increasing sophistication and technical detail of activities in this field of endeavor have now mandated that a diligent search be made for those Contributing Authors who have previously made significant contributions, demonstrated leadership, exhibited the necessary credibility, and are in the process of making important contributions in this public health arena. The medical specialists selected for this volume have presented valuable information based on their own personal clinical experience, evaluation of extensive research findings, and unique knowledge gained from close familiarity with the specialized field of asbestos disease. Their review articles and others currently in preparation represent a major advance in our understanding and capability of responding in a manner destined to save many lives.

DISCLAIMER

As Editor of this volume it was requested that I prepare introductory commentaries for these medical research review chapters to help the reader bridge the various chapters and perceive the overall purpose and organization of the book. As a non-medical specialist, I was naturally quite hesitant, despite the fact that lawyers must know enough about medicine to be able to assess medical reports, request additional examinations and tests, and otherwise prepare for the direct or cross examination of medical specialists at time of trial on issues of medical causation and damages. But non-medical specialists need to understand and be able to demonstrate the inter-disciplinary character of the overall public health problems created by asbestos. Thus, with apologies for commentary remarks that some medical research specialists might find not properly worded, I must urge the readers to look at the exact words of the Contributing Authors for the truth of what is being said and to use the Editors' Commentaries as merely an example of how lawyers and other non-medical specialists perceive and understand what is happening in asbestos medical research.

A conscientious attempt has been made to assure that the contents of this book are technically accurate and complete. However, new facts are always emerging when dealing with the advancing forefront of knowledge and some typographical errors inevitably will occur despite the best efforts of all concerned with the publication process. To help assure the accuracy and completeness of revisions to this book, readers are requested to send the authors or editors any recommended corrections or additions that they believe will enhance the accuracy and usefulness of this book.

This published work deals with an area in which there is much technical controversy, vigorously contested litigation, and persistent honest disagreement about fact and opinion. The editors and authors have attempted to be as fair as possible to all sides of the current controversies and to present information useful to everyone. In particular, comments have been made that might be useful to scientists attempting to resolve conflicts in research data or conclusions.

The publisher, editors, and authors must disclaim any liability in whole or in part, arising from the information in this volume. The reader is urged to verify the referenced material prior to any detrimental reliance thereupon. Since this material deals with legal, medical, and engineering information, the reader is urged to consult with an appropriate licensed professional prior to taking any action that might involve any interpretation or application of information within the realm of a licensed professional practice.

1

The Range of Medical Abnormalities Resulting from Asbestos Exposure

(AN OVERVIEW)

LEON S. GOTTLIEB, M.D., M.S. (MED.), F.C.C.P.

County Health Services Agency
Santa Cruz, California, U.S.A.

Synopsis

E. PLEURAL AND PERITONEAL DISEASE
F. MESOTHELIOMA
  1. Clinical Features
  2. Radiologic Features
  3. Management
  4. Benign Localized Mesothelioma
G. DIFFUSE PLEURAL THICKENING
  1. Pathologic Features
  2. Clinical Features
  3. Pulmonary Function
  4. Radiologic Features
H. DISCRETE PLEURAL THICKENING
  1. Pathologic Features
  2. Clinical Features
  3. Radiologic Features
I. ROUNDED ATELECTASIS
J. BENIGN ASBESTOS PLEURAL EFFUSION
  1. Clinical Features
  2. Pathologic Features
  3. Clinical Manifestations
  4. Radiologic Features
K. IMMUNOLOGIC CORRELATION
L. OTHER ASBESTOS-RELATED NEOPLASIA
M. REFERENCES

BIOGRAPHY

Dr. Leon S. Gottlieb has been interested in occupational lung disease for many years. He was previously Associate Professor of Medicine, University of Southern California School of Medicine (Pulmonary Disease Section), and Chief of Bronchoscopy, Los Angeles County—University of Southern California Medical Center, Los Angeles, California. He has published 2 books and 35 articles related to medicine and pulmonary disease. Currently, he is a clinician at the Santa Cruz (California) County Health Services Agency, and is Medical Advisor and Chairman of the Scientific Committee of Asbestos Victims of America. He may be contacted at 2-1161 East Cliff Dr., Santa Cruz, California 95062 (408-475-3888).

EDITORS' COMMENTARY

After harmful exposure to asbestos, the human body reacts. Distinctive disease processes may be initiated and progressive functional disability may gradually occur. Because of the time interval between exposure and development of symptomology, the causal connection and diagnosis by a physician may not be immediately obvious. It is increasingly important, to the medical specialist and to the exposed individual, that early specific diagnosis be made, possible palliative or curative treatment be initiated, and an informed prognosis be communicated to the patient as to the details of his probable future life. This is also increasingly important in terms of administrative and common law remedies or compensation plans for those disabled by asbestos.

This Chapter, on the range of abnormalities resulting from asbestos exposure, presents an overview of the clinical aspects of those who have already developed a diagnosable disease. It provides some insight and information on the questions faced by the physician in his attempt to diagnose and treat an individual patient. For those readers needing some introductory or preliminary knowledge concerning asbestos diseases, they should review Chapter 2, Medical Aspects, of Volume 1 of the *Sourcebook on Asbestos Diseases* (1980). Many people believe that asbestos causes cancer, some believe it causes both cancer and asbestosis, but few recognize the fact that it can cause a range of abnormalities. Recent medical research is, in fact, further extending our knowledge of the causal relationship between asbestos and other disease entities as well as the specifics of the disease processes.

Any review chapter captures the essence of our knowledge and is only the tip-of-the-iceberg for those who hope to fully understand the interaction between asbestos and the human body. For those readers who need access to relevant publications in this dynamic unfolding area of medical research, they should-first check the 110 references cited in this Chapter by Dr. Gottlieb. They can refer to the Chronological Bibliographies in the *Sourcebook on Asbestos Diseases:* Chapter 7 of Volume 1 (1980) and Chapter 18 of Volume 2 (1986). Consideration should also be given to the personal difficulties and social consequences of the diseases as described in Chapter 10, "Personal Consequences", of Volume 2 (1986).

In reading this clinically oriented Chapter, the multidisciplinary nature of the asbestos public health problem should not be overlooked. Why are so many patients presently afflicted with asbestos disease and why are there projections that the number of such patients will increase after so many years of knowledge about the toxic properties of asbestos? Are there problems in terms of preventive medicine, undiagnosed cases, or fallacious beliefs among non-medical groups? Is payment of appropriate medical costs a problem when there are cost constraints by insurers, public entities, and victims (who generally cannot pay since their compensation for injuries is generally meager and insufficient to pay the medical costs incurred). If there are public policy considerations that directly effect the diagnosis and treatment of asbestos disease, what are they? A few examples might provide insight.

Current risk assessments, ostensibly performed for an objective quantifiable presentation and evaluation of the relative risks and benefits of asbestos abatement options, are often seriously flawed and easily biased. One bias may be found in the inherent underreporting of asbestos disease and this results in underestimates of the actual risk. One flaw is in the risk assessment analyst's tendency to overestimate costs, so that asbestos removal is not economically feasible. High cost estimates, in situations where severe budget constraints exist may be considered administratively desirable (since the risk assessment may be intended for use in justifying a no-action decision). There may be a bias as to which costs are considered, since the eventual societal costs may be quite different than the immediate facility cleanup costs or the resultant patient medical costs. Who pays and when, may be the underlying forcing function in the selection of the attributes and variables considered in the risk assessment model. Thus, there can be manipulation so that the perception of risk may be minimized or the benefits may appear to be outweighed by the high costs of asbestos exposure controls.

Risk assessment is crucial to the formulation and implementation of public health oriented asbestos abatement policy, regulations, rules, plans, specifications, procedures, technology, audits, training, and management controls. Acceptability of the health risks, individual perception of risk of injury, the cost of abatement, and the effectiveness of abatement are important considerations in preventive medicine. Given all of these considerations and the problems in objective risk assessment, it seems as if there will be a constant flow of patients to be diagnosed and treated for many decades in the immediate future. The treating physicians will become more experienced and sophisticated by this activity and by the medical research now coming to fruition.

Let us consider an example of the practical aspects of risk assessment. The dyes used to enhance radiographic imaging of the circulatory system is claimed to produce about 10,000 severe adverse reactions and 100 deaths a year in the United States. Safer dyes reduce the adverse reactions from 13% to only 4% and are used in other countries such as Japan and West Germany. But, the cost is greater and their use may increase the cost of coronary x-rays by 10% and neurological scans by 50%. So they are not considered cost effective, particularly by those who reimburse such costs. It is believed that the cost outweighs the benefits, despite the health risk reduction. Similar decisions are made relative to the reduction of the risks of inducing asbestos related diseases.

There appears to be serious ethical, moral, value, and societal consequence implications in elevating cost-benefit risk assessments to decisional primacy. The prime consideration or credo should be the elimination of any risk of serious injury or premature death if a reasonable alternative exists. For asbestos induced injury, the reasonable alternatives do exist. The flow of patients to the clinician indicates a breakdown or perversion in "the system" that can either permit or prevent such injuries. The clinical consequences should be apparent from the following chapter.

A. HISTORICAL PERSPECTIVE

The extraordinary attributes of fibrous asbestos were recognized many years ago. The early Greek civilization, about 430 B.C., spoke of lamps made with incombustible wicks. The Romans used cremation clothes combined with asbestos to conserve the ashes of the deceased nobility. A popular legend

Accepted for publication 5 December 1988.

tells of the French emperor, Charlemagne, who would impress his audience by passing an asbestos tablecloth through fire to clean it. These amazing features endowed this strange mineral with the name "asbestos," which means "inextinguishable."

The fact that asbestos had the potential to be a health hazard was established in the first century. Pliny the Elder, the Roman naturalist, and Strabo, the Greek geographer, reported a lung disorder in slaves whose occupation was the weaving of asbestos into cloth.

The first detailed account of a worker's death from asbestosis and subsequent autopsy was reported by a British physician, H. Montague Murray, in 1907. (1) The man, an asbestos spinner, died in 1900. Extensive scarring of the lung was revealed at autopsy, attributed to the breathing of asbestos dust.

From 1907 to 1917, scattered reports on the ill effects of asbestos dust appeared in the medical literature from the United States, United Kingdom, France, Italy, Canada, and Germany. In 1917, Pancoast and colleagues reported on the radiological aspects of inhaled dust on the lung. (2) Cooke in 1924 called attention to the presence of particles of mineral matter in the fibrotic lungs of a woman, who had died after working for 20 years in an asbestos factory. (3) He referred to his finding as fibrosis of the lung due to the inhalation of asbestos dust. In 1927, Cooke first used the term " pulmonary asbestosis" to describe this type of pneumoconiosis. (4)

B. PUBLIC HEALTH ASPECTS

Interest in the public health aspects of asbestos exposure was heightened by the epidemiological studies of Merewether and Price, in 1930. In this classic report to the British Parliament, the study stressed the effects of asbestos dust on the lungs and methods of dust suppression. (5) This study resulted in the introduction of safety measures and medical supervision for asbestos workers. In 1934, Legge, a British specialist of occupational diseases, advised that asbestosis be added to the list of occupational diseases. (6) The 1930s and 1940s brought forth a substantial number of studies published in the United States, pertaining to asbestosis.

The cancer-producing potential of asbestos was initially recognized by Gloyne, a British pathologist, in 1935. (7) His report described the occurrence of squamous carcinoma of the lung associated with asbestosis. Further evidence linking asbestos with lung cancer was published in the United States, also in

1935. (8) In 1949, the certainty of the presence of lung cancer among asbestotics was established. Merewether, of the United Kingdom, in an Annual Report to the Chief Inspector of Factories for the year 1948, found that more than 13 percent of asbestotics had died of lung cancer. (9) Doll, in 1955, in a study of asbestos textile workers found a tenfold increase in lung cancer. (10) A study in the United States by Selikoff and colleagues, in 1964, found a striking excess in the death rate from lung cancer among insulation workers. (11,12)

There is abundant evidence to consider pleural and peritoneal mesothelioma as a signal neoplasm of exposure to asbestos. Uncommon in the past, this malignant tumor now appears with increasing frequency in persons with occupational and nonoccupational exposure to asbestos. An early report of a pleural neoplasm associated with asbestos exposure appeared in 1933. (13) Other brief reports on pleural neoplasms related to asbestos exposure were noted in the 1940s and 1950s, but in 1960 a definitive study was published that linked mesothelioma with asbestos exposure. (14) In this study from South Africa, Wagner and his co-workers reported that of 33 patients with mesothelioma, 32 elicited a history of occupational exposure to asbestos or residence in a crocidolite mining region. Brief, minimal, or casual exposure to asbestos does not guarantee protection from mesothelioma. Newhouse reported on 76 patients with mesotheliomas of which approximately half had either occupational or nonoccupational exposure. (15) Of the nonoccupational group, the patients either lived with an asbestos worker or lived in close proximity to an asbestos factory. The incidence of mesothelioma has been increasing in the United States. The incident rate for males ranges from 4–11 cases per million per year; for females from 1–4 per million per year. (16) The incidence of mesothelioma peaks to 60 per million per year among white men over 70. Evidence does not exist that smoking increases the risk for mesothelioma. (17)

About 81 percent of all reported mesotheliomas are pleural and 15 percent are peritoneal. Mesotheliomas of other organs: pericardium, ovaries, and testes account for approximately 4 percent. Peritoneal mesothelioma appears to be associated with heavier asbestos exposures and with asbestosis.

An important aspect of mesothelioma related to asbestos exposure is the development of mesothelioma following low levels of exposure for brief periods in the distant past. Childhood exposure to fibers from nearby asbestos factories, or to friable asbestos in schools, or to asbestos dust on clothing brought home for laundering may eventually lead to mesothelioma thirty years later. See Table 1-1 below for the Range of Abnormalities Resulting from Asbestos Exposure.

Table 1-1 Range of Abnormalities Resulting From Asbestos Exposure

- Lung
  - Parenchymal
    - Asbestosis (fibrosis)
    - Bronchogenic carcinoma
  - Pleural
    - Malignant mesothelioma
    - Diffuse pleural thickening
    - Discrete pleural thickening (plaques)
      - Calcified
      - Noncalcified
    - Rounded atelectasis (combined pleural-parenchymal)
    - Benign pleural effusion
- Peritoneum
  - Malignant mesothelioma
- Other neoplasia
  - Rectal, Colon, Laryngeal (evidence of increased risk)

C. ASBESTOSIS

Asbestosis is one of a number of diseases categorized as occupational lung disease, or environmental lung disease. The term pneumoconioses has also been used to characterize these disorders. A common pathological feature of this group consists of a diffuse, interstitial, fibrotic pulmonary reaction. A unique aspect of asbestosis that distinguishes it from other fibrotic diseases (silicosis, coal-worker's pneumoconiosis, berylliosis) is the presence of asbestos bodies and fibers predominantly in lung tissue.

Asbestos fibers invade the body by inhalation or ingestion. When inhaled, the fibers are ultimately deposited in the distal airways and lung tissue. Some fibers may be expectorated, or swallowed, and enter the gastrointestinal tract. Other fibers could be transported to the pleural and peritoneal cavities by lymphatic drainage.

Within the lung tissue, an alveolitis results from the interaction between the alveolus and the asbestos fiber, usually around respiratory bronchioles. The alveoli and fibers are invaded by phagocytic macrophages. (18) Some of these cells disintegrate, then become organized, fibrin is deposited and collagen formation ensues. These changes represent the beginning of the fibrotic process and gradual extension of this process leads to widespread fibrosis.

Asbestos bodies are significantly increased in workers with parenchymal asbestosis. Within the lung, asbestos bodies as well as fibers are found in the alveoli or interstitial tissue.

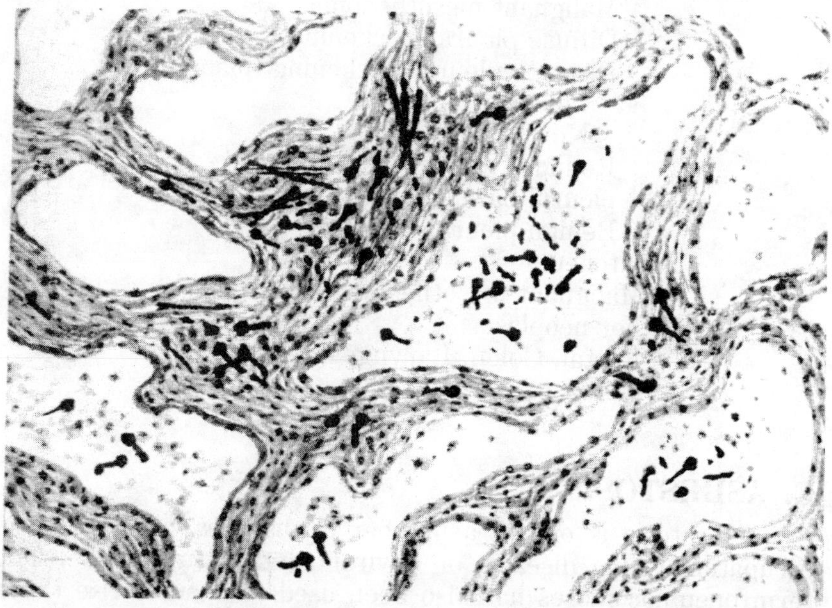

Fig. 1-1 Asbestos fibers and bodies in lung tissue. Club-shaped asbestos bodies are seen in the alveoli, and asbestos fibers in the interstitial tissue. There is extensive fibrosis.

Occasionally asbestos bodies are found in the sputum. The asbestos body may measure between 50–100 microns in length and 2–5 microns in width, and has a clubbed end or is dumbbell shaped. The structure may have a beaded or segmented appearance and is golden-brown in color. The core of the asbestos body is surrounded by a smooth layer of iron-containing glycoprotein with a high ferritin content. (19) The term "ferruginous" body refers to the ferritin contained in the coating of an asbestos body. Asbestos bodies and fibers have been detected in small numbers beyond the lung: in tonsils, thoracic and abdominal lymph nodes, pleura, peritoneum, liver, spleen, pancreas, kidneys, adrenals, and small and large intestines. (20)

Generally, asbestos workers with asbestosis carry the highest burden of asbestos fibers; higher concentrations of lung fibers are found among persons with pleural plaques than those without plaques; the number of asbestos bodies in sputum correlates with risk for pleural thickening. (21,22)

1. Pathological Features

The abnormalities relating to asbestos exposure include a wide spectrum of distinct manifestations. The pathologic process may vary from the small, irregular pulmonary opacity to colon-rectal cancer. The major lesions of asbestos-associated diseases concern the pulmonary parenchyma and the pleura. The effect of inhaling a considerable amount of asbestos fibers results in fibrosis. The fibrosis is predominantly seen in the lower lobes, and, initially is scattered, but with progression becomes more diffuse with upward extension. As the fibrotic process spreads, bronchioles retract causing a honeycombing pattern; with time, bronchiectasis and bullous emphysema may develop.

Early mircoscopic changes focus around respiratory bronchioles and alveolar ducts, where asbestos fibers, macrophages, and fibrin accumulate resulting in a peribronchiolar fibrosis. Extension of this process leads to diffuse fibrosis with areas of solid scarring.

2. Clinical Features

The clinical features of asbestosis are similar to the clinical findings of other disease processes of diffuse interstitial fibrosis. The symptoms include:

- shortness of breath
- dry cough

Breathlessness and dry cough occur rarely before a decade of exposure. The dyspnea appears first only after exertion and subsequently occurs at rest. The cough is dry and irritating, and becomes troublesome as the disease progresses. The dyspnea and cough are more common among asbestos workers who are cigarette smokers. By the time the early symptoms of dyspnea and cough appear, asbestosis is well-entrenched.

The physical signs of advanced asbestosis consist of:

- End-inspiratory crepitant rales at the lung bases
- Tachypnea
- Cyanosis
- Clubbing of the fingers
- Signs of cor pulmonale

A characteristic sign of asbestosis is the presence of crackles heard on auscultation at the lung bases and axilae. Usually, crackles are heard best at the end of the inspiratory phase. As the disease progresses, rales become more widespread and are heard throughout the inspiratory cycle. Tachypnea and cyanosis are indicative of impaired blood oxygenation resulting from advanced pulmonary fibrosis. Clubbing of the fingers is a late feature of asbestosis. Typical clubbing refers to a broadening of the distal phalanges, an increased curvature of the nail, and a softening of the nail bed.

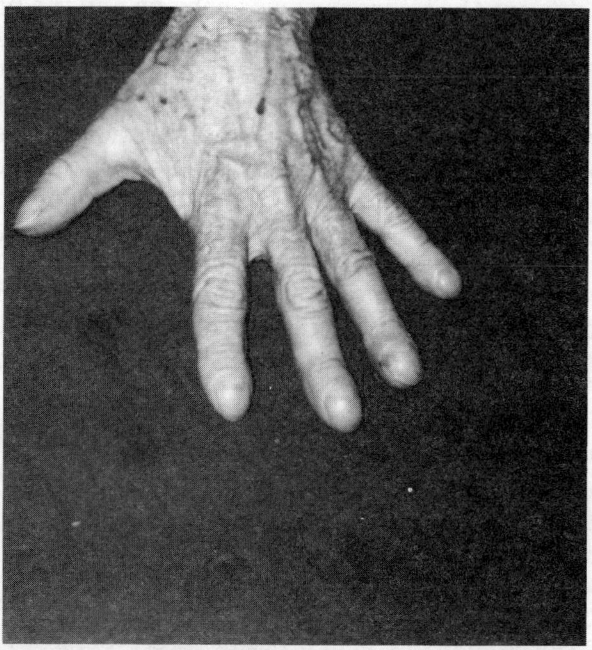

Fig. 1-2 Clubbing of the fingers.

Cor pulmonale may appear as a late manifestation of advanced asbestosis. Right ventricular hypertrophy and dilatation reflect severe alterations in the pulmonary circulation. Eventually, the sequelae of ventricular failure appear: hepatomegaly and peripheral edema.

3. Radiologic Features of Asbestosis

The radiologic signs of asbestosis resemble the radiologic pattern of other diseases included under diffuse interstitial fibrosis (idiopathic interstitial pneumonitis, scleroderma, rheumatoid lung, aspiration pneumonitis, and sarcoidosis, etc.). However, the appearance of pleural changes, notably pleural thickening and plaques suggests the possibility of asbestos exposure. The radiographic diagnosis of asbestosis is based on the presence of predominantly linear and irregular small opacities located chiefly in the lower lung fields.

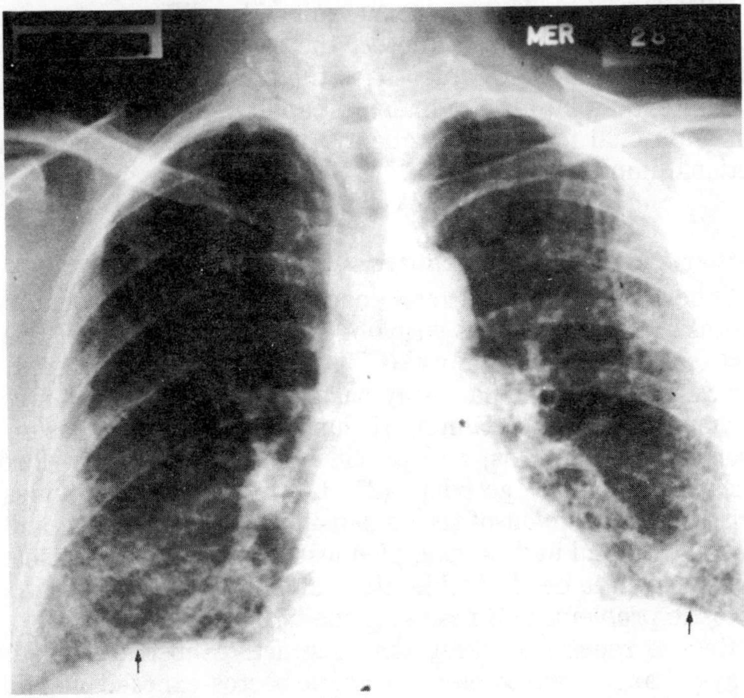

Fig. 1-3 Advanced fibrosis of both lungs with honeycomb changes of both lung bases.

Kerley B-lines, short, horizontal, linear septal lines in the periphery of the lower lung field often appear. With advanced asbestosis the outline of the diaphragm and heart become obscured (shaggy heart). By international agreement, the ILO 1980 International Classification of Radiographs of the Pneumoconioses has been recognized as the standard to grade and describe the radiologic features of asbestosis and other pneumoconioses. (23)

4. Pulmonary Function

Pulmonary function abnormalities in asbestosis are mainly those changes observed with a restrictive lung process. Spirometry usually shows progressive reduction in the forced vital capacity (FVC), decrease in the flow rate in one second (FEV_1) proportional to the FVC, and almost normal FEV_1/FVC ratio. Although, those with asbestosis who smoke or have bronchitis may show an obstructive component reflected by a reduced FEV_1/FVC ratio. The carbon monoxide diffusing capacity (DLCO), a sensitive test to detect the early stage of fibrosis, is often helpful. The DLCO measures the transfer of gas from the distal air spaces into the pulmonary capillaries. Exercise testing is an additional modality frequently used to assess pulmonary functional impairment.

5. Other Diagnostic Procedures

Other procedures recommended to enhance detection of asbestosis are chest x-rays with oblique views, Gallium-67 scans, and Computed Tomography (CT). The oblique films aid in visualizing plaques and parenchymal changes behind the domes of the diaphragm. (24) Gallium-67 lung uptake is increased in persons with asbestosis, and provides an indicator of peribronchiolar inflammatory activity. (25) CT of the lung provides a sensitive measurement of tissue density at various levels, and is extremely helpful in detecting plaques and parenchymal disease. CT has proven to be of considerable value in evaluating equivocal diagnostic problems and resolving medical-legal questions.

Recent reports suggest that distinctive obstructive small airways changes may occur in some asbestos-exposed individuals. (26)

D. BRONCHOGENIC CARCINOMA

Bronchogenic carcinoma is included with the asbestos-related abnormalities that involve the lung parenchyma. One of the earliest cases of asbestosis associated with carcinoma of the lung, proven at autopsy, was reported in 1935. (27) The man had been an asbestos mill weaver for twenty-one years. An extensive study in 1955, (28) showed that the actual risk of carcinoma of the lung was increased 10-fold over the general population for asbestos workers employed for 20 years or more, between 1922 and 1953. A significant study in 1964 of insulation workers found that malignant disease was the major complication of asbestos exposure with 45 percent dying of cancer. (29,30) In another study of 17,800 asbestos insulation workers, 20 percent died of lung cancer. (31)

There is ample evidence available to suggest an increased risk of bronchogenic carcinoma in asbestos workers that smoke cigarettes. Heavy asbestos exposure alone increases the risk of bronchogenic carcinoma by a factor of 5; cigarette smoking alone increases the risk of bronchogenic carcinoma by a factor of about 10; the combination increases the risk by a factor of about 50. In one group of asbestos workers who smoked, the risk of bronchogenic carcinoma was approximately 90 times compared to persons who neither smoked nor worked with asbestos. (32)

The latent interval for asbestos-related bronchogenic carcinoma is generally about 15 to 35 years. These carcinomas are more often seen in the periphery of the lung bases. There appears to be no specifity of cell types, all types are found. (33) Bronchogenic carcinoma has occurred in asbestos-exposed individuals in the absence of radiologic evidence of asbestosis. A situation of this nature would require detailed supportive procedures in order to attribute the bronchogenic carcinoma to asbestos exposure.

1. Clinical Presentation

The clinical features of asbestos-related bronchogenic carcinoma are contingent on whether the tumor presents early or late in the course of the disease. Detection of the carcinoma at an early stage enhances the prospect of surgical cure. The presence of severe associated asbestosis, however, could preclude surgical intervention. Cough is the most common of the primary symptoms, especially change in the pattern of a chronic cough. Chest pain may or may not be present, and is usually related to the late stage. A localized wheeze or hemoptysis may occur. The chest x-ray or CT may define a new opacity or a significant change in a preexisting opacity, or tissue change suspicious of malignancy. The tumor may not be visible on chest x-ray until it is at least 1.0

cm in diameter. Sputum cytology or cytology obtained by bronchoscopic aspiration or brushing may reveal malignant cells. Central lesions may be visualized and biopsied with a flexible bronchoscope; peripheral lesions can also be biopsied with the aid of fluoroscopy. Bronchogenic carcinoma presenting in the late stages generally infers that the tumor has extended beyond the stage of resection or curative surgery. In this stage, typical symptoms, signs, and syndromes of advanced carcinoma emerge.

2. Management

The management of bronchogenic carcinoma is dependent on the staging of the tumor. Operability implies that the patient can withstand a surgical procedure, and that pre-operative assessment insures adequate pulmonary reserve and cardiovasculature function. Early diagnosis and surgical resections of lesions increase the survival rate. Radiation and chemotherapy may be helpful in the overall therapeutic program.

E. PLEURAL AND PERITONEAL DISEASE

Asbestos-related pleural and peritoneal disease have a wide spectrum of manifestation. The diseases include mesothelioma, a malignant involvement of the pleura and peritoneum, and benign abnormalities of the pleura. The non-malignant pleural diseases consist of diffuse pleural thickening, discrete pleural thickening (plaques—calcified, noncalcified), rounded atelectasis, and benign pleural effusion.

F. MESOTHELIOMA

Malignant pleural mesothelioma has a long latency, the period between first exposure and development of mesothelioma has an average duration of 30–35 years, (34) or longer. In diseases with long latent periods, the incident of first exposure, often the only exposure, especially if nonoccupational, may have been forgotten. Because of the long latency, childhood exposure to asbestos confers the important implication that mesothelioma may develop at an age concomitant with the prime of life. Patients with mesothelioma between the ages of 20 and 40 usually had a parent employed in an asbestos-related occupation. (35,36) In a study of two groups of asbestos workers, deaths of mesotheliomas have been 8 percent (insulators) to 11 percent (asbestos factory workers). (37)

1. Clinical Features

The usual clinical features of mesothelioma comprise chest pain, shortness of breath, and cough. The pain may be localized or diffuse, and is frequently referred to the shoulder or upper abdomen. As the disease progresses, pain becomes severe demanding the increasing use of analgesics. Breathlessness is progressive and reflects compression of the lung by the enlarging tumor and related pleural effusion. Peritoneal mesotheliomas manifest abdominal cramps and pain, swelling of the abdomen, and weight loss. Initial abdominal examination may reveal a mass or swelling consistent with ascites. (38) Median survival for localized mesothelioma has been reported as 16 months, and extensive disease as 5 months. In some instances, the tumor may invade and grow through the diaphragm.

With progression of the mesothelioma, the effusion tends to subside, although in others the effusion is persistent and requires frequent removal of fluid. Thoracentesis yields an exudate that may be straw-colored or hemorrhagic. Pleural fluid hyaluronic acid levels may be elevated; levels above 0.8 mg per milliliter support the diagnosis of mesothelioma. However, the test lacks specificity except at higher concentrations; lower levels are frequently seen in metastatic carcinoma. (39)

There may be an element of controversy in establishing a pathological diagnosis of mesothelioma. About half of the malignant mesotheliomas consists of epithelial or tubulopapillary histology; the remainder have a mixed epithelial and sarcomatous histology. (40) The epithelial type may cause confusion with peripheral anaplastic lung carcinomas or metastatic carcinomas. Examination of a large biopsy specimen or the gross tumor at surgery, and the use of special stains or electron microscopy can aid in the differentiation. Ample tissue samples are advisable and may be obtained through thoracotomy or thoracoscopy for pleural mesothelioma, or laparotomy or peritoneoscopy for peritoneal mesothelioma.

As the tumor advances, the lung becomes encased with a thick, nodular layer that involves both the visceral and parietal pleura. The lung becomes entrapped and the pleural space is obliterated. (41)

The spread of peritoneal mesothelioma is more by direct invasion than by lymphatic or blood-borne metastasis. (42) As implied previously, the tumor may invade upward through the diaphragm resulting in bilateral pleural and pulmonary infiltration. (43)

2. Radiologic Features

The radiologic features of mesothelioma are composed of two components: a unilateral pleural effusion and a thickened, nodular pleura. The grossly thickened pleura and lobulated masses are

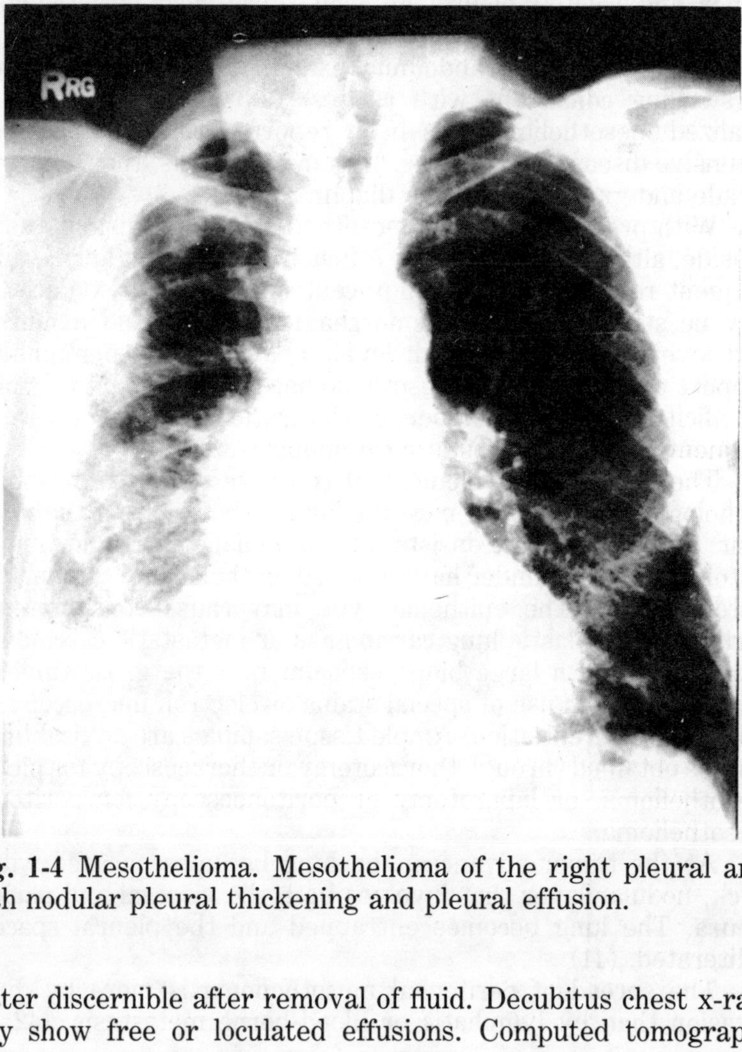

Fig. 1-4 Mesothelioma. Mesothelioma of the right pleural area with nodular pleural thickening and pleural effusion.

better discernible after removal of fluid. Decubitus chest x-rays may show free or loculated effusions. Computed tomography enhances conventional radiography in identifying the extent of disease. (44) CT may also reveal undisclosed pleural plaques, which could suggest the diagnosis of asbestos-associated mesothelioma. Chest wall involvement, rib destruction, and parenchymal asbestosis are additional findings demonstrated by CT; spread to the pericardium and the contralateral lung may also be demonstrated by this modality. (45)

3. Management

There is no standard therapeutic plan that is preferable in the treatment of mesothelioma. The treatment should be tailored to the individual problem. The extent of the disease measured by staging offers a rational approach to type of therapy, as well as prognosis. (46) Distinctive differences in the presentation of this tumor require an appraisal for the need of aggressive intervention or palliative measures. In general, relief of pain and dyspnea are of prime consideration. Narcotic analgesics are effective in alleviating pain; intracostal and intervertebral nerve blocks may be used to allay discomfort.

The distress arising from large pleural effusions can be relieved by aspiration. To control recurrent pleural effusions, pleural sclerosis using intrapleural sclerosing agents has been effective. (47)

More aggressive therapeutic procedures include surgery, chemotherapy, radiation of the involved hemithorax, intrapleural instillation of radioactive compounds, and combined therapy. For most patients, since an open thoracotomy is often required to obtain sufficient tissue for a specific diagnosis, the surgeon could couple this procedure with definitive surgical resection, if indicated. Pleuroscopy, with direct visualization, offers an alternative method to obtain a biopsy sample. (48)

Surgical intervention for malignant mesothelioma still remains controversial. There are proponents who believe the probability of cure is negligible, therefore the only surgery advised is that necessary to establish an accurate diagnosis. Some surgical centers, however, recommend pleuropneumonectomy or pleurectomy, when feasible. The Memorial Sloan-Kettering Cancer Center, Chest Surgery Group advocates pleurectomy preferably performed at the time of diagnostic thoracotomy. (49–51) With pleurectomy, three desirable features are achieved: adequate tissue for definitive diagnosis, retention of maximum lung volume and pulmonary function, and effective retardation of recurrent pleural effusions. (52) More extensive surgery involves radical extrapleural pneumonectomy and replacement of the diaphragm with plastic mesh. (53,54) Pleurectomy or pneumonectomy also appear to provide considerable palliation of recurrent pleural effusions and chest pain. (55) Survival may be prolonged in patients that have had these extensive surgical procedures, (56) but in most situations, thoracotomy reveals a tumor beyond resection. Very low five-year survivals have been reported resulting from surgical intervention.

The response rate of malignant mesothelioma to cytotoxic chemotherapy is low, but may be effective in prolonging survival. Treatment protocols utilizing doxorubicin (Adriamycin) have helped in selected cases. (57) Studies have also shown a response to doxorubicin and platinum analogues, with responding patients surviving longer (17 to 27 months). (58) A longer survival in some patients has been achieved with the instilliation of radioactive compounds into the diseased tissue or placed into the intrapleural space.

Radiation therapy has been useful in controlling pain and pleural effusion. High-dose radiotherapy of the involved hemithorax has shown some benefit; although the residual effect of radiation pneumonitis or radiation pneumonectomy may result. (59)

Combined therapy for advanced mesothelioma including surgery supplemented with radiation and/or chemotherapy has yielded good results in a small number of patients. These patients must be able to tolerate intensive treatment and cope with undesirable side effects. The combined modality approach using investigational protocols is now under study at a number of cancer centers. (60,61)

4. Benign Localized Mesothelioma

Benign localized or solitary mesotheliomas should be differentiated from diffuse malignant mesotheliomas. There is no evidence to support a causal relationship between asbestos exposure and benign mesothelioma. (62) This form of mesothelioma can be treated by surgical removal.

G. DIFFUSE PLEURAL THICKENING

Pleural changes are suggestive markers associated with an asbestos-exposed population. The changes may be diffuse or discrete (plaques). There appeared to be an almost comparable prevalence of diffuse and discrete pleural abnormalities in one series of over 500 asbestos-exposed workers of those at least 30 years from first exposure to asbestos. (63)

1. Pathologic Features

Diffuse pleural thickening, almost always associated with asbestos exposure, (64,65) is the result of fibrosis and thickening of the visceral pleura, which may be unilateral but usually is bilateral. The fibrotic process may involve the parietal pleura as well, and extend into the interlobar fissures and costophrenic angles. The pathogenesis of diffuse pleural thickening remains vague, however, a preexistent asbestos-related pleural effusion is postulated. Other causes for pleural thickening should be considered and excluded, notably tuberculosis, previous empyema, hemothorax, and pleurisy; albeit these diseases are generally unilateral, whereas asbestos-associated pleural thickening is usually bilateral. (66)

2. Clinical Features

The clinical manifestations of diffuse pleural thickening relate to the extent of involvement. A vast number of patients are asymptomatic; those with marked pleural thickening may complain of chest discomfort and shortness of breath. On auscultation, diminished breath sounds are found over the chest. Restricted movement of the chest wall on deep inspiration frequently occurs, often expressed as chest tightness.

3. Pulmonary Function

Pulmonary function abnormalities in diffuse pleural thickening exhibit a restrictive pattern. The forced vital capacity (FVC) and diffusing capacity (DLCO) tend to be decreased, but the DLCO/TLC is increased. (67) The static compliance is decreased. These changes reflect a lung that is relatively normal but has become encased. (68)

4. Radiologic Features

The radiographic features of diffuse pleural thickening entail an ill-defined thickening of the pleura greater than 1 mm, below the fourth intercostal space. (69) A width greater than 3 mm is more apt to identify true pleural thickening from the normal pleural line. (70) There may be some difficulty in separating plaques from diffuse pleural thickening. To distinguish the two

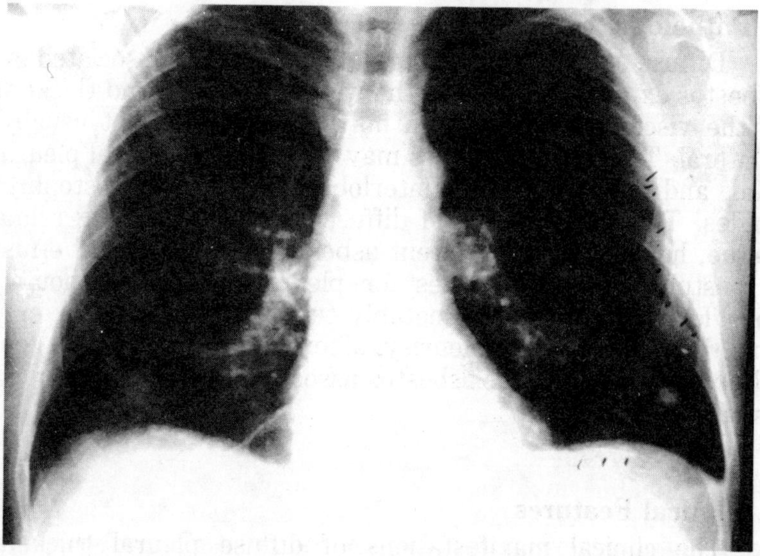

Fig. 1-5 Pleural thickening and calcification. Left pleural thickening and calcification of the left diaphragm.

entities, it has been suggested that the chest x-ray in diffuse disease usually shows bilateral pleural thickening along the lateral chest wall, and may involve the costophrenic sulcus; rarely calcifies; and has a graded increase in density from medial to lateral border and widens inferiorly. (71) Oblique films and computed tomography help delineate diffuse pleural thickening from pleural plaques and extrapleural fat tissue.

H. DISCRETE PLEURAL THICKENING (PLAQUES)

1. Pathologic Features

Asbestos-related pleural plaques occur as discrete, elevated, grey-white lesions on the parietal pleura of the rib cage and diaphragm. These lesions progress slowly and can calcify. Microscopically, the plaques are composed primarily of dense fibrous tissue, often containing deposits of calcium. With electron microscopy, small asbestos fibers may be found in the plaques. (72) Calcification becomes visible in the later stages.

2. Clinical Features

Pleural plaques generally appear about 20 years after first exposure to asbestos, and most plaques occur after 30 years or later. The presence of plaques are related to exposure; longer and heavier exposures to asbestos account for formation of more extensive plaques, although short exposures can result also in plaques. (73) The radiographic prevalence of pleural plaques in the general population ranges from none to 3 percent. (74–76) Occupationally asbestos-exposed populations show the highest prevalence of pleural plaques, with those of 40 or more years from time of first exposure having prevalences as high as 80 percent. (77) Reports vary in the proportion of noncalcified and calcified plaques. In one study, calcified plaques were present in about 15 percent of those with radiologic pleural asbestos-associated abnormalities. (78) Nonoccupational asbestos exposure (cryptic, bystander, household) has been associated with pleural plaques. (79) However, the majority of those with pleural plaques have had occupational exposure to asbestos.

Pleural plaques more often are indicative that parenchymal fibrosis will develop than those similarly exposed without plaques. Studies have shown that in the presence of pleural plaques the risk for bronchogenic carcinoma was increased more than two-fold. (80,81) Asbestos-related pleural disease should not be regarded only as a static or unchanging pleural lesion, but as a harbinger of further involvement and impairment. (82) In a report consisting of a four-year follow-up study, about 30 percent of patients showed radiologic progression of their pleural disease, with progression more common among patients with associated parenchymal fibrosis. (83)

Pleural plaques are usually asymptomatic unless extensive pleural involvement is present. Physical findings are seldom associated with plaques; physical signs if present relate to other co-existing abnormalities. Plaques alone do not yield pulmonary function changes, unless the involvement is widespread.

3. Radiologic Features

The radiologic features of pleural plaques are more evident when the plaques are calcified. On PA chest x-ray, plaques tend to show increasing density from faint medial to dense lateral shadow.

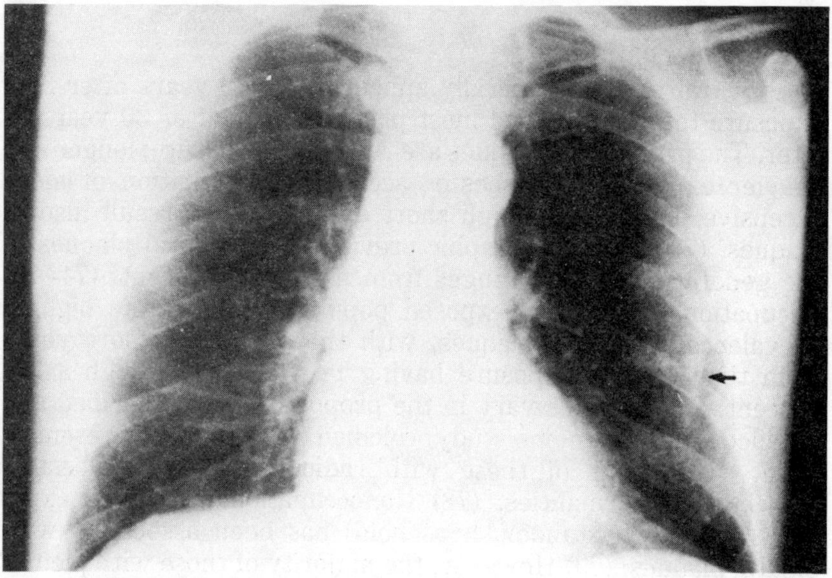

Fig. 1-6 Pleural plaque. Large left pleural plaque of the left midlung zone.

Plaques are often best seen tangentially. Oblique films enhance the identification of plaques by changing plaques from en face to profile views. Fluoroscopy may be of help, with rotation of the patient, the plaques may be viewed tangentially. (84) The pattern of plaques on PA chest x-rays may resemble a leaf with a rolled and nodular edge. Plaques are most frequently seen in the midzones and bases of the lung. Calcifications of the diaphragm offer a diagnostic clue of past asbestos exposure, as this unique finding almost never results from other disease processes. The plaques can be unilateral or bilateral, thick or thin; diaphragmatic plaques generally do not limit movement of the diaphragm. Various combinations may exist in conjunction with plaques, either plaques solely, or combined changes that include diffuse pleural thickening and parenchymal fibrosis. (85)

The radiologic differential diagnosis of pleural plaques includes pleural fat pads, healed rib fractures, metastatic disease, myeloma, and residuals of trauma and infection. Pleural plaques,

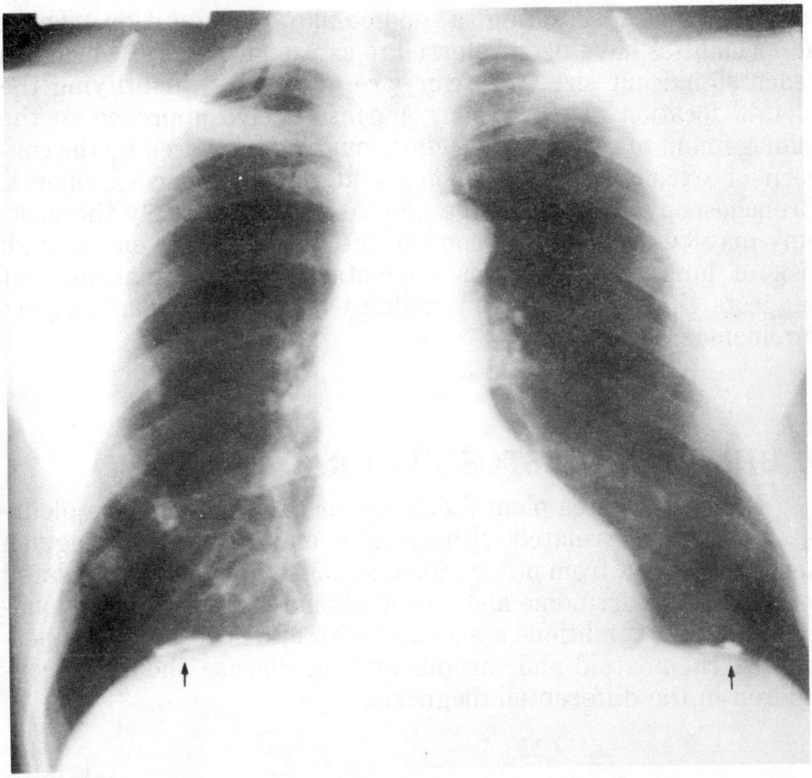

Fig. 1-7 Calcifications of both hemidiaphragms.

however, due to asbestos exposure are usually bilateral, whereas the above lesions are unilateral.

Crow's feet is a singular term that describes fibrous strands seen on chest x-ray films of some asbestos-exposed persons. The fibrous strands converge to a central point forming the pattern of a bird's foot. (86) These fibrous strands are not plaques. As seen on a CT scan, the strands involve the parietal and visceral pleura and may penetrate deep into the lung. (87)

I. ROUNDED ATELECTASIS

Rounded atelectasis is an unusual radiologic presentation associated with asbestosis and thickening of the parietal and visceral pleura. (88) This lesion consists of an infolding of asbestotic, atelectatic lung by overlying fibrotic thickening of the visceral pleura, creating a nodule-like configuration. These abnormalities have been referred to as pseudotumors, which can reach significant size. CT scans are of value in identifying the pleural location of the lesion. A conservative approach to the management of rounded atelectasis must be tempered by the concern of excluding mesothelioma and bronchogenic carcinoma. Bronchoscopy and fine-needle biopsies, and ultimately thoracotomy may be necessary to confirm the diagnosis. Given the high risk of lung cancer in this population, prudent management suggests that these solitary nodules be considered as suspect carcinomas. (89)

J. BENIGN ASBESTOS PLEURAL EFFUSION

Benign asbestos pleural effusion or benign exudative pleurisy are terms correlated with asbestos exposure. To distinguish benign effusions from other effusions caused by asbestos-related bronchogenic carcinoma and mesothelioma requires careful evaluation. Other conditions associated with effusions such as tuberculosis, rheumatoid and thromboembolic disease should be considered in the differential diagnosis.

1. Clinical Features

Benign asbestos pleural effusion may appear within the first decade after first exposure. More commonly, the effusion occurs within the first two decades after exposure, (90) but may also develop much later. (91) In a study of 57 patients with asbestosis or asbestos exposure, 12 or 21 percent were found to have asbestos pleural effusion. (92)

Asbestos effusions may be unilateral or bilateral, and tend to be recurrent. To establish the effusion as asbestos-related, three criteria are suggested: exclusion of other causes especially tuberculosis and malignancy; at least a two year follow-up to verify that it is benign; and a positive history of exposure to asbestos. (93) Spontaneous remissions have occurred.

2. Pathologic Features

Examination of the pleural fluid shows a sterile exudate but can be hemorrhagic, serous, or fibrinous. Cytologic examination and culture of aspirated fluid are usually negative.

3. Clinical manifestations

The physical examination reveals the usual signs of effusion: dullness to percussion, decreased breath sounds, and basilar rales may be heard if asbestosis is present. Chest pain, elevated temperature, leukocytosis, and an increased sedimentation rate may also accompany the effusion.

4. Radiologic Features

Chest roentgenography may show, in addition to the fluid, other manifestations of asbestos-related disease, namely asbestosis, diffuse pleural thickening, and calcified pleural plaques. CT scans are helpful in disclosing these abnormalities.

Abnormal pulmonary function, if present, may be attributed to pleural disease or associated parenchymal disease.

Therapy of asbestos pleural effusion is aimed primarily at providing relief of symptoms.

K. IMMUNOLOGIC CORRELATION

Exposure to asbestos fibers has been implicated with immunologic changes. The immunologic alterations associated with asbestosis and pleural diseases are reflected in peripheral blood and bronchoalveolar lavage. An increased prevalence of antinuclear and rheumatoid factors, (94,95) and immunoglobulins (96) has been observed. Asbestos may cause depressed interferon induction, (97) and altered lymphocyte function. (98) These immunologic changes are of great interest and merit further evaluation.

L. OTHER ASBESTOS-RELATED NEOPLASIA

Other asbestos-associated neoplasms have been reported among those exposed to asbestos fibers. Studies have shown a twofold to threefold increase in the prevalence of gastrointestinal cancer among insulation workers, miners, millers, and factory workers. (99,100) Tumors of the oropharynx, larynx, and esophagus occurred more frequently among asbestos workers who smoke; tumors of the stomach, colon-rectum, and kidney were not influenced by smoking. (101) A problem with some of the studies of cancers of the digestive tract has been the inclusion of peritoneal mesotheliomas making it difficult to document an increased risk of cancer of gastrointestinal system origin from that of mesothelioma. (102) Sufficient evidence currently exists to justify an adequate colon-rectal examination and stool test for occult blood in all asbestos-exposed persons. (103,104)

Reports linking asbestos exposure and laryngeal cancer are highly suggestive. The increased risk has been underlined in various studies. (107–109)

Studies of women asbestos workers have noted possible increases in cancers of the ovary and uterine cervix. (105,106) These reports require further investigation.

REFERENCES

1. Murray HM: Departmental Committee on Compensation for Industrial Diseases, Minutes of Evidence, appendices and index, pp. 127–128. London: Wyman and Sons, 1907.
2. Pancoast HK, Miller TG, Landris HRM: A roentgenologic study of the effects of dust inhalation on the lung. Trans Soc Am Physicians 32:97–108, 1917.
3. Cooke WE: Fibrosis of the lungs due to the inhalation of asbestos dust. Br Med J 11:147, 1924.
4. Cooke WE: "Pulmonary Asbestosis." Br Med J 11:1024–1025, 1927.
5. Merewether ERA, Price CW: Report on effects of asbestos dust on the lungs and dust suppression in the asbestos industry. London: H.M. Stationary Office, 1930.
6. Legge T: Asbestosis: Industrial maladies. London: Oxford University Press, pp. 190–194, 1934.
7. Gloyne SR: Two cases of squamous carcinoma of the lung occurring in asbestosis. Tubercle 17:5–10, 1935.
8. Lynch KM, Smith WA: Pulmonary asbestosis III: Carcinoma of lung in asbesto-silicosis. Am J Cancer 24:56–64, 1935.
9. Merewether ERA: Asbestosis and carcinoma of the lung. In Annual Report of the Chief Inspector of Factories for the Year 1948. London: H.M. Stationary office, 1949.
10. Doll R: Mortality from lung cancer in asbestos workers. Br J Ind Med 12:81, 1955.
11. Selikoff IJ, Churg J, Hammond EC: Asbestos exposure and neoplasia. JAMA 188:22–26, 1964.
12. Selikoff IJ: Disability Compensation for Asbestos-Associated Disease in the United States. Environmental Sciences Laboratory, Mount Sinai School of Medicine of the City University of New York, 1982.
13. Gloyne SR: The morbid anatomy and histology of asbestosis. Tubercle 14:550–558, 1933.
14. Wagner JC, Sleggs CA, Marchand P: diffuse pleural mesothelioma and asbestos exposure in the North Western Cape Province. Br J Ind Med 17:260–271, 1960.

15. Newhouse ML, Thompson H: Mesothelioma of pleura and peritoneum following exposure to asbestos in the London area. Brit J Indus Med 22:261–269, 1965.
16. Hinds MW: Mesotheliomas in the United States: Incidence in the 1970s. J Occ Med 20:469–471, 1978.
17. Becklake MR: Asbestos-related diseases of the lungs and other organs: Their epidemiology and implications for clinical practice. Am Rev Respir Dis 114:187–227, 1976.
18. Davis JMG: Electron microscope studies of asbestosis in man and animals. Ann NY Acad Sci 132:98, 1965.
19. Das RM, Holt PF, Horne MC: The formation of asbestos bodies. Med Lav 68:431, 1977.
20. Langer AM, Mackler AD, Pooley, FD: Electron microscopical investigation of asbestos fibres. Environ Health Perspect 9:63–80, 1974.
21. Doniach I, Swettenham KV, Hawthorn KS: Prevalence of asbestos bodies in a necropsy series in East London: Association with disease, occupation and domiciliary address. Br J Ind Med 32:16–30, 1975.
22. McLarty JW, Greenberg D, Hurst GA, et al.: The clinical significance of ferruginous bodies in sputa. J Occ Med 22:92–6, 1980.
23. International Labor Organization, International Classification of Radiographs of the Pneumoconioses. Geneva, ILO, 1980.
24. Parkes WR: Occupational Lung Disorders, 2nd ed., 1982.
25. Cantin A, Drapeau G, Lamoureux G, Begin R: Gallium-67 lung scanning in asbestos workers. (Abs.) Occupational Lung Disease. Gee JBL, Morgan WKC, Brooks SM (eds.), p. 211. Raven Press, New York, 1984.
26. Wright JL, Churg A: Morphology of small airway lesions in patients with asbestos exposure. Hum Pathol 15:68–74, 1984.
27. Lynch KM, Smith WA: Pulmonary asbestosis III: Carcinoma of lung in asbestos-silicosis. Am J Cancer 24:56–64, 1935.
28. Doll R: Mortality from lung cancer in asbestos workers. Br J Ind Med 12:81–86, 1955.
29. Selikoff IJ, Hammond EC, Seidman H: Cancer risk of insulation workers in the United States. Proc of the Working Group to Assess the Biological Effects of Asbestos, Int Agency for Research on Cancer, Lyon, France, 1972.
30. Selikoff, IJ, Churg J, Hammond EC: Asbestos exposure and neoplasia. JAMA 204:106–112, 1968.
31. Selikoff IJ, Hammond EC, Seidman H: Mortality experience of insulation workers in the United States and Canada, 1943–1976. Ann NY Acad Sci 330:91–116, 1979.
32. Selikoff IJ, Hammond EC, Churg J: Asbestos exposure, smoking and neoplasia. JAMA 204(2):106–112, 1968.
33. Kannerstein M, Churg J: Pathology of carcinoma of the lung associated with asbestos exposure. Cancer 30:14, 1972.

34. Legha SS, Muggia FM: Pleural mesothelioma: Clinical features and therapeutic implications. Ann Intern Med 87:613–621, 1977.
35. Selikoff IJ: Cancer risk of asbestos exposure. In Hiatt HH, Watson JD, Winsten JA, eds. Origins of human cancer. Cold Springs Harbor, NY. Cold Springs Harbor Laboratory. 1765–1784, 1977.
36. Antman KH, Blum RH, Greenberger JS, et al.: Multimodality therapy for malignant mesothelioma based on a study of natural history. Am J Med 68:356–362, 1980.
37. Newhouse ML, Berry G: Predictions of mortality from mesothelial tumours in asbestos factory workers. Br J Ind Med 33:147, 1976.
38. Moertel CG: Peritoneal mesotheliomas. Gastroenterology 63:346–350, 1972.
39. Antman KH: Malignant mesothelioma. N Engl J Med 303:200–202, 1980.
40. Legha SS, Muggia FM: Pleural mesothelioma: Clinical features and therapeutic implications. Ann Intern Med 87:613–626, 1977.
41. Legha SS, Muggia FM: Pleural mesothelioma: Clinical features and therapeutic implications. Ann Intern Med 87:613–621, 1977.
42. Winslow DJ, Taylor HB: Malignant peritoneal mesotheliomas. A clinicopathological analysis of 12 fatal cases. Cancer 13:127, 1960.
43. Morgan WKC, Seaton A: Occupational Lung Diseases, p. 358. Philadelphia: W.B. Saunders Co., 1984.
44. Grant DC, Sellzer SE, Antman KH, et al.: Computed tomography of malignant pleural mesothelioma. J Comp Ass Tom 7:626–632, 1983.
45. Elmes PC, Simpson MJC: The clinical aspects of mesothelioma. Q J Med 45:427–449, 1976.
46. Butchart EG, Ashcroft T, Barnsley WC, et al.: Pleuropneumonectomy in the management of diffuse mesothelioma of the pleura: Experience with 29 patients. Thorax 31:15–24, 1976.
47. Rosenstock L, Hudson LD: The pleural manifestations of asbestos exposure. In Rosenstock L (ed.) Occupational Pulmonary Disease. Philadelphia: Hanley and Belfus, p. 400, 1987.
48. Boutin C, Viallat JR, Cargnino P: La biopsie sous thoracoscopie dans la diagnostic des pleuresies. Le Concours Medical 23:4213–4218, 1979.
49. Brenner J, Sordillo PP, Magill, GB, et al.: Malignant mesothelioma of the pleura: Review of 123 patients. Cancer 49:2431–2435, 1982.
50. McCormack P, Nagasaki F, Hilaris BS, et al.: Surgical treatment of pleural mesothelioma. J Thorac Cardiovas Surg 84:834–842, 1982.
51. Wanebo HJ, Martini N, Melamed MR, et al.: Pleural mesothelioma. Cancer 38:2481–2488, 1976.
52. Antman KH, Corson JM: Benign and malignant pleural mesothe-

lioma. In Clinics in Chest Medicine, Pleural Diseases. Light RW (ed.) Philadelphia: W.B. Saunders Co., 6:127–140, 1985.
53. Butchart EG, Ashcroft T, Barnsley WC, et al.: Pleuropneumonectomy in the management of diffuse malignant mesothelioma of the pleura: Experience with 29 patients. Thorax 31:15–24, 1976.
54. DeLaria GA, Jensik R, Faber, et al.: Surgical management of malignant mesothelioma. Ann Thorac Surg 26:375–382, 1978.
55. Martini N, Manjit SB, Beattie EJ: Indications for pleurectomy in malignant effusion. Cancer 35:734–738, 1975.
56. Butchart EG, Ashcroft T, Barnsley WC, et al.: The role of surgery in diffuse malignant mesothelioma of the pleura. Semin Oncol 8:321, 1981.
57. Yap B, Benjamin RS, Burgess A, et al.: The value of Adriamycin in the treatment of diffuse malignant pleural mesothelioma. Cancer 42:1692–1696, 1978.
58. Zidar B, Pugh R, Schiffer L, et al.: Treatment of six cases of mesothelioma with doxorubicin and cis-platinum. Proc A.S.C.O. 2:225 (C–880), 1983.
59. Antman KH, Corson JM: Benign and malignant pleural mesothelioma. In Clinics in Chest Medicine, Pleural Diseases. Light RW (ed.) Philadelphia: W.B. Saunders Co., 6:127–140, 1985.
60. Antman KH: Malignant mesothelioma. N Engl J Med 303:200–202, 1980.
61. Antman KH, Corson JM: Benign and malignant pleural mesothelioma. In Clinics in Chest Medicine, Pleural Diseases. Light RW (ed.) Philadelphia: W.B. Saunders Co., 6:127–140, 1985.
62. Legha SS, Muggia FM: Pleural mesothelioma: Clinical features and therapeutic implications. Ann Intern Med 87:613–621, 1977.
63. Reger RB, Ames RG, Merchant JA, et al.: The detection of thoracic abnormalities using (PA) vs. PA and oblique roentgenograms. Chest 81:290–295, 1982.
64. Becklake M: Asbestos-related diseases of the lung and other organs: Their epidemiology and implications for clinical practice. Am Rev Respir Dis 114:187, 1976.
65. Parkes WR: Asbestos related disorders. Br J Dis Chest 67(4):260, 1973.
66. Hillerdal G: Non-malignant asbestos pleural disease. Thorax 36:669, 1981.
67. Rosenstock L, Hudson LD: The pleural manifestations of asbestos exposure. In Rosenstock L (ed.). Occupational Pulmonary Disease. Philadelphia: Hanley and Belfus, p. 396, 1987.
68. Wright PH, Hanson A, Kreel L, Capel LH: Respiratory function changes after asbestos pleurisy. Thorax 35:31–36, 1980.
69. Sargent EN, Gordonson J, Jacobson G, et al.: Bilateral pleural thickening: A manifestation of asbestos dust exposure. Am J Roentgenol 131:519–85, 1978.

70. Rosenstock L, Hudson LD: The pleural manifestations of asbestos exposure. In Rosenstock L (ed.) Occupational Pulmonary Disease. Philadelphia: Hanley and Belfus, p. 391, 1987.
71. Fletcher DE, Edge JR: The early radiographic changes in pulmonary and pleural asbestosis. Clinical Radiol 21:355–365, 1970.
72. Hertzog P, Toty L, Personne C, et al.: Plaques pleurales, parietales, fibrohyalines. J Fr Med Chir Thorac 26:59–70, 1972.
73. Hillerdal G: Pleural plaques in a health survey material: Frequency, development, and exposure to asbestos. Scand J Respir Dis 59:257–263, 1978.
74. Anderson HA, Selikoff IJ: Pleural reactions to environmental agents. Fed Proc 37:2496–2500, 1978.
75. Hillerdal G: Pleural plaques: Occurrence, Exposure to Asbestos and Clinical Importance. Doctoral Thesis at Uppsala University, 1980.
76. Hillerdal G, Lindgren A: Pleural plaques: Correlation of autopsy findings to radiographic findings and occupational history. Eur J Respir Dis 61:315–319, 1980.
77. Anderson HA, Selikoff IJ: Pleural reactions to environmental agents. Fed Proc 37:2496–2500, 1978.
78. McMillian GHG, Rosseter CE: Development of radiological and clinical evidence of parenchymal fibrosis in men with nonmalignant asbestos-related pleural lesions. Br J Ind Med 39:54–59, 1982.
79. Meurman LO: Pleural fibrocalcific plaques and asbestos exposure. Environ Research 2:30–46, 1968.
80. Edge JR: Asbestos-related disease in Barrow-in Furness. Environ Res 11:244–247, 1976.
81. Fletcher DE: A mortality study of shipyard workers with pleural plaques. Br J Ind Med 29:142–145, 1972.
82. Rosenstock L, Hudson LD: The pleural manifestations of asbestos exposure. In Rosenstock L (ed.) Occupational Pulmonary Disease. Philadelphia: Hanley and Belfus, p. 385, 1987.
83. Souranta H, Huuskonen MS, Zitting A, et al.: Radiographic progression of asbestosis. Am J Ind Med 3:67–74, 1982.
84. Hillerdal G: Nonmalignant pleural disease related to asbestos exposure. In Symposium on Pleural Diseases. Light R (Ed.) Clinics in Chest Medicine. Philadelphia: W.B. Saunders Co., 6:141–152, 1985.
85. Rom NR, Palmer PES: The spectrum of asbestos-related diseases. West J Med 121:10–21, 1974.
86. Mackenzie FAF, Harries PG: Changing attitudes to the diagnosis of asbestos disease. JR Nav Med Serv 56:116–123, 1970.
87. Hillerdal G: Nonmalignant pleural disease related to asbestos exposure. In Symposium on Pleural Diseases. Light R (Ed.) Clinics in Chest Medicine. Philadelphia: W.B. Saunders Co., 6:145, 1985.
88. Mintzer RA, Cugell DW: The association of asbestos-induced pleural disease and rounded atelectasis. Chest 81:457–460, 1982.

89. Rosenstock L, Hudson LD: The pleural manifestations of asbestos exposure. In Rosenstock L (ed.) Occupational Pulmonary Disease. Philadelphia: Hanley and Belfus, p. 393, 1987.
90. Mackenzie FAF, Harries PG: Changing attitudes to the diagnosis of asbestos disease. JR Nav Med Serv 56:116–123, 1970.
91. Hillerdal G: Nonmalignant asbestos pleural disease. Thorax 36:669–675, 1981.
92. Gaensler EA, Kaplan AI: Asbestos pleural effusion. Ann Intern Med 74:178–191, 1971.
93. Hillerdal G: Nonmalignant pleural disease related to asbestos exposure. In Symposium on Pleural Diseases. Light R (Ed.) Clinics in Chest Medicine. Philadelphia: W.B. Saunders Co., 6:143, 1985.
94. Doll NJ, Diem JE, Jones RN, et al.: Humoral immunologic abnormalities in workers exposed to asbestos cement dust. J Allergy Clin Immunol 72:509–512, 1983.
95. Turner-Warwick M, Parkes WR: Circulating rheumatoid and antinuclear factors in asbestos workers. Br Med J 3:492–495, 1970.
96. Kagan E, Solomon A, Cochrane JC, et al.: Immunological studies of patients with asbestosis II. Studies of circulating lymphoid cell numbers and humoral immunity. Clin Exp Immunol 28:268–275, 1977.
97. Hahon N, Eckert HL: Depression of viral interferon induction in cell monolayers by asbestos fibers. Environ Res 11:52, 1976.
98. Haslam PL, Lukoszek JA, Merchant JA, Turner-Warwick M: Lymphocyte responses to phytohemagglutinin in patients with asbestosis and pleural mesothelioma. Clin Exp Immunol 31:178, 1978.
99. Selikoff IJ, Hammond EC: Multiple risk factors in etiology of environmental cancer. In Fraumeni JF (ed.). Persons at high risk of cancer: An approach to cancer etiology and control. New York: Academic Press, pp. 467–483, 1975.
100. Elmes PC, Simpson MJC: Insulation workers in Belfast, 3. Mortality 1940–66 Br J Ind Med 28:226–36, 1971.
101. Hammond EC, Selikoff IJ, Seidman H: Asbestos exposure, cigarette smoking and death rates. Ann NY Acad Sci 330:473–490, 1979.
102. Craighead JE, Mossman BT: The pathogenesis of asbestos-associated diseases. N Engl J Med 306:1446–1455, 1982.
103. Selikoff IJ, Hammond EC, Seidman H: Mortality experience of insulation workers in the U.S. and Canada: 1943–1976. Ann NY Acad Sci 330:91–116, 1979.
104. Cook PM: Review of published studies on gut penetration by ingested asbestos fibers. Environ Health Perspect 53:121–130, 1983.
105. Becklake MR: Asbestos-related diseases of the lung and other

organs: Their epidemiology and implications for clinical practice. Am Rev Respir Dis 114:187–227, 1976.

105. Newhouse ML, et al.: A study of the mortality of female asbestos workers. Br J Ind Med 29:134–141, 1972.
106. Stell PM, McGill T: Asbestos and laryngeal carcinoma. Lancet 2:416–417, 1973.
107. Morgan RW, Shettigara PT: Occupational asbestos exposure, smoking, and laryngeal carcinoma. Ann NY Acad Sci 271:309–310, 1976.
108. Daum SM, Seidman H, Selikoff IJ: Laryngeal and bucco-pharyngeal cancers in asbestos workers. In Proceedings of Third International Symposium on the Detection and Prevention of Cancer. New York, 1976.
109. Newhouse ML, Berry G: Asbestos and laryngeal carcinoma. Lancet 2:615, 1973.

2

Asbestos and Disability

JAMES G. DAHLGREN, M.D.

University of California
Los Angeles, California, U.S.A.

Synopsis

BIOGRAPHY

Dr. James G. Dahlgren is an Assistant Clinical Professor of Medicine at the University of California School of Medicine, Los Angeles (UCLA). He also has his own private practice of occupational medicine. His research interests include occupational lung disease and industrial toxicology. He has published numerous articles and given many presentations. He is the founder of the Pacific Toxicology Laboratories in Los Angeles. He is the founder and was the first president of the California Society of Industrial Medicine and Surgery (CSIMS). He serves as the medical consultant to the International Chemical Workers Union. Dr. Dahlgren may be contacted at 6333 Wilshire Boulevard, Suite 202, Los Angeles, California 90048. (telephone: 213-653-9110) (FAX: 213-655-2825)

EDITORS' COMMENTARY

For some time, many specialists have believed that there must be a biological process, that has significant adverse effect, long before a definite lung fibrosis becomes manifest in chest radiographs or disability becomes manifest in pulmonary function tests. But, those "early" or "minor" cases have been routinely classified as *non-disabled* and the injuries *non-compensable*. Perhaps the questions we should ask are: Is there an objective basis for detecting, classifying, and dealing with such "marginal" cases from a medical, technical, or legal perspective? Would some kind of "early detection" permit a reduction in dose and response? Would removal from further exposure slow the process, rather than cumulatively antagonizing the injured tissue? If possible, perhaps in the future, prevention by engineering controls and personal protective measures could be supplemented by preventive medicine countermeasures.

One unique aspect of asbestos-induced diseases is that a very high proportion of those exposed develop some abnormality or disability over a long period of time. Is the disease actually latent or is it biologically active in a predictable discernable manner? Should greater focus be on the latent phase rather than the disabled phase of the disease? If brief low levels of asbestos exposure could produce an asbestos-related disease, then the focus, logically, should shift to early detection, susceptibility, precise characterization of the biological processes, and development of corrective or preventive countermeasures.

The following review chapter should provide considerable food for thought as to how many people are actually exposed to harmful quantities and types of asbestos, the possible health effects, and the true magnitude of this public health problem. Apparently, from the reports cited by Dr. Dahlgren and the inferences that can be made, the problems seem more widespread than previously believed.

The chapter differentiates between pleural and parenchymal (interstitial) asbestosis, since this is a common confabulation or source of confusion in research reports and their interpretation. In particular, Dr. Dahlgren discusses the problems in identifying parietal pleural plaques and suggests consideration of alternates to the International Labour Organization classification procedure. He discusses the disability associated with asbestos-induced pleural effusion and its progression.

He discusses the apparent lack of a relationship between pleural asbestosis and subradiographic parenchymal asbestosis. Small airways disease is considered indicative of an abnormal health problem that becomes manifest even before radiographic changes are detectable.

Disputes regarding the reading of chest x-rays have not been resolved by the ILO criteria nor the certification of readers. Dr. Dahlgren suggests the possible use of more sensitive imaging techniques. The effects of cigarette smoking, long a subject of controversy, is examined critically.

This interesting and provocative chapter clearly presents information that merits careful consideration by all disciplines involved in asbestos health problems. If no other reading is accomplished, the conclusions alone should demonstrate that there have been many misconceptions (as judged by current research knowledge), that have significantly effected the approach to this public health problem. If science involves ever closer discoveries and approximations of the truth, this chapter provides the basis for many issues that could be subject to further scientific inquiry. If clarification of issues and incentives for research are the hallmark of worthwhile scholarly work, this chapter should serve to highlight and motivate the quest for further understanding of the truth.

A. ASBESTOSIS AND DISABILITY

Most published criteria for the diagnosis of asbestosis requires an abnormal chest x-ray showing definite interstitial fibrosis of grade 1/1 or greater. If the person has a normal chest x-ray or only pleural changes, that person does not qualify for disability.[1–3] The history of significant asbestos exposure and appropriate time interval between exposure and detection of the disease

Accepted for publication on 10 February 1989.

is the basis for diagnosing asbestosis.[3,5] At this point in time a "classical" diagnosis of asbestosis rests on abnormal interstitial x-ray results and the presence of restriction on pulmonary function studies. These criteria will miss many if not most early and modest cases of asbestos induced lung disease.

Asbestos dust exposure causes fibrosis or scarring of the lung parenchyma and pleura with resultant decrease in the forced vital capacity and in the gas exchanging properties of the lung. Even low-level asbestos exposure can cause both parenchymal and pleural asbestosis. Both types of asbestosis can result in significant pulmonary disability even in the absence of chest x-ray manifestations.

Asbestos causes x-ray manifestations of pleural fibrosis in up to 65% of exposed persons if examined 40 years after the onset of exposure.[9,10]

There should be serious doubt about reliance on the chest x-ray as a case finding tool or as the basis for compensation because there are studies showing severe asbestosis with normal chest x-rays,[6,7] and radiologists cannot agree on the x-ray findings in a majority of asbestosis cases.[8]

This chapter will review the current x-ray criteria for diagnosis of asbestosis, discuss the limitations of that criteria, propose alternative criteria, review the studies demonstrating small airways dysfunction in asbestos-exposed workers, review the studies demonstrating significant disability in workers with pleural asbestosis alone, review the studies demonstrating disability in parenchymal asbestosis, and finally examine the role of cigarette smoking.

B. LOW-LEVEL ASBESTOS EXPOSURE

There is no agreement on what defines a safe level of exposure to asbestos and therefore any exposure to asbestos can cause disease.[5] Even short-term exposure for a day, a week, or a month if excessive can result in pleural fibrosis.[11] Asbestos fibers remain in the lung and are highly resistant to digestion and removal. Most retained asbestos fibers will remain in the lung until death although there is some breakdown and removal, particularly of chrysotile fibers.[12] High levels of asbestos dust in an occupational setting can be assumed if there is visible dust in the air. When there is visible dust in the air, it is likely that the fiber levels are unsafe and are in excess of the current United States-OSHA limit of 0.5 fibers per ml.[5] Urban environmental contamination has been demonstrated utilizing electron microscopy techniques with average values being 10 nanograms per cubic meter but air close to asbestos using facilities has much higher levels. Asbestos fibers smaller than 5 microns in length are usually not seen by the naked eye and the small fibers are hazardous.

Studies on asbestos workers' families, car mechanics, and shipyard workers demonstrate the danger of very low-level and brief asbestos exposure.

Asbestos workers can carry dust home on their clothing and hair, which exposes their families to the dust in the home environment. A high percentage of family members, mainly wives who give a history of washing their husband's asbestos-covered clothing, develop asbestosis, both pleural and parenchymal.[13–18]

In one study 490 family members of amosite asbestos workers showed a 39.6% incidence of pleural and parenchymal asbestosis (21.4% pleural only and 18.2% parenchymal).[14]

Kilburn et al studied 274 wives of shipyard workers with low-level asbestos exposure. In those who were over 20 years from the onset of exposure, abnormal x-rays with either pleural or parenchymal asbestosis was seen in 7.3%.[18] Kilburn notes that time elapsed from the onset of the exposure rather than the level or duration of exposure correlated with the prevalence of fibrosis.[16]

Sider studied 117 wives of insulation workers; 19.4% demonstrated pleural asbestosis (i.e., pleural plaques, diaphragmatic plaques, pleural calcification, or diffuse pleural thickening). The usual finding was pleural plaques on the lateral chest wall. On close questioning, the wives' only asbestos exposure was the shaking of their husband's work clothing prior to washing.[17]

Low-level intermittent asbestos exposure occurs from the removal of asbestos dust from brake drums and can cause asbestosis.[19–23]

The common practice of blowing the asbestos dust off of the brake drum and wheel with compressed air leads to fiber exposures as high as 29.2 fibers per ml. A study of brake workers in Hong Kong revealed that an average of 0.13 fibers per ml (highest 0.83) occurred in the breathing zone of mechanics.[23] The technique of blowing the dust off of the brakes is used in 65% of all brake repair establishments.[20]

Mineralogic studies of the asbestos dust from brakes revealed that 2% to 15% of the brake drum dust was chrysotile asbestos.[21]

Marcus studied 925 auto mechanics with asbestos exposure and compared them to office workers. As shown in Table 2-1, the rate of pleural asbestosis increased as the mechanics aged. None of the office workers had pleural asbestosis.

Table 2-1 Pleural Asbestosis in Auto Mechanics

Under age 40	0.4%
41–49	6%
50–59	25%
60–69	42%

World War II shipyward workers have a significant incidence of asbestosis and cancer from their exposure to asbestos insulation. Often the exposures in the shipyards were only for a few months and in workers without primary involvement with asbestos. Significant disease has developed in welders, pipefitters, and others who have worked in the vicinity where the asbestos insulation was used.[24]

C. PLEURAL ASBESTOSIS

Although asbestosis is a term that some reserve for cases of parenchymal or interstitial asbestosis, the textbook on asbestos-related disease by Selikoff and Lee uses the term pleural asbestosis to refer to those cases where there is pleural fibrosis only.[5] The most common consequence of asbestos exposure is pleural asbestosis. Pleural disease unlike lung cancer occurs independently of whether the exposed person has used cigarettes or not.[38] Londorf showed a dose-dependent response effect for pleural asbestosis among railway maintenance and repair shop workers. As the amount of exposure to asbestos increased, so did the prevalence of pleural disease.[39] Pleural disease alone in the absence of parenchymal involvement is commonly felt to not result in significant disability. Yet numerous studies, which will be detailed in the sections below, belie this common incorrect view.

Navratil described a series of patients with pleural asbestosis. The most striking feature in these 50 cases was the high incidence of death in those who had extensive pleural fibrosis.[41]

Hillerdal has divided asbestos-induced pleural reactions into four categories[26] (see Table 2-2). These categories will be used to examine pleural asbestosis.

1. Parietal Pleural Plaques

Parietal pleural plaquing is the most common form of pleural asbestosis. The usual explanation for formation of these plaques is that the asbestos fibers migrate from the lung via lymphatics and

Table 2-2 Types of Pleural Asbestosis

1. Parietal plaques and thickening
2. Pleural effusion
3. Visceral pleural thickening
4. Progressive pleural thickening

eventually protrude through the visceral pleura. With respiratory movement there is an irritation of the parietal pleura from the protruding asbestos fiber. Over time the plaques become confluent and create lateral chest wall pleural thickening. Pleural plaques are raised white, shiny, fibrous, hypoceullar lesions that grow and become confluent on the parietal pleura. They are most common on the posterolateral chest wall in a bilateral distribution affecting the middle one-third of the chest wall. They are next most common on the diaphragm. With progression they are more likely to be seen on the lower one-third of the chest wall.

General population surveys show the prevalence of pleural thickening will range from 0.05% to as high as 3.5% in males above the age of 40. Eighty percent of those who have definite pleural plaques by x-ray will recall an exposure to asbestos.[28,29] Albelda found pleural thickening to be a very specific indicator of asbestos exposure. Only 19% of pleural thickening cases fail to report a source of significant asbestos exposure.[30] There are many fewer cases of pleural thickening among female patients in the population surveys.

Plain film chest x-rays are inadequate to diagnose pleural plaques both because of a lack of sensitivity and a lack of specificity. Many pleural plaques will be missed by plain film chest x-ray and other diagnoses can be demonstrated for apparent pleural plaques.

The great majority of plaques do not show on plain chest x-ray. One autopsy study found only 12.5% of pleural plaques in asbestos exposed workers had been seen on plain x-ray.[27]

Other possible causes of radiographic pleural thickening and pleural plaques are subcostal adipose tissue, chest trauma, rib fractures, tuberculosis, allergic reactions, pulmonary emboli, emphysema, thoracic surgery, mineral oil pneumonia, and severe rheumatoid arthritis. Sargent has emphasized the importance of pleural fat as a cause of the pleural thickening on plain x-ray and recommended C.T. scanning to differentiate the fat from scarring.[31]

The ILO classification for thickening and pleural plaques utilizes quarters of the chest wall and rates the presence of pleural disease by the extent and width of the plaques regardless of location on the chest wall.[32] Yet when the pleural plaque is unilateral or involves only the upper portions of the lung, the likelihood of attribution to asbestos is less. Calcified pleural plaques on the diaphragm are almost always due to asbestos.

It is for this reason that some experts feel that the current ILO classification should be modified.

Bohlig has proposed a new scheme for describing pleural asbestosis which emphasizes the relative rarity of upper portions of the pleura being involved in pleural asbestosis.[9] Consideration to usage of this scheme should be given.

2. Pleural Effusion

Pleural effusion or pleural exudation commonly occurs in asbestos-exposed persons. The latency period for asbestos effusion is shorter than it is for the other asbestos-related disorders. Therefore effusion is the most common asbestos-related complication within the first 20 years after onset of exposure. A pleural effusion is attributable to asbestos exposure if there is no other explanation (i.e., cancer, infection, trauma, or embolism) in an asbestos-exposed person. The possibility of mesothelioma must be considered although some experts such as Gaensler have suggested that aggressive evaluation to diagnose mesothelioma is probably not warranted in view of the poor prognosis for treating mesothelioma.[37]

In a pleural effusion the pleural space is filled with fluid that is thick and frequently bloody. Pleural biopsies reveal fibrosis and inflammatory reaction with fibrinous exudates. Pleural effusions from asbestos are often asymptomatic although pain has been described. Some reports describe the common occurrence of asbestos-induced pleurisy.[43,44]

The prevalence of asbestos effusion is dose related. In one study, heavy exposure resulted in a prevalence of benign pleural effusion of 7% indirect exposure, 3.7% in peripheral or extremely low level 0.2%.[33] Another study indicates an incidence of approximately 9.2 effusions per thousand person years following heavy exposure, 3.9 effusions for intermediate-level exposure, and 0.7 for low-level exposure.[33]

Pleural effusions may be transient or may go on to develop into progressive pleural fibrosis with persistent exudate. In one study effusions had an average duration of 4.3 months.[26] In approximately 10 out of 22 pleural effusion cases described by

Hillerdal, there were preexisting pleural plaques.[26] One case in four will experience a recurrent effusion.[33] Pleural effusions in the absence of other pulmonary abnormalities can result in significant disability. Mattson described 25 persons with pleural effusions secondary to asbestos dust exposure.[40] Six of them were troubled by shortness of breath and three had reduced ability to work as a result of their pleural disease.

The onset of pleural effusion can occur within a few years of exposure or as late as 46 years after exposure.[34] Overall pleural effusion is a very common complication of asbestos exposure. Gaensler and Kaplan described pleural effusion in 21% of their asbestos worker population.[34] Obliteration of a single costophrenic angle (i.e., secondary to silent asbestos effusion) was seen in 84 out of 891 cases described by Hillerdal.[27] Asbestos pleural effusion must be added to the long list of causes for pleural effusion.

3. Visceral Pleural Thickening

Thickening of the visceral pleura alone is relatively uncommon and is usually seen only in the fissures, mainly the minor fissure. It is usually associated with heavy exposure.

4. Progressive Pleural Thickening

Progressive pleural thickening is defined by involvement of the parietal and visceral pleura by and progression to severe disability. Progressive pleural fibrosis can result in a very severe pulmonary disability. Hillerdal described a number of patients with this problem. In some patients it began as a pleural effusion with progression over the next few years.[26,34] Localized scarring (Crow's feet) can occur but the post effusion fibrosis usually becomes confluent and bilateral.[35] Unlike other types of asbestos pleural disease (i.e., pleural plaques), the progressive process can involve the lung apices.

Shrinking asbestos pleuritis or rounded atelectasis is probably a form of progressive pleural fibrosis with localized shrinking of the visceral pleural into the lung tissue causing a rounded nodule. Dernevik used sutures on the visceral pleura of animals to recreate the lesion of shrinking pleuritis.[36] This is a possible explanation of the pathophysiologic method by which asbestos fibers cause shrinking pleuritis.

Miller describes seven patients in ventilatory failure with severe pleural fibrosis but no evidence of parenchymal involvement. Four died in ventilatory failure. Gallium uptake in the pleura demonstrated active inflammatory process.[42]

Extensive scarring associated with this fourth form of pleural asbestosis results in a severe impairment of lung function. For this reason pleurectomy has been performed on a number of patients with mixed results. Patients with underlying fibrosis in the parenchyma do not experience significant improvement in breathing capacity. Some authors have recommended early pleurectomy in an attempt to preserve lung function before the degree and extent of the scarring becomes severe.[42]

In an experimental study on rabbits, the inflammatory response induced by the presence of asbestos fibers in the pleural space was inhibited by colchicine.[35]

Unfortunately treatment of this type of pleural asbestosis remains experimental, controversial, and limited. As in pleural effusions the possibility of mesothelioma must be considered.

D. PLEURAL ASBESTOSIS AND RESPIRATORY IMPAIRMENT

Radiographic pleural asbestosis in the absence of radiographic evidence of parenchymal disease is associated with significant pulmonary disability. In 1980 Wright described respiratory function in patients who had experienced asbestos pleural effusion noting insidious onset and a tendency to recur.[45] Wright's pleural asbestosis patients had significant shortness of breath with severe pleural thickening but no evidence of parenchymal fibrosis. Pressure volume curves and static recoil pressures showed that the lungs were stiffened by the scar tissue around the lung; hence, greater than normal negative pressure was required to move air into the lung.[45]

Hedenstierna describes reduced vital capacity and diffusion capacity plus small airways dysfunction in a group of patients who had pleural plaques but no evidence of interstitial fibrosis by plain x-ray. This author thought the pulmonary function abnormalities were due to parenchymal asbestosis but the plain x-ray focal point was too wide to see the parenchymal scarring.[46] Frederickson described 45 cases of pleural asbestosis detected at a health screening center, with an average latency of 39 years. Decreased lung volumes and compliance were noted in patients with pleural plaques. The more extensive the pleural fibrosis, the more severe the functional abnormalities.[47]

In another study by Britton, lung function studies in 88 asbestos workers whose chest radiograms showed only pleural changes showed a definite worsening of lung function as their degree of pleural involvement increased. Normal diffusion capacity and normal x-ray including CT scan of the chest are described. Britton concluded that the pleural scarring itself led to decreased vital capacity with resultant disability.[48]

Thirty-seven asbestos workers with diffuse pleural fibrosis were analyzed by McGavin.[49] As the degree of pleural thickening increased, the forced vital capacity decreased with no change in diffusion capacity. McGavin noted the more extensive the pleural involvement, the more severe the decline in forced vital capacity (FVC).

Frederickson and Hedenstierna opine that pleural plaques are a marker of subradiographic parenchymal fibrosis rather than disease arising from pleural scarring per se. Britton and McGavin are of the opposite opinion.

Baker describes 314 members of a sheet metal workers union who had low-level asbestos dust exposure. He found 70% of the workers with more than 30 years of employment had radiographic evidence of pleural disease. As the degree of pleural involvement increased, the forced vital capacity decreased. There was no similar effect on FEV-1 as a percent of forced vital capacity. The functional significance of asbestos-induced pleural disease alone was confirmed in this study. Only 4% of the workers had parenchymal opacities, thus confirming that low-level asbestos exposure leads to a high rate of pleural disease and a low rate of interstitial lung disease by plain x-ray. Dr. Baker could not distinguish between subradiographic interstitial lung disease or pleural fibrosis as the cause for the decreased forced vital capacity.[50]

Pleural plaques and respiratory function were studied by Jarvholn who described 202 non-smoking, low-level asbestos-exposed shipyard workers. Of these, 87 had pleural plaques but no other findings on x-ray. The remaining 115 workers had completely normal chest x-rays. Thirteen of the 87 with pleural plaques had forced vital capacity below reference ranges, and overall the workers with pleural plaques on x-rays had 6.9% lower forced vital capacity than the non-smoking individuals with normal chest x-rays.[51]

Among 200 subjects under the age of 70 with pleural plaques only on their chest x-rays, Hilt found an increased prevalence of breathlessness and lower forced vital capacity compared to a control population. Hilt concluded that pleural plaques alone are an important cause of disability.[52]

Hillerdàl emphasized that severe disability associated with pleural scarring occurs more commonly than has previously been recognized. Benign asbestos pleural effusion was described in 60 patients with several relapses. Even brief remote exposure to asbestos can be associated with the development of pleurisy with resultant fibrosis and significant disability.[34]

As can be seen from these studies, there is controversy among the experts as to the interpretation of abnormal lung function in patients with pleural asbestosis alone. One side maintains that the lung dysfunction indicates that there is subradiographic parenchymal disease. The other side maintains that the lung dysfunction is caused by pleural fibrosis in the absence of parenchymal disease. The work of Picado addresses this debate.

Six subjects with asbestos-related fibrosis of the pleura with the subjective complaint of shortness of breath were studied by Picado with exercise studies.[53] Overall limitation of maximal exercise capacity was noticed. Objective increases in minute ventilation, frequency of breathing, and respiratory flow rates were present. The patient's exercise tidal volume as a percentage of forced vital capacity is decreased. Abnormal dead space/tidal volume ratios during the exercise indicates abnormally high wasted ventilation. Fatigue of the diaphragm or chest wall muscles was ruled out by appropriate studies. The perception of shortness of breath is attributed to an abnormal breathing pattern caused by the pleural fibrosis (see Table 2-3).

Picado's subjects were exercised on a bicycle while O_2 and CO_2 partial pressures were continuously monitored. Ventilation was estimated every 15 seconds. Arterial carbon dioxide tension was estimated from end tidal carbon dioxide tension and a ratio of dead space to tidal volume was calculated. Arterial oxygen saturation was estimated by ear oximetry. The initial workload was 32.8 watts and was increased by a factor of 16.2 watts each minute. Exercise was stopped when the subjects could no longer continue. The patient was then asked to rest and then a second stage steady-state exercise test was performed at two workloads, 30% and 60% of the patient's VO_2 max. On the average, the maximum VT/VC (tidal volume divided by forced vital capacity) ratio was only 0.44

Table 2-3 Pleural Fibrosis and Impaired Exercise Performance

1. Abnormal breathing mechanics.
2. Tidal volume as a present of FVC on exercise is lower than normal 44%, normal 60%–70%.
3. Inspiratory time is shortened due to stiffness of chest wall.
4. High minute volume for the workload due to wasted ventilation, exercise VD/VT of 0.28.
5. Sense of breathlessness out of proportion to reduction in blood gases or oxygen consumption due to chest wall stiffness.

(predicted ratios for normal subjects 0.6–0.7). Tidal volume at peak exercise only reached 64% of predicted. The chest wall stiffness imposed by the pleural thickening led to the abnormal breathing pattern of small tidal volume relative to the forced vital capacity. Exercise dead space to tidal volume ratio (VD/VT) was elevated to an average value of 0.28, which is abnormal, in these six patients, indicating increased wasted ventilation. The amount of ventilation required to maintain a given workload is elevated above normal, again due to wasted ventilation.

In these patients computerized tomography, plain x-rays, and diffusion studies were normal indicating that the pleural fibrosis, not subradiographic parenchymal asbestosis, is the cause of these abnormalities.

Picado's studies give valuable new insight into the mechanism of the subjective complaint of dyspnea or shortness of breath in asbestosis. There are abnormalities in lung breathing mechanics seen only during exercise that can contribute significantly to disability. The debate about whether subradiographic parenchymal fibrosis or pleural fibrosis causes the dysfunction in these cases has been partially answered by Picado and colleagues. More studies of breathing mechanics in predominantly pleural asbestosis are needed.

E. ASBESTOS AND SMALL AIRWAYS DYSFUNCTION

Asbestos-exposed workers may have significant impairment in their lung function and have normal chest x-rays. Numerous studies have indicated that small airways dysfunction is one of the earliest indicators of pulmonary disease. Jodoin studied 24 asbestos workers who had normal plain chest x-rays. Thirteen had normal lung compliance as shown by an increase in the static recoil of the lung tissue. There was a correlation between the duration of exposure and the presence of the abnormal lung compliance. These patients with stiff lungs also had reduced vital capacity compared to normal. Many had reduced peak flow at low lung volumes. This abnormal air flow resistance occurred in the respiratory bronchiole. The findings indicated the presence of functionally significant small airways dysfunction and resultant disability in subradiographic or x-ray negative asbestosis.[54]

Rodriguez-Roisin described pulmonary function changes in 40 x-ray negative asbestos workers. Maximal expiratory flow volume curves were abnormal and correlated with asbestos exposure, not cigarette smoking. Non-smokers had significant impairment of their flow rates from asbestos alone and there was a defect in the smoking asbestos-exposed workers greater than expected from cigarettes alone. These authors recommended that recognizing small airways dysfunction was useful in order to remove workers who were experiencing early defect in lung function from further exposure.[55]

Begin described 17 non-smoking asbestos workers with 28 years average exposure to asbestos who did not have chronic bronchitis or other lung disability. Seven of these workers had x-ray evidence of asbestosis and ten did not. Significantly increased upstream resistance at low lung volumes was present in those with the diagnosis of asbestosis only. The normal chest x-ray group had less small airway dysfunction than the ones with abnormal x-rays. Lung biopsy in three of the patients revealed peribronchial alveolitis and fibrosis confirming the location of the asbestos lesion seen by others. Distortion of airways from parenchymal fibrosis causing dilatation of the larger bronchi was the explanation for the normal flow rates at high lung volumes. The workers who did not yet show asbestosis by x-ray and had normal flow rates had been exposed for a very short time.[56]

Siracusa et al confirmed the presence of asbestos-induced small airways dysfunction by comparing asbestos workers with controls. Even short-term (i.e., less than 10 years) occupational exposure results in significant pulmonary dysfunction. A combination of smoking and asbestos causes a more rapid decline in pulmonary dysfunction. Shortness of breath was significantly higher in the exposed group with more than 5 years of exposure to 2 fibers per cc of ambient air. The pulmonary function test results that indicated the presence of obstruction were raised residual volume and a decrease in the flow rate at 75% of the vital capacity. These workers had exposure to other occupational respiratory irritants as well, making comparisons with other studies somewhat difficult.[57]

Kilburn describes the small airways function in 97 non-smoking insulators, compared to a reference population. Seventy-seven subjects had normal chest x-rays. Seven had parenchymal fibrosis of 1/1 or greater and 13 had pleural asbestosis on plain chest x-ray. Distortion of the small airways (>2 mm) was indicated by the low FEF 25%–75%. Radial traction on the airways over 2 mm in diameter from interstitial fibrosis led to an increase in the flow rate of large airways. A decrease in the flow rate at FEF 75%–85% indicated a lesion in the respiratory bronchiole.[61]

Fifteen out of 45 non-smoking x-ray positive asbestos workers had abnormal maximum mid-expiratory flow rates, MMFR (FEF 25%–75%) in another study.[61]

Pathologic studies have confirmed disease in the small airways. Autopsies on 64 asbestos miners revealed diffuse peribronchial fibrosis and pigmentation in the small airways. In cigarette smokers lung disease, the membranous bronchioles show fibrosis and the respiratory bronchioles are spared, but in asbestosis there is fibrosis in the respiratory and membranous bronchioles. Another study describes Mineral Dust Airway Disease (MDAD) consisting of marked fibrosis and pigmentation of the respiratory (alveolar) bronchioles in 13 of 53 workers with occupational dust exposure (mostly asbestos) and in only 1 out of 121 controls. Age and smoking were adjusted in the two groups. The finding of MDAD is specific to asbestos or other mineral dust exposure.[59]

The pathology and pulmonary function studies reveal that asbestos dust leads to fibrosis in the small airways, predominantly the respiratory bronchioles. This small airway effect probably contributes significantly to the physiologic abnormalities and disability seen in some asbestotics. The detection of changes in small airways should alert the physician that an abnormal process is occurring in the lung even before the chest x-ray is found to be abnormal.

F. RADIOLOGIC TECHNIQUES IN PLEURAL AND PARENCHYMAL ASBESTOSIS

The standard plain chest x-ray is inadequate for documenting asbestosis both because of lack of sensitivity and also because of difficulty in interpretation. Even with ILO standardization, studies of observer variation have proven that there is very poor agreement in reading of plain chest x-ray changes for asbestos.[8]

Rockoff has emphasized the lack of value of plain chest x-rays in diagnosing asbestosis. He noted that interstitial changes in early cases are difficult to distinguish because of the size of the subject, x-ray technique, experience of the reader, and bias of the reader. A very large number of fibrotic lesions are needed to coalesce in order for the plain x-ray to detect their presence.[64]

Rockoff performed a statistical analysis that revealed a 10%–20% likelihood that a chest x-ray would miss significant asbestosis. Epler and Kipen reported numerous cases of severe parenchymal asbestosis with normal plain chest x-rays.[6,7]

Ducatman studied 105,000 x-ray interpretations on asbestos workers and found a 300-fold variation in readings of 1/1 films.

Various readers had a prevalence of 1/1 grade fibrosis ranging from 0.02% to 7.55% on populations with similar incidence of real disease. It is concluded that no decision on presence or absence of asbestosis should rest on a chest x-ray alone.[8]

The frequency and density of abnormal x-ray shadows on plain x-ray in interstitial fibrosis is insufficient to create an abnormal x-ray in many cases. An accurate diagnosis of asbestosis requires a complete history, physical examination, pulmonary function testing including exercise testing. The new imaging techniques such as CT or HRCT may prove a valuable tool in assessing the difficult case.

G. OTHER IMAGING TECHNIQUES

The chest x-ray as a tool for diagnosis of asbestosis is insensitive as shown by the studies cited above. The introduction of high resolution computerized tomography (HRCT) and regular CT scanning may be helpful in resolving the presence or absence of asbestosis in a given case.[31,62,63]

Friedman described the use of HRCT scanning in 60 workers who had occupational exposure to asbestos. HRCT of the lung is an advancement from regular computerized tomography because it involves taking thinner slices and thus increasing the accuracy of detecting small abnormalities in the lung tissue and pleura. All of Friedman's cases showed pleural plaques or thickening on plain x-ray. They found 17 out of 60 had pleural fat to explain the pleural shadows seen on plain film. In 14 cases with parenchymal asbestosis by plain film, the HRCT scan found the scars and shadows to be caused by other diseases. Two cases with negative plain x-ray for parenchymal disease were found to have interstitial fibrosis.[63]

Aberle studied the comparison between HRCT and regular CT scanning and found a HRCT to be significantly more accurate in distinguishing shadows caused by emphysema, focal inflammatory disease, and pleural plaques.

Curvilinear subpleural lines, thickened interlobular septal and intralobular core lines, subpleural non-specific density, parenchymal bands, and honeycombing are the five features (see Table 2-4) compatible with but not pathognomonic of parenchymal asbestosis. A history of exposure and other confirmation are necessary in order to finalize the diagnosis of asbestosis. For example, fibrosing alveolitis could cause similar HRCT changes. A history of asbestos exposure or the presence of asbestos fibers in tissue or

Table 2-4 Changes on High Resolution Computerized Tomography (HRCT) in Asbestosis

1. Curvilinear sub-pleural lines
2. Thickened interlobular septal and intralobular core lines
3. Subpleural (non-specific) density
4. Parenchymal bands
5. Honeycombing

sputum is necessary in order to distinguish the cause of these changes.[62]

Sargent describes the use of regular CT scanning to distinguish pleural asbestosis from pleural thickening due to adipose tissue, noting the need for computerized tomography whenever there is doubt about the cause of pleural shadows.[31]

H. CIGARETTE SMOKING AND ASBESTOSIS

The effect of cigarette smoking on the development of pulmonary fibrosis in asbestos workers remains controversial with some studies reporting increased rates of pulmonary fibrosis in cigarette smokers and other studies reporting no difference between smokers and non-smokers. In 1967 Weiss reported on a population survey of 999 persons. He found 4.2% (23/552) prevalence of pulmonary fibrosis (i.e., increased markings on 70 mm x-ray film) among cigarette smokers and a 1.5% (6/393) prevalence in a never-smoked population.[65] In 1971 he reported the age-adjusted prevalence of x-ray pulmonary fibrosis present in smoking asbestos textile workers as 40%, while only 24% of the non-smokers had increased lung shadows, suggesting an adverse effect on the chests x-ray findings of smoking.[66]

Weiss later wrote a review article on cigarettes and asbestos and concluded that the effect of cigarettes was additive to asbestos in producing parenchymal fibrosis. The cigarette smoke was thought to inhibit normal clearing mechanisms, leading to a larger internal dose. Weiss notes the lack of good external dose data in all of the studies to date and recommends more study of the question.[67]

Samet studied 383 asbestos workers and found no increase in x-ray evidence of fibrosis among smokers. Unexpectedly the non-smokers had more rapid decline in lung function. The authors speculate that the more severely affected non-smokers may have been exposed to more asbestos.[67]

Another study from Great Britain evaluated 1,009 shipyard

workers and noted that all workers with parenchymal asbestosis had been or were cigarette smokers but the numbers of non-smokers was too small to be conclusive.[68]

In an editorial in 1981, Kilburn noted the lack of firm evidence for increased pulmonary fibrosis in smokers.[69] Pearle studied 131 shipyard workers and concluded that cigarette smoking caused greater deficits in forced vital capacity, forced expiratory volume diffusion capacity, and pleural disease but had no influence on the prevalence of parenchymal fibrosis, but the numbers in each group were too small to be definitive. Asbestos exposure in Pearle's study was not assessed except by noting years of work in the shipyard.[70]

Sue studied 73 smoking and 73 never-smoking shipyard workers. The never-smoked group had slightly higher forced vital capacity, forced expiratory volume at one second (FEV_1), and diffusion capacity. Maximal oxygen (O_2) uptake and oxygen pulse was lower in smokers. The cause for impairment of O_2 uptake was cardiac disease in 16 of 33 smokers. Obstructive lung disease, rather than asbestosis, reduced O_2 consumption in 2 smoking workers. No data on asbestos exposure differences among the workers makes these conclusions difficult to interpret but do confirm a probable additive adverse effect of asbestos and cigarette smoking on exercise capacity.[71]

A 1988 autopsy study on 487 asbestos miners revealed no increase in the rate of histologic asbestosis among cigarette smokers. In reviewing the x-rays taken before death, more irregular opacities were seen in the smokers. Hnizdo and Sluis-Cremer conclude that smoking causes increased shadows on x-ray that are wrongly interpreted as being due to asbestosis.[72]

I. PARENCHYMAL ASBESTOSIS AND RESPIRATORY IMPAIRMENT

Parenchymal asbestosis is a diffuse pulmonary fibrosis of the lung parenchyma. It can present in a severe form without x-ray evidence of fibrosis[6,7] or present with classical x-ray changes. Chest x-rays are an insensitive method of detecting early parenchymal asbestosis. Almost all studies of asbestosis indicate a decline in forced vital capacity and gas exchanging capacity even before breathlessness or x-ray abnormalities are noted. Table 2-5 summarizes data from seven different studies.

Even resting pulmonary function tests may not adequately demonstrate early abnormalities. It may be necessary to perform exercise testing in order to detect abnormalities or to differentiate

Table 2-5 Asbestosis and Pulmonary Function Tests

	Number of Subjects	Decreased Vital Capacity	Abnormal Arterial Oxygen Exercise	Abnormal Wasted Ventilation on Exericse	Abnormal Diffusion Capacity	Correlation Fibrosis on Chest X-ray
Wright[45]	57	Yes	Yes	Yes	—	No
Bader[7]	598	Yes	Yes	Yes	Yes	No*
Williams[76]	38	Yes	—	Yes	Yes	Yes
Arzt[89]	195	Yes	Yes	Yes	—	No
Mai-Ling[90]	155	Yes	—	Yes	Yes	Yes
Wollmer[92]	137	Yes	Yes	—	—	No
Sue[93]	276	No	Yes	Yes	No	No

* Delayed 10–15 years

disability arising from asbestosis versus disability arising from other disease processes.

Early studies described patients with asbestosis. On the initial examination normal or slightly reduced FVC was seen but exercise testing showed distinct abnormalities indicative of mechanical changes in lung tissue. The physiologic changes will precede chest x-ray abnormalities.[73,74] Bader and colleagues described reduced forced vital capacity and abnormal arterial oxygen exchange due to "alveolar-capillary" block syndrome as the typical abnormality in asbestos. A poor correlation between chest x-ray abnormalities and the degree of physiologic impairment was seen.[74]

Later, Bader describes spirometric and x-ray changes among 598 actively employed insulation workers. The data supports a relationship between years of exposure to asbestos dust and the incidence of pulmonary function abnormalities. The higher asbestos exposures caused a greater decrement in forced vital capacity. Serial measurements of forced vital capacity will detect damage to lung tissue before the chest x-ray becomes abnormal. Pleural fibrosis without parenchymal involvement was the cause of impairment of forced vital capacity in 37%. Only 23% of insulation workers with reduced forced vital capacity had either pleural or parenchymal fibrosis by plain x-ray. Conversely, 16.8% of the workers had parenchymal fibrosis and normal vital capacity. Only a small percentage of the workers had evidence of obstructive airway disease as shown by a reduced FEV-1/FVC ratio indicating a minor contribution to pulmonary dysfunction from cigarette smoking. Bader concluded that chest x-rays are an insensitive method of detecting early asbestosis in this group of working men. The forced vital capacity on a serial basis detected disease before the patients experienced symptoms and before the chest x-ray becomes abnormal. In the workers with over 40 years of exposure, the rate of x-ray abnormality correlated with functional abnormality. In the 40+ year group, chest x-ray may be a useful tool for detecting fibrosis but in earlier years the chest x-ray cannot be used alone. In the first 20 years the forced vital capacity abnormalities were relatively common, about 30% of the workers have reduced forced vital capacity; yet only a few have abnormal x-rays[75] (see Table 2-6). The chest becomes abnormal 10–15 years *after* the pulmonary functions are abnormal. Thirty years after onset of exposure the chest x-ray and pulmonary function will correlate.[69]

Williams' studies on workers with asbestosis found diffusion capacity to be reduced as an early and sensitive indicator of pul-

Table 2-6 Exposure Pulmonary Chest

Years of Exposure	Abnormal Function Tests	Abnormal of Parenchymal Asbestosis
0–4	0	0
5–9	28%	2%
10–19	32%	3%
20–29	42%	21%
39–39	48%	42%
40+	47%	54%

monary dysfunction. A good correlation between chest x-ray abnormality and the degree of pulmonary impairment was seen in this study. Furthermore, the degree of dyspnea is also correlated with a decline in diffusion capacity. He concludes that diffusion capacity is useful in detecting the presence of asbestos-induced lung abnormality.[76]

Becklake describes 1,069 asbestos miners without parenchymal fibrosis on x-ray. Slight reductions in forced vital capacity and exercise minute ventilation compared to normal were present. The increased minute ventilation reflected ventilation-perfusion mismatching and is compatible with the studies of others that showed increased wasted ventilation in asbestosis. Becklake found forced vital capacity to be the most practical and sensitive test. Forced vital capacity declines significantly before there are parenchymal x-ray changes. Diffusion capacity was not significantly reduced in these x-ray negative asbestos miners. In those with only pleural fibrosis, there was a decrease in diffusion capacity, lung volumes, and flow rates even in the cases with parietal pleural involvement without visceral adhesions. As the parenchymal changes appear on the plain x-ray, the forced vital capacity and ventilation abnormalities worsened.[77]

Leathart reports clinical experience with a group of asbestos workers that emphasizes the progressive loss of lung function even after removal from exposure has occurred. Leathart believed the serial diffusion capacity would probably turn out to be a useful test for early diagnosis of asbestosis. He noted that rales in the lungs sometimes preceded a significant drop in the diffusion capacity and could also be an early warning sign.[78]

Zeda utilized diffusion capacity at rest and during exercise. This technique detected important physiologic impairment in asbestos-exposed workers who had normal chest x-rays.[79]

Murphy opined that the forced vital capacity and diffusion

capacity are sufficient to detect advanced cases of asbestosis. An annual incidence of 1.1% of severe, x-ray positive asbestosis is expected in a group of low-level asbestos-exposed workers such as shipyard workers. Medical surveillance of asbestos-exposed workers should include the following: physical examination for rales, spirometry for forced vital capacity, single breath carbon monoxide test for decreased diffusion capacity, and history for presence of breathlessness. Workers found to be suffering from definite early asbestosis by these parameters should be removed from further exposure because they are more susceptible to damage from continued exposure.[24]

Weill describes low-level asbestos-exposed asbestos-cement workers with small airway impairment and decreased forced vital capacity before chest x-rays become abnormal. He recommends serial physical examinations and spirometry for the same reason as Murphy. Cigarette smoking had little effect on the physiologic derangements in this study.[80]

Pearle describes x-ray positive asbestosis prevalence of 2.3% among 88 shipyard workers evaluated for the U.S. government because of breathlessness and fear of asbestosis. Exercise testing was found to be essential in order to differentiate asbestosis from other causes of exercise impairment, such as cigarette-induced obstructive lung disease.[81]

Ohlson describes low-level asbestos-exposed workers and concluded there was only a minor decrease in lung function, but this group were studied after a short latency. A statistically significant but small decrease in forced vital capacity was noted. The average decrease in forced vital capacity of 55 ml per year was elevated above normal. The presence of pleural plaques on chest x-ray did not increase the forced vital capacity abnormality versus those that had normal chest x-rays.[82]

In an Italian study low-level asbestos-exposed workers experienced a serial decline in forced vital capacity that increased with the number of years from onset of exposure. With less than 15 years from onset of exposure, the decline in forced vital capacity averaged 24 ml per year and in workers with more than 15 years from onset of exposure, they averaged a 52 ml per year decline in forced vital capacity. Cigarette smoking did not have *any* effect on the forced vital capacity decline.[83]

Ohlson's follow-up study noting forced vital capacity averaged 7% less in exposed workers when compared to the reference population. There was no evidence of parenchymal asbestosis and the presence of pleural plaques did not correlate with pulmonary function impairment.[84]

Lerman studied insulation workers' symptoms and noted a high percentage with dyspnea on exertion. The physical examination revealed many cases with rales. Cigarette smoking did not cause an increased prevalence of shortness of breath or rales.[85]

In the pulmonary function studies by Lerman, forced vital capacity was significantly decreased. Cigarettes did not cause any increase in the abnormalities on forced vital capacity but did have a noticeable effect on a reduction in forced expiratory volume at 1 second (FEV_1). Host factors are important since 46% of these insulation workers have normal forced vital capacity 30 years after the onset of exposure.[86]

Siracusa notes a decline in forced vital capacity that correlates with a degree of low-level asbestos exposure. Cessation of asbestos exposure for 10 years did not change the decline in lung function indicating that the changes induced by asbestos continue even when exposure ceases. Heavy cigarette smokers had a lower forced vital capacity and FEV_1.[87]

Oren describes the need for exercise testing in order to separate the effects of asbestos-induced restrictive disease as a cause of work impairment versus cigarette effects.[88]

Arzt describes forced vital capacity and arterial oxygen level as good indicators of the presence of asbestosis. Arzt found lung compliance to be useful in distinguishing those patients that had fibrosis affecting the parenchyma versus those who had fibrosis affecting the pleura. If the patients had only scar tissue involving the pleura, they would have a decline in forced vital capacity, but their compliance studies would be normal. Arzt found a statistically significant decline in forced vital capacity in patients with pleural disease only. Exercise blood gas measurement is useful in estimating degree of impairment. The serial changes in forced vital capacity is a sensitive indicator of parenchymal and pleural fibrosis.[89]

Mai-Ling describes Chinese asbestos workers with normal chest x-rays who had a decline in forced vital capacity correlated to their asbestos exposure. As the magnitude of the parenchymal asbestosis increases or more time passes, the chest x-rays become abnormal. Longitudinal studies by Mai-Ling revealed that serial declines in forced vital capacity occurred as a sensitive index of exposure. The higher the level of exposure, the more rapid the decline in forced vital capacity. Low-level asbestos exposure causes an average decline of 52 ml per year in forced vital capacity. Heavy dust exposure was associated with 84 ml per year decline.[90] Non-exposed controls experienced a 30 ml forced vital capacity yearly decline that is similar to other reports of normal annual decline in forced vital capacity of 18-33 ml (see Table 2-7).

Table 2-7 Annual Average Decline in Forced Vital Capacity (FVC) in Asbestosis

	Low Dust Exp.	High Dust Exp.	Normal
Mai-Ling[90]	52 ml	84 ml	30 ml
Siracusa[83]	54 ml*	N/A	20 ml
Ohlson[82]	55 ml	N/A	20 ml

* After 15 years latency.

Wollmer studied 137 workers with low-level asbestos exposure. The authors selected workers with normal chest x-rays and either shortness of breath, rales in their chest, or forced vital capacity below 80% of predicted. A high percentage of these patients had abnormal compliance of their lung as well as reduced arterial oxygen levels upon exercise. The abnormalities were greater in cigarette smokers. The decreased exercise capacity is mainly due to the air flow obstruction associated with tobacco consumption and that asbestos exposure by itself does not cause a significant decline in exercise ability.[92]

A research group in California studied a volunteer group of shipyard workers with possible low-level asbestos exposure who were self-selected on the basis of breathlessness. Some of these workers had reduced exercise capacity that the authors attribute most often as due to cigarette induced obstructive disease or cardiac dysfunction.[71,88]

Sue et al reported additional data on the same group of shipyard workers. The gas exchange abnormalities (see Table 2-8) are present in many cases within normal diffusion studies. The authors conclude that diffusion capacity and chest x-rays are of limited value in predicting significant abnormalities of gas exchange on exercise. Chest x-ray and diffusion capacity were usually normal in cases of significant abnormalities in gas exchange not always due to asbestosis.[93] Epler reported on 44 patients with

Table 2-8 Signs of Abnormality of Gas Exchange on Exercise in Parenchymal Asbestosis[58]

1. Decline in arterial oxygen or $PaO_2 < 80$ mmHg.
2. Widening of P(A-a) O_2 gradient above 35.
3. Arterial pCO_2 minus end-tidal CO_2 above zero. (P(a-ET) $CO_2 > 70$)
4. Wasted ventilation on exercise (V_D/V_T above 0.30).

severe interstitial fibrosis on biopsy who had normal plain chest x-rays. Six of the 44 had asbestosis.[6]

Kipen reported on 25 cases with significant histologic evidence of asbestosis but normal chest x-rays. The study describes 9.6% of patients with all types of severe interstitial fibrosis who had normal chest x-rays. Among asbestosis they noted 18% are x-ray negative.[7]

Becklake reviews the literature with 231 references in 1976. In combining her extensive experience with a detailed review of the literature, she concluded on page 207:

> The important conclusion for clinical practice that in the individual case, disability cannot be predicted with reliability from symptoms, function, or radiographic changes. It should therefore be evaluated by appropriate exercise tests, if necessary at more than one load, for each case individually.[93]

Wright noted in 1955 the poor correlation between x-ray, resting spirometry, and asbestosis and recommended exercise testing. It is still apparent that exercise testing is necessary to assess pulmonary impairment in asbestosis.

J. PUBLISHED CRITERIA FOR DIAGNOSIS OF PARENCHYMAL ASBESTOSIS

Murphy describes a criteria for making a diagnosis of asbestosis.

1. The history of significant exposure to asbestos.
2. A forced vital capacity of less than 80% of predicted.
3. A chest x-ray showing a degree of parenchymal fibrosis of 2/1 (ILO/UC classification) or greater.
4. A diffusion capacity that is less than 80% of predicted.

If the patient has three of the four criteria, they would be considered to have asbestosis.[24]

Selikoff and Lee's textbook gives more general criteria for the diagnosis. A history of exposure of sufficient duration (i.e., more than a few months of heavy exposure) followed by adequate latency (i.e., more than 10 years from the onset of exposure) with typical changes, either by x-ray or pulmonary function, of interstitial fibrosis and no other cause, makes the diagnosis. Demonstrating asbestos fibers in the tissues or in the sputum is a method of confirming exposure. If lung tissue were available for examination, certain characteristic changes in the pathologic picture are indicative of asbestosis (i.e., peribronchial fibrosis and asbestos bodies or fibers in the tissue).[5]

Parkes describes the criteria for diagnosis in his textbook to include a history of exposure; the presence of pleural plaques on x-ray or asbestos bodies in the sputum; dyspnea on exertion; persistent basal crepitations with or without clubbing; appearance on the chest x-ray compatible with diffuse interstitial fibrosis; and finally reduction below normal in either forced vital capacity, total lung capacity, or diffusion capacity. In early stages of the disease, the patient may not have very much dyspnea on exertion nor abnormal chest x-ray. Rales (crepitations) at the end of inspiration are felt to be the earliest sign by Pares.[1]

In the text by Cotes and Steel they list their criteria for parenchymal asbestosis a history of exposure; fine basilar rales (i.e., crepitations); reduced lung distensibility or reduced diffusion capacity; and abnormal chest x-ray. All are required to be present for diagnosis! Cotes feels that a history of heavy asbestos exposure for 2 years is more convincing although shorter exposure is possible. At least 10 years should have elapsed from the onset of exposure before the disease was manifest noting that only rarely do shorter latencies result in disease. All other causes of the patient's abnormal pulmonary function should be excluded.[2]

The American Thoracic Society ad hoc committee on Asbestosis recognized the problem of using conventional techniques for definitive diagnosis of asbestosis and therefore gave very loose and general guidelines for the doctor to follow. The primary criteria is history of exposure with sufficient latency. The diagnosis of asbestosis should be based on physical findings, pulmonary function, and plain x-rays. Exercise testing was not considered and pleural fibrosis was ignored.[3]

K. CONCLUSIONS

1. Asbestos-exposed, susceptible persons will experience subradiographic peribronchial fibrosis and pleural scarring within a few years after onset of exposure. There will be a decline in forced vital capacity and other pulmonary function parameters usually 10–15 years before x-ray changes or significant symptoms appear. Even very low-level and brief asbestos exposure is associated with significant, progressive decline in the lung function even after exposure ceases.

2. In medical surveillance, forced vital capacity on a serial basis is a sensitive and economical indicator of early disease.

3. In assessing disability, plain chest x-ray, resting spirome-

try, and diffusion studies alone will miss many cases of asbestosis or misdiagnose other conditions.

4. Exercise ventilation and blood gas studies are necessary to detect significant asbestos-induced physiologic impairment and exclude other causes of breathlessness such as cardiac disease or obstructive lung disease. A complete history, physical examination, chest x-rays, spirometry, diffusion exercise, ventilation, and blood gas studies are needed in order to detect and accurately measure effects of asbestos on lung function.

5. The usual published criteria for parenchymal asbestosis is not relevant to partial disability or subradiographic cases.

6. Pleural asbestosis can cause significant disability in some cases. Persons with only pleural abnormalities should be assessed by appropriate exercise studies to detect the adverse effect on the mechanics of breathing.

7. High resolution computerized tomography (HRCT) can improve the accuracy and sensitivity in assessing pleural and parenchymal asbestosis.

REFERENCES

1. Gloag, D., "Asbestos—Can It Be Used Safely?", British Medical Journal, 282:551–553, 1981.
2. Parkes, W.R. Editor, Occupational Lung Disorders, Butterworths, London, 1974.
3. Cotes, J.E. and Steel, J., Work Related Lung Disorders, publisher Blackwell, Yearbook Medical Publishers, London, Boston, Palo Alto, 1987.
4. Murphy, R. L. et al, The Diagnosis of Non-Malignant Diseases Related to Asbestos, Am. Rev. Resp. Dis., 134:363–368, 1986.
5. Selikoff and Lee, Asbestos and Disease, Academic Press, New York, 1978.
6. Epler, G.R. et al, Normal Chest Roentgenograms in Chronic Diffuse Infiltrative Lung Disease, NEJM, 298:934–939, 1978.
7. Kipen, H.M. et al, Pulmonary HIstopathologic Evaluation, British Journal of Industrial Medicine, 44:96–100, 1987.
8. Ducatman, A.M., "B-Readers" and Asbestos Medical Surveillance, J.O.M., 30:644–647, 1988.
9. Bohlig, H. et al, Developmental, Radiological Zone Patterns and Importance of Diffuse Pleural Thickening in Relation to Occupational Exposure to Asbestosis, British Journal of Industrial Medicine, 44:673–681, 1987.
10. Selikoff, I.J., The Occurrence of Pleural Calcification Among Asbestos Insulation Workers, Ann. N.Y. Acad. Sci., 132:351–367, 1965.
11. Selikoff, I.J., "Asbestosis Disease in the United States 1918–1975", Rev. Fr. Mal. Resp., Supplement One, 4:7–24, 1976.
12. Begin, R. et al, Asbestos Exposure and Retention as Determinants of Airways Disease and Asbestos Alveolitis, Am. Rev. Resp. Dis., 134:1176–1181, 1986.
13. Anderson, H.A.R., Household Neoplastic Risk, Annals of New York Academy of Sciences, 271:311, 1976.
14. Anderson, H.A., Asbestosis Among Household Contacts of Asbestos Factory Workers, Annals of New York Academy of Sciences, 330:387–399, 1979.

15. Epler, G.R., Asbestos Related Disease from Household Exposure, Respiration, 39:229–240, 1980.
16. Kilburn, K.H., Pulmonary Functional Impairment and Symptoms in Women in Los Angeles Harbor Area, American Journal of Medicine, 79:23–28, 1985.
17. Sider, L. et al, Changes on Radiographs of Wives of Workers Exposed to Asbestos, Radiology, 164:723–726, 1987.
18. Kilburn, K.H., Asbestos Diseases and Pulmonary Symptoms and Signs in Shipyard Workers and Their Families in Los Angeles, Archives of Internal Medicine, 146:2213–2220, 1986.
19. Lorimer, W.V., Asbestos Exposure of Brake Repair Workers in the United States, Mt. Sinai Journal of Medicine, 43:207–218, 1976).
20. Castleman, B., Public Health Reports, 90:254–256, 1975.
21. Rohl, A.N., Asbestos Exposure During Brake Lining Maintenance and Repair, Environmental Research, 12:110–128, 1976.
22. Hickish, D.E. and Knight, K.L., Exposure to Asbestos During Brake Maintenance, Ann. Occup. Hyg., 13:17–21, 1970.
23. Cheng, V.K.I. and O'Kelly, F.J., Asbestos Exposure in Motor Vehicle Repair and Servicing Industry in Hong Kong, J. Soc. Occup. Med., 36:104–106, 1986.
24. Marcus, K. et al, Asbestos-Associated Lung Effect in Car Mechanics, SC and J Work Environ., Health, 13:252–254, 1987.
24. Murphy, R.L.H., et al, Diagnosis of Asbestosis—Observations from a Longitudinal Survey of Shipyard Pipe Coverers, American Journal of Medicine, 65:488–498, 1978.
25. Selikoff, I.J., Asbestos Disease in U.S. Shipyards, Ann. N.Y. Acad. Sci., 330:295–311, 1979.
26. Hillerdal, G., Non-Malignant and Asbestos Pleural Disease, Thorax, 36:669–675, 1981.
27. Hillerdal, G. and Lindgren, A., Pleural Plaques: Correlation of Autopsy Findings to Radiographic Findings and Occupation History, Eur. J. Resp. Dis., 61:315–319, 1980.
28. Hilt et al, Asbestos Related Findings from Chest Radiographs of the Male Population of the County of Telemark, Norway—A Cross Sectional Study, Scandinavian Journal of Work, Environmental Health, 12:567–573, 1986.
29. Londorf, E., Radiological Evaluation of Early Pleural and Pulmonary Changes in Light Asbestos Exposure, European Journal of Respiratory Disease, 70:145–149, 1987.
29. Gilson, J.C., Asbestos Health Hazards: Recent Observations in the United Kingdom. Proceedings of International Conf. on Pneumoconiosis, Johannesburg, South Africa, London: Oxford University Press, 1969.
30. Albelda, S.M., et al, Pleural Thickening: Its Significance and Relationship to Asbestos Dust Exposure, Am. Rev. Resp. Dis., 126:621–624, 1982.
31. Sargent, E.N. et al, Subpleural Fat in Patients Exposed to Asbes-

tos: Distinction from Non-Calcified Pleural Plaques, Radiology, 152:273–277, 1984.

32. ILO Guidelines for Use of ILO International Classification of Radiographs of Pneumoconioses, Rev. ed., Safety and Health Series No. 22 (rev. 80), General International Labor Office, 1980.
33. Epler, Prevalence and Incidence of Benign Asbestos Pleural Effusion in Working Population, JAMA, 247:617–622, 1982.
34. Hillerdal, G., Benign Asbestos Pleural Effusion: 73 Exudates in 60 Patients, European Journal of Respiratory Disease, 71:113–121, 1987.
34. Gaensler, E.A. and Kaplan, A.I., Asbestos Pleural Effusion, Ann. Int. Med. 74:178–191, 1971.
35. Shore, B.L., Benign Asbestos Pleurisy in the Rabbit, A Model for the Study of Pathogenesis, American Review of Respiratory Disease, 128:481–485, 1983.
35. MacKenzie, FAF, Changing Attitudes of the Diagnosis of Asbestos Disease, Journal of the Royal Naval Medical Service, 56:116–123, 1970.
36. Dernevik, L., Pathogenesis of Shrinking Pleuritis with Atelectasis—Rounded Atelectasis, European Journal of Respiratory Disease, 71:244–249, 1987.
37. Gaensler, E.A., Thoracic Surgical Problems in Asbestos-Related Disorders, Annals of Thoracic Surgery, 40:82–96, 1985.
38. Lilis, R., Asbestosis: Interstitial Pulmonary Fibrosis and Pleural Fibrosis in Asbestos Insulation Workers: Influence of Cigarette Smoking, American Journal of Industrial Medicine, 10:459–470, 1986.
39. Londorf, E., Radiological Evaluation of Early Pleural and Pulmonary Changes in Light Asbestos Exposure, European Journal of Respiratory Disease, 70:145–149, 1987.
40. Mattson, S. B., Monosymptomatic Exudative Effusion in Persons Exposed to Asbestos Dust, Scandinavian Journal of Respiratory Disease, 56:263–272, 1975.
41. Navratil, M. and Dobias, J., Development of Pleural Hyalinosis in Long Term Studies of Persons Exposed to Asbestos Dust, Environ. Res., 6:455–472, 1973.
42. Miller, A., Ventilatory Failure Due to Asbestos Pleurisy, American Journal of Medicine, 75:911–919, 1983.
43. Collins, T.F.V., Pleural Reaction Associated with Asbestos Exposure, British Journal of Radiology, 41:655–661, 1968.
44. Sluis-Cremer, J.K. and Webster, I., Acute Pleurisy in Asbestos Exposed Persons, Environ. Res., 5:380–392, 1972.
45. Wright, P.H., Respiratory Function After Asbestos Pleurisy, Thorax, 35:31–36, 1980.
46. Hedenstierna, G., et al, Pleural Plaques and Lung Function in Construction Workers Exposed to Asbestos, European Journal of Respiratory Disease, 62:111–122, 1981.
47. Frederickson, H.V., Increased Lung Stiffness in Persons with

Pleural Plaques, European Journal of Respiratory Disease, 62:412–424, 1981.

48. Britton, N.G., Asbestos Pleural Disease, British Journal of Diseases of the Chest, 76:1–10, 1982.
49. McGavin, C.R. et al, Diffuse Pleural Thickening in Asbestos Workers, Disability and Lung Function Abnormalities, Thorax, 39:604–607, 1984.
50. Baker, E.L., Respiratory Illness in the Construction Trade, The Significance of Asbestos Associated with Pleural Disease Among Sheet Metal Workers, Journal of Occupational Medicine, 27:483–489, 1985.
51. Jarvholn, B., Pleural Plaques and Respiratory Function, American Journal of Industrial Medicine, 10:419–426, 1986.
52. Hilt, B., Lung Function and Respiratory Symptoms in Subjects with Asbestos-Related Disorders, a Cross-Sectional Study, American Journal of Industrial Medicine, 11:517–528, 1987.
53. Picado, C., Mechanisms Affecting Exercise Performance in Subjects with Asbestos-Related Pleural Fibrosis, Lung, 165:35–37, 1987.
54. Jodoin, G. et al, Early Effects of Asbestos Exposure on Lung Function, American Review of Respiratory Disease, 104:525–535.
55. Gaensler, E.A. and Kaplan, A.I., Asbestos Pleural Effusion, Ann. Int. Med., 74:178–191, 1971.
55. Rodriguez-Roisin, R. et al, Maximal Expiratory Flow Volume Curves in Workers Exposed to Asbestos, Respiration, 39:158–165, 1980.
56. Begin R. et al, Airway Function in Lifetime Non-Smoking Older Asbestos Workers, American Journal of Medicine, 75:631–638, 1983.
57. Siracusa, A. et al, Small Airway Disease After Short Term Occupational Asbestos Exposure, Med. Lav., 74:13–22, 1983.
58. Wright, J.L. and Churg, A., Severe Diffuse Small Airways Abnormalities in Long Term Chrysotile Asbestos Miners, British Journal of Industrial Medicine, 42:556–559, 1985.
59. Churg, A. et al, Small Airways Disease in Mineral Dust Exposure, Prevalent Structure and Function, American Review of Respiratory Disease, 131:139–143, 1985.
60. Kilburn, K.H. et al, Airways Disease in Non-Smoking Asbestos Workers, Archives of Environmental Health, 40:293–295, 1985.
61. Mohsenifar, Z. et al, Asbestos in Air Flow Limitation, Journal of Occupational Medicine, 28:817–820, 1986.
62. Aberle, D.R. et al, Asbestos Related Pleural and Parenchymal Fibrosis: Detection of High Resolution CT, Radiology, 166:729–734, 1988.
63. Friedman, A.C. et al, Asbestos Related Pleural Disease in Asbestosis: A Comparison to CT and Chest Radiology, AGR, 150:269–275, 1988.
64. Rockoff, D.S. and Schawartz, A., Roentgenographic Underesti-

mation of Early Asbestosis by International Labor Organization Classification, Chest, 93:1088–1091, 1988.
65. Weiss, W.. Cigarette Smoking and Diffuse Pulmonary Fibrosis, Arch. Environ. Health, 14:564–568, 1967.
66. Weiss, W., Cigarette Smoking, Asbestos and Pulmonary Fibrosis, Am. Rev. Resp. Dis., 104:223–227, 1971.
67. Samet, J.M. et al, Absence of Synergism Between Exposure to Asbestos and Cigarette Smoking in Asbestosis, Amer. Rev. Resp. Dis., 120:75–82, 1979.
67. Weiss, W. Cigarette Smoke, Asbestos, and Small Irregular Opacities, Am. Rev. Resp. Dis, 130:293–301, 1984.
68. McMillan, G.H.G., Effect of Smoking on Attack Rates of Pulmonary and Pleural Lesions Related to Exposure to Asbestos Dust, Brit. J. Ind. Med., 37:268–272, 1980.
69. Kilburn, K.H., Cigarette Smoking Does Not Produce or Enhance the Radiographic Appearance of Pulmonary Fibrosis, Am. J. Ind. Med., 2:305–308, 1981.
70. Pearle, J.L., Smoking and Duration of Asbestos Exposure in the Production of Functional and Roentgenographic Abnormalities in Shipyard Workers, J.O.M., 24:370–40, 1982.
71. Sue, D.Y., Lung Function and Exercise Performance in Smoking and Non-Smoking Asbestos-Exposed Workers, American Review of Respiratory Disease, 132:612–618, 1985.
72. Hnizdo, E. and Sluis-Cremer, G.K., Effect of Tobacco Smoke on the Presence of Asbestosis at Post Mortem and on the Reading of Irregular Opacities on Roentgenograms in Asbestos-Exposed Workers, Am. Rev. Resp. Dis., 138:1207–1212, 1988.
73. Wright, G.W., Functional Abnormalities of Industrial Pulmonary Fibrosis, Archives of Industrial Health, 11:196–203, 1955.
74. Bader, M.E. et al, Asbestosis of the Lung, American Journal of Medicine, 30:235–242, 1961.
75. Bader, M.E. et al, Pulmonary Function and Radiographic Changes in 598 Workers with Varying Degrees of Exposure to Asbestos, Journal of Mt. Sinai Hospital, 37:492–500, 1970.
76. Williams, R. and Hugh-Jones, P., Significance of Lung Function Changes in Asbestosis, Thorax, 15:109–119, 1960.
77. Becklake, M.R., Lung Function in Relation to Chest Radiographic Changes in Quebec Asbestos Workers, Bulle. Physio-path Resp., 6:637–659, 1970.
78. Leathart, G.L., Pulmonary Function Tests in Asbestos Workers, Trans. Soc. Occup. Med., 18:49–55, 1968.
79. Zeda, S., et al, Lung Function in Relation to Radiographic Changes in Asbestos Workers, Respiration, 30:132–140, 1973.
80. Weill, H., Lung Function Consequences of Dust Exposure in Asbestos Cement Manufacturing Plants, Archives of Environmental Health, 30:88–97, 1975.
81. Pearle, J., Exercise Performance in Functional Impairment in Asbestos-Exposed Workers, Chest:701–705, 1981.

82. Ohlson, C.G., et al, Decreased Lung Function in Long Term Asbestos Cement Workers, a Cross Sectional Study, American Journal of Industrial Medicine, 5:359–366, 1984.
83. Siracusa, A., Lung Function Among Asbestos Cement Factory Workers, A Cross Sectional and Longitudinal Study, American Journal of Industrial Medicine, 5:315–325, 1984.
84. Ohlson, C.G. et al, Ventilatory Decrements in Former Asbestos Cement Workers, A Four-Year Follow-Up, British Journal of Industrial Medicine, 42:612–616, 1985.
85. Lerman, Y. et al, American Journal of Industrial Medicine, 10:449–458, 1986.
86. Lerman, Y., Spirometric Abnormalities Among Asbestos Insulation Workers, Journal of Occupational Medicine, 30:228–233, 1988.
87. Siracusa, A., An Eleven-Year Longitudinal Study of Occupational Dust Exposure and Lung Function of PVC's, Cement and Asbestos Cement Factory Workers, Scandinavian Journal of Work Environmental Health, 14:181–188, 1988.
88. Oren, A., The Role of Exercise Testing Impairment Evaluation, American Review of Respiratory Disease, 135:230–235, 1987.
89. Arzt, G.H., Review of Lung Function Data in 195 Patients with Asbestosis of the Lung, International Archives of Occupational Environmental Health, 45:63–79, 1980.
90. Mai-Ling, W. and Pei-Lian, L., Lung Function Studies of Asbestos Workers, Scandinavian Journal of Work Environmental Health, 11:Supplement 4, 34–42, 1985.
91. Hansen, J.E. and Wasserman, K., Disability Evaluation, Murray, J.F. ed., Textbook of Respiratory Medicine, W.B. Saunders, pp. 699–719, 1980.
92. Wollmer, P., Relation Between Lung Function, Exercise Capacity and Exposure to Asbestos Cement, British Journal of Industrial Medicine, 44:542–549, 1987.
93. Sue, D.Y., Diffusion Capacity for Carbon Monoxide as a Predictor of Gas Exchange During Exercise, New England Journal of Medicine, 316:1301–1306, 1987.
93. Becklake, M.R., Asbestos Related Disease of the Lung and Other Organs, Their Epidemiology and Implications for Clinical Practice, American Review of Respiratory Disease, 114:187–227, 1976.

3

Early Diagnosis of Malignant Mesothelioma: The Contribution of Effusion and Fine Needle Aspiration Cytology and Ancillary Techniques

DARREL WHITAKER, PH.D., F.I.M.L.S., A.A.I.M.L.S., C.F.I.A.C.
GREG STERRETT, M.B.B.S., F.R.C.P.A., F.I.A.C.
KEITH SHILKIN, M.B.B.S., F.R.C.P.A., F.R.C.PATH.

Department of Pathology,
University of Western Australia,
Nedlands, Western Australia

Department of Histopathology,
Sir Charles Gairdner Hospital,
Nedlands, Western Australia

Synopsis

BIOGRAPHY

Dr. Darrel Whitaker, is a cytologist with the Cytology Unit of the Combined Anatomical Pathology Services, at the Queen Elizabeth II Medical Centre, Nedlands, Western Australia. He is Honorary Visiting Cytologist of Sir Charles Gairdner Hospital and a member of the Mesothelioma Panel of the Royal College of Pathologists of Australasia and National Secretary of the Australian Society of Cytology. His research interests include mesothelial healing and the cytopathology of asbestos related lung disease. He has published both on the mesothelium and mesothelioma and is co-author of a "Manual and Atlas of Fine Needle Aspiration Cytology". Dr. Whitaker was awarded the International Cytotechnology Award of the International Academy of Cytology in 1986, partly in recognition of his work on mesothelioma. Dr. Darrel Whitaker may be contacted at the Department of Pathology, Hospital and University Pathology Services, Sir Charles Gairdner Hospital and University of Western Australia, The Queen Elizabeth II Medical Centre, Nedlands 6009, WESTERN AUSTRALIA.

Dr. Greg Sterrett, is a cytopathologist in the Department of Histopathology at the Sir Charles Gairdner Hospital and Head of the Cytology Unit of the Combined Anatomical Pathology Services at The Queen Elizabeth II Medical Centre. He has a special interest in fine needle aspiration cytology, and is a co-author of a "Manual and Atlas of Fine Needle Aspiration Cytology". He has served on the Executive of the Australian Society of Cytology as Vice-President and President, and has interests in education and research in cytology as well as in diagnostic aspects.

Dr. Keith Shilkin, is a pathologist and Head of the

Department of Histopathology at the Sir Charles Gairdner Hospital, the teaching Hospital of the University of Western Australia in Perth, Western Australia. As well as his general interests in pathology, having been President of the Australasian Division of the International Academy of Pathology and a Visiting Associate Professor of Pathology at the Albert Einstein College of Medicine, New York, he has researched and published on pathological aspects of mesothelioma. He is a Member of the Pathology Panel of the Australian Mesothelioma Surveillance Programme and Consultant Pathologist to the Pneumoconiosis Medical Panel of Western Australia. Dr. Keith B. Shilkin may be contacted at the Department of Histopathology of the Sir Charles Gairdner Hospital, Verdun Street, Nedlands, Western Australia 6009 (telephone: 09-389-3333; telex: AA 93446).

EDITORS' COMMENTARY

Of all of the cancers, mesothelioma is among the most feared because of its rapid progression and the current absence of effective treatment. It seems unique to asbestos exposure, despite the "Turkish Affair", although current intensive research may produce greater insight as to how it is initiated, triggered, facilitated, gene suppressed, or accelerated. Just recently (October 1988), we have seen misdiagnosed mesothelioma, despite what seemed like grossly apparent clinical symptoms. This may reflect unfamiliarity or uncertainty in diagnosis. It also suggests underreporting in epidemiological studies. The following Chapter clarifies objective diagnosis. It provides a basis for early cytodiagnosis and describes techniques, tests, criteria, cell features, and ancilliary procedures. There are concerns as to diagnostic sensitivity and accuracy, particularly when influenced by information content and the purpose of clinical, laboratory, panel, or project evaluations. There are issues as to the reproducibility and precision of differential diagnosis where inexperience, technical meticulousness, and professional interest may be not sufficient to avoid pitfalls. There is the promise of productive research as to possible etiology, types, growth, and treatment. But, great future promise should not detract from the urgency of prerequisite and practical early diagnosis, such as that based on cytomorphological criteria applied to serous effusion samples and needle aspirates.

A. INTRODUCTION

Malignant mesothelioma is a common, uniformly fatal neoplasm. Therapeutic intervention has not proven to be of value in

Accepted for publication 28 December 1988.

saving life or in significantly altering the progression of the disease. Much of the difficulty in addressing the problem clinically has been that diagnosis has only been possible in the late stages of the disease. Part of the reason for this lies in the acknowledged difficulty of diagnosis. Despite the ever increasing incidence of malignant mesothelioma, intense study of the disease and the better definition of its diagnostic criteria, there is still controversy over what constitutes an adequate sample on which to make a confident morphological diagnosis.

Some authors have maintained that nothing short of full post mortem is needed to establish the diagnosis of mesothelioma beyond doubt, (1,43) although as Hillerdal (47) succinctly pointed out, from a clinical point of view, this is not a fruitful approach. Some have demanded at least open thoractomy with generous tissue sampling (19,93) while others, recognising the need for earlier and less invasive methods, advocate thoroscopy. (10,68) We would contend that when mesothelioma is being considered, the first line diagnostic approach, providing certain conditions are met, should include the proper evaluation of serous effusions as well as a closed needle biopsy. Using the information derived from this small biopsy and the effusion, most mesotheliomas can confidently be diagnosed. (26,86,118,125,127)

There are several compelling clinical reasons for this approach. Up to 90% of mesotheliomas present with a serous effusion, (15,43) requiring drainage for relief of discomfort. A ready source of material for various analyses is thus available. From the physician's stand point, thoracentesis is a relatively simple and safe procedure and it is widely accepted that cytodiagnosis of effusions is a quick, inexpensive and reliable tool with which to diagnose malignancy. (52,61) In addition, although "early" diagnosis by cytology as yet provides no advantage in terms of survival from disease, this modality is at least relatively painless and complication free. There is proportional increase in the rate of complications, mainly local painful growth of tumour at the incision site, the more invasive the technique used to obtain a sample; (10,31) even thoroscopy is associated with this complication at a higher rate than simple thoracentesis and needle biopsy. (10,68)

Our aim in this chapter is to attempt to dispel some of the unwarranted lack of confidence in cytodiagnosis as expressed in some of the literature on mesothelioma, and to put this method into its proper clinical perspective; firstly, by reviewing the literature on the cytodiagnosis of mesothelioma and examining the reasons why some workers find the technique valuable and others unrewarding; secondly, by outlining the ideal conditions, the techniques used, and the diagnostic criteria which can be applied to the successful cytological diagnosis of mesothelioma; and thirdly, by exploring the value of ancillary diagnostic tests used in support of the cytological findings and placing them in diagnostic sequence.

B. CYTODIAGNOSIS—THE CONTROVERSIES

1. The Accuracy of Cytodiagnosis

There is an extraordinary variation in opinions expressed in the scientific literature about the value of cytodiagnosis of mesothelioma. Some (52,53,97) maintain simply that such a diagnosis cannot be made, while others state that the technique is of uncertain or questionable value. (3,11,15,47,57,105) Claims have been made that cytodiagnosis is associated with large numbers of false positives and false negatives. (105) The technique has been described as "difficult to use", (16,29,40,70,104) and "helpful", (22,54,75) and suggestions that more attention should be given to this modality (39) have been made. However, other acknowledged experts recognize that cytodiagnosis can be especially accurate in experienced hands. (28,55,74)

a. Sensitivity of Diagnosis

Figure 1 details the results of cytodiagnosis in a number of series of mesothelioma and shows a variation in sensitivity (the percentage of cases diagnosed by cytology) of diagnosis from 5–93%. In a retrospective analysis of our own results (123) in 1986, there were only 12 cases of mesothelioma reported as negative on effusion cytology out of 125 cases. On review, 7 of the 12 did not contain any mesothelial cells on the slides. When we examined the histopathology of these cases, four showed a sarcomatous growth and three a biphasic pattern. Of the five negative reports that did contain mesothalial cells, one was, in retrospect, a true false negative, in which criteria of malignancy were evident, but not recognized, while in the other four, the mesothelial cells did not show any obvious cytological criteria for malignancy. The true false negative diagnosis was made in 1974, before we had accumulated any significant experience in mesothelioma diagnosis. Our ability to correctly diagnose mesothelioma has risen with experience. An analysis of the period 1986–1988 shows our sensi-

MALIGNANT MESOTHELIOMA: Diagnosis in Serous Effusions

SERIES DETAILS						CYTOLOGY RESULTS						
						Tumour Typing					Sensitivity of diagnosis %	
YEAR	AUTHOR	ORIGIN OF PATIENTS/SERIES	TOTAL Nr. OF CYTOLOGY CASES	PERIOD (YRS)	RATE (PER YEAR)	MALIG. DIAGN.	MESO.	MESO/ ADENO.	? MESO.	NEG.	MESO.	MALIG.
1962	Klempman [58]	South African Asbestos Mines	27	?	?	24	24	-	-	3	89	89
1963	Naylor [80]	Uni. of Michigan Ann Arbor	7	4	1.7	6	4	2	-	1	57	86
1971	Oels [82]	Mayo Clinic I	25	22	0.88	15	(15)		1	9		60
1972	Roberts [91]	Ship Yards (Glasgow)	14	18	0.7	10	8	2	2	2	57	71
1973	Butler [12]	Many referrals	27	5	5.4	25	25	-	1	0	93	93
1976	Sherrin [97]	General Hospital	15	24	0.16	1	(1)		(14)			7
1976	Elmes [31]	Collected referred series	127	9	14.1 *	26	7	19	(101)		5	20
1977	Jara [48]	Hospital	20	19	1.0	8	1	7	2	11	5	40
1978	Whitaker [128]	Asbestos Mine (Western Australia) I	12	3	4.0	10	8	2	1	1	60	83
1978	Edge [27]	Ship Yards (Barrow)	26	10	2.6	20	20	-	-	6	77	77
1979	Tao [105]	General Hospital	22	11	2.0	17	17	-	-	5	77	77
1980	Antman [3]	Ship Yards	28	13	2.1	8	1	7	(20)		4	28
1981	Lewis [69]	Local Asbestos Industry	46	9	5.1	3	3	?	?	?	6	6
1981	Brenner [11]	Memorial Hospital	60	31	1.9	22	7	15	(38)		12	37
1982	Nauta [79]	Hospital	26	17	1.5	9	4	3	(17)		15	35
1984	Law [67]	London Chest Hospitals	80	9	8.8	20	-	20	21	39	0	25
1984	Triol [107]	Asbestos Factory	75	16	4.6	50	42	8	23	4	56	67
1984	Martensson [70]	Mainly Ship Yards (Sweden)	31	3	10.3	11	1	10	(14)		3	35
1985	Matzel [73]	Chest Hospital (Bulgaria)	51	7	7.8	39	21	18	-	12	41	76
1986	Adams [1]	Mayo Clinic II	69	30	2.3	22	18	4	9	38	26	32
1987	Whitaker [123]	Asbestos Mine (Western Australia) II	103	10	10.0	83	74	8	10	9	72	81
1987	Strankinga [104]	Hospital (Amsterdam)	25	3.5	7.1	0	0	-	(25)		0	0
1988	Riback [88]	Asbestos Insulation Workers	182	17	10.1	50	(50)		51	81		31
1988	Whitaker	Authors Update 1986 - 1988	30	2	15.0	27	24	3	2	1	80	90

MALIG: DEFINITE DIAGNOSIS OF MALIGNANCY
MESO: MESOTHELIOMA
MESO/ADENO: DEFINITELY MALIGNANT - EITHER MESOTHELIOMA OR ADENOCARCINOMA
? MESO: ATYPICAL CELLS - EITHER MESOTHELIOMA OR REACTIVE PROLIFERATION
NEG: NEGATIVE

( ) Distinction not made between catagories
* Series referred from many centres

$$\text{SENSITIVITY} = \frac{\text{Number of cases diagnosed}}{\text{Total number of cases}} \%$$

Fig. 3-1

tivity to be 80% compared with 72% in 1973–1986 and 60% in the period 1973–1977. We attribute much of this improvement to better technical preparation of effusions. For example, we would now regard bloodstained smear preparations without mesothelial cells as unsuitable for diagnosis rather than negative, and make every effort to apply cell concentration techniques or to obtain further or more voluminous effusion samples for study. There are still cases where mesothelial cells cannot be identified in smears even after careful preparation (particularly so in sarcomatous tumours), but these can be minimized. Finally, caution must be advised in categorising benign asbestos pleurisy (35) on the basis of a negative cytology report as a few cases have subsequently developed mesothelioma.

b. False Positive Diagnosis of Malignancy

For the experienced, well-trained cytopathologist false positive diagnoses of malignancy in serous effusion cytology are exceedingly rare. (54,61) As Dekker and Bupp (21) have stated "in the past" small reactive clusters of mesothelial cells, particularly after pulmonary infarction, were occasionally a problem for the pathologist; however, such findings are now well described and recognized and the notion that benign mesothelial cell aggregates are still a frequent source of diagnostic error especially in the pleura, is false. While large, benign mesothelial aggregates have occasionally been found in pericardial (5,100) or peritoneal effusions, (61,94,116) they are exceedingly rare in pleural effusions. Spriggs (101) says "In 30 years of reporting by Mr. M. N. Boddington and myself, no false positive report of carcinoma has been given as a result of finding cell balls in aspirations of serous fluid". We would concur with this opinion. We have not made a false positive diagnosis of malignant mesothelioma in our clinical practice and cannot find a single example of such a mistake in the literature. Diagnosis based on cell aggregates, particularly when they are accompanying nuclear abnormalities, is extremely reliable. Diagnosis of malignancy based on the finding of small numbers of single atypical cells in effusions is much more difficult and here a more cautious approach should be adopted and ancillary testing such as immunoperoxidase staining for Epithelial Membrane Antigen (EMA) performed (see later). Clinicians should also be careful in labelling a case a "false positive diagnosis of malignancy", without either a long follow-up or strong morphological evidence. We have seen several cases of mesothelioma in which there were periods of good health up to 18 months after cytodiagnosis, before recurrence of effusion or symptoms.

c. Incorrect Tumour Typing

We have not personally seen nor are aware of an example in the literature of a case of adenocarcinoma being incorrectly labelled mesothelioma on cytology. However, some mesotheliomas have erroneously been identified as adenocarcinomas on the basis of effusion cytology. This error has usually been associated with lack of awareness or experience in mesothelioma cytodiagnosis, or the omission of ancillary testing such as staining for mucin or carcino-embryonic antigen or ultrastructural study. On review, we found that cases most likely to fall into this category are those where the cytological picture consists only of cell aggregates with no free mesothelial cells. In such a situation ancillary testing is obligatory to determine the true tumour type.

In summary, much of the literature on the accuracy on cytodiagnosis of mesothelioma is unduly pessimistic. An uncritical examination might lead to an incorrect view of what can be achieved with due care and attention. The overall performance of centres with reasonable experience in the diagnosis of mesothelioma is as good as that in the best centres reporting on the accuracy of cytodiagnosis metastatic adenocarcinoma. (20,21,51,61,78)

2. Reasons for Variations in Accuracy

a. Technical Considerations

Over the years we have certainly become more familiar with the cytologic picture seen in mesothelioma; however, we believe that much of the clarification of this characteristic picture was made easier by improvements in our technical approach. The ficol-hypaque gradient method of cell concentration is invaluable for blood stained effusions. Smear preparation is technically quite simple, but exacting regard to detail can produce magnificent cytomorphology. To us, the cell block technique is indispensible for the evaluation of any effusion, and particularly so for mesothelioma diagnosis. We have now introduced an extended laboratory protocol for use when mesothelioma is suspected. Ancillary testing can make the diagnosis easier in formerly

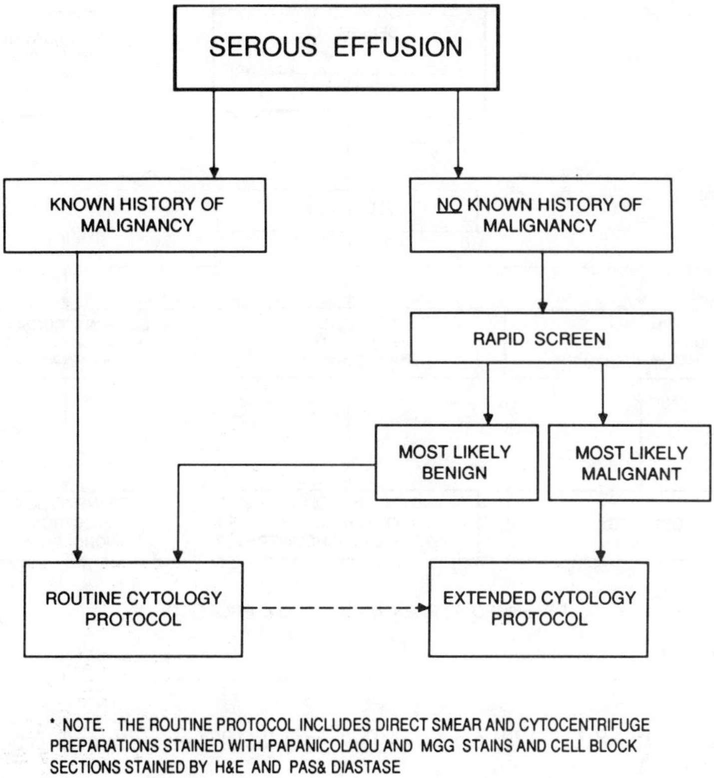

SEROUS EFFUSION PROTOCOL

Fig. 3-2

difficult cases. The value of attention to detail in regard to technical approach (in respect of mesothelioma cytodiagnosis) has been stressed by others. (18,38,40)

b. Experience

Any attempt to analyse the reasons behind other authors' results is fraught with difficulty as in most cases we are not aware of the techniques used, whether the material was seen by one or many pathologists, or whether they were experienced in effusion cytodiagnosis of mesothelioma. However, some general comments can be made about the value of experience. At least three ways for accumulating such experience are evident:

(1) Substantial rapidly acquired local experience is often associated with a high local incidence of mesothelioma, linked with asbestos

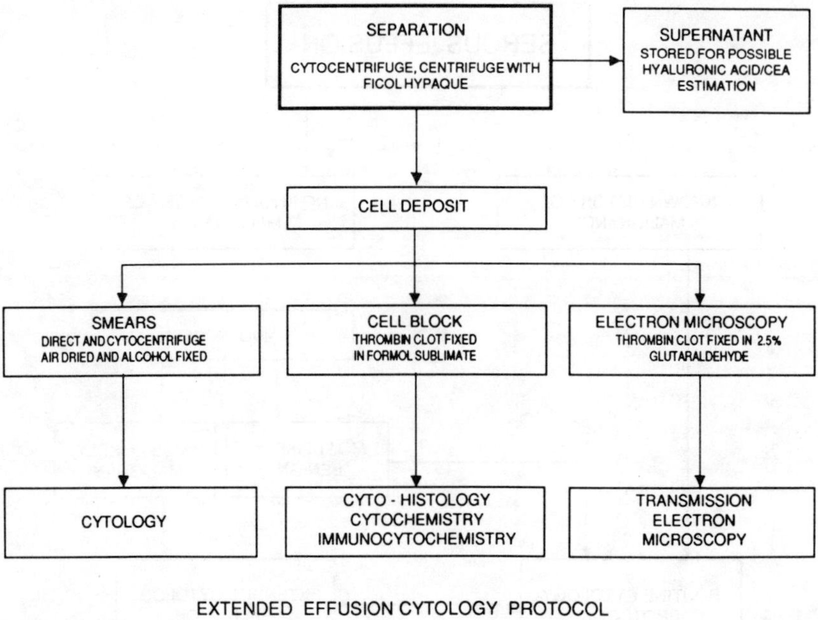

Fig. 3-3

mining, (12,58,117,120) asbestos factory (38,107) or shipyard exposure. (6,7,27,91)

(2) By having a particular interest in the cytodiagnosis of this disease, certain authorities have attracted referrals of cases of mesothelioma from many centres. (12,27)

(3) By a more gradual process, viewing material derived from a general hospital over many years, some groups can accumulate a large number of cases.

Most laboratories will fall into the third category, that is, only gaining experience gradually.

An examination of Figure 1, shows that experience or exposure to cases of mesothelioma alone is not necessarily associated with good results as some of the largest series are associated with poor results. For example, in 1984, Law et al. (67) reported on a large series of mesotheliomas from the London Chest Hospitals over nine years. Eighty cases had cytology performed, yet in no case was the diagnosis of mesothelioma made and in only 20 was malignancy established using cytology.

In 1971 Oles et al. (82) reported 37 cases of mesothelioma seen at the Mayo Clinic between the years 1945–1967. Effusions were present in 31 and cytology was performed in 25. Fifteen of these were called malignant, either mesothelioma or adenocarcinoma, one was reported as atypical and nine as negative. Almost 20 years laters, Adams et al. (1) from the same Institute reported on a larger series of cases, including the earlier reported material and covering the period 1945–1986. On this occasion 22 were reported as malignant, (11 mesothelioma, 7 possible mesothelioma and 4 adenocarcinoma), nine atypical and 38 negative. The sensitivity of diagnosis of malignancy therefore fell from 60% over the period 1945–1967 to 16% over the latter period (1977–1986), even though more cases (22:44) were seen in the latter period. The reasons for this disparity remain unclear.

Because it was one of the earliest and largest series of mesotheliomas, the paper of Elmes and Simpson (31) is frequently quoted as an example of where cytodiagnosis was of little value in determining the diagnosis of mesothelioma. (2,67,70) Elmes and Simpson, in a detailed paper on 327 cases, reported that in only 7 cases out of 172 was effusion cytology suggestive of malignant mesothelioma. This begs the question as to why the cytologic modality was so insensitive in this series; this only becomes clear after fully reading the paper. The cohort was, in fact, a collected series gathered from hospitals throughout the United Kingdom over a 9 year period. The information on the cytologic results was obtained by studying the originating hospital's medical records. The cytology slides were apparently not reviewed, whereas the histopathology was. Hence, it seems likely that the relative experience with cytodiagnosis of malignant mesothelioma of the individually contributing laboratories may have been quite limited. There is also an indication from an earlier report (32) that laboratory technique may have been a problem. We read "in the half the cases with free fluid the exudate was heavily blood stained and sometimes difficult to distinguish from pure blood. In these cases cytological examination for malignant cells was fruitless". Cell concentration techniques, such as ficol hypaque gradients, to extract the cell component from heavily blood contaminated samples were not in general use at that time.

In contrast, when samples, rather than simply reports, have been referred to a single cytopathologist having a particular interest in mesothelioma, the situation is reversed and a very high degree of sensitivity has been achieved. (27) It is of interest that many of the series with the best results (Figure 1) are either found in the cytological literature or are reported by well-known cytopathologists, further suggesting that a commitment to cytopathology as a discipline may be an important factor.

In company with reports of good results in diagnosis over the years, there has also been a shift towards confidence in cytodiagnosis in general in this area. Dr. Leopold Koss, considered by many to be the doyen Cytopathologist for the past thirty years, writing in 1961 (62) suggested that—"An accurate cytologic diagnosis of mesothelioma is exceedingly difficult, and, perhaps, one should not attempt more than a provisional diagnosis". In 1968 (63) he wrote "a suspicion of mesothelioma was expressed in a few cases" but by 1979 (61) "it was possible to establish the diagnosis of a primary mesothelioma in several personally observed cases".

While there are still dissenters among experienced cytopathologists, and some still hold the view that cytodiagnosis of this condition is rarely possible (51,53), we content that good results can be obtained by a combination of factors including a commitment to the discipline of cytopathology, confidence that cytodiagnosis of mesothelioma is possible, and adequate exposure to cases of mesothelioma.

3. Portability of Diagnostic Accuracy

This then raises an important question: is the knowledge gained by cytopathologists with wide experience in the cytodiagnosis of mesothelioma, portable to those without such direct working experience? The characteristics and criteria for diagnosis of mesothelioma and its various pitfalls are now widely known and described in the literature. Careful critical analysis of these criteria has also been provided by pathologists who support this approach as a method of refining diagnosis and increasing reproducibility between pathologists (29), although it has been very reasonably suggested that simply applying the criteria enunciated by others will not be as effective as personal experience. (46) Within the discipline of cytology in general, scientific meetings, lectures, tutorials and workshops are recognized as essential additional educational exercises forming an important part of Quality Assurance Programmes. Certainly these direct "hands on" processes, especially workshops, are bound to be educationally more rewarding than reading scientific reports and attempting to apply the criteria alone in what is essentially a pattern recognition diagnostic exercise.

There are some indications, however, that portability of diagnostic accuracy is likely to be possible. Within the workings of the Australian Mesothelioma Panel, increased confidence in cytodiagnosis has become evident. Whereas as a few years ago, pathologists were more circumspect in cytodiagnosis, many now write such comments on reports of panel cases as "shows typical cytologic pattern". Within the workings of our own department, pathology registrars, rotating through the Cytology Unit as part of their pathology training and trainee cytotechnologists have soon learned the criteria for diagnosis and have been able to apply them successfully in the routine diagnostic situation.

4. The Influence of Knowledge of Asbestos Exposure

There is some dispute as to whether or not pathologists should have available to them information about asbestos exposure when attempting to diagnose malignant mesothelioma. Wright et al. (126) and Adams et al. (1) maintain that such information may bias the pathologist and therefore should not be available while others (29,74) including ourselves (117) believe it is essential. There are two issues here—firstly, the setting in which the diagnosis is being made, and secondly, how such information is used. For example, there is a difference between the clinical setting and a review process such as a mesothelioma panel or research project.

We maintain that, with any hospital case, all relevant available clinical information should be known by the interpreting pathologist. Moreover, it is a medical truism that the likelihood of a correct pathological diagnosis (of any condition) is heightened by evaluating the morphologic findings within its correct clinical setting.

We consider that details such as history of asbestos exposure, previous history of carcinoma, pulmonary infarction, to be important background knowledge against which to evaluate the cytologic picture. What is even more relevant, is not that such information will influence the diagnosis towards mesothelioma, but, that, in the absence of a consistent clinical picture, the diagnostician should be very cautious. When the cytomorphology suggests mesothelioma yet there is no history of asbestos exposure, a request should be made for more information including a detailed occupational history; other evidence from ancillary testing should also be considered.

C. CYTOLOGICAL SAMPLES, TECHNIQUES AND TESTS

1. Sample

Mesotheliomatous effusions are usually voluminous and recur after tapping. An adequate sample should be no less than 200mls but preferably as much as a clinician can provide the cytology laboratory. Some investigators have commented about the fact that cellular material was degenerate and diagnosis was not possible. This should not be the case in a routine hospital practice, as the cells of serous effusions (unlike CSF) do not undergo rapid degeneration. We have found by using a special preservative/anti-coagulant fixative in which to collect the serous effusion (122), cell preservation and clot formation are no longer a problem. As many effusions are heavily blood stained in mesothelioma, separation by the ficol hypaque gradient technique is of great value in selectively collecting the malignant cells. Occasionally, high viscosity of the fluid due to high levels of hyaluronic acid may give a hint to the diagnosis even before examining the smears.

2. Techniques

Our experience with the cytodiagnosis of malignant mesothelioma has clearly demonstrated to us the importance of the sample and how it is prepared. We firmly believe that our present confidence in diagnosing mesothelioma is due, in no small part, to our improved technical approach. In reviewing the early cytologic material in the 1960's from our hospital, we could rarely make a diagnosis of mesothelioma. The cytomorphological criteria discussed below have been defined using adequate, well-preserved effusion samples and employing several techniques.

3. Tests

Given an adequate sample the cellular deposit should be separated from the supernatant and following tests performed.

a. Cell Deposit

Direct smears and cyto-centrifuge smears for air-dried May Grunwald Geimsa (MGG) staining and wet-fixed for Papanicolaou

ANCILLARY TESTING

PHASE I - POTENTIAL AIDS TO THE DIAGNOSIS OF MALIGNANCY

TEST PERFORMED	RESULTS	
	Benign	Malignant
IMMUNOPEROXIDASE (IP)		
EMA	Usually negative	Strongly Positive
CEA	Invariably negative	Adenocarcinoma - Mostly positive Mesothelioma - Negative
EFFUSION BIOCHEMISTRY		
Hyaluronic Acid	Below 40ng/ml	Adenocarcinoma- below 40 ng/ml
CYTOGENETICS		
Structural & numerical Chromosomal Abnormalities	Absent	Present

Fig. 3-4

staining; a cell block using the thrombin clot method fixed in formal sublimate for cytomorphology, immunoperoxidase and cytochemical staining. Some of the cell deposit is placed into gluteraldehyde for electron microscopy.

ANCILLARY TESTING

PHASE II - TUMOUR TYPING

TEST PERFORMED	RESULTS	
	Adenocarcinoma	Mesothelioma
CEA (IP)	90 % positive	Negative
Epithelial Mucin Stains	Often positive	Negative
Effusion CEA	Often above 15ng/ml	Below 5.0ng/ml
* Ultrastructure		
Microvilli	Variable in length & shape	Abundant, long - thin
Basal rootlets	Often present	Absent
Glycogen	Variable	Abundant
Mucin like granules	Variable	Absent
Terminal web	Present	Absent

* after Henderson (1982)

Fig. 3-5

b. Supernatant

This can be stored at −20C for possible hyaluronic acid and carcinoembryonic antigen (CEA) estimation. Full technical details of our laboratory procedures have been previously published. (122)

D. DESCRIPTIVE CYTODIAGNOSIS

1. Effusions

(6,7,12,29,38,54,58,61,64,73,80,91,105,106,107,108,117,120, 124,127)

Heterogeneity in tumour morphology is well recognized in mesothelioma there being a spectrum of differentiation from epithelial to spindle cell growth with many tumours showing a biphasic pattern of histology. The degree of differentiation also varies and a proportion of anaplastic mesotheliomas defy easy characterization. As far as the cytomorphology is concerned there are two quite distinct pictures: one that is readily recognizable in effusions from growths with an epithelial component; and one that is not, the sarcomatous variety.

a. Epithelial or Biphasic Mesothelioma Cytology

Our experience, like that of others, suggests that most mesotheliomatous effusions are found in association with epithelial mesotheliomas or have an epithelial component that freely sheds many cells into the fluid bathing them. The cytodiagnosis of mesothelioma is a *two-stage process.* The first is to establish malignancy and then to recognize the mesothelial characteristics of the malignant cells.

i. Criteria of Malignancy

The normal criteria for malignancy including nuclear irregularity, hyperchromasia, and enlargement still apply. However, these usual cytologic features of malignancy are not always present in malignant mesothelioma. Within this context other criteria are useful.

As McCaughey recently stated (74), "In mesothelioma (as opposed to reaction) you get more cells, larger cells, and bigger clusters". Larger cells are frequently found, sometimes up to 4 times the size of reactive mesothelial cells. These are not seen in benign reactive conditions. The finding of many large cell clusters (see later) in pleural effusions is almost diagnostic of malignancy. We have also seen a few cases of malignant mesothelioma where the sole malignant criterion was the presence of solitary central macronucleoli. Given an adequate cell sample, it is usually easy to establish the malignant nature of an effusion.

ii. Mesothelial Criteria

Having established the diagnosis of malignancy, the next important step is to determine the mesothelial nature of the malignant cell population. No single observation is entirely specific, but a combination of findings will enable a tumour to be correctly classified in most cases.

Aggregates: Cell aggregates are plentiful and common in serous effusions from mesothelioma. They may accompany single malignant cells, or the cell sample may simply consist of aggregates. On direct smears these often have a "nobbly" or "berry-like" external contour. In section they may be solid or in the form of a pseudoacinus, and are composed of cuboidal rather than columnar cells (characteristic of adenocarcinoma). Some may have a small, central, stromal core. (107,108,121) Small clusters of 5 to 10 cells are frequently arranged in a peculiar "floret" arrangement.

Cell cytoplasm: The optical density of mesothelial cytoplasm is a fairly consistent finding and this is a useful distinguishing feature from adenocarcinoma cells which are usually less dense and more foamy. Mesothelial cytoplasm is basophilic and on MGG staining appears dark blue. With the Papanicolaou stain the cytoplasm is a dense green or with an unusual tinctorial change ranging from red/orange surrounding the nucleus to green at the periphery. On H&E sections of cell block preparations the cytoplasm also stains darkly, with a deep red hue. A peripheral arrangement of small vacuoles can sometimes be seen on MGG-stained smears, and some larger vacuoles may be present (see glycogen and hyaluronic acid).

Cell periphery: Normal mesothelial cells are endowed with a rich microvillous border and in malignancy this is frequently accentuated. This feature is one of the ultrastructural hallmarks of mesothelioma and in optimally prepared smears the microvilli can also be seen at the light microscope level, appearing as a brush-like border. Cytoplasmic blebbing is also a fairly common feature of mesothelioma cell surfaces. This is probably an artefact of cell preparation, but is a common enough feature to be of some value in mesothelial identification. It is not, however, specific.

Cell-to-cell aposition: When mesothelial cells lie in close aposition, a window-like gap (Figures 3-6.4 and 3-6.5) is often seen between the cells. This effect has been attributed to the prominent microvillous border between the two adjacent cells pushing them slightly apart.

Cell engulfment: A widely recognized and variously described feature is the finding of one cell being partially or wholly wrapped around another (Figure 3-6.4). Such terms as "embracement", pincer-like grip, cell engulfment, and even "cannibalism" have been used to describe this feature. It is certainly much more common in mesothelioma than in proliferative mesothelial reactions. Multinucleation is also a commonly seen feature in malignant mesothelioma.

These five features are to be found in most cytologic descriptions of mesotheliomas. There are a few "finer" points of recognition which, while not often seen, are fairly specific for mesothelioma.

Glycogen: Mesotheliomatous cells often have very large amounts of glycogen. Sometimes this is randomly dispersed throughout the cytoplasm, but it may be present as large, crescent-shaped lakes occupying a large area of the cell. In Papanicolaou-stained smears this appears as a yellow, refractile material and cytopathologists will easily equate this picture with the glycogenated navicular cells sometimes seen in cervical smears. The lakes of glycogen can be easily seen in electron micrographs of mesothelioma cells.

Small degenerate cells: In Papanicolaou-stained smears, in marked contrast to the main population of green staining cells, a few very small, pink/red staining cells with pyknotic nuclei are occasionally seen. These closely resemble degenerate squamous epithelial cells. These particular cells are exceedingly rare, in other types of malignant serous effusion, and while they are not often seen they are a good marker of mesothelioma. It may well be that this appearance is due to the large amount of keratin filaments present in mesothelioma cell cytoplasm.

Hyaluronic acid in the background: Some mesotheliomas secrete a large amount of hyaluronic acid, and occasionally this substance can be found in the smear background. It can be identified in the thicker parts of Papanicolaou stained smears where it presents as an unusual "network" pattern. (124)

Vacuoles: Besides the ring of small peripheral vacuoles already described, occasionally mesothelioma cells may have a

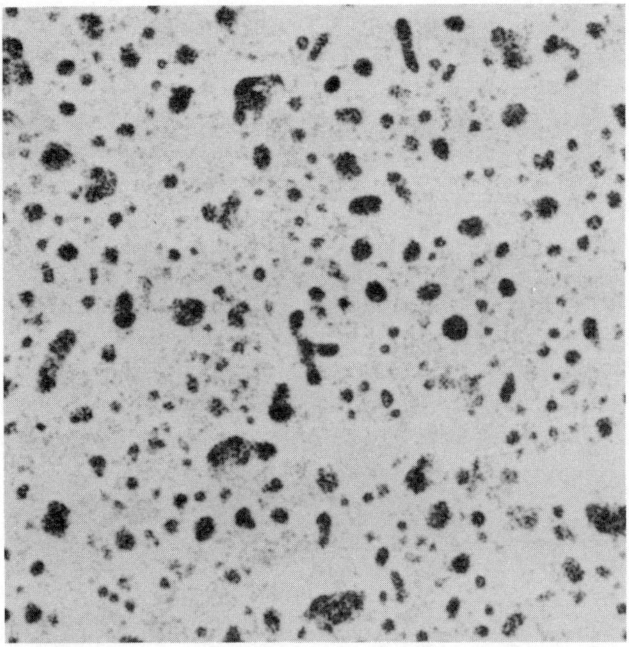

Fig. 3–6.1 A cellular smear with many aggregates of varying size; Papanicolaou smear ×43

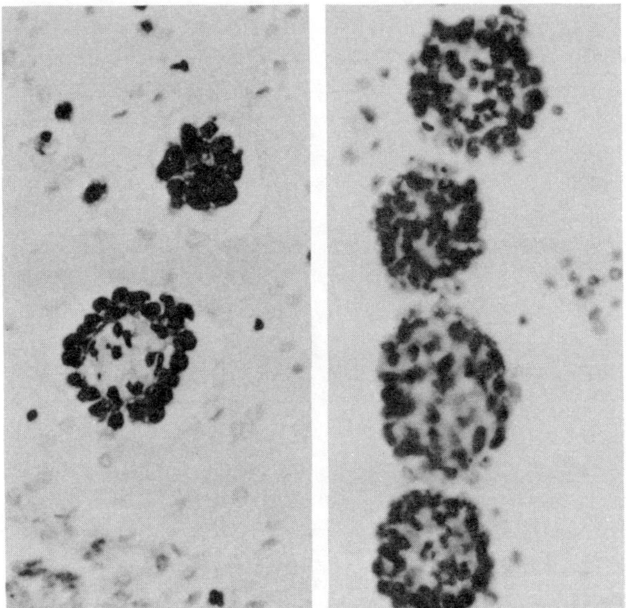

Fig. 3–6.2 Cell aggregates: Right – four rounded large cell aggregates. Papanicolaou smear ×270. Left – cell block section of aggregate. Haematoxylin and eosin ×270.

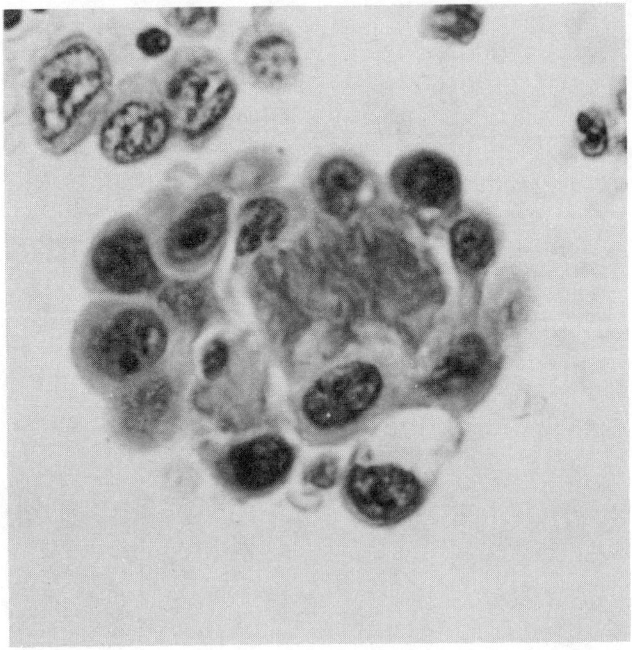

Fig. 3–6.3 Aggregate with a central core of collagen van Gueson ×480

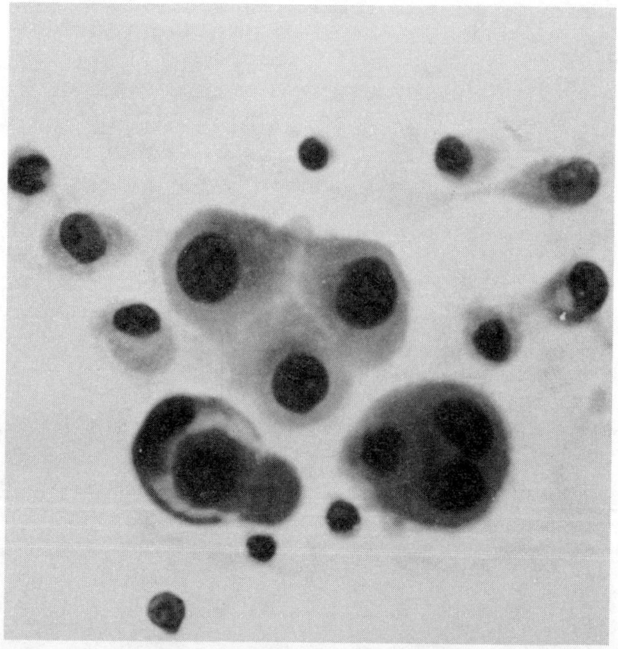

Fig. 3–6.4 Mesothelioma cells showing dense cytoplasmic staining, cell engulfment, fine microvillous border, and window-like gap between cells. Papanicolaou smear ×480.

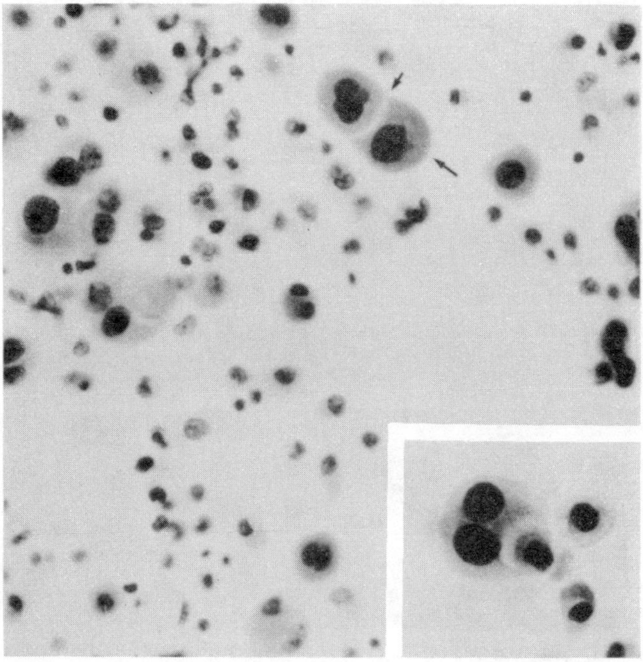

Fig. 3–6.5 Mesothelioma cells showing a prominent window (small arrow) and fine microvillous border (arrow). Inset, cell engulfment. Papanicolaou smear ×280 (Inset ×320)

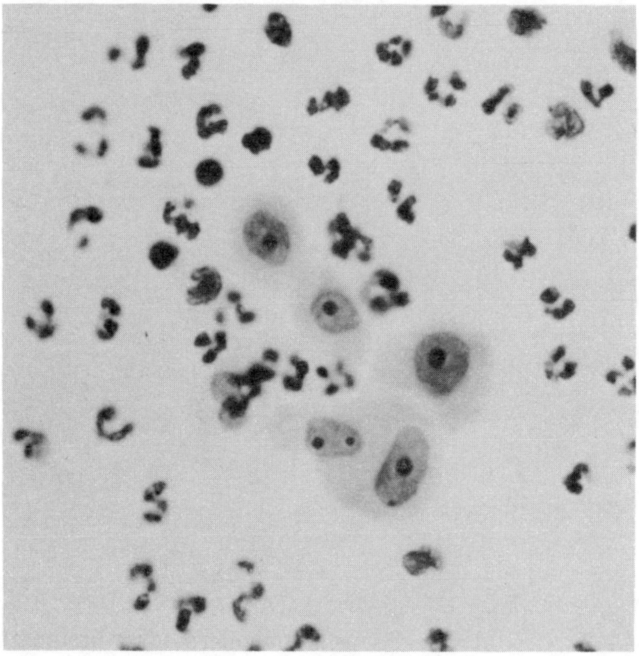

Fig. 3–6.6 A group of five mesothelioma cells, the main malignant criteria is the presence of large nucleoli. Papanicolaou smear ×690.

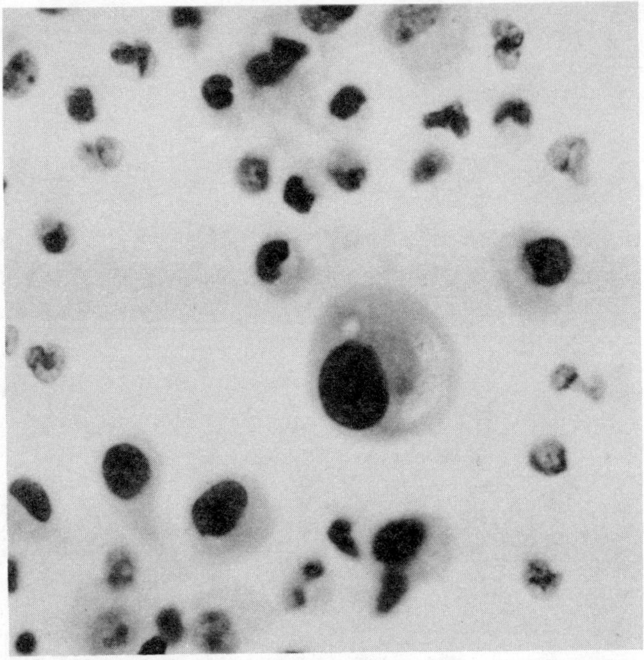

Fig. 3–7.1 Mesothelioma: a few small malignant cells and one large mesothelioma cell with a refractile, crescent shaped cytoplasmic inclusion (glycogen). Papanicolaou smear ×480.

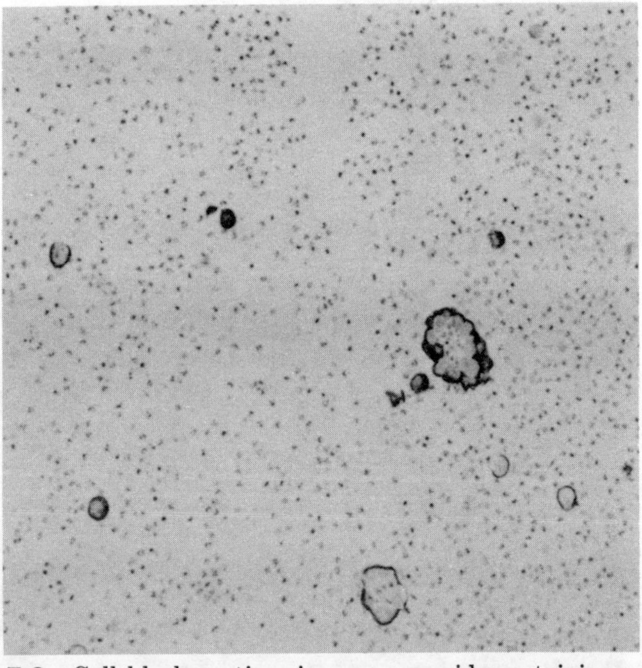

Fig. 3–7.2 Cell block section: immunoperoxidase staining with epithelial membrane antigen; both the cell clusters and the single mesothelioma cells are strongly decorated with reaction product. Epithelial membrane antigen ×270.

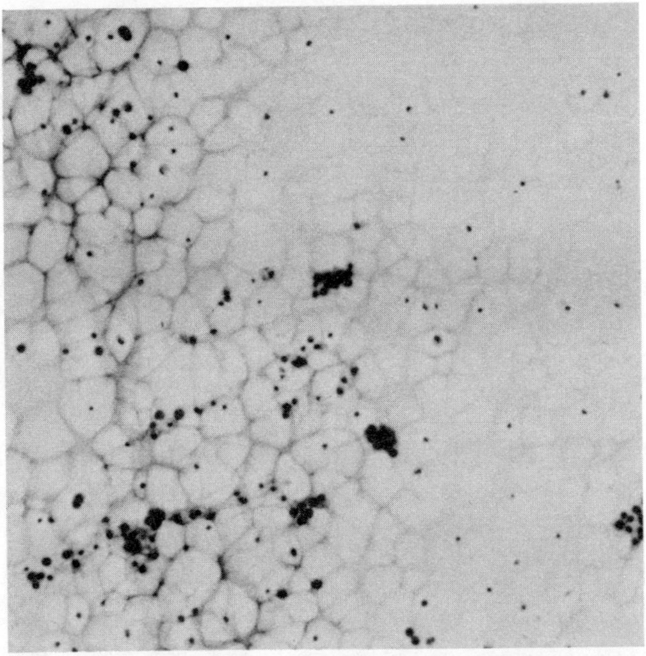

Fig. 3–7.3 Papanicolaou smear showing a few small clusters of mesothelioma cells and a prominent net-like or soap bubble pattern in the background (hyaluronic acid). Papanicolaou smear ×44.

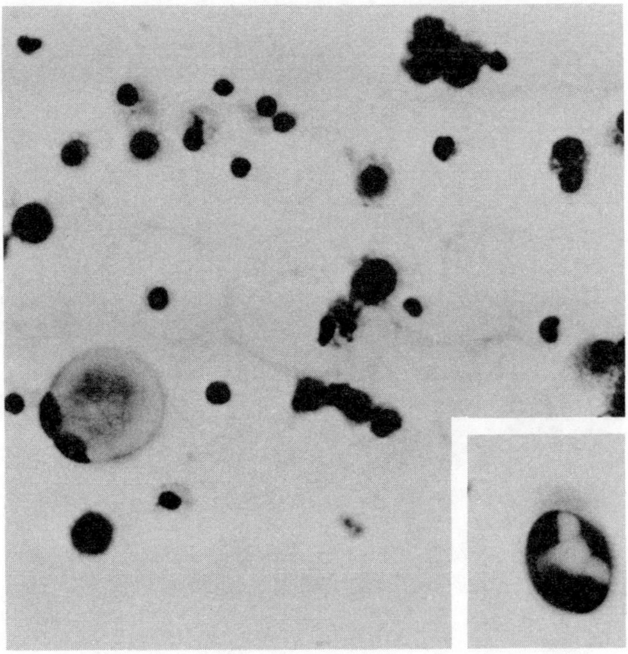

Fig. 3–7.4 Papanicolaou smear showing vacuoles. One binucleate cell has a large vacuole containing a granular substance thought to be hyaluronic acid. The inset has three hard edged vacuoles. Papanicolaou smear ×270 (Inset ×290)

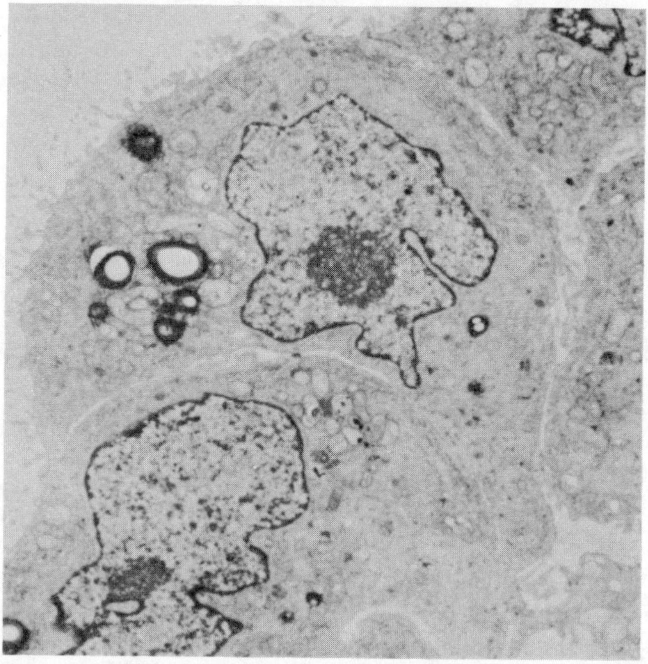

Fig. 3–7.5 Electron micrograph. Mesothelioma cells showing close apposition and abundant surface mircovilli. Magnification ×3360.

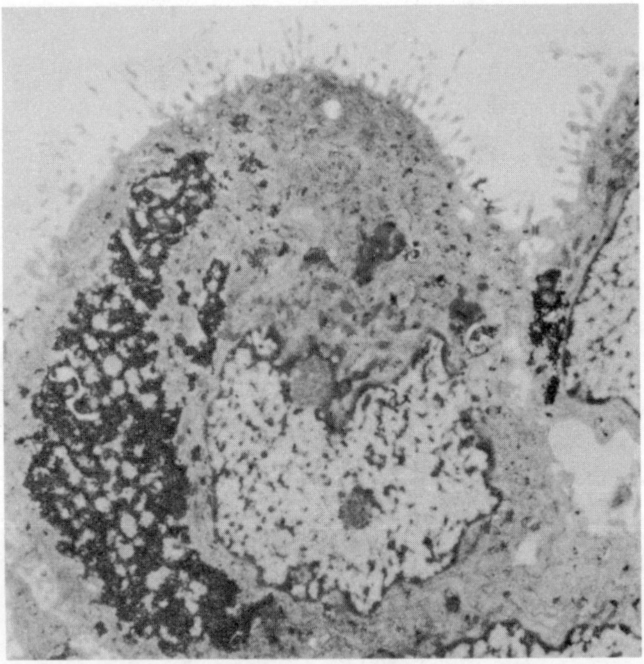

Fig. 3–7.6 Electron micrograph. Mesothelioma cells showing abundant long thin microvilli and a large crescent of glycogen. Magnification ×3600.

large, solitary, hard-edged vacuole. It has been suggested (29,54) that these probably result from degeneration; we believe they represent hyaluronic acid secretion. The substance within the vacuoles often assumes a greyish hue and can be compared with similar vacuoles more readily identified in fine needle aspirates from mesotheliomas stained with alcian blue and removed by hyaluronidase treatment.

b. Sarcomatous Mesothelioma Cytology

Serous effusions are far less commonly seen in sarcomatous mesothelioma. If an effusion does form they shed into the fluid infrequently. (73,106) When present, the malignant cells occur as single spindle cells or small aggregates of sarcomatous growth. Such malignant spindle cells in effusion should always prompt the consideration of mesothelioma and if found in a patient with a history of asbestos exposure they may permit a definite cytologic diagnosis to be made. However, in our experience this is very uncommon. Fortunately, most mesotheliomas are not of the sarcomatous variety.

c. Effusion Cytodiagnosis—Update

In analysing effusion cytodiagnosis, of our most recent 30 cases of malignant mesothelioma, we examined the criteria used above to decide which were most valuable in establishing the diagnosis. Further, we paid particular attention to those cases where we failed to make a definite diagnosis of mesothelioma or those which gave a negative result.

We made the following observations:

(1) Given an adequate cellular sample the correct diagnosis was invariably made.

(2) Many tumours without diagnostic cellular material in effusions were sarcomatous mesotheliomas.

(3) The easiest samples to interpret correctly contained many epithelial aggregates together with many free malignant cells.

(4) Cell aggregates were of most value in allowing a diagnosis of malignancy.

(5) Single cells or clusters of two to six cells were of most value in determining the mesothelial nature of the malignant cells.

(6) When the cytologic picture consisted only of aggregates, cell block sections and ancillary tests, such as mucin stains, immunoperox-

idase stains and electron microscopy, were sometimes necessary to distinguish mesothelioma from adenocarcinoma with absolute certainty.

2. Fine Needle Aspiration (FNA) Cytodiagnosis of Mesothelioma

The advent of this technique has meant that many previously inaccessible lesions throughout the body are now amenable to sampling. (60,83) In this regard, malignant mesotheliomas without serous effusion or in unusual places or as secondary deposits may now be sampled. (73) In 1987 (103) we reported our findings in 19 cases and suggested that fine needle aspiration cytology might become the first line diagnostic approach in patients suspected of having a pleural mesothelioma without an effusion or with an atypical clinical presentation. This opinion has since been reiterated by Obers et al. (81) from another location having a high incidence of mesothelioma. These authors agree that, in the correct clinical setting and using ancillary testing, a confident diagnosis can be made on which to base clinical management. Butler (54) observed that fine needle aspirates of mesothelioma have a similar appearance to imprint smears taken from tissue of that tumour.

This technique has also been usefully applied to the detection of peritoneal mesotheliomas. (50,89) Koss (60) has also suggested this dual cytological approach—exfoliative cytopathology for effusions and fine needle aspiration for solid lesions. He was also of the opinion that the former technique was better for detecting epithelial mesotheliomas and the latter for biphasic and sarcomatous tumours. However, it has been our experience that all histological subtypes of mesothelioma may be seen in fine needle aspirates of solid lesions and that epithelial and biphasic mesotheliomas may both shed diagnostic epithelial cells into effusions with equal frequency. In the past 18 months, we have seen a further three cases of mesothelioma where a cytologic diagnosis was made on fine needle aspirates. All three patients gave a history of asbestos exposure and presented with pleural lesions without effusion. Of the last 10 cases subjected to FNA, we have been able to diagnose 9 with confidence. One aspirate contained only a few spindle cells of uncertain nature, this case subsequently being shown to be a sarcomatous mesothelioma. Ancillary testing on FNA material includes cell block preparation and electron microscopy (see later). In addition the alcohol-fixed smears of FNA material in several cases have provided good material for the demonstration of intracellular hyaluronic acid.

E. ANCILLARY TESTS ON EFFUSIONS

We have previously stressed the value of performing a range of ancillary tests (including histochemistry, immunohistochemistry, electron microscopy, and supernatant fluid analysis) in support of the cytologic findings. (117) This suggested approach has now found common acceptance. (29,41,74,127)

It is important to stress here that the whole effusion sample is of value and that the cytology department has a pivotal role in the decision making process as to whether or not ancillary tests should be ordered.

1. Cytochemistry

Of the so-called "special stains" three need to be considered when applying this form of ancillary test to distinguish mesothelioma from metastatic malignancy. The first and probably most important is the use of the periodic acid Schiff stain (PAS) without and with (PAS-D) digestion. With this stain it is possible to demonstrate intracytoplasmic glycogen with PAS and when material has been pre-digested with the enzyme diastase any residual staining may well represent epithelial mucin. Providing adequate digestion has taken place, then the large solitary magenta stained inclusions are almost certainly epithelial mucin thus indicating adenocarcinoma and excluding malignant mesothelioma. The second form of special stain we use is the van Gieson stain. When many large aggregates are found in the cell block section it is sometimes possible to demonstrate a central, stromal core within some of these aggregates, indicating the true papillary nature of the tumour clusters. Both we (121) and Triol (107) have found this to be a valuable discriminating test, in that aggregates containing a collagen core are seen in mesothelioma, but rarely in adenocarcinoma. The third stain which is often advocated but is seldom of practical value in effusion cytology is that for hyaluronic acid. While in fine needle aspiration cytology (using alcohol-fixed smears) it is possible to demonstrate secretory vacuoles of hyaluronic acid, in cell block effusion samples, most of hyaluronic acid is dissolved; hence we have found this test to be of little practical value.

2. Immunocytochemistry

In discussing the subject of immunocytochemical characterization of mesotheliomas and their distinction from other tumours, Holden and Churg (76) said "the current state of the art in immunocytochemical staining is to some extent one of the methodological overload". There still remains much controversy about whether or not mesotheliomas can be reliably separated firstly from other tumours and secondly from reactive proliferations of the benign mesothelial tissue using immunocytochemical testing. As has been suggested before, much of the disparity results from variation in tissue samples, fixation, technique and antibodies used. It appears that, whereas a particular institution can produce relatively reproducible results useful in the practical diagnostic situation, portability of findings cannot be guaranteed and each laboratory needs to develop its own techniques and methods of interpretation.

Because serous effusions provide a ready source of fresh cells, good material is available for immune testing. Here again there are several ways in which material can be tested. Some workers use cytospin or direct air-dried smears, (37) some wet-fixed smears, (33) and some both. (36) Others, (17,66) including ourselves, have preferred to use the cell block technique. The clear advantage of cell block is that it provides the opportunity of cutting multiple sections of the same cell group for comparative analysis. That is, with a particular aggregate of cells, it is possible not only to study morphology with H&E section, but to see how it reacts with conventional special stains such as PAS and diastase, and what its immunocytochemical profile is. We have found two anti-sera to be helpful routinely. Firstly, carcinoembryonic antigen (CEA) for distinguishing between mesothelioma and adenocarcinoma and secondly, epithelial membrane antigen (EMA) for helping distinguish between mesothelioma and reactive mesothelial cells.

a. Carcino-Embryonic Antigen (CEA)

Over the last decade the impact of immunocytochemistry in the problem area of tumour typing has been enormous. In respect to the differential diagnosis of lung tumours (including mesotheliomas) various antisera have now been widely tested. The onco-foetal antigen (CEA) has emerged as having a pivotal role in distinguishing mesothelioma from adenocarcinoma. Some earlier reports found CEA positivity in a significant proportion of mesotheliomas as well as adenocarcinomas. (4,48,96) In reviewing the subject Bosman (8) still advocates caution when interpreting immunoperoxidase results, especially CEA positivity as the sole criterion used to distinguish between mesothelioma and adenocarcinoma. Controversy still exists about the nature of CEA-like substance being found in mesotheliomatous tissue. (76) However, there has been an increase in the body of evidence that supports the view that most mesotheliomas are negative for CEA. (17,25,30,66,98) As far as cytodiagnosis is concerned several authors have suggested the use of CEA as a help in diagnosing malignancy on cellular material especially when confronted with a few atypical cells with positive staining. (84) Certainly in this context benign mesothelial cells are always negative for CEA and hence strong CEA positivity, especially in cell aggregates, means malignancy. Over many years we have found the demonstration of CEA, to be an extremely reliable discriminant between mesothelioma and adenocarcinoma both in histopathologic material and effusion cells. (117,119)

b. Epithelial Membrane Antigen (EMA)

There are conflicting reports as to whether or not reactive mesothelial cells stain with EMA (or the related antigen HMFG2). Ghosh and colleagues (37) found that in at least half of their cases reactive mesothelial cells stain positive for EMA, whereas Epenetos et al. (33) found such cells were negative. We recognize that the use of this antibody to help establish a malignant diagnosis may be controversial. However, antibody using mercury fixed, cell block sections of effusion cells, we have found that the monoclonal EMA (Dako Patts Inc., Denmark) to be of particular value. In hundreds of effusions tested (117) we have never seen strong membrane staining reaction *in most of the cell clusters* in any benign situation. Occasionally a few single mesothelial cells may show some membrane staining in a reactive situation. On two occasions we found what was thought at the time to be a false positive EMA reaction. However, both of these patients subsequently proved to have malignant mesothelioma. More recent reports on the use of EMA on cytologic material have supported our findings, (66,98,109,111) that is, rarely, if ever, do clusters of reactive mesothelial cells stain strongly for EMA. EMA staining is thus particularly useful in "screening" where, for example, an effusion appears to contain reactive mesothelial cells, but where there are some small mesothelial cell clusters. Strong EMA staining in these cases would warrant a careful re-evaluation of the cytological findings and clinical features. We would not issue a negative report in this situation, but would advise close follow-up.

While in the past, mesothelioma cells have been reported to react variably for EMA, (4) we have found that most of malignant mesothelioma cells in any given effusion are EMA positive. This observation has been recently confirmed by most investigators. (66,109,111) In one recent paper, however, Mason et al. (71) reported that all four cases of malignant mesothelioma tested by them were negative for EMA. Why this should be so is uncertain; however, the authors reported variability in reaction product between smears and cell blocks using the same antisera.

EMA has also recently been demonstrated at the ultrastructural level on the surface of mesothelioma cells (109,111) and from these studies it seems likely that the observed differences in EMA expression at the light microscope level, between benign mesothelial cells and malignant cells, (including mesothelioma) may simply reflect a quantitative difference in the amount of reaction product. (111) However, this observation does not negate the differential diagnostic value of EMA on routine cytological material.

In summary, as a result of the search for the elusive unique immune marker for malignant mesothelioma, (24,99,102) the literature abounds with a plethora of suggestions of antisera or panels of antisera that should help distinguish mesothelioma from adenocarcinoma and a mesothelial reaction. Despite this ever increasing spectrum of tests, for the practising diagnostic cytopathologist, we, like Silverman et al., (98) view the state of the art in 1988 to be a simple choice, viz. the pair of antisera to CEA and EMA.

3. Electron Microscopy

Ultrastructural assessment of tissue has greatly helped in the correct typing of many tumours and, despite technical limitations, such as sampling and considerations of expense and availability, its use has grown in the area of tumour diagnosis. It is of some value in typing poorly differentiated malignancies and of considerable value in distinguishing between well-differentiated tumours having a similar morphology at the light microscope level. (44) Distinguishing between mesothelioma and adenocarcinoma may be such a problem. The ultrastructural features of mesothelioma have been documented for several years, (112,113) (Figure 3-5) but problems of tissue sampling still exist. It is clear that, once again, effusion cells provide a good source of sample for electron microscopy and in our own institution, the preservation of such samples is much better than any other type of cytology sample submitted for ultrastructural analysis, including fine needle aspirates. There have been several reports as to the usefulness of ultrastructural examination of effusion cells and that this technique frequently permits the distinction between malignant mesothelial cells and metastatic adenocarcinoma cells. (23,77) There has also been a suggestion that the distinction between benign reactive mesothelial cells and malignant mesothelioma could also be made; (13) however, this has not been substantiated. Recently, Kobzik, Antman, and Warhol (59) in an excellent detailed study clearly showed that certain ultrastructural criteria could be very reliable in distinguishing between adenocarcinoma and mesothelioma; however, the same criteria could not be applied to the distinction of benign reactive pleurisy from mesothelioma. In their own words—"these cases (2 false positives) illustrate the perils of the diagnostic EM outside the context of routine histopathology and clinical history". With this we would wholly concur, the place of electron microscopy in the diagnostic sequence is *after* the cytologic diagnosis of malignancy has been made.

In summary, we, like Warhol, (114) believe that electron microscopy has a useful role to play in the differential diagnosis of mesothelioma and is best done on effusion cells. Using this technique it is nearly always possible to distinguish between mesothelioma and adenocarcinoma.

4. Cytogenetics

There have been few reports on the use of this technique in the investigation of mesothelioma. (69,115,117) However, there has been some further investigation in this field and Bousfield et al., (9) in a dual approach of identifying both structural and numerical chromosomal abnormalities, were able to identify two cases of epithelial mesothelioma using this cytogenetic approach. However, equivocal results were obtained in a single case of sarcomatous mesothelioma. (9) These authors correctly place this sophisticated tool in the diagnostic sequence as an adjunct to cytodiagnosis. If available, this test will have a particular role in helping confirm the malignant nature of those mesotheliomas that lack the normal morphologic malignant criteria. In collaboration with the Western Australian State Health Laboratory Services' Cytogenetics Unit we are currently investigating mesothelioma cell lines and mesotheliomatous effusions for their cytogenetic profile.

5. Supernatant Analysis

Two tests can be performed which may help in the differential diagnosis of malignant mesothelioma. Effusion levels of CEA can be of value as these are found to be high in many adenocarcinomas; and hyaluronic acid level measurement may also be of value as high levels of this substance is found in association with many malignant mesotheliomas (Figure 3-4).

a. Serous Effusion CEA Levels in the Exclusion of Malignant Mesothelioma

Initially, the biochemical assessment of serous effusion CEA was suggested as an adjunct to cytology in the diagnosis of serosal malignancy. (34,87,110) Faravelli (34) and ourselves (118) noted that only low levels of CEA substance were present in the serous effusions from mesotheliomas; and when used in the specific situation of having established malignancy by the demonstration of malignant cells, it is a good discriminant between mesothelioma and adenocarcinoma in that 67% of adenocarcinomas tested contained levels of above 15 ng/ml of CEA. No mesothelioma had levels above 2.9 ng/ml. (118)

In their recent detailed paper Pinto et al. (87) confirmed the usefulness of this method in diagnosing adenocarcinoma, and they further noted that "in males presenting with (apparent) adenocarcinoma in pleural fluid, a negative fluid CEA would suggest mesothelioma". In limiting this assertion to males, the authors highlighted the fact that some female genital tract carcinomas do not secrete CEA and would therefore would have low levels of this substance in serous effusions. In fact the distinction of metastatic serous adenocarcinoma of the ovary from mesothelioma in effusions usually requires ultrastructural examination.

b. Hyaluronic Acid Levels in Serous Effusions

It has long been recognized that some mesotheliomas secrete large amounts of hyaluronic acid. (42) Not only has this observation led to this muco-substance being demonstrated in mesotheliomatous tissue, but also to its quantitation in serous effusion. The value of estimating levels of hyaluronic acid as a means of diagnosing malignant mesothelioma is somewhat controversial (14,41). Cut-off levels of hyaluronic acid to ensure specificity range from 212–800 mg/litre. (72,88) Using the technique of Rowley et al. (95) we have performed hyaluronic acid estimations on cases of mesothelioma and effusions due to benign processes and metastatic adenocarcinoma. Initially we used a cut off point of 200 mg/litre, but now have adjusted this to 400 mg/litre. Using these various cut-off points ranging from 212–400 mg/litre the sensitivity of these biochemical tests in diagnosing mesothelioma ranges from 33–42%. A recent report by Roboz (92) using high performance electrophoresis is interesting. They examined a series of effusions from mesotheliomas and metastatic tumours. They found that 13 out of 14 mesotheliomas had levels of hyaluronic acid greater than 250 mg/litre and no detectable hyaluronic acid in any of the 56 control effusions. In the context of the differential diagnosis, the test appears to have a very real potential in the situation of distinguishing between a reactive pleurisy and mesothelioma.

F. APPROACH TO DIAGNOSIS

As early as 1977 Kannerstein et al. (56) recommended a systematic approach to the diagnosis of malignant mesothelioma using various samples and techniques. We and others (65,117) have advocated a similar approach using a battery of ancillary tests in a systematic way to support the morphological findings found in effusions and pleural needle biopsies. No survey of the

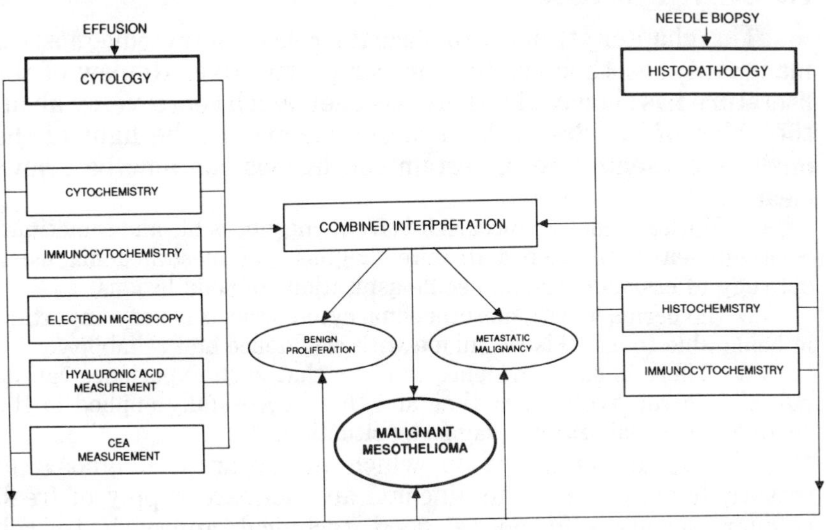

POSSIBLE PATHWAYS OF APPROACH TO THE EARLY DIAGNOSIS OF MALIGNANT MESOTHELIOMA.

Fig. 3-8

early diagnosis of malignant mesothelioma would be complete without at least mention of small sample tissue biopsies. A discussion of this is beyond the scope of this chapter, but nevertheless, in early diagnosis both cytological and micro-histological samples may be available. Using a combination of the two may enhance the diagnostic accuracy. (117) A simple but eminently sensible approach has recently been advocated by McCaughley, Kannerstein and Churg (74) in a chapter devoted to the early diagnosis of mesothelioma (Fig. 3-9). Here the authors stress and illustrate a sequential approach to the diagnosis. We would add electron microscopy to their list of adjuncts used on serous effusions. The advent of fine needle aspiration cytology with its easy sampling of chest wall, thoracic, and other metastatic lesions now makes this technique an important part of the early diagnostic armoury in the diagnosis of mesothelioma. Not only does it fill an important gap in conventional cytodiagnosis by enabling the sampling of those cases of mesothelioma presenting without effusions, it also is an approach involving minimal discomfort or complication to the patient. By using this two-pronged cytodiagnostic approach: FNA for solid lesions and exfoliative cytology for serous effusions, most mesotheliomas will be successfully diagnosed quite early.

G. CONCLUSION

This chapter attempts to place the role of the cytodiagnosis of malignant mesothelioma in a proper perspective. Review of the literature has shown why there has been much controversy about the value of cytodiagnosis of mesothelioma. In the light of the analysis presented here, certain conclusions can now be drawn clearly.

(1) With a modern approach it is frequently possible and sometimes relatively easy to make a definite diagnosis of mesothelioma using cytology of effusions or fine needle aspirations of solid lesions.

(2) Experience with mesothelioma cytodiagnosis is very important in being able to use this technique with confidence and reliability.

(3) There is some evidence to show that such experience can be gained in a relatively short time and then successfully applied in the routine clinical/laboratory diagnostic situation.

The ideal conditions in which an accurate diagnosis of mesothelioma can be made include an adequate supply of fresh cellular serous effusion, a good technical approach to cell concentration, and the setting aside of portions of the cell samples to prepare cell blocks for special tests and electron microscopy. Of all the ancillary tests available the most valuable are:

ELEMENTS IN THE DIAGNOSIS OF DIFFUSE MESOTHELIOMA

1. History and clinical
2. Fluid cytology – with cell histochemistry, immunohistochemistry and fluid biochemistry as adjuncts
3. Studies excluding other sources of tumor – i.e., physical, radiographic, endoscopic
4. Gross morphology of the tumor – radiographic, endoscopic, exploratory surgery
5. Microscopic morphology of the tumor (needle or open biopsy) – histochemistry and electron microscopy as adjuncts
6. Autopsy

From: Tumors and Pseudotumors of the Serous Membranes.
McCaughey, Kannerstein and Churg.
(Courtesy of the A.F.I.P.)

Fig. 3-9

(1) For tumour typing—immunoperoxidase demonstration of CEA, PAS-D for epithelial mucin, and electron microscopy.

(2) For supporting a diagnosis of malignancy—immunoperoxidase demonstration of EMA.

Given adequate experience there is no doubt that the serous effusion sample, and especially its cytodiagnosis, can provide a solid foundation on which to base a confident and reliable diagnosis of malignant mesothelioma. However, we have found that the optimal situation in which to establish a diagnosis of mesothelioma on minimal material is when the serous effusion findings are assessed in conjunction with those of a needle tissue biopsy.

REFERENCES

1. Adams VI, Unni KK, Huhm JR, Jett JR, Ilstrup DM, Bernantz PE. Diffuse malignant mesothelioma of pleura: Diagnosis and survival in 92 cases. Cancer 1986; 58:1540–1551
2. Antman KH, Blum RH, Greenberger JS, Flowerdew GS, Karin AT, Canellos GP. Multimodality therapy for malignant mesothelioma based on a study of natural history. Am J Med 1980; 68:356–362
3. Antman KH. Malignant mesothelioma. N Engl J Med 1980; 303:200–202
4. Battifora H & Kopinski BS. Distinction of mesothelioma from adenocarcinoma. Cancer. 1985; 55:1679–1685.
5. Becker SN, Pepin DW, Rosenthal DL. Mesothelial papilloma: a case of mistaken identity in a pericardial effusion. Acta Cytol 1979; 20:266–268.
6. Boon ME, Kwee WS, Alons CL, Morawetz F, Veldhuizen RW. Discrimination between primary pleural and primary peritoneal mesotheliomas by morphometry and analysis of vacuolization pattern of the exfoliated mesothelial cells. Acta Cytol 1982; 26:103–108
7. Boon ME, Weldhuizen RW, Ruinaard C, Snieders MW, Kwee WS. Qualitative distinctive differences between the vacuoles of mesothelioma cells and of cells from metastatic carcinoma exfoliated in pleural fluid. Acta Cytol 1984; 28:443–449
8. Bosman FT. Immunocytochemical Assessment of Lung Tumors In: McVie, Bakker, Wagenaar, Carney Eds. Clinical and Experimental Pathology of Lung Cancer Lancaster, Martinus Nijhoff, 1986, 75–89
9. Bousfield LR, Greenberg ML, Pacey F, Cytogenetic Diagnosis of Cancer from Body Fluids. Acta Cytol 1985. 29:768–774
10. Boutin C, Viallat JR, Rey F. Thoroscopy in the diagnosis, prognosis and treatment of mesothelioma. In: Antman, Aisner. Ed. Asbestos related malignancy. Orlando, Grune & Stratton. 1986:301–322
11. Brenner J, Sordillo PP, Magill GB, Golbey RB. Malignant mesothelioma of the pleura: review of 123 patients. Cancer 1982; 49:2431–2435

12. Butler EB, Berry AV. Diffuse mesotheliomas. Diagnostic criteria using exfoliative cytology. In: Bogovski P, Gilson JC, Timbrell V, Wagner JC, eds. Biological effects of asbestos. Lyon: International Agency for Research on Cancer. 1973; 68–73.
13. Butler EB, Johnson JF. The use of electron microscopy in the diagnosis of diffuse mesotheliomas using human pleural effusions. In: Wagner JC, ed. Biological Effects of Mineral Fibres. Lyon: IARC Sci Publ 1980; 30:409–418
14. Castor CW, Naylor B. Acid mucopolysaccharide composition of serous effusions. Cancer 1967; 20:462–466
15. Chahinian AP, Pajak TF, Holland JF, Norton L, Ambinder RM, Mandel EM. Diffuse malignant mesothelioma. Prospective evaluation of 69 patients. Ann Int Med 1982; 96:746–755
16. Churg A, Golden J. Current problems in pathology of asbestos-related disease. Pathol Ann 1982; 17(part 2):33–66
17. Cibas ES, Corson JM, Pinkus GS. The distinction of adenocarcinoma from malignant mesothelioma in cell blocks of effusions: the role of routine mucin histochemistry and immunohistochemical assessment of carcinoembryonic antigen, keratin proteins, epithelial membrane antigen, and milk fat globule-derived antigen. Hum Pathol. 1987; 18:67–74.
18. Corson JM. Pathology of malignant mesothelioma. In: Antman, Aisner Eds. Asbestos related malignancy. Orlando, Grune & Stratton Inc. 1987:179–200
19. Craighead JE. Asbestos-Associated Diseases. Arch Path Lab Med. 1982; 106:588.
20. Cretien J, Jaubert F. Pleural response in malignant metastatic tumours. In: Cretien J, Bignon J, Hirsch A, eds. The pleura in health and disease. New York, Dekker, 1985:489
21. Dekker A, Bupp PA. Cytology of serous effusions. An investigation into the usefulness of cell blocks versus smears. Am J Clin Pathol 1978; 70:855–860
22. Dimitrov NV, McMahon S. Presentation, diagnostic methods, staging and natural history of malignant mesothelioma. In: Antman, Aisner Eds. Asbestos related malignancy, Orlando, Grune & Stratton. 1986:225–238
23. Domagala W, Woyke S. Transmission and scanning electron microscopic studies of cells in effusions. Acta Cytol. 1975; 19:214–224.
24. Donna A, Betta PG, Bellinger D, Marchisini A. New marker for mesothelioma: an immunoperoxidase study. J Clin Pathol. 1986; 39:961–968.
25. Duggan MA, Masters CB, Alexander F. Immunohistochemical differentiation of malignant mesothelioma, mesothelial hyperplasia and metastatic adenocarcinoma in serous effusions using staining for carcinoembryonic antigen, keratin and vimentin. Acta Cytol. 1987; 31:807–814.
26. Dunhill MS. Pulmonary pathology. 2nd Edit. Edinburgh: Churchill Livingstone, 1987:516

27. Edge JR, Choudhury SL. Malignant mesothelioma of the pleural in Barrow-in-Furness. Thorax 1978; 33:26–30
28. Edge JR. Mesothelioma. Br J Hosp Med 1983; 29:521–530; 535–536
29. Ehya H. The cytologic diagnosis of mesothelioma. Sem Diag Pathol 1986, 3:196–203
30. Elema JD, De Leij L, Postmus P, Popema S, The T.H. Critical Evaluation of New Techniques in the Morphological Diagnosis of Lung Cancer, McVie, Bakker, Wagenaar, Carney Eds. Clinical and Experimental Pathology of Lung Cancer. Lancaster, Martinus Nijkoff 1986; 91–103
31. Elmes PC, Simpson MJC. The clinical aspects of mesothelioma. Quart J Med 1976; 45:427–429
32. Elmes PC. The natural history of mesothelioma of the pleura. J Irish Coll Physn & Surg 1972; 1:117–123
33. Epenetos AA, Canti G, Taylor-Papadimitriou J, Curling M, Bodmer WF. Use of two epithelium-specific monoclonal antibodies for diagnosis of malignancy in serous effusions. Lancet. 1982; ii; 1004–1006.
34. Faravelli B, Diamore E, Nosenzo M et al. Carcinoembryonic antigen in pleural effusions. Diagnostic value in malignant mesothelioma. Cancer 1984; 53:1194–7.
35. Gaensler EA, Kaplan AI. Asbestos pleural effusion. Ann Inter Med. 1974; 74:178–191.
36. Ghosh AK, Spriggs AI, Curling M. Tumour markers in serous effusions. Lancet. 1984;i;338.
37. Ghosh AK, Spriggs Ai, Taylor-Papadimitriou J, Mason DY. Immunocytochemical staining of cells in pleural and peritoneal effusions with a panel of monoclonal antibodies. J Clin Pathol. 1983; 36:1154–1164.
38. Greenberg SD. Recent advances in pulmonary cytopathology. Hum Pathol 1983; 14:901–912
39. Griffiths MH, Riddell RJ, Xippell JM. Malignant mesothelioma. A review of 35 cases with diagnosis and prognosis. Pathology. 1980; 12:591–603.
40. Gupta PK, Frost JK. Cytologic changes associated with asbestos exposure. Semin Oncol 1981; 8:283–289
41. Hammar SP, Bolen JW. Pleural neoplasms. In: Dail DH, Hammar SP. eds Pulmonary Pathology. New York. Springer-Verlag. 1987; 1012–1020.
42. Harrington JS, Wagner JC, Smith M. The detection of hyaluronic acid in pleural fluids of cases with diffuse pleural mesotheliomas. Br J Exp Pathol 1963; 44:81
43. Hassan FN, Nash G, Kazeni H. The significance of asbestos exposure in the diagnosis of mesothelioma: A 28 year experience from a major urban hospital. Am Rev Resp Dis 1977; 115:761–768
44. Henderson DW, Papadimitriou JM. Ultrastructural appearances

of tumours: A diagnostic atlas. Edinburgh: Churchill Livingstone. 1981; 109–115

45. Henderson DW. Asbestos-related pleuropulmonary diseases: asbestosis, mesothelioma and lung cancer. Pathology. 1982; 14:239–243.
46. Herbert A. The diagnosis of malignant mesothelioma (Editorial). J Path. 1984; 143:145–146.
47. Hillerdal G. Malignant mesothelioma 1982: Review of 4710 published cases. Br J Dis Chest 1983; 77:321–343
48. Holden J, Churg A. Immunohistochemical staining for keratin and carcinoembryonic antigen in the diagnosis of malignant mesothelioma. Am J Surg Pathol 1984 8:277–279
49. Jara F, Hiroshi T, Uma NMR. Malignant mesothelioma of pleura. N.Y. State J Med. 1977; 77:1885–1888.
50. Jayaram G, Ashok S. Fine needle aspiration cytology of well-differentiated papillary peritoneal mesothelioma. Acta Cytol 1988; 32:563–566
51. Johnston WW. Perspectives in cytological diagnosis. In: Cretien J, Bignon J, Hirsch A, eds. The pleura in health and disease. New York, Dekker, 1985:777
52. Johnston WW. The malignant pleural effusion. Cancer. 1985; 56:905–909.
53. Johnston WW. Cytologic Correlations In: Dail DH, Hammer SP. eds Pulmonary pathology. Berlin: Springer Verlag, 1987: 1071
54. Jones JSP, Lund C, Planteydt HT. Colour Atlas of Mesothelioma. Lancaster, MTP Press Ltd. 1985 20–23
55. Kannerstein M, Churg J, McCaughey WT. Asbestos and mesothelioma: A review. Pathol Ann 1978; 13(part 1):81–129
56. Kannerstein M, McCaughey WTE, Churg J, Selikoff IJ. A critique of the criteria for the diagnosis of diffuse malignant mesothelioma. Mt Sinai J Med 1977; 44:485–494
57. Kittle CF. Mesothelioma, diagnosis and management. Chicago. Year Book Medical Publishers Inc. 1987:21–23
58. Klempman S. The exfoliative cytology of diffuse pleural mesothelioma. Cancer 1962; 15:691–704
59. Kobzik L, Antman KH, Warhol MJ. The distinction of mesothelioma from adenocarcinoma in malignant effusions by electron microscopy. Acta Cytol. 1985; 29:219–225.
60. Koss LG, Woyke S, Olezewski W. Aspiration biopsy—cytologic interpretation and histologic basis. New York, Igaku-Shoin, New York, 1984:331–333
61. Koss LG. Diagnostic Cytology and its Histopathologic Bases. 3rd ed. Philadelphia: Lippincott, 1979
62. Koss LG. Diagnostic Cytology and its Histopathologic Bases. 1st ed. Philadelphia: Lippincott, 1961
63. Koss LG. Diagnostic Cytology and its Histopathologic Bases. 2nd ed Philadelphia: Lippincott, 1968

64. Kwee WS, Veldhuizen RW, Alons CL, Morawetz F, Boon ME. Quantitative and qualitative differences between benign and malignant mesothelial cells in pleural fluid. Acta Cytol 1982; 26:401–406
65. Kwee WS. Quantitative and qualitative studies of malignant mesothelioma. Amsterdam, Netherlands: Vrije Universiteit TE Amsterdam. 1982. Thesis.
66. Lauritzen AF. Distinction between cells in serous effusions using a panel of antibodies. Virchows Arch A. 1987; 411:299–304.
67. Law MR, Hodson ME, Turner-Warwick M. Malignant mesothelioma of the pleura. Clinical aspects and symptomatic treatment. Eur J Resp Dis 1984; 65:162–168
68. Lewis RJ, Sisler GE, MacKenzie JW. Diffuse, mixed malignant pleural mesothelioma. Ann Thor Surg 1981; 31:53–60.
69. Mark J. Three chromosomal abnormalities observed in cells of two malignant mesotheliomas studied by banding technique. Acta Cytol. 1978; 22:298–401.
70. Martensson G, Hagmar B, Zettergren L. Diagnosis and prognosis in malignant pleural mesothelioma: A prospective study. Eur J Respir Dis 1984; 65:169–178
71. Mason RM, Bedrossian CWM, Fahey CA. Value of immunocytochemistry in the study of malignant effusions. Diagn Cytopath. 1987; 3: 215–221.
72. Matzel W, Schubert G. Hyaluronic acid in pleural fluids: An additional parameter for clinical diagnosis on diffuse mesothelioma. Arch fur Gesch 1979; 49:146–154
73. Matzel W. Biochemical and cytological features of diffuse mesotheliomas of the pleura. Arch Geschwulstforsch 1985; 55:259–264
74. McCaughey WTE, Kannerstein M, Churg J. A.F.I.P. fascicle: No. 20. Tumours and Pseudotumours of the Serous Membranes, 1985
75. Morgan WKC, Seaton A. Occupational lung diseases. 2nd Edit. Philadelphia: WB Saunders, 1984:532
76. Mukai K. Malignant mesothelioma and CEA staining. Am J Surg Pathol. 1985; 9:159–160.
77. Murad TM. Electron microscopic studies of cells in pleural and peritoneal effusions. Acta Cytol. 1973; 17:401–409.
78. Naib ZN. Exfoliative Cytopathology, 2nd Edit. Boston: Little Brown. 1976; 301.
79. Nauta RJ, Osteen RT, Antman KH, Koster JK. Clinical staging and the tendency of malignant pleural mesotheliomas to remain localized. Ann Thorac Surg. 1982; 34:66–70.
80. Naylor B. The exfoliative cytology of diffuse malignant mesothelioma. J Pathol Bacteriol 1963; 86:293–298
81. Obers VJ, Leiman G, Girdwood RW, Spiro FI. Primary malignant pleural tumors (mesotheliomas) presenting as localized masses. Acta Cytol 1988; 32:567–575
82. Oels HC, Harrison EG, Carr BT, Bernatz PE. Diffuse malignant mesothelioma of the pleura: a review of 37 cases. Chest 1971; 60:564–570

83. Orell SR, Sterrett GF, Walters MN-I, Whitaker D. Manual and Atlas of Fine Needle Aspiration Cytology. Edinburgh: Churchill Livingstone, 1986:141
84. Orell, SR, Dowling KD. Oncofetal Antigens as Tumor Markers in the Cytologic Diagnosis of Effusions. Acta Cytol. 1983; 27:625–629.
85. Osteen RT. Peritoneal mesothelioma. In: Antman K, Aisner J, ed. Asbestos related malignancy. Orlando, Grune & Stratton Inc. 1986:339–356
86. Parkes WR. Occupational lung disorders. 2nd Edit. London: Butterworth, 1982:290
87. Pinto MM, Bernstein LH, Brogan DA, Criscuolo EM. Carcinoembryonic Antigen in Effusions. A Diagnostic Adjunct to Cytology. Acta Cytol 1987; 31:113–118
88. Rasmussen KN, Faber V. Hyaluronic Acid in 247 Pleural Fluids. Scand J Resp Dis 1967; 48:366–371
89. Reuter K, Raptopoulos V, Reale F, Krolikowski FJ, D'Orsi CJ, Graham S, Smith EH. Diagnosis of peritoneal mesothelioma: computed tomography, sonography, and fine-needle aspiration biopsy. AJR 1983; 140:1189–1194
90. Ribak J, Lilis R, Suzuki Y, Penner L, Selikoff IJ. Malignant mesothelioma in a cohort of asbestos insulation workers: Clinical presentation, diagnosis, and causes of death. Br J Ind Med 1988; 45:182–187
91. Roberts GH, Campbell GM. Exfoliative cytology of diffuse mesothelioma. J Clin Pathol 1972; 25:577–582
92. Roboz J, Greaves J, Silides D, Chahinian AP, Holland JF. Hyaluronic acid content of effusions as a diagnostic aid for malignant mesothelioma. Cancer Res 1985; 45:1850–1854
93. Roggli VL, Kolbeck J, Sanfilippo F, Shelburne JD. Pathology of human mesothelioma. Etiologic and diagnostic considerations. Pathol Annu. 1987; 22:91–131.
94. Rosai J, Dehner LP. Nodular mesothelial hyperplasia in hernia sacs: a benign reactive condition simulating a neoplastic process. Cancer 1975; 35:165–175
95. Rowley G, Antonas KN, Hilbert J. Quantitation of hyaluronic acid in equine synovia. Am J Vet Res 1982; 43:1096–1099
96. Said W, Nash G, Tepper G, Banks-Schlegel S. Keratin proteins and carcinoembryonic antigen in lung carcinoma: An immunoperoxidase study of fifty-four cases, with ultrastructural correlations. Human Pathol. 1983, 14:70–76
97. Sherrin JC, Jackson P. Malignant pleural mesothelioma. J Thorac Cardiovasc Surg. 1976; 71:621–627.
98. Silverman JF, Nance K, Phillips B, Norris MT. The use of immunoperoxidase panels for the cytologic diagnosis of malignancy in effusions. Diagn Cytopathol. 1987; 3:134–140.
99. Singh G, Whiteside TL and Dekker A. Immunodiagnosis of mesothelioma: use of antimesothelial cell serum in an indirect immunofluorescence assay. Cancer. 1979; 43:2288–2296.

100. Spriggs AI, Jerome DW. Benign mesothelial proliferation with collagen formation in pericardial fluid. Acta Cytol 1979; 23:428–430
101. Spriggs AI. The architecture of tumour cell clusters in serous effusions. In: Koss LG, Coleman DV. Advances in clinical cytology. Vol 2. New York. Masson. 1984; 287–289.
102. Stahel RA, O'Hara CJ, Waibel R & Martin A. Monoclonal antibodies against mesothelial membrane antigen discriminate between malignant mesothelioma and lung adenocarcinoma. Int J Cancer. 1988; 41:218–223.
103. Sterrett GF, Whitaker D, Shilkin KB, Walters MN. Fine needle aspiration cytology of malignant mesothelioma. Acta Cytol 1987; 31:185–193.
104. Strankinga WF, Sperber M, Kaiser MC, Stam J. Accuracy of diagnostic procedures in the initial evaluation and follow-up of mesothelioma patients. Respiration 1987; 51:179–187
105. Suzuki Y. Pathology of human malignant mesothelioma. Semin Oncol 1980; 8:268–282
106. Tao LC. The cytopathology of mesothelioma. Acta Cytol 1979; 23:209–213
107. Triol JH, Conston AS, Chandler SV. Malignant mesothelioma. Cytopathology of 75 cases seen in a New Jersey community hospital. Acta Cytol 1984; 28:37–45
108. Triol JH, Conston AS, Chandler SVD. Distinguishing adenocarcinoma from mesothelioma in effusions. Hum Pathol 1987; 18:969
109. Van der Kwast TM, Versnel MA, Delahaye M, de Jong A, Zondervan PE, Hoogstden H. Expression of epithelial membrane antigen in malignant mesothelioma cells—an immunocytochemical and immunoelectron microscopic study. Acta Cytol. 1988; 32:169–174.
110. Vladutiu AO, Brason FW, Adler RH. Differential diagnosis of pleural effusions—clinical usefulness of cell marker quantitation. Chest 1981; 79:297–301.
111. Walts AE, Said JW, Shintaku PT. Epithelial membrane antigen in the cytodiagnosis of effusions and aspirates. Diagn Cytopathol. 1987; 3:41–49.
112. Wang NS. Electron microscopy in the diagnosis of pleural mesotheliomas. Cancer. 1973; 31:1046–1054.
113. Warhol MJ, Hickey WF, Corson JM. Malignant mesothelioma. Ultrastructural distinction from adenocarcinoma. Am J Surg Pathol. 1982; 6:307–314.
114. Warhol MJ. Electron microscopy in the diagnosis of mesothelioma with routine biopsy, needle biopsy and fluid cytology. In: Antman, Aisner eds. Asbestos related malignancy. Orlando, Grune & Stratton Inc. 1987; 201–220.
115. Watts KC, Boyo-Ekwueme H, To A, Posnansky M, Coleman DV.

Chromosome studies on cells cultured from serous effusions: use in routine cytologic practice. Acta Cytol. 1983; 27:38–44.
116. Whitaker D, Papadimitriou JM, Walters MN-I. The mesothelium and its reactions: a review. CRC Crit Rev Toxicol 1982; 10:81–144
117. Whitaker D, Shilkin K. Diagnosis of pleural malignant mesothelioma in life—a practical approach. J Pathol 1984; 143:147–175.
118. Whitaker D, Shilkin KB, Stuckey M, Nieuwhof WN. Pleural fluid CEA levels in the diagnosis of malignant mesothelioma. Pathology 1986; 18:328–329
119. Whitaker D, Sterrett GF, Shilkin KB. Detection of tissue CEA-like substance as an aid in the differential diagnosis of malignant mesothelioma. Pathology 1982; 14:255–258
120. Whitaker D, Shilkin KB. The cytology of malignant mesothelioma in Western Australia. Acta Cytol 1978; 22:67–70
121. Whitaker D. Cell aggregates in malignant mesothelioma. Acta Cytol 1977; 21:236–239
122. Whitaker D. Serous effusion diagnosis of malignant mesothelioma. Broadsheet No. 13. Australian Institute of Medical Laboratory Scientists. 1989.
123. Whitaker D. The validity of a cytological diagnosis of mesothelioma. Aust NZ J Med 1987; 17:519
124. Whitaker D. Hyaluronic acid in serous effusion smears. Acta Cytol. 1986; 30:90.
125. Whitaker D. Pleural effusions in Mesothelioma. Impulse. 1987; 26:1–6
126. Wright WE, Sherwin RP, Dickson EA, Burnstein L, Fromm JB, Henderson BE. Malignant Mesothelioma: Incidence, asbestos exposure, and reclassification of histopathology. Br J. Ind Med 1984; 41:39–45
127. Young JA. Colour atlas of pulmonary cytopathology. Oxford University Press. Oxford. 1985; 116

4

Immunohistochemical and Histochemical Markers in Lung Carcinomas and Mesotheliomas

HELMUT H. POPPER, M.D.

Laboratory of Environmental Pathology
Institute of Pathology
University of Graz, School of Medicine
Auenbruggerplatz 25
A-8036 Graz/Austria

Synopsis

D. CARCINOEMBRYONIC ANTIGEN (CEA)
E. S-100 PROTEIN
 1. Surfactant Aprotein
 2. Pregnancy Specific Glycoprotein 1 (SP1)
 3. LeuM1 Antibodies
 4. B72.3 Antibody
 5. ATPases
 6. Ferritin
 7. Lectins
F. RECOMMENDATIONS FOR MESOTHELIOMA DIAGNOSIS

BIOGRAPHY

Helmut H. Popper is a staff member at the Department of Pathology, University of Graz, School of Medicine, Graz, Austria. He has done two years postgraduate research work at the Department of Pharmacology and Toxicology, University of Graz, and then moved to the Department of Pathology. He finished his postgraduate training in Pathology in 1985, got a degree of a Dozent (Associate Prof. of Pathology) in the same year. His interests were first focused on inflammation with special emphasis on the role of eosinophils. Besides this he specialized in lung and respiratory tract pathology and did some research work in immunohistochemical markers in malignant lung and pleura tumors. Since 1986 his interests are shifted toward inhalation toxicology and pathology. Then laboratories for Environmental Pathology were installed at the Department of Pathology. Dr. Popper is a member of the Austrian, German, and European societies of Pathology, the Austrian branch of the Int. Academy of Pathology, the Int. Soc. of Toxicology, the Austrian and European societies of Immunology and Allergy. The author may be contacted at the Institute of Pathology, University of Graz, Medical School, Auenbruggerplatz 25, A-8036 Graz, Austria.

EDITORS' COMMENTARY

The differential diagnosis of malignant tumors is important for both medical and legal specialists (as well as for the patient!). A lawsuit may involve allegations that the plaintiff is suffering from mesothelioma caused by exposure to asbestos, whereas the defense may respond that it is just another disease process, such as adenocarcinoma, that may not be associated with asbestos. While specific differential diagnosis is often difficult, it could assure the best possible treatment under the circumstances. The effort to achieve greater specificity and certainty also could lead to better understanding of the pathology and its causes, progression, alternative treatment, prognosis, and possible prevention. The pathologist may be relied upon to examine tissue samples to provide more objective information to facilitate a differential diagnosis. By morphological appearance and the relative effects of panels of enzymes, antibodies, and proteins, increased certainty can be achieved in the characterization of the cell and the specific disease process. The following chapter provides important information regarding cell staining techniques that could be extremely useful in the differential diagnosis of mesothelioma. It reflects some significant advances in one area of medical research that contributes to the mosaic by which we are rapidly gaining a better overall understanding and more effective approach in dealing with the complex problems that have arisen from the unsafe use of asbestos. The increasingly productive medical research should be extremely helpful for treating physicians, research scientists, government regulators, attorneys at law, safety engineers, industrial hygienists, occupational physicians, and abatement contractors.

A. INTRODUCTION

Tumors of the visceral and parietal serous membranes (pleura, peritoneum, pericardium) were recognized in the 19th century but not well defined. In 1931 Klemperer and Rabin first related these neoplasms to the mesothelial cells and classified them into localized and diffuse forms. Since then this division has been accepted by pathologists and clinicians. Localized tumors are usually fibrous and benign, diffuse tumors are often epithelial and nearly always malignant.

Diffuse malignant mesotheliomas originate from mesothelial cells of either the visceral or parietal pleura or peritoneum, less frequently of pericardium. In early stages they form a thin cellular film on the serosa and easily single cells or groups of tumor cells detach, float freely in the serous fluid, spread, adhere to other areas and continue to grow. Richly cellular and hemorrhage effusions are common in this early stage. By conventional cytologic evaluation, tumor cells and reactive proliferating mesothelial cells, e.g., associated with most inflammatory disorders, cannot be differentiated (Koss, 1979). All cytologic criteria that had been proposed as being specific for malignancy, e.g., pink centers, nuclear atypia, distinct cell membrane, coarse chromatin, etc., can also be found in benign proliferations (Koss, 1979) (Fig. 4-1). Therefore, recurrent pleural (peritoneal effusions associated with mesothel cell proliferation should be investigated by biopsy.

Malignant mesothelioma has a wide morphologic spectrum: The spectrum comprises tumors that are entirely of epithelial or mesenchymal type as well as a range of intermediate (biphasic) forms. As in other neoplasms, cytologic and architectural features may vary from well differentiated to anaplastic. The epithelial part can be squamoid, tubulo-papillary (Figs. 4-2 and 4-3), signet ring cell-like, spindle cell-like, or solid anaplastic; the mesenchymal part may exhibit myxoid, angiosarcomatous, fibrosarcomatous, or desmoplastic features (Fig. 4-4) (McCaughey et al., 1985; Mark, 1984; Carter, Otis, 1988). A new lymphoid type has been recently described (Henderson et al., 1988). The majority of the reported cases have been epithelial ranging from 54% to 75%, whereas biphasic and sarcomatous forms account for 25% and 21%, respectively (Legha and Maggia, 1977; Kannerstein and Churg, 1977).

Asbestos was established to be an important etiologic factor for mesotheliomas, but also for the induction of pulmonary neo-

Accepted for publication 15 May 1989

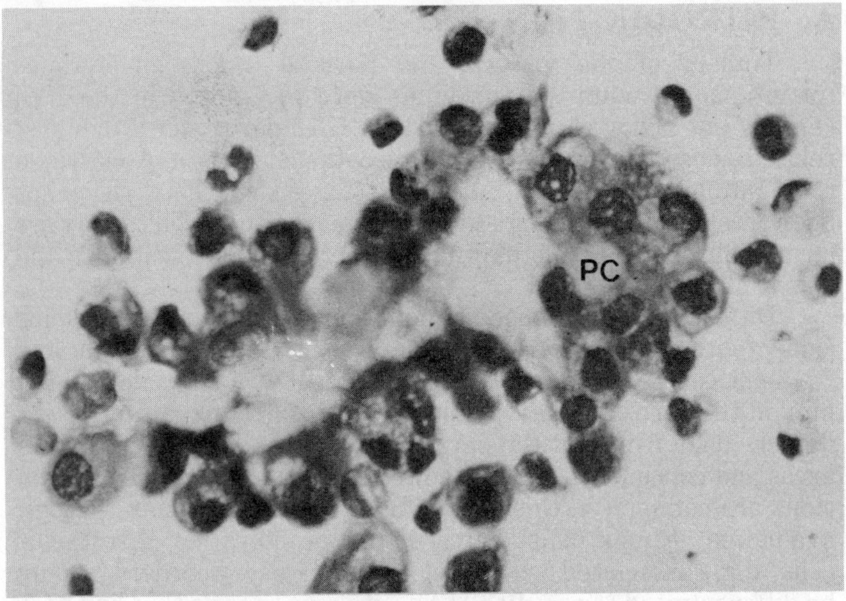

Fig. 4-1 Cytology of malignant epithelial mesothelioma. Cells are large with mild atypic nuclei. It is impossible to differentiate these cells from proliferating reactive mesothelial cells. PC = pink center; May-Grünwald-Giemsa, ×625.

plasms. Diffuse mesothelioma of pleura and peritoneum and lung carcinoma following lung asbestos (among other carcinomas from other organs) are accepted as neoplastic consequences of asbestos exposure in man (Norseth, 1980; McCaughey et al., 1985; Kannerstein et al., 1978). It should be mentioned, however, that mesotheliomas and more often pulmonary neoplasms may arise without relation to previous asbestos exposure.

Lung carcinoma is the other tumor entity that can be induced by asbestos fibers, although the majority of them is caused by tobacco smoke inhalation (Doll, 1978). Lung carcinomas are divided into squamous, large, and small cell types and adenocarcinomas (WHO, 1981). There is usually no problem in differentiating squamous, small, and large cell carcinomas from diffuse malignant epithelial mesotheliomas, but the differential diagnosis of pulmonary adenocarcinoma and adenocarcinomas derived from other organs, esp. papillary, tubular (Figs. 4-5 and 4-6) and solid types, and mesothelioma is difficult. Because of the differences in therapy of mesothelioma and adenocarcinoma, a clear-cut differential diagnosis is essential. Various methods have been used to

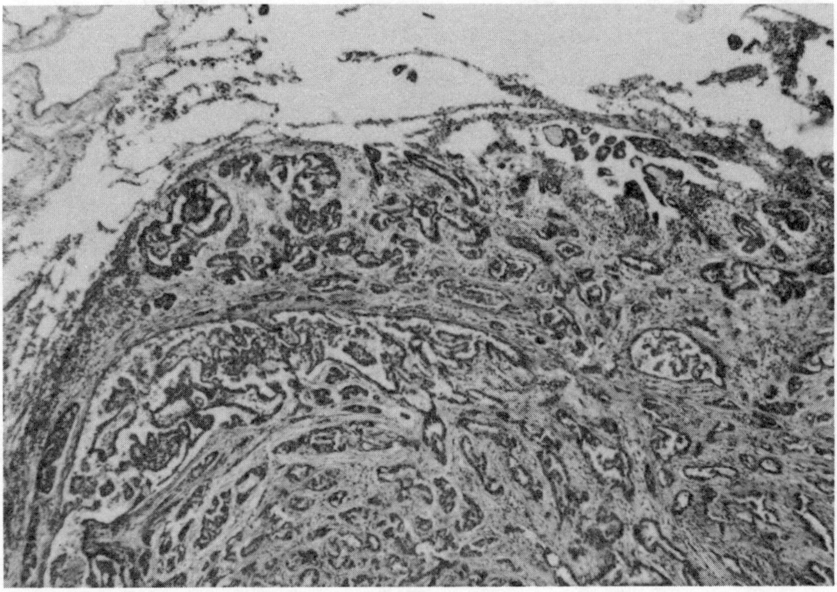

Fig. 4-2 Tubular mesothelioma. HE ×80.

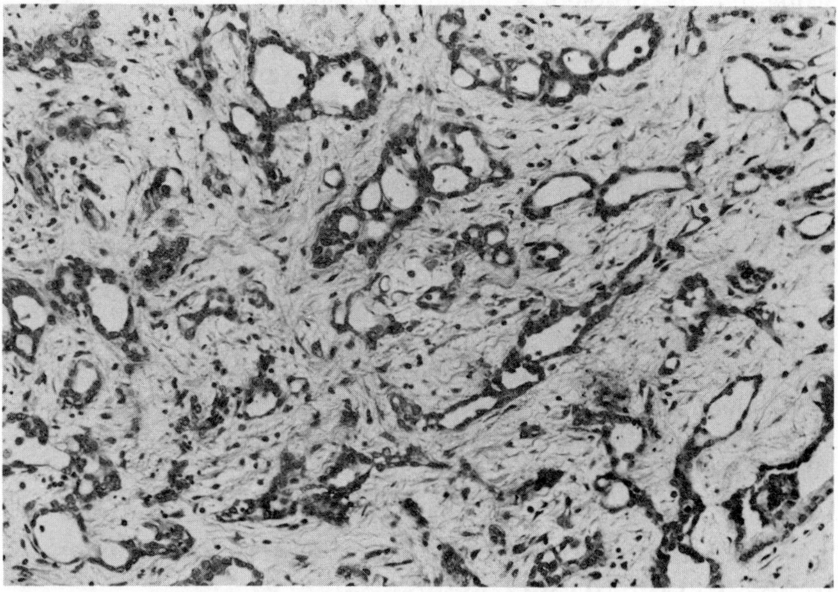

Fig. 4-3 Tubulo-papillary mesotheliomas. HE: ×150.

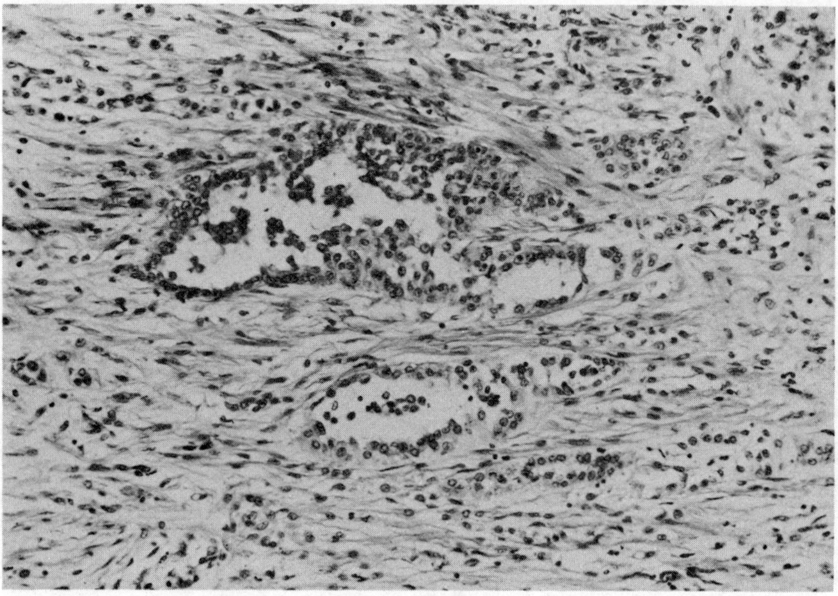

Fig. 4-4 Epithelial tubular mesothelioma with extensive desmoplastic reaction of the fibrous stroma. HE: ×160.

overcome this problem including mucin stains and electron microscopy, but the problem is still unresolved.

B. MESOTHELIOMA: GROSS EXAMINATION

In early stages diffuse mesothelioma is usually represented by multiple neoplastic foci involving parietal and/or visceral serous membranes. With progression the foci fuse and form thicker tumor plaques and layers, sometimes several centimeters in thickness. Infiltration of diaphragm is often found. Invasion of the lungs is often noted. It is superficial in most cases, but may also form large masses or multiple nodules within the lung parenchyma. Mesotheliomas frequently metastasize to mediastinal, hilar, abdominal, cervical and axillar lymph nodes, but also hematogenous dissemination is frequently noted at autopsy (Roberts, 1976; Cantin et al., 1982).

1. Glycosaminoglycans and Other Mucin Substances in Mesothelioma and Adenocarcinoma

In the cytoplasm of mesothelioma and adenocarcinoma cells periodic acid Schiff reagents (PAS) positive material is regularly

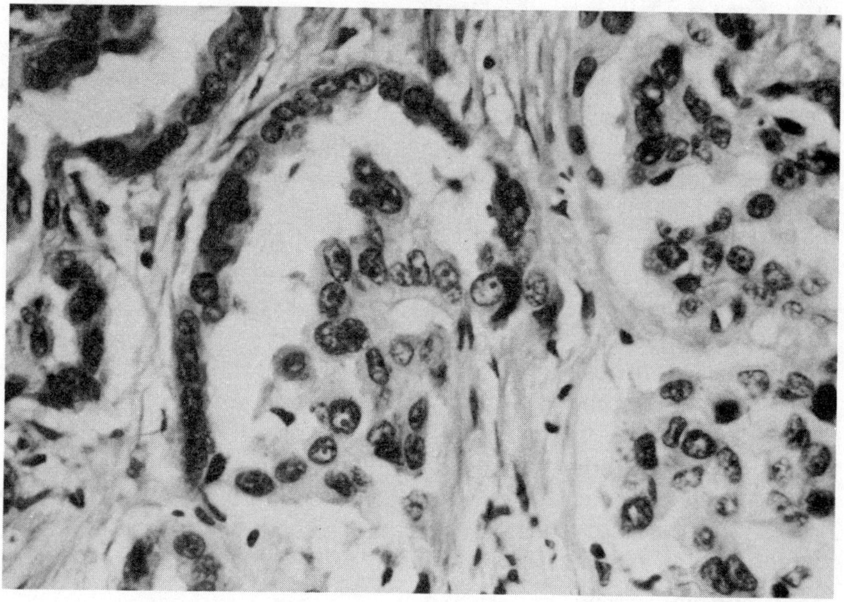

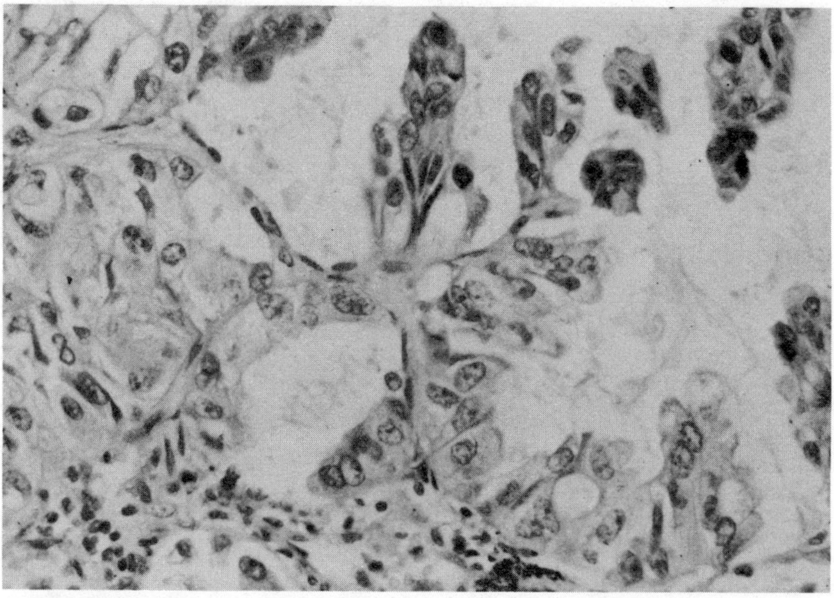

Figs. 4-5 and 4-6 Two cases of tubular and tubulopapillary adenocarcinomas of the lung. Comparing their features with those of mesotheliomas (Figs. 4-2 and 4-3) there are no specific differences in light microscopy. HE: ×310, ×400, respectively.

found. If the sections are preincubated with diastase to remove glycogen, mesothelioma cells are often unstained in contrast to adenocarcinomas (Fig. 4-7). But in some mesotheliomas diastase-resistant PAS-positive epithelial mucin was found (McCaughey et al., 1985). Therefore, the presence of diastase-resistant epithelial mucin is not specific for adenocarcinomas.

The demonstration of acidic mucin by alcian blue stain (or equivalent stains), which can be removed by pretreatment with hyaluronidase, favors a mesothelioma (Arai et al., 1979). But hyaluronic acid, the substratum for this enzyme reaction, is leached out of tumor tissue by aqueous fixatives and therefore this reaction is limited to unfixed tumor tissue (Kannerstein et al., 1973). Unfixed tumor tissue is unfortunately seldom available to pathologists. The glycosaminoglycans present in malignant epithelial mesotheliomas usually contain large amounts of hyaluronic acid (Waxler et al., 1979) and chondroitin-6-sulfate (Iozzo et al., 1981), and these glycosaminoglycans (Kawai et al., 1985) can be demonstrated by electrophoretic analysis. But again this requires fresh unfixed tissue.

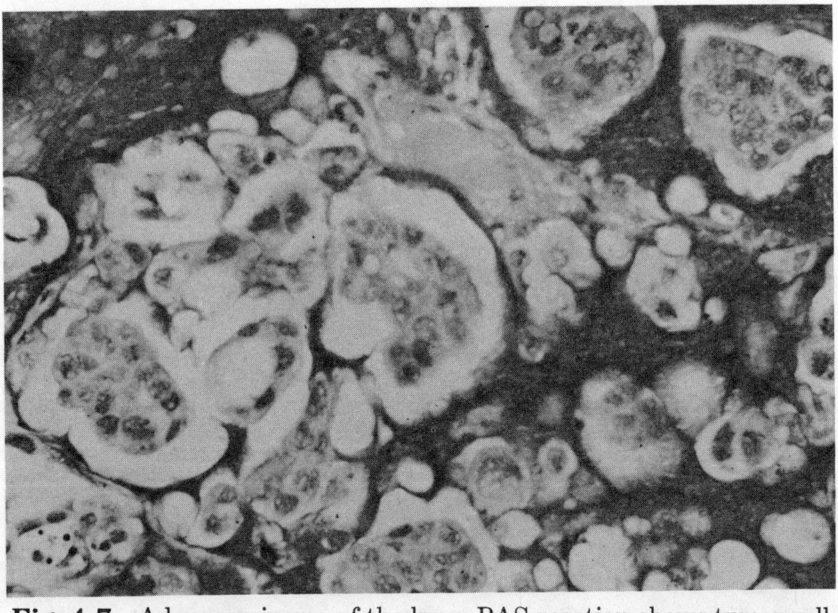

Fig. 4-7 Adenocarcinoma of the lung. PAS reaction shows tumor cell complexes lying within dark stained epithelial mucin substances. PAS with diastase pretreatment, ×310.

C. ELECTRON MICROSCOPY

Different cell types have been described in diffuse mesotheliomas: epithelial- and fibroblasts-like cells, and myofibroblasts. In well-differentiated mesotheliomas the epithelial cells usually present long microvilli, well-developed desmosomes and tight junctions. In the cytoplasm microfilaments, a well-developed rough endoplasmic reticulum, prominent vacuoles and glycogen granules are found. In less well-differentiated mesotheliomas one or several of these features may be absent. One of the characteristic features, e.g., "bushy" microvilli (Wang, 1973) are often inconspicuous in moderate and poorly differentiated mesotheliomas and, therefore, the distinction between adenocarcinomas and mesotheliomas is difficult.

1. Intermediate Filaments: Cytokeratins and Vimentin

Intermediate filaments are composed of proteins that are very resistant to solubilization. They form the major components of the cytoskeleton of eukariotic cells (Franke et al., 1978a, 1978b, 1979). Different proteins were found, among them cytokeratin (CK) proteins and vimentin. These proteins have become very important markers of cell differentiation (for review see Osborn and Weber, 1983; Schliwa, 1986) and antibodies directed against these proteins are among the most important markers in immunohistochemistry today.

A large amount of antibodies reacting with pan-CK proteins, different subtypes of cytokeratins and with vimentin are now available, most are monoclonal antibodies, some of them also usable for immunohistochemistry on formaldehyde fixed paraffin embedded tissue. Most monotypic antibodies, e.g., antibodies reacting exclusively with one CK protein, cannot be used on fixed paraffin embedded tissue because antigenic structures are changed or obscured and in part destroyed by this procedure (Altmannsberger et al., 1981; Blobel et al., 1985).

Numerous investigations have been reported in the last years demonstrating the use of these antibodies as an aid in the differential diagnosis of malignant tumors. In the first reports CK antibodies seemed to be valuable tools to differentiate pulmonary adenocarcinomas (Figs. 4-8–4-10) from mesotheliomas because the CK antibodies used preferentially recognized high molecular weight (MW) CK proteins and did not react with adenocarcinomas, whereas most mesotheliomas were stained (Schlegel

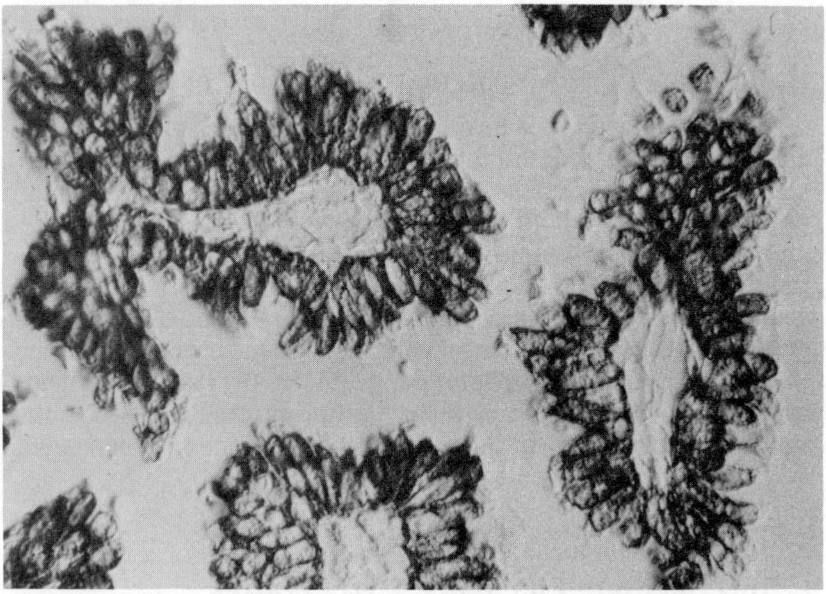

Figs. 4-8–4-10 Different pulmonary adenocarcinomas were reacted with different antibodies for low MW CK components. 4-8: reaction with TPA-antibodies (a fragment of CK 18), ×310; 4-9: reaction with CK 310 antibodies (reacts only with low MW CK components), ×200; 4-10: reaction with PKK1 antibodies (a commercially available CK antibody), ×310.

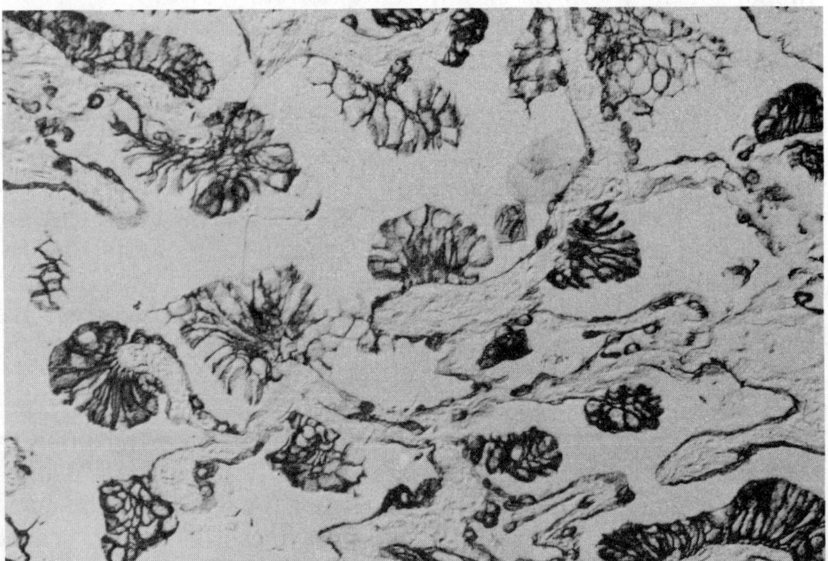

Fig. 4-9

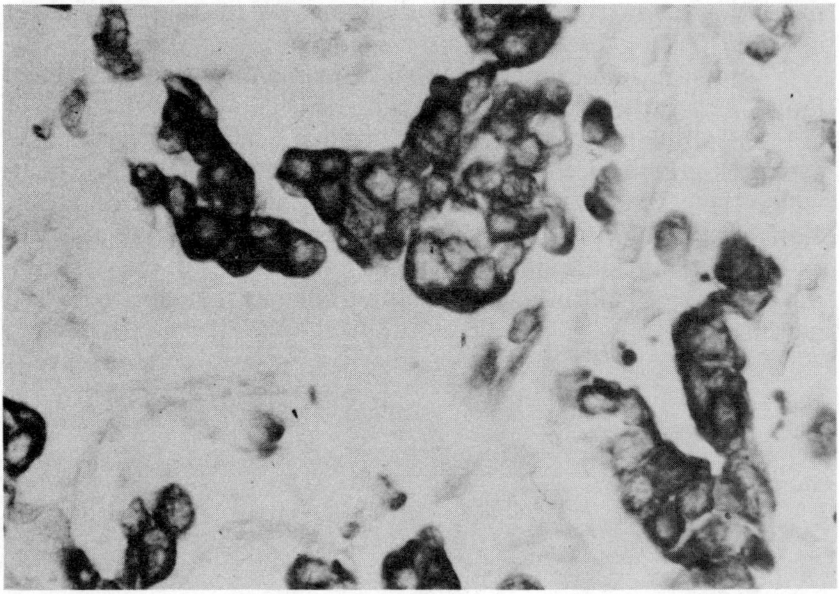

Fig. 4-10

et al., 1980; Corson, Pinkus, 1982; Said et al., 1983a, 1983b). Later it was shown that CK antibodies derived from low MW CKs stained mesotheliomas as well as pulmonary adenocarcinomas (Loosli, Hurlimann, 1984; Holden, Churg, 1984; Kahn et al., 1984; Bejui et al., 1984; Gibbs et al., 1985; Blobel et al., 1984, 1985; Battifora, Kopinski, 1985; Churg, 1985). It has been demonstrated that the composition of CK filaments in mesotheliomas is different from that of most pulmonary adenocarcinomas. Mesotheliomas usually contain CKs 4, 5, and 6 (MW 56–59 kDa). Those cytokeratins were found in all 5 epithelial and some biphasic mesotheliomas investigated by gel electrophoresis and immunohistochemistry and were not found in pulmonary adenocarcinomas (Wu et al., 1982; Blobel et al., 1985). CKs 7, 8, 18, and 19 are found in all adenocarcinomas and nearly all mesotheliomas (Figs. 4-11–4-15). But unfortunately most monoclonal and monotypic ABs directed against one CK protein do not give reproducible reactions on fixed paraffin embedded tissue. Therefore, the use of these CK antibodies is limited to scientific investigations and at the moment cannot be extended to routine pathological examinations. CKs are usually found in epithelial and in epithelial parts of biphasic mesotheliomas, whereas sarcomatous mesotheliomas are unstained (Pfaltz et al., 1987).

Vimentin, another intermediate filament protein, has been found in mesotheliomas (Blobel et al., 1985; Churg, 1985; Jasani et al., 1985; Bolen et al., 1986; Pfaltz et al., 1987), in part being coexpressed with CKs (Ramaekers et al., 1983; LaRocca, Rheinwald, 1984; Blobel et al., 1985; Jasani et al., 1985; Pfaltz et al., 1987; Azumi and Battifora, 1987; Kawai et al., 1988a) (Figs. 4-16 –4-18). But the suitability of vimentin antibodies in the differential diagnosis of mesotheliomas versus adenocarcinomas is limited because:

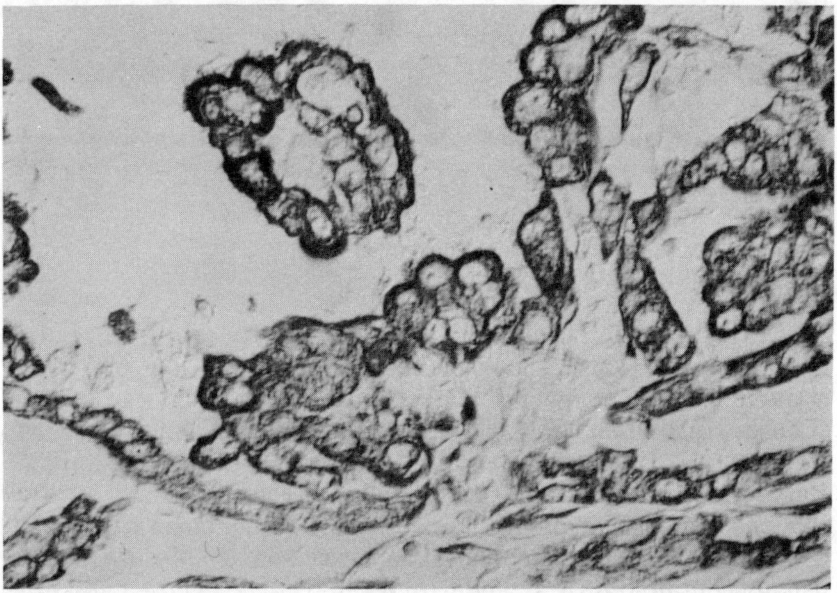

Figs. 4-11–4-15 Reaction of mesotheliomas with different CK antibodies. 4-11: reaction with TPA antibodies, ×310; 4-12: reaction with Lu5 antibodies, which stained all mesotheliomas, ×160; 4-13: reaction with CK antibodies AE 1 + 3—in one mesothelioma the cells are unstained, whereas remnants of alveolar and bronchiolar epithelia are positively decorated by the reaction, ×160; 4-14 and 4-15: reaction with CK antibodies AE 1 + 3; epithelial mesotheliomas with extensive desmoplastic reaction and a pseudosarcomatous reaction; epithelial tumor cells are isolated by a dense fibrous stroma and can be mistaken for sarcomatous part on H&E-sections, whereas immunohistochemical reactions showed a positive expression of CK polypeptides. Magnification in both, ×160.

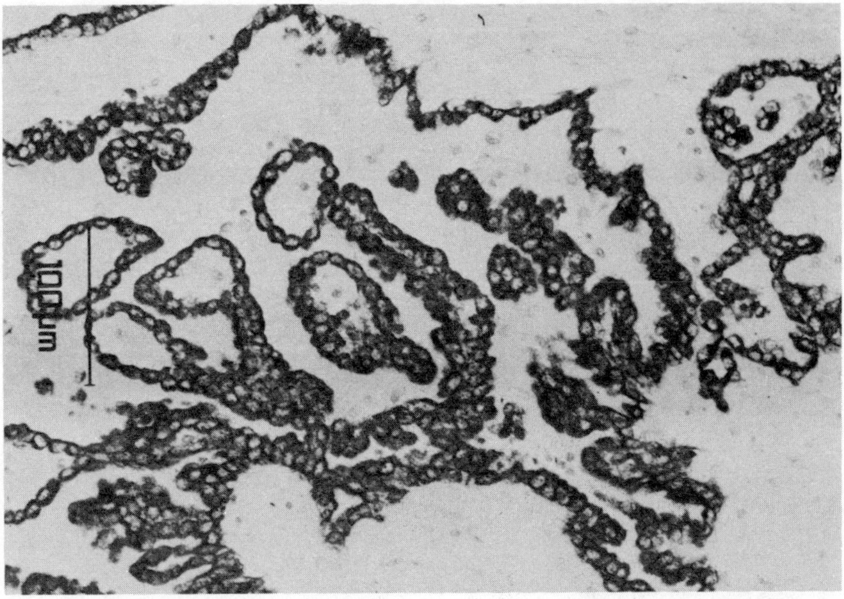

Fig. 4-12

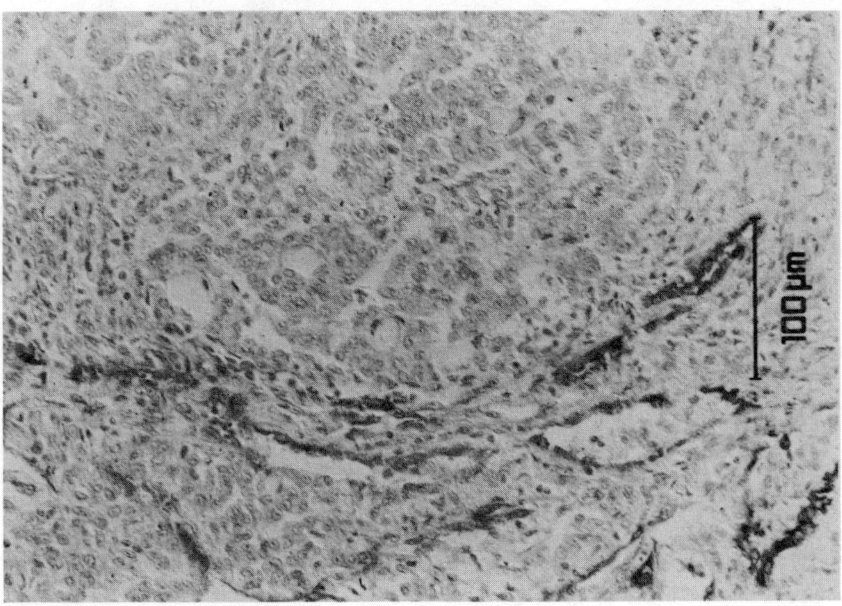

Fig. 4-13

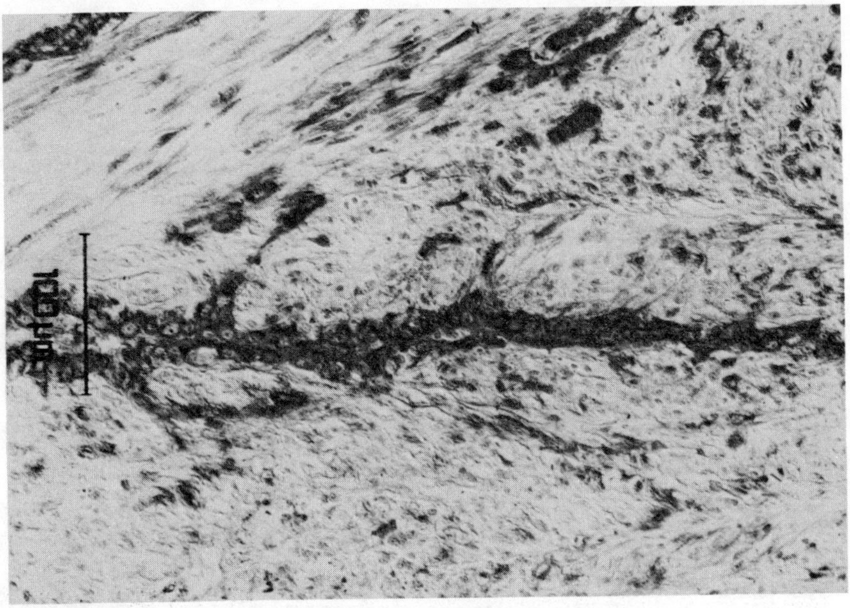

Fig. 4-14

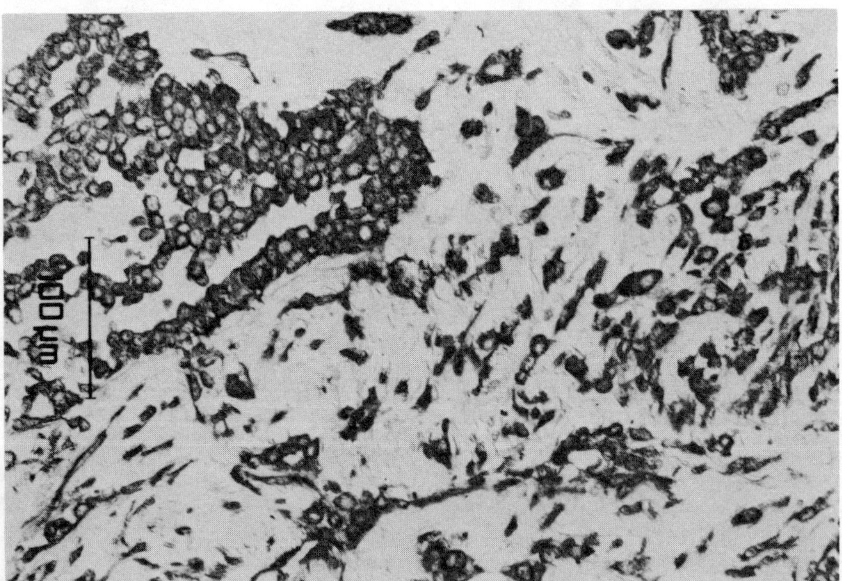

Fig. 4-15

1. Only 27%–57% of epithelial mesotheliomas coexpress vimentin and CKs (Kawai et al., 1988a; Jasani et al., 1985).

2. Some carcinomas coexpress CKs and vimentin like thyroid carcinomas (Miettinen et al., 1984), renal cell carcinoma (Holthofer et al., 1983), and others, e.g., anaplastic carcinomas.

3. Some adenocarcinomas, pulmonary and others, also exhibit a coexpression of CKs and vimentin when present within the pleura and pleural cavity (Ramaekers et al., 1983).

In the near future the use of different monospecific antibodies reactive with only one CK component and applicable for formaldehyde fixed paraffin embedded tissue might be available commercially. Then CK antibodies might become important in the differential diagnosis of pulmonary adenocarcinomas and mesotheliomas.

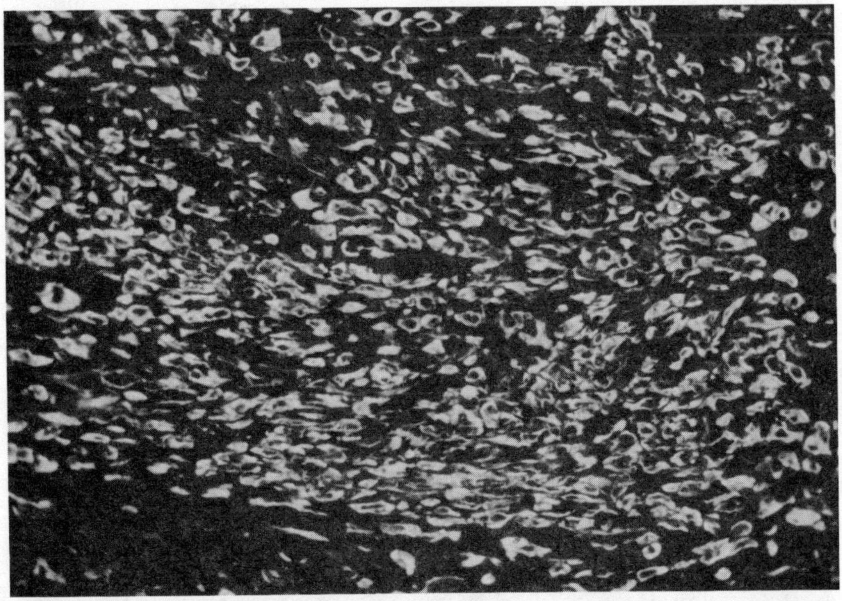

Figs. 4-16–4-18 Reaction with vimentin antibodies. In 4-16 and 4-17, fresh frozen material had been available and the mesothelioma cells showed a coexpression of vimentin and in parallel sections also CK polypeptides with the appropriate antibodies: 4-16 ×200; 4-17 ×400. Fig. 4-18 shows a reaction with vimentin antibodies on formaldehyde fixed paraffin embedded epithelial mesothelioma; some mesothelioma cells are positively decorated but the reaction is weak. Magnification, ×320.

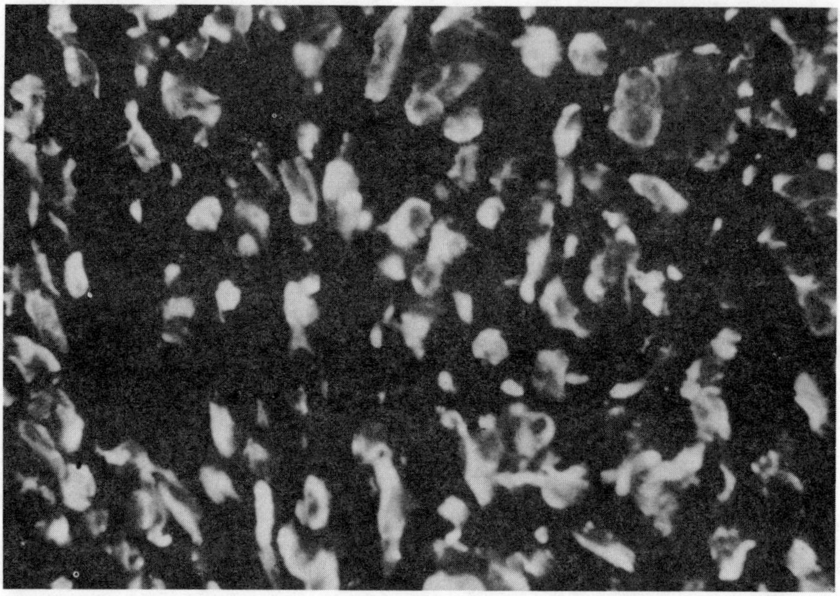

Fig. 4-17

2. Epithelial Membrane Antigen and Human Milk Fat Globule Membrane Protein

Antibodies directed to epithelial membrane antigen (EMA antibodies) and human milk fat globule membrane protein antibodies (HMFG antibodies) were studied for their suitability to differentiate adenocarcinomas and mesotheliomas. EMA antibodies stained most adenocarcinomas, esp. pulmonary ones (Sloane, Ormerod, 1981; Loosli, Hurlimann, 1984; Marshall et al., 1984; Battifora, Kopinski, 1985) and mesotheliomas (Ernst, Brooks, 1981; Sloane, Ormerod, 1981; Loosli, Hurlimann, 1984; Marshall et al., 1984; Pfaltz et al., 1987; Van der Kwast et al., 1988), but reactive mesothelial proliferation remained unstained. However, in the research of other authors all mesotheliomas were negative (Battifora, Kopinski, 1985). The reaction of HMFG antibodies was quite similar. Both antibodies were useful to separate mesotheliomas and reactive mesothelial cells but not adenocarcinomas and mesotheliomas, unless this reaction was combined with staining for carcinoembryonic antigen (CEA). A positive reaction with CEA and EMA antibodies is a strong indication for adenocarcinomas and makes the diagnosis of mesothelioma less reliable.

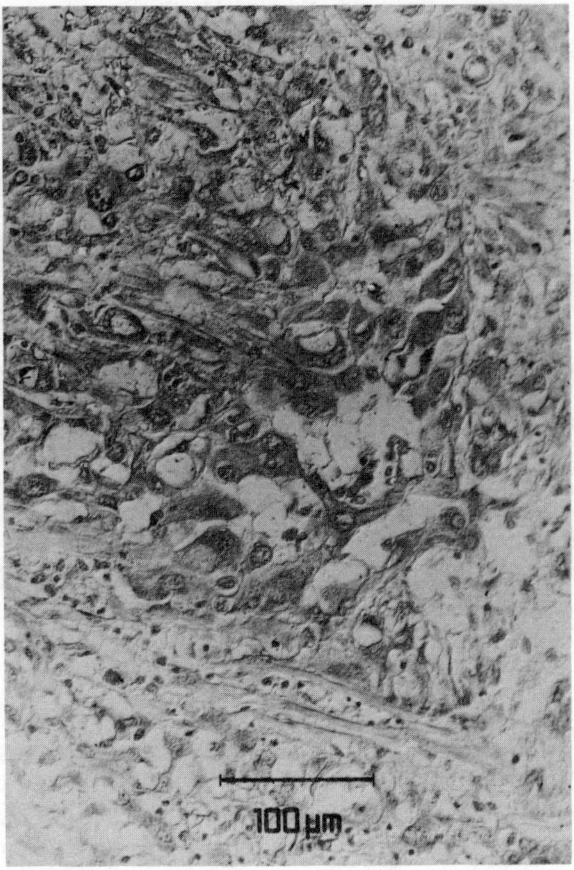

Fig. 4-18

D. CARCINOEMBRYONIC ANTIGEN (CEA)

CEA was first thought to be a characteristic marker for carcinomas derived from the large intestine (Gold and Freedman, 1965). Antibodies directed against CEA usually stain gastrointestinal carcinomas, and CEA is often found to be elevated in serum. But it has been shown, that CEA antibodies also react with lung adenocarcinomas (Fig. 4-19), while leaving mesotheliomas unstained (Fig. 4-20) (Wang et al., 1979; Kwee et al., 1982; Whittaker et al., 1982; Marshall et al., 1984; Gibbs et al., 1985; Friemann et al., 1986). But in 15%–35% of cases these antibodies stained mesotheliomas (Corson, Pinkus, 1982; Said et al., 1983a; Holden, Churg, 1984; Loosli, Hurlimann, 1984; Battifora,

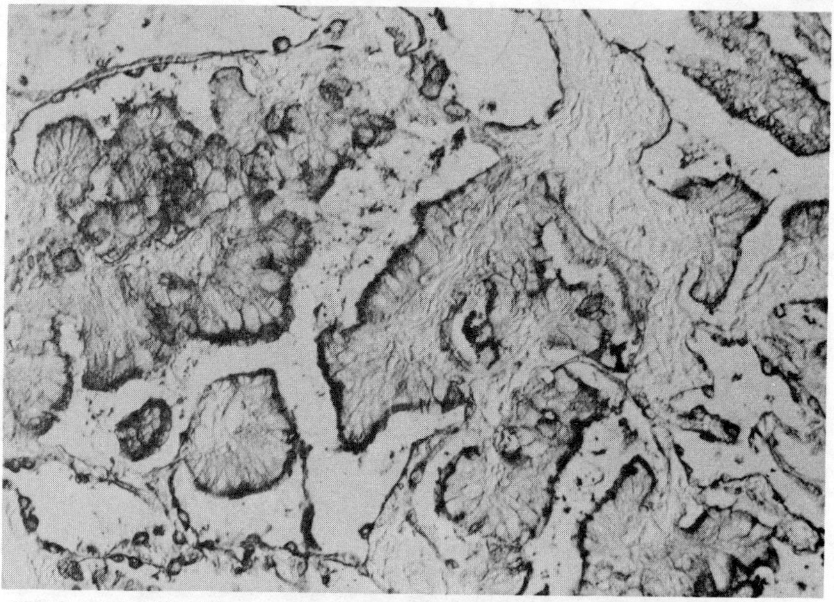

Fig. 4-19 Papillary pulmonary adenocarcinoma giving positive reaction with CEA antibodies. Magnification, ×200.

Kopinski, 1985; Otis et al., 1987; Pfaltz et al., 1987; Wirnsberger et al., 1988). In many cases this positive reaction with commercially obtained CEA antibodies was due to cross reactivity with nonspecific cross-reacting antigen (NCA) (Nap et al., 1983).

Therefore, a positive reaction with CEA antibodies does not necessarily exclude mesotheliomas. Even, some of the newly developed monoclonal antibodies, although showing no cross-reaction with NCA, stain some mesotheliomas (Figs. 4-21 and 4-22). Wirnsberger et al. (1988) investigated 26 epithelial mesotheliomas with 4 different CEA antibodies. Two of the antibodies were characterized to cross-react with NCA (Behring, BAM 130a, cross reacts strongly with a 55 kDa; the other one, BAM 130b, strongly cross reacts with a 95-kDa NCA component), whereas two other monoclonal antibodies (Ortho Diagnostics; Behring, BAM 130c) showed no crossreaction with NCA. But one of these antibodies (Behring, 130c) reacted with 4 out of the 26 mesotheliomas, although only few tumor cells were positively stained. In addition, not all pulmonary adenocarcinomas reacted positively with CEA antibodies (Pascal et al., 1977; Whittaker et al., 1982; Gibbs et al., 1985). Therefore, newly produced CEA antibodies should be investigated with a fairly large number of proven mesotheliomas until used in routine immunohistochemistry.

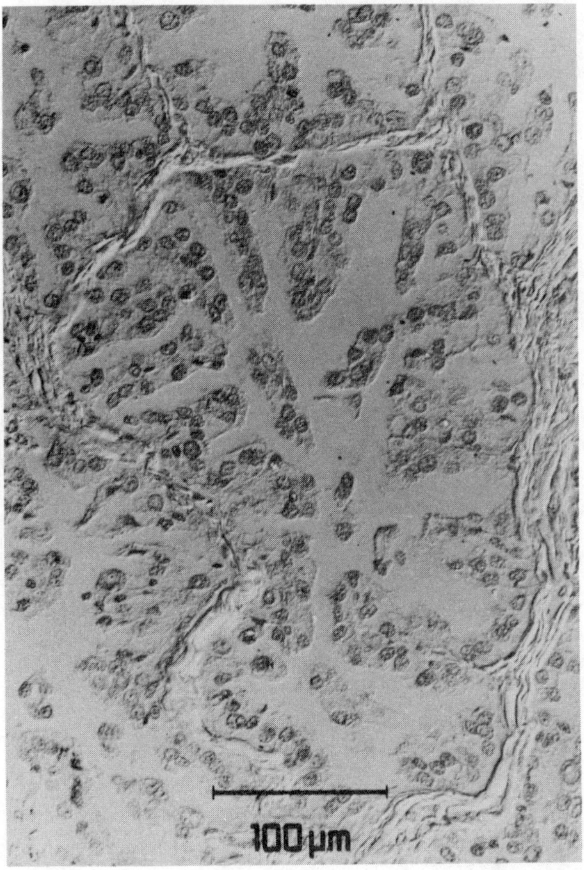

Fig. 4-20 Malignant epithelial mesothelioma, tubulopapillary type; the reaction with CEA antibodies (Ortho Diagnostics, monoclonal) was negative. Magnification, ×180.

E. S-100 PROTEIN

S-100-protein, a 20–25-kDa protein, was first isolated from rabbit brain and thought to be a specific marker for neural tissue and neural tumors (Moore and Perez, 1966), like schwannomas, neurofibromas, gliomas (Dohan et al., 1977; Haglid et al., 1978; Jacque et al., 1979; Yamaguchi, 1980). Within a few years many other non-nervous cells and tumors were shown to react with S-100 protein antibodies—e.g., reticulum cells in lymphoid tissue (Takahashi et al., 1981), Langerhans cells in skin (Cocchia et al., 1981; Nakajima et al., 1982a, 1982c), melanomas (Nakajima et al., 1982b), some lymphomas and histiocytosis X cells (Nakajima et

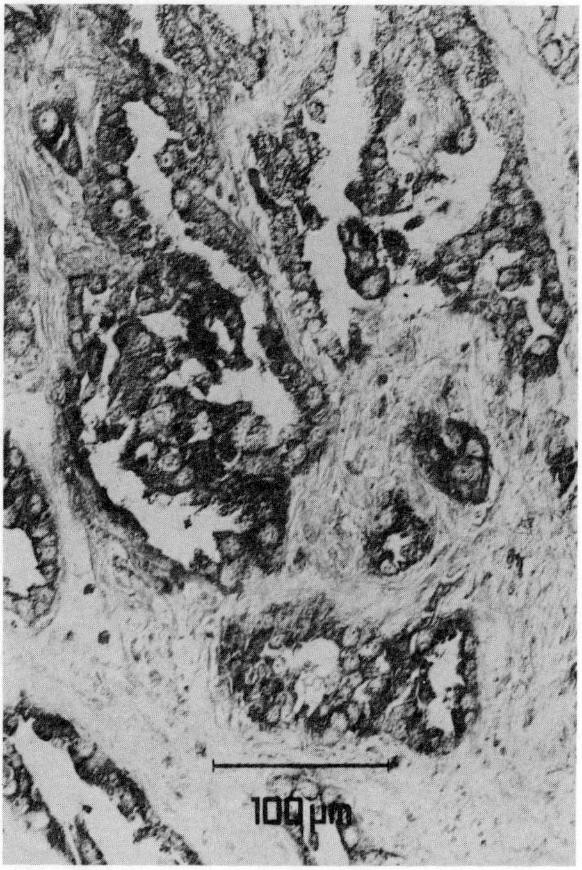

Figs. 4-21 and 4-22 Different CEA antibodies were tested for their reactivity with proven mesotheliomas; both monoclonal antibodies were characterized to give no cross-reaction with NCA; both antibodies reacted positively with larger or smaller groups of mesothelioma cells. Magnification in both, ×160.

al., 1982c). With respect to the differential diagnosis between pulmonary adenocarcinomas infiltrating the pleura and diffuse malignant mesotheliomas spreading into the lung, S-100 protein antibodies may aid in distinguishing these two neoplasms: It was independently shown by two groups of investigators (Popper et al., 1987; Herrera et al., 1988) that in pulmonary adenocarcinomas, esp. papillary and bronchioalveolar types, Langerhans cells of the lungs proliferate. Numerous benign cells can be demonstrated within the carcinoma by S-100 protein antibodies (Figs. 4-23 and 4-24), whereas proliferation of Langerhans cells could not be found in mesotheliomas extending into the lungs. But the number of cases presented were to small to allow reliable conclusions

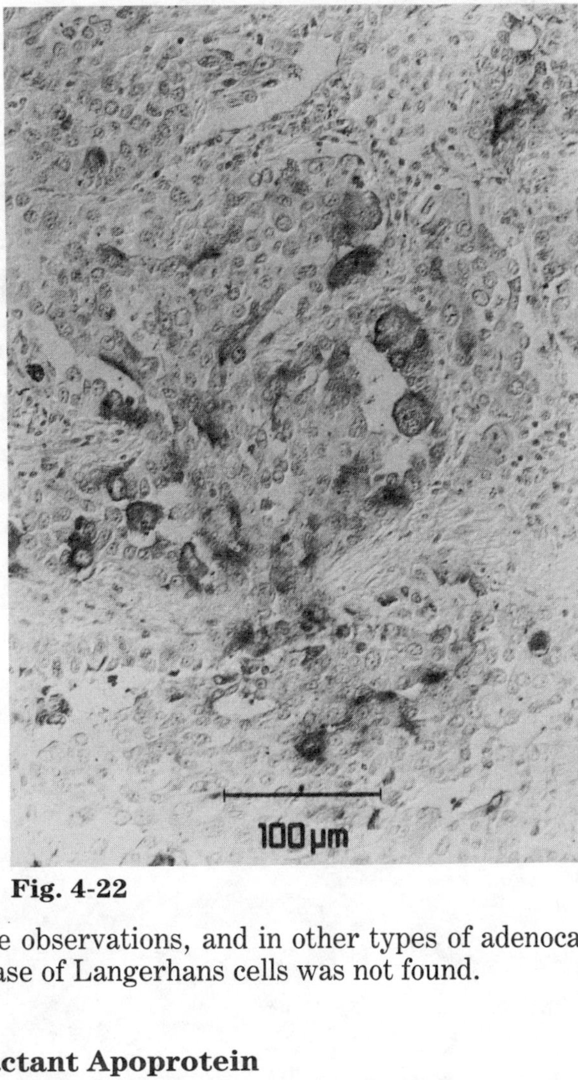

Fig. 4-22

from these observations, and in other types of adenocarcinomas this increase of Langerhans cells was not found.

1. Surfactant Apoprotein

Surfactant apoprotein is a 35-kDa protein produced by normal pneumocytes type II. It was also found in Clara cells by immunohistochemistry with surfactant apoprotein antibodies. Recently a study was reported (Mizutani et al., 1988) showing that 36 out of 75 pulmonary adenocarcinomas were stained by these antibodies and that other types of lung carcinomas, other adenocarcinomas metastasing into the lungs, and mesotheliomas were untreated. A second 10-kDa protein isolated from Clara cells was found recently (Bedetti et al., 1987) but was not tested for its discriminating ability between mesotheliomas and primary and secondary lung adenocarcinomas.

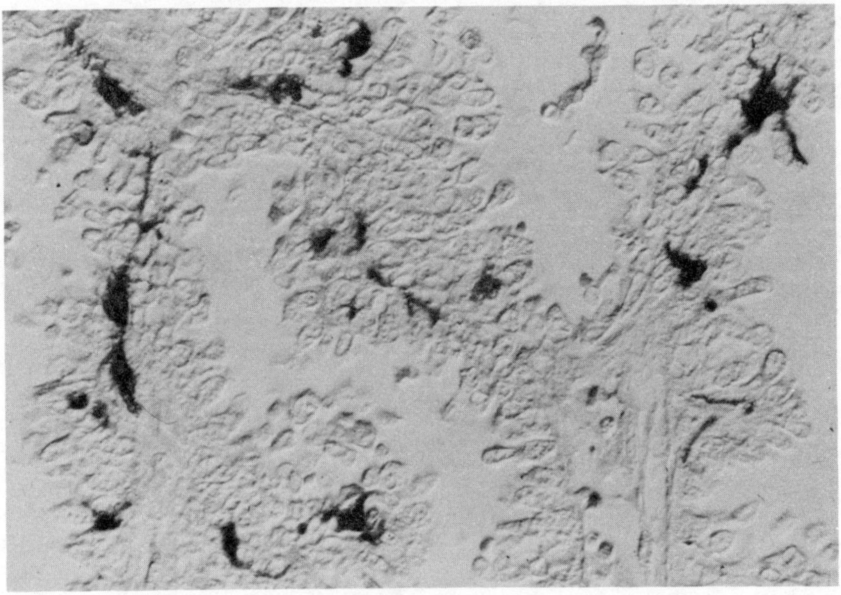

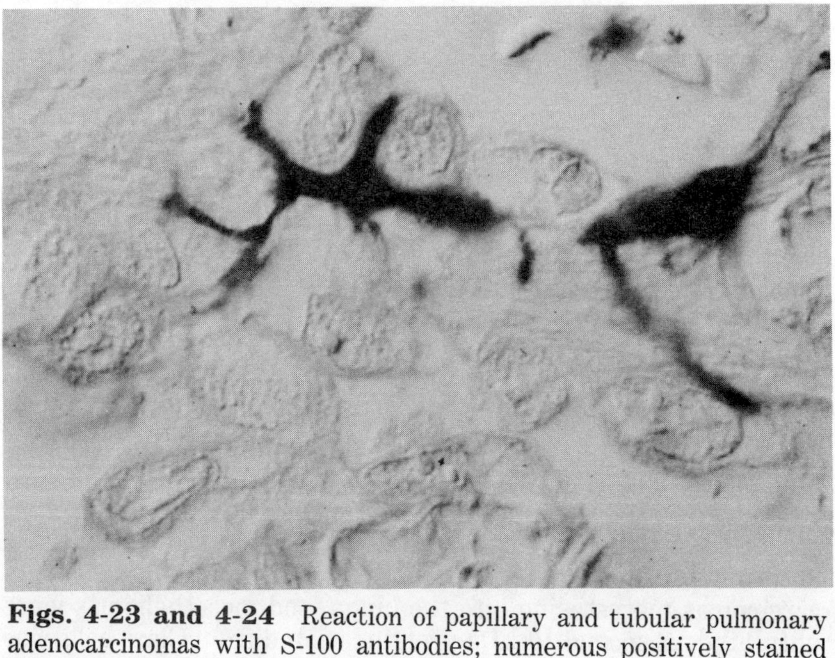

Figs. 4-23 and 4-24 Reaction of papillary and tubular pulmonary adenocarcinomas with S-100 antibodies; numerous positively stained Langerhans cells could be found within the tumor and in the surrounding stroma. Magnifications, ×200 and ×800, respectively.

2. Pregnancy Specific Glycoprotein 1 (SP1)

In one study 22 pulmonary adenocarcinomas and 47 proven mesotheliomas were investigated with SP1 antibodies (Pfaltz et al., 1987). Thirteen out of 22 adenocarcinomas and 3 out of 47 mesotheliomas were stained. In another study all adenocarcinomas reacted positively, whereas all mesotheliomas were unstained (Gibbs et al., 1985). Because of these conflicting results the SP1-antibody reaction does not seem to be useful for the differential diagnosis of adenocarcinoma and mesothelioma at the present time.

3. LeuM1 Antibodies

LeuM1 antibodies originally produced by immunizing with a human-derived monocytic cell line was used in typing white blood cells (Hanjan et al., 1982). A few studies have been reported recently that described these antibodies as being useful in discriminating mesotheliomas and pulmonary adenocarcinomas. This LeuM1 antibody was shown to react with about 50%–90% of adenocarcinomas tested but left all mesotheliomas unstained (Sheibani et al., 1986, 1988; Strickler et al., 1987; Warnock et al., 1988).

4. B72.3 Antibody

Similar results were reported in a study with B72.3 antibodies, an antibody that detects a high MW mucin-like glycoprotein (>1,000,000 Da), derived from immunizing with a membrane-enriched fraction of human breast cancer and termed tumor-associated glycoprotein 72 (Johnson et al., 1986). In three different investigations 50%–86% of adenocarcinomas were stained and mesotheliomas were unstained (Szpak et al., 1986; Gold and Mattes, 1988; Warnock et al., 1988).

5. ATPases

ATPases are enzymes located in different organelles and within the cytosol of mammalian cells. Three different types are known and named according to the kation necessary for its activation: calcium-, magnesium-, and sodium/potassium-activated ATPase. These enzymes provide the energy for different functions (Gibbons, 1987). Ca^{++}-activated ATPase is normally found in ciliated cells of the bronchus, in mesenchymal cells and also in mesothelial cells, but so far was not found in pulmonary adenocarci-

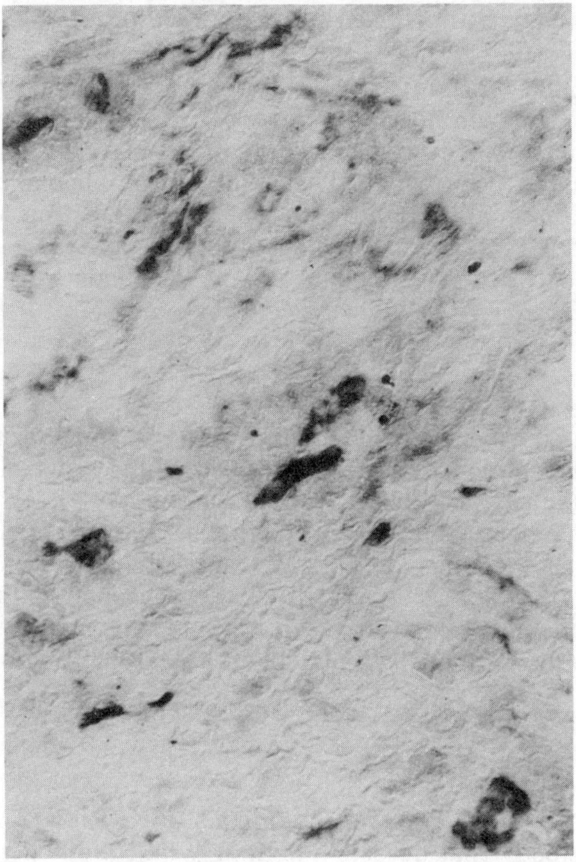

Figs. 4-25 and 4-26 Histochemical reaction for calcium-activated ATPase in mesotheliomas: positive reaction of the epithelial and sarcomatous parts: 4-25: frozen histological section, mixed type, ×130; 4-26: cytology specimen, ×500. The reaction in pulmonary adenocarcinomas was negative.

nomas (12 cases tested) where Mg^{++}-activated ATPase was found (Popper et al., 1986, 1987). In epithelial mesotheliomas, esp. papillary and tubular types, Ca^{++}-activated ATPase was demonstrable in 5 out of 5 cases (Figs. 4-25 and 4-26).

So far the lack of Ca^{++}-activated ATPase favors the diagnosis of pulmonary adenocarcinoma and a positive reaction that of a mesothelioma. Unfortunately, fresh unfixed tissue is necessary for the histochemical reaction, and this is rarely available. For this reason the number of cases investigated is fairly small, and the usefulness of this histochemical reaction is limited.

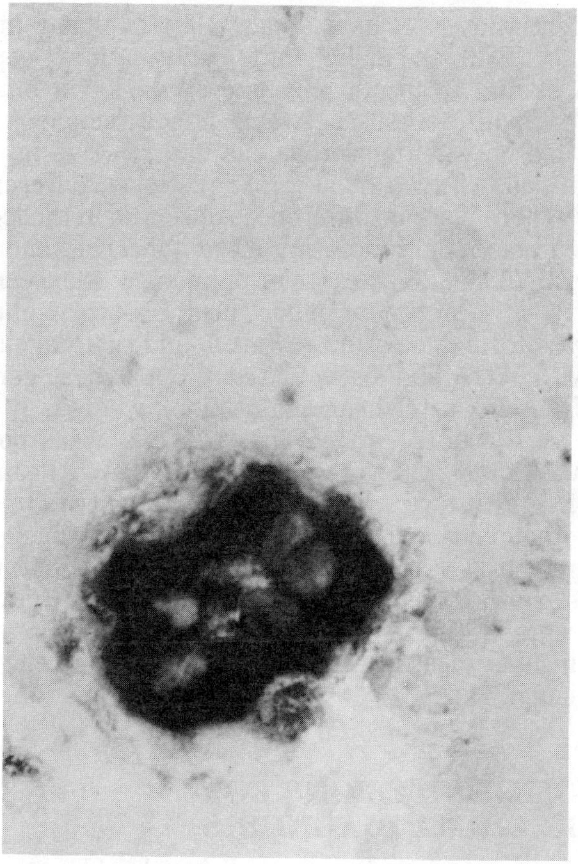

Fig. 4-26

6. Ferritin

Also ferritin antibodies were tested for their ability to react with mesothelial cells. A positive reaction was reported with all mesothelial cells, including proliferating reactive cells (Neubauer et al., 1987), but ferritin antibodies were not tested in a controlled retrospective study with clearly defined tumor types for their ability to discriminate between adenocarcinomas and mesotheliomas.

7. Lectins

Lectins are glycoproteins that specifically bind to different carbohydrate groups. Their binding sites are important in embryonic differentiation (Teshima et al., 1984), cellular maturation (Reano et al., 1982), and malignant transformation (Cooper, 1982; Yonezawa et al., 1982). In only one study lectin binding was investigated to differentiate between adenocarcinomas and mesotheliomas and between mesothelioma and reactive proliferating mesothelial cells (Kawai et al., 1988b). Seven different lectins were used. There were no differences observed in the lectin binding between reactive proliferating mesothelial cells and mesotheliomas. In 22/28 and 26/28 cases of pulmonary adenocarcinomas, respectively, N-acetyl-neuraminic acid, N-acetyl-glucosamine and β-D-galactosamine residues were found that gave a positive reaction with WGA and succinylated WGA (wheat germ agglutine) and RCA-I (Caster bean agglutinine); whereas 13/23 mesotheliomas were positive with WGA, 1/23 was weak positive for succinyl-WGA, and 2/23 were positive for RCA-I. Peanut agglutinine (PNA) with neuraminidase pretreatment was positive in 13/23 mesotheliomas and 27/28 adenocarcinomas suggesting that D-galactosyl-β-1,3-N-acetyl-D-galactosamine is present in most tumor cells of either type. Therefore Suc-WGA and RCA-I may be useful markers in differentiating mesotheliomas from pulmonary adenocarcinomas, although negative reactions do not rule out adenocarcinomas.

F. RECOMMENDATIONS FOR MESOTHELIOMA DIAGNOSIS

A tumor suggestive of a mesothelioma should be examined by conventional histological stains and immunohistochemical evaluation should be included with a panel of antibodies directed against CEA, EMA, high MW CKs, vimentin, B72.3, and LeuM1. A negative reaction with CEA, EMA, high MW CK, vimentin, B72.3, and LeuM1-antibodies would favor the mesothelioma diagnosis. If unfixed frozen tissue is available different MW CK antibody and Ca-ATPase reactions as well as differentiation for epithelial mucin should be performed by diastase-PAS reaction and alcian blue stain with/without hyaluronidase pretreatment.

ACKNOWLEDGEMENTS

The author is indebted to Dr. H. Denk for critical reading of the manuscript and to Mr. I. Georgiev for photographic assistance. Part of this investigation was funded by the Österreichische Fonds zur Förderung der Wissenschaftlichen Forschung, project No. P6065, which is gratefully acknowledged.

REFERENCES

1. Altmannsberger M, Osborn M, Schauer A, Weber K: Antibodies to different intermediate filament proteins. Cell type-specific markers on paraffin-embedded human tissues. Lab.Invest.45, 427–434, 1981.
2. Arai H, Kang KY, Sato H, Satoh K, Nagai H, Motomiya M, Konno K: Significance of the quantification and demonstration of hyaluronic acid in tissue specimens for the diagnosis of pleural mesothelioma. Am.Rev.Respir.Dis. 120, 529–532, 1979.
3. Azumi N, Battifora H: The distribution of Vimentin and Keratin in epithelial and nonepithelial neoplasms: A comprehensive immunohistochemical study on formalin- and alcohol-fixed tumors. Am.J.Clin.Pathol. 88, 286–296, 1987
4. Battifora H, Kopinski MI: Distinction of mesothelioma from adenocarcinoma an immunohistochemical approach. Cancer 55, 1679–1685, 1985
5. Bedetti CD, Singh J, Singh G, Katayal SL, Wong-Chong ML: Ultrastructural localisation of rat Clara cell 10 kD secretory protein by the immunogold technique using polyclonal and monoclonal antibodies. J.Histochem.Cytochem. 35, 789–794, 1987
6. Bejui-Thrivolet FB, Patricot LM, Vauzelle JL: Keratins in malignant mesotheliomas and pleural adenocarcinomas: comparative immunohistochemical analysis with polyclonal and monoclonal antibodies. Path.Res.Pract. 179, 67–73, 1984.
7. Blobel GA, Moll R, Franke WW, Kayser KW, Gould VE: The intermediate filament cytoskeleton of malignant mesotheliomas and its diagnostic significance. Am J Pathol. 121, 235–247, 1985
8. Blobel GA, Moll R, Franke WW, Vogt-Moykopf I: Cytokeratin in normal lung and lung carcinomas. I Adenocarcinomas, squamous cell carcinomas and cultured cell lines. Virchows Arch Cell Pathol. 45, 407–429, 1984
9. Bolen JW, Hammar SP, McNutt MA: Reactive and neoplastic serosal tissue. A light-microscopic, ultrastructural and immunocytochemical study. Am.J.Surg.Pathol. 10, 34–47, 1986.
10. Cantin R, Al-Jabi M, McCaughey WTE: Desmoplastic diffuse mesothelioma. Am.J.Surg.Pathol. 6, 215–222, 1982.

11. Carter D, Otis CN: Three types of spindle cell tumors of the pleura. Fibroma, sarcoma, and sarcomatoid mesothelioma. Am.J.Surg. Pathol. 12, 747–753, 1988
12. Churg A: Immunohistochemical staining for vimentin and keratin in malignant mesothelioma. Am J Surg Pathol. 9, 360–365, 1985
13. Cocchia D., Michetti F., Donato R.: Immunochemical and immunocytochemical localization of S-100 antigen in normal human skin. Nature 294, 85–87, 1981.
14. Cooper H.S.: Peanut lectin-binding sites in large bowel carcinoma. Lab Invest 47, 383–390, 1982
15. Corson JM, Pinkus GS: Mesothelioma: Profile of keratin proteins and carcinoembryonic antigen. An immunoperoxidase study of 20 cases and comperison with pulmonary adenocarcinomas. Am J Pathol. 108, 80–87, 1982
16. Dohan F.C., Kornblith P.L., Wellum G.R., Pfeiffer S.E., Levine L.: S-100 protein and 2′,3′-cyclic nucleotide-3-phosphohydrolase in human brain tumors. Acta Neuropathol. 40, 123–128, 1977.
17. Doll R: Atmospheric pollution and lung cancer. Environ. Health Perspect 22, 23–31, 1978.
18. Ernst CS, Brooks JJ: Immunoperoxidase localization of secretory component in reactive mesothelium and mesotheliomas. J. Histochem.Cytochem. 29, 1102–1104, 1981.
19. Franke WW, Appelhans B, Schmid E, Freudenstein C, Osborn M, Weber K: Identification and characterization of epithelial cells in mammalian tissues by immunofluorrescence microscopy using antibodies to prekeratin. Differentiation 15, 7–25, 1979.
20. Franke WW, Schmid E, Osborn M, Weber K: Different intermediate-sized filaments distinguished by immunofluorescence microscopy. Proc.Natl.Acad.Sci. USA 76, 5034–5038, 1978a.
21. Franke WW, Weber K, Osborn M, Schmid E, Freudenstein C: Antibody to prekeratin: Decoration of tonofilament-like arrays in various cells of epithelial character. Exp.Cell Res. 16:429–445, 1978b.
22. Friemann J, Otto H, Müller KM: Immunhistochemische Befunde zur Differentialdiagnose primärer und sekundärer Pleuratumoren. Verh.Dtsch.Ges.Pathol. 70, 311–316, 1986.
23. Ghosh AK, Gatter KC, Dunnill MS, Mason DY: Immunohistological staining of reactive mesothelium, mesothelioma, and lung carcinoma with a panel of monoclonal antibodies. J.Clin.Pathol. 40, 19–25, 1987
24. Gibbs AR, Harach R, Wagner JC, Jasani B: Comparison of tumor markers in malignant mesotheliomas and pulmonary adenocarcinoma. Thorax 40, 91–95, 1985.
25. Gibbons IR: New jobs for dynein ATPases. Nature 330, 600, 1987.
26. Gold D.V., Mattes M.J.: Monoclonal antibody B72.3 reacts with a core region structure of O-linked carbohydrates. Tumor Biol. 9, 137–144, 1988.

27. Gold P., Freedman S.O.: Specific carcinoembryonic antigens of the human digestive system. J. Exp. Med. 122, 467–481, 1965.
28. Haglid K., Hamberger A., Hansson H.A., Stavrou D.: An immunohistochemical study of human brain tumors concerning the brain specific proteins S-100 and 14-3-2. Acta Neuropathol. 24, 187–196, 1978.
29. Hanjan SNS, Kearney JF, Cooper MD: A monoclonal antibody (MMA) that identifies a differentiation antigen on human myelomonocytic cells. Clin.Immunol.Immunopathol. 23, 172–188, 1982.
30. Henderson DW, Attwood HD, Constance TJ, Shilkin KB, Steele RH: Lymphohistiocytoid mesothelioma: a rare lymphomatoid variant of predominantly sarcomatoid mesothelioma. Ultrastruct. Pathol. 12, 367–384, 1988
31. Herrera G.A., Turbat-Herrera E.A., Lott R.L.: S-100 protein expression by primary and metastatic adenocarcinomas. Am. J. Clin. Pathol. 89, 168–176, 1988.
32. Holden J, Churg A: Immunohistochemical staining for keratin and carcinoembryonic antigen in the diagnosis of malignant mesothelioma. Am J Surg Pathol. 8, 277–279, 1984
33. Holthofer H, Miettinen A, Paasivuo R, Letho VP, Linder E, Alfthan O, Virtanen I: Cellular origin and differentiation of renal carcinomas. A fluorescence microscopic study with kidney-specific antibodies, antiintermediate filament antibodies, and lectins. Lab.Invest. 49, 317–325, 1983.
34. Iozzo RV, Goldes IA, et al: Glycosaminoglycans of pleural mesothelioma: A possible biochemical variant containing chondroitin sulfate. Cancer 48, 89–97, 1981
35. Jacque C.M., Kujas M., Poreau A., Raoul M., Collier P., Racadot J., Bauman N.J.: GFA and S-100 protein levels as an index for malignancy in human gliomas and neurinomas. J. Natl. Cancer Inst. 62, 479–483, 1979.
36. Jasani B, Edwards RE, Thomas ND, Gibbs AR: The use of vimentin antibodies in the diagnosis of malignant mesothelioma. Virchows Arch Pathol Anat. 406, 441–448, 1985
37. Johnson VG, Schlom J, Paterson AJ, Bennett J, Magnani JL, Colcher D: Analysis of a human tumor-associated glycoprotein (TAG-72) identified by monoclonal antibody B72.3. Cancer Res. 46, 850–857, 1986.
38. Kahn HJ, Huang S, Hanna WM, Baumal R, Phillips MJ: Immmunohistochemical localization of epidermal and mallorybody cytokeratin in undifferentiated tumors. Comparison with ultrastructural features. Am.J.Clin.Pathol. 81, 184–191, 1984.
39. Kannerstein M, Churg J, Magner D: Histochemistry in the diagnosis of malignant mesothelioma. Ann.Clin.Lab.Sci. 3, 207–211, 1973.
40. Kannerstein M, Churg J, McCaughey WTE: Asbestos and mesothelioma: A review. Path Ann. 13, 81–129, 1978.

41. Kannerstein M, Churg J: Peritoneal mesothelioma. Hum.Pathol. 8, 83–94, 1977.
42. Kawai T, Suzuki M., Shinmei Y., Maenaka Y., Kageyama K.: Glycosaminoglycans in malignant diffuse mesothelioma. Cancer 56, 567–574, 1985
43. Kawai T, Greenberg SD, Truong LD, Mattioli CA, Klima M, Titus JL: Differences in lectin binding of malignant pleural mesothelioma and adenocarcinoma of the lung. Am.J.Pathol. 130, 401–410, 1988b.
44. Kawai T, Torikata C, Suzuki M: Immunohistochemical study of pulmonary adenocarcinomas. Am.J.Clin.Pathol. 89, 455–462, 1988a.
45. Klemperer P, Rabin CB: Primary neoplasms of the pleura. Arch.Pathol. 11, 385–412, 1931.
46. Koss LG: Diagnositc Cytology and its histopathologic basis. 3rd ed., Vo. 2, p 911 ff. J.B. Lippincott Comp., Philadelphia - Toronto, 1979
47. Kwee WS, Veldhuizen RW, Golding R, Mullink H, Stam J, Donner R, Boon ME: Histologic distinction between mesothelioma, benign pleural lesions and carcinoma metastasis. Evaluation of the application of morphometry combined with histochemistry and immunostaining. Virchows Arch.Pathol.Anat. 397, 287–299, 1982.
48. LaRocca PJ, Rheinwald JG: Coexpression of simple epithelial keratins and vimentin by human mesothelium and mesothelioma in vivo and in culture. Cancer.Res. 44, 2991–2999, 1984.
49. Legha SS, Muggia FM: Pleural mesotheliomas: Clinical features and therapeutic implications. Ann.Intern. Med. 87, 613–621, 1977
50. Loosli H, Hurlimann J: Immunohistological study of malignant diffuse mesotheliomas of the pleura. Histopathology 8, 793–803, 1984
51. Mark EJ: Lung Biopsy Interpretation. p 151–159. William & Wilkins, Baltimore - London, 1984.
52. Marshall RJ, Herbert A, Braye SG, Jones DB: Use of antibodies to carcinoembryonic antigen and human milk fat globule to distinguish carcinoma, mesothelioma and reactive mesothelium. J Clin Pathol. 37, 1215–1221, 1984
53. McCaughey WTE, Kannerstein M, Churg J: Tumors and pseudotumors of the serous membranes. Atlas of Tumor Pathology, Fasc. 20, p 39 ff. Armed Forces Institute of Pathology, Washington D.C., 1985
54. Miettinen M, Franssila K, Letho VP, Paasivuo R, Virtanen I: Expression of intermediate filament proteins in thyroid gland and thyroid tumors. Lab.Invest. 50, 262–269, 1984.
55. Mizutani Y, Nakajima T, Morinaga S, Gotoh M, Shimosato Y, Akino T, Suzuki A: Immunohistochemical localization of pulmonary surfactant apoproteins in various lung tumors. Special reference to nonmucus producing lung adenocarcinomas. Cancer 61, 532–537, 1988
56. Moore B.W., Perez V.J.: Specific acidic proteins of the nervous

system. In: Physiological and Biochemical Aspects of Nervous Integration, pp 343–359, ed. F.D. Carlson, Prentice Hall, Englewood Cliffs, NJ, 1966.

57. Nakajima T., Sato Y., Watanabe S., Shimosato Y., Ishihara K., Isobe T.: Immunoelectron microscopic demonstration of S-100 protein in epidermal Langerhans' cells. Biomed.Res. 3, 226–231, 1982a.
58. Nakajima T., Watanabe S., Sato Y., Kameya T., Shimosato Y., Ishihara K.: Immunohistochemical demonstration of S-100 protein in malignant melanoma and pigmented nevus, and its diagnostic application. Cancer 50, 912–918, 1982b.
59. Nakajima T., Watanabe S., Sato Y., Shimosato Y., Motoi M., Lennert K.: S-100 protein in Langerhans' cells, interdigitating reticulum cells, and histiocytosis X cells. Gan. 73, 429–432, 1982c.
60. Nap M, tenHoor KA, Fleuren GJ: Cross reactivity with normal antigens in commercial anti-CEA sera used for immunohistology: The need for tissue control and absorption. Am.J.Clin.Pathol. 79, 25–31, 1983.
61. Neubauer A, Thalmann U, Musch R, Grosser H., Loddenkemper R, Huhn D: Prospective comparison of the diagnostic value of cytology and immunocytology in pleural effusion studied by thoracoscopy and biopsy. Klin.Wochenschr. 65, 44–406, 1987.
62. Norseth T: Asbestos and metals as carcinogens. J.Toxicol.Environ.Health 6, 1021–1028, 1980
63. Osborn M, Weber K: Tumor diagnosis by intermediate filament typing: A novel tool for surgical pathology. Lab.Invest. 48, 372–394, 1983.
64. Otis CN, Carter D, Cole S, Battifora H: Immunohistochemical evaluation of pleural mesothelioma and pulmonary adenocarcinoma. A biinstitutional study of 47 cases. Am.J.Surg.Pathol. 11, 445–456, 1987
65. Pascal RP, Mesa-Tejada R, Bennett SJ, Garces A, Fenoglio CM: Carcinoembryonic antigen. Immunohistologic identification in invasive and intraepithelial carcinomas of the lung. Arch.Pathol. Lab.Med. 101, 568–571, 1977.
66. Pfaltz M, Odermatt B, Christen B, Ruttner JR: Immunohistochemistry in the diagnosis of malignant mesothelioma. Virchows.Arch.A 411, 387–393, 1987
67. Popper HH, Wirnsberger G, Denk H: Immunohistochemical and histochemical markers of primary lung cancer, lung metastases and pleural mesotheliomas. Cancer Detect. Prevent 10, 167–174, 1987
68. Popper HH, Wirnsberger G, Reisenhofer E: Tumormarker in der Differentialdiagnose maligner Lungen- und Pleuratumoren. Verh.Dtsch.Ges. Path. 70, 317–320, 1986
69. Ramaekers FCS, Haag D, Kant A, Moesker O, Jap PHK, Vooijs GP: Coexpression of keratin- and vimentin-type intermediate filaments in human metastatic carcinoma cells. Proc.Natl. Acad.Sci.USA 80, 2618–2622, 1983.

70. Reano A., Faure M., Jacques Y., Reichert U., Schaefer H., Thirolet J.: Lectins as markers of human epidermal cell differentiation. Differentiation 22, 205–210, 1982
71. Roberts GH: Distant visceral metastases in pleural mesothelioma. Br.J.Dis.Chest. 70, 246–250, 1976.
72. Said JW, Nash G, Banks-Schlegel S, Sassoon AF, Murakami SD, Shintaku IP: Keratin in human lung tumors.Patterns of localization of different molecular weight keratin proteins. Am.J.Pathol. 113, 27–32, 1983b.
73. Said JW, Nash G, Tepper G, Banks-Schlegel S: Keratin proteins and carcinoembryonic antigen in lung carcinoma: an immunoperoxidase study of fifty-four cases, with ultrastructural correlations. Hum Pathol. 14, 70–76, 1983a.
74. Schlegel R, Banks-Schlegel S., McLeod JA, Pinkus GS: Immunoperoxidase localisation of keratin in human neoplasms. Am.J. Pathol. 101, 41–50, 1980.
75. Schliwa M: The cytoskeleton. An introductory survey. Cell Biol. Monographs, Vo 13, p 82ff, Springer Verl., New York, Vienna, 1986.
76. Sheibani K, Battifora H, Azumi N: Further evidence demonstrating the value of Leu-M1 antigen in differential diagnosis of malignant mesothelioma and adenocarcinoma: An immunohistologic evaluation of 395 cases. Lab.Invest. 84A, 1988
77. Sheibani K, Battifora H., Burke J.S.: Antigenic phenotype of malignant mesotheliomas and pulmonary adenocarcinomas: An immunohistochemical analysis demonstrating the value of Leu M1 antigen. Am. J. Pathol. 123, 212–219, 1986.
78. Sloane JP, Ormerod MG: Distribution of epithelial membrane antigen in normal and neoplastic tissues and its value in diagnostic and tumor pathology. Cancer 47, 1786–1795, 1981.
79. Strickler J.G., Herndier B.G., Rouse R.V.: Immunohistochemical staining in malignant mesotheliomas. Am. J. Clin. Pathol. 88, 610–614, 1987.
80. Szpak C.A., Johnston W.W., Roggli V., Kolbeck J., Lottich S.C., Vollmer R., Thor A., Schlom J.: The diagnostic distinction between malignant mesothelioma of the pleura and adenocarcinoma of the lung as defined by a monoclonal antibody (B 72.3). Am. J. Pathol. 122, 252–260, 1986.
81. Takahashi K., Yamaguchi H., Ishizeki J., Nakajima T., Nakazato Y.: Immunohistochemical and electron microscopic localization of S-100 protein in the interdigitating reticulum cells of the human lymph node. Virchows Arch. Cell Pathol. 37, 125–135, 1981.
82. Teshima S., Hirohashi S., Shimosato Y., Kishi K., Ino Y., Matsumoto K., Yamada T.: Histochemically demonstrable changes in cell surface carbohydrates of human germ cell tumors. Lab.Invest. 50, 271–277, 1984.
83. van der Kwast TH, Versnel MA, Delahaye M, de Jong A, Zondervan PE, Hoogsteden H: Expression of epithelial membrane antigen

on malignant mesothelioma cells. An immunocytochemical and immunoelectron microscopic study. Acta.Cytol. 32, 169–174, 1988
84. Wang NS, Huang SN, Gold P: Absence of carcinoembryonic antigen-like material in mesothelioma. Cancer 44, 937–943, 1979.
85. Wang NS: Electron microscopy in the diagnosis of pleural mesotheliomas. Cancer 31, 1046–1054, 1973.
86. Warnock ML, Stoloff A, Thor A: Differentiation of adenocarcinoma of the lung from mesothelioma. Periodic acid-Schiff, monoclonal antibodies B72.3, and Leu M1. Am.J.Pathol. 133, 30–38, 1988.
87. Waxler B, Eisenstein R, Battifora H: Electrophoresis of tissue glycosaminoglycans as an aid in the diagnosis of mesothelioma. Cancer 44, 221–227, 1979.
88. Whittaker D, Sterrett GF, Shilkin KB: Detection of tissue CEA-like substance as an aid in the differential diagnosis of malignant mesothelioma. Pathology 14, 255–258, 1982.
89. WHO: Histological typing of lung tumours. International Histological Classification of Tumours, No. 1, 2nd. ed. World Health Organization, Geneva, 1981.
90. Wirnsberger G, Friemann J, Popper HH, Müller KM: The use of immunohistochemical and histochemical markers in the differential diagnosis of epithelial mesotheliomas. Proceedings of the 8. Congress of SEP, Budapest, 1988.
91. Wu YJ, Parker LM, Binder NE, Beckett MA, Sinard JH, Griffiths CT, Rheinwald JG: The mesothelial keratins: A new family of cytoskeletal proteins identified in cultured mesothelial cells and nonkeratinizing epithelia. Cell 31, 693–703, 1982
92. Yamaguchi Y.: Studies on immunohistochemical localization of S-100 and GFA proteins in the rat nervous system and in human brain tumors. Brain Nerve 32, 1055–1064, 1980.
93. Yonezawa S., Nakamura T., Tanaka S., Sato E.: Glycoconjugate with Ulex europaeus agglutinin-I binding sites in normal mucosa, adenoma and carcinoma of the human large bowel. J. Natl. Cancer Inst. 69, 777–785, 1982.

5

Malignant Mesothelioma: Studies of Immunological Anti-Cancer Processes

BRUCE W.S. ROBINSON, M.D.
LINDA S. MANNING, M.D.
RAYLEEN V. BOWMAN, M.D.
DARREL S. WHITAKER, PH.D., F.I.M.L.S., A.A.I.M.L.S., C.F.I.C.
JAMES FLEXMAN, M.D.
ANTHONY W. MUSK, M.D.

University of Western Australia
Nedlands, Australia

Synopsis

BIOGRAPHY

Bruce W.S. Robinson is a respiratory physician and senior lecturer in the University Department of Medicine, University of Western Australia. He has a long-standing interest in pulmonary immunology and cell biology, particularly of the occupational lung diseases, asbestosis and malignant mesothelioma. He is director of a laboratory that has established a large number of malignant mesothelioma cell lines and has evaluated the tumour immunology of mesothelioma patients with a view to establishing immunotherapy treatment regimes. In addition he has conducted a large number of studies of the immunological and inflammatory processes underlying asbestosis. Dr. Robinson may be contacted at the University Department of Medicine, Queen Elizabeth II Medical Centre, Nedlands, Perth, 6009, Western Australia (telephone: 06-389-2098; telex: 9344C).

Dr. Linda S. Manning is a post-doctoral scientist in the Department of Respiratory Medicine at the Sir Charles Gairdner Hospital. She has a long-standing interest in tumour immunology, particularly the role of natural killer cells, lymphokine-activated killer cells and interleukin-2 in malignant mesothelioma.

Dr. Rayleen V. Bowman is a respiratory physician in the Department of Respiratory Medicine at the Sir Charles Gairdner Hospital. Her research interests include the use of cytokines such as tumour necrosis factor to boost cytolytic lymphocyte effector mechanisms in cancer. She has also conducted clinical studies using lymphokine-activated killer cells and interleukin-2 intrapleurally in patients with malignant pleural mesothelioma. She also has ongoing research interests in the pathogenic mechanisms underlying pulmonary asbestosis.

Dr. Darrel S. Whitaker is a cytopathologist in the Department of Pathology at the Queen Elizabeth II Medical Centre. He has a long-standing interest in the cytological evaluation of malignant mesothelioma and in animal models of mesothelioma.

Dr. James Flexman is a physician and post-doctoral scientist whose research interest is in the area of tumour immunology, particularly natural killer cells and their regulation. He has conducted a number of studies evaluating routes of interleukin-2 administration and their effect on host anti-cancer defences.

Dr. Arthur W. Musk is a respiratory physician in the Sir Charles Gairdner Hospital. His research interests include the clinical and epidemiological evaluation of malignant mesothelioma in crocidolite-exposed workers in Western Australia. He also has interests in asbestosis and other occupational lung diseases.

EDITORS' COMMENTARY

Mesothelioma has been a dreaded disease entity among those involved in asbestos activities because it has been considered as a possible outcome of low-level exposure (no safe level), with rapid progression (½ to 1½ years of life expectancy), affecting all age groups (including children), and with no effective treatment (even palliative for the painful effects). It has been a consideration in establishing asbestos abatement policies and practices, government regulations, and courtroom access. There seemed to be no hope in terms of surgery, radiation, chemotherapy, or immunotherapy. In 1984, hope was created for pulmonary cancer regression by the use of recombinant interleukin-2 and lymphokine activated killer cells. In 1989, there has been some renewed hope for enhancing the tumor fighting capability of the immune system by the use of tumor infiltrating lymphocytes (site specific) that are proliferated by interleukin-2 and then enhanced by the immunosuppressant cyclophosphamide. The hope is not yet proven reality, but it is a powerful stimulus on the road of medical discovery. Meanwhile, at the University of Western Australia, research studies were being conducted on the immunological anti-cancer process dealing specifically with malignant mesothelioma. The following chapter presents evidence that there are immunological treatment possibilities for malignant mesothelioma in terms of tumor suppression and enhancing anti-cancer defense mechanisms. While there is *promise* in finding appropriate combinations and doses, while controlling side effects, there is substantial *progress* in our understanding of why some who are exposed to asbestos develop cancer and of the mechanisms by which the adverse health effects can be retarded or for remission to be enhanced.

A. INTRODUCTION

Malignant mesothelioma is a relatively rare tumour in most centers. Because of its causal relationship with inhalation of asbestos fibers, particularly amphiboles such as crocidolite, it occurs in increased frequency in areas where individuals are exposed to asbestos (1). In Western Australia, a crocidolite mine operated between 1948 and 1966. Large numbers of workers were exposed to crocidolite in the mining, milling, or transport of crocidolite; others were incidentally exposed in the township of Wittenoom Gorge (2). The number of cases of malignant mesothelioma in Western Australia is increasing at an alarming rate (Fig. 5-1).

Previous therapeutic approaches to malignant mesothelioma have proved fruitless. Neither chemotherapy, radiotherapy, nor surgery has proven to be widely effective and currently there is no established therapy for this disease (3).

Over the past few years there has been considerable interest in host anti-cancer defences. It is known that a variety of cells exert the capacity to destroy tumour cells, including the cytolytic lymphocytes natural killer (NK) (4) and lymphokine-activated killer (LAK) cells (5). NK cells are present in the normal individual's blood and circulate in relatively large numbers. They are able to destroy a variety of malignant cells without requiring any prior sensitization (in contrast to antigen-specific cytotoxic T-cells) and without requiring long-term exposure to interleukin-2 (in contrast to LAK cells). LAK cells represent lymphocytes that have a broad range of tumoricidal activity, being able to lyse a variety of NK-resistant cell lines and NK-resistant tumour targets. They are derived from normal peripheral blood lymphocytes following exposure to interleukin-2 for several days. The major precursor populations are NK cells. Recent studies utilizing LAK cells and interleukin-2 in patients with otherwise treatment-resistant malignancies have shown some partial and complete responses (6, 7).

In patients with advanced cancer, suppression of a variety of immunological processes has been described, including those responsible for anti-cancer activity (8). In addition, asbestos exposure is also known to alter systemic immune activity (9). For these reasons, we have evaluated host anti-cancer activity in patients with malignant mesothelioma and also in those individuals exposed to asbestos who do not have malignant mesothelioma.

Accepted for publication on 9 February 1989.

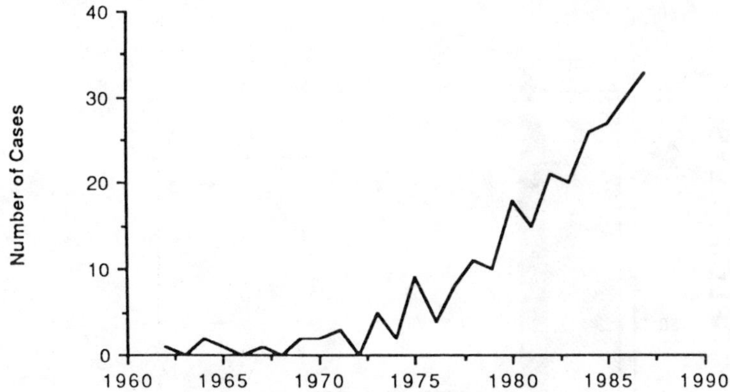

Fig. 5-1 Number of Cases of Malignant Mesothelioma Occurring in Western Australia, 1962–1987.

B. IN VITRO TUMOUR IMMUNOLOGY OF MESOTHELIOMA

1. NK-Resistence of Mesothelioma Cells

In order to determine whether malignant mesothelioma cells were susceptible to normal host anti-cancer surveillance mechanisms, we established a number of malignant mesothelioma cell lines from the pleural fluid of patients with proven malignant mesothelioma. These cell lines were cultured in standard medium containing 10% fetal calf serum and characterized by cytological, ultrastructural, and karyotypic analysis. Six of these cell lines have been designated NO3, HA5, DHA3, JU7, DEH2, and MO5. In addition, frozen banks of fresh malignant mesothelioma cells have been preserved from these patients at −135°C in 90% FCS/10% DMSO.

In order to evaluate the susceptibility of these cells to NK-mediated lysis, a standard NK assay was performed. Target cells were labelled with ^{51}Cr and a 4 hour cytotoxicity assay performed using peripheral blood mononuclear cells obtained from normal volunteers. Malignant mesothelioma cells were shown to be resistant to NK-mediated lysis when compared to a standard NK-sensitive target, K562 cells (Fig. 5-2).

As LAK cells have been shown to lyse a variety of NK-resistant malignant targets, we evaluated the susceptibility of these NK-resistant malignant mesothelioma lines to LAK cell mediated lysis. As with most other tumour targets, these meso-

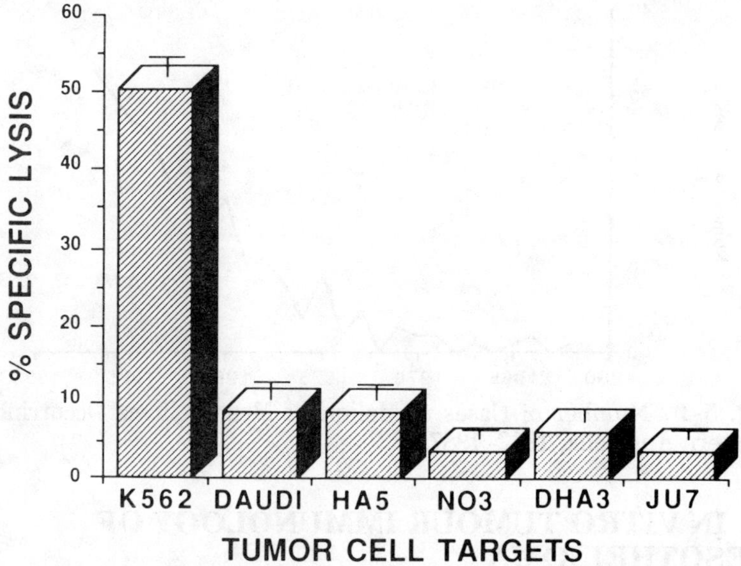

Fig. 5-2 Susceptibility of Human Cultured Malignant Mesothelioma Cells to Lysis by NK Cells. Human malignant mesothelioma cells, established in culture for at least 1 month, were assessed for susceptibility to NK cell lysis in a 4 hour-^{51}Cr release assay. The data is presented as the mean % specific lysis (±SEM) for the 2 standard NK and LAK cell targets (K562 and Daudi) and 4 cultured mesothelioma cell targets (HA5, NO3, DHA3, and JU7) for 12–38 experiments.

thelioma cells were shown to be sensitive to LAK cells (Fig. 5-3). The levels of lysis for each of the mesothelioma cell lines was similar to that seen with the standard LAK-sensitive target Daudi. Kinetic studies of LAK cell generation demonstrated that 3 to 10 days in culture produced optimum levels of target cell lysis (Fig. 5-4). The effect of the serum source on the generation of LAK cells was evaluated by culturing them in either autologous serum, pooled human AB serum or fetal calf serum. Autologous serum was more effective than either of the other two sources of serum (Fig. 5-5).

As in vitro culture conditions can alter cell characteristics and cytotoxic lymphocyte susceptibility, we studied the capacity of LAK cells to lyse fresh, non-cultured tumour targets in the presence or absence of interleukin-2. These targets were also NK-resistant and LAK-sensitive (Fig. 5-6).

These studies demonstrate that, at least in vitro, human malignant mesothelioma cells can be destroyed by immunological effector cells following exposure to interleukin-2.

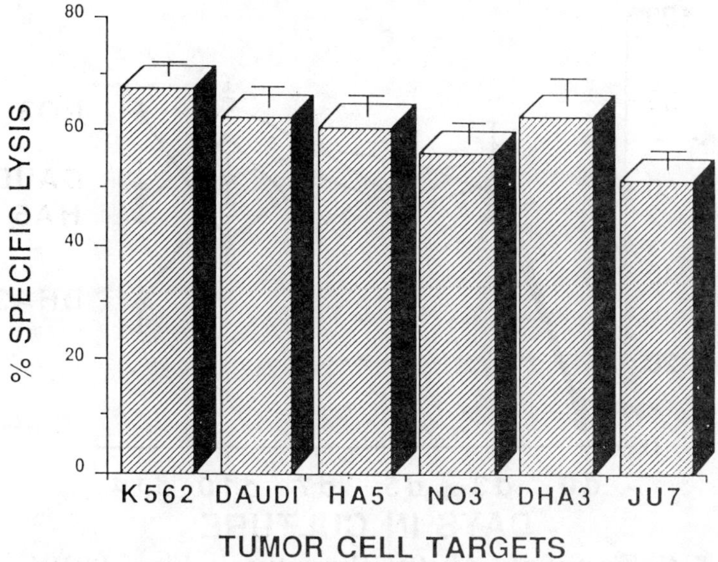

Fig. 5-3 Susceptibility of Human Cultured Malignant Mesothelioma Cells to Lysis by LAK Cells. Human malignant mesothelioma target cells were evaluated as in Fig. 5-1 for susceptibility to LAK cell killing in a 4 hour-^{51}Cr release assay (11–47 experiments).

C. IN VIVO TUMOUR IMMUNOLOGY OF MALIGNANT MESOTHELIOMA

In order to determine whether patients with malignant mesothelioma have deficient anti-cancer cellular activity, we evaluated NK cell activity and LAK cell generation in 22 patients with malignant mesothelioma and compared the results to those from 80 healthy volunteers (10). NK cell activity was comparable in the two groups (43 ± 4% versus 49 ± 3% lysis respectively, Fig. 5-7). LAK cell activity against malignant mesothelioma targets was 55 ± 4% in patients with mesothelioma compared to 66 ± 2% in control individuals ($p < 0.01$, Fig. 5-7).

1. Effects of Asbestos Exposure

In order to determine whether asbestos exposure itself was capable of inducing these changes, we evaluated NK cell activity and LAK cell generation in a further 52 individuals occupationally exposed to asbestos who did not have malignant mesothelioma. As in the other two groups, NK cell activity was not reduced

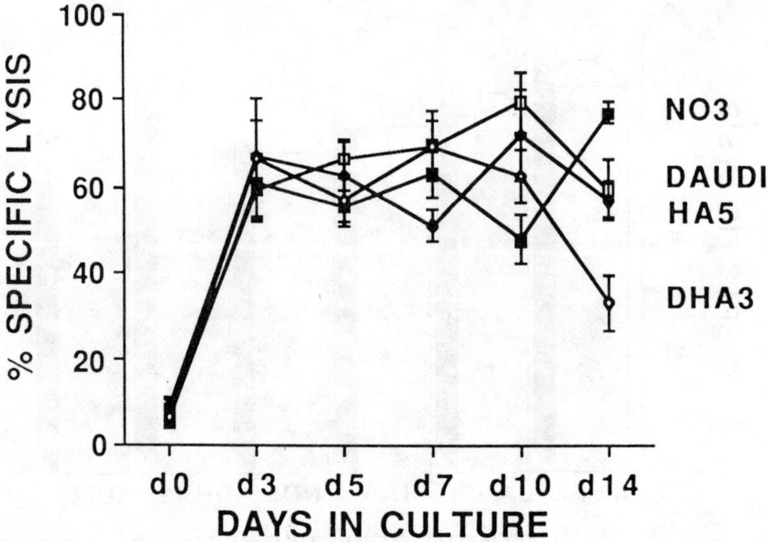

Fig. 5-4 Kinetics of LAK Cell Generation In Vitro. PBMNs were incubated for 0–14 days in the presence of 1,000 units/ml IL-2 and then assessed for LAK cell activity in the 4 hour-^{51}Cr release assay. The data is presented as the mean % specific lysis of 3–8 experiments for each time point for the standard LAK cell target, Daudi, and 3 cultured mesothelioma cell lines (NO3, HA5, and DHA3).

(50 ± 5% lysis). LAK cell generation was also similar (62 ± 2% lysis).

2. Effects of Indomethacin

As previous studies have demonstrated, that suppressed immunological processes in patients with advanced cancer may be mediated in part by the release of E-series prostaglandins, we evaluated the capacity of indomethacin, an agent that suppresses prostaglandin production, to reverse the suppression of LAK cell generation in patients with malignant mesothelioma. At a dose of 10 μg/ml, indomethacin restored normal LAK cell activity in these patients (52 ± 6% lysis of cultured human mesothelioma cells, no significant difference compared to controls) (Fig. 5-8). Indomethacin had no significant effect on LAK cell generation in normal individuals.

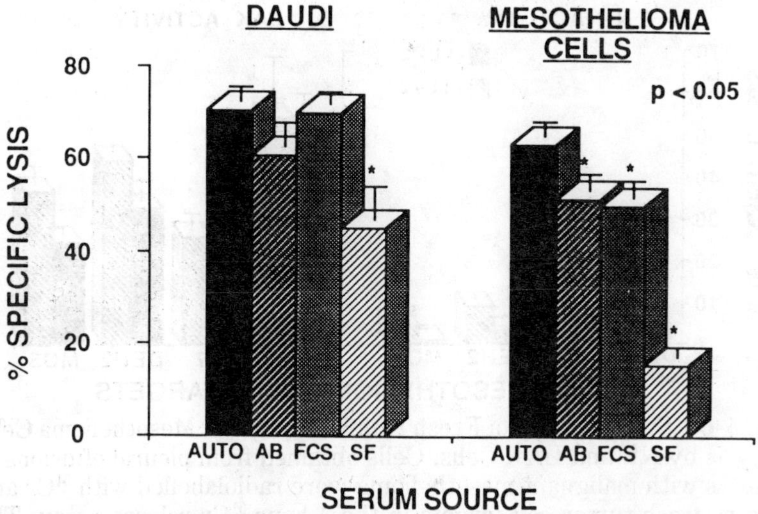

Fig. 5-5 Effect of Different Serum Sources on LAK Cell Generation In Vitro. PBMNs were incubated for 3–10 days in culture medium containing 1,000 units/ml IL-2 and either 10% autologous serum (Auto), 10% Human AB Serum (AB), 10% FCS (FCS), or serum-free medium (SF). LAK cell activation was assessed in the 4 hour-^{51}Cr release assay. The data is presented as the mean % specific lysis (±SEM) for 4–35 experiments for the standard LAK cell target, Daudi, and the 6 cultured mesothelioma cell lines (pooled data).
* $p < 0.05$ cf autologous serum.

D. EFFECTS OF ASBESTOS FIBERS ON ANTI-CANCER ACTIVITY

1. Effects on NK Activity

The addition of asbestos fibers to a standard NK assay produced suppression of NK activity in a dose-dependent fashion (Fig. 5-9), and was more marked with chrysotile asbestos compared to other forms of asbestos (11). No significant suppression of NK activity was seen when comparable doses of glass wool fibers and ceramic fibers were utilized. This suppressive effect on NK cell activity was not due to cytotoxicity of the effector cells, as cell viability (trypan blue exclusion) was not altered by asbestos fibers, and the cytotoxic activity of NK cells could be restored following removal of the asbestos fibers by passage through nylon wool filters. The suppressor effect was exerted directly on the NK

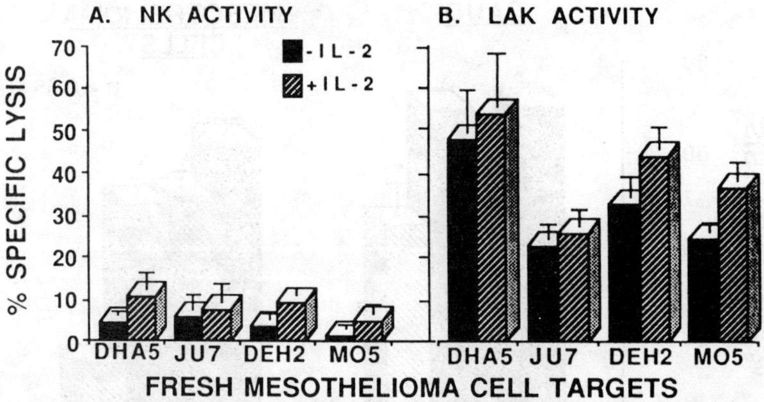

Fig. 5-6 Susceptibility of Fresh Human Malignant Mesothelioma Cells to Lysis by NK and LAK Cells. Cells obtained from pleural effusions of patients with malignant mesothelioma were radiolabelled with ^{51}Cr and used as fresh tumor cell targets in the 4 hour-^{51}Cr release assay. The data is presented as the mean % specific lysis (±SEM) by NK cells (panel A) and LAK cells (panel B) against 4 fresh mesothelioma cell targets (DHA3, JU7, DEH2, and MO5) for 3–17 experiments.

effector cell in that purified large granular lymphocytes were suppressed by NK asbestos fibers.

2. Effect of Interleukin-2

Interleukin-2 exposure for 18 hours was able to partially reverse asbestos-mediated suppression of blood and lung NK activity, producing a level of NK activity that was comparable to that seen in lymphocyte populations not exposed to asbestos fibers (Fig. 5-10). Similarly, lung lymphocytes obtained from individuals with sarcoidosis who were exposed to large amounts of interleukin-2 in vivo were resistant to suppression by asbestos fibers (data not shown).

E. EFFECT OF IN VIVO INTERLEUKIN-2

1. Animal Studies

In preparation for a clinical trial using recombinant human interleukin-2 intrapleurally in patients with malignant mesothelioma, we conducted animal studies evaluating the capacity of intra-

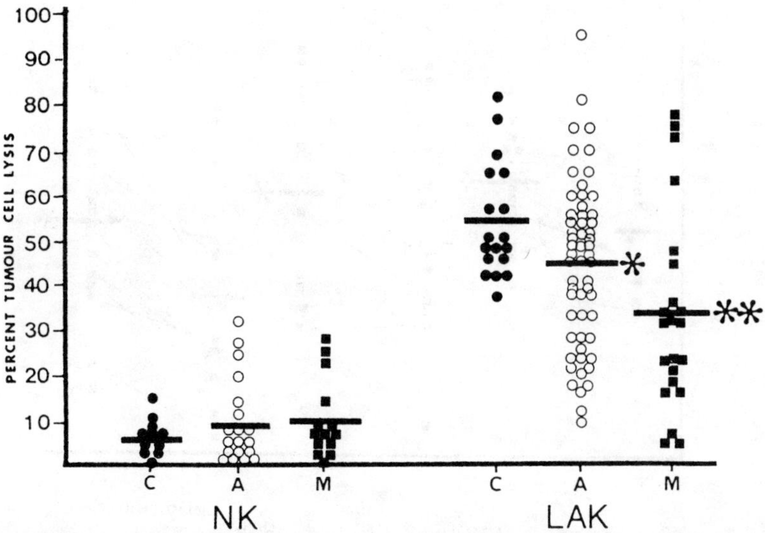

Fig. 5-7 NK/LAK Cell Activity Against Cultured Human Malignant Mesothelioma Cells. Controls (C, ●), asbestos-exposed individuals (A, ○) and patients with MM (M, ■). The percent tumour cell lysis is shown for each individual with the mean percent lysis for each group indicated by the bar.
* $p < 0.05$
** $p < 0.01$ (Tukey-Kramer studentised range test) comparing LAK activity by asbestos-exposed individuals and patients with MM, respectively, to controls.

pleural interleukin-2 to boost host anti-cancer defences (12,13). Five daily doses of 50,000 units of interleukin-2 were administered to CBA mice (5 per group) intrapleurally and the effect on boosting of pulmonary NK activity and systemic (splenic activity) was evaluated using a ^{51}Cr release assay using the NK-sensitive YAC-1 target.

Following intrapleural therapy with interleukin-2 and/or LAK cells, a 3-fold increase in pleural cell yields was seen compared to control (saline) animals. In addition, whereas pleural cells in control animals showed only <3% cytotoxicity to the YAC-1 cells at 25:1 effector:target rates, pleural cells from mice injected with LAK cells alone showed 30% toxicity to the YAC-1 cells, and those from mice injected with LAK cells plus interleukin-2 or interleukin-2 alone showed 66% cytotoxicity against the YAC-1 cells (Table 5-1). Intrapleural interleukin-2 also boosted pulmonary and systemic NK activity and LAK activity to levels comparable to those seen with either intraperitoneal or intrave-

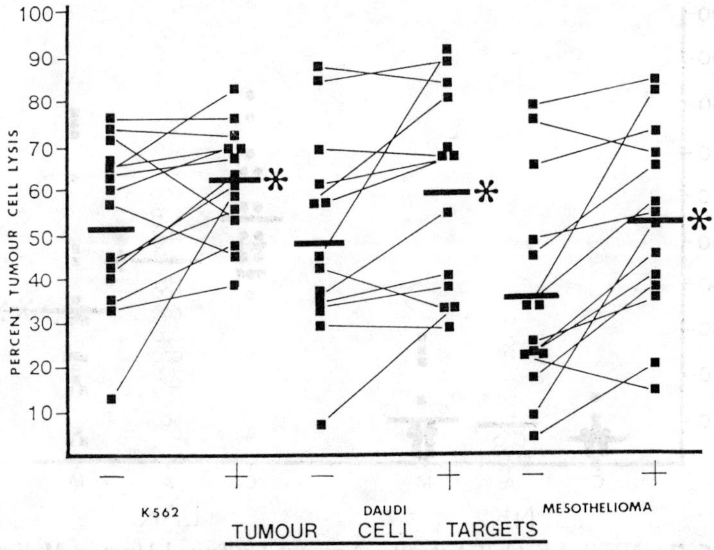

Fig. 5-8 Effect of Indomethacin on LAK Cell Activity by Patients with MM. PBMNs from 14 patients with MM were cultured for 3–7 days in media plus IL-2 in the absence (−) or presence (+) of 10 μg/ml indomethacin. LAK activity against K562, Daudi, and 6 cultured human MM cell lines was assessed using the ^{51}Cr release assay. Percent tumour cell lysis by each individual is shown (0) and the mean percent lysis for the 2 groups (−/+ indomethacin) against each target is indicated by the bar.

* $p < 0.05$ (paired Student's t test) comparing LAK cell activity generated in the absence or presence of indomethacin.

nous interleukin-2 administration. These studies demonstrated that intrapleural interleukin-2 was able to boost both local pleural and systemic anti-cancer activities.

2. Human Studies

We have recently commenced a clinical trial using recombinant human interleukin-2 plus LAK cells intrapleurally in patients with malignant mesothelioma. Thus far 4 patients have been entered for a total of eleven cycles of therapy. Each cycle consists of a single leukapheresis following which the recovered lymphocytes (approximately 2 × 10^9 cells) are cultured in autologous serum and interleukin-2 (1,000 units/ml for 4 days). These LAK cells are then injected intrapleurally along with interleukin-2. Two further

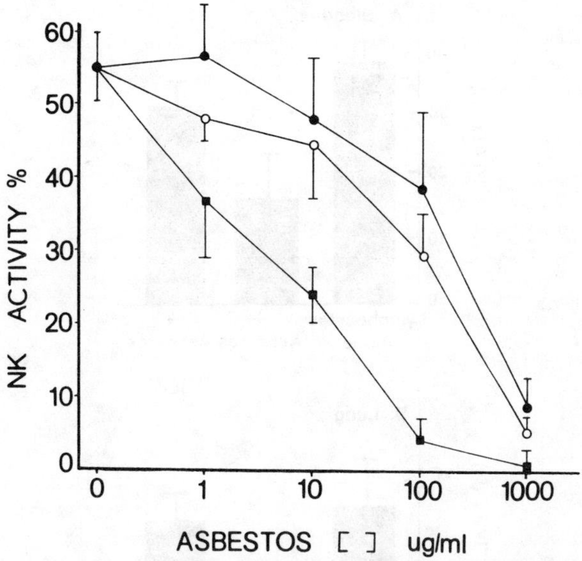

Fig. 5-9 Suppression of Normal Human Blood NK Activity by Asbestos Fibers. Asbestos [amosite (●), crocidolite (○), chrysotile (intermediate length, ■)] were added in various concentrations to a standard NK assay (effector:target ratio = 50:1).

doses of interleukin-2 are given intrapleurally on each of the subsequent 2 days. Cycles are given three times per week.

Toxicities seen have been similar to those observed with intravenous administration—i.e., fevers, chills, fluid retention, skin rash, and CNS changes. In addition, local pleural problems (fluid accumulation, loculation, and infection) have been encountered.

Boosting of blood NK and LAK cell activity has been observed with higher doses of therapy and parallels systemic toxicity.

The trial is in its early stages and response rates have not been evaluated.

F. CONCLUSIONS

These studies demonstrate that patients with malignant pleural mesothelioma have suppressed anti-cancer defences. The capacity of lymphocytes from these patients to destroy malignant

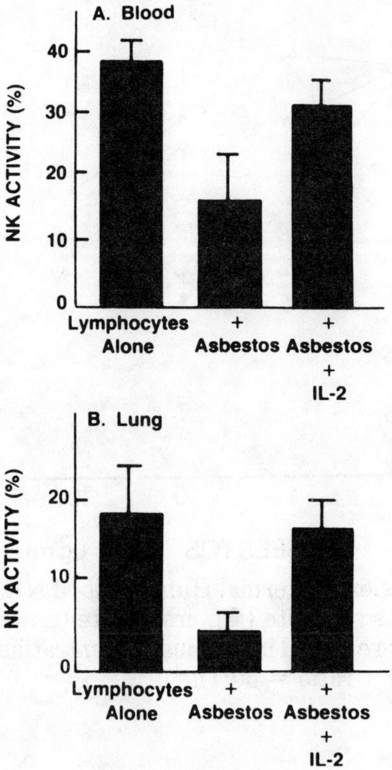

Fig. 5-10 Capacity of Interleukin-2 (IL-2) to Reverse Asbestos-Mediated Suppression of Blood and Lung NK Activity. Blood (A) or lung (B) lymphocytes were cultured in IL-2 or medium alone for 24 hours then asbestos (chrysotile 100 μg/ml) added and NK activity assayed.

Table 5-1 NK and LAK Activity of Pleural and Splenic Leucocytes Following 5 Daily Doses of 50,000U of IL-2 Intrapleurally

Cell Source	Group*	Average Cell Yield/mouse	Cytotoxic Units + SD YAC-1	Cytotoxic Units + SD P815
Pleural cavity	Control	2.3×10^6	2.5 ± 1.4	0.2 ± 0.3
	Intrapleural IL-2	6.1×10^6	65.7 ± 5.1	13.5 ± 1.9**
Spleen	Control	5.9×10^7	18.0 ± 2.0	2.1 ± 0.6
	Intrapleural IL-2	7.9×10^7	35.7 ± 2.9**	3.0 ± 1.1

*For both groups the cells from 10 CBA mice were pooled for the 4 hour ^{51}Cr release assay against the targets shown.
**$p < 0.001$.

mesothelioma cells can be boosted by exposure to interleukin-2 in vitro and by reversing a prostaglandin-mediated suppression by the addition of indomethacin.

Intrapleural interleukin-2 boosts local and systemic anti-cancer activity in animals and we are currently conducting a Phase I/II clinical trial using intrapleural interleukin-2 plus LAK cells in patients with malignant pleural mesothelioma.

REFERENCES

1. Wagner, J.C., Sleggs, C.A., and Marchand, P., Diffuse pleural mesotheliom a and asbestos exposure in the North Western Cape Province. Br. J. Ind. Med. 17:260–271, 1960.
2. Cookson, W.O.C.M., de Klerk, N.H., Musk, A.W., Clancy, J.J., Armstrong, B.K., and Hobbs, M.S.T. Benign and malignant pleural effusions in former Wittenoom crocidolite millers and miners. Aust. N.Z. J. Med. 15:731–737, 1985.
3. Musk, A.W., and Woodward, S.D. Conventional treatment and its effect on survival of malignant pleural mesothelioma in Western Australia. Aust. N.Z. J. Med. 12:229–232, 1982.
4. Robinson BWS, Pinkston P, Crystal RG. Natural killer cells are present in the normal human lung but are functionally impotent. J.Clin Invest 74:942–50, 1984.
5. Manning L., Robinson BWS. Susceptibility of fresh and cultured malignant mesothelioma cells to lysis by NK and LAK cells. In press. Am Rev Respir Dis. 1989.
6. Rosenberg, S.A., Lotze, M.T., Muul, L.M., Leitman, S., Chang, A.E., Ettinghausen, S.E., Matory, Y.L., Skibber, J.M., Shiloni, E., Vetto, J.T., Seipp, C.A., Simpson, C., and Reichert, C.M. Observations on the systemic administration of autologous lymphokine-activated killer cells and recombinant interleukin-2 to patients with metastatic cancer. N. Engl. J. Med. 313:1485–1492, 1985.
7. Rosenberg, S.A., Lotze, M.T. Cancer immunotherapy using interleukin-2 and interleukin-2 activated lymphocytes. Ann. Rev. Immunol. 4:681–709, 1986.
8. Sibbits, W.L., Bankhurst, A.D., Jumonville, A.J., Saiki, J.H., Saiers, J.H., and Doberneck, R.C. Defects in natural killer cell activity and interferon response in human lung carcinoma and malignant melanoma. 44:852–856, 1984.
9. Kagan, E., Soloman, A., Cochrane, J.C., Beissner, E.I., Gluckman, J., Rocks, P.H. and Webster, I. Immunological studies of patients with asbestosis. Studies of cell-mediated immunity. Clin. Exp. Immunol. 28:261–267, 1977.
10. Manning LS, Bowman R, Darby S, Musk AW, Robinson BWS.

Lymphokine-activated killer (LAK) cells generated from patients with malignant mesothelioma (MM) are less effective against cultured MM cells than LAK cells from control individuals. Aust. N.Z. J. Med. 18:A553, 1988.

11. Robinson BWS. Asbestos and cancer: human natural killer cell activity is suppressed by asbestos fibres but can be restored by recombinant interleukin-2. In press. Am Rev Respir Dis. 1989.
12. Flexman J, Manning L, Robinson BWS. Augmentation of lung natural killer (NK) cell activity by administration of recombinant interleukin-2 (IL-2): comparison of different routes of administration. Aust. N.Z. J. Med. 17:515, 1987
13. Flexman J, Manning L, Robinson BWS. Local therapy of pleural malignancy: evaluation of intrapleural interleukin-2 (IL-2) and/or lymphokine-activated killer (LAK) cell administration. Aust. N.Z. J. Med. 17:516, 1987.

6

The Epidemiology of Asbestos Tumours

MURIEL L. NEWHOUSE, M.D., F.R.C.P.
KEITH R. SULLIVAN, M.Sc., A.F.I.M.A.

Occupational Health Unit
Department of Public Health and Policy
London School of Hygiene and Tropical Medicine
University of London
London, England, U.K.

Synopsis

BIOGRAPHY

Dr. M. L. Newhouse worked in the old Department of Occupational Health at the London School of Hygiene and Tropical Medicine since the 1960s. Research into the biological effects of asbestos exposure has been her main interest. She is best known for her studies of mesothelioma and her cohort studies of asbestos workers, but she also has wide interests in other occupational health problems. Dr. Newhouse can be contacted at the Occupational Health Unit, Department of Public Health and Policy, London School of Hygiene and Tropical Medicine, University of London, Keppel Street, London WC1E 7HT, England, U.K. (telephone: 01-636-8636; Fax: 01-436-5389; telex: 8953474).

Mr. K. R. Sullivan is a medical statistician who has worked in the field of occupational health statistics for the past 10 years and has a particular interest in asbestos-related diseases.

EDITORS' COMMENTARY

Much of the history of asbestos disease has centered around England; and significant issues continue to emerge from the research, practice, and evaluations conducted in that country. The following chapter presents epidemiological evidence on the risk of mesothelioma and cancers of the lung, larynx, gastro-intentinal tract, ovaries, pancreas, brain, and esophagus. Issues relating to fiber type, effects of smoking, and exposure limits are mentioned. In terms of risk assessment, predictive models are discussed based on factors such as dose, duration, and age at first exposure. Epidemiological research has identified and illuminated many issues for further medical research. However, earlier studies sometimes grossly estimated exposure level or dose, whereas improved instrumentation now permits careful monitoring of airborne asbestos levels (which still may be highly variable for each worker since dust clouds may be localized, transient, and vary by a factor of ten in addition to sampling and analytical errors). Without some precision about past and present dose, response is less predictable. What is being measured is also important. For example, if fibers below 5 microns in length are ignored, the results may be misleading (so transmission election microscopy and other new imaging devices are an important supplement or replacement for PLM microscopy). The interest and ability to identify, diagnose, make a differential diagnosis, and to report a particular disease entity is improving. Better understanding of the background risk or standard population, used to make comparisons and obtain estimates of excess risk, is now better understood. Other chapters in this book present evidence dealing with dose, duration, age, diagnosis, and reporting that should help clarify some of the past conflicts, differences in opinion, and ambiguities. However, the critical importance of earlier epidemiology deserves special emphasis. It had a profound effect on regulatory, technical, and legal matters. Epidemiology has and will be an important stimulus for further research and discovery in dealing with this worldwide public health problem.

A. INTRODUCTION

The association between exposure to asbestos dust and the development of cancer has been recognized for more than 60 years. In the 1930s, case reports of asbestos workers suffering from lung cancer, not at that time a common disease, began to appear in the literature. In 1960 mesothelioma was defined and its association with crocidolite asbestos was described in a survey from South Africa. Within a short time further studies of asbestos workers in addition to quantifying the excess deaths from lung cancer and mesothelial tumours also suggested that there were excess deaths from gastro-intestinal tumours, cancer of the larynx, and also a possible association with cancer of the ovary, pancreas, and brain. Epidemiological studies of groups of workers have advanced the understanding of the circumstances that contribute to the development of these diseases. The majority of the studies described here are mortality studies in which a group of asbestos workers are defined and their cause of death over a period of years are compared with the mortality of a standard population not exposed to asbestos. Most generally the population used for comparison is that of the whole country for which national figures are available and in which an asbestos risk, if present at all, is so diluted as to be insignificant.

Certain case control studies will also be cited. These studies have been used to explore the aetiology of diseases as well as for other purposes such as drug trials. Ideally the cases and controls should be closely matched for age and sex and socio-economic status and be derived from similar sources. The trial should be conducted blind—i.e., the investigator does not know whether he is interviewing a case or control.

Clinically, occupational cancers cannot be differentiated from cancers of other or unknown aetiology. Characteristically the latent period, that is the period from first exposure to onset of the disease, is long. For asbestos-induced lung cancer the latent period is 15–25 years; in mesothelioma this is often much longer, taking between 20 to 40 or even 50 years. Evidence of a dose-response relationship between the degree of exposure to the suspected carcinogenic agent and the frequency of occurrence of the tumours is strong, supporting evidence when assessing the probability of any cancer being occupationally related.

Accepted for publication 10 April 1989

B. LUNG CANCER

The first asbestos textile factories in England opened in Manchester in 1888 and in East London in 1905. Respiratory effects were noted within a few years and the prevalence of asbestosis became a matter of considerable concern. In 1929 a survey of the East London textile factories by Merewether and Price resulted in the legislation of 1931, which made asbestosis a compensatable disease and required an autopsy before compensation could be granted.[1,2] There was increasing interest in asbestosis and evidence of other asbestos-related diseases began to accumulate. In the early 1930s Gloyne, and Lynch and Smith, reported on cases of carcinoma of the lung in workers with asbestosis.[3,4] Further reports from Germany and other countries confirmed these findings. In the 1947 Annual Report of the Chief Inspector of Factories published in 1949, Merewether reviewed 235 autopsies of patients with asbestosis and found a prevalence of cancer of the lung of 13% in the asbestos workers compared to 1.3% in workers with silicosis.[5] Carcinoma of the lung was found in 17.3% of the males autopsied and 8.4% of the females. However, in spite of considerable disquiet there was no general acceptance that cancer of the lung in asbestos workers was an occupational cancer.

In 1955 the case was much strengthened by a classical cohort study by Doll of workers at a textile factory.[6] The group selected for study were those with 20 or more years of employment in areas of the factory designated as "scheduled." Under the 1931 asbestos industry regulations, these jobs were scheduled as dusty and workers were required to be under medical surveillance. There were 113 men in the cohort. The deaths were grouped in 6 categories: lung cancer (1) with or (2) without asbestosis; other respiratory diseases (3) with or (4) without asbestosis; (5) other neoplasms; and (6) all other diseases. The number of deaths in each category was compared with the number to be expected in men of the general population of England and Wales of the same age using the person-years method first described by Case in 1955 (Table 6-1).[7] There were 11 deaths from lung cancer with less than 1 expected. All the cases of lung cancer were confirmed histologically and all were associated with the presence of asbestosis. Doll concluded that "lung cancer was a specific industrial hazard of certain asbestos workers."

Studies of other groups of workers soon followed. Mancuso and Coulter in Pittsburgh in 1963 identified workers in a factory where the principal exposure was to asbestos.[8] The Bureau of Old Age and Survivors Insurance (BOASI) was used to identify all workers employed at the plant in 1937 and 1938. Details of the birthdate, sex, and color of each worker were available as well as

Table 6-1 Causes of Death Among Male Asbestos Workers Compared with Mortality Experience of All Men in England and Wales (Doll, 1955)

Cause of death	No. of Deaths: Observed	No. of Deaths: Expected	Test of Significance of Differences Between Observed and Expected (Value of P)
Lung Cancer:			
with mention of asbestosis	11	—	<0.000001
without mention of asbestosis	0	0.8	
Other respiratory diseases (including pulmonary tuberculosis) and cardiovascular diseases:			
with mention of asbestosis	14	—	<0.001
without mention of asbestosis	6	7.6	
Neoplasms other than lung cancer	4	2.3	>0.1
All other disease	4	4.7	
All causes	39	15.4	<0.000001

the occupational records. All death certificates were traced. The number of deaths to be expected was calculated from the vital statistics of the population of the state of Ohio. Their methods were described in great detail and are worth studying by those with a special interest in epidemiological techniques. The ratio of observed to expected deaths for lung cancer was 2.75:0 in males and 4.40:0 in females, giving an overall standardised mortality ratio of 338. In 1964 Selikoff, Hammond, and Churg published their study of New York insulation workers.[9] A list was prepared of all men in the metropolitan locals of the Asbestos Workers Union who were members of the Union from December 31, 1942, to December 31, 1962. The 1942 list included 632 men who joined before 1942. The Union records gave detailed work histories. Three hundred and thirty-nine men had 20 or more years of exposure to asbestos by January 1943. Copies of death certificates were obtained for those who had died. In the period 1943–1962, 45 men died of cancer of the lung, whereas less than 7 were expected to have died based on United States national figures. The 370 from this study of survivors were the subject of a further 4-year investigation, as the earlier results had indicated a very high incidence of deaths from cancer of the lung in those who smoked.[10] The survirors were interviewed, smoking habits were recorded, and each was given a clinical examination, including a chest x-ray. These examinations were repeated annually. Ninety-four men died during the period of investigation, 24 from bronchogenic carcinoma. All these 24 deaths occurred in men who had a history of regular cigarette smoking (Table 6-2). The authors calculated that the combined risk of lung cancer in a smoking asbestos worker was ×92 that of a non-smoker not exposed to asbestos.

Other important cohort mortality studies were also underway in the United States, England, and Canada. Newhouse in 1969 studied male workers at an East London textile factory, establishing the vital statistics of past workers through the Department of Health and Social Security and the National Health Service Central Register.[11] As far as possible, the cause of death on the death certificate was validated by histological examination obtained at autopsy or by biopsy during life. Later in 1972 a cohort of women workers were also traced.[12] The particular difficulties of tracing women, because of the change of name on marriage, were overcome by selecting all women employed in the war time period during which all residents in the United Kingdom received an identity number that later became the National Health Service Number, so the searches were undertaken by the National Health Service Central Register. In both the male and female cohorts the

Table 6-2 Lung Cancer Mortality of Asbestos Workers by Smoking Habit (Selikoff et al, 1968)

Smoking Habits	No. of Men	No. of Deaths	
		Observed	Expected
Never smoked regularly	48	0	0.05
History of pipe or cigar smoking only	39	0	0.13
History of regular cigarette smoking*	283	24	2.98
Total	370	24	3.16

*Includes cigarette smokers who also smoked pipe or cigar.

workers were grouped into two exposure categories, "low-moderate" and "severe," each category was divided by length of exposure, less than 2 years and more than 2 years. These studies revealed an increasing risk of lung cancer with increasing length and severity of exposure. In Canada, McDonald et al studied the mortality of Quebec chrysotile asbestos miners and millers.[13] In this work there was sufficient information from counts of dust in air dating from 1904 to attach a dust index to each subject and the dose-response relationship was confirmed (Fig. 6-1). It also highlighted the lesser risk of workers exposed only to chrysotile asbestos, compared to those working with amphibole and mixed fiber exposure.

The smoking habits of a sub-group of the East London workers were also examined for a 10-year period.[14] The figures were not conclusive (Table 6-3) but seemed to favour the theory that asbestos exposure and cigarette smoking act in a synergistic or multiplicative manner.

There is considerable interest in the cell type of asbestos

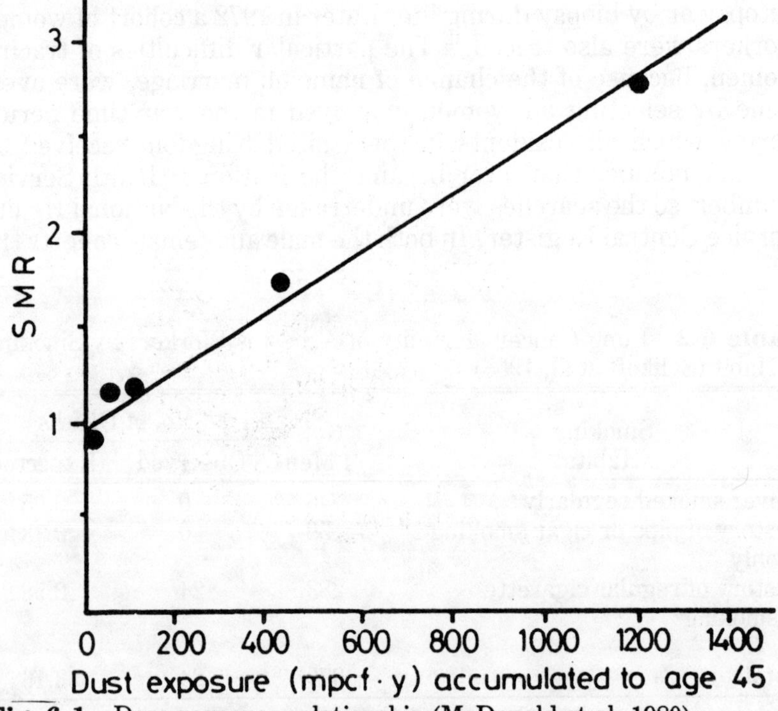

Fig. 6-1 Dose-response relationship (McDonald et al, 1980).

Table 6-3 Distribution of Lung Cancers in Asbestos Workers by Smoking Habit (Berry et al, 1972)

Smoking Habits	Observed Deaths	Expected Non-Occupational Deaths	Expected Occupational and Non-Occupational Deaths	
			Additive model	Multiplicative model
Males:				
Smokers	32	12.0	31.4	33.1
Non-smokers	0	0.0	1.2	0.1
Females:				
Smokers	18	1.9	14.0	17.8
Non-smokers	2	0.2	5.4	2.2

induced bronchial carcinomas, particularly if there is difficulty in attributing the disease to asbestos exposure or to cigarette smoking. A study of the histological types of lung cancer in patients with asbestosis dying in the United Kingdom was made by Whitwell, Newhouse, and Bennett in 1974.[15] In the United Kingdom up until recently all patients dying of a pneumoconiosis were the subject of an autopsy. Records and histological specimens of 88 patients dying of asbestosis were collected, 34% of the specimens showed an adenocarcinoma (Table 6-4). Smoking habits were known in 69 patients; there were none who had never smoked. Again while the findings are not decisive, an adenocarcinoma in a smoking asbestos worker suggests the probability of the tumour being asbestos induced.

Review of the available evidence seems to suggest that the risk of bronchial carcinoma is less in mining than in manufacture

Table 6-4 Histological Type of Tumour (Whitwell et al, 1974)

	Male		Female	Total
	No.	%		
Squamous	19	21.6	2	21
Oat	23	26.1	3	26
Adenocarcinoma	30	34.1	3	33
Simplex	12	13.6	1	13
Mixed	4	4.6	—	4
Total	88		9	97

and less with chrysotile exposure than with mixed exposures or amphibole exposure alone. This is supported by McDonald's study of miners and millers[13] and studies of cement factories[16,17] and friction material factories[18] where only chrysotile asbestos has been used. Accurate estimates of risk were not possible in all of these studies because in many cases there is lack of detailed exposure information at the relevant period. However, in the work of Hughes et al, which reviewed 8 mortality studies from cement factories,[17] where chrysotile is predominantly used with varying amounts of crocidolite, 3 studies exhibited no excess risk of lung cancer whereas the relative risk in the other 5 ranged from 1.46 to 4.90.

In the United Kingdom bronchial carcinoma in asbestos workers became a compensatable disease in December 1983. In view of the difficulties in distinguishing between the influence of cigarette smokng and asbestos exposure in the aetiology of the cancer, the prescription is limited to primary carcinoma of lung where there is accompanying evidence of asbestosis or bilateral diffuse pleural thickening, both conditions giving incontrovertible evidence of past asbestos exposure.

C. MESOTHELIOMA OF THE PLEURA AND PERITONEUM

It was not until the mid 1950s that the mesothelial tumour, a rare tumour in the general public, was recognized as a definite pathological entity. At that same time the various histological types were defined and those definitions agreed to among pathologists. Case reports of cancer of the pleura and peritoneum in asbestos workers started to appear in the literature. Bonner, Faulds, and Stewart in 1955 found 12 cases of lung cancer, 2 cases of pleural cancer, and 4 cases of peritoneal cancer in 72 autopsies of workers with asbestosis.[19] However, it was the classical paper of Wagner, Sleggs, and Marchand in 1960 that established the association of this tumour with exposure to crocidolite asbestos.[20] This investigation describes a survey undertaken in the Transvaal in South Africa. Here crocidolite asbestos was mined in open-cast mines. The male workers isolated the asbestos ore; women often accompanied by their children were employed in cobbing, that is, breaking up pieces of ore to isolate bands of fiber. One of the authors had been concerned by the large number of patients in his practice suffering from this unusual and fatal tumour. In all, 33 patients alive and deceased were identified. Careful details of age, sex, race, and evidence of asbestos exposure were collected. The majority of the patients in this series had been born in the vicinity of the crocidolite mine or had lived there for some years during childhood. Several had actually worked as miners, others had been employed transporting the asbestos. Four of the patients had no association with the mines or the mining area but had worked with crocidolite asbestos on locomotive bodies or on steam pipes. For only one was there no history of asbestos exposure.

The publication of this paper stimulated workers in other centers to collect and examine the characteristics of other series of patients dying of mesothelial tumours. Important papers came from Northern Ireland,[21] from Germany,[22] and from England.[23]

In the English investigation Newhouse and Thompson were able to obtain the occupational and residential histories of 76 patients who had died at the London Hospital between 1936 and 1962 who had also been the subjects of autopsy. A spouse or other relative was interviewed. Thirty-one of the patients had had occupational exposure to asbestos either in asbestos factories or as laggers or insulators. Nine had family members working in asbestos factories in their childhood, and 11 had lived as children within half a mile of an asbestos factory. In 25 of the patients in the series no evidence of asbestos exposure could be obtained. This paper emphasized the importance of non-occupational exposure, either through exposure in the home from asbestos dust bought home on the clothes of a factory worker or by environmental contamination of the atmosphere from an asbestos source such as a factory. In approximately one-third of the series no asbestos contact could be traced; similar results were obtained in other surveys. The latent period in this series varied between 29 and 49 years (mean 37.5 years). The majority of deaths occurred between 1955 and 1964, probably reflecting the increasing use of asbestos in manufacturing after 1920.

Cohort studies also demonstrated the frequency of occurrence of this tumour in asbestos workers. Selikoff's study of insulators,[9] now extended to cover all insulators in North America, identified 31 deaths from mesothelial tumours among 1,249 insulators followed between 1963 and 1974. These men were largely exposed to amphibole asbestos, particularly amosite. Newhouse followed a cohort of asbestos factory workers exposed to all three types of asbestos, but many of them to only crocidolite asbestos, and found that over the period of followup, 1933–1980, there had been 98 deaths among 3,000 men from mesothelial tumours.[24] In contrast, among more than 11,000 chrysotile miners in Canada studied by McDonald, there were 11 deaths from mesothelial tumours between 1910 and 1970.[25] In a factory producing friction materials, that is, brake and clutch linings and employing >13,000 male and female workers, over a 40-year period, there were 11 deaths from pleural mesothelioma.[18] In this factory, chrysotile asbestos was predominantly used, with crocidolite used for only 2 short periods for a specific job. Eight of the 11 workers dying from mesothelioma had been exposed to the crocidolite asbestos; in the other three there was a possibility of asbestos exposure elsewhere.

The geographical distribution of the mortality from mesothelial tumours was studied in England and Wales by Gardner, Acheson, and Winter in 1982.[26] Deaths occurred predominantly in manufacturing areas and ports with ship and dockyards, probably reflecting occupational exposure of the workers many years previously. In the East London survey by Newhouse already mentioned, tales were told of piles of asbestos tailings left where children played outside the factory. This was in the 1920s and the 1930s when little was known of the biological effects of asbestos exposure.

Useful techniques for examining the fiber content of lungs were developed by Langer, Machler, and Pooley in 1974.[27] These were used by Wagner et al in 1988 to examine the lungs of 38 patients dying of asbestos-related diseases who had been employed at the East London factory.[28] Crocidolite and amosite contents were strongly associated with mesothelioma, asbestosis, and cancer of the lung; no such correlation was evident with chrysotile fibers.

The particular role of crocidolite and amosite asbestos in the causation of mesothelioma is recognized in the United Kingdom by regulation. Crocidolite and amosite in air must not exceed 0.2 fibers per milliliter (0.2 f/ml), whereas the level for chrysotile is 0.5 f/ml. In effect the standard for crocidolite and amosite is impossible to achieve and these materials are no longer imported. However, they are present in the lagging of buildings and other structures and strict regulations govern any process where they are handled. The different types of asbestos are not recognized in the regulations of the United States.

McDonald has carefully reviewed the available data on mesothelioma incidence both in the United States and the United Kingdom.[29] He concludes that for females the incidence rate is approximately 2 per million of the population, with little change since 1970. The cause of this background level is uncertain, but some cases are probably due to occupational or domestic exposure. For males there has been a steep rise in incidence to more than 15 per million, which is likely to continue until the end of the century, reflecting the expansion of the asbestos industry in the 1950s and 1960s.

D. CANCER OF THE LARYNX

Cancer of the larynx is an uncommon tumour in the general population and occurs most frequently in elderly males. Alcohol consumption and cigarette smoking are recognized aetiological factors. An excess risk of this tumour was observed by Stell and McGill in Liverpool in 1973.[30] In this study 100 patients with squamous carcinoma of the larynx and 100 patients suffering from non-malignant diseases were questioned about possible exposure to asbestos; 31 of the cancer patients compared to 3 of the controls were found to have been exposed to asbestos, frequently as shipyard workers. Morgan in a case-control study in Canada found 10 out of 43 patients with laryngeal cancer with positive asbestos histories compared to none of the 43 controls.[31] Later case-control studies gave less dramatic results. Data from cohort studies summarized by Doll and Peto indicate a lower relative risk of the order of 1.6–2.7.[32] Study of patients is probably more satisfactory than mortality studies as the condition is not infrequently cured by operation, but it is difficult to reconcile the very high risk found in the first two studies quoted with the lower risks or negative results of later studies. Nevertheless the condition has been accepted as an asbestos-related tumour and accepted as compensatable under the Industrial Injuries Act in the United Kingdom.

E. G-I CANCERS

Suspicion that asbestos exposure is related to an excess of cancer of the alimentary tract dates from Selikoff's earliest analysis of the insulation workers' mortality, which showed more than a 2:1 excess of these tumours.[9] Newhouse's earlier analysis of the East London factory workers also suggested excess mortality from these causes.[17] However, later work indicated that underdiagnosis of peritoneal mesothelioma was probably responsible. For example, the review of post mortem material in 14 deaths that had been certified as due to gastro-intestinal tumours, lead to 7 of the deaths being reclassified as due to peritoneal mesothelioma.[33] Doll and Peto support this theory strongly, however, they suggest the possibility that cancer of the oesophagus may indeed be an asbestos-related tumour.[32]

Other cancers have also been implicated, particularly cancer of the ovary. There have been positive findings in studies of women who had been exposed to crocidolite asbestos, but here again there is a possibility of confusion in diagnosis with peritoneal mesothelioma.

F. RISK ASSESSMENT

It is often of use to be able to quantify the risk to the individual of the particular exposure he has experienced.

For mesothelioma there has been one main approach to this, that is, to model the risk in relation to time since first employment in an asbestos exposed job.[34,35] Newhouse and Berry in 1976, reporting on a group of workers exposed to chrysotile and a mixture of amphiboles used this simple model to predict mesothelioma mortality rates in man to the year 2000.[34] They estimated a mortality rate of 7%–11% for male and 9%–12% for female asbestos textile workers by 2000 AD. Peto et al in 1982 refined this basic model showing that for brief asbestos exposure the risk of mesothelioma was the cube of time since first exposure, and that for continuous exposure it was raised to the fourth power.[35] The current model used by several regulatory agencies predicts that mesothelioma risk begins to increase 10 years after the start of exposure and increases at a rate proportional to the cube of the elapsed time for the next 10 years and then increases quadratically.[36]

For lung cancer the accepted model indicates that the resulting incidence of cancer in asbestos workers is equal to the product of normal lung cancer incidence among unexposed individuals of the same age and smoking history times the average exposure level in fibers/ml (f/ml) a factor for fiber size and type, and also duration of exposure of the asbestos workers.

Factors in determining dose-response and risk in cancer incidence among asbestos workers should be considered. It is known that mesothelioma incidence rises sharply with time since first exposure to asbestos but appears to be unrelated to age at first exposure or smoking habit. However, it seems to be more strongly dependent on the type of asbestos used than lung cancer. Lung cancer in contrast is strongly related to smoking, age, and time since first exposure. Peto in 1985 using published data calculated risk models for lung cancer and mesothelioma.[37] The ratio of mesothelioma to excess lung cancer is more than 4:1 in non-smokers, and approximately 1:2 in smokers first exposed to asbestos before age 25, and 1:4 in smokers first exposed at age 25 or over. The observed-to-expected risk of lung cancer is the same regardless of age or cigarette smoking. This confirms that asbestos exposure multiples lung cancer risk.

Doll and Peto maintain that asbestos acts at the first stage of carcinogenesis in mesothelioma, in lung cancer it acts at a later stage.[32] Direct observations show that about 20 years exposure to an average 10 f/ml causes a substantial risk, and a working lifetime exposure to 2 f/ml might cause a risk of 1 in 10 for asbestos-related cancers in an asbestos textile factory. Studies in other working environments suggest lower dose-specific risks.

In summary there appears to be incontrovertible evidence that lung cancer and mesothelioma of the pleura and peritoneum are strongly related to exposure to asbestos; for mesothelioma the role of crocidolite asbestos is particularly important. For the other cancers considered there is a strong case for cancer of the larynx and possibly for cancer of the oesophagus. The case is much weaker for gastro-intestinal tumours and requires further study with pathological evidence to support the epidemiological findings.

REFERENCES

1. Merewether ERA, Price CW (1930) "Report on Effects of Asbestos Dust on the Lungs and Dust Suppression in the Asbestos Industry" London:HMSO.
2. Asbestos Industry Regulations (1931) "Statutory Rules and Orders, 1931, No. 1140" London:HMSO.
3. Gloyne SR (1933) "The Morbid Anatomy and Histology of Asbestosis" Tubercle **14:**445–451, 493–497, 550–558.
4. Lynch KM, Smith WA (1935) "Pulmonary Asbestosis III: Carcinoma of Lung in Asbesto-Silicosis" Amer J Cancer **24:**56–64.
5. Annual Report of the Chief Inspector of Factories for 1947 (1949) London:HMSO.
6. Doll R (1955) "Mortality from Lung Cancer in Asbestos Workers" Brit J lndust Med **12:**81–86.
7. Case RAM, Lea AJ (1955) "Mustard Gas Poisoning, Chronic Bronchitis and Lung Cancer" Br J Prev Soc Med **9:**62–72.
8. Mancuso TF, Coulter EJ (1963) "Methodology in Industrial Health Studies. The Cohort Approach, With Special Reference to an Asbestos Company" Arch Environ Health **6:**210–226.
9. Selikoff IJ, Hammond EC, Churg J (1964) "Asbestosis and Neoplasia" J A M A **188:**22–26.
10. Selikoff IJ, Hammond EC, Churg J (1968) "Asbestos Exposure, Smoking, and Neoplasia" J A M A **204:**104–110.
11. Newhouse ML (1969) "A Study of the Mortality of Workers in an Asbestos Factory" Brit J Indust Med **26:**294–301.
12. Newhouse ML, Berry G, Wagner JC, Turok ME (1972) "A Study of the Mortality of Female Asbestos Workers" Brit J Indust Med **29:**134–141.
13. McDonald JC, McDonald AD, Gibbs GW, Siemiatycki J, Rossiter CE (1971) "Mortality in the Chrysotile Asbestos Mines and Mills of Quebec" Arch Environ Health **22:**677–686.
14. Berry G, Newhouse ML, Turok ME (1972) "Combined Effect of Asbestos Exposure and Smoking on Mortality from Lung Cancer in Asbestos Workers" Lancet **2:**476–479.
15. Whitwell F, Newhouse ML, Bennett D (1974) "A Study of the

Histological Cell Types of Lung Cancer in Workers Suffering from Asbestosis in the United Kingdom" Brit J Indust Med **31**:298–303.
16. Thomas HF, Benjamin IT, Elwood PC, Sweetnam PM (1982) "A Further Follow-up Study of Workers from an Asbestos Cement Factory" Brit J Indust Med **39**:273–276.
17. Hughes JM, Weill H, Hummad YY (1987) "Mortality of Workers Employed in 2 Asbestos Cement Manufacturing Plants" Brit J Indust Med **44**:161–174.
18. Berry G, Newhouse ML (1983) "Mortality of Workers Manufacturing Friction Materials Using Asbestos" Brit J Indust Med **40**:1–7.
19. Bonner GM, Faulds JS, Stewart MJ (1955) "Occupational Cancer of the Urinary Bladder in Dyestuffs Operatives and of the Lung in Asbestos Textile Workers and Iron-Ore Miners" Amer J Clin Path **25**:126–134.
20. Wagner JC, Sleggs CA, Marchand P (1960) "Diffuse Pleural Mesothelioma and Asbestos Exposure in the North Western Cape Province" Brit J Indust Med **17**:260–271.
21. Elmes PC, Simpson MJC (1971) "Insulation Workers in Belfast. 3. Mortality 1940–1966" Brit J Indust Med **28**:226–236.
22. Konig J (1960) "Uber die Asbestose" Archiv fur Gewerbepathologie und Gewerbehygiene **18**:159–204.
23. Newhouse ML, Thompson H (1965) "Epidemiology of Mesothelial Tumors in the London Area" Ann N Y Acad Sci **132**:579–588.
24. Newhouse ML, Berry G, Wagner JC (1985) "Mortality of Factory Workers in East London, 1933–80" Brit J Indust Med **42**:4–11.
25. McDonald JC, Liddell FDK, Gibbs GW, Eyssen GE, McDonald AD (1980) "Dust Exposure and Mortality in Chrysotile Mining 1910–70" Brit J Indust Med **37**:11–24.
26. Gardner MJ, Acheson ED, Winter PD (1982) "Mortality from Mesothelioma of the Pleura during 1968–78 in England and Wales" Brit J Cancer **46**:81–88.
27. Langer AM, Machler AD, Pooley FD (1974) "Election Microscopical Investigation of Asbestos Fibres" Environ Health Perspectives **9**:63–80.
28. Wagner JC, Newhouse ML, Corrin B, Rossiter CE, Griffiths DM (1988) "Correlation between Fibre Content of the Lung and Disease in East London Asbestos Factory Workers" Brit J Indust Med **39**:273–276.
29. McDonald JC (1985) "Health Implications of Environmental Exposure to Asbestos" Environ Health Perspectives **62**:319–328.
30. Stell PM, McGill T (1973) "Asbestos and Laryngeal Carcinoma" Lancet **2**:416–417.
31. Morgan RW, Shettigara PT (1976) "Occupational Asbestos Exposure, Smoking and Laryngeal Carcinoma" Ann N Y Acad Sci **271**:308–310.
32. Doll R, Peto J (1985) "Asbestos: Effects on Health of Exposure to Asbestos" London:HMSO.

33. Newhouse ML, Wagner JC "Validation of Death Certificates in Asbestos Workers" Brit J Indust Med **26**:302–307.
34. Newhouse ML, Berry G (1976) "Predictions of Mortality from Mesothelial Tumours in Asbestos Factory Workers" Brit J Indust Med **33**:7–151.
35. Peto J, Seidman H, Selikoff IJ (1982) "Mesothelioma Mortality in Asbestos Workers: Implications for Models of Carcinogenesis and Risk Assessment" Brit J Indust Med **45**:124–135.
36. Crump KS, Allen BC, Howe RB, Crockett PW (1987) "Time-Related Factors in Quantitative Risk Assessment" J Chronic Dis **40**:101–111.
37. Peto J (1985) "Problems in Dose-Response and Risk Assessment: The Example of Asbestos" In "Risk Quantification and Regulatory Policy, Banbury Report 19" eds: Hoel DG, Merrill RA, Perera FP; Cold Spring Harbor, New York, Cold Spring Harbor Laboratory pp. 89–101.

7

The Analysis and Meaning of Asbestos Burden in Lung Tissue and Fluids

(AN OVERVIEW)

RONALD F. DODSON, Ph.D., F.C.C.P.

University of Texas Health Center
Tyler, Texas, U.S.A.

Synopsis

I. QUANTITATIVE TECHNIQUES IN DETERMINING TISSUE BURDEN OF ASBESTOS
J. ASBESTOS PRESENCE IN SPUTUM
K. ASBESTOS PRESENCE IN LAVAGE
L. HEALTH HAZARD OF NONASBESTOS FIBERS
M. REFERENCES

BIOGRAPHY

Dr. Ronald Dodson is the Professor and Chairman of the Department of Cell Biology/Environmental Sciences and the Associate Director for Research at The University of Texas Health Center at Tyler. He also serves as the Administrative Director of Environmental Research Institute, Inc. in Tyler.

Dr. Dodson held a graduate college fellowship in Electron Microscopy at Texas A&M University, College Station, Texas. After serving on the faculty at Baylor College of Medicine at Houston, Texas, he joined the faculty at the Health Center.

Dr. Dodson's research is in the area of asbestos related diseases with a particular emphasis addressing tissue burden of dust as determined by electron microscopy analysis. His laboratories have participated in the Oxford International Counting Trials and are certified under the Asbestos Hazard Emergency Response Act (AHERA) guidelines for asbestos analysis.

Dr. Dodson lectures on the health effects of asbestos in a number of EPA and OSHA approved training programs. He is a member of the Asbestos Advisory Committee of the Texas Department of Health. He also serves on numerous other state, university and national committees which deal with asbestos issues.

Dr. Dodson has published over a hundred scientific articles and is a reviewer for several scientific journals. He is a member of the American Thoracic Society, the New York Academy of Sciences, Electron Microscopy Society of America and holds a status of fellow in the American College of Chest Physicians. Professor Dodson can be contacted at the *Department of Cell Biology/Environmental Sciences, The University of Texas Health Center, P.O. Box 2003, Tyler, Texas 75710 U.S.A. (telephone: 214-877-7552 or 214-877-3451 ext. 2504).*

EDITORS' COMMENTARY

Fundamental to an appropriate understanding of asbestos-induced disease processes is an appreciation for what actually happens when asbestos fibers enter the lung, its fluids, its tissues, and interactions at the cell level. Visualization of structure and dynamics, from explicit microphotography, provides an essential factual basis for valid and meaningful comprehension of the events that occur prior, during, and after the clinical manifestation of a disease process. The following chapter reviews and illustrates the current status of knowledge pertaining to what transpires from a significant burden of inhaled asbestos fibers. This is important for medical research, diagnosis, and treatment endeavors. It is also important in terms of regulatory actions, abatement specifications, and the requirements for personal protective devices. It is important to remember that there have been recent (1988) publications that have simplistically concluded that asbestos fibers less than 8 microns in length have no adverse effect in the human lungs, despite evidence to the contrary. Such conclusions could have a dramatic effect in terms of what fibers are counted (safe limits) and what means (microscopy) are used for compliance with government standards, regulations, and rules. Similarly, other recent publications have concluded that chrysotile fibers are harmless compared to the amphibole fibers (such as crocidolite) that are straight, rigid, and pointed in shape. Such conclusions, if accepted at face value, could have dramatic effects in terms of asbestos abatement (i.e., don't bother to remove or isolate white asbestos). Thus, a factually based appreciation of what really occurs in the lung is of great practical importance. Whatever the truth, it will be revealed by the scientific method and the objective facts produced by the diligent inquiry of respected research scientists. A fair and objective summary of current knowledge is presented in the following chapter and, hopefully, it will tend to highlight and provide a better understanding of the significant issues in dealing with the asbestos public health problem. Such issues include: the differentiation of ferruginous bodies; the capability of laboratory instruments used for fiber counting to determine exposure levels and building clearance; the specific physiologic transport, retention, and reaction that is associated with various disease mechanisms, the procedures used for particulate isolation from tissue samples; the background burdens and dose-response relationships for various pathological events at various body sites; and fiber length toxicity for various tissue changes and disease entities. Of particular significance is the increasing sophistication in method and the promise implicit in this interesting work.

A. ASBESTOS—CHEMICAL AND PHYSICAL FEATURES

The word "asbestos" is defined in Webster's as "a mineral (as amphibole) that readily separates into long flexible fibers suitable for use as a noncombustible, nonconducting, chemically resistant material" (1). It is of little surprise, therefore, that such versatility would lead to asbestos being given the status of a "magic or miracle mineral." These properties were appreciated by ancient societies and were the basis for the use of asbestos in fire resistant wicks and in cloth (2). These same properties are the reason for its inclusion in many of the 3000 plus products used by our society.

The word "asbestos" has become synonymous with increasing perceptions of potential threats to health and elicits strong overall emotionalism as an issue. In order to make judgments based on the best available facts, one must begin with an understanding of the nature of asbestos, a general concept of how the normal respiratory system functions and how pulmonary responses to asbestos alter the functional state of the respiratory system. In this chapter, we will draw on a composite of information to give an overview of problems associated with asbestos exposure. We will also introduce questions for which only partial answers presently exist, pointing out the necessity for further research in these crucial areas.

Asbestos is a general name given to six fibrous forms of

Accepted for publication 23 December 1988.

minerals. These six forms are classified in two different groups, amphibole and serpentine. There is only one serpentine type of asbestos—chrysotile. It is of most importance because it constituted over 90% of the world's production (3) and was the major asbestos fiber used commercially within the United States during the peak years of asbestos utilization (4). This type of asbestos has a magnesium hydroxide layer on a silicate matrix. Due to its "scroll" morphology, a chrysotile fibril appears as a "hollow tube" in the transmission electron microscope. The longer chrysotile fibers will display a more "flexed" posture. This is an important physical factor when compared with the straighter nature of amphibole fibers of the same length. This feature also impacts on the overall theoretical diameter of chrysotile thereby effecting its potential for respirability.

The other five types of asbestos—amosite, actinolite, anthophyllite, tremolite, and crocidolite are classified under the amphibole type of asbestos (5). These fibers contain tetrahedron layers of silicon dioxide which form parallel chains cross linked by

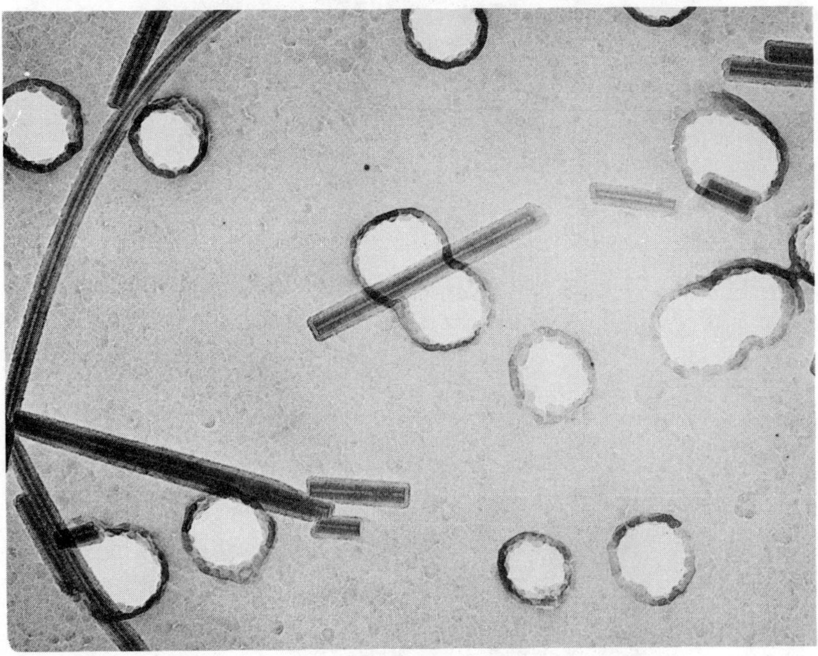

Fig. 7-1 The "scroll" morphology of chrysotile asbestos causes the fibrils to appear tubular by transmission electron microscopy. 66,000× magnification

various cations. The result of this crystalline structure is seen as a reproducible internal pattern in the electron microscope.

Of the amphibole types of asbestos, amosite and crocidolite are often loosely labeled the "commercial forms" since these were used in industrial production in the United States. The other amphiboles may in fact be found in many manufactured goods as well. They often occupy the same rock formation as the primary mineral and therefore appear as a contaminant in the final product. This fact, as well as a concern for the health risk from exposure to any type of asbestos, has resulted in the inclusion of all of the asbestos types by name in our present OSHA and EPA regulatory documents which are directed toward protection of workers (6–8).

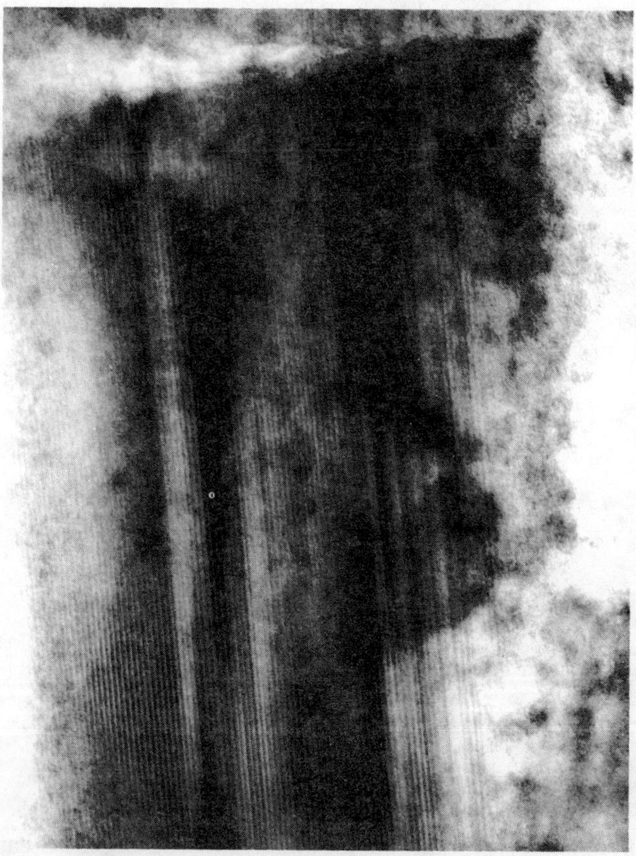

Fig. 7-2 This thin section reveals the internal lattice of amosite asbestos. 300,000× magnification

Every facet of production, from the mining process to the abatement procedures, results in breaking the fibers into smaller units of asbestos. The concept of how asbestos occurs in nature lends itself to this continual separation into smaller components. In essence, asbestos exists as stacks of pencils, but unlike pencils, when disturbed, the asbestos breaks apart into both shorter and thinner fibers. The crystalline structure of both groups of asbestos contain planes along which these fractures occur (9).

The smaller units may be designated as fibers (several pencils) or fibrils (a single pencil). The diameter of most chrysotile fibrils is less than 50 nm while the smallest amphibole units are below 500 nm (10).

As will be discussed in subsequent sections, these individual fibrils as well as the smaller fibers are well within the diameter of respirable particulates. Taking this comparison of size to another level, the single units of chrysotile and of amphibole asbestos are approximately 25 and 0.4 respectively, the diameter of a human hair.

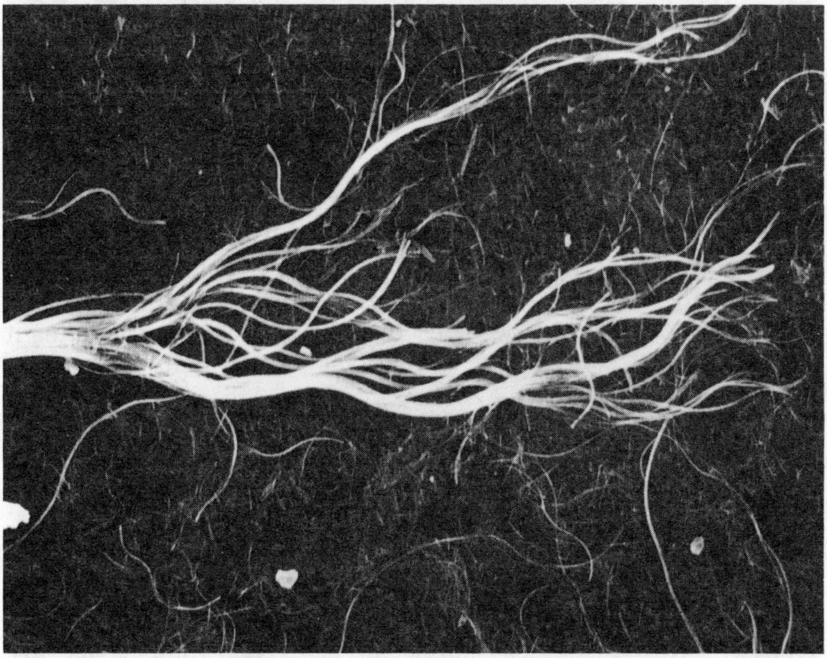

Fig. 7-3 The tendency of asbestos to break into both shorter and thinner units when disturbed is typified in this scanning electron micrograph. 8,000× magnification

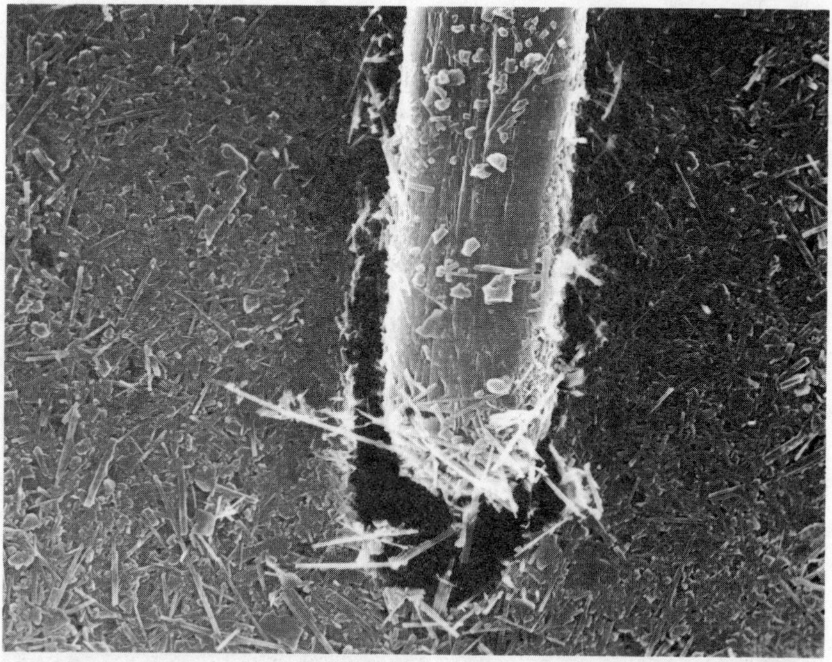

Fig. 7-4 This scanning electron micrograph shows the comparative size of amosite fibers and a human hair. 1,200× magnification

B. THE RESPIRATORY SYSTEM: ITS DESIGN, DEFENSES AND SUSCEPTIBILITY

Of the three surfaces (digestive, skin, respiratory) in the human body that are directly exposed to our environment, only the respiratory surface is a closed system. This design makes it particularly susceptible to permanent entrapment of aerosol particles. To understand the regions of susceptibility, it is appropriate to look at each level of this system and define its general function.

The major conducting portion of the respiratory system includes the nasal cavities, pharynx, larynx, bronchi, and bronchioles. Most of these divisions are lined with a unique mucous membrane. The functions of the conducting portion include keeping the air moist and warm and acting as the first line of defense against inhaled particulates. These objectives are achieved through a combination of factors. For example, in the entrance to the nasal cavities are numerous hairs that assist in filtration and create turbulence causing particles to strike the walls and to become entrapped. The design of the multibranching system of airways further enhances the creation of turbulence and, thus, increases the chance that particles in the airstream will strike a wall and be entrapped. The design of the multibranching system also leads to particle removal through sedimentation. Most particles greater than 5 μm in diameter are trapped on the surface of these larger airways (11,12). This method of clearance is extremely important because the mucous membrane is constantly being moved toward the back of the throat for either swallowing or expelling, thereby removing these particles from the respiratory system. This upward movement of the mucous is caused by special ciliated cells which are part of the epithelial lining layer of these conducting airways. The hair-like projections called "cilia" extend from the surface of these cells into the airway and into the adjacent mucous layer. The cilia, numbering approximately 250 per cell surface, beat with a rhythmic pattern (1000 times per minute) and thus propel the mucous layer upward creating what is commonly called the mucociliary pathway (13).

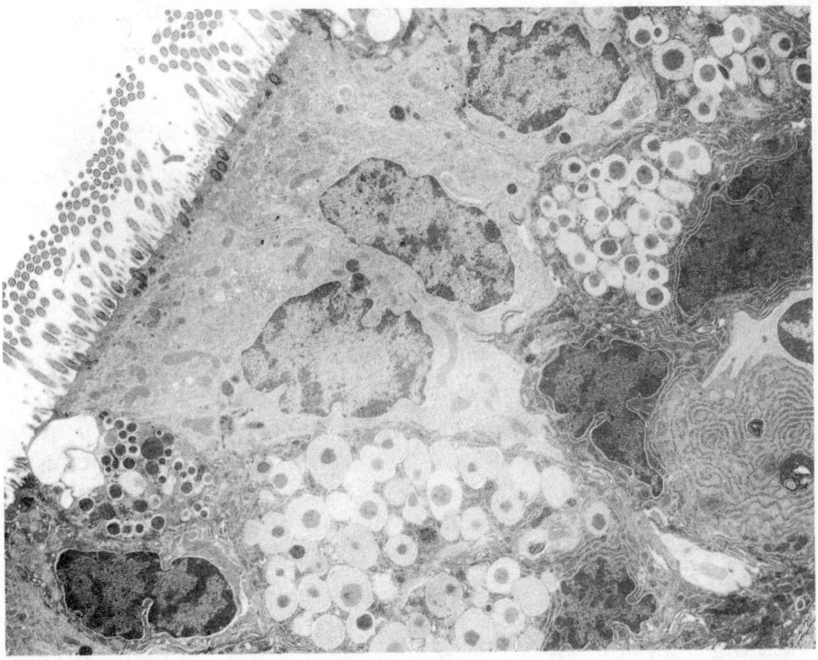

Fig. 7-5 Numerous hair-like projections (cilia) coat the surface of many of the cells which line the larger airways. 10,000× magnification

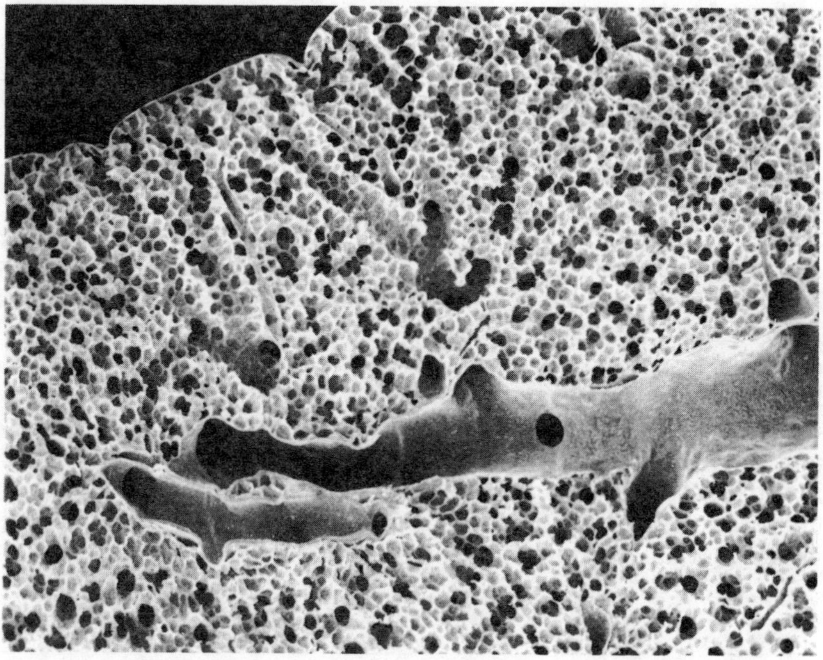

Fig. 7-6 The lungs are sponge-like in texture and the parenchyma is largely composed of air sacs (alveoli). 36,000× magnification

At the end of the multibranched, larger conducting airways are the lung acini or parenchyma. These are defined as "the unit of lung tissue in man" (14). It is at this level, which is composed primarily of air sacs called alveoli, that gas exchange between the air and the blood occurs (15). The outward, sponge-like appearance of the lung parenchyma is due to these alveoli. The large number of air sacs (from 150 to 300 million per lung (16)) provides a tremendous surface area (17,18). This surface area has been projected by light microscopy data to be between 50 to 70 square meters or the equivalent of the floor area of a room measuring 30′ by 20′ (19). Electron microscopy studies by Weibel (20) have shown these figures to be conservative and expanded the surface area to between 100–190 m^2. The thin walled membrane which constitutes the lining of the air sac is approximately 0.1 μm to 1 μm in width (19). Questions as to whether this delicate part of the lung was cellular and what types of cells might be present were heartily debated until electron microscopy resolved the alveolar ultrastructure.

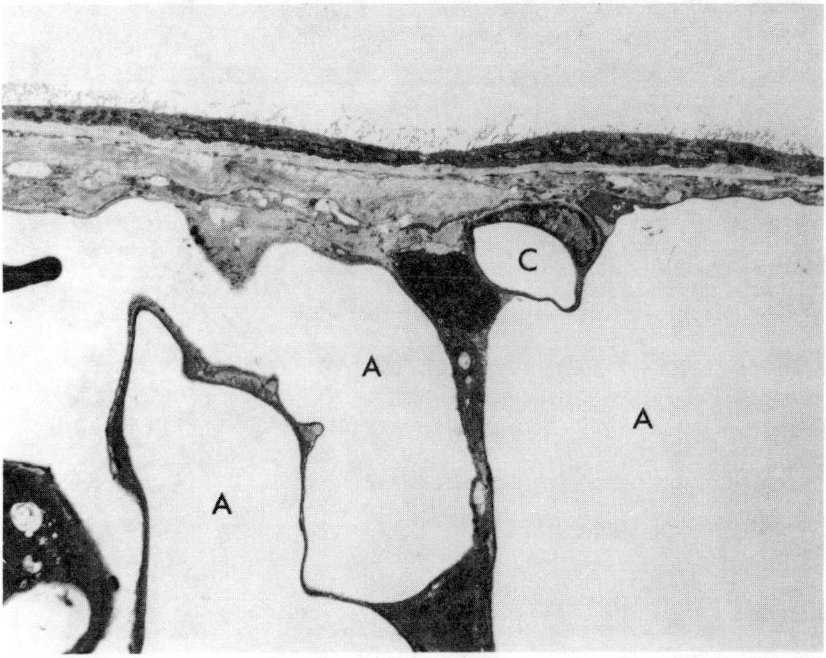

Fig. 7-7 This transmission electron micrograph shows the delicate thin membrane which separates the air compartments in the alveoli from the vascular lumen of the capillary. A = alveolus, C = capillary. 2,200× magnification

The lining of the air sac was shown to be comprised of the alveolar epithelium, capillary endothelium, and interstitial spaces (21). Alveoli are the most susceptible components of the respiratory system to inhaled particulates. The reason for increased susceptibility is a less efficient clearance mechanism compared to that associated with the conducting airways. At the gas exchange level, no mechanism equivalent to cilia assists in the rather rapid movement of the surface layer into the larger airways and thus out of the lung. The major physiologic response to inhaled particulates deposited in the alveoli consists of the recruitment of macrophages and neutrophils to alveolar surface. While these phagocytic cells are important scavengers, acting to keep the surface of the air sacs cleared of particles, their presence may create an early and potentially chronic alveolitis. Fortunately, many of the macrophages and neutrophils, containing phagocytized particles, do reach the conducting airways and are eventually cleared via the mucociliary pathway.

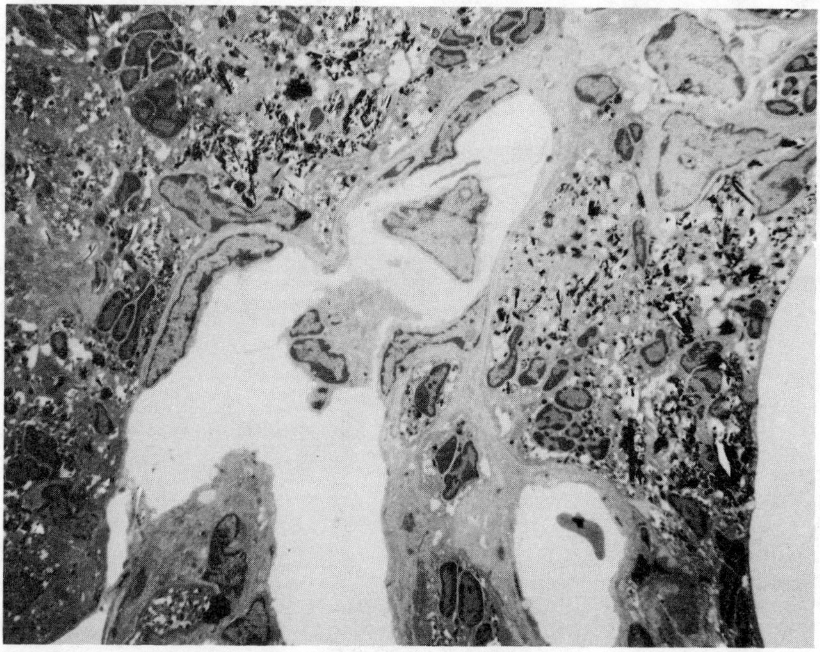

Fig. 7-8 The alveolitis associated with asbestos exposure involves a callup of the defense cells which can congest the air chambers. Only the capillaries remain open. 4,000× magnification

C. MECHANISMS FOR ASBESTOS INDUCED DAMAGE IN THE LUNG

If the overall clearance system is overwhelmed by the sheer volume of dust, then a chronic inflammatory state occurs. Generations of macrophages and neutrophils migrate out the blood on to the gas exchange surfaces to interact with dust particles liberated when the previous generation of phagocytes dies. This process results in a cyclic phenomenon that contributes to the ongoing disease mechanisms. While these reactions between cells and particulates are occurring, chemicals within the phagocytic cells are being released at the site of inflammation. These secretions in turn cause a triggering of events which include: 1) stimulation of fibroblasts (a major contributor to development of a connective tissue and fibrotic response) 2) localized release of chemical irritants, and/or 3) callup of additional macrophages and neutrophils, which can in turn continue to contribute to these events (22–29).

As discussed, the effectiveness of the larger airways for entrapping particles above 5 μm in diameter by either electrostatic attraction, interception, impaction, or gravitational factors, provides a highly efficient first line of defense. However, with decreasing particle diameter, there occurs an increasing potential for the dust to stay in the airstream thereby reaching the smallest airways and the alveoli (11). As previously described, much asbestos dust breaks down into fibers with diameters that easily enable it to reach this less protected level of the respiratory system. However, our overall defense mechanisms are highly efficient in removing even these smaller particles. Gross offered a projection that the combined effectiveness of our inherent defenses against dust was 98–99% efficient (30). The implication is, therefore, that pneumoconioses (dust related diseases) are caused by the 1–2% of the inhaled dust that remains in the lung. As with dust in general, there is an effective entrapment and/or clearance of inhaled asbestos as shown by the studies of Evans (31). This study reports that two thirds of the inhaled fibers were trapped in the larger airways, which greatly limited the peripheral burden. It was further noted that by the end of the first month, clearance had eliminated three fourths of the particles that reached the distal airways. Unfortunately, there remains some threshold for any given dust that, when exceeded, triggers events that can result in pathological changes in the lung.

D. SMOKING AND ASBESTOS

Before continuing a further discussion of how asbestos contributes to the development of disease, it is appropriate to discuss an environmental exposure that makes individuals more susceptible to any dust exposure, smoking. Cigarette smoke over time induces alterations in normal respiratory functions in the upper airways. These include a decrease in the efficiency of ciliary function and actual alteration in the cellular makeup of the epithelial lining of the airways. The smoke residue, furthermore, contributes its own types of particulates. These "dust particles" are in the respirable range and result in a deposition seen as pigments in the parenchyma.

As with any increased exposure to any dust, phagocytic cells are called in from the blood stream to isolate the particulates. Likewise, as with many dusts, the ingested particles can pose toxic threats to the phagocytic cell. Cigarette smoke further

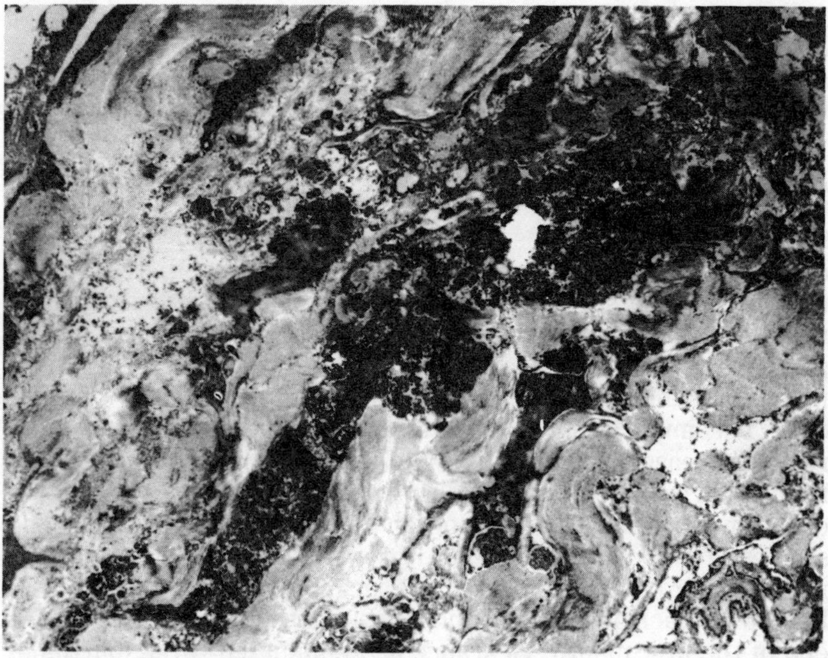

Fig. 7-9 Characteristic anthracotic pigments in this electron micrograph are the results of accumulation of particles associated with cigarette smoke. 3,000× magnification

alters lung defense by inducing changes at the immunological, clearance, and functional levels (32). Smoke has been shown to decrease the fast clearance phase and to increase the half time of the slower clearance phase (33).

The combination of these influences results in an overall compromise of clearance efficiency. Less dust of any type is cleared from the lungs of a cigarette smoker (34). Tissue analyses have shown that particulates from all sources are retained in greater numbers in lungs of patients who had been smoking than in a nonsmoker's lung (35). Recent data from animal models have further shown that cigarette smoke may increase the penetration of fibers into the airway walls (36). Cigarette smoke and asbestos are both recognized as carcinogens and while the numbers for risk factors may vary from one study to another, the synergistic effect of cigarette smoke and asbestos consistently results in a greater cumulative risk than the combined additive risks from either. Numbers given in a recent physicians' guide noted the risk factor for lung cancer in an asbestos worker was five times that of a control while the risk factor for an asbestos worker who smoked was 53 times that of a control (37).

E. DUST AND DISEASE—PHYSICAL AND CHEMICAL EVENTS

Thus far, we have addressed the issues of how asbestos reaches the more vulnerable parts of the respiratory system, how various factors effect the rate of its elimination from the lung, and have suggested that some threshold level of residual asbestos must be reached to induce a disease. But how does asbestos actually render its toxic effects? The toxicity of any dust, including asbestos, must be determined by first answering several known criteria. 1) What is the morphology of the dust? Asbestos is fibrous in habit and also breaks down into thin, respirable fibers. Stanton (38), Pott (39) and Bonneau (40) have shown that physical features are important factors in determining the carcinogenic potential of any dust and that these factors include the parameters of dimension (long thin fibers) and durability. It should be noted that their studies were carried out using nonasbestos fibers, an important consideration to be discussed in greater detail later in the chapter. 2) At what level in the respiratory system does the dust deposit (with an emphasis on depth of penetration)? Asbestos breaks down into units that can reach all levels of the respiratory system including the alveoli. 3) Does there seem to be a dose relationship to diseases? Levels of exposure for any dust, fibrous or nonfibrous, will dictate when the level of clearance efficiency and/or overall defense mechanisms are overwhelmed. Obviously, the toxicity of a given dust, as well as the exposure period, as factors used to estimate the tissue burden that results in a pathological response. 4) Are there special features about a specific dust? A number of features about asbestos fibers make them candidates for interactions with biological systems. The amphibole forms of asbestos have negative surface charges while the magnesium hydroxide (brucite layer) of chrysotile results in a positive surface charge. The availability of charged surfaces provides reactive sites for the absorption of other toxic agents from the environment, thereby letting the asbestos fiber act as a carrier for these other toxic agents (41).

Once asbestos is in the lung, these same charged surfaces can interact through various biochemical mechanisms to create radicals and other chemical compounds deleterious to health. (40–45) Because the surface characteristics of asbestos have been shown to vary from the central to peripheral areas (42), there may be increasing complex interactions between a single fibril, the environment, and the biosystem.

The surface features of chrysotile may be changed by another factor—the cleaving of magnesium or the brucite surface layer (46–48). In fact, as will be discussed in greater detail in the section dealing with particulate burden in tissue, some investigators hypothesize that the degeneration of chrysotile may progress in a biosystem to the level of partial to total dissolution of the chrysotile fiber (49). This overview of variables which can influence how an asbestos fiber reacts with tissue, suggests it is reasonable that numerous yet undefined mechanisms also exist.

F. INSTRUMENTS AND ASBESTOS DETECTION

In order to accurately assess asbestos content in air, water or tissue, one must first choose an instrument which permits visualization of asbestos at the level needed for the given purpose. The first-line instrument for working with asbestos analysis in the past has been the light microscope. For example, the polarizing light microscope technique, incorporating dispersion staining oils, provides a useful approach for determining the presence, type, and approximate percent of asbestos in bulk samples of material. This technique bases its validity on the larger fibers in the sample. The light microscope is also used for counting individual fibers in an air or water sample as collected on a filter. However, since the light microscope has an approximate 0.25 μm limit of resolution, the usefulness of phase contrast microscopy for counting fibers (such as the NIOSH 7400 method) is limited (49).

The next level of instrumentation used for fiber counting and analysis is the electron microscope. The newer scanning electron microscopes (SEM) have a resolution limit of approximately 5 nm and, thus, with appropriate user expertise and preparative skills, smaller fibers can be seen than would be observed in the light microscope. There will still be appreciable numbers of fibers at/or below this instrument's practical working resolution. One additional advantage of the SEM is the capability to generate X-ray energy dispersive elemental (XEDS) analyses from fibers and particulates of interest. This enables one, within certain technical limits, to obtain the elemental composition of the fibers and thus assists in determining whether their composition is consistent with asbestos. The transmission electron microscope (TEM) offers resolution limits of 0.2 nm (lattice image) and thus enables the users to see even the smallest "fibril" of asbestos. Likewise, information as to elemental composition can be obtained by X-ray energy dispersive techniques (50), as in the SEM. In addition, another identifier of the fiber, an electron diffraction pattern, can be obtained by TEM. The diffraction pattern results from the interaction of the electron beam with the crystalline structure of asbestos. This forms a pattern which is a specific "finger print" for the mineral. Under the Asbestos Hazard Emergency Response Act, TEM is classified as "state of the art" instrumentation for analysis of air samples for asbestos. This act (Title II of the Toxic Substance Control Act 15, U.S.C. Sections 2641 through 2654) requires use of a specified interim analytical method using TEM. The interim method specifies sample preparation, analysis procedures (51), quality control methods, and reporting procedures (6). Many of these same guidelines could be equally applied to quantitative analysis of biological samples.

Fig. 7-10(a) Shown are typical selected area electron diffraction patterns from chrysotile (10a) and amosite (10b) asbestos.

Fig. 7-10(b)

A thorough understanding of the capabilities of instruments used in asbestos analysis is an important facet in many of the following sections. The limit of the significance of the data in any study is often related to limits of detectability of the instrumentation used to generate the data.

G. RESIDUAL ASBESTOS IN THE LUNG

The mechanisms of asbestos deposition and clearance from the lung have been discussed in prior sections. However, what happens to the asbestos that remains in the parenchyma? Some fibers and fibrils, of course, are trapped within the inflammatory cells as phagocytized material within macrophages and to a lesser degree, neutrophils. Those fibers that are shorter in length will

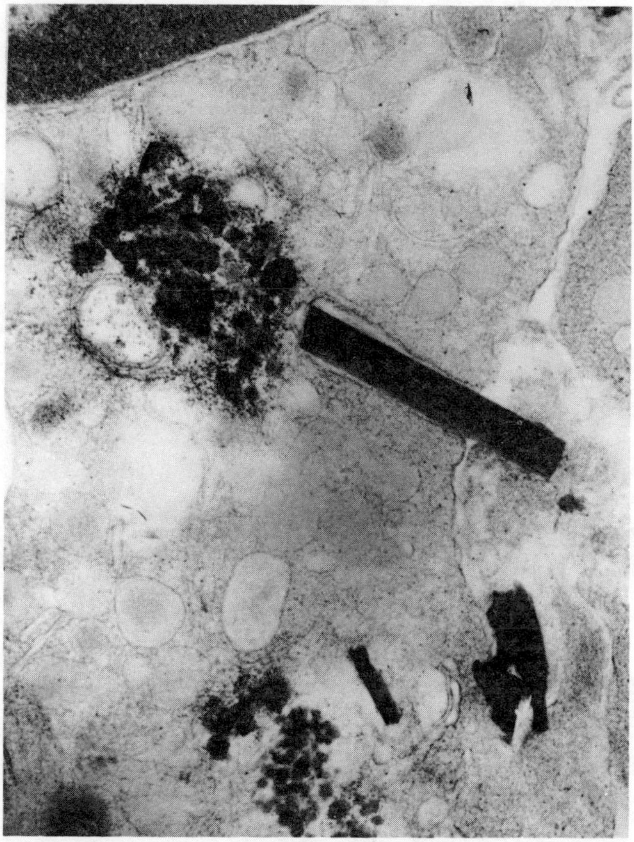

Fig. 7-11 Macrophages and neutrophils are called to the surface of the airways in response to the asbestos stimulus and attempt to phagocytize and, therefore, isolate the asbestos from the lung. 83,000× magnification

be found in a single phagocytic cell within phagolysosomes whereas several macrophages may simultaneously interact with the longer fibers. By virtue of their size, the shorter fibers have been shown to penetrate small airways (52), interstitium (53), as well as airway walls (36). Animal studies have shown these smaller inhaled fibers are also found in lymph nodes and pleura and have been reported in other parts of the body as well (54). Also, ingested amphibole fibers have been shown to be eliminated in human urine indicating a passage across several tissue barriers (55). The suggested mechanisms for transport of asbestos fibers in the body are: 1) as free fibers in blood or lymph, 2) as phagocytized fibers (within cells), and 3) as free fibers that simply

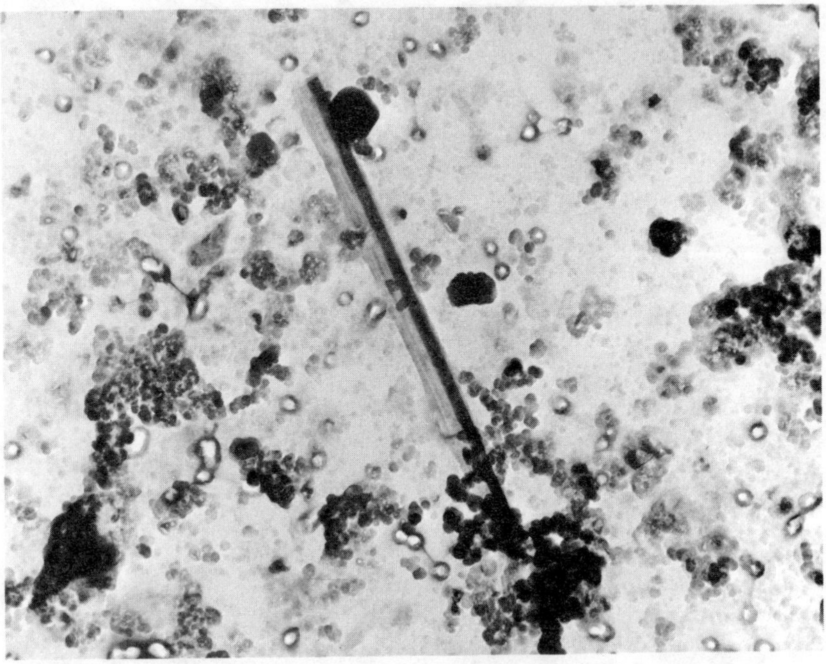

Fig. 7-12 The uncoated amosite fiber was isolated from a lymph node. 14,000× magnification

penetrate various tissues and therefore are capable of constant relocation.

Those fibers remaining in the lung parenchyma are the sites of two different types of physiologic reactions that are generally dictated by fiber length and asbestos type. The majority of the shorter fibers are isolated within cells (phagocytes). Continual and multiple macrophage interactions with some of the longer fibers (≤ 8 μm) result in the eventual coating of all or parts of the fiber surfaces. This coating material is an iron/protein complex that is deposited over time by generations of macrophages (56). These marcophages have tried to isolate or phagocytize these fibers but because of the fiber length, were physically unable to do so. Asbestos fibers that have been coated are classified with other types of similarly coated fibers as ferruginous bodies.

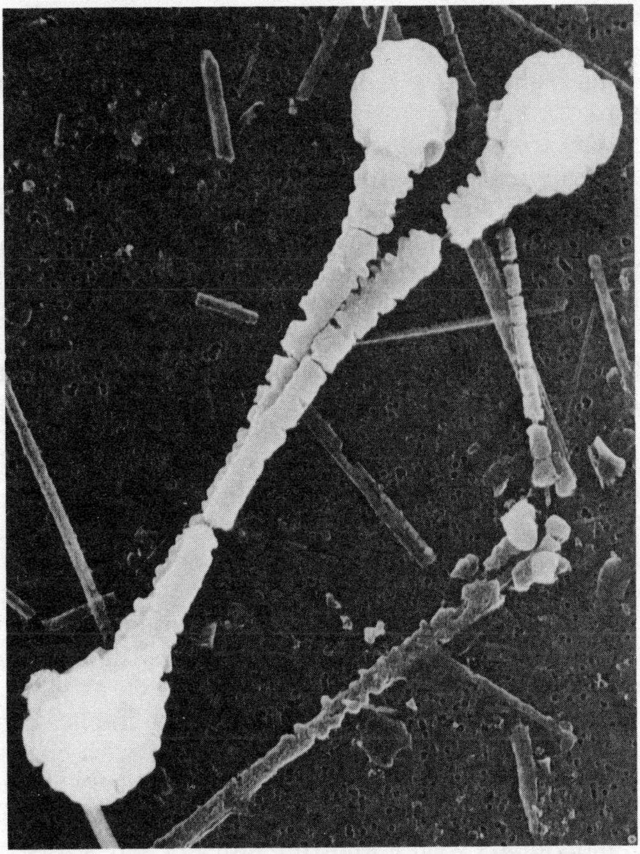

Fig. 7-13 Partial or total coating of the longer asbestos fibers result in the formation of asbestos bodies such as these isolated from an asbestos worker's lung. 5,200× magnification

H. THE MEANING OF FERRUGINOUS BODIES IN THE LUNG

When such ferruginous material is found on asbestos fibers, the term asbestos body is appropriately used. The presence of asbestos bodies in tissue denotes various levels of past exposure to amphibole asbestos and, in some special cases, to chrysotile. When the identity of the core material has not been confirmed, the more general term ferruginous body was recommended by Gross (57). This recommendation was supported by the observation that the formation of ferruginous bodies could be induced in animal lungs with fibrous aluminum silicates, silicon carbide whiskers, cosmetic talc, and glass fibers. Gross noted these ferruginous bodies were indistinguishable from those produced by asbestos fibers.

The data from human studies supports the concept that when classical ferruginous bodies are seen at the light microscopy level, the vast majority are formed on asbestos cores. In one study, samples of digested tissue from the general population were evaluated by light microscopy for the presence of ferruginous bodies (58). Material from 252 urban autopsy or surgical patients was examined by light microscopy. Samples from eight individuals that had been shown by light microscopy to contain atypical ferruginous bodies were examined by electron microscopy using XEDS and electron diffraction patterns. Of 83 bodies from the patients screened by TEM, 43 were proven to have an asbestos core, 22 with black cores were determined to be of an amorphous material (presumably carbon), and 13 were noted to be platy or a yellowish color by light microscopy and shown through energy dispersive and X-ray analysis to be formed on sheet silicates (58). Black cored ferruginous bodies were also noted in three individuals in a recent report by Masse (59). While the data from the analytical EM analysis is rather unclear, the cores were considered by the authors to be silicon carbide. The implication seems rather clear that "typical" ferruginous bodies with clear central cores as determined by light microscopy most likely are asbestos bodies. Certainly the accuracy of this statement goes up appreciably in individuals with a known history of asbestos exposure. Of course, this can easily include everyone in the general population since each of us has asbestos fibers in our lungs (60–67). Indeed, most quantitative studies have been carried out on former workers who either had a primary or suspected secondary exposure to asbestos or on tissue from members of the general population.

The question must remain open as how often "classical nonasbestos cored" ferruginous bodies may exist in special exposure settings. If such tissue were analyzed by light microscopy with no supportive core analysis by analytical electron microscopy, such ferruginous bodies could be misclassified as asbestos bodies. A case was referred to our center for TEM analysis of the particulate burden and core analysis of ferruginous bodies that had been detected by light microscopy. The referral included a diagnosis of "asbestos induced disease" since mild fibrosis and "clear cored-typical" ferruginous bodies had been found by light microscopy. Some of the ferruginous bodies did,

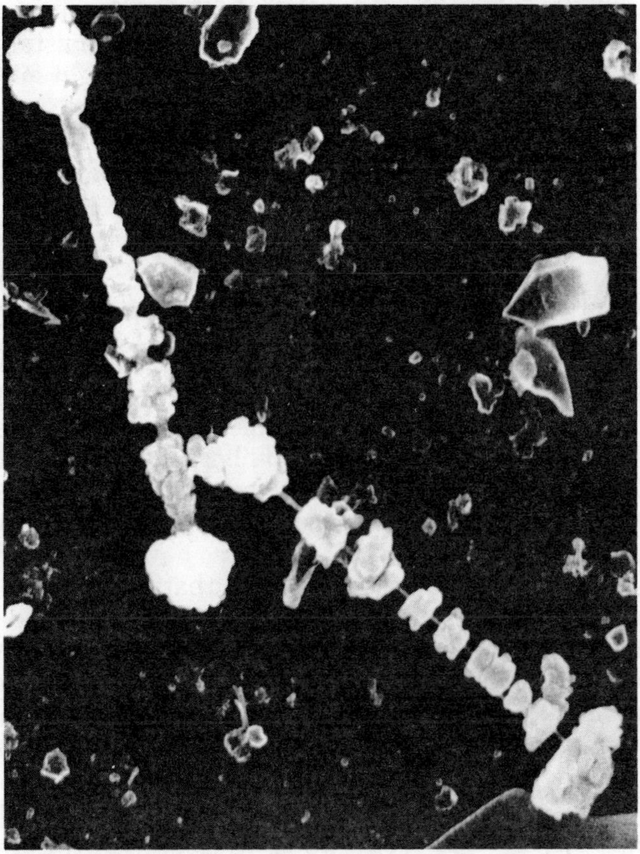

Fig. 7-14 The ferruginous bodies in this field were formed on a naturally occurring iron-rich fiber. 2,300× magnification

however, contain readily visible cores. Others looked very much like asbestos bodies because the core was clear. Both types were definitely on fibrous cores. The tissue burden was determined to be 110,000 ferruginous bodies/gm of wet weight. Isolation and analysis of the core material (68) as well as an analysis of uncoated fibers in the tissue proved the material in both to be a naturally occurring iron-rich nonasbestos fiber (69).

Certainly, this type of occurrence is not commonly found among the work groups previously evaluated in much of the literature, particularly where electron microscopy techniques were used for analysis. However, such nonasbestos FBs may be quite common in selected settings where a particular cohort is exposed to the type of nonasbestos mineral fiber noted in our study (69), the fibers listed by Gross (57), or the fibers not yet recognized as nonasbestos because they are being mistaken to be asbestos bodies based on their appearance at the light microscopy level.

I. QUANTITATIVE TECHNIQUES IN DETERMINING TISSUE BURDEN OF ASBESTOS

The clinical conditions caused by asbestos include asbestosis, pleural fibrosis, and effusion, as well as the malignancies—lung and gastrointestinal cancer and/or mesothelioma. These conditions result from the accumulation of fibers in tissue. As has been noted, ferruginous bodies can be seen and to an appreciable degree be classed as asbestos bodies by light microscopy. The quantitation of uncoated asbestos fibers, however, requires the use of electron microscopy. It is evident that tissue sections from paraffin or plastic embedded material must be evaluated with an awareness of problems associated with such sections. There are the problems of random sampling errors and problems with orientation of the fibers within a given plane of section. All of these variables can result in visible fibers being interpreted as nonfibrous.

In an attempt to overcome the problems of working with tissue sections, various approaches have been tried to isolate the particulates from tissue. Preparative procedures have included sample filtration (70), low temperature (71), and high temperature (72,73) ashing. Digestion procedures using ozone (74,75), strong bases (76,77), and hydrogen peroxide (65,78,79) have been tested. A different series of chemical treatments were also tried for dissolving tissue in bleach (57,58,65,80–82). Concern exists for many of the procedures because they can potentially create fiber fragmentation, thus giving unrealistic data. Other procedures are thought to lose fibers through various stages of the process, and some procedures decompose the fibrous material and ferruginous bodies. Some of these procedures work reasonably well by allowing visualization of larger structures such as ferruginous bodies but leave appreciable residue which obstructs the surface of the collection filter and thus obscures smaller uncoated fibers. The bleach method offers the best opportunity for minimizing fiber loss since the digestion procedure is relatively straightforward and can be carried out, if desired, on material deposited on the filter. With modifications added to the procedure by Williams (83), the problems associated with organic debris, particularly in mucus rich material such as lavage or sputum, were overcome.

Studies using digestion techniques for quantitative analysis of FBs and uncoated asbestos fibers in lung tissue have offered additional information about exposure in man. Churg and Warnock (65) reported that 80% of the fibers in a general population study were chrysotile asbestos and that 90% of these were less than 5 μm long. The predominance of short fibers is a consistent finding in individuals of the general population who have no occupational exposure. The number of uncoated asbestos fibers tends to stratify according to past exposures between three groups of the society: 1) general population, 2) blue collar workers, and 3) occupationally exposed individuals. Churg reported a mean number of asbestos fibers in a general population group to be 1×10^6 fibers/g dry lung while patients with asbestosis or mesothelioma were reported to have $100–200 \times 10^6$ fibers/g dry lung (84). The levels of tissue burden in blue collar workers lies somewhere in between. Blue collar workers are individuals exposed to asbestos somewhere in the work place but not as an "asbestos worker." It should be noted that these data are based on the use of TEM for analysis and used a counting procedure that included all asbestos fibers. A procedure which provides data based only on fibers ≤ 5 μm excludes the majority of the tissue burden represented by the smaller fibers.

There are arguments for excluding shorter fibers from analytical data. Instrumentation (TEM) that allows for detection of small fibers is expensive and technically more complex than light microscopy techniques. In addition, there are data that suggest that long fibers are the more toxic portion of the inhaled dust. The latter argument is based on data that indicated the longer fibers have increased carcinogenic potency. The relationship of carcinogenicity and fiber dimensionality and durability is well covered in a recent review (85) and is similar to the relationship shown by the Stanton hypothesis (38). Long fibers are also the fibers that are less likely to be cleared from the lung. This population thus makes up a permanent source of irritation and reaction in the lung.

The shorter fibers, which are the predominant portion of the inhaled dust, are cleared more readily from the lung. The shorter fibers are also the fibers that more readily move into the interstitium, lymphatics, and pleura.

Table 7-1 Asbestos Bodies and Fibers in Various Populations

Ref.	*Population*	*FB/gm Wet*	*FM/gm Dry*	*ASB. Type*	*F/gm Wet*	*F/gm Dry*
109	10 nonurban general population	-	17.9	chry	-	$.058\times10^6$
				amp	-	$.204\times10^6$
	12 amosite workers (av. exposure: 3.7yrs)	-	208×10^3	chry	-	1.2×10^6
				amp	-	45×10^6
108	male accident victims from general population:					
	15 ≤18yrs	-	120	chry	-	50×10^3
				amp	-	6×10^3
	33 19–40yrs	-	270	chry	-	33×10^3
				amp	-	14×10^3
	19 41–60yrs	-	350	chry	-	89×10^3
				amp	-	113×10^3
	14 61+yrs	-	530	chry	-	62×10^3
				amp	-	24×10^3
64	no occupational exposure:					
	14 males with lung cancer (11 blue collar; av. age:63)	-	-	chry	-	$.4\times10^6$
				amp	-	$.72\times10^6$
	14 male controls (av. age:63)	-	-	chry	-	$.2\times10^6$
				amp	-	$.61\times10^6$
107	9 chrysotile miners with early asbestosis (av. exposure: 34yrs; av. age:66)	-	46×10^3	chry	-	47×10^6
				amp	-	106×10^6
	9 chrysotile miners without asbestosis (av. exposure:32yr av. age:61)	-	20×10^3	chry	-	23×10^6
				amp	-	58×10^6
106	general autopsy population:					
	29 with plaques (28 males, 1 female; av. age:65)	1732	-	chry	51×10^3	-
				amp	63×10^3-	-
	25 no occupational exposure (24 males, 1 female; av. age:65)	42		chry	68×10^3	-
				amp	30×10^3	-

FB/gm = ferruginous bodies/gram wet or dry tissue weight
F/gm = fibers/gram wet or dry tissue weight

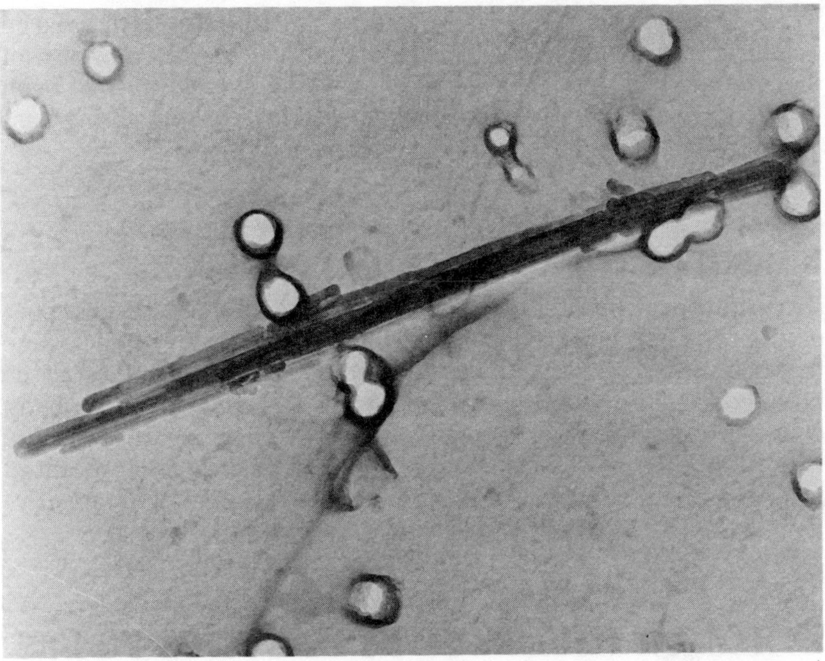

Fig. 7-15 The short chrysotile fibers in this field are typical of those found in pleural plaques. 39,000× magnification

A count that ignores fibers below 5μm makes an assumption that they are of little importance. This is a stance for which we have no conclusive proof.

The combination of data that includes uncoated asbestos fibers and ferruginous body load in tissue are a better basis for establishing a relationship of asbestos burden to tissue changes than data relying only on ferruginous body burden. Because chrysotile is less likely to cause FB formation and because 80% of the fibers in the general population are reported to be chrysotile asbestos (65), collecting data only on FB formation could be extremely misleading. Furthermore, some individuals may be poor formers of FBs even when adequate amphibole fibers of appropriate length are present in tissue (86,87).

J. ASBESTOS PRESENCE IN SPUTUM

Asbestos bodies found in sputa are reported to be a highly sensitive indicator of occupational exposure to amphibole asbestos (88,89) because they are not seen in samples from a large urban cohort from the general population (88). Evaluation of digested sputum samples for uncoated fibers recently has been shown to be an even more sensitive procedure for indicating past occupational levels of amphibole exposure (90).

K. ASBESTOS PRESENCE IN LAVAGE

Another potentially useful approach for assessing past occupational level of exposure is through the analysis of lavage material. DeVuyst (91) has reported a correlation of asbestos body content in bronchoalveolar lavage and lung asbestos body concentration. Work in progress in our Center again indicates that combined evaluation of ferruginous bodies and uncoated asbestos fibers in digested lavage increases the level of sensitivity in confirming past occupational levels of exposure.

L. HEALTH HAZARD OF NONASBESTOS FIBERS

As with asbestos and other dusts, the first issue that determines whether nonasbestos fibers are a threat to man is whether they break down into respirable dust. Once the dimensions are shown to permit inhalation of the fibers, the common factors of dose, durability, toxicity, and other unique features will determine whether reversible or irreversible reactions occur in the lung.

At present, much of our understanding of potential hazards from nonasbestos fibers comes from animal experiments. The studies by Pott (92), Stanton (38), Wagner (93) and Muhle (94) all indicate that a ceramic fiber, manmade mineral fibers, and various other fibers which are long, thin, and durable are potentially carcinogenic.

Although little is known about their potential threat to health, a variety of nonasbestos fibers have been reported in analyses of dust burdens in lung tissue (59,87,95,96). These fibers have been shown to occur in large numbers and an appreciable percentage of the particle population fall within the more "carcinogenic" range of dimensions.

Masse (59) concluded that the presence of long, thin silicon carbide fibers within lung tissue of two workers with lung cancer could reflect the findings of the Stanton hypothesis (38,97) by demonstrating nonasbestos fibers in association with cancer in

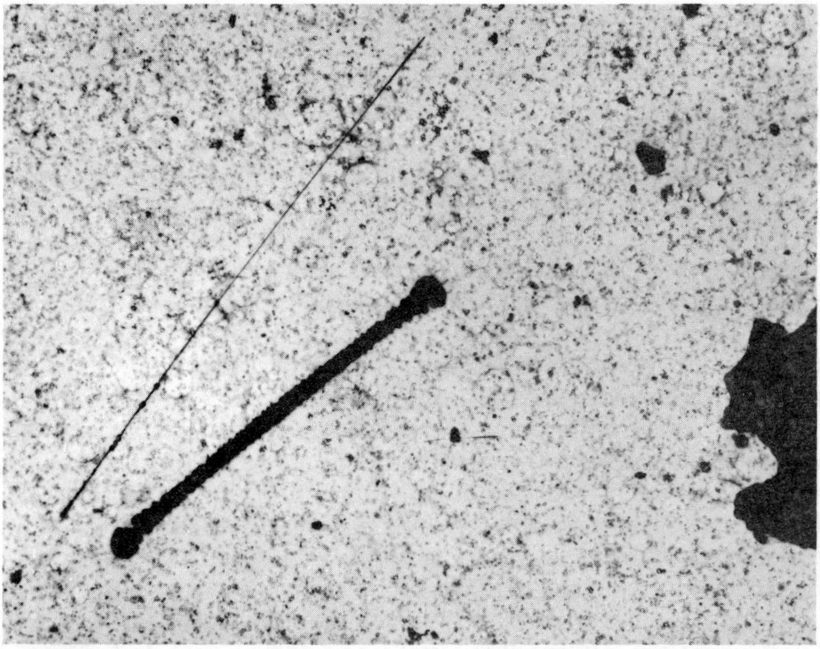

Fig. 7-16 the ferruginous bodies in this micrograph were isolated from lavage material of an asbestos worker. 1,600× magnification

man. Another example of a nonasbestos fiber suspected of producing cancer in man was reported by Sebastien (96), Long, thin fibers of erionite were found in the environment, in lung tissue, and in sputum of individuals living in an area of rural Turkey. The material was a natural occurring fiber within the soil and was suggested as the cause of a high incidence of mesothelioma among the populus (98).

Mesothelioma in the United States and much of the world is generally linked to some past asbestos exposure (99,100). This is not a difficult relationship to prove since there are widespread opportunities for exposure to asbestos. This relationship between exposure within our society and incidence of mesothelioma has posed increasing concerns, especially because lower or minimal exposure to asbestos has been related to some cases of mesothelioma (101,102).

The risk factors for human exposure to manmade mineral fibers (MMMF) (fiberglass, rockwool, slag fibers) and ceramic fibers have been tempered with several observations. These include the fact that many of these fibers were simply of a sufficiently large diameter that fragmentation resulted in nonrespirable particles. This is in part due to the fact that MMMFs, cannot fragment along their long axis, thus the original diameter remains a permanent feature unless the fibers have been partially dissolved. Another complication in assessing the effects of past exposure to MMMFs is that only a minority of the fibers of most samples manufactured prior to the last 10–15 years had diameters in the respirable size range. Thus, the "risk" should be less than exposure to a fibrous dust with many respirable size particles, such as asbestos. Further compounding the issue of assessing risk associated with inhaled MMMF is the unknown factor of the length of latency periods. In asbestos exposure, for example, an interval of 15–25 years after first exposure is usually required before diseases are observed.

The concern for such exposure to nonasbestos fibers has continued because these were the exact type of fibers shown to produce cancer by Stanton in 1972 (103). The level of this concern has increased because the level of small diameter fiber production has increased in the last decade. While exposure to such products has been limited in the recent past, Weill has noted that exposure to manmade vitreous fibers of small diameter may lead to a low level profusion of small opacities as seen on roentgenograms (104).

Even more ominous overtones arose from the conclusion issued at a symposium on manmade mineral fibers (105). Doll concluded that data presented from the meeting indicated "an occupational hazard of lung cancer as was demonstrated in rock and slag wool section of the industry and possibly in the glass wool section" (105).

The purpose of this chapter and the role of this volume is to provide the latest overview of our understanding of the asbestos hazard and how it affects the health of man.

If we are wise, however, we will draw even more from the lessons of asbestos and, in the future, heed the statement of Dr. Margaret Becklake (11). "It is now difficult to accept that any airborne dust inhaled into the lung is truly inert."

ACKNOWLEDGEMENTS

The author wishes to thank Dr. Susan Walker, Mrs. Carolyn Tuley and Mr. Glenn Williams for their editorial assistance in the development of this chapter.

REFERENCES

1. Woolf HB. Webster's New Collegiate Dictionary. Springfield: G. & C. Merriam Company, 1976: 65.
2. Selikoff IJ, Lee DHK. Historical background. In: eds, Lee DHK, Hewson EW, Okun D, Asbestos and Disease. New York: Academic Press, 1978:3–8.
3. Hendry NW. The geology, occurrences, and major uses of asbestos. In: ed, Boland B, Annals of the New York Academy of Sciences. 132th ed. New York: The New York Academy of Sciences, 1965:12.
4. Clifton RA. Asbestos. In: ed, Bureau of Mines, Bureau of Mines Minerals Yearbook. Washington, D.C.: United States Department of the Interior, 1973:1–5.
5. Vallyathan V, Green FHY. The role of analytical techniques in the diagnosis of asbestos-associated disease. CRC Crit Rev Clin Lab Sci 1985:22:1–42.
6. Environmental Protection Agency. 40 CFR Part 763 (Subpart E 763.80–763.99) Asbestos-containing materials in schools. In: ed, Environmental Protection Agency, Federal Register, Vol. 52, No. 210, Friday, October 30, 1987. Washington, D.C.: Environmental Protection Agency, 1987:1857–1897.
7. Occupational Safety and Health Administration. Title 29 CFR Part 1910.1001. In: eds, Federal Register, Vol. 51, No. 119, Friday, June 20, 1986. Washington, D.C.: U.S. Department of Labor, Occupational Safety and Health Administration, 1986:22733–22755.
8. Occupational Safety and Health Administration. Title 29 CFR Part 1926.58. In: eds, Federal Register, Vol. 51, No. 119, Friday, June 20, 1988. Washington, D.C.: U.S. Department of Labor, Occupational Safety and Health Administration, 1986:22758–22790.
9. Veblen DR, Buseck PR, Burnham CW. Asbestiform chain silicates: new minerals and structural groups. Science 1977; 1989:359–364.
10. Mueller PK, Stanley RL. Asbestos fiber atlas. Washington, D.C.: U.S. Environmental Protection Agency, 1975: 9–19.

11. Becklake MR. Asbestos-related diseases of the lung and other organs: their epidemiology and implications for clinical practice. Am Rev Respir Dis 1976; 114:187–227.
12. Morgan WKC. The effects of particles, vapours, fumes and gases. Eur J Respir Dis 1982; 123S:7–12.
13. Breeze R, Turk M. Cellular structure, function and organization in the lower respiratory tract. Environ Health Perspect 1984; 55:3–24.
14. Spencer H. The anatomy of the lung. In: eds, Pathology of the Lung. 4th ed. Oxford: Pergamon Press Ltd., 1985:17–17.
15. Dunnill MS. Postnatal growth of the lung. Thorax 1962; 17:329–333.
16. Rhodin JAG. Respiratory system. In: eds, Histology. New York: Oxford University Press, 1974:608–608.
17. Charnock EL, Doershuk CF. Developmental aspects of the human lung. Pediatr Clin North Am 1973; 20:275–292.
18. Davies G, Reid L. Growth of the alveoli and pulmonary arteries in childhood. Thorax 1970; 23:669–681.
19. Guyton AC. Pulmonary ventilation. In: eds, Textbook of Medical Physiology. 3rd ed. Philadelphia: W. B. Saunders Company, 1966:555–555.
20. Weibel ER. Morphometry of the human lung: the state of the art after two decades. Bull Eur Physiopathol Respir 1979; 15:999–1013.
21. Weibel ER. Stereological methods for biological morphometry. In: eds, Stereological Methods. London: Academic Press, 1979:322–322.
22. Donaldson K, Slight J, Brown GM, Bolton RE. The ability of inflammatory bronchoalveolar leucocyte populations elicited with microbes or mineral dust to injure alveolar epithelial cells and degrade extracellular matrix in vitro. Br J Exp Pathol 1988; 69:327–338.
23. Hunninghake GW, Gadek JE, Fales HM, Crystal RG. Human alveolar macrophage-derived chemotactic factor for neutrophils. J Clin Invest 1980; 66:473–483.
24. Worthen GS, Haslett C, Rees AJ, Gumbay RS, Henson JE, Henson PM. Neutrophil-mediated pulmonary vascular injury. Am Rev Respir Dis 1987; 136:19–28.
25. Fantone JC, Ward PA. Polymorphonuclear leukocyte-mediated cell and tissue injury. Hum Pathol 1985; 16:973–978.
26. Harada RN, Bowman CM, Fox RB, Repine JE. Alveolar macrophage secretions. Chest 1982; 81S:52S–54S.
27. Bowden DH. The alveolar macrophage. Environ Health Perspect 1984; 55:327–341.
28. Rola-Pleszycynski M, Gouin S, Begin R. Asbestos-induced lung inflammation. Inflammation 1984; 8:53–62.
29. Brain JD. Macrophage damage in relation to the pathogenesis of lung diseases. Environ Health Perspect 1980; 35:21–28.

30. Gross P, Detreville RT. The lung as an embattled domain against inanimate pollutants. Am Rev Respir Dis 1972; 106:684–691.
31. Evans JC, Evans RJ, Holmes A, Hounam RF, Jones DM, Morgan A, Walsh M. Studies on the deposition of inhaled fibrous material in the respiratory tract of the rat and its subsequent clearance using radioactive tracer techniques. Environ Res 1973; 6:180–201.
32. Green GM, Jakab GJ, Low RB, Davis GS. Defense mechanisms of the respiratory membrane. Am Rev Respir Dis 1977; 115:479–514.
33. Bohning DE, Atkins HL, Cohn SH. Long-term particle clearance in man: normal and impaired. Ann Occup Hyg 1982; 26:259–271.
34. Cohen D, Arai SF, Brain JD. Smoking impairs long-term dust clearance from the lung. Science 1979; 204:514–517.
35. Churg A, Wiggs B. Mineral particles, mineral fibers, and lung cancer. Environ Res 1985; 37:364–372.
36. McFadden D, Wright J, Wiggs B, Churg A. Cigarette smoke increases the penetration of asbestos fibers into airway walls. Am J Pathol 1986, 123:95–99.
37. Barclay WR, Craighead JE, Cugell DW, Dolan WD, Jones RJ, Kagan E, Shimkin MB, Tomashefski F, Wheater RH. A physician's guide to asbestos-related diseases. JAMA 1984; 252:2593–2597.
38. Stanton MF, Layard M, Tegeris A, Miller E, May M Kent E. Carcinogenicity of fibrous glass: pleural response in the rat in relation to fiber dimension. J Natl Cancer Inst 1977; 58:587–603.
39. Pott F. Problems in defining carcinogenic fibres. Ann Occup Hyg 1987; 31:799–802.
40. Bonneau L, Malard C, Pezerat H. Studies on surface properties of asbestos II. Role of dimensional characteristics and surface properties of mineral fibers in the induction of pleural tumors. Environ Res 1986; 41:268–275.
41. Jolicoeur C, Poisson D. Surface physico-chemical studies of chrysotile asbestos and related minerals. Drug Chem Toxicol 1987; 10:1–47.
42. Bonneau L, Suquet H, Malard C, Pezerat H. Studies on surface properties of asbestos I. Active sites on surface of chrysotile and amphiboles. Environ Res 1986; 41:251–267.
43. Hamilton JA. Asbestos fibers, plasma and inflammation. Environ Health Perspect 1983; 51:281–285.
44. Eberhardt MK, Roman-Franco AA, Quiles MR. Asbestos-induced decomposition of hydrogen peroxide. Environ Res 1985; 37:287–292.
45. Kennedy TP, Ky H, Rao NV, Hopkins C, Tolley E, Dodson RF, Hoidal JR. Asbestos and kaolin cause red cell hemolysis by acting as fenton reagents. Am Rev Respir Dis 1987; 135:A166.
46. Jaurand MC, Bignon J, Sebastien P, Goni J. Leaching of chrysotile asbestos in human lungs. Environ Res 1977; 14:245–254.

47. Hahon N, Vallyathan V, Booth JA, Sepulveda MJ. In vitro biologic responses to native and surface-modified asbestos. Environ Res 1986; 39:345–355.
48. Beck EG, Holt PF, Nasrallah ET. Effects of chrysotile and acid-treated chrysotile on macrophage cultures. Br J Ind Med 1971; 28:179–185.
49. Becklake MR. Asbestos-related diseases of the lungs and pleura. Am Rev Respir Dis 1982; 126:187–194.
50. Champness PE, Cliff G, Lorimer GW. The identification of asbestos. J Micros 1976; 108:231–249.
51. Yamate G, Agarwal SC, Gibbons RD. Methodology for the measurement of airborne asbestos by electron microscopy. Washington, D.C.: Office of Research and Development, U.S. Environmental Protection Agency. Contract No. 68–02–3266., 1984:
52. Filipenko D, Wright JL, Churg A. Pathologic changes in small airways of the guinea pig after amosite asbestos exposure. Am J Pathol 1985; 119:273–278.
53. Pinkerton KE, Pratt PC, Brody AR, Crapo JD. Fiber localization and its relationship to lung reaction in rats after chronic inhalation of chrysotile asbestos. Am J Pathol 1984; 117:484–498.
54. Kaczenski JH, Hallenbeck WH. Migration of ingested asbestos. Environ Res 1984; 35:531–551.
55. Cook PM, Olson GF. Ingested mineral fibers: elimination in human urine. Science 1979; 204:195–198.
56. Davis JMG, Gross P, deTreville RTP. "Ferruginous bodies" in guinea pigs. Arch Pathol 1970; 89:364–373.
57. Gross P, deTreville RTP, Cralley LJ, Davis JMG. Pulmonary ferruginous bodies. Arch Pathol 1968; 85:539–546.
58. Churg A, Warnock ML, Green N. Analysis of the cores of ferruginous (asbestos) bodies from the general population. Lab Invest 1979; 40:31–38.
59. Masse S, Begin R, Cantin A. Pathology of silicon carbide pneumoconiosis. Mod Pathol 1988; 1:104–108.
60. Dodson RF, Greenberg SD, Williams MG, Corn CJ, O'Sullivan MF, Hurst GA. Asbestos content in lungs of occupationally and nonoccupationally exposed individuals. JAMA 1984; 252:68–71.
61. Dodson RF, Williams MG, Corn CJ, Rankin TL. A comparison of asbestos burden in non-urban patients with and without lung cancer. Cytobios 1988;
62. Breedin PH, Buss DH. Ferruginous (asbestos) bodies in the lungs of rural dwellers, urban dwellers and patients with pulmonary neoplasms. South Med J 1976; 69:401–404.
63. Churg A, Warnock ML. Analysis of the cores of ferruginous (asbestos) bodies from the general population. I. Patients with and without lung cancer. Lab Invest 1977; 37:280–286.
64. Churg A, Warnock ML. Correlation of quantitative asbestos body counts and occupation in urban patients. Arch Pathol Lab Med 1977; 101:629–634.

65. Churg A, Warnock ML. Asbestos fibers in the general population. Am Rev Respir Dis 1980; 122:669–678.
66. Churg A, Warnock ML. Asbestos and other ferruginous bodies. Am J Pathol 1981; 102:447–456.
67. Churg A, Wood P. Observations on the distribution of asbestos fibers in human lungs. Environ Res 1983; 31:374–380.
68. Dodson RF, Williams MG, Hurst GA. Method for removing the ferruginous coating from asbestos bodies. J Toxicol Environ Health 1983; 11:959–966.
69. Dodson RF, O'Sullivan MF, Corn C, Williams MG, Hurst GA. Ferruginous body formation on a nonasbestos mineral. Arch Pathol Lab Med 1985; 109:849–852.
70. Millette JR, Twyman JD, Hansen EC, Clark PJ, Pansing MF. Chrysotile, palygorskite, and halloysite in drinking water. Scan Electron Microsc 1979; 1:579–586.
71. Berkley C, Churg J, Selikoff IJ, Smith WE. The detection and localization of mineral fibers in tissue. In: eds, Boland B, Hitchcock J, Kates S, Biological effects of asbestos. 132th ed. New York: The New York Academy of Sciences, 1965:48–63.
72. Carter RE, Taylor WF. Identification of a particular amphibole asbestos fiber in tissue of persons exposed to a high oral intake of the mineral. Environ Res 1980; 24:85–93.
73. Pooley JD. Electron microscope characteristics of inhaled chrysotile asbestos fibers. Br J Ind Med 1972; 29:146–153.
74. Chatfield EJ. Preparation and analysis of particulate samples by electron microscopy, with special reference to asbestos. ScanElectron Microsc 1979; 1:563–578.
75. Chatfield EJ, Dillon MJ. Some aspects of specimen preparation and limitations of precision in particulate analysis by SEM and TEM. Scan Electron Microsc 1978; 1:487–496.
76. Ashcroft T, Heppleston AG. The optical and electron microscopic determination of pulmonary asbestos fiber concentration and its relation to the human pathological reaction. J Clin Pathol 1973; 26:224–234.
77. Langer AM, Rubin IB, Selikoff IJ. Chemical characterization of asbestos body cores by electron microprobe analysis. J Histochem Cytochem 1972; 20:723–734.
78. Stasny JT, Husach C, Albright FR, Schumacher DV, Sweigart DW, Boyer K. Development of methods to isolate asbestos from spiked beverages and foods for SEM characterization. Scan Electron Microsc 1979; 1:587–595.
79. Sundius N, Bygden A. Isolation of the mineral dust in lungs and sputum. J Ind Hyg Toxicol 1938; 20:351–359.
80. Gloyne SR. The presence of the asbestos fibre in the lesions of asbestos workers. Tubercle 1929; 10:404–407.
81. Smith MJ, Naylor B. A method of extracting ferruginous bodies from sputum and pulmonary tissue. Am J Clin Pathol 1972; 58:250–254.
82. Sebastien P, Masse R, Bignon J. Recovery of ingested asbestos

fibers from the gastrointestinal lymph in rats. Environ Res 1980; 22:201–216.
83. Williams MG, Dodson RF, Corn C, Hurst GA. A procedure for the isolation of amosite asbestos and ferruginous bodies from lung tissue and sputum. J Toxicol Environ Health 1982; 10:627–638.
84. Churg A. Fiber counting and analysis in the diagnosis of asbestos-related disease. Hum Pathol 1982; 13:381–392.
85. Lippman M. Asbestos exposure indices. Environ Res 1988; 46:86–106.
86. Warnock ML, Wolery G. Asbestos bodies or fibers and the diagnosis of asbestosis. Environ Res 1987; 44:29–44.
87. Dodson RF, Williams MG, O'Sullivan MF, Corn CJ, Greenberg SD, Hurst GA. A comparison of the ferruginous body and uncoated fiber content in the lungs of former asbestos workers. Am Rev Respir Dis 1985; 132:143–147.
88. Modin BE, Greenberg SD, Buffler PA, Lockhart JA, Seitzman LH, Awe RJ. Asbestos bodies in a general hospital/clinic population. Acta Cytol 1982; 26:667–670.
89. McLarty JW, Greenberg SD, Hurst GA, Spivey CG, Seitzman LH, Hieger LR, Farley ML, Mabry LC. The clinical significance of ferruginous bodies in sputa. J Occup Med 1980; 22:92–96.
90. Dodson RF, Williams MG, Corn CJ, Idell S, McLarty JW. Asbestos fibers in sputum—an indicator of past occupational exposure. Lab Invest 1988; 58:144. (Abstract)
91. De Vuyst P, Dumortier P, Moulin E, Yourassowsky N, Roomans P, de Francquen P, Yernault JC. Asbestos bodies in bronchoalveolar lavage reflect lung asbestos body concentration. E Resp Journal 1988; 1:362–367.
92. Pott F, Roller M, Ziem U, Reiffer FJ, Bellmann B, Rosenbruch M, Huth F. Carcinogenicity studies on natural and man-made fibres with the intraperitoneal test in rats. In: eds, Symposium on Mineral Fibres in the Non-occupational Environment, Lyon, September 8–10, 1987. Lyon:, 1988:1–4.
93. Wagner JC, Berry G, Timbrell V. Mesothelioma in rats after inoculation with asbestos and other materials. Br J Cancer 1973; 28:173–185.
94. Muhle H, Pott F, Bellmann B, Takenaka S, Ziem U. Inhalation and injection experiments in rats to test the carcinogenicity of MMMF. Ann Occup Hyg 1987; 31:755–764.
95. Churg A. Nonasbestos pulmonary mineral fibers in the general population. Environ Res 1983; 31:189–200.
96. Sebastien P, Bignon J, Barris YI, Awad L, Petit G. Ferruginous bodies in sputum as an indication of exposure to airborne mineral fibers in the mesothelioma villages of Cappadocia. Arch Environ Health 1984; 39:18–23.
97. Stanton MF, Layard M, Tegeris E, Miller E, May M, Morgan E, Smith A. Relation of particle dimension to carcinogenicity in

amphibole asbestos and other fibrous materials. J Natl Cancer Inst 1981; 67:965.

98. Lilis R. Fibrous zeolites and endemic mesothelioma in Cappadocia, Turkey. J Occup Med 1981; 23:548–550.
99. Aisner J, Wiernik PH. Seminars in oncology. Semin Oncol 1981; 13:241–242.
100. Wagner JC. Mesothelioma and mineral fibers. Cancer 1986; 57:1905–1911.
101. Chen W, Mottet NK. Malignant mesothelioma with minimal asbestos exposure. Hum Pathol 1978; 9:253–258.
102. Garrahan K. Mesothelioma: has patient had contact with even small amount of asbestos?. JAMA 1987; 257:1569–1570.
103. Stanton MF, Wrench C. Mechanisms of mesothelioma induction with asbestos and fibrous glass. J Natl Cancer Inst 1972; 48:797–821.
104. Weill H, Hughes JM, Hammad YY, Glindmeyer HW, Sharon G, Jones RN. Respiratory health in workers exposed to man-made vitreous fibers. Am Rev Respir Dis 1983; 128:104–112.
105. Doll R. Symposium on MMMF, Copenhagen, October 1986: Overview and conclusions. Ann Occup Hyg 1987; 31:805–819.
106. Churg A. Asbestos fibers and pleural plaques in a general autopsy population. Am J Pathol 1982; 109:88–96.
107. Churg A. Asbestos fiber content of the lungs in patients with and without asbestos airways disease. Am Rev Respir Dis 1983; 127:470–473.
108. Case BW, Sebastien P, McDonald JC. Lung fiber analysis in accident victims: a biological assessment of general environmental exposures. Arch Environ Health 1988; 43:178–179.
109. Dodson RF, Hurst GA, Williams MG, Corn CJ, Greenberg SD. Comparison of light and electron microscopy for defining occupational asbestos exposure in transbronchial lung biopsies. Chest 1988; 94:366–370.

8

Pleural Plaques from Low Levels of Asbestos

MANFRED NEUBERGER, M.D.

Institute of Environmental Hygiene
University of Vienna
Wein, Austria

Synopsis

BIOGRAPHY

Dr. Manfred Neuberger is Professor and Chairman of Preventive Medicine at the Institute of Environmental Hygiene, University of Vienna. As the deputy director of this institute he teaches environmental and occupational medicine at the school of medicine and in post-graduate courses. As an internist he serves as a consultant for the Austrian Workers Compensation Board, and as an epidemiologist he was nominated deputy director of the institute of environmental medicine of the municipality of Vienna. He published 164 scientific articles, including chapters for WHO reference handbook on air pollution; participated in multicenter studies of the IARC on occupational cancer and advised national and international boards on air pollution effects (clinical and epidemiologic consultancy for United Nations Development Programme), standard setting, and in particular on prevention of asbestos-related disease (advisor of Austrian delegation at ILO conferences). For his scientific contribution to risk estimation and prevention of hazards from asbestos and other aerosols he has been awarded several prizes. Dr. Neuberger may be contacted at the Department of Preventive Medicine, Institute of Environmental Hygiene, University of Vienna, A-1095 Wien, Austria, Kinderspitalgasse 15 (telephone: 222/43 15 95).

EDITORS' COMMENTARY

If pleural plaques could be initiated by low-level exposure to asbestos fibers, this would be of considerable interest to attorneys handling such personal injury cases and to regulators attempting to determine "safe" levels of exposure. If it is a result of early age exposure, it would help to determine which exposure may be the initiating or causal event. Is it a true independent disease entity or is it a precursor or associated with some other diseases? Is it relatively benign, slowly developing, or limited in the lung area involved and disabled? The degree and rate of growth of pleural plaques is of interest to attorneys (damages) and to physicians (prognosis). There are many other questions relating to diagnosis: lung sensitivity, variability of growth, types, and the specificity of this disease process. Thus, the following chapter contains information of interest to research scientists, diagnostic and treating physicians, personal injury lawyers, and to those who might set new standards (TLV, PEL, etc.) for permissible exposure in various buildings and workplaces.

A. INTRODUCTION

Pleural thickening has been well known to pathologists for nearly 100 years. It was considered to be remnants of inflammation. The first description of pleural plaques in connection with asbestosis was probably made in 1931. Sparks (132) described small irregular calcareous deposits in the lower zone of the lungs. Epidemiological results, however, on the relations of asbestos differentiating diffuse pleural thickening and of circumscribed pleural plaque to inhalation had not been reported before 1950.

In 1975 Bohlig and Otto (14) reviewed the literature on pleu-

Accepted for publication 15 April 1989.

ral effects of asbestos and summarized them in a graph that showed plaques as the earliest sign of low-level asbestos exposure (Fig. 8-1). environmental studies confirmed the hypothesis that plaques are a sensitive indicator of past asbestos exposure, though we know today that fiber type, fiber dimension, and age at first exposure plays a more important role for pleural plaques on the one hand and mesothelioma on the other hand than does cumulative dose, which is more important for asbestosis and lung cancer (145).

B. DIAGNOSIS OF PLEURAL PLAQUES

1. Pathology

Macroscopically, pleural plaques are shiny white elevations with sharp borders. They can be situated on the chest wall, diaphragm, or pericardium, towards the mediastinum or interlobar. These circumscribed thickenings develop in the parietal layer of the pleura and only occasionally they can be found in the visceral layer also.

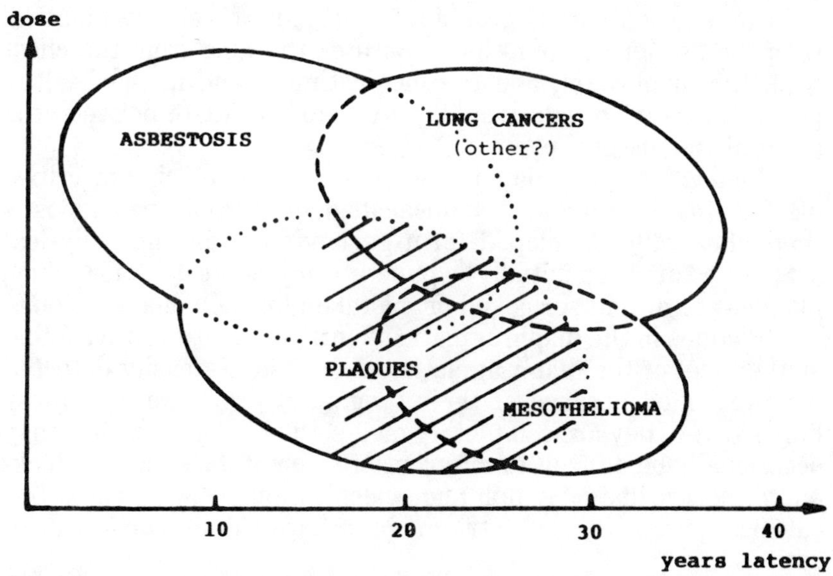

Fig. 8-1 Sequalae of asbestos exposures different in dose and latency. (Dashed part: pleural calcifications.)

Microscopically, they consist of fibro-hyaline connective tissue containing very few cells. There are no inflammatory cells within the pleural plaques, but small aggregates can be seen in their periphery, indicating a low-grade inflammation there. As a rule pleural plaques are covered with normal mesothelial cells (11, 14, 52, 65, 145).

In contrast to pleural plaques the diffuse pleural thickening primarily affects the visceral pleura. The pleura is found as a thickened seam, which may enclose the lung from all sides. In pleural thickening calcification is much less common than in pleural plaques.

Connective strands that emanate from the pleura can go far into the lung parenchyma. They are combined with diffuse pleural thickening, which is sometimes regional and usually also associated with a blunting of the sinus.

2. Radiology

The normal pleura is not visible radiographically, except as a companion shadow along the posterior portion of the lower border of the second rib, at most 2 mm wide, and as a delicate, slightly arcuate linear density, produced by the orthograde projection of an interlobar septum, and almost always visible in right mid-lung field.

As seen on the radiographic film the pleura is always identical with the border contour that separates the lung from the chest wall, the diaphragm, and the mediastinum, and in the healthy person there is no radiographic way to differentiate between the parietal and visceral pleura.

Pleural plaques may be present as simple, circumscribed pleural fibrosis or hyalinosis, uncalcified, or with calcified deposits that when fully developed form garlands or take on holly-leaf shapes and are seen initially as punctate or linear calcific foci. Such plaques are often overlooked or mistaken for pulmonary lesions.

Plaques in the diaphragmatic pleura are almost always found at the level of the diaphragmatic domes and are easily detected when calcified because of their tangential projection in survey films. When they are completely mediastinal in location they may occasionally be difficult to differentiate from diffuse pleural thickening, pericardial or lymph node calcifications, wall or thrombus calcifications in the left atrium, or atheromatous aortic calcifications.

In diffuse malignant pleural mesothelioma, pleural effusion usually develops very early and masks localized densities of the

Table 8-1 Advantages and Disadvantages of High- and Low-Voltage Techniques for Diagnosis of Pleural Shadows from Effusions and Calcifications (11)

	Pleural Shadows			
		Pleural Calcifications		
Voltage	Effusions	Diaphragm	Chest Wall	Mediastinum
High (100–150 kV)	Good	Very good	Poor	Very good
Low (65–85 kV)	Good	Poor	Very good	Poor

chest wall; by the time the broad, polycyclic border appears on the x-ray, it is too late for an early diagnosis. To make this diagnosis it seems most important to think immediately of the possibility of a malignant mesothelioma when an unexplained pleural effusion or other pleural findings are present, especially after asbestos exposure, to differentiate beginning effusion in asbestos workers from malignant disease and to attempt to make the diagnosis as early as possible, even if it requires the use of aspiration, diagnostic pneumothorax, thoracoscopy, and/or thoracotomy.

Invasive techniques are also required to tell malignant mesotheliomas from pleural cacinomatosis. Benign pleural tumors are more easily differentiated radiologically because they are localized and mostly isolated.

Diffuse pleural thickening is seen on x-ray as a long condensation between the ribs and the lung. It is regularly combined with an obliteration of the costophrenic angle, which forms a continuation of the diffuse pleural thickening. It can extend along part or all of the chest wall and can cover the entire lung. It is often combined with connective strands in the lung parenchyma (11, 43, 57, 65, 121).

Connective strands often converge towards a center. The strands can then, with a little imagination, be seen to resemble the tracks of a bird, and are sometimes called "crow's feet" (57, 65) which, however, have also been interpreted as thickened interlobar pleura, partly distorted from shrinkage (16).

The differential diagnosis of diffuse pleural thickening and pleural plaques is important for the prognosis of asbestos exposed persons. Table 8-2 summarizes the radiological criteria (11). Usually diffuse pleural thickening is detected with high-voltage technique only, because it rarely calcifies.

Table 8-2 Pleural Plaques and Diffuse Pleural Thickening

	Shape	Thickness	Borders	Calcium Distribution	Side Involved	Distribution	Diaphragma	Course
Plaques	Punctate to linear, with garland- or map-shaped configurations	Maximal 20 mm	Mound or flat-top shaped	Mostly inside the soft tissue densities only: centers frequently somewhat less dense	Mostly bilateral	More ventral, lateral, and mediastinal than dorsal; mostly parallel to the ribs	Calcium in the center of the diaphragmatic dome	Mostly slow increase of the lesions in number, size, and calcific density
Pleural thickening	Flat, shell-like compact	Up to several cm	Mostly parallel to the chest wall	Either along the border to aerated lung tissue or in clumpy distribution across the entire area of thickening	Mostly unilateral	Mostly following lobar or segmental borders	Calcium in the CP space or along the periphery	No further change after the calcific armor has developed

3. Computerized Tomography (CT) and Other Diagnostic Methods

With CT it is possible to observe the pleura all around the chest in a chosen section. The tissue contents within a process can be judged with great accuracy with CT. Fat can be distinguished from other types of soft tissue by direct determination at attenuation values (Hounsfield units) within a well-defined area. Calcifications are also easily identified (34, 39, 65). The reported incidence of pleural plaques is expected to increase with more abundant use of CT.

Unfortunately, CT examinations are expensive and time consuming and the x-ray dose is not negligible. Therefore, CT is not used for primary screening but in special cases when parenchymal diseases or tumors are suspected. Only in risk groups a primary CT-screening could be considered to improve early diagnosis, also of pleural plaques (34), which are invisible on x-ray (e.g., near the bone). Very important for all screening purposes is the elimination of false-positive radiological diagnosis by consecutive CT, which can differentiate between pleural thickening and subpleural fat (39).

The most important clinical use of CT in pleural disease is to decide where a lung or pleural biopsy must be done, especially in pleural changes suspect of mesothelioma.

Ultrasonic techniques (echography) which have been recommended (20) could be advantageous for followup of persons with pleural plaques. They cannot reveal plaques situated under the ribs and at present they seem to be less suited for screening purposes than radiological methods.

a. The ILO Classification

The radiological ILO classification of 1980 given below is under revision at present, and it is planned to separate pleural plaques from diffuse pleural thickening because of differences in aetiology and prognostic significance discussed in the following chapters. In the ILO classification in current use, both circumscribed and diffuse pleural thickenings of chest wall are graded as follows:

Maximum width:

1. Up to about 5 mm.
2. >5 mm and <10 mm.
3. >10 mm.

Extent (total length):

1. Up to one-quarter of the projection of the lateral chest wall.

2. Greater than one-quarter but not one-half of the projection of the lateral chest wall.

3. Greater than one-half of the projection of the lateral chest wall.

Extent of pleural calcifications:

1. An area of calcified pleura with greatest diameter up to about 20 mm, or a number of such areas the sum of whose greatest diameters does not exceed about 20 mm.

2. An area of calcified pleura >20 mm and <100 mm.

3. An area of calcified pleura >100 mm.

The ILO classification was originally developed for epidemiologic studies. Unfortunately, it was used at the same time for predicting the presence of early asbestosis-induced disease in the individual subject for which it seems to be of limited usefulness (115).

This mixing of purposes introduced bias to studies (e.g., readers whose attention focused on the individual case used to look at the exposure history before classifying the x-ray). Also studies on plaques were subject to some self-fulfilling prophecies.

A comprehensive proposal called "ILO-classification 1991" intends to increase sensitivity, specifity, and practicability (64). Diffuse pleural thickening (right/left, upper/middle/lower chest wall, costophrenic angle) will be recorded separately from pleural plaques.

In plaques only calcified, hyaline, and unsure plaques will be distinguished (right/left, upper/middle/lower chest wall, diaphragm) because the width is more important for classification of diffuse thickening. Several authors, however, require a plaque thickness of at least 5 mm.

Calcifications are easier to detect. Those of 2 mm width are usually sufficient for detection on posterior/anterior x-ray, and even smaller ones can be seen on the diaphragm but calcification usually occurs within areas of already thickened pleura. Apical caps, interlobar or mediastinal pleural thickenings, pleural strands with atelectasis, confluent pleural strands (crow's feet), and separate pleural strands will be recorded by special symbols. A localized flattening or irregularity of diaphragm that is not believed to be due to localized eventration but suspect of hyaline plaque should be recorded, too (58, 64, 122, 139).

b. Differential diagnosis (radiological)

i. Non-calcified plaques.

Oblique views of both lungs, properly coned-down, often provide more information, especially if there are bilateral hyaline plaques. This projection avoids the superposition of interfering soft tissue shadows (e.g., breasts) and does not cause magnification of the dimensions of examined parts (11). There are, however, many normal and pathological structures in the chest wall that may simulate plaques (65):

- Muscles in the chest wall and muscle attachments may occasionally have a plaque-like appearance. Misinterpretations may occur, particularly on oblique films that are taken too obliquely from the PA film. The muscle shadows characteristically disappear totally in one projection, while they are well seen in others. An experienced observer is usually able to make a distinction between muscle contours and plaques.
- Old rib fractures may cause a local thickening of the nearby pleura, which may resemble a plaque. Such post-traumatic changes are, however, seldom bilateral. If rib fractures are suspected, it is advisable to take a film on the area with low-voltage technique. On such a film, callus formation is easily detected.
- Subpleural fat may cause diagnostic problems if increased. Often, but not always, the pleural fat is seen as a diffuse thickening involving the whole lateral chest wall on both sides. With such fat formation, occurring most often in overweight subjects, it is very difficult to assess concomitant non-calcified plaques. With the aid of CT, the possibilities improve slightly, but it is obvious that the diagnosis of plaques is less sensitive in presence of subpleural fat.

ii. Calcified plaques.

When calcifications are present, the differential diagnostic problems are different.

The following diagnoses must be considered (11, 65):

- Residues from pleuritis, particularly of tuberculous nature; sometimes also from mycotic infections such as histoplasmosis and actinomycosis.
- Residues from tuberculosis treated with pneumothorax.
- Residues from hemothorax after chest trauma.
- Residues from empyema, e.g., postinfluenzal (Spanish flu).

All the above-mentioned conditions are usually unilateral. Furthermore, they are usually more widespread, and the calcifications have different localizations. They are closely connected with the lung parenchyma, and between the calcified area and the chest wall there is a markedly thickened non-calcified parietal pleural leaf.

The subject is also often aware of the previous illness. This means that the differential diagnosis is facilitated by a complete history of previous diseases.

c. Screening (Reliability and validity, sensitivity and specificity of the radiological diagnoses)

One can have the same radiologist read the same films on different occasions and study the variability in the readings (intraobserver reliability). One can also give the same films to different radiologists and study the discord between them (inter-observer reliability). The reproducibility also depends on the diagnostic criteria, the frequency of changes on the films, the skill of the readers and the quality of the films.

Sheers et al. (128) used films in which 30% were abnormal and found an intra-observer reliability of about 85% for pleural thickening and 94% for calcified plaques. Rossiter (120) found similar frequencies (87% intra-observer reliability for pleural thickening and 94% for calcified plaques). If 12 radiologists read 100 films the prevalence of pleural thickening varied from 20% to 55%. Thus the consistency between trained radiologists was found to be poor for pleural thickening but rather good for calcified plaques (32). If x-ray reader agreement is low, the diagnosis of plaque is questioned. Readers may agree, however, and still be incorrect in their interpretation (112). An initial reading of 566 films found 25% to be positive for pleural changes, while only 4% were considered positive by a panel of 3 readers under blind conditions.

It is easy to identify plaques at autopsy if desired. Different diagnostic procedures can be validated against the findings at autopsy. Using miniature and full-sized x-rays and strict radiological criteria, Hillerdal and Lindgren (59) found a sensitivity of 13% (which means that only 13% of plaques seen at autopsy were found by the radiologist) and specificity was 100%. Change of criteria increased the sensitivity to 46%, but decreased the specificity to 92% (which means that 8% of persons without plaques at autopsy were wrongly diagnosed radiologically as having plaques). Rubino et al. (123) found a sensitivity of 88% if only large plaques were considered, which decreased to 40% if all plaques were studied, with a specificity of 80%. Wain et al. (141) reported a sensitivity of 28% with a specificity of 100%.

From Bayes' theorem it is obvious that routine anterior/posterior x-rays have low validity for examination of groups with a low prevalence of pleural plaques (113). If we achieve a sensitivity of 75% and a specificity of 99% in an x-ray screening for pleural plaques and apply this screening to a population with a true plaque prevalence of 5%, then the likelihood to detect a person with plaques will be 80% in cases with radiological signs of plaques. If we apply the same screening to a population with a true plaque prevalence of 1%, however, the likelihood of finding a person with plaques among x-ray-positive cases will be only 43%. If we demand a minimal likelihood of 50% true plaques in persons with radiological signs of plaques, it is not possible to examine a population with a plaque prevalence below 1%; and this would still be true if not only specificity but also sensitivity could be raised to 99%.

C. PLEURAL PLAQUES AND ASBESTOS EXPOSURE

1. Plaques and Asbestos Disease (Importance of Fiber Type, Dose, and Age)

The pleura of most experimental animals will show granulomatous response after injection of asbestos, but similar reactions are produced by other mineral dusts (29), and inhalation experiments with asbestos failed to produce pleural plaques within the life span of the animals.

In man the most frequent pleural reaction to higher (occupational and paraoccupational) asbestos exposure is *diffuse pleural thickening* which tends to run parallel to the prevalence and severity of asbestosis (81). Diffuse pleural thickening, however, is no specific reaction to asbestos but a rather frequent response to different other noxae (infections, trauma) in persons not exposed to asbestos. Therefore, not all cases of pleural thickening in asbestos exposed can be attributed to exposure. Table 8-3 shows pleural and parenchymal changes in relatives of asbestos workers (126) for whom considerable paraoccupational (domestic) exposures can be assumed, which occurred earlier than occupational ones (e.g., in daughters cleaning the working clothes of their fathers). Pleural changes were found to be more frequent than parenchymal changes. The diffuse pleural thickening is more specific for asbestos if it includes two or more adjacent zones on each side (15) or at least the middle-third of each pleura (122). If diffuse thickening is bilateral it might be due to asbestos even if only the costophrenic angle is involved, and asbestos workers have a higher probability to develop a costophrenic-angle obliteration or a fissural thickening than pleural plaques visible on x-ray. Rockoff et al. (114) found a 50% chance of developing fissural thickening with 21 years of occupational asbestos exposure, while 31 years of exposure were needed for a 50% change of forming pleural plaques. Fissural thickening and obliteration of sinus, however, is less specific for asbestos exposure than pleural plaques. Therefore it cannot be used in screening the general population for signs of possible asbestos exposure.

Pleural plaques are a sensitive indicator of early asbestos exposure, more sensitive for past exposure than small opacities (68) and more specific than diffuse pleural thickening, especially when bilateral and calcified.

Calcified plaques, especially on the diaphragm, which are easily detected in routine x-ray, are considered more specific for past asbestos exposures than others. Hyaline diaphragmatic pla-

Table 8-3 X-Ray Abnormalities among 490 Family Members of Amosite Asbestos Workers (126)

Relative	Total Examined	Pleural Thickening Only	Pleural Calcification Only	Pleural Plaques Only	More than One Pleural Change Present	Irregular Opacities Only	Irregular Opacities and Some Type of Pleural Change	Total Abnormalities
Wives	114	19 (16.7%)	3 (2.6%)	4 (3.5%)	4 (3.5%)	15 (13.2%)	16 (14.0%)	61 (53.5%)
Daughters	163	15 (9.2%)	3 (1.8%)	4 (2.5%)	7 (4.3%)	10 (6.1%)	2 (1.2%)	41 (25.2%)
Sons	112	23 (20.5%)	4 (3.6%)	2 (1.8%)	6 (5.4%)	12 (10.7%)	13 (11.6%)	60 (53.6%)
Siblings	57	4 (7.0%)	0	0	0	6 (10.5%)	5 (8.8%)	15 (26.3%)
Other	44	4 (9.1%)	1 (2.3%)	1 (2.3%)	1 (2.3%)	4 (9.1%)	6 (13.6%)	17 (38.6%)
Total	490	65 (13.3%)	11 (2.2%)	11 (2.2%)	18 (3.7%)	47 (9.6%)	42 (8.6%)	194 (39.6%)

ques could be an earlier sign of past asbestos exposure, but in some locations they will hardly be detectable by x-ray. The possibility of calcified pleural lesions after infections like tuberculosis or trauma will usually be revealed by the patient's medical history and they will have different radiological appearances (11, 126). Tuberculosis commonly involves the apical areas, and calcified lesions resembling plaques can be shown to lie at various depths in the lung. When located in the pleura, they are nearly always posterior or posterolateral when located in the lower or middle portions of the chest (and very rarely diaphragmatic, mediastinal, or pericardial), and they are regularly combined with diffuse thickening secondary to pleurisy or empyema. Hyaline plaques are an earlier but probably a less specific sign of asbestos exposure then calcified plaques because hyaline plaques from other origins seem to be more common. In smokers, plaques were found more frequently (52), which could be explained, however, by the impairment of respiratory clearance and other effects of tobacco smoke modifying the effect of asbestos.

For medical surveillance after *high* asbestos exposures, the profusion of small opacities in the lung is the most important radiological parameter as an early sign of asbestosis. Diffuse pleural thickening, however, can be the most frequent (12, 53, 72, 124) and earliest detectable sequel of *moderate* exposure to asbestos, with earlier involvement of the upper and middle zones. The earliest signs of asbestos exposure, however, are the least specific. Bilateral diffuse thickening within the upper pleural zones, for example, was found in 71% of asbestos-exposed workers and in 40% of non-exposed controls (15). Even *low* asbestos exposures can be detected by x-ray screening if they occurred early, such as in paraoccupational and environmental exposures (145). In this case pleural plaques are the most important radiological screening parameter. They can only be diagnosed, however, 5 or more years after first exposure; while diffuse pleural thickening can be observed after 2 years of heavy asbestos exposure.

While cumulative dose is important for diffuse pleural thickening, asbestosis, and lung cancer, it seems to be of little importance for pleural plaques. The effect of *age* on the frequency of plaques is so pronounced that some authors described plaques as an "aging" of the pleura (51, 88, 138), which was contradicted, however, by the observed frequency distributions (14) and the observation that plaques develop at earlier ages in exposed subjects. Because plaques develop at earlier ages in exposed subjects, the increase of plaque prevalence with age seems to be more pronounced in men (109). In asbestos-induced plaques *age at first exposure* is much more important than cumulative dose. Therefore many investigators did not find clear dose-response relationships. Despite the fact that higher occupational exposures can shorten the latency time (52), plaques develop at an earlier age in persons exposed environmentally since birth to very much lower concentrations (89, 145).

Fiber type, fiber dimensions, and fiber-surface characteristics could decide which sequelae of asbestos exposure will develop. In epidemiological studies, it is difficult to find groups exposed to only one fiber type without considerable impurities and in comparable amounts and age. Amphiboles are more persistent in the lungs than chrysotile (145) and therefore have the highest chance to produce plaques as a late consequence of asbestos exposure, if they do not lead to premature death (e.g., from asbestosis or cancer) before. Early exposures to anthophyllite and tremolite have been associated with a high prevalence of plaques in the general population and there is some evidence that early exposure to long and thin amphiboles (crocidolite, amosite) and zeolites (erionite) cause mesothelioma, whereas early exposure to respirable but thick- and short-fibered amphiboles and perhaps even cleavage fragments cause only plaques (89, 140, 145). Some authors related plaques also to non-fibrous dust exposures (4, 14, 73, 80, 110, 134). Talcum associated with plaques was found to be contaminated with tremolite, and mining of pure talcum without fibrous contaminants could not be related to plaques. In Austria 1,279 small-size chest x-rays of talcum miners and the full-size chest x-rays of 92 talcum and leucophyllite miners compensated for pneumoconioses (talcosis, silicosis, silicotuberculosis, mixed pneumoconioses) did not reveal any pleural plaques (89). The same observation was made in China in 97 pneumoconiotics from a talc mine that also contains a very pure talcum (149).

2. Plaques in Working Populations

Plaques are not as frequent as diffuse thickening in working populations (68). In asbestos workers plaque prevalence varies with fiber type (52) and time since first exposure (63). Plaques prevalences reported for working populations have been summarized by several authors (4, 52, 82), but comparisons are difficult because different diagnostic methods have been applied, diagnostic criteria are not fully documented, and most studies using the ILO 1980 classification did not differentiate between circumscribed plaques, diffuse pleural thickening, and combined changes. Differences in reported prevalences are influenced by interobserver variation (15) but also group reading may introduce bias and lead to overdiagnosis of pleural changes (112). On the other hand radiographs showed plaques in only a small proportion of cases that had such lesions at autopsy (62, 141). Only a few studies compare the plaque prevalence in asbestos workers with the prevalence in appropriate reference groups (4). Differences in age-structure and in diagnostic methods and criteria used in different groups make comparisons impossible. In working populations results on rare symptoms like calcified plaques can be heavily biased by selection (97). In all retrospective approaches observer bias has to be taken into account, and even in prospective studies self-fulfilling prophecies may occur such as the diagnosis, grading, and reporting of asbestosis influenced by concomitant finding of pleural plaques that are regarded to "strongly suggest the diagnosis of asbestosis" (Varkey, 1983). The diagnostician can only be blinded with regard to exposure but not with regard to other asbestos associated signs. Therefore the association between parenchymal and pleural changes found in asbestos workers cannot be related to exposure alone. The presence of one sign (e.g., plaques) can influence the detection and grading of another sign (e.g., small opacities)—and vice versa—and can lead to an overdiagnosis of plaques in asbestosis. Diagnoses relying on combined symptoms are necessary in the individual case, but they limit the usability of diagnostic data for epidemiological studies investigating such combinations.

3. Plaques in the General Population

Pleural plaques are an important sign of past asbestos exposure in the general population because their prevalence increases at lower doses than the prevalence of small irregular opacities and diffuse pleural thickening (sensitivity) and because their prevalence related to asbestos is less confounded by smoking (69, 101), other dust exposures (16, 95, 103), infections (56), trauma, etc. (specificity).

In towns, industrial areas, harbours, etc., plaques have been related primarily to occupational asbestos exposure. Therefore they are more frequent in men. Hillerdal found 2.2% of men in Uppsala above age 40 had radiologically visible pleural plaques (53) and confirmed occupational exposures by history in 80% (52), mainly in building, plumbing, automobile industry, electricians, insulators, and other professions using asbestos occasionally and in small amounts. The highest percentages were found at autopsy series performed in shipyard areas. In the Monfalcone area of

Italy, where there has been considerable employment in shipyards, pleural plaques were found in 70% of men and 23% of women at autopsy. In women plaques were mainly associated with a history of domestic exposure to asbestos (9). In the vicinity of shipyards and other asbestos industries plaques and mesothelioma (see under "Plaques and Cancer," p. 258) have also been related to neighborhood exposures, but it proved to be difficult to separate them from occupational and household exposures (145).

In 1960 Kiviluoto (70) reported 77 cases of pleural plaques found in 35,000 routine chest x-rays in Finland. Thirty-five of 68 cases investigated were found to have had no occupational exposure to asbestos and a cluster of plaques (8% prevalence) was described for a farming population in eastern Finland, living on anthophyllite containing soil. Some of these farmers lived many kilometers away from anthophyllite mines. In consecutive studies (107), however, the prevalence of plaques was found to be higher in cities (52% of autopsies) than in the countryside (32% of autopsies). Radiographs of 8,000 Finns representative of the Finnish population aged 30 or over were classified according to the ILO 1980 scheme (150). The age-adjusted prevalences of pleural and parenchymal changes found in men and women by 2 radiologists is given in Table 8-4.

The different prevalences in men and women were related to working conditions and smoking habits. The high proportion of small opacities and diffuse pleural thickening could be an indication that occupational exposure to asbestos played an important role in Finland and that part of the increase in pleural plaques related to environmental exposure could be due to occupation, too, especially in men. The higher percentage of plaques reported for Finnish immigrants to Sweden compared to (occupationally exposed) Swedish residents might also be due to different types of occupational and paraoccupational exposure. There was, however, a disproportionally high number of 17

Table 8-4 Percentages of Pleural and Parenchymal Abnormalities Found in the Finnish Population >30 Years of Age

	Men	Women
Pleural plaques	10.2	2.6
Pleural calcifications	6.6	2.3
Diffuse pleural thickening	13.8	3.2
Small opacities ≥ 1/1	16.5	10.0

Finnish-born women among 42 female cases with pleural plaques, for whom occupational exposures could be excluded by interview (54).

In Bulgaria (151) and Austria (95) endemic pleural plaques in the vicinity of anthophyllite and tremolite mines and deposits have been related to non-occupational exposures of farmers from natural erosion of an asbestos-containing soil and the dust formation during its cultivation (18, 19, 89). Considering the participation rates of men and women in the screening examinations, the percentage of plaques in females was considerably higher than in the Finnish population, and occupational exposures to asbestos and other minerals of possible relevance (like wollastonite found in Finnish limestone quarries) were excluded by personal interviews and consecutive investigations.

In Bulgaria a plaque prevalence of 3.3% was found in areas with anthophyllite deposits, but less than 1% in tremolite and control areas (Table 8-5).

Burilkov related the endemic occurrence of pleural plaques in Bulgaria to anthophyllite and fibrous sepiolite (18, 19). Ginzburg et al. related a similar endemic occurrence in the Sowjet Union to a "small asbestos fiber" (44).

In Rechnitz, an Austrian agricultural town of 3,500 inhabitants living on tremolite-containing soil, x-ray screening revealed a prevalence of 5.3% definite and 4.7% unsure plaques in the adult population (mean age of participants, 58 years). This endemic occurrence of pleural plaques was verified by blind comparison of the miniature x-rays with controls from other areas screened and by consecutive examinations of persons with plaques with full-sized films (89, 95, 102). Tremolite was mined near the town until 1945, but only few cases recalled any occupational asbestos exposure at interview or were married to a former asbestos miner. Not the small, abandoned mine, covered by vegetation, but na-

Table 8-5 Pleural Plaques in Bulgaria (18)

Fiber	Villages, n	Persons with Plaques, % (Age >20)
Anthophyllite	32	3.29
Anthophyllite + tremolite	5	0.67
Tremolite	14	0.18
No asbestos	44	0.01

tural erosion and the work in the fields and vinyards were found responsible for present asbestos exposure to several thousands of fibers (>5 μm) per m^3 air (48, 83). Asbestos was also found in the dust of houses, and higher exposures have to be assumed before roads were covered with asphalt. Occasional higher exposures than from agricultural work have to be assumed when farmers built their own houses and wells. Childhood exposures could have resulted from playing with tremolite-containing sand. Because Neuberger found considerably lower frequencies of circumscribed pleural plaques in asbestos cement workers than in the general population of Rechnitz living on natural asbestos deposits, he related this endemic occurrence of plaques to the exposure since birth to a special fiber (short tremolite) and associated minerals (89, 95). Not only frequency of plaques in the adult population of Rechnitz but also their size and the number of plaques in the individual cases were extraordinary and they showed massive calcification with age (Fig. 8-2).

Recently endemic occurrences of pleural plaques and calcifications were reported for 4 villages in north-western Greece (26) with tremolite and other asbestos related fibers in the soil, and for 4 villages in north-eastern Corsica (10, 133) with tremolite and chrysotile deposits. In a hospital-based study patients with occupational exposure in the chrysotile mine in Corsica were excluded, and of 1,757 patients born in the eastern part 53 (3.7%) were found to have bilateral plaques, while from 264 patients born in the western part without asbestos deposits only 3 (1.2%) had such plaques (133). A significant difference of mean atmospheric asbestos concentrations between "plaque villages" and control villages could be proven for tremolite but not for chrysotile (10). Similar to the Rechnitz area in Austria, also in Corsica higher exposures than the recorded mean tremolite level of 24 ng/m^3 have to be taken into account in agricultural and building operations. In the past farmers in Corsica were reported to have made not only houses but also pottery with tremolite containing material, and the diversion of children living in villages close to a deposit of asbestos could have been to search for the largest fibers in order to make wicks and pottery (10).

Plaques have been reported also in other non-occupationally exposed persons living in the vicinity of asbestos factories (3, 28, 62, 89) in East and West Germany, Czechoslovakia, and England, but it is more difficult to separate neighborhood exposure in these studies from paraoccupational exposure. In Turkey 22.3% of adults from 4 villages on asbestos deposits (chrysotile and amphiboles) were found to have pleural calcification (60). Nearby

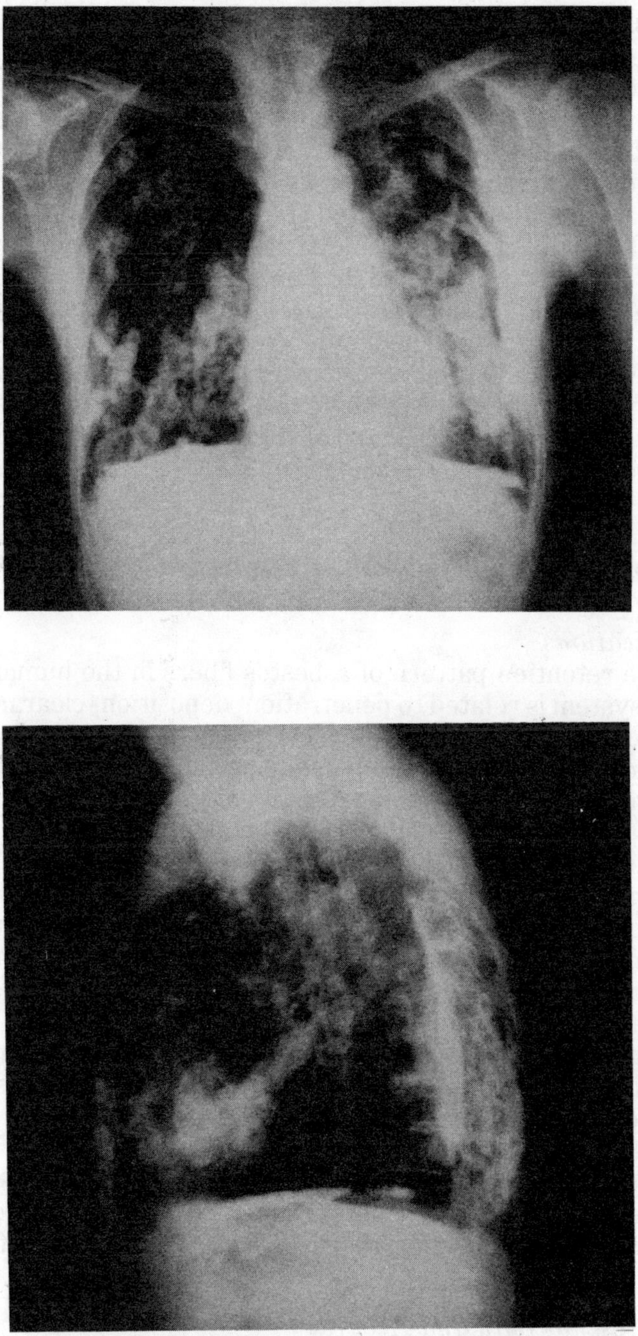

Fig. 8-2 X-rays of a woman from Rechnitz, Austria, with bilateral calcification both on the diaphragm and the costal pleura.

asbestos is mined for local use and for export on a small scale. Most of the exposure of the general population was to a short fibered tremolite used for making baby powder and to paint the walls and floors of the houses (147). From 2 villages on volcanic tuff, partially converted into long-fibered zeolites, 14.2% of adults were found to have pleural calcifications that have been described as "atypical" because they affected the visceral rather than the parietal pleura (5). Similar calcifications combined with blunted costophrenic angles and fissural thickening have been described from South Africa (131) and were related to a general population exposure to crocydolite. The amphibole crocydolite and the zeolite erionite are both long-fibered minerals that have been related to diffuse pleural thickening rather than to circumscribed plaques in the general population (60) and at the same time to mesothelioma (see under "Plaques and Cancer," p. 258).

4. Biological Assessment of Exposure

a. *Indications*

The retention pattern of asbestos fibers in the human respiratory system is related to penetration, deposition, clearance, and translocation (6). Occupational history and tissue analysis have to supplement each other in epidemiological research on the one hand and in decisions on compensation of occupational diseases on the other hand (35, 99, 116). Tissue analysis can reveal past exposures to fibers which have been persistent in the lung. They are most important for diseases related to cumulative dose. Time and length of exposure, however, cannot be derived from cumulated dose, and an occupational history is necessary for correct interpretation of results of tissue analysis, taking respiratory clearance and latency into account.

Light microscopy (LM) provides the most rapid examination method but is limited to diameters $>0.2\ \mu m$. Finer fibers can be identified by scanning electron microscopy (SEM) and transmission electron microscopy (TEM) aided by energy dispersive x-ray analysis (EDAX) and selective area electron difraction (SAED), but this requires time-consuming examinations and procedures of homogenization and preparation that may introduce artefacts.

b. *Representativity and Accuracy*

Both admission rates to hospitals and biopsy/autopsy-rates are influenced by diagnosis and exposure history. Unfortunately, errors due to Berkson' fallacy (97) were not quantified in any of the hospital-based studies reported in this chapter; and also in autopsy series, selection bias cannot be estimated from published results. Therefore generalizations of these results can only be made with great caution.

Accurate but expensive and time-consuming methods of exposure assessment can usually be applied to only small samples, which will be less representative. A small part of fibers in the lung is covered with a ferroprotein complex. They are called "ferruginous bodies" and "asbestos bodies" if asbestos fibers are coated. Asbestos bodies can mostly be found in the lungs of persons living in cities if their concentration is enriched by digestion techniques. After heavy occupational exposure, such as experienced by insulators, asbestos bodies will be found in all parts of the lung and in the sputum. After moderate exposure, however, biopsies can be false-negative and also small samples taken at surgery or autopsy may not reveal asbestos bodies in serial sections. Asbestos bodies also may not be revealed by digestion techniques (33), since asbestos concentration in lung is extremely inhomogenous (24) and only longer fibers are coated. Even after homogenization of whole lungs before digestion and application of statistical sampling strategies with estimation of asbestos body concentration by LM followed by counts of coated and uncoated fibers by SEM and TEM with EDAX and SAED for fiber identification, only crude estimates of asbestos concentrations can be given for the lung and the person in question (47, 83, 99).

c. *Results at Autopsy*

Neither asbestos fibers nor asbestos bodies are generally found in pleural plaques (84, 107). Some authors found both in digested hyaline pleura (37) and in calcified plaques (62, 77, 136), others reported that they are absent in the parietal pleura while they may be found in the visceral layer (77). When asbestos and other particles reach the pleural space, they are drained by the lymphatics of the parietal pleura (50), which could be important in the pathogenesis of plaques. For epidemiological purposes, however, the measurement of asbestos in the lung tissue of persons with plaques (82) proved to be more successful.

In an autopsy series Churg (22) found a median of 1,700 asbestos bodies per gram of wet lung in 29 cases with pleural plaques, compared to a median of 42 asbestos bodies in 25 normal lungs. The total number of fibers, chrysotile, and noncommercial amphiboles was not different; but persons with plaques had a median of 50,000 high-aspect ratio amphibole fibers, while in normal lungs only a median of 1,000 such fibers was found. The author concluded that about one-half of the patients with plaques had developed plaques from asbestos exposure. Amosite and crocydolite were found to be most abundant (22, 143). An increase of asbestos bodies in persons with plaques was also reported from other autopsy series (2, 142, 143), and an association between factors related to the fiber coating and to the pleural plaque formation has been discussed (2). Roggli et al. (118) described asbestos bodies as the hallmark of asbestos exposure, with the number of bodies highest in asbestosis, intermediate in mesothelioma, and lowest in parietal pleural plaques. In 48 patients with plaques, but without asbestosis or mesothelioma, LM revealed a median of 110 asbestos bodies (well above the author's upper normal value of 20 asbestos bodies) and SEM revealed a median of 1,700 asbestos bodies per gram wet lung. Total uncoated fibers were much less easily discriminated because of their shorter length and partly chrysotile nature. Stephens et al. (35) note that there may be a continuum between visceral plaques and diffuse pleural fibrosis and report on mineral fiber counts (crocydolite, amosite, mullite) in diffuse pleural fibrosis falling between those found with plaques and those with lung fibrosis.

In persons reported to mesothelioma registers, a correlation between asbestos bodies in the lung and pleural plaques at autopsy was found (85). Figure 8-3 shows such granular hyaline plaques at the diaphragm of a 71-year-old insulator who died of pleural mesothelioma. In cases of mesothelioma, longer- and higher-aspect ratio amosite fibers were found in the peripheral (subpleural) lung tissue of the upper lobe and in the central part of the lower lobe (24).

Of persons who resided in or near a Canadian chrysotile mining town and had never been employed in the chrysotile mining and milling themselves, 4 persons with plaques at autopsy were found to have an equal chrysotile content but had a fourfold elevation in median tremolite content compared to 9 persons from the same region without plaques (25). In Austria, in an area of endemic pleural plaques, the asbestos content of the lungs ranged from several thousand fibers in persons with environmental exposure to more than a million fibers per mg ash in a person with former occupational exposure in the mine (99); 70%–100% of fibers found in the lungs after plasmaincineration could be classified as tremolite (by STEM, EDAX, and SAED) and laser microprobe mass analysis (LAMMA) supported the results. Figure 8-4 shows typical LAMMA spectra from these investigations (31). Taking a decrease in magnesium, calcium, and aluminium into account, the

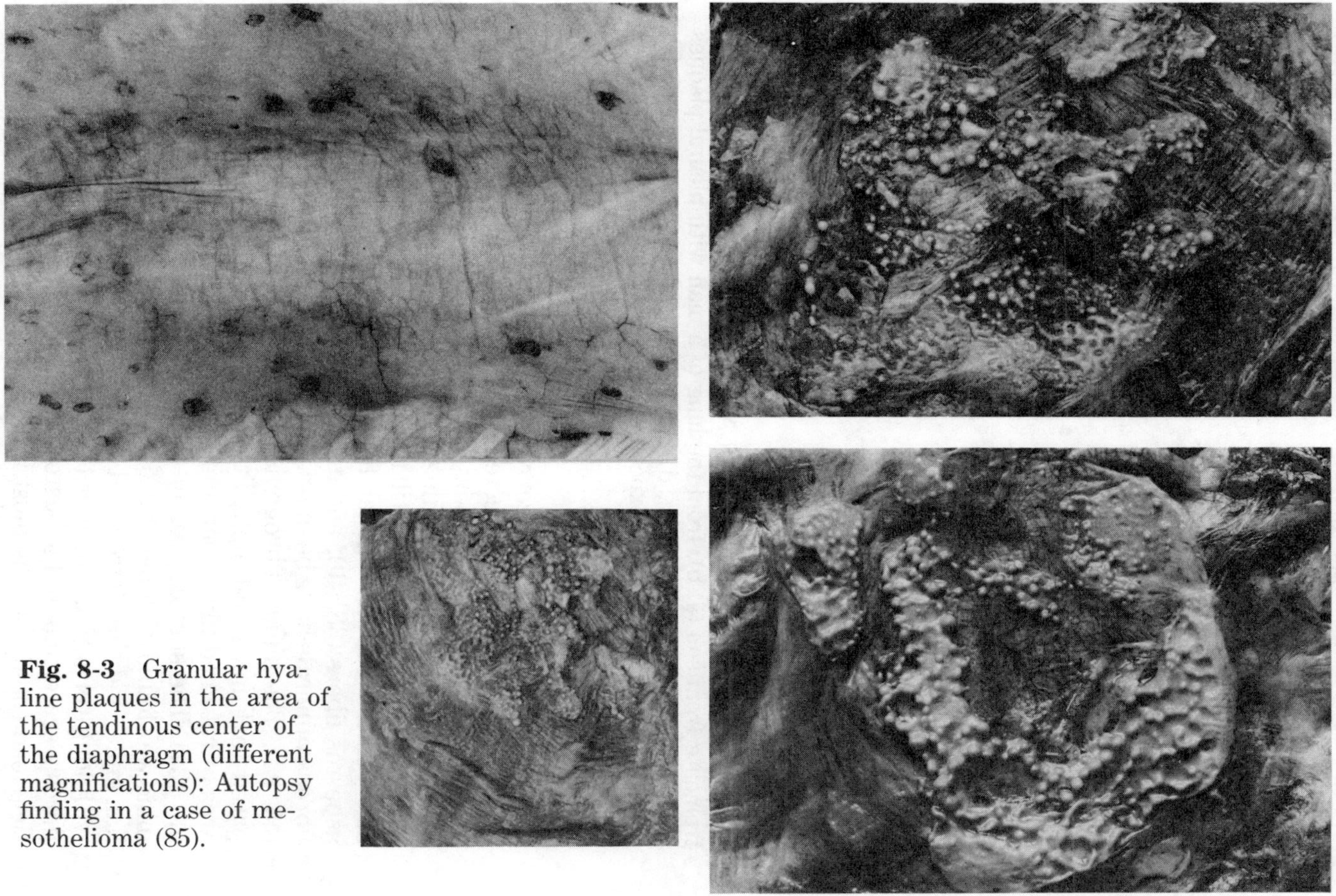

Fig. 8-3 Granular hyaline plaques in the area of the tendinous center of the diaphragm (different magnifications): Autopsy finding in a case of mesothelioma (85).

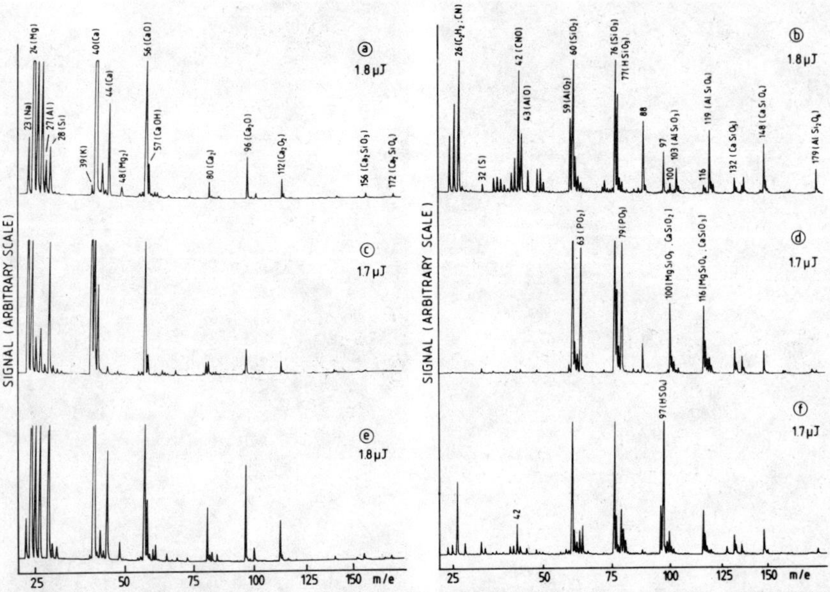

Fig. 8-4 Positive and negative LAMMA spectra (left and right) of tremolite from soil (a, b), from the lung of a man with pleural plaques from occupational exposure (c, d), and from the lung of a woman with plaques from environmental exposure (e, f) in Rechnitz, Austria.

three fingerprint spectra correspond closely, pointing to a common origin as was also detected by STEM (47).

Occasionally other fibers—e.g., titanium oxide (25, 99)—were also found in environmental cases of plaques, but the importance of these fibers is still uncertain (30). Animal experiments also related submesothelial fibrosis and mesothelioma to non-asbestos fibers (38, 40), and in epidemiological studies even non-fibrous minerals have been related to plaques, fibrosis, and cancer (45, 93). The higher fibrogenicity of Australian crocydolite compared to Finnish anthophyllite was related to the total surface area of retained fibers per unit weight of lung tissue (Timbrell et al., 137). The surface area of the average fiber from the Finnish mine was found 25 times that of the average fiber from the Australian mine, and the aggregated surface area of all mineral particles with long-term pulmonary retention showed closer relations to a fibrosis score than did asbestos or quartz. The total mineral particle load could play the most important role in lung cancer (105), with smoking influencing the total long-term retention of durable fibers and non-fibrous particles from all sources (23).

5. Clinical Relevance of Plaques

Clinically, plaques were described by Bohlig (13) as "harmless beauty mark[s]" since they were not considered to be precancerous lesions or considered to cause symptoms or loss of function. Numerous epidemiological studies tested this and the alternative hypothesis, mainly in persons with plaques from occupational and environmental asbestos exposure.

a. Plaques and Lung Function

From Finland (71) a reduction of vital capacity and diffusion capacity in 38 cases with plaques compared to 23 controls was reported. However, there were probably several cases with radiological signs of fibrosis included in this study (65). In Bulgaria no significant impairment of lung function could be found in 89 persons with plaques compared to persons without plaques from the same region, but vital capacity of all 632 persons from the area with endemic plaques was significantly lower than in 734 controls from another area (19), which, however, could also be due to other factors like a sub-roentgenologic fibrosis (66). In the Austrian area in which endemic plaques were found, lung function screening (including flow-volume-curves and resistance) revealed no significant impairment in persons with plaques compared to controls from the same region matched for sex, age, and smoking (102). Examinations of the decline in lung function with age among 302 persons examined showed a larger decrease of vital capacity and expiratory flow rates than predicted by reference values. This subnormal pulmonary function observed in older persons in Rechnitz could represent subclinical pathology including small-airway dysfunction from environmental asbestos exposure but may also reflect the underrepresentation of older persons in the studies from which lung function reference-values have been derived (98, 102).

Small-airway dysfunction was also found in non-smoking asbestos workers (125). Lung function impairment from smoking proved to be such an important confounder (116) that studies without appropriate smoking histories cannot prove lung function impairment related to asbestos or pleural plaques, especially if the decrements found are only small (7). Both restrictive and obstructive lung function impairments have been found in asbestos workers with normal x-ray, and it is still uncertain whether the lung function impairments found in several groups of asbestos workers with pleural plaques are due to heavier exposure to asbestos (65). In former asbestos-cement workers no significant correlations between pleural plaques and ventilatory function were found after adjustment for exposure (108). Gaensler et al. studied 385 persons with plaques who had worked in shipyards, papermills, and an asbestos plant for 8–22 years (42). Comparison with 100 unexposed men at preemployment examination and 223 asbestos workers without plaques showed that plaques by themselves had no perceptible effect on lung volumes and gas exchange (Table 8-6) and that neither their extent nor their degree of calcification was related to lung function.

This result was due to the careful exclusion of all persons with diffuse pleural thickening (from asbestosis, benign asbestos effusions, other effusions, or fat) by oblique films and sometimes CT. Diffuse pleural thickening, unlike plaques, caused a significant loss of lung function and, unlike plaques, this loss was strongly related to extent and thickness, with bilateral cases most markedly impaired (Fig. 8-5).

In summary, lung function impairment by low-level asbestos exposure may be observed in persons with normal x-rays as well as in persons with plaques. Though plaques can be a sign of asbestos exposure, they are not related to a decrease in lung function if they are not combined with diffuse pleural thickening or lung fibrosis. This is true also for extensive calcified plaques (Fig. 8-2) if they involve only the parietal pleura, do not cause adhesive pleuritis, and are patchy and interrupted structures that do not interfere with thoracic motion (14, 42, 102).

b. Plaques and Cancer

Extrapolations of pleural changes and cancer risk in asbestos workers to pleural changes and cancer risk in the general population (117) have been misleading because differences in specificity of pleural changes, etc., have not been taken into account. Distributions of risk factors (asbestos and other), exposures (fiber

Table 8-6 Mean Values (% Predicted) for Forced Vital Capacity (FVC) and Diffusing Capacity (DL)

Group	FVC	DL	Smokers
100 normal males, age >40 years	96	94	72
223 asbestos exposed >15 years, no plaques	96	98	76
255 asbestos exposed, plaques, asbestosis 0	95	97	74
86 asbestos exposed, plaques, asbestosis 1	82	77	79
28 asbestos exposed, plaques, asbestosis 2	60	58	82
16 asbestos exposed, plaques, asbestosis 3	55	40	83

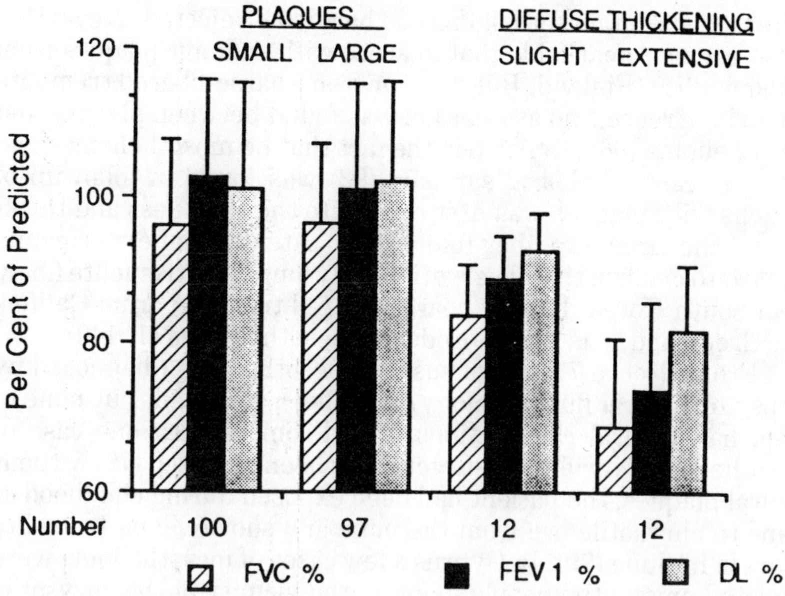

Fig. 8-5 Lung function in asbestos workers with plaques and diffuse thickening (42). Forced vital capacity (FVC) forced expiratory volume in one second (FEV_1) and diffusing capacity (DL).

types, age at first exposure), and type of pleural changes (circumscribed and diffuse) are so different in working and general population that reliable cancer risk estimations can only be derived from observations on the population involved.

In Austria, in the area where persons showing endemic pleural plaques from environmental asbestos exposure (89, 95) were found, lung cancer mortality was compared with national, provincial, and local rates and proved to be lower than expected. Even after adjustments for community size, agricultural index, and smoking habits from microcensus results, no significant lung cancer excess could be found (100). From the power of the study, however, only a relative lung cancer risk ≥2.04 can be excluded. In Canada a relative lung cancer risk >1.4 was excluded for the population of the chrysotile-mining area (145) and the excess in men could be attributed to occupational exposure (130). Power considerations lead to the conclusion that increased risk of mesothelioma can only be detected in areas with endemic plaques if large groups at risk are observed for very long periods or if the risk for mesothelioma in persons with plaques is extremely high. Therefore the hypothesis that plaques indicate populations with increased risk of mesothelioma can hardly be rejected. Nevertheless it seems remarkable that in areas with endemic plaques from anthophyllite (Finland, Bulgaria) or from coarse-fibered tremolite (Austria, Greece), no association was found between plaques and mesothelioma (96). In Austria the fact that no mesotheliomas and only one case of pleural sarcoma (92) was found in followup of persons with plaques was first related to the shortness and thickness of the tremolite fiber found (89). Later animal experiments seemed to confirm this observation: only long, thin tremolite fibers from South Korea, but not coarse-fibered tremolite from California, Greenland, and Italy, produced mesotheliomas (1, 140).

From Greece 7 cases of suspect mesothelioma (diagnosed by biopsy or pleural fluid cytology) have been reported, but none of them had pleural calcifications (27). From Corsica one case of mesothelioma (verified by surgery) has been reported (79) without pleural plaques; the patient had been exposed during childhood at home to chrysotile ore from the mine and showed long tremolite fibers in his lung (79). In Cyprus a few cases of mesothelioma were reported among the people living in the vicinity of the chrysotile mine and were associated with tremolite, some of which is fine-fibered. These people use the tremolite, which is separated from the chrysotile during the milling process (21), for stuccoing their houses (140). A similar situation exists in Turkey where in some areas tremolite and the very fine erionite used for stuccoing is associated with the incidence of pleural calcification, mesotheliomas, and bronchial cancers (60, 148). In the "asbestos villages" only a moderate increase in malignancies was found, but in the "erionite villages" the incidence of mesotheliomas was extremely high. Persons at high risk from cancer were found to develop calcification of the visceral rather than parietal pleura (5, 60). This "atypical" granular calcification affecting the pulmonary surface and leaving the bulk of the thickening and the parietal pleura uncalcified was found in 8 out of 10 cases from erionite villages, 3 of which were bilateral, and only in 3 out of 15 cases (all unilateral) from the asbestos villages where tremolite had been used for making baby powder and white washing the houses (60). No such pleural changes have been reported from Austria, Bulgaria, or Finland, where endemic circumscribed parietal plaques occurred without increase of cancer. Only in Turkey (Anatolia) and South Africa (northeast Cape Province) both mesothelioma and pleural plaques were raised and an association between the endemic pleural changes and mesothelioma was established (55, 131). Environmental exposures to crocydolite in South Africa and to erionite and other fibrous zeolites in Turkey have in common that both are exposures to very fine fibers (145) and that after inhalation, thin and rather long fibers will be persistent in the human lung for many years. Possibly certain types of tremolite such as found in South Korea could have similar effects. Plaques were also increased in areas with coarse-fibered tremolite, but this variety similar to amphibole cleavage fragments, seem to be not (or much less) carcinogenic (89, 140, 146), and the same applies to coarse anthophyllite, which has been reported to induce mesotheliomas in animals with the sarcomatous variant prevailing (74) but seems to be not (or much less) carcinogenic when inhaled by humans.

The clinical sign to indicate persons at risk of cancer is not the parietal plaque that develops slowly, probably from low-grade continous irritation, but the visceral and diffuse pleural thickening that can develop after acute pleurisy and benign effusion (41, 46, 76, 78, 81, 119). Three hundred and seventeen persons with pleural plaques from the endemic area of Finland showed costophrenic angle obliteration in only 4.7% (bilateral 0.9%), while the prevalence of sequelae of pleurisy was very much higher in persons with pleural plaques in Turkey (61), South Africa, and also in working populations with high risk of cancer (49, 78, 119, 127).

Early reports on associations between pleural plaques and cancer in asbestos workers (36) did not differentiate circumscribed and diffuse pleural thickening. In a nested case-control study Harber (49) found no association between pleural plaques and asbestos-associated malignancies that were independent of causative factors like duration of asbestos exposure, age, and cigarette smoking. Although occupational asbestos exposure can cause plaques and can also cause cancer, plaques per se are not causally related to subsequent cancer development, and any association between plaques and cancer is spurious, being a consequence of their associations with asbestos exposure. If workers are known to have had significant exposure, it appears unwise not to include them in cancer prevention and detection programs (94, 101) because plaques are not detected. On the other hand even asbestos workers with a history of only moderate exposure should be included in such programs if they show diffuse pleural thickening or lung fibrosis because these clinical signs indicate higher exposures and cancer risk. Careful exposure histories, however, should be taken in persons with only circumscribed plaques and if positive, these persons should be screened if they develop other pleural and parenchymal changes in the course of time (53) because hyaline plaques as revealed by CT-scan can also be the first sign of an exposure that later might lead to diffuse pleural thickening, lung fibrosis, and cancer, if it had been heavy. Unfortunately secondary prevention by screening for early lung cancer has not been very successful up to now, and chances for cure in cases of mesothelioma are even poorer (89). General population screening for plaques, however, can reveal occupational, paraoccupational, and environmental asbestos exposure (14, 28, 52, 145), which is important for primary cancer prevention because these exposures can only be reduced or eliminated when recognized.

For surveillance of working populations the screening for plaques is less important, but some unknown exposures like the tremolite contamination of talcum have been detected this way. Lung cancer risk in asbestos workers is determined by fiber-type, cumulative fiber dose, and cumulative tar dose from smoking (145). Both cumulative doses have little effect on the incidence of pleural plaques. In asbestos-cement production an increase of lung cancer risk was found with increasing profusion of small opacities, but no lung cancer excess showed up in persons with only plaques (63). A cohort study in the oldest asbestos-cement factory showed the predominant influence of smoking on lung cancer and associated increased risk with cumulative fiber doses, which also can cause lung fibrosis (104, 106). In the asbestos textile industry (using longer fibers) lung cancer risk was found to be higher than in the production of asbestos cement, brake lining, and friction products, and the highest risk was found in insulators using amosite and crocydolite (93). Here again the clinical sign to indicate persons at risk from cancer was lung fibrosis and diffuse pleural thickening (41, 81, 78, 126). Plaques are not related to increased risk of lung cancer unless they are combined with lung fibrosis and/or diffuse pleural thickening.

Amphibole doses too low to cause asbestosis or lung cancer can cause mesothelioma and plaques. Both mesothelioma and plaques were found to be more closely related to time since first exposure than to cumulative dose. Current regulations of fiber concentration at work places are expected to eliminate not only the risk of lung cancer but also the risk of mesothelioma if pure chrysotile is used or if tremolite impurities have been removed by milling (21, 93). Studies available so far on persons exclusively exposed to pure chrysotile indicate that mesotheliomas occur—if at all—only at high exposures. In amphibole exposure, however, the relative risk for mesothelioma is much higher and even small amounts of crocidolite used in the production of asbestos cement (104) or brake linings (8) led to mesotheliomas in these cohorts as had been shown by nested case-control studies. The exposure to crocydolite, amosite, or long-fibered tremolite can be so low in cases of mesothelioma that lung fibrosis and diffuse pleural thickening cannot be detected on x-ray. Lilis et al. (1987) found 20% of pleural and 12% of peritoneal mesotheliomas in insulators without radiologically detectable fibrosis of lung or pleura (78). In persons with low-level exposure, however, mesothelioma is a very rare event, and it is still uncertain whether it develops more frequently in those who also develop plaques.

Pleural mesotheliomas have been found also in persons without asbestos exposure (89, 91), sometimes after chronic irritations of the pleura (recurrent pleurisy, empyema, callosity, pneumothorax treatment, recurrent inflammations after shell fragment injuries, etc.), but pleural plaques per se do not seem to increase the risk for this tumor (119). The hypothesis that mesotheliomas develop from pleural plaques (144) could not be proven and the coincidence of plaques and pleural mesothelioma seems to be the result of parallel developments. In the general population both pleural plaques and mesothelioma are indicative of exposure to asbestos, and they can signal even low-level exposures to amphiboles such as domestic or neighborhood exposures around shipyards because childhood exposures are decisive when age at first exposure is more important than dose. Nevertheless an association between plaques and mesothelioma is difficult to prove in the general population because both are very rare events and cause no specific reaction to asbestos: Population-based case-control studies showed considerable proportions of non-asbestos-related mesotheliomas (75, 90); pleural plaques also were relatively abundant in areas where tuberculosis and other infectious diseases have been frequent in the past (87). Endemic plaques from environmental exposure to anthophyllite or coarse-fibered tremolite could not be associated with increased risk of malignant neoplasms, while endemic plaques from fine-fibered asbestos, such as crocydolite in South Africa, and from fine-fibered zeolites in Turkey are certainly associated with the risk of mesothelioma. This could be an indication that respirable and durable fibers can cause plaques but are less likely to cause mesothelioma if short and thick than if long and thin. It is possible, however, that completely different mineralogic parameters and surface characteristics of fibers are responsible for asbestos-induced mesotheliomas on the one hand and asbestos-induced pleural plaques on the other hand.

For general population screening it can be concluded that circumscribed plaques can only be indicative of past asbestos exposure but not for risk of malignant neoplasms. The diagnosis of plaques, however, can help to discover a history of asbestos exposure, interpret other less specific signs of asbestos exposure in the individual case, or detect other less sensitive signs at an earlier stage, and then relate the combination of these signs (in particular diffuse fibrosis of lung and pleural) to cancer risk.

D. SUMMARY

Pleural plaques are an important radiological sign of past asbestos exposure, which can be more sensitive and more specific than radiological signs of diffuse pleural thickening and pulmonary fibrosis. If asbestos exposure was early in life, even low levels can produce plaques that are easily detectable when they calcify with increasing age. A radiological screening for plaques, which seems feasible in populations with an expected prevalence of more than 1%, can help to discover occupational, para-occupational, and even environmental asbestos exposures such as from natural anthophyllite or tremolite deposits. Plaques seem to be of less importance for the surveillance of working populations, with higher age at onset of exposure, to mainly chrysotile and usually younger age at end of observation than the general population. Computer tomography could enable earlier diagnosis of plaques; however, this will only have preventive consequences because in the individual case other possible causes of plaques have to be considered, and without concommitant diffuse pleural thickening or parenchymal changes (lung fibrosis) no impairment of lung function was found.

In contrast to persons with diffuse pleural thickening or parenchymal changes no increase of cancer risk was detected in persons with only pleural plaques. Plaques are certainly no precancerosis but could be associated with mesothelioma from amphibole exposures. Such an association can hardly be proven by epdemiological methods because plaques from low-level asbestos exposure and mesothelioma are both rare events and they are not a specific reaction to asbestos. Possibly different mineralogic parameters are responsible for asbestos-induced mesotheliomas on the one hand and asbestos-induced pleural plaques on the other hand.

ACKNOWLEDGEMENTS

The author thanks Prof. Dr. M. Haider (Director of the Institute of Environmental Hygiene, Vienna), Dr. A. Raber (Austrian worker's compensation board), and Dr. P. Gross for their contributions to this work. He gratefully received valuable comments and data by Dr. H. Bohlig (Dormagen-Zons), Prof. Dr. E. A. Gaensler (Boston) and Prof. Dr. K. M. Müller (Bochum).

REFERENCES

1. Addison, J. (1988): Mesothelioma production by tremolite asbestos from Korea as compared to non-asbestiform tremolite from Italy. In: Abstracts of Communications, VIIth International Pneumoconiose Conference, August 23–26, Pittsburgh, p. 202.
2. Andrion, A., Bellis, D., Bertoldo, E., Mollo, F. (1984): Coated and uncoated lung mineral fibres in subjects with and without pleural plaques at autopsy. Pathol. Res. Pract. 178(6), 611–616.
3. Anspach, M. (1962): Sind Pleuraverkalkungen pathognomonisch für eine Asbestose? Int. Archiv. f. Gewerbepathologie und Gewerbehygiene, 19, 108–120.
4. Anspach, M. (1965): Zur Ätiologie von Pleuraverkalkungen. Radiol. Diagn. 6, 341.
5. Baris, Y., Artvinli, M., Sahin, A.A. (1979): Environmental mesothelioma in Turkey. Ann. N.Y. Acad. Sci., 330, 423–432.
6. Becklake, M.R., (1983): Clin. and Invest. Medicine, 6, 305.
7. Becklake, M.R., Gournier-Massey, G., McDonald, J.C., Sieiatycki, J., Rossiter, C.E. (1970): Lung function in relation to chest radiographic changes in Quebec asbestos workers. I. Methods, results and conclusions. Bull. Physiopath. Resp. 6, 637–659.
8. Berry, G., Newhouse, M.L. (1983): Mortality of workers manufacturing friction material using asbestos. Br. J. Ind. Med. 40, 1–7.
9. Bianchi, C., Brollo, A., Ramani, L. (1988): Hyalin Pleural Plaques and Asbestos Exposure. In: Abstracts of Communications, VIIth International Pneumoconiose Conference, August 23–26, Pittsburgh, p. 105.
10. Billon-Galland, M.A., Dufour, G., Gaudichet, A., Boutin, C., Viallat, J.R. (1988): Environmental Airborne Asbestos Pollution and Pleural Plaques in Corsica. Ann. Occup. Hyg. Vol. 32, Suppl. 1., 497–504.
11. Bohlig, H. (1980): Lung an Pleura, Georg Thieme Verlag Stuttgart, New York.
12. Bohlig, H. (1983): Interbeurteiler-Variation bei arbeitsmedizinischen Vorsorgeuntersuchungen von Asbestarbeitern in der Bundesrepublik Deutschland. In: Bergbau-Berufsgenossenschaft. Hrsg.: VI International pneumoconiosis conference. Bochum.

13. Bohlig, H., Dalquen, P., Hain, E. (1972): Epidemiologie asbestbedingter Gesundheitschäden. Der Internist 13, 318–325.
14. Bohlig, H., Otto, H. (1975): Asbest und Mesothelion. Arbeit und Gesundheit. In: Med. Schriftenreihe des BM für Arbeit und Sozialordnung, Hrsg.: Goetz, E., Wagner, R., Heft 89, Georg Thieme Verlag, Stuttgart.
15. Bohlig, H., Calavrezos, A. (1987): Development, radiological zone patterns, and importance of diffuse pleural thickening in relation to occupational exposure to asbestos. Br. J. Ind. Med. 44 (10), 673–681.
16. Bohlig, H., Otto, H. (1989): Die pleuralen Röntgenzeichen der Pneumokoniosen. In: Handbuch der medizinischen Radiologie. Vo. IX/5b, Springer, Berlin, 153–200.
17. Boutin, C., Vaillat, J.R., Steinbauer, J., Massey, D.G., Charpin, D., Mouries, J.C. (1986): Bilateral Pleural Plaques in Corsica: A non-occupational Asbestos Exposure Marker, Eur. J. Respir. Dis., 69.
18. Burilkov, T. (1971): Epidemiologie und Ätiologie der endemischen Pleura-Plaques in Bulgarien. 4. Internat. Pneumokoniose Konferenz, Bukarest, Apimondia Publ. House, 280–282.
19. Burilkov, T. (1985): Zur Kausalität von Pleura-Plaques und asbestinduzierten Tumoren. Wissenschaft und Umwelt 2, 146–148.
20. Burilkov, T., Krusteva, R. (1983): Ultrazvukova diagnostika na plevralnite izmeneniia pri azbestoza (Ultrasonic diagnosis of pleura changes in asbestosis). Vutr Boles, 22 (5), 90–93.
21. Churg, A. (1988): Chrysotile, Tremolite, and Malignant Mesothelioma in Man. Chest 93, 3, 621–628.
22. Churg, A. (1982): Asbestos Fibers and Pleural Plaques in a General Autopsy Population. Am. J. of Pathology, 109(1), 88–96.
23. Churg, A., Wiggs, B. (1985): Mineral Particles, Mineral Fibers and Lung Cancer. Env. Res. 37, 364–372.
24. Churg, A., Wiggs, B. (1987): Accumulation of Long Asbestos Fibers in the Peripheral Upper Lobe in Cases of Malignant Mesothelioma. Am. J. of Ind. Medicine, v. 11, no. 5, 563–569.
25. Churg, A., DePaoli, L. (1988): Environmental pleural plaques in residents of Quebec chrysotile mining town. Chest, 94(1), 58–60.
26. Constantopoulus, S.H., Goudevenos, J.A., Saratzis, N., Langer, A.M., Selikoff, I.J., Moutsopoulos, H.M. (1985): Pleural calcification and restrictive lung function in Northwestern Greece. Environmental exposure to mineral fiber as etiology. Environ. Res. 38, 319–331.
27. Constantopoulos, St., Malamou-Mitsi, V., Goudevenos, J., Papathanasiou, M., Pavlidis, N., Papadimitriou, C. (1987): High Incidence of Malignant Pleural Mesothelioma in Neighbouring Villages of Northwestern Greece. Respiration 51, 266–271.
28. Dalquen, P., Hinz, I., Dabbert, A.F. (1970): Pleuraplaques, Asbestose und Asbestexposition, eine epidemiologische Studie aus dem Hamburger Raum. Pneumonologie 143, 547–558.

29. Davis, J.M.G. (1972): The fibrinogenic effects of mineral dusts injected into the pleural cavity of mice. Br. J. Exp. Pathol. 53, 190–201.
30. Davis, J.M.G., Jones, A.D. (1988): Experimental studies in rats on the effects of asbestos inhalation coupled with the inhalation of titanium dioxide. In: Abstracts of Communications, VIIth International Pneumoconiose Conference, August 23–26, Pittsburgh, p. 13.
31. De Waele, J.K., Adams, F.C., Vermeire, P.A., Neuberger, M. (1986): Laser Microbe mass analysis for the identification of asbestos fibers in lung tissue and broncho-alveolar-washing fluid. Microchimia Acta, 3, 197–213.
32. Delclos, G.L., Wilson, R.K., Bradley, B.L. (1988): Interobserver Variability using the ILO (1980) Classification in Asbestos-Exposed Subjects Referred for Compensation Evaluation. In: Abstracts of Communications, VIIth International Pneumoconiose Conference, August 23–26, Pittsburgh, p. 110.
33. Dodson, R.F., Williams, M.G., O'Sullivan, M.F., Corn, C.J., Greenberg, S.D., Hurst, G.A. (1985): A Comparison of the Ferruginous Body and Uncoated Fiber Content in the Lungs of Former Asbestos Workers. Am. Rev. of Resp. Disease 132(1), 143–147.
34. Dongay, G., Levade, M., Lauque, D., Carles, P., Bollinelli, R. (1985): Tomodensitometrie de la pathologie pleuropulmonaire de l'amiante. (Computerized Tomography of pleuropulmonary pathology due to asbestos). Rev. Mal. Respir. 2 (1), 31–36.
35. Eitner, F., Otto, H. (1984): Zur Dignität von Asbestkörperzählungen im Lungengewebe. Sonderdruck aus Arbeitsmedizin Präventivmedizin. 19. Jg. Heft 1, Jan. 1984, 1–5.
36. Fletcher, D.E. (1972): A mortality study of shipyard workers with pleural plaques. Brit. J. Industr. Med. 29, 142.
37. Fondimare, A., Desorbes, J., Perrotey, J. (1976): Teneur des tissus en amiante et pathologie pleuro-pulmonaire. Ouest M-d. 29, 593.
38. Friemann, J., Voss, B., Weller, W., Müller, K.M. (1987): Asbestos induced fibrosis in the omentum of rats. Virchows Arch. A. 411, 403–408.
39. Friedman, A.C., Fiel, S.B., Fisher, M.S., Radecki, P.D., Levtoaff, A.S., Caroline, D.F. (1988): Asbestos-related pleural disease and asbestosis: a comparison of CT and chest radiography. AJR, 150 (2), 269–275.
40. Friemann, J., Brinkmann, O., Pott, F., Müller, K.M. (1988): Peritoneale Differenzierungsstörungen als Reaktion auf Asbest- und Asbestersatzstoffe. Tierexperimentelle Untersuchungen. Verh. Dtsch. Ges. Path. 72, 312–316.
41. Gaensler, E.A., Kaplan, A.I. (1971): Asbestos Pleural Effusion. An. Int. Med. 74, 178–191.
42. Gaensler, E.A., Jederlinic, P.J., McLoud, T.C. (1988): Lung Function with asbestos-related Circumscribed Pleural Plaques.

In: Abstracts of Communications, VIIth International Pneumoconiose Conference, August 23–26, Pittsburgh, p. 70.

43. Gefter, W.B., Epstein, D.M., Miller, W.T. (1984): Radiographic Evaluation of Asbestos-related Chest Disorders. CRC Crit. Rev. Diagn. Imaging, 21 (2), 133–181.
44. Ginzburg, E.A., Silova, M.V., Kornejefa, M.J., Levtonova, E.V., Sergeiev, A.M., Romanov, V.M., Folonenko, M.S., Ivanova, E.S., Altynova, M.P., Tolgeskaja, M.S. (1973): Röntgenbild der nichtberufsbedingten Asbestose der Pleura. Rad. diagn. 3, 307–312.
45. Goldsmith, D.F., Winn, D.M., Shy, C.M. (eds.) (1986): Silica, silicosis and cancer. Cancer research monographs, Vol. 2, Praeger, Philadelphia.
46. Grant, D.C., Seltzer, S.E., Antman, K.H., Finberg, H.J., Koster, K. (1983): Computered tomography of malignant pleural mesothelioma. J. Comput. Assist. Tomogr. 7(4), 626–632.
47. Grasserbauer, M., Neuberger, M., Müller, H.W., Schwaighofer, B. (1984): Quantitative studies on asbestos pollution with a combination of light and electron microscopy. Fresenius Z. Anal. Chem. 317, 293–299.
48. Haider, M., Neuberger, M. (1981): Pleuraplaques und Asbestexposition. In: Umweltbelastung durch Asbest. Beiträge des Bundesministeriums für Gesundheit und Umweltschutz 2, 1–66.
49. Harber, Ph. (1987): Pleural Plaques and Asbestos-associated Malignancy. J. Occup. Med., 29, 8, 641–644.
50. Hayek, Hv (1970): Die menschliche Lunge. Springer, Berlin, Heidelberg, New York.
51. Heine, F., Krickan, G. (1973): Verkalkte Pleuraplaques. Prax. Pneumol. 27, 11.
52. Hillerdal, G. (1980): Pleural Plaques. Occurrence, exposure to asbestos, and clinical importance. Acta Universitatis Upsaliensis. Uppsala.
53. Hillerdal, G. (1981): Non-malignant asbestos pleural disease. Thorax, 36, London, 669–675.
54. Hillerdal, G. (1983): Pleural Plaques in Sweden among immigrants from Finland—with an editorial note. Eur. J. Respir. Dis. 64 (5), 387–390.
55. Hillerdal, G. (1984): Pleural changes and exposure to fibrous minerals. Scand. J. Work. Environ. Health 10, 473–479.
56. Hillerdal, G. (1984): Asbestos related pleuropulmonary lesions and the erythrocyte sedimentation rate. Thorax 39(10), 752–758.
57. Hillerdal, G. (1985): Nonmalignant pleural disease related to asbestos exposure. Clin. Chest Med. 6(1), 141–152.
58. Hillerdal, G. (1988): A Proposal for Revision and Similification of the ILO classification of Pleural and Pleuro-Parenchymal Lesions. In: Abstracts of Communications, VIIth International Pneumoconiose Conference, August 23–26, Pittsburgh, p. 199.
59. Hillerdal, G., Lindgren, A. (1980): Pleural plaques: correlation of

occurrence at autopsy to radiographic findings and occupational history. Eur. J. Respir. Dis 61, 315–318.
60. Hillerdal, G., Baris, Y. (1983): Radiological study of pleural changes in relation to mesothelioma in Turkey. Thorax 38, 443–448.
61. Hillerdal, G., Zitting, A., v. Assendelft, A.H., Kuusela, T. (1984): Rarity of mineral fibre pleurisy among persons exposed to Finnish anthophyllite and with low risk of mesothelioma. Thorax 39(8), 608–611.
62. Hourihane, D.O.'B., Lessor, L., Richardson, P.C. (1966): Hyaline and Calcified Pleural Plaques as an Index of Exposure to Asbestos. A Study of Radiological and Pathological Features of 100 Cases with a Consideration of Epidemiology. Brit. M.J., 1069–1074.
63. Hughes, J.M., Weill, H. (1988): Pulmonary Fibrosis as a Determinant of Asbestos-Induced Lung Cancer. In: Abstracts of Communications, VIIth International Pneumoconiose Conference, August 23–26, Pittsburgh, p. 39.
64. Gilson, J.C., Bohlig, H., Murray, R., Rossiter, C.E. (1988): International Labour Organization: ILO 1991, Classification of Radiographs of the Pneumoconioses. 1–12.
65. Jaervholm, B., Arvidsson, H., Bake, B., Hillerdal, G., Westrin, C.G. (1986): Pleural plaques—asbestos—ill-health. Eur. J. Respir. Dis. 145, Vol. 68, 1–59.
66. Jaervholm, B., Larsson, S. (1988): Do pleural plaques produce symptoms? A brief report. J. Occup. Med. 30 (4), 345–347.
67. Jones, J.S.P., Sheers, G. (1972): Biological Effects of Asbestos. In: Biological Effects of Mineral Fibers, IARC, Lyon, Paper 37.
68. Jones, R.N., Diem, J.E., Ziskand, M.M., Rodriquez, M., Weill, H. (1984): Radiographic evidence of asbestos effects in American marine engineers. J. Occup. Med. 26 (4), 281–284.
69. Kasuga, H., Mikami, R., Tamura, M., Miyazaki, R., Narita, N. (1987): Effects of smoking on Asbestos-related Pulmonary and Pleural changes. Jpn. J. Ind. Health 29, 191–195.
70. Kivilouto, R. (1960): Pleural calcification as a roentgonologic sign of non-occupational endemic autophyllite-asbestosis. Acta Radiol. Suppl. 194.
71. Kiviluoto, R. (1965): Pleural plaques and asbestos: further observations on endemic and other non-occupational asbestosis. Ann. N.Y. Acad. Sci. 132, 235–239.
72. Kiviluoto, R., Bohlig, H. (1964): Die Pleura. In: Die Staublungenerkrankungen und ihre Differentialdiagnose. Hrsg.: Bohlig, H., G. Thieme, Stuttgart, 261–267.
73. Kleinfeld, M., et al. (1973): A study of workers exposed to asbestiform minerals in commercial talc manufacture. Environ. Res. 6, 132.
74. Kolev, K. (1988): Morphology, Character and Features of Antophyllite-induced Mesotheliomas. In: Abstracts of Commu-

nications, VIIth International Pneumoconiose Conference, August 23–26, Pittsburgh, p. 1.
75. Konetzke, G., et al. (1982): Asbestos related medotheliomas—results of a retrospective study. OLO Occupational Safety and Health Series 46, 104.
76. Lange, H., Becher, H. (1978): Verkalkte Pleurahyalinose und malignes Pleuramesotheliom—Bedeutung und Konsequenzen des Nachweises pleuraler Spätkomplikationen nach Asbeststaubexposition. Dt. Gesh. Wesen 33, 27, 1275–1279.
77. Le Bouffant, L., et al. (1973): Stucture and composition of pleural plaques. In: Biological Effects of Asbestos. Ed: Bogovski P., et al. IARC Sci. Publ. No. 8, 249, IARC Lyon.
78. Lilis, R., Ribak, J., Suzuki, Y., Penner, L., Bernstein, N., Seilkoff, I.J. (1987): Non-malignant chest x-ray changes in patients with mesothelioma in a large chohrt of asbestos insulation workers. Br. J. Ind. Med. 44(6), 402–406.
79. Magee, F., Wright, J.L., Chan, N., Lawson, L., Churg, A. (1986): Malignant Mesothelioma Caused by Childhood Exposure to Long-Fiber Low Aspect Ratio Tremolite. Am. J. Ind. Med. 9, 529–533.
80. Marsova, D. (1964): Beitrag zur Ätiologie der Pleuraverkalkungen. Z. Tuberk. 121, 329.
81. McLoud, T.C., Woods, B.O., Carrington, C.B., Epler, G.R., Gaensler, E.A. (1985): Diffuse Pleural Thickening in an Asbestos Exposed Population: Prevalence and Etiologies. Am. J. Roentgen. 144, 9–18.
82. Meurmann, L.O. (1968): Pleural fibrocalcific plaques and asbestos exposure. Environ. Res. 2, 30.
83. Müller, H.W., Neuberger, M., Riedmüller, G., Schwaighofer, B. (1982): Mineralogische Untersuchungen an Stäuben in Zusammenhang mit endemischen Pleuraverkalkungen. Staub Reinh. Luft 42, 415–418.
84. Müller, K.M. (1983): Pleura. In: Spezielle pathologische Anatomie, Pathologie der Lunge. Bd. 16. Hrsg.: Doerr, W., Seifert, G., Springer Verlag, 1295–1398.
85. Müller, K.M. (1989): personal communication (Director of the Institute of Pathology, Berufsgenossenschaftliche Krankenanstalten Bergmannsheil, Universitätsklinik Bochum, BRD).
86. Navratil, M. (1970): Occurrence of pleural calcifications in workers exposed to asbestos dust. Studia Pneumologica et Phtiseologica Cechoslovaca 30, 48–54.
87. Navratil, M., Moravkova, K., Trippe, F. (1975): Study on the development of pleural hyalinosis in the population as compared to subjects exposed to asbestos dust (Czech). Casopis L-karu Cesk'ych 114 (46), 1433–1438.
88. Neef, W. (1963): Beidseitige Pleuraverkalkungen im Alter. Fortschr. Röntgenstr. 99, 632.
89. Neuberger, M. (1979): Epidemiological Contributions to Risk Evaluation. Facultas, Wien (English Translation, 2. Edition, Facultas, Vienna 1981).

90. Neuberger, M. (1984): Mesotheliome und Krebsrisiko durch Asbest in Österreich. In: Zur Beurteilung der Krebsgefahr durch Asbest. Hrsg.: Fischer, M., Meyer E., Bga Schriften, MMV Medizin Verlag München, S. 107–109.
91. Neuberger, M. (1986): Untersuchungen über Pleuramesotheliome in Österreich. In: Tagungsbericht der Österr. Ges. f. Lungenerkrankungen 1985. Hrsg.: Sighart, H., Klech, H., Hoffmann, Wien, 85–88.
92. Neuberger, M. (1986): Zur Epidemiologie von Plaques und malignen Mesotheliomen der Pleura in Osterreich. In: Staubbekämpfung und Staublungenerkrankungen, Internat. Symposium, Sliven, Bulgarien.
93. Neuberger, M. (1987): Zur gesundheitlichen Bewertung krebserzeugender Arbeitsstoffe. Sichere Arbeit 2, 12–18.
94. Neuberger, M. (1988): Möglichkeiten und Grenzen der Frühdiagnose von Berufskrankheiten in der Asbestindustrie. In: Gesundheitsbeeinträchtigungen und Arbeit. Hrsg.: Baumgartner, E., Maudrich, Wien, 128–132.
95. Neuberger, M., Gründorfer, W., Haider, M., Königshofer, R., Müller, H.W., Raber, A., Riedmüller, G., Schwaighofer, B. (1978): Umweltbedingte endemische Pleuraplaques. Zbl. Bakt. Hyg. I. Abt. Orig. B 167, 391–404.
96. Neuberger, M., Raber, A., Friedl, H.P. (1982): Epidemiologie asbestassoziierter Pleuraerkrankungen in Österreich. In: 16. Tagung d. Österr. Ges.f. Lungenerkrankungen, Hrsg.: Denck, H., Neumann, M., Hoffman, Wien, 127–129.
97. Neuberger, M., Raber, A. (1983): Unterschiedliche Selektionsraten—falsche Schlüsse bei epidemiologischen Untersuchungen. Zbl. Bakt. Hyg. Orig. 1B, 177, 539–561.
98. Neuberger, M., Ambrosch, P. (1984): Asbest, Pleuraplaques und Lungenfunktion. In: Arbeitstagung 1983. Arbeitsgemeinschaft für klin. Atemphysiologie, Hrsg.: Feldner, H., Schlick, W., Wr. Med. WoSchr., 134. Jg., Suppl. 80, 16–17.
99. Neuberger, M., Grasserbauer, M., Müller, H.W., Schwaighofer, B. (1984): Die Bedeutung der Lungenstaubanalyse im Feststellungsverfahren von Berufskrankheiten. In: Tagungsbericht d. 17. Tagung der Österr. Ges.f. Lungenerkrankungen und Tuberkulose. Hrsg.: Schindl, R., Neumann, M., Klech, H., Hoffmann, Wien, 49–51.
100. Neuberger, M., Kundi, M., Friedl, H.P. (1984): Environmental Asbestos Exposure and Cancer Mortality. Arch. of Env. Health, Vol. 39, No. 4, 261–265.
101. Neuberger, M., Ambrosch, P., Kundi, M. (1985): Prävention von Berufskrebs am Beispiel der Asbestzementindustrie. Zbl. Bakt. Hyg. I. Abt. Orig. B 181, 81–86.
102. Neuberger, M., Ambrosch, P. (1985): Lungenfunktionsuntersuchungen in einer Population mit endemischen Pleuraplaques und unweltbedingter Asbestexposition. Wr. Klin. WoSchr., 97. Jg., Heft 6, 289–293.

103. Neuberger, M., Sluka, F. (1985): Österreichischer Ringversuch zur Röntgen-Frühdiagnose der Asbestose. Arbeitsmed. Sozialmed. Präventivmed., 20. Jg., Heft 7, Gentner Verlag, 159–162.
104. Neuberger, M., Kundi, M., Friedl, H.P., Haider, M. (1988): Asbestos Exposure, Smoking and Lung Cancer—Results of a Cohort Study in the Asbestos Cement Industry. In: Abstracts of Communications, VIIth International Pneumoconiose Conference, August 23–26, Pittsburgh, p. 38.
105. Neuberger, M., Westphal, G., Bauer, P. (1988): Long-term effects of occupational dust exposure. Jpn. J. Ind. Health 30, 362–370.
106. Neuberger, M., Kundi, M. (1989): Zum Berufskrebsrisiko durch Asbest in Österreich. In: 2. Asbestkolloquium des Bundesgesundheitsamtes Berlin 1987, Hrsg.: Fischer, M., Meyer, E., BGA-Berichte, im Druck.
107. Nezrnabm K,I, (1966): Asbestos bodies and pleural plaques in a Finnish series of sutopsy cases. Acta Pathol. Mirociol. Scand., Suppl. 181.
108. Ohlson, C.G., Bodin, L., Rydman, T., Hogstedt, C. (1985): Ventilatory decrements in former asbestos cement workers: a four year follow up. Br. J. Ind. Med. 42, 612–616.
109. Ohyagi, S., Kagamimori, S., Toda, K. (1981): A Comparative Study of the prevalence of pleural thickening related with asbestos exposure. Jpn. J. Ind. Health 23, 366–376.
110. Ollino, P. (1955): Le reazioni pleuriche nel quadro radiologico dell asbestosi pulmonare. Arch. Sci. Med. 100, 403.
111. Otto, H. (1984): Erfahrungen mit dem Mesotheliomregister in Dortmund. In: Zur Beurteilung der Krebsgefahr durch Asbest. Hrsg.: Fischer, M., Mayer, E. BGA-Schriften 2/84, Medizin Verlag München, 94–101.
112. Parker, D.L., Bender, A.P., Williams, A.N., French, L.R., Hankinson, S. (1988): Public Health Implications of the Variability of the Interpretation of “B” Readings. In: Abstracts of Communications, VIIth International Pneumoconiose Conference, August 23–26, Pittsburgh, p. 18.
113. Raber, A. (1982): Die Formel von Bayes—ein Hilfsmittel bei der Planung epidemiologischer Untersuchungen. Sichere Arbeit, 24–26.
114. Rockoff, D., Kegan, E., Path, Ch., Schwartz, A., Kriebel, D., Hix, W., Rohatgi, P. (1987): Visceral pleural thickening in asbestos exposure: The occurrence and implications of thickened interlobar fissures. J. Thorac. Imag. 2 (4), 58–66.
115. Rockoff, S., Schwartz, A. (1988): Roentgenographic Underestimation of Early Asbestosis by International Labor Organization Classification. Chest 93, 1088–1091.
116. Rödelsperger, K., Woitowitz, H.J., Manke, J., Brückel, B., Giesen, T. (1985): Die postmortale Lungenstaubanalyse als beweismittel einer beruflichen Asbeststaubgefährdung. Zbl. Arbeitsmed. 35, 1, 10–17.

117. Rogan, W.J., Gladen, B.C., Ragan, N.B., Anderson, H.A. (1987): US prevalence of occupational pleura thickening. A look at chest X-rays from the first National Health and Nutrition Examination Survey. Am. J. Epidemiol. 126 (5), 893–900.
118. Roggli, V.L., Pratt, P.C., Brody, A.R. (1986): Asbestos content of lung tissue in asbestos associated disease: a study of 110 cases. Brit J. of Ind. Med. 43, 18–28.
119. Rom, W.N., Lockey, J.E. (1982): Diffuse malignant mesothelioma: A review. West. J. Med. 137/6, 548–554.
120. Rossiter, C.E. (1972): Initial repeatability trials of the UICC/Cincinnati classification of the radiograpchic appearance of pneumoconioses. Br. J. Ind. Med. 29, 407–419.
121. Rossiter, C.E., Browne, K., Gilson, J.C. (1988): International classification trial of AIA set of 100 radiographs of asbestos workers. Br. J. Ind. Med. 45, 538–543.
122. Rossiter, C.F., Gilson, J.C., Bohlig, H., Murray, R. (1988): The ILO 1980 International Classification of Radiographs of the Pneumoconioses: Proposal for Revision. In: Abstracts of Communications, VIIth International Pneumoconiose Conference, August 23–26, Pittsburgh, p. 198.
123. Rubino, G.F., Scansetti, G., Pira, E., Piolatto, G., Mollo, F., Andrino, A., Colomba, A., Bertasso, L. (1980): Pleural plaques and lung asbestos bodies in the general population: an autoptical and clinico-radiological survey. IARC Publ. 30, 545–551.
124. Sargent, E.N., Boswell, W.D., Ralls, W.P., Markovitz, A. (1984): Subpleural fat pads in patients exposed to asbestos: distinction from non-calcified pleural plaques. Radiology 152, 273–277.
125. Secker-Walker, R.H., Ho, J.E. (1982): Regional Lung Function in Asbestos Workers: Observation and Speculations. Respiration 43, 8–22.
126. Selikoff, J., Lee, H.K. (1978): Asbestos and Disease. Academic Press Inc., New York.
127. Selikoff, I.J., Seidman, H., Lilis, R., Lerman, Y. (1988): Predictive Significance of Lesser Degrees of Pleural Fibrosis. Prospective Study of 1,117 Asbestos Insulation Workers, January 1, 1963–January 1, 1988. Mortality Experience. In: Abstracts of Communications, VIIth International Pneumoconiose Conference, August 23–26, Pittsburgh, p. 71.
128. Sheers, G., Rossiter, C.E., Gilson, J.C., MacKenzie, A.F. (1978): UK naval dockyards asbestosis study: radiological methods in the surveillance of workers exposed to asbestos. Br. J. Ind. Med. 35, 195–203.
129. Sheers, G. (1979): Asbestos-associated disease in employees of Devonport dockyard. Ann. N.Y. Acad. Sci. 330, 281–287.
130. Siemiatychi, J. (1982): Mortality in the general population in asbestos mining areas. World Symposium on Asbestos, Session 5, Montreal, Canada.
131. Solomon, A., Sluis-Cremer, G.K., Goldstein, B. (1979): Visceral pleural plaque formation in asbestosis. Envir. Res. 19, 258–264.

132. Sparks, J.W. (1931): Pulmonary asbestosis. Radiology 17, 1249–1257.
133. Steinbauer, J., Boutin, C., Viallat, J.R., Dufour, G., Gaudichet, A., Massey, D.G., Charpin, D., Mouries, J.C. (1987): Plaques pleurales et environnement asbestosisque en Corse du Nord. Rev. Mal. Respir. 4(1), 23–27.
134. Stephanopoulos, C. (1962): Pleural calcification following dust exposure. Acta tuberc. scand. 42, 228.
135. Stephens, M., Gibbs, A.R., Pooley, F.D., Wagner, J.C. (1987): Asbestos induced diffuse pleural fibrosis: pathology and mineralogy. Thorax 42, 583–588.
136. Thomson, J.G. (1970): The pathogenesis of pleural plaques. Pneumoconiosis. Proc. Int. Conf., 3rd, 1969. Ed.: Shapiro, H.A., Oxford Univ. Press, Cape Town, 138.
137. Timbrell, V., Taikina-Aho, O., Paakko, P., Ashcroft, T., Meurman, L.O., Shilkin, K.B. (1988): Similarities in the Fibrogenicity of Asbestos Fibres and other Mineral Particles retained in Human Lungs. In: Abstracts of Communications, VIIth International Pneumoconiose Conference, August 23–26, Pittsburgh, p. 17.
138. Ulrich, P. (1971): Pathologische Anatomie der hyalinen Pleuraplatten. Pneumologie 146, 159.
139. Vinci, F., Falappa, P., Romano, C., Castellino, N. (1988): ILO international classification of radiographs of Pneumoconioses (1980): proposals for innovations. In: Abstracts of Communications, VIIth International Pneumoconiose Conference, August 23–26, Pittsburgh, p. 201.
140. Wagner, J.C., Chamberlain, M., Brown, R.C., Berry, G., Pooley, F.D., Davies, R., Griffiths, M. (1982): Biological Effects of Tremolite. Br. J. Cancer 45, 352–360.
141. Wain, S.L., Roggli, V.L., Foster, W.J. (1984): Parietal pleural plaques, asbestos bodies, and neoplasia. A clinical, pathologic, and roentgenographic correlation of 25 consecutive cases. Chest 86, 707–713.
142. Wain, S.L., Roggli, V.L., Foster, W.L. (1986): Parietal pleural plaques, asbestos bodies, and neoplasia. A clinical pathologic, and roentgenographic correlation of 25 consecutive cases. Chest 86/5, 707–713.
143. Warnock, M.L., Prescott, B.T., Kuwahara, Th. (1982): Numbers and Types of Asbestos Fibers in Subjects With Pleural Plaques. Am. J. Pathol. 109(1), 37–46.
144. Webster, I. (1977): Method by which mesothelioma can be diagnosed. Proc. Asbestos Symposium 8, Dpmt. of Mines, Joannesburg.
145. Who (1986): Asbestos and Other Natural Mineral Fibres. Environmental Health Criteria 53, World Health Organization, Geneva.
146. Wylie, A.G. (1988): Discriminating Amphibole Cleavage Fragments from Asbestos: Rationale and Methodology. In: Abstracts

of Communications, VIIth International Pneumoconiose Conference, August 23–26, Pittsburgh, p. 124.

147. Yazicioglu, S. (1976): Pleural Calcification Associated with Exposure to Chrysotile Asbestos in Southeast Turkey. Chest 70, 1, 43–47.

148. Yazicioglu, S., Ilcayto, R., Balci, K., Sayli, S., Yorulmaz, B. (1980): Pleural calcification, pleural mesotheliomas, and bronchial cancers caused by tremolite dust. Thorax, 35, 564–569.

149. Zaho Jinduo, Z., Zhong, L. (1988): Radiographical Appearance of Talcosis and Composition of Talc. In: Abstracts of Communications, VIIth International Pneumoconiose Conference, August 23–26, Pittsburgh, p. 47.

150. Zitting, A.J., Kuuselka, T., Impivaara, O., Maatela, J., Aromaa, A. (1988): Prevalence of radiographic small lung opacities and pleural abnormalities in a representative sample of adult Finns. In: Abstracts of Communications, VIIth International Pneumoconiose Conference, August 23–26, Pittsburgh, p. 99.

151. Zolov, C., Bourilkov, T., Babadjov, L. (1967): Pleural asbestosis in agricultural workers. Environ. Res. 1, 287.

9

Evaluation of Pulmonary Inflammatory Processes in Asbestos-Exposed Individuals

BRUCE W.S. ROBINSON, M.D.
ALISON H. ROSE, M.D.
ANTHONY HAYES, M.D.
RAYLEEN BOWMAN, M.D.
ANTHONY W. MUSK, M.D.

University of Western Australia
Nedlands, Australia

Synopsis

C. MEDIATOR PRODUCTION IN ASBESTOS-EXPOSED INDIVIDUALS
   1. Neutrophil Chemotactic Factor
   2. Gamma Interferon (IFN) Release

D. GALLIUM LUNG SCANNING

E. PULMONARY INFLAMMATION IN ASBESTOS-EXPOSED INDIVIDUALS WITH NORMAL CHEST RADIOGRAPHS

F. CONCLUSIONS

BIOGRAPHY

Dr. Bruce W. S. Robinson is a senior lecturer in the University Department of Medicine at the Queen Elizabeth II Medical Centre and a Consultant Respiratory Physician at the Sir Charles Gairdner Hospital. He is a pulmonary physician with a major research interest in asbestos-induced lung diseases, particularly asbestosis and malignant mesothelioma. He did postgraduate studies in the pulmonary branch of the National Institutes of Health and is currently working in the Queen Elizabeth II Medical Centre studying interstitial lung diseases and human pulmonary tumor immunology. Dr. Robinson may be contacted at the University Department of Medicine, Queen Elizabeth II Medical Centre (G Block), Nedlands, Perth 6009, Western Australia (telephone: 06-389-2098; telex: AA 93446).

Dr. Alison H. Rose is a research scientist in the Department of Respiratory Medicine at the Sir Charles Gairdner Hospital. She has a long-standing interest in the evaluation of inflammatory changes in the human lower respiratory tract utilizing bronchoalveolar lavage and assays of disordered cellular immunity.

Dr. Anthony Hayes is a pulmonary physician and physician in nuclear medicine. He has conducted a number of studies into neutrophil chemotaxis in asbestosis and gallium lung scan changes in asbestos-exposed individuals.

Dr. Rayleen Bowman is a pulmonary physician with an interest in mediator production in human interstitial lung diseases. She has conducted a number of studies of the potential role of the multifunctional cytokine tumour necrosis factor alpha in asbestosis.

Dr. Arthur W. Musk is a pulmonary physician with a long-standing interest in the epidemiology, radiology, clinical features and underlying mechanisms of occupational lung diseases.

EDITORS' COMMENTARY

Early detection of pulmonary inflammatory and immunological disorders, specifically associated with asbestos exposure, would be important, particularly if it were possible at some subclinical stage and prior to any detectable radiological manifestation of a disease process. Appropriate detection techniques could significantly improve early differential diagnoses and might suggest some treatment or control options. The following chapter provides important information on characteristic activated macrophage and elevated neutrophil counts identified by gallium uptake and bronchoalveolar lavage studies. The associated cellular immune events and chemical byproducts could provide both a better understanding of the underlying pathogenic processes and some objective signals or markers of destructive disease entities. Objective information is highly desirable in terms of screening efficiency, detection sensitivity, and accuracy; as well as item counts, rates, proportions, subpopulations, subtypes, and phases. The following chapter provides data and methodology holding great promise in terms of scientific discovery and utility in terms of public health applications.

A. INTRODUCTION

Inflammation is known to be present in many human interstitial lung diseases (1). Animal studies of asbestosis have demonstrated inflammation within the pulmonary tissue as well as in lavage samples (2). Histologic appearances of lung tissue in humans with asbestosis also demonstrate pulmonary inflammation (3). It is thought that in the lung, as in other organs, chronic

Accepted for publication on 9 February 1989.

inflammation leads to ongoing tissue damage and leads to a healing process with deposition of excessive amounts of collagen leading to scarring, i.e. pulmonary fibrosis (1)

One of the most sensitive ways of studying inflammatory processes within the human lower respiratory tract is by the use of a technique known as bronchoalveolar lavage (BAL). This is a simple and safe procedure that samples inflammatory cells in the lower respiratory tract (4). Differences in the number or type of inflammatory cells present as well as in their function have led to insights into the pathogenic mechanisms of a variety of diseases and have also provided useful information for clinical staging and therapeutic decisions (1).

In addition to changes in the respective proportions of different cell types, BAL provides an opportunity for assaying a variety of functions of recovered cells. This is largely achieved by culturing the BAL cells and measuring their ex-vivo production of cytokines and other mediators. These studies have provided insights into the pathogenesis of a variety of diseases (1, 5).

Gallium lung scanning is also used to evaluate pulmonary inflammation. Injected gallium is retained in the lung by activated cells, particularly macrophages and neutrophils, and the distribution and intensity of pulmonary gallium uptake, determined by gamma camera scanning 48 hours after injection, has proven useful as a marker of disease activity in a variety of clinical situations (1).

B. BAL PATTERNS IN ASBESTOSIS

1. Differential Cell Counts

BAL studies have been performed in small numbers of chrysotile-exposed individuals and have demonstrated increased BAL neutrophil counts (6, 7). We have studied the changes in both crocidolite- and chrysotile-exposed workers and have found similar changes with both types of asbestos (8). Most individuals with asbestosis have elevated BAL neutrophil proportions (Fig. 9-1), ranging from approximately 4%–17% using cytospin preparations. The majority of patients with asbestosis also exhibit modest increases in eosinophil proportions (1%–9%; Fig. 9-1). Occasionally patients also exhibit elevated lymphocyte proportions, but this represents only a minority of patients.

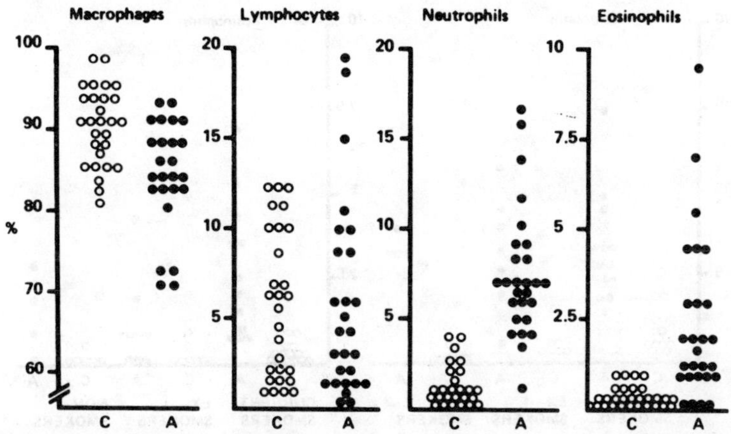

Fig. 9-1 Proportions of macrophages, lymphocytes, neutrophils, and eosinophils in bronchoalveolar lavage samples from 29 non-asbestos-exposed control subjects (C) and 27 individuals with pulmonary asbestosis (A). Cell counts were performed on May-Grunwald-Giemsa-stained cytospin preparations. Each point represents the proportion of that cell type expressed as a percentage of all recovered cells, excluding bronchial epithelial cells.

2. Relationship Between BAL Changes and Cigarette Smoking

Although cigarette smoking itself can induce a modest increase in BAL neutrophil proportions (up to 4%) our studies have shown that elevated BAL neutrophil proportions in asbestosis patients is not restricted to those who are current or ex-smokers (Fig. 9-2). Similar conclusions can be drawn from studies of eosinophil proportions in current, ex- and non-smokers (Fig. 9-2).

3. Airway versus Alveolar Inflammation in Asbestosis

The BAL technique that we utilize involves the initial installation of a 50 ml aliquot of normal saline that is then aspirated as the "airway" sample (9). The fluid recovered from the remaining five 50 ml aliquots represents the "alveolar" sample. Patients with asbestosis, like patients with other diffuse chronic inflammatory conditions of the lower respiratory tract such as cryptogenic fibrosing alveolitis/idiopathic pulmonary fibrosis and rheumatoid lung, exhibit higher proportions of neutrophils in the airway sample compared to the alveolar sample (Table 9-1). Lymphocyte and eosinophil proportions, however, are comparable in both airway

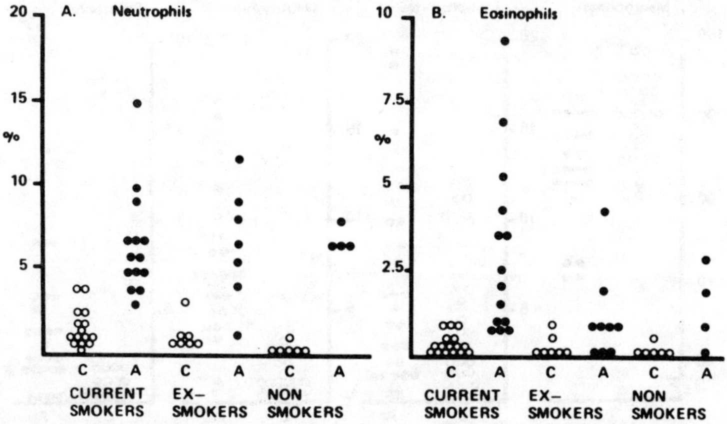

Fig. 9-2 Relationship between cigarette smoking and asbestos-induced alveolitis. A. Neutrophil proportions in recovered lavage fluid from control subjects (C) and patients with asbestosis (A) who were current smokers, ex-smokers or nonsmokers. B. Eosinophil proportions in recovered lavage fluid from the same individuals as in Fig. 9-3A. Results are recorded as in Fig. 9-1.

and alveolar samples. This is consistent with the known feature of inflammation of the small airways with asbestosis. Again, this increase in airway inflammation in asbestosis is not restricted to current or ex-smokers (Fig. 9-3).

4. BAL Lymphocyte Subpopulations

Evaluation of the subtypes of lymphocytes present in interstitial lung diseases has been studied using monoclonal antibodies (10). The presence of increased proportions of the helper/inducer (CD4) subpopulation is characteristic of pulmonary sarcoidosis, whereas elevated proportions of the suppressor/cytotoxic subpopulation (CD8) is seen in patients with extrinsic allergic alveolitis/hypersensitivity pneumonitis. We have evaluated BAL lymphocyte subpopulations using direct immunofluorescence using a UV microscope.

Fluoresceinated anti-Leu3 and anti-Leu2 (Becton Dickinson) were studied in 30 patients with non-sarcoidosis diffuse interstitial lung disease, of whom 10 had asbestosis, and compared to 20 patients with untreated pulmonary sarcoidosis and 8 control subjects.

All but one of the asbestosis patients exhibited a normal or reduced CD4/CD8 ratio, as did the other patients with non-

Table 9-1 Volumes and Total Cell Numbers Recovered from Each of Two Sequential 50 ml Bronchoalveolar Lavages (BAL) in a Single Subsegment in Patients with Interstitial Lung Disease

	Vol Recovered		Cell number	Vol Recovered		Cell Number		
	(ml)	(%)[d]	($\times 10^6$)	(%)[c]	(ml)	(%)	($\times 10^6$)	(%)[d]
CFA	11 ± 3[d]	38 ± 5[d]	1.3 ± 0.6[d]	28 ± 13[d]	17 ± 4	62 ± 5	4.6 ± 1.5	72 ± 8
RL	13 ± 1[d]	35 ± 2[d]	1.4 ± 0.3[d]	22 ± 6[d]	23 ± 8	65 ± 5	7.2 ± 0.3	78 ± 6
ASB	11 ± 1[d]	37 ± 3[d]	1.9 ± 0.3[d]	26 ± 4[d]	17 ± 2	63 ± 3	5.6 ± 0.2	74 ± 4
SARC	12 ± 3[d]	29 ± 3[d]	1.4 ± 0.5[d]	23 ± 4[d]	28 ± 3	71 ± 4	4.4 ± 1.8	77 ± 2
Controls	13 ± 3[d]	28 ± 5[d]	1.4 ± 0.5[d]	20 ± 6	28 ± 4	72 ± 5	3.9 ± 0.4	80 ± 10

Abbreviations: CFA, cryptogenic fibrosing alveolitis; RL, rheumatoid lung; ASB, asbestosis; SARC, sarcoidosis

[a] The first of two sequential 50 ml BALs in a single lung subsegment

[b] The second of two sequential 50 ml BALs in a single lung subsegment

[c] % of the total recovery (sample I plus sample II)

[d] P = Ω 0.05 compared to sample II. Table 9-2

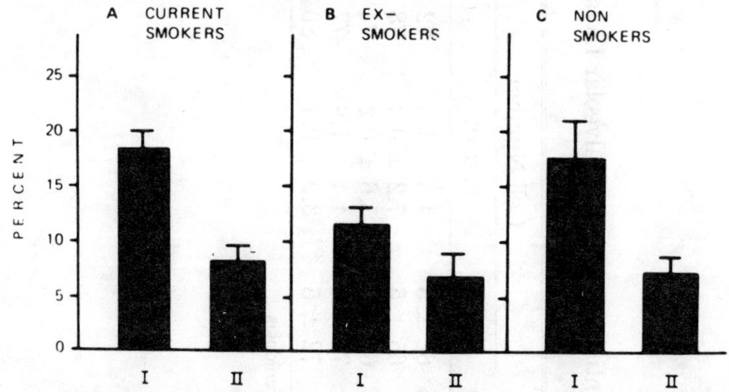

Fig. 9-3 Relationship between neutrophil proportions in airway and alveolar samples and smoking history: neutrophil proportions in fluid recovered from two sequential 50 ml bronchoalveolar lavages in a single lung subsegment in 19 patients with asbestosis, of whom 10 were current smokers (A), 4 ex-smokers (B), and 5 life-time non-smokers (C).

sarcoidosis interstitial lung disease. This contrasted with the findings in the sarcoidosis patients, the majority of whom exhibited an elevated CD4/CD8 ratio, the mean value being 4.4 ± 1 (Fig. 9-4).

5. BAL Asbestos Body Counts

While examination of the sputum for asbestos bodies has routinely been used as an indicator of exposure, we have found that BAL is a much more sensitive method of determining the presence of asbestos bodies (11). We have quantified asbestos body counts using cytospin preparations and filter preparations on 75 crocidolite-exposed individuals and compared them to counts in 412 non-exposed individuals. Asbestos bodies were detected in 58% of the asbestos-exposed individuals compared to 2% in the non-exposed individuals. Furthermore, those individuals not known to have been exposed to asbestos exhibited less than 10 asbestos bodies per ml of lavage fluid compared to the asbestos-exposed individuals who exhibited up to 200 asbestos bodies per ml of lavage fluid. When BAL and sputum examination were compared (n = 57) we found that when BAL is positive, only 37% of those individuals will be sputum positive for asbestos bodies (Table 9-2). As cytospin preparations sample approximately 1% of the total BAL, we evaluated the filter method, which uses increased volumes of fluid, to determine whether or not it increases

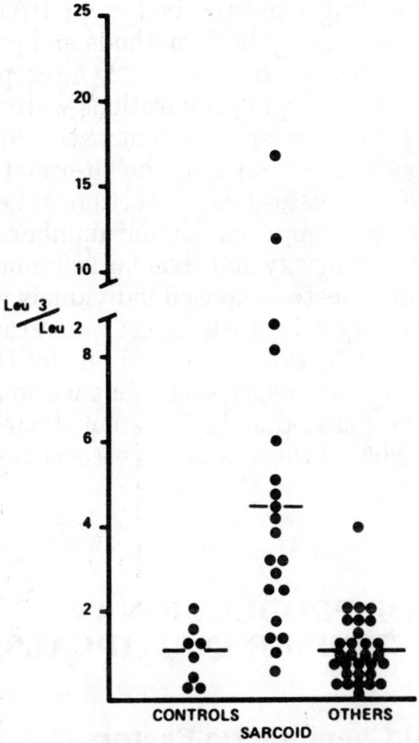

Fig. 9-4 Bronchoalveolar lavage helper/suppressor (Leu3/Leu2) T-cell ratios in the same individuals as in Fig. 9-1. Data are expressed as percentage of lymphocytes bearing Leu3/percentage bearing Leu2, determined using direct immunofluorescence and fluorescence microscopy. The mean value in each group is marked with a horizontal bar.

Table 9-2 Comparison of Sensitivity of Bronchoalveolar Lavage (BAL) and Sputum Analysis for Detection of Asbestos Bodies (AB) in 57 Crocidolite-Exposed Workers

		BAL	
		Present	Absent
Sputum	Present	13	0
	Absent	20	24

the chances of finding asbestos bodies in BAL fluid. Fifty-six samples were examined by both methods and both cytospins and filter preparations were positive in 22, filter preparations only were positive in 12, cytospin preparations were positive in 0, and in 22 samples neither preparation demonstrated asbestos bodies.

Thus, using a larger sample by the filter method increases the sensitivity of BAL asbestos body detection. When the airway and alveolar samples are compared, similar numbers of asbestos bodies are located in the airway and alveolar fractions. When asbestos body counts from asbestos-exposed individuals were evaluated in those with pulmonary asbestosis (chest radiograph with irregular opacities of grade 1/0 or greater, based on the ILO classification) versus those with asbestos exposure but without radiological asbestosis, we have found that BAL demonstrates presence of asbestos bodies in 80% of those with asbestosis versus 44% of those with exposure only.

C. MEDIATOR PRODUCTION IN ASBESTOS-EXPOSED INDIVIDUALS

1. Neutrophil Chemotactic Factor

As neutrophils are found in BAL samples in patients with asbestosis, we evaluated the potential mechanisms of neutrophil accumulation in asbestosis by assaying spontaneous neutrophil chemotactic factor (NCF) release in asbestos-exposed individuals compared to control individuals (12). While there was no spontaneous NCF released by control individuals, a known positive signal for NCF release, opsonized zymosan, could induce release (Fig. 9-5). In contrast, however, alveolar macrophages from individuals with asbestosis demonstrated spontaneous release of NCF (Fig. 9-5). Furthermore, we evaluated an additional 13 asbestos-exposed individuals who did not have radiological asbestosis and found that those with increased BAL neutrophil proportions ($n = 7$) released more NCF (93 ± 24 neutrophils per HPF) compared to those who have a normal neutrophil count ($n = 6$; 11 ± 6 neutrophils per HPF, $P < 0.02$). Thus, a neutrophil chemotactic factor is spontaneously released by alveolar macrophages in patients with asbestosis and in those asbestos-exposed individuals who have elevated BAL neutrophil proportions.

To determine whether asbestos fibres could directly induce pulmonary macrophages to release a neutrophil chemotactic fac-

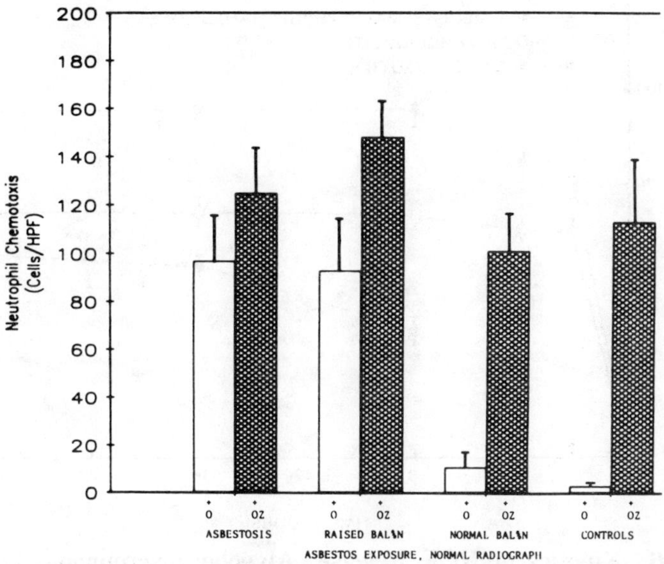

Fig. 9-5 Release of neutrophil chemotactic factor (NCF) by alveolar macrophages (AM) in medium alone (+0) and following addition of opsonized zymosan (+OZ) in subjects with radiographic asbestosis, asbestos-exposed individuals with normal chest radiographs (raised or normal BAL neutrophils), and control subjects. Normal BAL neutrophil proportions were taken as <2% for non-smokers, <3% for ex-smokers, and <4% for current smokers.

tor, we incubated control alveolar macrophages with asbestos fibres for several hours and then assayed the supernatants for NCF activity (13). These studies demonstrated that alveolar macrophages were very sensitive to the presence of asbestos fibres, releasing large amounts of NCF shortly after exposure to asbestos fibres (Fig. 9-6). This NCF is of low molecular weight (approximately 600 daltons), based on gel filtration analysis (Fig. 9-7).

2. Gamma Interferon (IFN) Release

Direct activation of alveolar macrophages with the release of NCF may explain some of the ongoing damage to the lungs seen in this disease. Because of data from animal models of asbestosis and from systemic studies of humans with asbestosis, that there is disordered immunological activity, we reasoned that there may also be disordered immune events within the lungs of humans exposed to asbestos, i.e., at the primary site of disease. IFN is spontaneously released by activated T cells during cellular im-

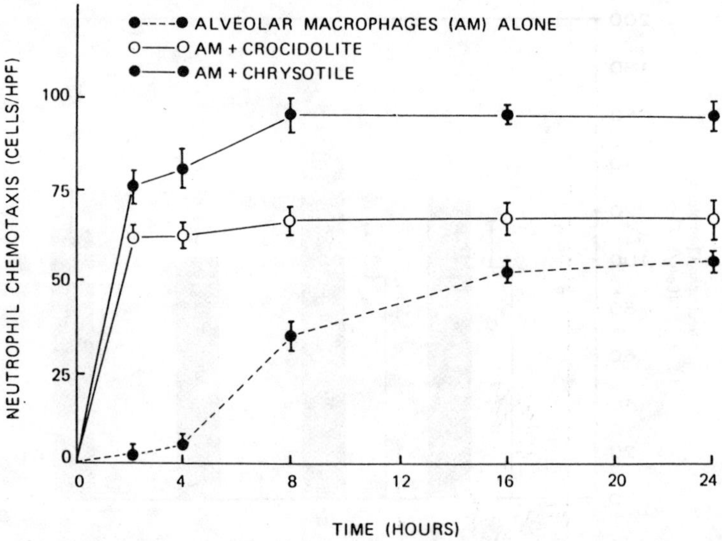

Fig. 9-6 Kinetics of NCF Release. Alveolar macrophages (10^6/ml) were placed in 24 well plates and cultured with medium alone or medium containing crocidolite 1 mg/ml or chrysotile 1 mg/ml and supernatants collected at various time points over a 24-hour period and tested for NCF activity. Results are expressed as in Fig. 9-1.

mune processes and has been shown to be increased in interstitial lung diseases associated with increased cellular immune activity (e.g., sarcoidosis) (5) and in some patients with other diffuse interstitial lung diseases (e.g., CFA/IPF and rheumatoid lung) (14).

We, therefore, measured spontaneous IFNγ production by BAL cells in 26 persons with asbestosis using a bioassay (EMC virus on human amniotic WISH cells) (15). IFNγ release in asbestosis was compared to control individuals (n = 18) and in 7 patients with active pulmonary sarcoidosis, a disease known to be associated with spontaneous IFNγ production. Thirty-five percent of the patients with asbestosis released increased amounts of IFNγ, up to 320 units/ml, the levels seen in the sarcoidosis patients (Fig. 9-8). In contrast all control subjects released less than 10 units/ml. All the interferon released was IFNγ based on monoclonal antibody suppression studies. In the asbestosis patients, IFNγ production was not related to a history of cigarette smoking (Table 9-3). IFN production was related to serum IgG levels ($P < 0.001$; Table 9-4) but not with the levels of IgM, IgA, antinuclear factor, or rheumatoid factor (Table 9-5). These data sug-

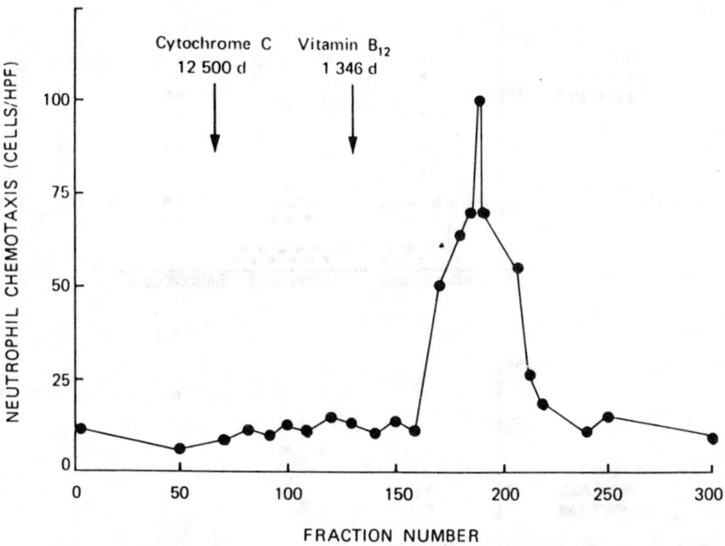

Fig. 9-7 Partial Characterization of NCF. Sephadex G-25 fine gel filtration of a neutrophil chemotactic factor (NCF) test sample generated by incubating human alveolar macrophages (10^6/ml) with crocidolite 1 mg/ml (37°, 4 hours). Molecular weight markers: Cytochrome C (12,500 daltons) and Vitamin B12 (1,346 daltons). Results are expressed as in Fig. 9-1.

gest a role for activated cellular immune processes in the lungs of some individuals with asbestosis.

D. GALLIUM LUNG SCANNING

In view of the role of gallium lung scanning in the evaluation of pulmonary inflammation in patients with interstitial lung disease, and in view of the fact that increased gallium uptake is noted in patients with elevated neutrophil proportions (e.g., CFA/IPF) and in patients with spontaneous IFNγ production (e.g., sarcoidosis), we evaluated gallium uptake in 35 asbestos-exposed individuals (16).

In individuals with radiographic evidence of asbestosis (n = 15), 13 had a positive gallium lung scan. In those asbestos-exposed individuals with equivocal radiological changes (⁰⁄₁ based on the ILO classification, n = 12), 6 (50%) had a positive gallium lung scan. In those individuals with a normal chest x-ray (n = 8) only 2 (25%) had a positive gallium lung scan. These data dem-

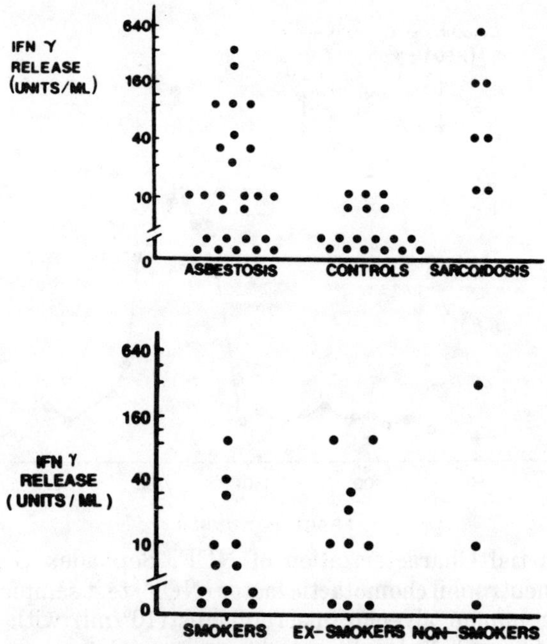

Fig. 9-8 Spontaneous Gamma Interferon Production in Patients with Asbestosis Compared to Control and Sarcoidosis Patients. Cells recovered using bronchoalveolar lavage were cultured at 5×10^6/ml for 24 hours, and the spontaneous release of IFNγ was determined. Each dot represents data from a separate subject.

Table 9-3 Relationship Between Bronchoalveolar Lavage Data and Smoking History in Subjects with Asbestosis

	Smoking History		
Parameter	Current	Ex	Non
Fluid recovery (%)	44 ± 5[a]	62 ± 3	66 ± 8
Cell number ($\times 10^6$)	57 ± 14	24 ± 3[b]	11 ± 6[b]
Cell proportions			
Macrophages (%)	87 ± 2	77 ± 3	82 ± 9
Lymphocytes (%)	4 ± 1[b]	15 ± 4	17 ± 11
Neutrophils (%)	5.5 ± 0.9	5.9 ± 2.2	3.0 ± 2.5
Eosinophils (%)	3.2 ± 0.7	1.7 ± 1.1	0.2 ± 0.1

[a] Mean ± SEM
[b] $P < 0.05$ compared to current smokers.

Table 9-4 Relationship between Gamma Interferon (IFNγ) Production and Asbestos Exposure

Parameter	IFNγ Producers[a]	Non-IFNγ Producers[b]
Number of subjects	7	11
Duration of exposure (yrs)	2.6 ± 0.5[c]	2.2 ± 0.7
Interval since initial exposure (yrs)	25 ± 1[c]	27 ± 2
No. of asbestos bodies per 10^5 cells[d]	61 ± 45[c]	39 ± 19
No. of asbestos bodies per μl[e]	71 ± 49[c]	80 ± 31

[a] Spontaneous production of ≥20 units/ml.
[b] Production of ≤10 units/ml. N.B. All Control subjects produced ≤10 units/ml.
[c] No significant difference compared to non-IFNγ-producers.
[d] Evaluated on cytospin preparations.
[e] Evaluated as in "d" and corrected for recovered lavage volume.

onstrate that most subjects with crocidolite-induced asbestosis have an abnormal gallium lung scan and that, in addition, many individuals with asbestos exposure, particularly those with equivocal radiological changes, have an abnormal gallium lung scan. This suggests the presence of active subclinical pulmonary inflammation in these individuals.

E. PULMONARY INFLAMMATION IN ASBESTOS-EXPOSED INDIVIDUALS WITH NORMAL CHEST RADIOGRAPHS

A significant proportion of asbestos-exposed individuals who have normal chest x-rays demonstrate features of underlying pulmonary inflammation. We have studied 93 asbestos-exposed individuals who have normal chest x-rays, evaluating BAL differential cell counts, gallium lung scan results, and spontaneous production of IFNγ and a macrophage cytokine, TNFα. BAL cell differential counts were abnormal in 40% of these individuals, most exhibiting increased neutrophil and/or eosinophil proportions. IFNγ and TNFα were spontaneously released in 40% and 50% respectively (all $P < 0.05$ compared to controls). In addition, 25% had abnormal gallium lung scans. These results demonstrate that inflammatory and immunological lung processes can be detected in many persons exposed to asbestos in the absence of detectable x-ray changes and suggest that radiological features do not detect low levels of pulmonary inflammation associated with asbestos exposure.

Table 9-5 Relationship between IFNγ Production and Systemic Immunological Parameters

Parameter	IFNγ Producers[a]	Non-IFNγ Producers[a]
WBC count ($\times 10^9$/L)	6.8 ± 0.7[b]	9.0 ± 0.9
IgG (G/L)	16.1 ± 1.4[c]	12.1 ± 0.9
IgM (G/L)	1.2 ± 0.5[b]	1.2 ± 0.4
IgA (G/L)	4.5 ± 1.1[b]	2.6 ± 0.3
Antinuclear factor[d]	0/5	0/7
Rheumatoid factor[e]	2/5	1/6

[a] As in Table 9-3. N.B. All control subjects produced <10 units/ml.
[b] No significant difference compared to non-IFNγ producers.
[c] $P < 0.001$ compared to non-IFNγ producers.
[d] Elevated if >7 units.
[e] Elevated if >30 units.

F. CONCLUSIONS

These data demonstrate that active pulmonary inflammation is present in most individuals with pulmonary asbestosis. This inflammation is characterized by the presence of increased numbers of neutrophils and eosinophils and, in some patients, by increased cellular immune processes and spontaneous IFN production.

This study establishes the standard pattern of BAL cell differential abnormalities in crocidolite-exposed individuals and describes the sensitivity of BAL in measuring the presence of asbestos bodies within the lungs.

This study also clearly demonstrates that asbestos-exposed individuals who have normal chest x-rays may have features of underlying pulmonary inflammation based on BAL differential cell counts, mediator production, and gallium lung scanning. In view of the fact that pulmonary inflammation can lead to the development of progressive pulmonary fibrosis, further follow-up studies are necessary to determine whether or not those exposed individuals with normal chest x-rays who have features of inflammation will exhibit progression of radiological and physiological interstitial lung disease, as has been suggested elsewhere (13).

REFERENCES

1. Crystal RG, Bitterman PB, Rennard SI, Hance AJ, Keogh BA. Interstitial lung diseases of unknown cause: disorders characterized by chronic inflammation of the lower respiratory tract. N Engl J of Med 1984;310:154–166 and 235–244.
2. Schoenberger CI, GW Hunninghake, O Kawanami, VJ Ferrans, RG Crystal. Role of alveolar macrophages in asbestosis: modulation of neutrophil migration to the lung following acute asbestos exposure. Thorax 1982;37:803–809.
3. Parkes WR. Silicates and lung disease. In Occupational Lung Disorders, 1984. Butterworths, London, 233–332.
4. Hunninghake GW, Gadek JE, Kawanami O, Ferrans VJ, Crystal RG. Inflammatory and immune processes in the human lung in health and disease: evaluation of bronchoalveolar lavage. Am J Pathol 1979;97:149–206.
5. Robinson B.W.S. McLemore TL, Crystal RG. Gamma interferon is spontaneously produced by lung T-lymphocytes and alveolar macrophages in patients with pulmonary sarcoidosis. J Clin Invest 1985;75:1488–1495.
6. Bignon J, K Atassi, MC Jaurand, J Yamine, H Kaplan, P Geslin, R Solle, M Bientz. Etude cytologique et biochemique du liquide du lavage broncho-alveolaire (LBA) dans la fibrose pulmonaire idiopathique et l'asbestose. Rev Fr Mal Resp 1978;6:353–358.
7. Begin R, Cantin A, Drapeau G, Lamoreux G, Boctor M, Masse S, Rola-Pleszczynski M. Pulmonary uptake of gallium-67 in asbestos exposed humans and sheep. Am Rev Respir Dis 1983;127:623–630.
8. Robinson BWS, A Rose, A Hey, D Whittaker, AW Musk. Alveolitis of pulmonary asbestosis: bronchoalveolar lavage studies in crocidolite- and chysotile-exposed individuals. Chest 1986;90: 3986–402.
9. Robinson BWS, A James, A Rose, G Sterret, AW Musk. Accurate processing of bronchoalveolar lavage samples requires separate processing of airway and alveolar samples. Br J Dis Chest 1988;82:45–55.
10. Robinson BWS, A Rose, PJ Thompson, A Hey. Comparison of lung

helper/suppressor ratios in pulmonary sarcoidosis versus other interstitial lung diseases. Aust NZ J Med 1987;17:9–15.
11. Rose AH, Whitaker D, Musk AW, Hayes A, Robinson BWS. Evaluation of lung alveolar asbestos body (AB) load using bronchoalveolar lavage (BAL). Aust NZ J Med 1987;17:519.
12. Hayes A, Rose AH, Musk AW, Robinson BWS. Neutrophil chemotactic factor release and neutrophil alveolitis in asbestos-exposed individuals. Chest 1988;94:521–525.
13. Hayes A, Robinson BWS, Musk AW. Neutrophil chemotactic factor is spontaneously released by alveolar macrophages in patients with asbestosis. Am Rev Respir Dis 1986;133:198.
14. Robinson BWS, Rose AH, Musk AW. Lung cells from some patients with chronic non-granulomatous interstitial lung diseases spontaneously release gamma interferon. Aust NZ J Med 1986;16:633.
15. Robinson BWS, Rose AH, Hayes A, Musk AW. Increased pulmonary gamma interferon production in asbestosis. Am Rev Respir Dis 1988;138:278–283.
16. Hayes A, Mullan B, Lovegrove FT, Robinson BWS, Musk AW. Gallium lung scanning and bronchoalveolar lavage in crocidolite-exposed workers. In press. Chest 1989.

10

Possible Protective Agents Against Asbestos Toxicity

SIGMUND A. WEITZMAN, M.D.
MARC M. DUNN, M.D.

Department of Medicine
Northwestern University Medical School
Chicago, Illinois, U.S.A.

PHILIP GRACEFFA, PH.D.

Department of Muscle Research
Boston Biomedical Research Institute
Boston, Massachusetts, U.S.A.

Synopsis

BIOGRAPHY

Dr. Sigmund A. Weitzman is the Chief of the Section of Hematology/Oncology in the Department of Medicine at Northwestern University Medical School and is Deputy Director of the Northwestern University Cancer Center. He has been interested in the carcinogenic and cytotoxic properties of reactive oxygen species, particularly those produced by phagocytes. He may be contacted at the Section of Hematology/Oncology, Northwestern University Medical School, 303 East Chicago Avenue, Chicago, Illinois 60611, U.S.A. (telephone 312-908-5284).

Dr. Marc M. Dunn is a pulmonary physician and a member of the Section of Pulmonary Medicine at Northwestern University Medical School in Chicago. His research interests include studies of mechanism of lung injury. He may be contacted at the Northwestern University Medical School, 303 East Chicago Ave., Chicago, Illinois 60611, U.S.A.

Dr. Philip Graceffa is a physical chemist and a member of the Department of Muscle Research at the Boston Biomedical Research Institute. His research interests include studies of free radical mechanisms, and the use of electron paramagnetic resonance spectroscopy in the study of these mechanisms. He may be contacted at the Boston Biomedical Research Institute, 21 Staniford Street, Boston, Massachusetts 02114, U.S.A.

EDITORS' COMMENTARY

The following chapter is an interesting and provocative review of some of the research presently underway at the Northwestern University Medical School. It reflects an attempt to better understand the adverse reactions that occur between the human body and asbestos fibers that result in disabling disease processes. For many years there have been discussions of the physical properties of asbestos fibers: their sharp pointed ends, hollow tubule stagnancy, irritant shape, and very small size. Similarly, there have been discussions of asbestos fiber physiochemical properties: macrophage accumulation and byproducts, the accumulation or depletion of iron and magnesium, enzyme and acid reactions, and induced genetic changes. Sometimes such discussions may seem to be speculative, occasionally they may seem superficial, and often they are without implications for beneficial application.

Is there a "chemical remedy" that is both explanatory as to the adverse biological processes and utilitarian in terms of interrupting or controlling the basic disease processes? Is there a "silver bullet" that can be used therapeutically with patients or that can be added for preventive purposes to wetting agents in asbestos removal projects, to encapsulants, and even to waste disposal site stabilizers?

One important biochemical approach emphasizes oxygen radical formation in the pulmonary inflammatory process and the study of antioxidants. It may be combined with anti-chelating agents, dealing with lipid cell propensities or interfering with adverse genetic effects. What is needed are systematic analyses that are theoretically insightful that can produce hypotheses or issues that can be tested experimentally and clinically and that have the potential for beneficial applications. The following chapter presents the logic, results, and promise of an approach that inherently suggests hope and remedies for this major public health problem.

A. INTRODUCTION

Asbestos-induced lung diseases remain prevalent despite the reduced industrial use of this mineral. These diseases continue to be common due to the long latency between exposure and disease recognition as well as the continued use or presence of asbestos. Protective measures directed toward the prevention of asbestos toxicity can be prophylactic or therapeutic. Prophylactic measures have primarily been aimed at reducing industrial exposure to the worker by altering the ventilation and instituting remote handling of asbestos. The risk of inhaling asbestos has also been reduced with the use of NIOSH-approved face masks or respirators if used properly. There is currently no specific treatment of asbestos-induced lung disease once it occurs. Specifically, there are no clinically available approaches directed toward reducing the toxicity of the asbestos fiber once it is deposited in the lung. The biochemical basis of asbestos toxicity has been partially clarified and new approaches to the prevention of asbestos toxicity or reduction of toxicity once it occurs may be proposed.

B. TOXIC AND CARCINOGENIC FACTORS OF ASBESTOS

Physical properties of the asbestos fiber were the focus of theories of the pathogenesis of asbestos-related pulmonary disorders for many years (2,26,45,46,48,50). Although the size or shape of asbestos fibers do appear to have a significant role in the pathogenesis of these disorders, more recent studies have demonstrated the additional importance of some of the chemical properties intrinsic to the structure of these fibers. In particular, asbestos-induced oxygen radical formation is a prominent mechanism in recent proposals of toxicity. The biochemical structure of asbestos is particularly suited for propagation of biochemical reactions resulting in the formation of these potent radicals. The as-

Accepted for publication 25 April 1989.

bestos minerals comprise a group of fibrous hydrous silicates that contain any of a number of metal cations as counterions, depending on the type of asbestos (24,56). However, all types of asbestos contain iron cations as an integral part of the ideal mineral crystal structure or as a substitute cation and surface impurity (3,24,25,42,47,56). In biological systems, iron catalyzes chemical reactions resulting in the formation of the potent oxidant, hydroxyl radical, and superoxide (6,21–23). Recent evidence suggests that the iron in asbestos can also catalyze these reactions (4,30,51). The oxygen radicals can then damage biological macromolecules such as proteins, cell membrane lipids, deoxyribonucleic acid (DNA), and ribonucleic acid (RNA). Damage to these essential cellular components can then result in altered cellular function or death. Therefore these reactions can play a role in the toxicity and carcinogenicity of asbestos.

C. POSSIBLE PROTECTIVE AGENTS

1. Deferoxamine

There is experimental evidence implicating oxygen radicals in the pathogenesis of asbestos-induced injury and the prevention of this injury with agents that interfere with oxygen radical formation or action. This evidence is derived from studies of biochemical reactions in which asbestos may be involved—e.g., cell damage experiments or the assessment of injury *in vivo*. Unfortunately, minimal supporting evidence is currently available from the last source. As mentioned, the combination of asbestos and physiologically relevant concentrations of hydrogen peroxide results in the formation of hydroxyl radical (4,51). This reaction can be inhibited by treating the asbestos with deferoxamine (51), an iron chelator (17,22,23). Deferoxamine binds avidly to asbestos *in vitro* and *in vivo* and inactivates the catalytic activity of the iron in asbestos (15,30,51,53). The hydrogen peroxide necessary for the above reaction may be derived *in vivo* from several sources. First, when lung macrophages ingest asbestos, hydrogen peroxide is produced (12). These cells are commonly found lining the lung and are considered to be the initial cellular defense of the lung. Cigarette smoke also contains hydrogen peroxide (36). This is one mechanism whereby the combination of cigarette smoking and asbestos exposure may interact to promote toxicity. It has also been reported that under certain conditions the combination of asbestos and oxygen generates the hydroxyl radical (54,55) and that deferoxamine inhibits this reaction (see Fig. 10-1) (55). Asbestos can also catalyze the formation of lipid peroxides (7,10,18–20,28,52). The peroxidation is also thought to occur through the iron in asbestos, since iron alone can cause lipid peroxidation (22,23) and prewashing the asbestos with deferoxamine inhibits the formation of lipid peroxides (52). Other antioxidants and chelators also inhibit the formation of lipid peroxides: ethylenediaminetetraacetic acid (EDTA), butylated hydroxytoluene (BHT), and others (19,20). However, not all studies have demonstrated a protective effect from antioxidants (7). The formation of lipid peroxides has important implications, since lipids are essential components of cell membranes and alteration of this component may result in cellular injury. Furthermore, lipid peroxides have been implicated as carcinogens.

2. SOD, Catalase, and Deferoxamine

Oxygen radicals and iron have been implicated as the toxins in several studies of asbestos-induced cytotoxicity. In one study macrophages produced oxygen radicals when exposed to asbestos, which were then toxic to these cells (12). Superoxide dismutase (SOD), catalase, and deferoxamine decreased the cytotoxicity. SOD and catalase degrade the oxidants superoxide and hydrogen peroxide, respectively. SOD, catalase, and deferoxamine also inhibited asbestos-induced toxicity to fibroblasts, cells that produce collagen (43). Dimethlythiourea (DMTU), an inhibitor of the hydroxyl radical, also inhibited cytotoxicity. SOD and inhibitors of hydroxyl radical also reduce asbestos-induced tracheal epithelial cell injury (34,35). DNA damage has also occurred following incubation with asbestos (49). Cell death and carcinogenesis are among the potential implications of damage to genetic material.

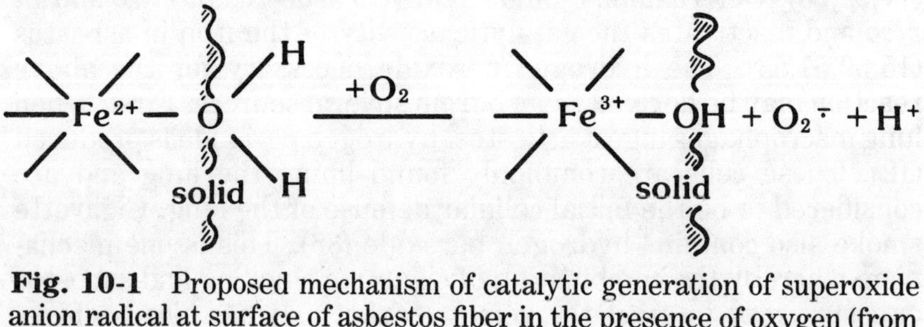

Fig. 10-1 Proposed mechanism of catalytic generation of superoxide anion radical at surface of asbestos fiber in the presence of oxygen (from reference 54).

Oxygen radicals have been implicated in asbestos-induced DNA damage and deferoxamine washing of the asbestos limits the damage. Two other studies have demonstrated that hydrogen peroxide and asbestos causes DNA damage (27,29). This damage is inhibited by incubating asbestos with the chelators 1,10-phenanthroline or desferrithiocin (an iron chelator related to deferoxamine). Asbestos-induced damage to DNA may occur without hydrogen peroxide (31), which is consistent with the observation that the iron in asbestos can catalyze the generation of the hydroxyl radical in the absence of hydrogen peroxide (54,55). These studies demonstrate the role of oxygen radicals in damage to essential cellular lipid and genetic structures. Furthermore, this damage can be ameliorated with iron chelators, which inhibit the formation of hydroxyl radical or antioxidants.

There is also some evidence for the role of oxygen radicals in asbestos toxicity *in vivo*. In experimental animals asbestos induces an inflammatory reaction composed variably of neutrophils and activated alveolar macrophages. These cells are among the most potent producers of oxygen radicals. Lung homogenates and lysosomes of rats exposed to a single intratracheal dose of asbestos demonstrated increased lipid peroxidation 1, 3, and 7 months following the inoculation (28). A single intraperitoneal injection of asbestos is toxic to the mesothelial cells of the diaphragm, as well as macrophages (14). Macrophages that were isolated 3 days following intraperitoneal asbestos inoculation spontaneously produced hydrogen peroxide. Prevention of diaphragmatic toxicity was demonstrated when mice were injected with SOD or catalase, complexed to polyethylene glycol for stability. Finally, deferoxamine-washed asbestos also ameliorated the damage seen with asbestos alone. Thus, although there is not a large body of information from *in vivo* models, there is a suggestion for the role of oxygen radical-induced damage following asbestos exposure and protection by agents that interfere with the generation of these toxins.

D. IRON CHELATION EFFECTIVE AGAINST ASBESTOS-TOBACCO SYNERGY

In addition to the disease processes that may directly be attributed to asbestos fibers, such as asbestosis and mesothelioma, these fibers also exhibit a potent synergistic carcinogenic effect with tobacco smoke in the production of bronchogenic carcinoma. There is considerable evidence that the catalytic properties of asbestos may be important to this synergy. First, asbestos catalyzes other redox reactions (which may or may not involve iron). For example, asbestos catalyzes the reduction of tetracyanoethylene (1), and the oxidation of 6-hydroxybenzo[a]pyrene to the 6-oxobenzo[a]pyrene free radical (16). This latter reaction may, in fact, be related specifically to potentiation of bronchogenic carcinoma since 6-hydroxybenzo[a]pyrene is a metabolite of benzo[a]pyrene, a major polycyclic aromatic hydrocarbon carcinogen found in significant amounts in tobacco smoke. The 6-hydroxybenzo[a]pyrene catalytic reaction is not inhibited by deferoxamine and, therefore, not likely to involve the iron contained in the fibers or on the surface. Furthermore, this reaction does not appear to require molecular oxygen.

In contrast, asbestos also catalyzes other reactions that are probably very important in amplifying tobacco smoke carcinogenesis but which are likely dependent on iron (27). When cigarette smoke and asbestos fibers were co-incubated with DNA, 78% of the DNA developed strand breaks. If, however, DNA was exposed to either asbestos fibers alone or tobacco smoke alone, only 4.3% or 9.8%, respectively, of the DNA developed strand breaks (27). In these experiments, the ability of asbestos plus tobacco smoke synergistically to cause strand breaks in DNA appears to require asbestos iron, since the effect is reversed by the presence of the iron chelators, 1,10-phenanthroline and desferrithiocin. Thus, some of the effects of asbestos in amplifying the carcinogenic properties of tobacco smoke could potentially be prevented by iron chelation.

E. OTHER METHODS

As noted above, there are likely to be multifactorial mechanisms for the production of asbestos-induced lung diseases. Even if iron catalyzed reactions and size and shape considerations prove to be of dominant importance, other properties also appear significant. Therefore, the investigation of other approaches directed toward reducing toxicity has also been described. For example, asbestos can induce hyperplasia and squamous metaplasia in the epithelium of explants of hamster tracheas. This process could be inhibited by incubation with the retinoid retinylmethylether (33). The mechanism for this protection is uncertain, but the authors speculated that inhibition of cell division might be involved. Since retinoids can also be free radical scavenging antioxidants, this might be another potential mechanism of protection.

In another study, protein derivitization of asbestos inhibited cytotoxicity to lung cells (5). This may be related to alteration of either surface charge or catalytic activity of the fibers. Other groups have also looked at surface modification as a potential mechanism for inhibition of asbestos toxicity. In some of these experiments, asbestos toxicity was defined by the ability of asbestos fibers to induce hemolysis of red blood cells, and a protective effect defined by an inhibition of hemolysis. Since it is not clear whether red cell hemolysis can be related directly to the damage caused to nucleated cells, however, it is uncertain whether these effects could pertain to injury *in vivo*. Substances that have been used to treat and coat asbestos fibers in an effort to make them less hemolytic include EDTA, polyvinylpyridine N-oxide, versenate, phosphate, and aluminum (32), as well as certain acidic polymers (44). Pieper (37) also suggests that polyvinlypyridine N-oxide treatment may also reduce the risks of asbestosis. Pezzoli has reported treating asbestos with metal tungstates, metal sulfides, a metal ferrocyanide, or metal molybdates can all inhibit the hemolytic activity of asbestos (38–41). Flowers has described methods for coating asbestos fibers with metal-micelle polymer coatings, including a metal-weak base-strong acid aqueous ion system or a metal-strong base-weak acid ion system (8,9). Despite the fact that these fibers may actually have increased total iron and other metal contents, this treatment of the fibers is reported to reduce cytotoxicity to lung macrophages. It is possible that this treatment may have altered the surface catalytic properties of the fiber so that even though the total metal content was increased, that fraction available for catalysis was reduced. This aspect was not tested, however.

F. CONCLUSION

In summary, diseases due to asbestos continue to occur in significant numbers, both in the United States and elsewhere in the world. Asbestos usage is currently declining rapidly, but some industrial exposure still takes place. However, more important perhaps are the vast quantities of asbestos materials present in public buildings and private homes. These represent potential threats of accidental exposure to occupants as well as threats to those exposed (especially if unknowingly) as a consequence of their jobs or hobbies (such as repairing or remodeling old buildings). In addition, removal, or disposal of asbestos are other potential sources of exposure. For all of these reasons, further investigation directed toward reducing the toxicity of asbestos continues to have genuine relevance. It seems probable now that the capacity of asbestos fibers to cause disease is related to the chemical nature of the fiber as well as the physical dimensions. In recent years, the chemical and catalytic properties of the fibers have received considerable attention, as discussed above. With respect to the possibility of making asbestos exposure safer, we would favor further investigation into the use of deferoxamine, which has had extensive clinical use for other purposes and is safe to humans. As we have proposed previously (53), this agent might have two potential applications for prevention of asbestos toxicity. First, there could be utility in the asbestos removal industry. Regulations currently require the spraying of asbestos with certain wetting chemicals before removal. Deferoxamine (or certain of the other agents we have reviewed above) might be added to these wetting agents. We would currently favor deferoxamine for this purpose because we have shown that it stays bound to asbestos in the body (53). A second possibility, theoretical at present, is that deferoxamine could be administered to individuals felt to be at high risk for asbestos disease due to known heavy prior exposure. Some groups are investigating the possibility of identifying such individuals (11), suggesting that this may be a realistic possibility in the future.

REFERENCES

1. Bonneau L and Pezerat H. (1983) *J Chim Phys* 80:275 280.
2. Craighead JE and Mossman BT. (1982) *N Engl J Med* 306:1446–1456.
3. De Waele JK and Adams FC. (1988) *Scanning Microscopy* 2:209–228.
4. Eberhardt MK, Roman-Franco AA, and Quiles MR. (1985) *Environ Res* 37:287–292.
5. Evans PH, Brown RC, and Poole A. (1983) *J Toxicol Environ Health* 11:535–543.
6. Fenton HJH. (1894) *J Chem Soc* 899–910.
7. Fontecave M, Mansuy D, Jaouen M, and Pezerat H. (1987) *Biochem J* 241:561–565.
8. Flowers ES. (1982) *U.S. Patent* #4328197.
9. Flowers ES. (1983) *U.S. Patent* #4401636.
10. Gabor S and Anca Z. (1975) *Brit J Ind Med* 32:39–41.
11. Gellert AR, Langford JA, and Winter RJD, et al. (1985) *Brit J Dis Chest* 79:37–42.
12. Goodglick LA, and Kane AB. (1986) *Cancer Res* 46:5558–5566.
13. Goodglick LA and Kane AB. (1987) *Amer Rev Resp Disease* 135, A163.
14. Goodglick LA and Kane AB. (1988) *Proceedings of the VIIth International Pneumonconioses Conference.*
15. Graceffa P and Weitzman SA. (1984) *U.S. Patent* #4,474,742.
16. Graceffa P and Weitzman SA. (1987) *Arch Biochem Biophys* 257:481–484.
17. Graf E, Mahoney JR, Bryant RG and Eaton JW. (1984) *J Biol Chem* 259:3620–3624.
18. Gulumian M, Sardianos F, Kilroe-Smith T, and Ockerse G. (1983) *Chem Biol Interactions* 44:111–118.
19. Gulumian M and Kilroe-Smith TA. (1987) *Environ Res* 43:267–273.
20. Gulumian M and Kilroe-Smith TA. (1987) *Environ Res* 44:257–259.
21. Haber F and Weiss J. (1934) *Proc Roy Soc Lond* (A) 147:332–335.
22. Halliwell B and Gutteridge JMC. (1984) *Biochem* J 219:1–14.
23. Halliwell B and Gutteridge JMC. (1986) *Arch Biochem Biophys* 246:501–514.

24. Hodgson AA. (1979) in *Asbestos* (Michaels L and Chissick SS, eds), Vol I, Chap 3, Wiley, New York.
25. Harrington JS. (1965) Ann N.Y. *Acad Sci* 132:31–47.
26. Harrington JS. (1981) *J Natl Cancer Inst* 67:977–989.
27. Jackson JH, Schraufstatter IU, Hyslop PA, Vosbeck K, Sauerheber R, Weitzman SA, and Cochrane CG. (1987) *J Clin Invest* 80:1090–1095.
28. Jajte J, Lao I and Wisniewska-Knypl JM. (1987) *Brit J Ind Med* 44:180–186.
29. Kasai H and Nishimura S. (1984) *Gann* 75:841–844.
30. Kennedy TP, Dodson NV, Rao NV, Ky H, Hopkins C, Baser M, Tolley E, and Hoidal JR. (1989) *Arch Biochem Biophys* 269:359–364.
31. Leanderson P, Soderkvist P, Tagesson C, and Axelson O. (1988) *Brit J Ind Med* 45:309–311.
32. McNab G and Harrington JS. (1967) *Nature* 214:522–523.
33. Mossman BT, Craighead JE, and MacPherson BV. (1980) *Science* 207:311–313.
34. Mossman BT, Marsh JP, and Shatos MA. (1986) *Lab Invest* 54:204–212.
35. Mossman BT, Marsh JP, Shatos MA, Doherty J, Gilbert R, and Hill S. (1987) *Drug and Chemical Toxicology* 10:157–180.
36. Nakayama T, Kodama M, and Nagata C. (1984) *Gann* 75:95–98.
37. Pieper G. (1976) *German Patent* #1642022.
38. Pezzoli PA. (1979) *U.S. Patent* #4168346.
39. Pezzoli PA. (1979) *U.S. Patent* #4171405.
40. Pezzoli PA. (1980) *U.S. Patent* #4,234,377.
41. Pezzoli PA. (1982) *U.S. Patent* #4,309,477.
42. Pooley FD. (1981) *Semin Oncol* 8:243–249.
43. Shatos MA, Doherty JM, Marsh JP, and Mossman BT. (1987) *Environ Res* 44:103–116.
44. Schnitzer RJ and Pundsack F. (1970) *Environmental Res* 3:1–14.
45. Stanton MF and Wrench C. (1972) *J Natl Cancer Inst* 48:797–821.
46. Stanton MF, Layard M, Tegeris A, Miller E, May M, Morgan E, and Smith A. (1981) *J Natl Cancer Inst* 67:965–975.
47. Timbrell V. (1970) in Pneumonconiosis: *Proceedings of the International Conference*, Johannesburg (Shapiro HA, ed.), pp 28–36.
48. Timbrell V, Griffiths DM, and Pooley FD. (1971) *Nature* 232:55–56.
49. Turver CJ and Brown RC. (1987) *Brit J Cancer* 56:133–136.
50. Wagner JC, Berry G, and Timbrell V. (1973) *Brit J Cancer* 28:173–185.
51. Weitzman SA and Graceffa P. (1984) *Arch Biochem Biophys* 228:373–376.
52. Weitzman SA and Weitberg AB. (1985) *Biochem J* 225:259–262.
53. Weitzman SA, Chester JF, and Graceffa P. (1988) *Carcinogenesis* 9:1643–1645.

54. Zalma R, Bonneau L, Guignard J, and Pezerat H. (1987) *Can J Chem* 65:2338–2341.
55. Zalma R, Bonneau L, Guignard J, and Pezerat H. (1987) *Toxicol Environ Chem* 13:171–181.
56. Zussman J. (1979) in *Asbestos* (Michaels L and Chissick SS, eds.), Vol I, Chap 2, Wiley, New York.

11

Radiology of Asbestos-Related Thoracic Disease

DAVID LYNCH, M.D.

Department of Radiology
University of Colorado Health Sciences Center
Denver, Colorado 80262

GORDON GAMSU, M.D.

Department of Radiology
University of California Medical Center
San Francisco, California 94143-0628

Synopsis

- c. Pleural Abnormalities
  - i. Pleural Thickening
  - ii. Pleural Calcification
- d. Symbols

D. THE ILO AND ASBESTOS-RELATED DISEASE

E. ASBESTOS-RELATED DISEASE

1. Asbestos-Related Pleural Plaques
   - a. Chest Radiographs
   - b. Conventional CT
   - c. HRCT
   - d. Fissural Pleural Plaques
   - e. Diffuse Visceral and Parietal Pleural Thickening (Fibrosis)
   - f. Pleural Effusion
   - g. Visceral Pleural Thickening
   - h. Mesothelioma
2. Asbestosis
   - a. Chest Radiographs
   - b. Conventional CT
   - c. High Resolution CT
3. Benign Asbestos-Related Lung Masses
4. Asbestos-Related Neoplasms

F. CONCLUSIONS

BIOGRAPHY

Dr. David Lynch is Assistant Professor of Radiology and Chief, Chest Radiology at the University of Colorado Health Sciences Center and the National Jewish Hospital for Immunology and Respiratory Medicine in Denver, Colorado. He graduated from University College in Dublin, Ireland, in 1979 and completed residencies in internal medicine and radiology in Dublin before becoming a Clinical Instructor in Chest Radiology at the University of California, San Francisco, in 1987. His interests include the use of high resolution CT in detection and characterization of interstitial lung disease. Dr. Lynch may be reached at the University of Colorado Health Sciences Center, Department of Radiology, Campus Box C277, 4200 East Ninth Avenue, Denver, Colorado 80262 (telephone: 303-270-7711).

Dr. Gordon Gamsu is Professor of Radiology and Medicine and Director of Thoracic Imaging in the Department of Diagnostic Radiology at the University of California San Francisco. He is a consultant to the Navy, Army, and Veteran's Administration. Dr. Gamsu is active in clinical thoracic imaging, teaching, and research. His research in the imaging of patients with asbestos-related pleuroparenchymal disease has been documented in approximately ten publications and editorials. He has published more than 150 peer-reviewed scientific articles, 45 book chapters, and has edited several books. Dr. Gamsu is active in numerous societies, is on review panels and editorial boards of several journals. His major interests at this time include computed tomography, magnetic resonance imaging of the thorax, and diffuse lung diseases. Dr. Gamsu is a NIOSH-certified B-reader. Dr. Gamsu may be reached at the University of California Medical Center, Department of Radiology, San Francisco, California 94143-0628 (telephone: 415-476-1451).

EDITORS' COMMENTARY

The detection of asbestos-related diseases by radiographic methods is dependent on appropriate imaging, whether by conventional or computerized methods. The following chapter provides worthwhile recommendations to improve detection, quality, reliability, and interpretation of the thoracic abnormalities that are the result, sign, and evidence of an asbestos-related disease process. Differential diagnosis and the assessment of asbestos disease can be enhanced based on the techniques and criteria presented by these Contributing Authors. This chapter may be supplemented by the information contained in Chapter 19 (the ILO classification system for radiographs), Chapter 20 (the list of certified B-readers), and references to chest x-rays in many other chapters.

A. INTRODUCTION

The chest radiograph has for many years been the mainstay in the epidemiological investigation of the pneumoconioses. It remains the primary means of detecting the effects of the pulmonary retention of certain dusts, e.g., silica, coal, and asbestos, and has contributed much to our understanding of the course of these diseases. An abnormal chest radiograph is frequently accepted as the major legal evidence of dust exposure in workmen's compensation situations and occupational litigation. Seldom, however, is the chest radiograph useful in the assessment of pulmonary impairment.

Chest radiographs are increasingly being supplemented by conventional computed tomography (CCT) (1, 2) and more re-

Accepted for publication 3 June 1989.

cently by high resolution CT (HRCT) (3, 4) for the detection and imaging of asbestos-related diseases.

B. RADIOGRAPHIC TECHNIQUES

As in all aspects of radiology, careful attention to technique is important, so that one may reliably and reproducibly detect abnormalities.

1. Chest Radiography

The technical standards for chest radiographs were published in the Federal Register [1978;43(148)], as defined by NIOSH, LOC, PHS, and HEW. The specifications apply only to a posteroanterior radiograph of the chest and cover machine performance and the requirement for a film:screen combination. The variable cited is the time of exposure, which should generally not exceed 50 msec, and all modern x-ray equipment should conform to these standards. The voltage requirement for the exposure is not defined, but most modern medical radiographs of the chest are obtained at high kilovoltage (usually 120 to 140 kVp). To enhance the fine interstitial lines seen in asbestosis, a lower kilovoltage (80 to 90 kVp) may be better. The detection of pleural disease is much better at the higher energy. We recommend three views of the thorax for detection of asbestos-related thoracic disease. We suggest the best exposures are a low kilovoltage (80 to 90 kVp) for the posteroanterior radiograph and a higher kilovoltage (120 to 140 kVp) for two 45° oblique views of the thorax. All radiographs should be obtained at full inspiration. Expiratory radiographs may give a false appearance of disease.

2. Computer Tomography

Computed tomography (CT) is a widely available modality that first came into medical imaging in the early 1970s. It is used for obtaining images of the thorax and other regions of the body.

A CT scanner is composed of several parts, including:

1. A gantry, which contains the x-ray source and detector array. It is shaped like a donut. The patient is placed inside the hole of the donut and the x-ray source revolves around the inside perimeter of the donut hole.
2. A motorized table on which the patient lies is placed within the center of the gantry.
3. A CT viewing and control console for the technician.

4. A computer data acquisition and reconstruction system, including computer peripherals such as line magnetic tape storage units for storage of CT data.

In CT, a highly collimated fan beam of x-rays passes through the chest and the attenuation of the x-rays is recorded by 600 to 1200 detectors. The information is fed into a computer that reconstructs the information into an image. The resultant picture is a thin slice through the body, depicting the tissues dependent on their x-ray attenuation or CT density. Air is dark, and more dense tissues are progressively whiter.

The CT display consists of different shades of gray, black, or white either on a video screen or on film producing the CT image. An image is made up of points (pixels) of light and dark that when viewed together form a picture, like the points of gray, black, and white that when seen together make a newspaper photograph. Newer scanners have displays made up of a matrix of 512 × 512 pixels. Current CT scanners can resolve structures as small as 0.6 to 1 mm. The range of density recorded on a CT image is from −1000 to +1000 units, the units being referred to as Hounsfield units (HU). Water is given a CT density of 0 HU, while air is −1000 HU.

The full HU scale cannot be shown on a video screen or film because the display shows only a limited number of shades of gray, typically only 16, while the computer in the CT scanner stores a range of 2000 HU. The operator selects the part of the CT density scale to be viewed by adjusting the "window level." The range of CT densities depicted on the image is varied by chaning the "window width."

CT scans of the thorax are now considered either "conventional" or "high resolution" in type.

3. Conventional CT

CCT uses contiguous slices 8–10 mm thick and are usually obtained from the lung apices to the lung bases. Technical factors (kVp, mA, and time of acquisition) will vary, depending on patient size and scanner capabilities, but the scan time should usually be less than 3 sec. Intravenous contrast can be administered when there is a need to outline the vascular structures of the thorax. This is particularly important when there is a question of hilar or mediastinal mass, or in order to stage a bronchogenic carcinoma or mesothelioma. For routine scanning for asbestos-related pleural or parenchymal disease, intravascular contrast is not required.

4. High Resolution CT

High resolution CT (HRCT) is used to delineate fine interstitial structures within the lung. This is achieved by using thin slices (1–1.5 mm thick) and a "high resolution" reconstruction algorithm that accurately reconstructs high-contrast lung detail at the cost of a moderate increase in background noise. Adherence to appropriate image acquisition parameters is essential for good quality HRCT (6). Since one cannot hope to examine the entire chest using a 1 or 1.5 mm thick slice, HRCT is essentially used as a sampling method (Table 11-1). For asbestosis, we perform 5 to 6 scans through the mid and lower zones of the lungs, where asbestos-related pleural disease and lung fibrosis is most likely to be found (3, 4). One may therefore miss significant lung masses or

Table 11-1 Technique for High Resolution CT of the Lungs for Asbestosis

Technical Factors	
kVp:	120 to 140
Scan Time:	2 to 3 sec
mA:	140 to 170
Collimation:	1.0–2.0 mm
Positioning	
Series #1: Supine	
Series #2: Prone	
Scout	
AP–Whole Lung	
Scan Area	
Series #1: Done supine on full suspended inspiration	
Scan 1. through carina	
Scan 2. midway between carina and right diaphragmatic dome	
Scan 3. midway between scan 2 and right diaphragmatic dome	
Scan 4. at right diaphragmatic dome	
Scan 5. at base of lungs	
Series #2: Done prone	
Repeat the scan at the same levels as supine scans	
Reconstruction	
All scans reconstructed using a high resolution algorithm	
Photography	
6 on 1 format	
3 separate windows:	1. window width 400 level +40 (for pleura & mediastinum)
	2. window width 1000 level −700 (for lung detail)
	3. window width 2000 level −700 (relationship: lung & pleura)

other abnormalities that are not included in the selected slices. Thus, a conventional chest radiograph should always be obtained in addition to the HRCT. Scans must be performed both in supine and prone positions, to fully expand the lungs and eliminate the artifacts produced in dependent areas of the lungs.

B. CLASSIFICATION

1. International Labour Organization (ILO) Classification of Chest Radiographs (Modified from Reference 7)

The first ILO classification of the radiographic appearance of pneumoconiosis was published by the ILO, Geneva, Switzerland, in 1930. The most recent modifications to the classification were published by the ILO in 1980 (8) and replace the 1971 International Classification of Radiographs. Each new classification published by the ILO has brought modifications and changes based on the international experience gained in the use of earlier classifications.

The 1980 classification consists of a written text, a set of standard reference radiographs, and a series of explanatory notes. The guidelines for its use contain both the complete and short classifications. The publication also includes information for recording the radiographic abnormalities that are provoked by the inhalation of dusts.

In order to classify chest radiographs properly in accordance with the ILO 1980 classification, one must be familiar not only with the features of the classification, but also with the explanation, background data, and recommendations provided in the guidelines published by the ILO. The radiograph being classified must be compared with the actual standard radiographs that can be obtained in North America from the regional center of the International Labour Office, 1750 York Avenue NW, Washington, DC 20006. In other parts of the world they may be purchased from the International Labour Offices, Geneva, Switzerland.

No features seen in a radiograph of the chest are pathognomonic of dust exposure. Recommendations for classifying a posteroanterior radiograph of the chest are that if any appearances of the pleura or the parenchyma are consistent with pneumoconiosis, the radiograph is classified. Any appearances that are definitely not consistent with pneumoconiosis are recorded using symbols and comments in accordance with the instructions of the ILO classification. If *all* the appearances are the result of some other etiology, they are recorded using the symbols and comments of the ILO classification. If the appearances *might* be due to pneumoconiosis, the observations are recorded according to the classification and other considered etiologies are noted.

For most purposes, a standard form should be used for classification of the radiograph for pneumoconiosis.

a. Technical Quality

The 1980 ILO classification requires an assessment of the technical, or radiographic, quality of the posteroanterior radiograph of the chest being classified. The four grades used to record technical quality are:

1. Good;
2. Acceptable, with no technical defect likely to impair classifying the radiograph for pneumoconiosis;
3. Poor, with some technical defect but still acceptable for the purpose of classification;
4. Unacceptable. If the technical quality is not Grade 1, the reader should make a comment about the technical defects.

b. Parenchymal Abnormalities

i. Small Opacities

These are classified according to profusion, extent, size, and shape.

Profusion. This category is based on an assessment of the concentration of opacities by comparison with the standard radiographs. The following definitions are a guide for recording purposes, but the standard radiographs take precedence:

- Category 0: Small opacities absent or less profuse than the lower limit of Category 1.
- Categories 1, 2, 3: Increasing profusion of small opacities as defined by corresponding standard radiographs.

A 12-point scale first adopted in the 1971 classification is retained in the 1980 classification. It recognizes the existence of a continuum of change from normal to the most advanced category. The four major categories (0, 1, 2, and 3) as defined by standard radiographs remain, but the scale permits subdivision of the categories, providing a more refined scoring system (Figs. 11-1 and 11-2).

Extent. Each lung (right or left) is divided into three zones:

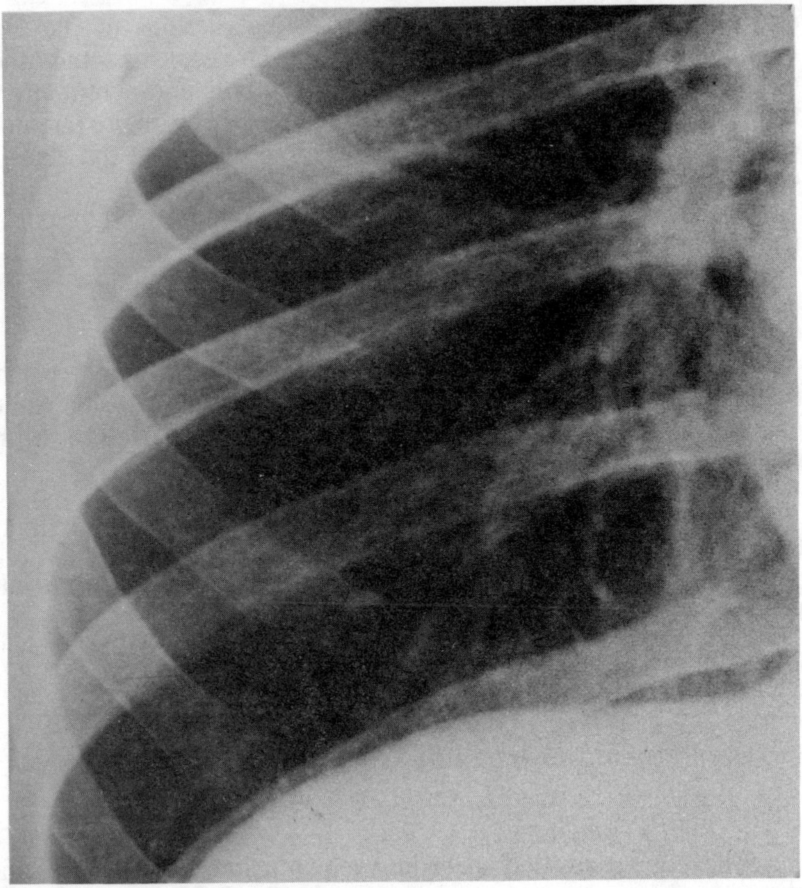

Fig. 11-1 Detail from chest radiograph shows normal (0/0) lung parenchyma.

upper, middle, and lower. The zones in which the opacities are seen are recorded.

Determination of the category of profusion of small opacities is based on a consideration of the profusion as a whole over the affected zones of the lungs. When there is a marked difference (three or more minor categories) in different zones of the lungs, the zone(s) showing the lesser degree of profusion is ignored for classifying profusion.

Shape and size. Both the shape and size of the small opacities are recorded. Two kinds of shape are recognized: rounded and irregular. Three sizes are differentiated for each of these shapes. The shapes and the sizes are illustrated by the standard radiographs.

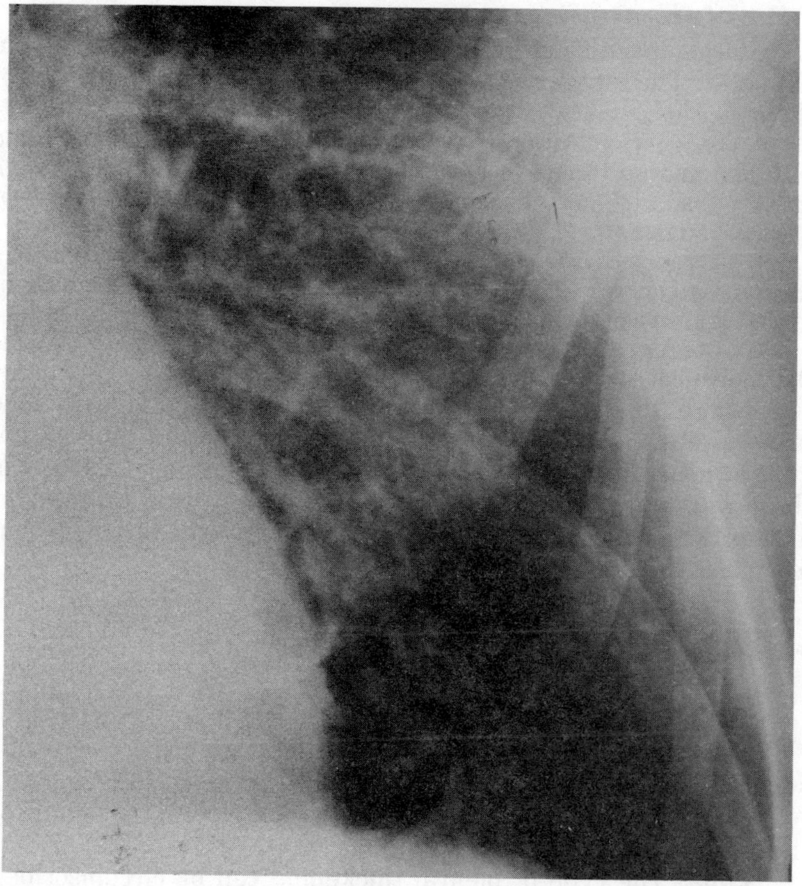

Fig. 11-2 Detail from chest radiograph shows abnormal lung parenchyma, with small irregular opacities of size s/t and profusion 1/1.

The letters **p, q,** and **r** denoted small *rounded* opacities. **p** is the diameter up to ≈1.5 mm. **q** is the diameter exceeding ≈1.5 mm up to ≈3 mm. **r** is th diameter exceeding ≈3 mm and up to ≈10 mm.

The letters **s, t,** and **u** denote small *irregular* (linear) opacities. **s** is the width up to ≈1.5 mm. **t** is the width exceeding ≈1.5 mm and up to ≈3 mm. **u** is the width exceeding ≈3 mm and up to ≈10 mm. The small opacities in asbestosis are all of the irregular variety.

Two letters are used to record shape and size. If all or virtually all the small opacities are of one shape and size, the letter is recorded twice. If a second shape or size is also present, the second shape or size is recorded as the second letter (Fig. 11-2). This permits the recording of a combination of small opacities.

ii. Large Opacities

Large opacities in the standard radiographs exceed 10 mm in diameter. The categories are defined in terms of the dimensions of the opacities.

- Category A: An opacity having a greatest diameter exceeding ≈10 mm and up to and including ≈50 mm, or several opacities each greater than ≈10 mm the sum of whose greatest diameters does not exceed ≈50 mm.
- Category B: One or more opacities larger or more numerous than those in Category A whose combined area does not exceed the equivalent of the right upper zone.
- Category C: One or more opacities whose combined area exceeds the equivalent of the right upper zone.

Large opacities were originally defined for upper lobe massive fibrosis found with silicosis. However, large lung parenchymal opacities are found in asbestos-related disease, usually in the lower lobes in combination with diffuse pleural thickening. Theoretically, these could be recorded under large opacities, but are usually described under comments.

c. Pleural Abnormalities

i. Pleural Thickening

The site, width, and extent of pleural thickening are recorded separately.

Chest wall. The type, site, and width of pleural thickening of the chest wall are recorded.

Type. The type of pleural thickening can be circumscribed (plaques), diffuse, or both circumscribed and diffuse.

Width. The measurement of the maximum width of pleural thickening along the lateral wall of the chest is from the inner line of the chest wall to the inner margin of the thickening. **a** is a maximum width up to ≈5 mm. **b** is maximum width greater than ≈5 mm and up to ≈10 mm. **c** is maximum width greater than about 10 mm.

Pleural thickening seen face on is recorded even if it is also in profile. If pleural thickening is face on only, the width cannot be measured.

Extent. The extent of pleural thickening is defined in terms of the maximum length of pleural involvement or as the sum of maximum lengths whether it is seen in profile or face on. **1** is the total length up to one-quarter of the projection of the lateral chest wall. **2** is the total length greater than one-quarter but one one-half of the projection of the lateral chest wall. **3** is the total length greater than one-half of the projection of the lateral chest wall.

Diaphragm. A plaque involving the diaphragmatic pleura is recorded separately as present or absent, right or left.

Costophrenic Angle Obliteration. This thickening is recorded separately from thickening at other sites. If the thickening extends up the chest wall, the radiograph is classified both for obliteration of the costophrenic angle and pleural thickening. Obliteration of the costophrenic angle is recorded as present or absent, and the site (right or left) is specified.

ii. Pleural Calcification

The site and extent are recorded separately.

Site. The sites of pleural calcification recorded are the chest wall, the diaphragm, and "other." Other includes calcification of the mediastinal and the pericardial pleura.

Extent. **1** is a site of calcified pleura with greatest length up to ≈20 mm, or a number of such sites the sum of whose greatest lengths does not exceed ≈20 mm. **2** is a site of calcified pleura with greatest length exceeding ≈20 mm and up to ≈100 mm, or a number of such sites the sum of whose greatest length exceeds ≈20 mm but does not exceed ≈100 mm. **3** is a site of calcified pleura with greatest length exceeding ≈100 mm, or a number of such sites the sum of whose greatest lengths exceeds ≈100 mm.

d. Symbols

Symbols are used to record radiographic features of importance and cover a range of chest abnormalities. Their use is obligatory.

D. THE ILO AND ASBESTOS-RELATED DISEASE

The initial development of the ILO system was for epidemiological study and not litigation. It initially applied to coal- and gold-mine workers and modifications have been made for its application to asbestos workers. Several problems are therefore present for asbestos-related diseases. The classification does not allow for oblique radiographs to be used, whereas these may frequently show pleural plaques not detected on a posteroanterior radiograph. The classification does not include honeycombing as a primary finding in pneumoconiosis, although this is distinctly part of asbestosis. Focal lung findings of asbestosis, such as rounded atelectasis, are also not part of the classification.

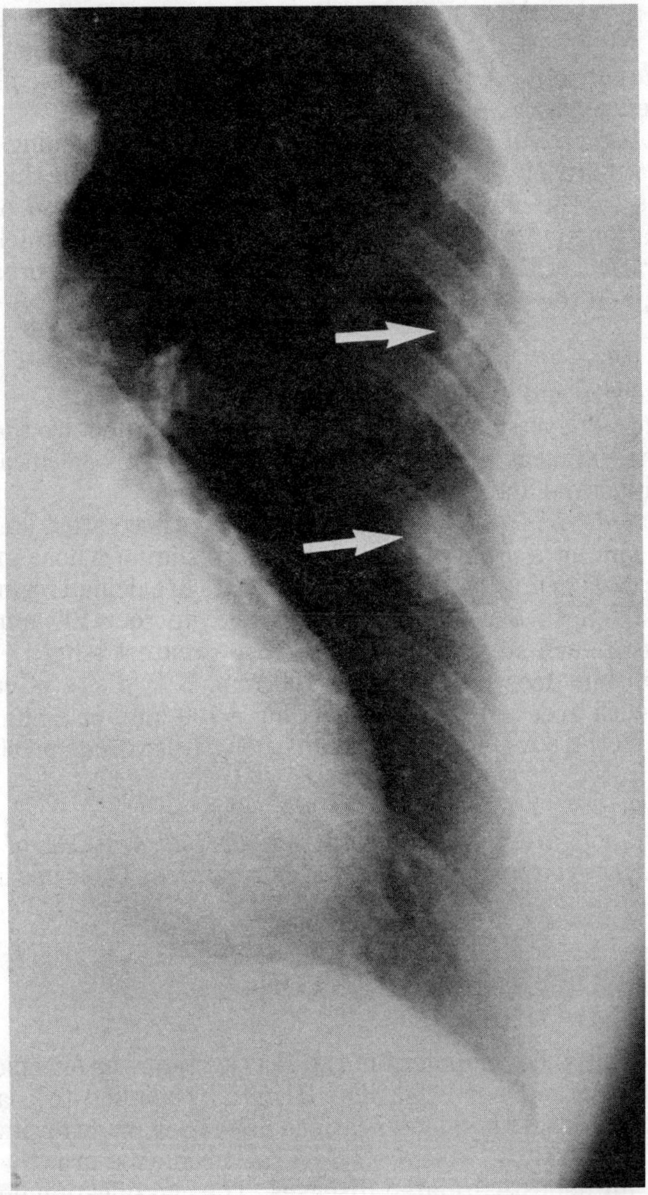

Fig. 11-3 Oblique chest radiograph shows multiple noncalcified pleural plaques (arrowheads) not evident on the frontal radiograph.

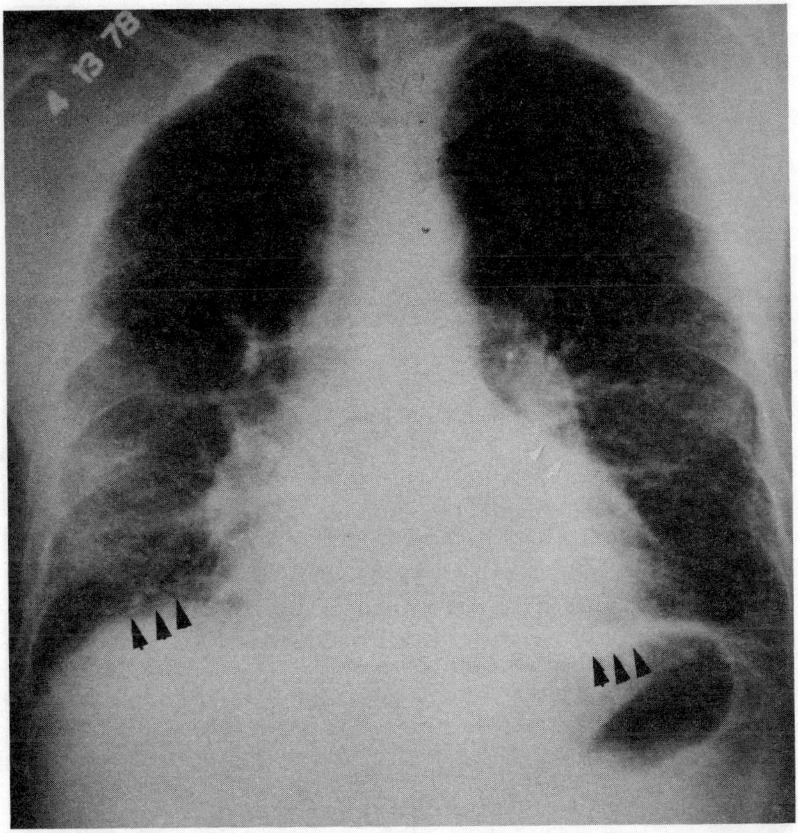

Fig. 11-4 Chest radiograph in a patient with honeycombing shows fine calcification of pleural plaques (arrowheads).

E. ASBESTOS-RELATED DISEASE

The following thoracic asbestos-related disorders will be described: pleural plaques; benign asbestos pleural effusion; diffuse pleural thickening; asbestosis; benign pulmonary masses, including rounded atelectasis; malignant mesothelioma; and bronchogenic carcinoma.

1. Asbestos-Related Pleural Plaques

a. Chest Radiographs

Pleural plaques are identified on the chest radiograph most commonly as an irregular thickening between the lateral chest wall and the adjacent lung (Fig. 11-3). They are most readily

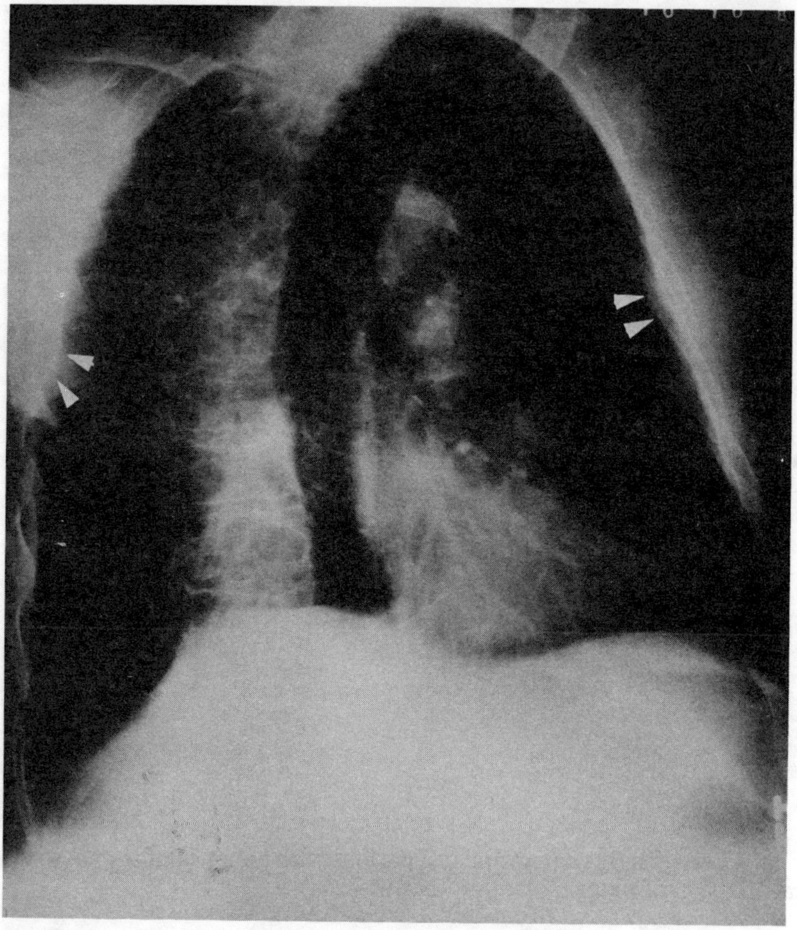

Fig. 11-5 Frontal chest radiograph shows multiple calcified pleural plaques (arrows) in a female asbestos-exposed patient.

demonstrated between the fifth and tenth ribs and are usually bilateral and more common against the inner margin of the ribs. They may also occur over the diaphragms, next to the spine, and over the heart. Noncalcified pleural placques are considerably more frequent but are more difficult to detect on chest radiographs than calcified plaques. They are best seen in profile, as a localized area of soft tissue 1–15 mm thick, deep to the chest wall or as localized bulges along the diaphragm. In the ILO system, pleural plaques are coded in terms of their thickness (seen in profile) and the total length of chest wall involvement. Calcified plaques may be identified either in profile, when the x-ray beam passes tangential to the calcified plaque, or face on. In profile, they are seen as linear opacities that parallel the chest wall or diaphragm (Fig. 11-4). Face on, they are seen as irregularly geographic opacities that often attain a considerable size (Fig. 11-5). Many calcified plaques will have a noncalcified component. Pleural calcification and diaphragmatic plaques are recorded separately from noncalcified plaques in the ILO classification. Pleural plaques will be detected with greater frequency if oblique chest radiographs are performed in addition to the standard PA projection (Fig. 11-3). The x-ray beam passes through more tissue in the oblique projection, so well-penetrated high kVp radiographs are optimal for this projection.

Noncalcified plaques must be differentiated from normal anatomic shadows, especially the serratus anterior muscle, from fat deposits, and from other causes of localized pleural thickening. The slips of origin of the serratus anterior muscle are seen as symmetric triangular opacities with their apices directed inferomedially, arising near the lateral aspects of the fifth through ninth ribs. Pleural plaques will be less angular and less symmetric. A "companion shadow," appearing as a thin white line paralleling the medial surface of the upper 3 or 4 ribs, may occasionally be mistaken for a pleural plaque. Noncalcified diaphragmatic plaques can be difficult to differentiate from normal diaphragmatic lobulation. The development of squared-off or plateau opacities on the diaphragm on serial radiographs over several years is good evidence of diaphragmatic plaques. They are most commonly shown on radiographs over the middle third of the diaphragm.

A diagnostic problem is posed by the frequent presence of extrapleural fat, especially in overweight people (9). These fat deposits are characteristically seen on chest radiographs as a wavy, continuous band of soft tissue thickening, most often posterolaterally in location, sparing the lung bases and costophrenic angles. This soft tissue band may have a lower density component, suggestive of fat, but this is often subtle. Accurate differentiation between subpleural fat deposition and noncalcified pleural plaques on the plain chest radiograph may be straight-forward or may be impossible. In particular, the presence of plaques superimposed on extrapleural fat may be difficult to discern. Extrapleural fat is not coded in the ILO system. When extrapleural fat is a differential consideration, CT scans will readily make the correct diagnosis.

The chest radiograph has a high specificity and low sensitivity for detecting pleural plaques found at autopsy (10). If less strict criteria are used for the presence of plaques, the sensitivity increases but the specificity goes down. Likewise, most pleural plaques seen on CT are not identified on chest radiographs (4).

b. Conventional CT

On CTT scans pleural plaques are readily identified as discontinuous lines or bands of increased density, ranging from 1 mm to more than 5 mm in thickness (1, 4). Their density is usually greater than that of muscle. CT will readily show plaques along the spine, mediastinum, posterior rib cage, and anterior rib cage, that are usually not seen on frontal chest radiographs. In our study of 100 asbestos-exposed individuals, we found that CCT was more sensitive than chest radiographs for detecting plaques (Table 11-2) (4). CT also greatly improves determining the extent of plaques and increasing the confidence with which they can be diagnosed. The ability of CT to differentiate between plaques and extrapleural fat has already been mentioned. Subpleural fat deposition is seen as a continuous band of decreased density that may invaginate the interlobar fissures (11). Plaques superimposed on subpleural fat may be readily identified (Fig. 11-6). Calcification within plaques is also more readily diagnosed with CCT than with chest radiographs (Table 11-2). Occasionally, very mild degrees of pleural thickening may not be apparent on CCT.

c. HRCT

HRCT reveals the anatomy of the pleural and subpleural tissues with superb detail (Fig. 11-6). Even minor pleural plaques are readily identified and can be distinguished from underlying intercostal vessels and muscle layers. In our study of 100 asbestos-exposed workers, we identified pleural plaques in 56 subjects by CCT, while 64 had definite plaques on HRCT (Table 11-2) (4).

Table 11-2 Comparison of Imaging Modalities for Detecting Asbestos-Related Pleural Disease (4)

100 Subjects	HRCT	CCT	CRX
Plaques	64 (+29 min)	56 (+25 min)	49
Calcification	20	16	13

min = minimal pleural abnormality

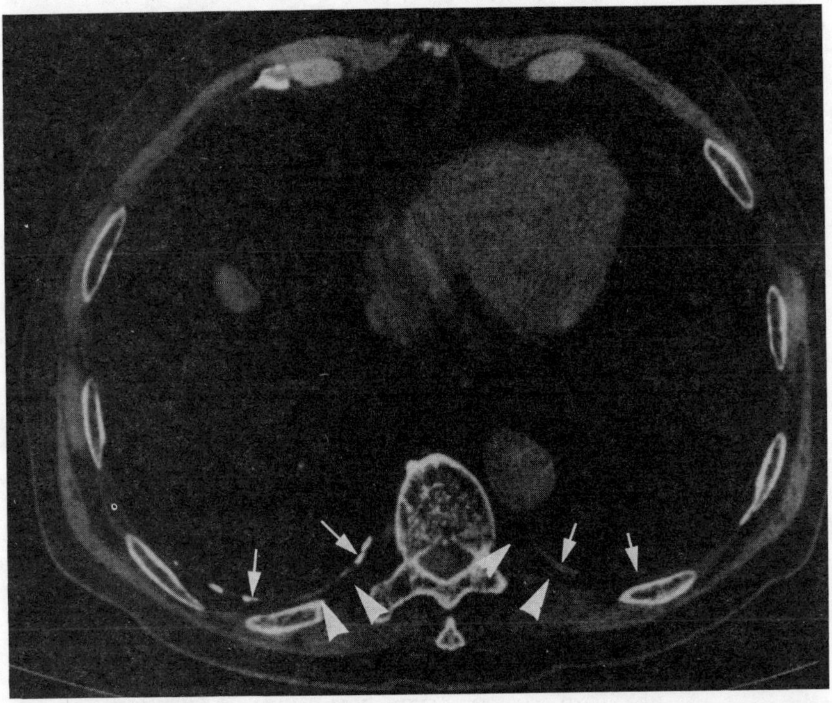

Fig. 11-6 Supine HRCT shows calcified and noncalcified pleural plaques (arrows) superimposed on a layer of extrapleural fat (arrowheads).

Thus, HRCT is more sensitive for pleural abnormality than CCT, despite the fact that it samples only 10 thin slices per patient. We have encountered the occasional subject in whom CCT demonstrated pleural plaques not identified by HRCT.

d. Fissural Pleural Plaques

Pleural plaques are much more common on the parietal pleura (the outer pleural layer against the chest wall), but may also occur on the visceral pleura (the inner pleural layer enveloping the lungs). Therefore, plaques may uncommonly be seen in the interlobar fissures that consist entirely of visceral pleura (2, 12). These may be confused with a lung nodule on chest radiographs or CCT. A lateral chest radiograph may show the fissural plaque lying along the major or minor interlobar fissure (2). In cases of doubt, HRCT will show the precise relationship of the plaque to the fissure. An interlobar pleural plaque is coded as “pi” in the ILO classification, but this notation does not distinguish between interlobar pleural plaques and more diffuse visceral pleural thickening.

e. Diffuse Visceral and Parietal Pleural Thickening (Fibrosis)

Combined diffuse visceral and parietal pleural thickening is most commonly due to prior pleuritis with or without effusion (14). Its differentiation from large pleural plaques on chest radiographs is essentially one of extent and may be difficult. The most recent working definition (14) is a smooth uninterrupted pleural density extending over at least one quarter of the chest wall, with or without obliteration of the costophrenic angle (Fig. 11-7). The ILO classification of pleural thickening records the total length of pleural thickening, its width, and the presence or absence of costophrenic angle obliteration.

Patients with diffuse combined pleural thickening provide a history of a prior benign pleural effusion in about 50% of instances (14). In a minority of cases, confluent pleural plaques, previous trauma, or infection can produce an appearance of diffuse thickening of the pleura. On CCT and HRCT, we have defined diffuse pleural thickening as pleural thickening more than 3 mm thick, at least 8 cm in cephalocaudal extent, and at least 5 cm thick in transverse extent (2, 4). On CT, diffuse pleural thickening is different from large pleural plaques because it usually has an irregular inner margin, a lower CT density, and does not calcify.

f. Pleural Effusion

Benign, asbestos-related pleural effusion occurs in 3% to 7% of asbestos-exposed individuals, often within 10 years from initial exposure (15). Radiologically, the effusions are often small, may persist or recur, and may be simultaneously or sequentially bilateral. The clinical presentation ranges from a mild short episode of malaise to an acute illness with fever, chest pain, and an elevated white blood cell count. The effusions are most frequently exudative and blood-tinged. There is nothing specific about the radiographic appearance of these effusions, and the diagnosis is one of exclusion of malignancy or other causes of an exudative effusion. The major differential possibilities are mesothelioma, metastatic cancer, and, less likely, infection. The most difficult to exclude is malignant mesothelioma, and indeed cases of "benign asbestos-related pleural effusions" have been found to develop mesothelioma at intervals of up to 7 years from initial presentation. We have encountered three patients in whom the effusion resolved, who developed mesothelioma within 3 years. Asbestos-related pleural effusions are likely to be associated with rounded atelectasis and with linear, fibrotic strands radiating into the surrounding lung (16). However, these findings may occur in relation to any chronic pleural fibrosis. Benign asbestos-related pleural effusion must be differentiated clinically from other causes of chornic pleural effusion such as infection (including tuberculosis) and trauma. The majority of benign asbestos-related pleural effusions lead to diffuse, combined pleural thickening, with consequent restriction of pulmonary function.

g. Visceral Pleural Thickening

Diffuse thickening localized to the visceral pleura is most commonly from subpleural fibrosis extending from lung fibrosis. On the chest radiograph, it is manifested as increased thickness of the interlobar fissures, a finding that increases with increased latency (13). On chest radiographs, it is not possible to distinguish costal visceral pleural thickening from parietal pleural thickening. On HRCT, visceral pleural thickening is different in appearance from combined diffuse pleural thickening or pleural plaques. It is seen as a thin, irregular pleural line, usually associated with changes of lung fibrosis in the subjacent lung (Fig. 11-8). Parietal pleural thickening or plaques, in contrast, are usually well defined and smooth or lumpy on CT.

h. Mesothelioma

Although the relationship between asbestos exposure and mesothelioma has been known for only 30 years, the number of cases has escalated in the last 10 years. The relationship to asbestos exposure is not dose-related (17). Slight or transient exposure can cause tumor induction. The risk of mesothelioma is related to the type of asbestos fiber to which a person has been exposed. Crocidolite poses a much higher risk than amosite or chrysotile. The incidence of mesothelioma can have a 30- to 40-year latency and rises exponentially with latency (18). About half of all patients with mesothelioma have had an occupational exposure to asbestos. The incidence in the USA may be as high as 10,000 per year for the next 30 years. Malignant mesothelioma most frequently presents as a large unilateral pleural effusion (18, 19). Virtually all cases will have pleural fluid at some stage in their disease. Other presentations include pleural thickening that is commonly nodular or lobulated (Fig. 11-9) or, less commonly, a solitary pleural mass. The ipsilateral hemothorax is often decreased in volume, in contrast to most pleural effusions. Nodular invasion of the fissures is

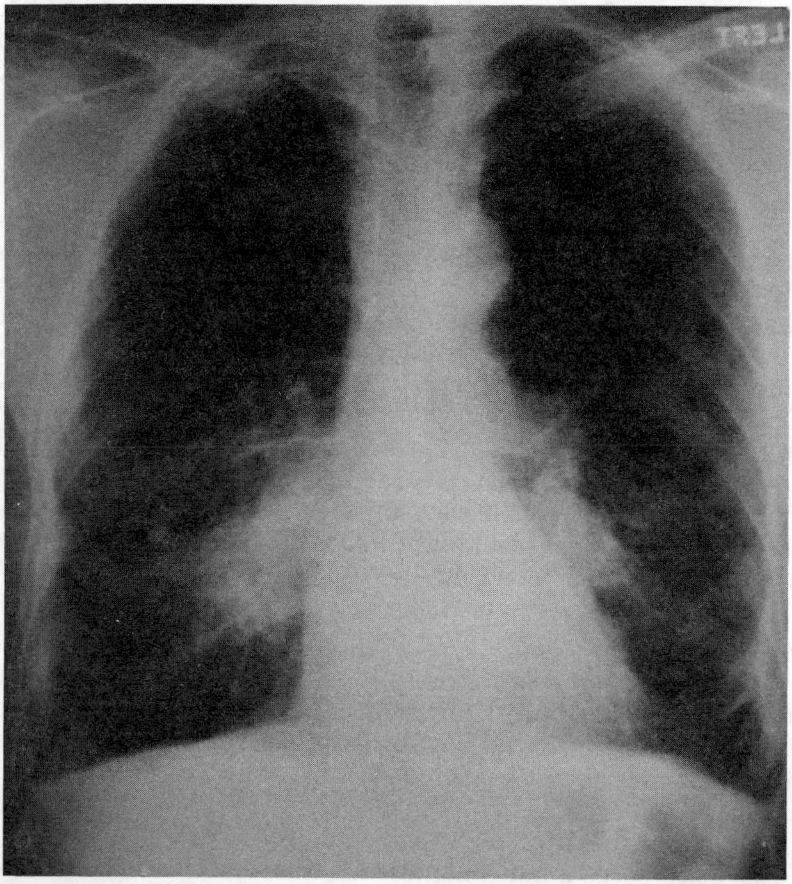

Fig. 11-7a Frontal chest radiograph shows bilateral pleural thickening with obliteration of both costophrenic angles. Bilateral lower lobe masses are seen.

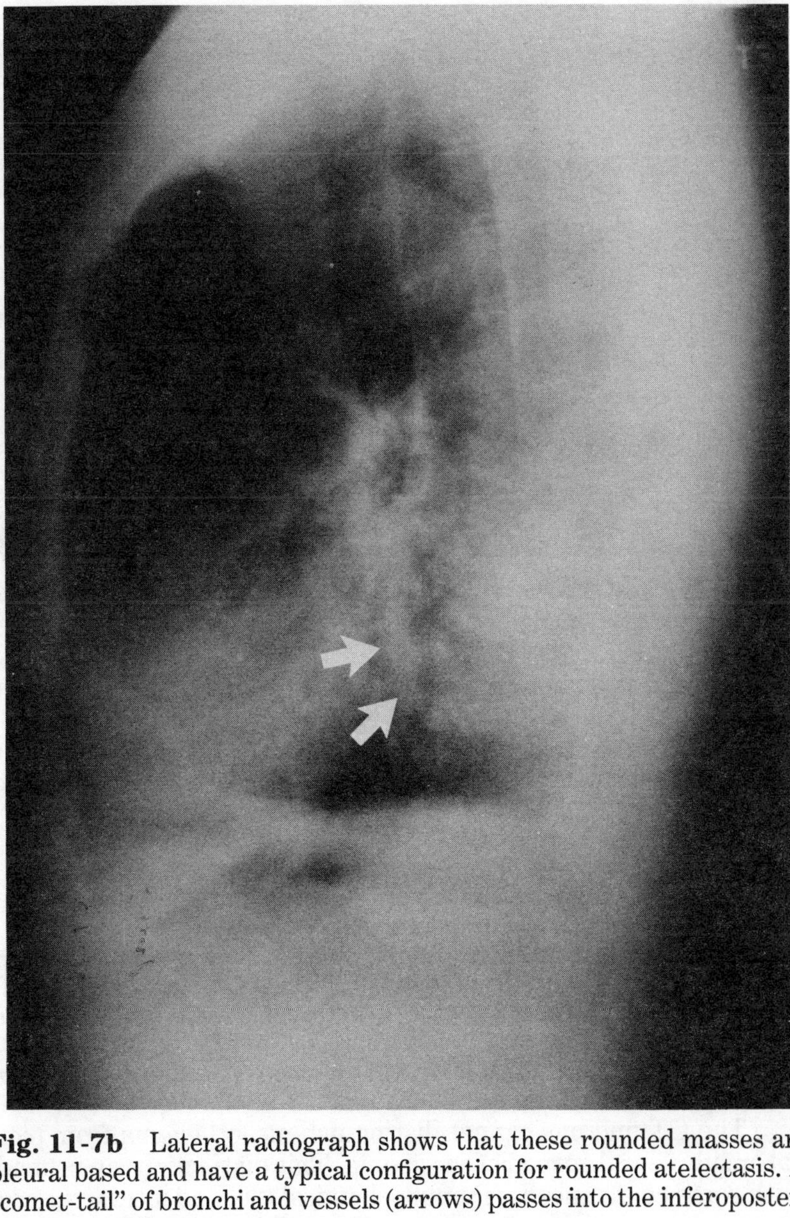

Fig. 11-7b Lateral radiograph shows that these rounded masses are pleural based and have a typical configuration for rounded atelectasis. A "comet-tail" of bronchi and vessels (arrows) passes into the inferoposterior aspect of the mass.

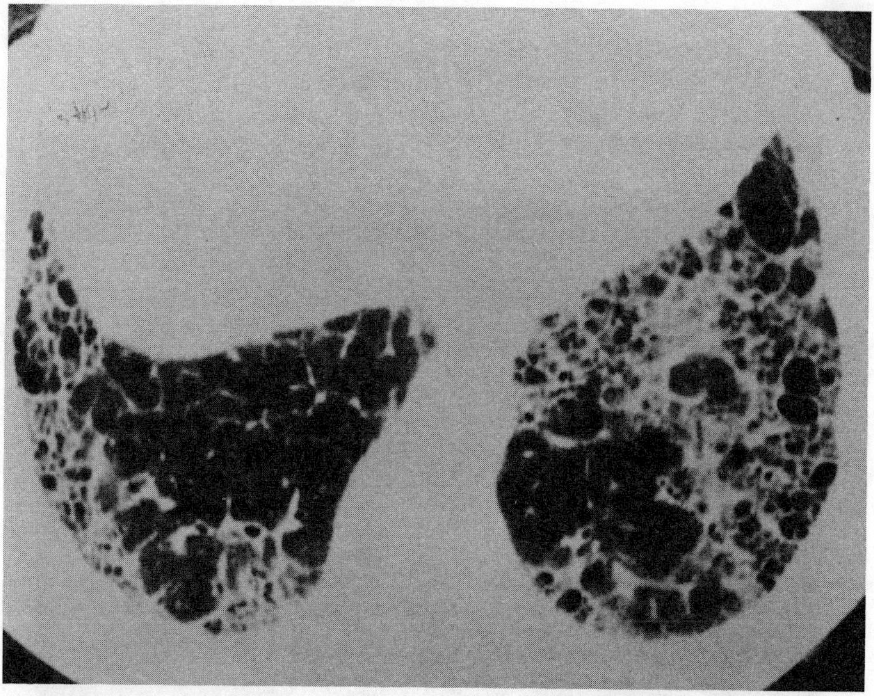

Fig. 11-8 HRCT seen at the level of the diaphragm shows marked bilateral honeycombing.

common and is better demonstrated with CT than on plain radiographs.

The CT features of mesothelioma (18, 19) include (Fig. 11-9):

1. Focal, nodular, or plaquelike pleural thickenings that tend to be larger and more numerous than asbestos-related hyaline pleural plaques.
2. Pleural effusions of various sizes (in 80% to 95% of patients).
3. Pleural encasement that later becomes circumferential.
4. Ipsilateral intrapulmonary nodules (in about 60% of patients).
5. Spread of the tumor to hilar and mediastinal nodes, through the chest wall, and across the diaphragm, all of which can be detected by CT.
6. Shrinkage of the involved hemithorax as the tumor becomes circumferential.
7. Distant metastases. (Though common at autopsy, these are rarely apparent clinically before death.)

The CT findings cannot distinguish mesothelioma from pleural or subpleural spread of carcinoma. This distinction can be made with some confidence by immunochemical (20) and ultrastructural examination. CT is of value in determining the extent of the mesothelioma when surgery (pleurectomy or radical pneumonectomy) is being considered (17, 18). If surgery is contemplated, CT is indicated to demonstrate possible spread through the chest wall, into the mediastinum, through the diaphragm, or metastatic nodules most commonly in the ipsilateral or contralateral lung. CT can also help follow the response to chemotherapy or radiotherapy.

CT may identify focal areas of pleural thickening suitable for biopsy in patients with pleural effusions. Initial experience with magnetic resonance imaging suggests that it may be able to differentiate malignant mesothelioma from longstanding pleural fibrosis and may be sensitive for detecting invasion of the mediastinum and chest wall.

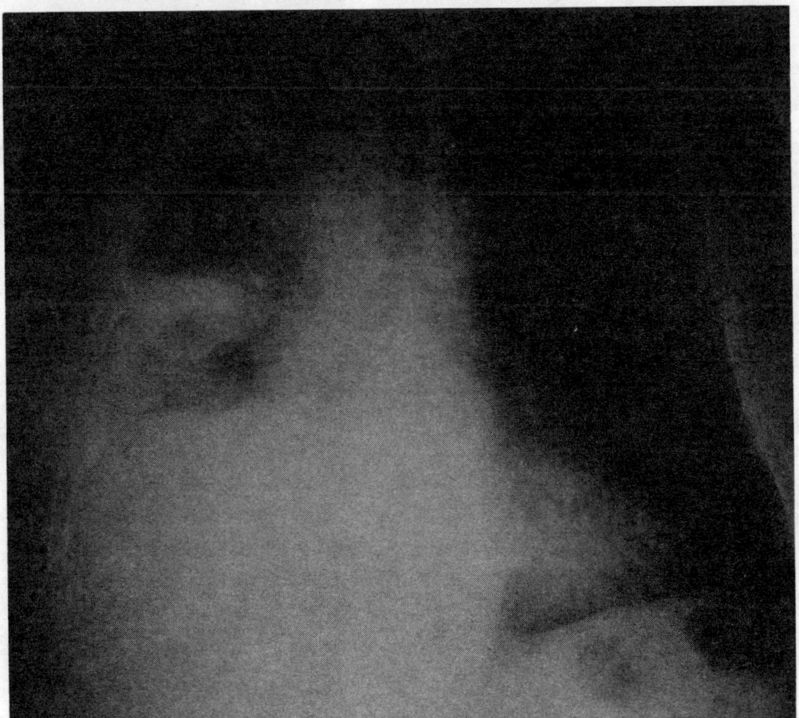

Fig. 11-9a Chest radiograph of a patient with advanced malignant mesothelioma shows a right pleural effusion with decreased size of the right hemithorax and multiple pleural nodules.

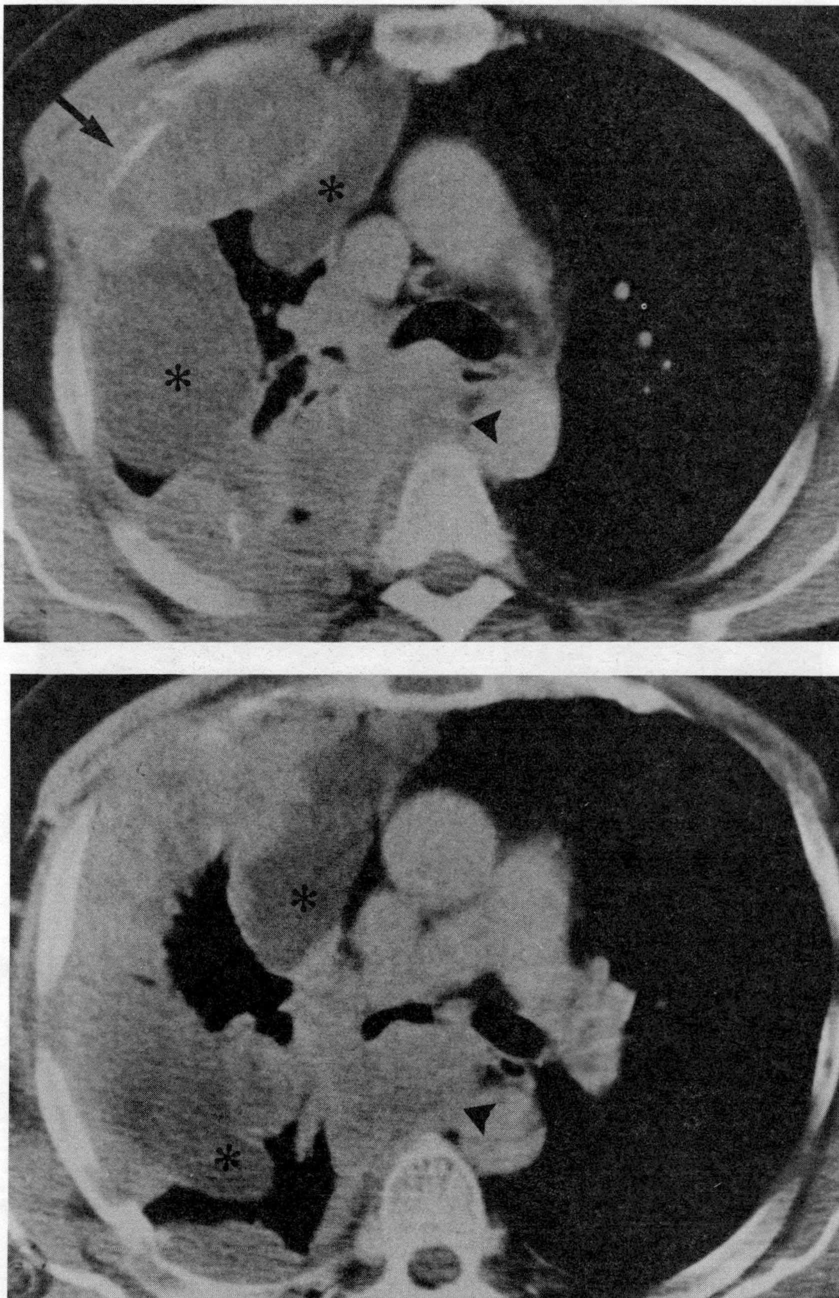

Fig. 11-9b and c Conventional CT scans of the same patient show multiple soft-tissue masses with rib destruction (arrow) and extension into mediastinum (arrowheads). There is a large amount of loculated pleural fluid (asterisks).

2. Asbestosis

a. Chest Radiographs

Asbestos-related lung fibrosis is characterized on the chest radiograph by small irregular opacities, septal lines, and in more advanced cases by linear bands of fibrosis and honeycombing. Associated pleural abnormalities are common but may be absent in 15% to 20% of cases (21). The small irregular opacities are coded in the ILO classifications as **s, t,** or **u** according to their size and are rated for profusion on a 12-point scale from 0/− to 3/+ by comparison with standard radiographs (Figs. 11-1 and 11-2) (6). Though the ILO classification has proven value as an epidemiologic tool in the study of pneumoconioses, it is basically descriptive rather than interpretive in nature, and was never intended to be a diagnostic scale. Correlation with pulmonary function tests shows wide interindividual variation within the same ILO grade (22, 23).

The lower limits of the ILO profusion score for an acceptable diagnosis of asbestosis has remained controversial. In the legal arena a score of 1/1 is accepted by virtually all as clearly compatible with pulmonary asbestosis. Many authorities will accept 1/0 as indicative of parenchymal lung disease. These narrow differences do not take into account the subject nature of the observations or the real interobserver error in radiographic interpretation. In general, interpretation of the ILO standard radiographs is conservative as would be expected with an epidemiologic, as opposed to a diagnostic, classification.

It is generally recognized that between 10% and 25% of patients with histologically demonstrable interstitial pulmonary fibrosis will have a normal chest radiograph (22, 24, 25). Thus, while the presence of small irregular opacities on the chest radiograph, with an appropriate exposure history, is compatible with and strongly suggestive of asbestosis, a normal radiograph does not exclude asbestosis.

The pulmonary parenchymal changes found in asbestosis may be pathologically and radiologically indistinguishable from those in idiopathic pulmonary fibrosis. Asbestosis has a basal predominance, while idiopathic fibrosis does not. Without a biopsy, the diagnosis of asbestosis will always have an element of presumption. The 1986 American Thoracic Society Statement on the Diagnosis of Asbestosis (26) indicates that the diagnosis is not excluded by a normal chest radiograph but should be made with caution.

A further significant difficulty in radiographic interpretation is that asbestos-exposed smokers demonstrate an increased incidence of small irregular opacities on chest radiographs (27, 28). However, there is no corresponding increase in functional abnormalities indicating restrictive lung disease in this group. Therefore, in asbestos-exposed smokers, the presence of **s, t,** or **u** opacities on the radiograph may be deceptive. Evidence suggests HRCT may now more precisely detect lung fibrosis in exposed smokers (29).

b. Conventional CT

CCT scanning will readily demonstrate honeycombing and parenchymal bands of fibrosis in moderate or severe asbestosis (1). In general, its resolution does not permit the detection of the fine interstitial thickening characteristic of asbestosis. For this reason, it has been supplanted by HRCT.

c. High Resolution CT

The signs of asbestosis on HRCT (Table 11-3) are based on an understanding of the anatomy of the secondary pulmonary lobule (30). This is the basic functional subunit of the lung and is supplied by a small bronchus and accompanying pulmonary artery branch. These reach the center of the lobule as "core structures" and their branches radiate out toward the periphery. The interlobular septa that mark the boundaries of each lobule contain the pulmonary veins and lymphatics that drain the lobule. These septa are best defined at the periphery of the lung. On HRCT of the normal lung (Fig. 11-10), the interlobular septa and core structures are identified as very fine linear structures. The earliest HRCT evidence of asbestosis is the presence of core structure thickening and thickening of interlobular septa (3–5). These features appear to correspond to histologic peribronchiolar fibrosis (31) and septal fibrosis. The HRCT findings of asbestosis are (4):

1. *Interstitial Thickening* (Fig. 11-11). Abnormal interstitial thickening is due to either thickened septal lines or core structures. Thickened septal lines are evident as linear densities 1 to 2 cm in length, usually extending to the pleura. Thickened core structures are branching lines radiating from a central core, originating about 1 cm from the pleura within the secondary pulmonary lobule. Thickening of the interlobular septa in pulmonary asbestosis is due to interstitial fibrosis. Prominent core structures seen radiating from the center of the secondary pulmonary lobule represent peribronchiolar fibrosis.

Prone images are critical for confirming the fixed structural nature of thickened septal lines and core structures in asbestosis (4). Prominent dependent septal lines can be due to vascular distention and may be

Table 11-3 HRCT Features of Asbestosis

Sign	Description	Significance	Probable Pathologic Correlate
Core structure thickening	Radiating fine lines within 1–2 cm of pleural surface in nondependent lung	Suggestive of early	Probably peribronchiolar lung fibrosis
Septal thickening	Parallel short lines perpendicular to pleura, extending 1–2 cm into lung	Suggestive of early lung fibrosis septa	Fibrous thickening of interlobular or intralobular
Curvilinear subpleural line	1–10 cm line within 1 cm of pleura, and parallel to it	Common in dependent lung; suggests fibrosis when persistent in nondependent lung	Peribronchiolar fibrosis
Haze	Persistent "ground-glass" increased density of nondependent lung	Uncommon; may indicate active lung inflammation	May represent alveolitis
Parenchymal bands	2–5 cm lines contacting pleural surface, extending into lung parenchyma	Indicates lung fibrosis	Fibrotic bands
Honeycombing	Cystlike spaces <1 cm diameter with walls 1–3 mm	End-stage lung destruction	Destroyed lung, with air cysts and dilated bronchioles
Visceral pleural thickening	Thickened irregular pleural surface	Advanced fibrosis (usually with other signs)	Subpleural fibrosis

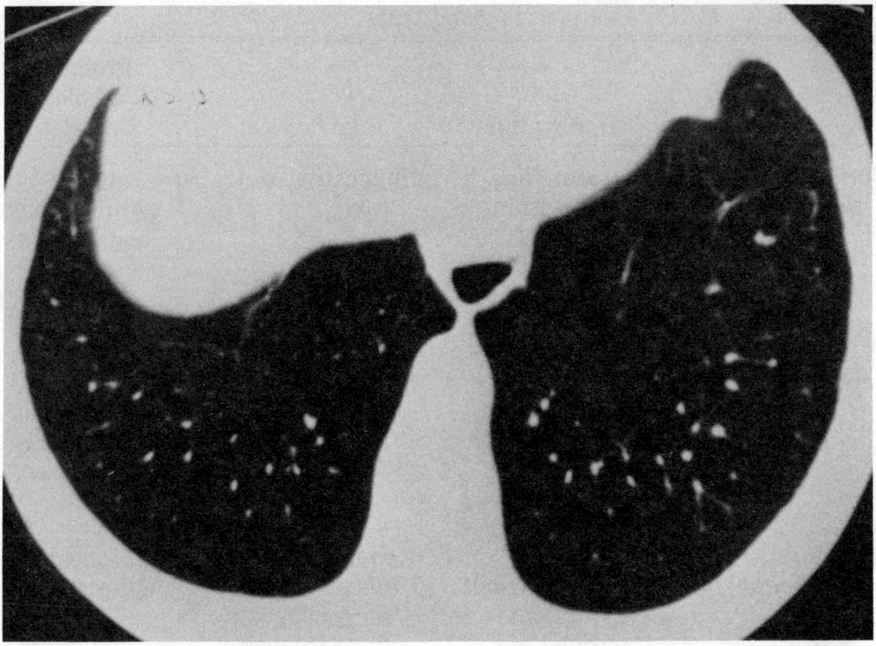

Fig. 11-10 Prone HRCT scan shows normal lung parenchyma. The fine branching structures near the periphery of the lung represent normal pulmonary arteries and veins.

misinterpreted as pulmonary fibrosis. Septal thickening in the nondependent lung is invariably abnormal and, in the correct clinical setting, is usually due to fibrosis. However, cellular infiltration of the interstitium, unrelated to asbestosis, can produce similar fixed abnormalities (32, 33). Interstitial thickening is seen in virtually all patients with asbestosis.

2. *Honeycombing* (Figs. 11-8–11-12). On CT, honeycombing appears as multiple cystic spaces 1 to 15 mm in diameter, with thick walls. Most commonly, the honeycomb pattern is subpleural in distribution and predominates in the posterior lower lobes. The adjacent pleura is frequently thickened. Dilation of small bronchi and bronchioles may be evident within the honeycombing.

In general, the honeycomb pattern on HRCT corresponds to histologic honeycombing. The pattern is seen in about 20% of patients with the HRCT finding of asbestosis.

3. *Parenchymal Bands* (Fig. 11-13). These bands are linear densities 2 to 5 cm in length, running through the lung, generally not in the direction of pulmonary blood vessels, and usually extending to the pleural surface.

Parenchymal bands represent fibrosis of connective tissue septa, extending deep into the pulmonary parenchyma. Parenchymal bands are

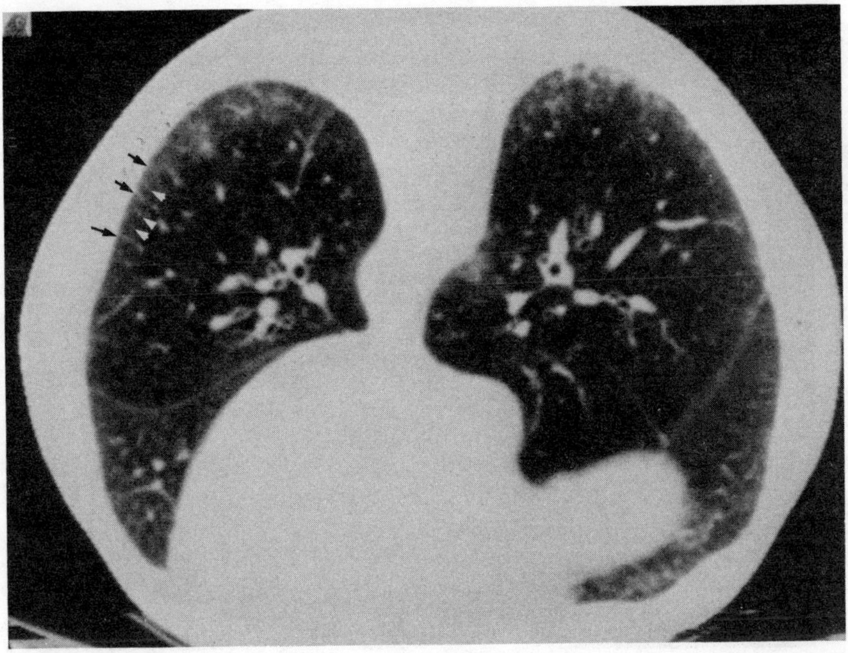

Fig. 11-11 Prone HRCT scan shows bilateral interlobular septal thickening (arrows) and prominent core structures (arrowhead).

fixed, structural abnormalities and do not vary when the subject moves from the supine to the prone position.

4. *Subpleural Lines* (Fig. 11-14). These linear densities are within 1 cm of the pleura and parallel to it (34). Subpleural lines occur in the dependent lung in about 30% of patients with asbestosis and in an equal percentage of normal subjects. They often clear in asbestosis and always clear in normal lungs when the lung is nondependent. A subpleural line that persists in the prone position is usually seen with other features of asbestosis and is probably indicative of distorted interlobular septal fibrosis. In our experience, only subpleural lines in the nondependent lung are significant. In some instances, subpleural honeycomb cysts are marginated by a subpleural line. The subpleural line in such instances represents the innermost extent of the row of subpleural honeycomb cysts.

5. *Subpleural Dependent Density* (Fig. 11-15). This is a 2 to 30 mm thick band of poorly marginated, increased pulmonary density paralleling the dependent pleura and obscuring the underlying pulmonary morphology. The dependent density usually clears when the region is nondependent. It may be found in subjects without pulmonary abnormalities.

The zone of the subpleural density in the dependent lung seen

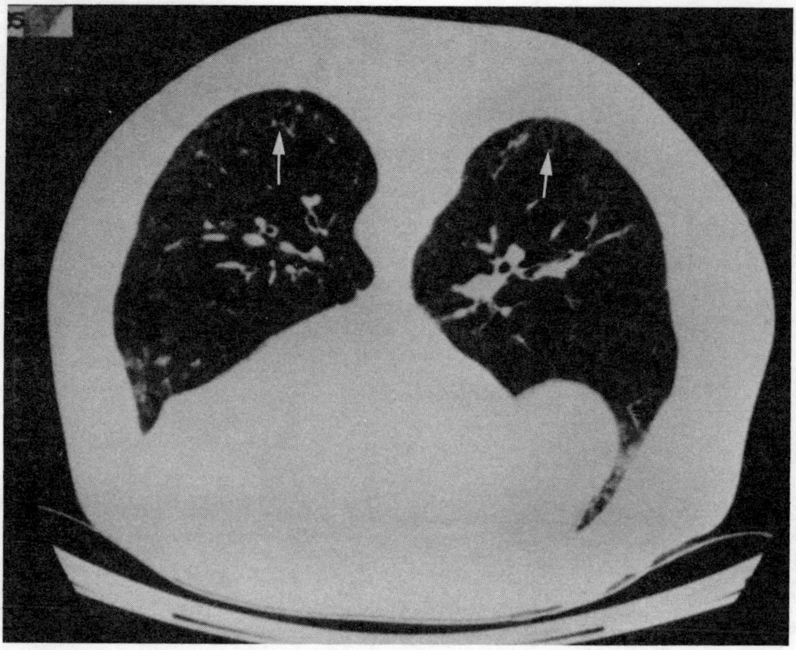

Fig. 11-12 Prone HRCT scan of a patient with asbestosis shows bilateral focal honeycombing, seen as small (less than 1.0 cm) air-filled cysts (arrows).

on HRCT in patients with asbestosis may reflect decreased pulmonary compliance, but dependent density has no pathologic correlate. Subpleural dependent density occurs in about 60% of asbestos-exposed persons and in 30% of persons without pulmonary disease (4). In asbestosis, the density may persist when that pulmonary region is nondependent but it more commonly clears (Fig. 11-15), revealing septal thickening or other architectural abnormalities. In normal persons, dependent density always clears and reveals a normal underlying pulmonary structure.

Thus, the optimal HRCT evaluation of the pulmonary parenchyma necessitates supine and prone scans. The major sites of fibrosis in the pulmonary parenchyma are the posterior bases. On supine scans, the lung bases are compressed, are at a lower lung volume than the nondependent lung, and have a larger blood volume. The persistence of abnormalities when the involved lung is nondependent is an important distinguishing feature of abnormality in the diagnosis of asbestosis, as it is in the diagnosis of other interstitial diseases.

HRCT has a strong, positive relationship to radiographic and clinical asbestosis. The vast majority of patients (over 95%) who

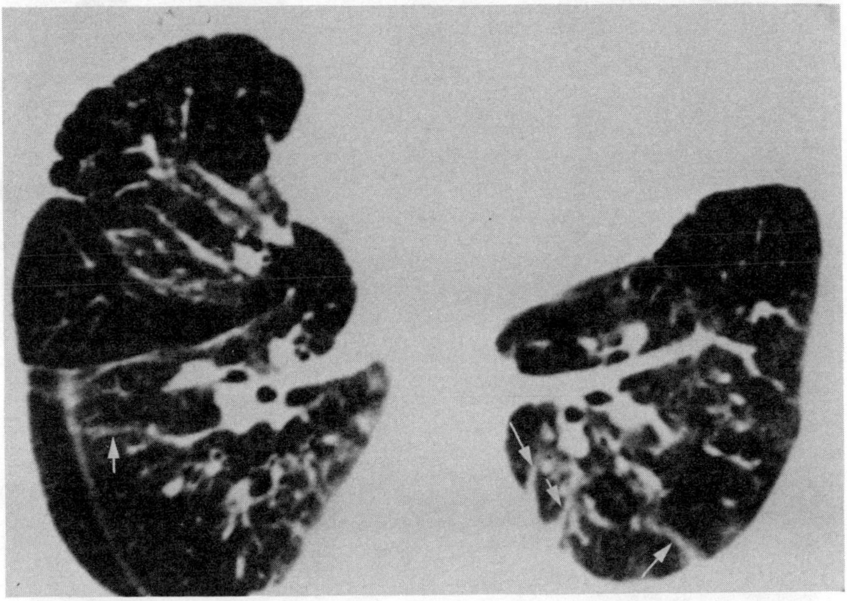

Fig. 11-13 Prone HRCT scan shows multiple parenchymal bands of fibrosis traversing both lungs (arrows). These cannot represent vessels because of their thickness, lack of branching, and abnormal course.

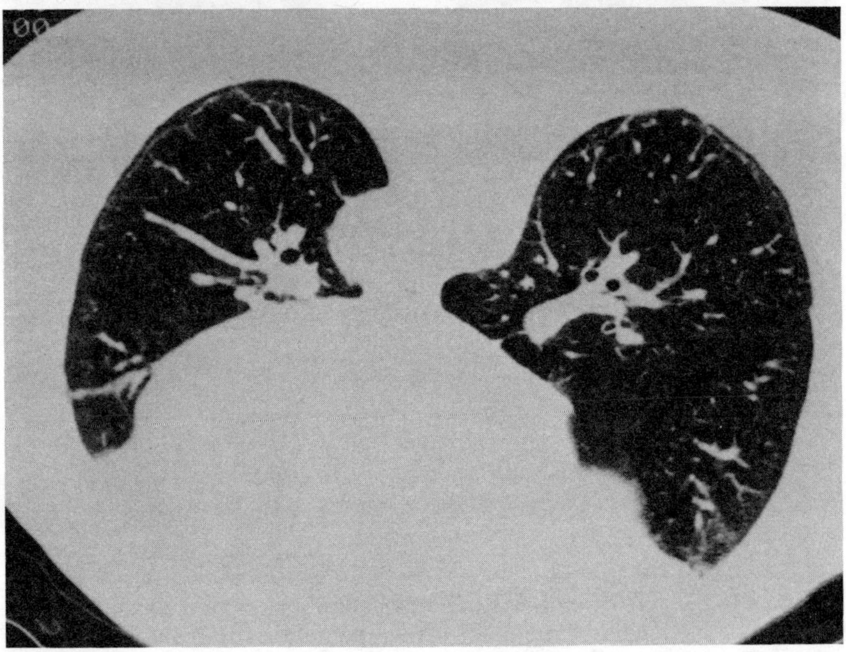

Fig. 11-14 Prone HRCT scan shows bilateral subpleural curvilinear lines.

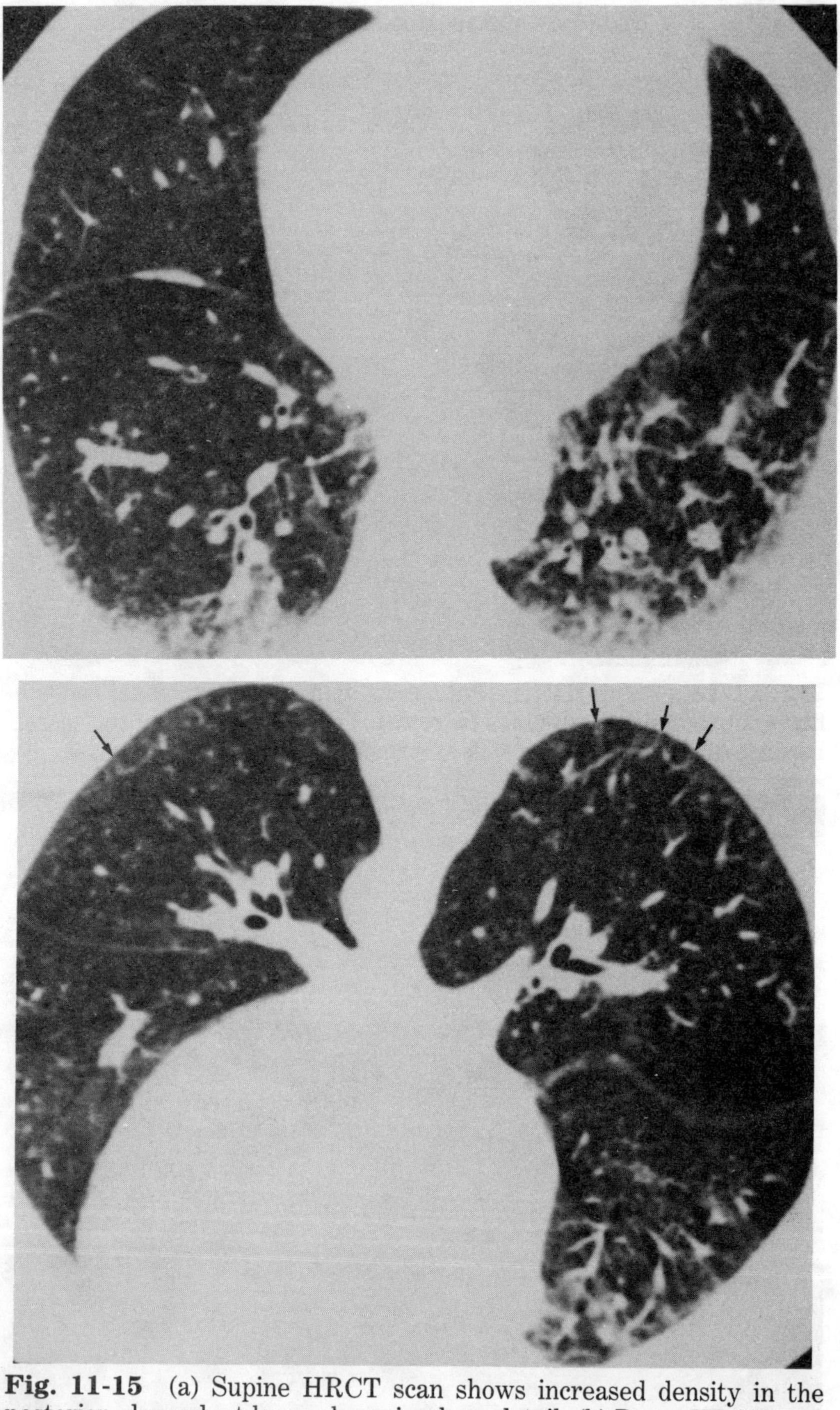

Fig. 11-15 (a) Supine HRCT scan shows increased density in the posterior, dependent lung, obscuring lung detail. (b) Prone HRCT scan shows widespread thickening of interlobular septa in the posterior lung (arrows).

have positive radiographs for asbestosis (ILO profusion ≥1/0) will have abnormal HRCT scans that are compatible with asbestosis (Table 11-4). The scans will demonstrate the previously described abnormalities throughout the lower lobes. In up to 30% of subjects who have had heavy occupational exposure to asbestos and who have radiographic or CT evidence of pleural plaques but normal-appearing pulmonary parenchyma, the HRCT is abnormal and highly suggestive of asbestosis. The high spatial resolution of HRCT seems to allow detection of asbestosis that is unapparent on chest radiographs.

HRCT is sensitive for early detection of abnormality in many types of interstitial lung disease, including sarcoidosis (35), idiopathic pulmonary fibrosis (32), lymphangitis carcinomatosis (33), and many others. Correlation between the radiologic and pathologic abnormalities is excellent. It seems likely that HRCT will become a mainstay of the diagnosis of asbestosis when radiographs are normal or inconclusive, probably in association with sensitive pulmonary function tests, such as tests during exercise.

3. Benign Asbestos-Related Lung Masses

Asbestos exposure may be associated with a variety of benign lung masses (2). Rounded atelectasis is the best known (36–39), but small benign pleural-based masses, intrafissural plaques (11), and masslike fibrotic sheets also occur. We have found that CT will detect asymptomatic benign masses in up to 10% of workers with significant asbestos exposure and that more than 90% of these masses will be benign (2).

Detection of asbestos-related lung masses from chest radiographs may be impaired by the presence of pleural disease and parenchymal fibrosis. Careful comparison with previous radiographs is essential. CT scanning, by eliminating confusing superimposed shadows, may be helpful in confirming the presence of a significant lung mass and may also aid in differential diagnosis.

Table 11-4 Correlation between CXR and HRCT in Asbestos-Exposed Workers (4)

		HRCT		
		Severely Abnormal	Moderately Abnormal	Normal
CXR	Abnormal	30	4	1
	Normal	29	10	26

Rounded atelectasis is probably the most common lung mass in an asbestos-exposed population. This is seen as a mass of airless lung, always adjacent to an area of pleural thickening. The lung may re-expand when the pleural adhesions are divided at thoracotomy. Rounded atelectasis is virtually always associated with diffuse pleural thickening (2) and is probably due to pleural adhesions with contraction of the pleura and progressively decreased aeration of the subjacent lung. On chest radiographs, rounded atelectasis is seen as a smooth pleural-based mass adjacent to pleural thickening, often with evidence of loss in volume of the lobe. A "comet-tail" of vessels and bronchi often radiates into the inferoposterior aspect of the mass (Fig. 11-7) (37, 39).

On CT, rounded atelectasis is a masslike lesion adjacent to a site of diffuse pleural thickening (Fig. 11-16) (3, 40). "Rounded" atelectasis is most common in the posteromedial part of the lung, where diffuse pleural thickening is also most common. Additional CT findings include a loss of lobular volume and a gentle curving of the bronchi and vessels toward the mass from the hilum. Rounded atelectasis may actually be wedge shaped or lentiform and may be well or poorly marginated. It is uncommonly round. On CT, air

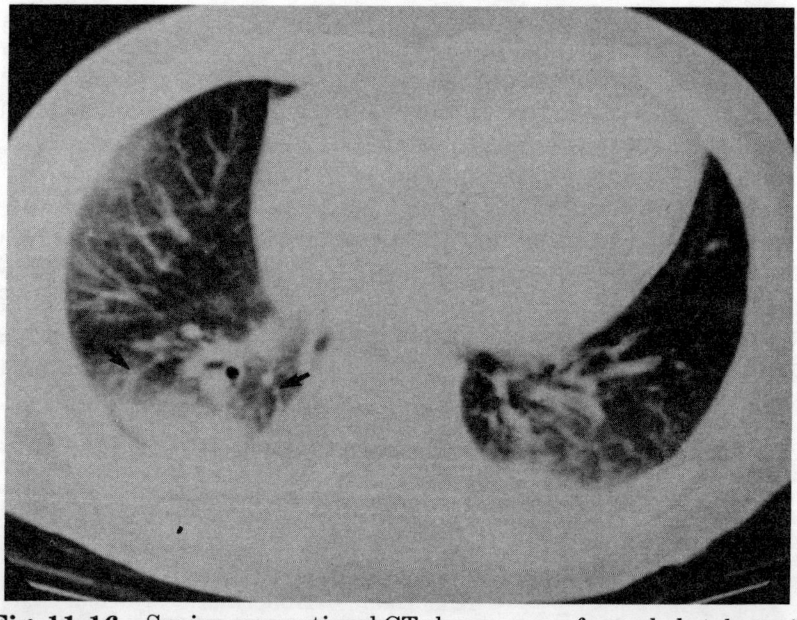

Fig. 11-16 Supine conventional CT shows mass of rounded atelectasis adjacent to a site of pleural thickening. Vessels are seen to curve into the medial and lateral aspects of the mass (arrows).

bronchograms and calcification may be seen in the mass. Fibrotic parenchymal bands often radiate from the mass into the surrounding lung. Multiple masses are not uncommon (Fig. 11-7). The CT features of rounded atelectasis are sufficiently characteristic to preclude a biopsy in classic cases. If any doubt exists as to the diagnosis, a biopsy should be undertaken.

Other small benign pleural-based masses that do not meet the classic criteria for rounded atelectasis are also found with asbestos exposure (2). These are usually less than 2 cm in diameter, are adjacent to an area of pleural abnormality, and are usually wedge shaped or lentiform.

In advanced asbestosis, masslike sheets of fibrosis can extend through the lung, usually from an area of pleural abnormality (2). Condensation of fibrotic scars and bands of fibrosis cause cicatricial crowding of bronchi and vessels that can simulate a mass on CT and chest radiography. Careful retrospective scrutiny of old chest radiographs may reveal that the abnormality was present earlier but not appreciated. The possibility of a neoplasm must be strongly considered (2) if the mass is neither adjacent to pleural thickening nor caught up in an area of radiating scars or cicatricial condensation of the lung. On CT, the spiculations of a neoplasm (40) should be distinguishable from the long fibrotic bands of a benign mass.

With CCT, fissural plaques usually appear as bandlike or nodular masses. The fissure is often visible as an avascular zone or ill-defined density, and the precise relationship of the plaque to the fissure is not apparent. On HRCT, the normal fissure is visible and the plaque can be precisely localized within the fissure (2).

4. Asbestos-Related Neoplasms

Occupational exposure to asbestos predisposes to bronchogenic carcinoma, pleural and peritoneal mesothelioma (17, 31), and other neoplasms, including cancer of the esophagus and stomach, the head and neck (17), and possibly the breast and colon. The first case of death from bronchogenic carcinoma in a person with asbestosis was reported in 1935. Numerous major cohort studies have all shown an excess of lung cancer in exposed workers (16, 42, 43). An association between mesothelial tumors and asbestos exposure was first reported in 1959 and by 1963 it was recognized that most commercial fibers were implicated (31).

The role of CT in asbestos-related neoplasms is similar to its role in thoracic neoplasms in general (44). CT can assist in defining the intrathoracic and extrathoracic extent of the disease, in determining the most appropriate routes for biopsy, in planning a resection or radiation therapy, and in following patients for possible recurrence. Concomitant pulmonary fibrosis and pleural calcification can make the radiographic detection of a bronchogenic carcinoma difficult. In this circumstance, CT can readily discriminate between a parenchymal mass and pleural plaques. HRCT can demonstrate the interlobar fissures and define the nature of an intrafissural pleural plaque (2). HRCT is of value in assessing the solitary pulmonary nodule (41). In many instances, CT can distinguish between benign subpleural masses within the spectrum of rounded atelectasis, and masses suggestive of a neoplasm.

Early detection of lung cancer is important so that curative resection may be considered, though this may be poorly tolerated in those with significant lung fibrosis. Since small carcinomas may be obscured by lung or pleural disease, careful comparison of serial radiographs is necessary for early diagnosis. Any interval change on radiographs should be aggressively investigated with more sophisticated imaging studies and biopsy, where appropriate.

F. CONCLUSIONS

Imaging studies are central to the diagnosis and assessment of the asbestos-exposed worker. Chest radiography, though still the primary investigation, has shortcomings (45) including lack of sensitivity for lung and pleural fibrosis, considerable interobserver variations, and generally poor radiographic-physiologic correlations. CT is useful for differential diagnosis of asbestos-related lung masses. HRCT is more sensitive than chest radiographs and CCT for detecting pulmonary fibrosis and pleural disease, but a standard technique and standardized scoring system must be achieved if the method is to gain widespread medical and legal acceptance.

REFERENCES

1. Katz D, Kreel L. Computed tomography in pulmonary asbestosis. Clin Radiol 1979;30:207–213.
2. Lynch DA, Gamsu G, Ray CS, Aberle DR. Asbestos-related focal lung masses: Manifestations on conventional and high resolution CT. Radiology 1988;169:603–607.
3. Aberle DR, Gamsu G, Ray CS, Feuerstein IM. Asbestos-related pleural and parenchymal fibrosis: Detection with high resolution CT. Radiology 1988;166:507–510.
4. Aberle DR, Gamsu G, Ray CS. High resolution CT of benign asbestos-related diseases: Clinical and radiographic correlations. AJR 1988;151:883–891.
5. Friedman AC, Fiel SB, Fisher MS, Radecki PD, Lev-Toaff AS, Caroline DF. Asbestos-related pleural disease and asbestosis: A comparison of CT and chest radiography. AJR 1988;150:269–275.
6. Mayo JR, Webb WR, Gould R. High resolution CT of the lungs: An optimal approach. Radiology 1987;163:507–510.
7. Russell AR (ed) Classification of radiographs of the pneumoconioses. Medical Radiography & Photography (Eastman Kodak, Rochester, NY) 1981;57 (1):1–18.
8. International Labour Office: Guidelines for the use of ILO International Classification of Radiographs of Pneumoconioses. Geneva ILO 1980, ILO Occupational Safety and Health Series No. 22 (rev. 80).
9. Sargent EN, Boswell WD, Ralls PW, Markovitz A. Subpleural fat pads in patients exposed to asbestos: Distinction from noncalcified pleural plaques. Radiology 1984;152:273–277.
10. Hourihane DOB, Lessof I, Richardson PC. Hyaline and calcific pleural plaques as an index of exposure to asbestos. A study of radiological and pathological features of 100 cases with a consideration of epidemiology. Br Med J 1966;1:1069–1079.
11. Gale ME, Grief WL. Intrafissural fat: CT correlation with chest radiography. Radiology 1986;160:333–336.
12. Sargent EN, Felton JS, Barnes LT. Calcified interlobar pleural plaques. Visceral pleural involvement due to asbestos. Radiology 1981;140:634.

13. Solomon A, Irwig LM, Sluis-Cremer GK, Thomas RG, Dutoit RS. Thickening of pulmonary interlobar fissures: Exposure-response relationship in crocidolite and amosite miners. Br J Ind Med 1979;36:195–198.
14. McLoud TC, Woods BO, Carrington CB, Epler GR, Gaensler EA. Diffuse pleural thickening in an asbestos-exposed population: Prevalence and causes. AJR 1985;144:9–18.
15. Epler GR, McLoud TC, Gaensler EA. Prevalence and incidence of benign asbestos related pleural effusion in a working population. JAMA 1982;247:617–622.
16. Martensson G, Hagberg S, Petterson K, Thringer G. Asbestos pleural effusion: A clinical entity. Thorax 1987;42:646–651.
17. Selikoff IJ (ed). Cancer risk of asbestos exposure. In *Origins of Human Cancer*. Cold Spring Harbor Laboratory, New York, 1977, pp 1765–1784.
18. Mirvis S, Dutcher JP, Haney PJ, Whitley ND, Aisner J. CT of malignant pleural mesothelioma. AJR 1983;140:665–670.
19. Grant DC, Seltzer S, Antman KH, Finberg HJ, Koster K. Computed tomography of malignant pleural mesothelioma. J Comput Assist Tomogr 1983;7:626–632.
20. Szpak CA, Johnston WW, Roggli V. The diagnostic distinction between malignant mesothelioma and adenocarcinoma of the lung as defined by a monoclonal antibody (B72-3). Am J Pathol 1986;122:252–260.
21. Soutar CA, Simon G, Turner-Warnick M. The radiology of asbestos-induced diseases of the lungs. Br J Dis Chest 1974;68:235–252.
22. Rockoff SD, Schwartz A. Roentgenographic underestimation of early asbestosis by International Labour Organization Classification. Chest 1988;93:1088–1091.
23. Rossiter CE. Initial repeatability studies of the UICC/Cincinnati Classification of the radiographic appearance of pneumoconiosis. Br J Ind Med 1972;29:407–419.
24. Epler GR, McLoud TC, Gaensler EA, Mikus JP, Carrington CB. Normal chest roentgenograms in chronic diffuse infiltrative lung disease. N Engl J Med 1978;298:936–939.
25. Kipen HM, Lilis R, Suzuki Y, Valcuikas JA, Selikoff IJ. Pulmonary fibrosis in asbestos insulation workers with lung cancer. A radiological and histopathological evaluation. Br J Ind Med 1987;44:96–100.
26. American Thoracic Society Statement. The diagnosis of nonmalignant diseases related to asbestos. Am Rev Respir Dis 1986;136:363–368.
27. Blanc PD, Golden JA, Gamsu G, Aberle DR, Gold WM. Asbestos exposure–cigarette smoking interactions among shipyard workers. JAMA 1988;259:370–373.
28. Weiss W. Cigarette smoke, asbestos and small irregular opacities. Am Rev Respir Dis 1984;130:293–301.

29. Blanc PD, Gamsu G. The effect of cigarette smoking on the detection of small radiographic opacities in inorganic dust diseases. J Thorac Imaging 1988;3:51–56.
30. Heitzman ER (ed). Subsegmental anatomy of the lung. In *The Lung, Radiographic-Pathologic Correlations*. CV Mosby, St. Louis 1984, pp 50–69.
31. Craighead JE, Abraham JC, Churg A, Green FH, Kleinerman J, Pratt PC, Seemayer TA, Vallyathan V, Weill H. The Pathology of asbestos-associated diseases of the lungs and pleural cavities: Diagnostic criteria and proposed grading system. Arch Pathol Lab Med 1982;106:544–596.
32. Mueller NL, Miller RR, Webb WR, Evans KG, Ostrow DN. Fibrosing alveolitis: CT-pathologic correlations. Radiology 1986;160:585–588.
33. Stein MG, Mayo J, Muller N, Aberle DR, Webb WR, Gamsu G. Pulmonary lymphangitic spread of carcinoma: Appearance on CT scans. Radiology 1987;162:371–375.
34. Yoshimura H, Hatakeyama M, Otsuji H, Maeda M, Ohishi H, Uchida H, Katsuta H, Katada H, Narita N, Mikami R, Konishi Y. Pulmonary asbestosis: CT study of subpleural curvilinear shadow. Work in progress 1986;158:653–658.
35. Bergin CJ, Mueller NL. CT in the diagnosis of interstitial lung disease. AJR 1985;145:505–510.
36. Mintzer RA, Cugell DW. The association of asbestos-induced pleural disease and rounded atelectasis. Chest 1982;81:457–460.
37. Hanke R, Kretzschmar R. Round atelectasis. Sem Roentgenol 1980;15:174–182.
38. Hillerdal G, Hemingsson A. Pulmonary pseudotumors and asbestos. Acta Radiol Diagn 1980;21:615–620.
39. Schneider HJ, Felson B, Gonzalez L. Rounded atelectasis. AJR 1980;134:225–232.
40. Doyle TC, Lawler GA. CT features of rounded atelectasis of the lung. AJR 1984;143:225–228.
41. Siegelman SS, Khouri NF, Leo FP, Fishman EK, Braverman RM, Zerhouni EA. Solitary pulmonary nodules: CT assessment. Radiology 1986;160:307–312.
42. Berry G, Newhouse ML, Antonis P. Combined effect of asbestos and smoking on mortality from lung cancer and mesothelioma in factory workers. Br J Ind Med 1985;42:12–18.
43. Fletcher DR. A mortality study of shipyard workers with pleural plaques. Br J Ind Med 1972;29:142–145.
44. Mann H. CT in the management of lung cancer. Sem US, CT, MR 1988;9:40–52.
45. Gefter WB, Conant EF. Issues and controversies in the plain film diagnosis of asbestos-related disorders in the chest. J Thorac Imaging 1988;3:11–28.

12

High Risk Asbestos Workers Groups: Selected Review with Emphasis on the Tyler Asbestos Workers Program

GEORGE A. HURST, M.D., F.A.C.P., F.C.C.P.
RONALD F. DODSON, PH.D., F.C.C.P.
DAVID E. GRIFFITH, M.D.
JERRY W. MCLARTY, PH.D.

University of Texas Health Center
Tyler, Texas, U.S.A.

Synopsis

G. TYLER ASBESTOS WORKERS PROGRAM (TAWP)
H. PATIENT MANAGEMENT
I. VENTILATORY STUDIES
J. CHEST RADIOGRAPHY
K. SPUTUM CYTOPATHOLOGY
L. ASBESTOS BODIES AND UNCOATED FIBERS IN SPUTUM AND LUNG

BIOGRAPHY

Dr. George A. Hurst is the Director of The University of Texas Health Center at Tyler, and a Professor of Clinical Medicine. He is a graduate of Southwestern Medical School and holds board certification in internal medicine and pulmonary disease. Dr. Hurst has special interest in asbestos-related diseases and was the principal investigator of The Tyler Asbestos Workers Program. Dr. Hurst may be contacted at the Office of the Director, University of Texas Health Center, U.S. Highway 271 at State Highway 155, P.O. Box 75710, East Texas Chest Hospital, Tyler, Texas 75708, U.S.A. (telephone: 214-877-7750).

Dr. Ronald F. Dodson is Associate Director for Research, Chairman, Department of Cell Biology and Environmental Sciences, and Professor of Cell Biology and Environmental Sciences at The University of Texas Health Center at Tyler. Dr. Dodson is also the Director of Environmental Research Institute.

Dr. David E. Griffith is Assistant Professor of Clinical Medicine. He is a graduate of Baylor University College of Medicine and is board certified in internal medicine and pulmonary disease.

Dr. Jerry W. McLarty is Chairman of Epidemiology/Biomathematics and Professor of Epidemiology and Biomathematics at The University of Texas Health Center at Tyler. He is principal investigator of "Beta-Carotene and Lung Cancer Chemoprevention."

EDITORS' COMMENTARY

The following chapter begins with a detailed review of the historical development of our understanding of the disease processes associated with asbestos. Then it describes the procedures and results of a five-year program to serially study a large group of workers exposed to amosite. These high risk workers were examined and evaluated by use of pulmonary function tests, chest radiography, sputum cytopathology, questionnaires, and other sources of information. The results verify much of what has appeared in the literature, opens new areas of inquiry, and demonstrates the variability inherent in the factors used for diagnosis. The control group or background risk problem suggests the need for diligent inquiry into this confounding phenomena. The importance of early diagnosis, before any radiographic manifestations of a disease process, is emphasized for treatment possibilities. Issues such as coated asbestos bodies and use of TEM are discussed. This important study continues as part of a chemoprevention cancer effort, so further serial and correlation analysis data will be forthcoming.

A. INTRODUCTION

This chapter will focus on the increased danger of detrimental health effects to workers who are exposed to asbestos in air as compared to the hazard of developing the same health problems in the general population. The great bulk of available information on the environmental distribution, as well as untoward effects of asbestos, relates to its presence in air. In fact, most of the studies that have been described over the past 50 years have related to

Accepted for publication 17 April 1989.

respiring air contaminated with this mineral and its effect on the lung and adjacent structures. Some of the non-pulmonary effects of asbestos, specifically gastrointestinal malignancies, are thought to be related to the swallowing of salivary as well as pulmonary secretions that contained asbestos. Air is not the only source of asbestos contamination and, therefore, exposure of human body tissues and organs to this mineral can occur in other ways. There has been increasing information in the past 15 years about the presence of asbestos in water, food, and drugs, as well as other consumer products, but scarce data is available regarding the adverse health effects of the use or consumption of asbestos in these other substances (1).

B. OVERVIEW

Before discussing the health effects, we will review the types of asbestos, its historical uses, and the occupational groups who are at increased risk for asbestos exposure. Asbestos minerals fall into two major subdivisions: chrysotile, which belongs to the serpentines, and the amphiboles, which include the crocidolite, amosite and anthrophyllite, and tremolite. Asbestos has been identified in the clay of ancient pottery. It is possible it was intentionally added to the pottery to give increased strength to the finished product. In classical times, descriptions exist of an asbestos-like material that was used for wicks in ceremonial lamps and for weaving into funeral shrouds. In the former case, the mineral wick would persist after the oil had burned off and in the latter the asbestos cloth would not be consumed in the funeral fire and could be recovered after cremation of the body. The term asbestos itself may come from a Greek word meaning "unquenchable" although other possible origins exist (2). In more recent history, Benjamin Franklin may have presented a purse made from North American asbestos to an English friend in the early 1700s (3). While a purse from this era exists, it is impossible to verify whether it truly belonged to Benjamin Franklin.

C. ASBESTOS' HISTORY IN INDUSTRY

Overall, until the late 1800s, use of asbestos was intermittent and only anecdotally described with no confirmed adverse health consequences. With the advent of the Industrial Revolution, however, and the resulting demand for fibrous mineral with high tensile strength and significant resistance to heat and chemicals, asbestos found widespread use. In the late 1800s and early 1900s asbestos deposits were known to exist in the Soviet Union, Italy, Canada, South Africa, Rhodesia, and the United States. The first commercial production was attempted in Italy between 1850 and 1870 with the production of asbestos paper and cloth although a steady market for this material was not yet available (4). Other uses for asbestos at that time included asbestos yarns, ropes, and engine packing. Large scale use of asbestos followed exploitation of the Quebec deposits in the 1860s and South African deposits in the 1890s. Canadian asbestos production increased dramatically from 50 tons per year in 1878 to greater than 9,000 tons per year in 1891. After a temporary wane in production over the next few years, asbestos production again blossomed in 1896 and steadily increased to a level of over 900,000 tons in 1953 (5). In the United States, the manufacture of asbestos products began in the late 1860s and the early 1870s with the development of a pipe covering made from layers of felts, papers, and asbestos (6).

The number of products containing asbestos has grown steadily in the 20th century. World War II, particularly, provided a strong impetus for expanding the use of asbestos and dramatically increased its demand. The scope of asbestos uses can best be illustrated in terms of those stimuli against which it gives protection: weather, corrosion, fire, heat, cold, acid, alkali, electricity, noise, energy losses, vibration, accident, frost, bacteria, dust, and vermin.

Chrysotile is the most common form of asbestos consumed in the United States and approximately eight times as much chrysotile is utilized as compared to the amphibole asbestos (1). Of the asbestos consumed in the United States, approximately one-sixth or 100 short tons of asbestos is mined in this country and the rest of it is imported. Most of the imported chrysotile comes from Canada and the imported amphiboles from South Africa. Chrysotile has been mined in Vermont since the early part of this century and later deposits and mines were found in Arizona, California, Texas, and Alaska with California having the most active mining operation. Anthrophyllite deposits have been found in Georgia and North Carolina. The occupational exposure to asbestos may be seen in Table 12-1 (7).

Most of the asbestos mines are open pit operations utilizing power shovels and bulldozers with the transportation of the ore by truck or train to a nearby mill. Although these mining and milling operations were previously very dusty, there has been vast improvement over the years to control the dust and to protect work-

Table 1

Occupational Exposure*

Industry	Occupation
Mining, milling, transportation	Driller, heavy equipment operator, truck driver, blender, bagger, packer, palletizer, car loader, crusher, dryer operator, laboratory technician, foreman, laborer, maintenance worker, mill operator
Manufacturing of asbestos, cement products, friction materials, insulation products, paper products, textiles, floor tiles, roofing products, etc.	Bag opener, cutter, puncher of dry products, carder, spinner, weaver, other workers
Automobile repair	Brake repairman, auto mechanic, body repairman
Construction	Insulation worker, spray insulator, carpenter, lagger, painter, tile layer, mason, demolition, worker, janitorial worker, sheet metal and heating equipment worker, other workers (plumber, welder, electrician)
Shipbuilding or renovation	Sailmaker-lagger, lagger, sprayer, mason, painter, asbestos storeman, electrical fitter, welder, ship fitter, plumber, caulker, driller

*Modified from Table by Arai and Weill (7)

ers. Much of this has come as a result of standards developed by the Environmental Protection Agency and Occupational Safety and Health Administration (OSHA). California is responsible for two-thirds of the United States' production employing about one-half of the approximately 500 people engaged in mining and milling operations (1). It is estimated that approximately 3,000 or more products contain asbestos minerals (8). The United States produces about one-fourth of the world's asbestos products, and it has been estimated that the number of employees in the United States asbestos manufacturing industry is around 200,000 (1). The largest single use of asbestos in the United States is the manufacture of asbestos cement products (1, 9). They may contain up to 20–30% of asbestos, mostly chrysotile, and cement pipes constitute the largest volume of production, although flooring products, friction materials, insulation products, and roofing materials utilize large quantities of asbestos (8). The incorporation of asbestos fibers greatly increases the tensile strength of cement so that the weight of material required is correspondingly reduced. It has been technically manageable to regulate and monitor asbestos air contamination in manufacturing plants utilizing asbestos. It is far more difficult to attempt to do this in the field where asbestos-containing products are utilized. Labor unions for several groups such as insulators have effectively communicated to its members the health hazards of asbestos and how to protect themselves. The plant producing asbestos-containing insulation material in Tyler closed, and some other plants have substituted for asbestos other materials having similar properties or have moved outside of the continental USA to places such as Mexico to avoid scrutiny by regulatory agencies.

D. OPPORTUNITIES FOR EXPOSURE

The mechanics who repair automobiles, particularly those involved in servicing brakes, are exposed to asbestos when cleaning the brake drum with jet-compressed air. Construction workers, such as insulation workers, may be exposed to asbestos dust in the process of cutting and installing insulation material. Those companies that have expertise in demolition and removal of asbestos have to meet strict standards set out by OSHA. Many maintenance or janitorial workers may be involved in minor repairs and cleaning of buildings that contain asbestos in ceilings and wall boards, and around pipes. If the buildings are not public buildings, such as schools, there may be no knowledge of asbestos presence, and a greater likelihood of worker exposure.

Tens of thousands of men and women were involved during World War II in ship building or renovation and have evidence of pleural changes on x-ray. Many workers are unaware of their exposure to asbestos, and the burden for establishing such exposure falls upon the industrial or private physician, and increasingly the lawyers are becoming involved. Few physicians take a complete occupational history and many are not aware of common sources of exposure. Sometimes the exposure is distant, intermittent, or of short duration. A good exposure history should be taken carefully to include all occupations ever held including short-term and summer jobs, and military as well as other service exposures and should also include the start and stop dates, job titles, job descriptions including processes and agents used as well as plant health services and worker health experience (10).

There are a number of non-occupational exposure opportunities for asbestos including spouses and family members of workers. Anderson and co-workers suggested that asbestos-laden clothing worn at work resulted in the contamination of the air at home when clothes were laundered by family members (7, 11). Individuals residing or working in the neighborhood of nearby industrial plants fabricating asbestos-containing products, as well as mines and mills, have been shown to be exposed to asbestos by developing pleural plaques or less commonly developing mesothelioma. A number of products used by handymen who remodel their own homes such as caulking material, paints, plastics, floor tiles, etc., can be a source of exposure. Finally, asbestos fibers can be demonstrated in the lungs of practically everyone in major metropolitan areas (12). The risk for lung cancer and mesothelioma for exposure to asbestos in schools has been reviewed by Hughes and Weill (13).

E. EARLY EVIDENCE OF CONTAMINATION

Suspicion of the harmful health effects of asbestos arose in Europe, particularly Great Britain, at the turn of the century. Two formidable impediments existed in the recognition of the role of asbestos in the development of lung disease. First, other pneumononioses, including silicosis and coal workers pneumoconiosis, had been previously described and some cases of respiratory disease in asbestos workers was attributed to these other minerals. Second, tuberculosis was a frequent concomitant of pneumoconiosis and some deaths of asbestos workers were attributed to tuberculosis, although it was recognized that the inhalation of asbestos dust might potentially exacerbate tuberculosis itself. In spite of these difficulties, because of massive asbestos exposure in industry in the early 20th century, the development of asbestos-related disease became widely recognized and described over an approximately 30-year period.

In 1897, a Vienna physician noted emaciation and respiratory problems in asbestos weavers and their families and felt that dust inhalation was the cause. Although he did not recognize asbestos per se as the critical factor, he did recommend steps to ameliorate dust inhalation in these workers (14). In a series of reports between 1898 and 1906, the Lady Inspectors of Factories in Great Britain clearly noted the hazards of working with asbestos (15–17). In 1898, asbestos manufacturing processes were specifically mentioned "on account of their easily demonstrated danger to the health of workers and because of ascertained cases of injury to bronchial tubes and lungs medically attributed to the employment of the suffers" (15). In 1906, Lady Inspectors further noted: "Of all injurious dusty processes of which I again received complaints, none I believe surpass in injuriousness of the workers the sewing, preparing, carding and spinning processes in asbestos manufacture" (17). Although no firm cause and effect relationship between asbestos and disease had yet been developed, the severity of the problem was already obvious.

In 1906, Dr. Monteque Murray reported to a British Parliamentary Commission on compensation for industrial diseases on a fatal case of pulmonary fibrosis in an asbestos worker (18). The autopsy had actually been performed in 1900, but the case had not been previously reported in the medical literature. The case involved a 33-year-old man who worked 14 years in a "carding room" of an asbestos textile plant. Carding was the process of separating textile fibers and layering them in a parallel web removing impurities in the process. At autopsy, Murray found no evidence of tuberculosis and attributed the man's death to damage to the lung by asbestos dust. This is generally regarded as the first proven case of pulmonary disease from asbestos in modern times.

In 1906, Auribault reported 16 deaths from pulmonary fibrosis between 1890 and 1895 in a French asbestos spinning mill and weaving factory (19). In 1908, Scarpa, an Italian, reported the deaths of 30 patients employed in asbestos mining and spinning mills between 1894 and 1906 (20). These subjects died of pulmonary disease and did not respond to anti-tuberculosis measures. In 1911, Collis, in England, reported 5 deaths due to lung disease in a plant manufacturing asbestos mattresses (21). This report is significant in that it notes that workers in less dusty asbestos jobs conceivably were endangered by dust raised by their co-workers. In 1914, Fahr, a pathologist in Hamburg, autopsied a 35-year-old female asbestos worker (22). He described scarring in the lung and "a large number of crystals of a peculiar nature." The first extensive radiographic investigation of asbestos workers was carried out in the United States by Pancoast, Miller, and Landis who reported abnormal chest roentgenograms in 15 asbestos workers (23).

At about this time, a statistician with Prudential Insurance Company named Hoffman wrote a monograph on dusty trades (24). He cited previous work from the British literature but also cited some of Prudential's data that showed an excessive early mortality in asbestos workers. While he acknowledged that the data on adverse health effects of asbestos in the United States was lacking, he wrote that the mining and "dressing of asbestos unquestionably involves a considerable hazard." He also intimated that the life insurance company would not issue life insurance policies to asbestos workers. Again, without firm pathophysiologic evidence, the severe nature of this problem was strikingly evident.

In 1924, Cooke published a case report in the *British Medical Journal* of a 33-year-old female who died after 20 years of work in an asbestos factory with evidence of extensive fibrosis on chest roentgenogram (25). In 1927, he published details of the pathological examination that, on gross exam, showed a thickened pleura over the entire surface of the lung with dense adhesions to the chest wall and pericardium (26). Microscopic examination of the lung showed extensive fibrosis with thickening of the alveolar walls and foreign bodies of various shapes with sharp angles throughout the lungs which he initially termed "curious bodies." The 1927 report first coined the term "asbestosis" while the term "asbestos bodies" was used in a 1929 report to describe the "curious bodies" noted on the microscopic examination of the lung (27). In the ensuing years, a number of case reports were published primarily in the British literature, which further elucidated aspects of the disease asbestosis including symptoms, physical findings, radiographic features, and the distressing young age of onset of disease and subsequent death of the asbestos workers (28–32). One report from East London again emphasized the danger of asbestos exposure and subsequent asbestosis to patients not directly handling asbestos (31).

In 1930, Merewether and Price published a seminal study on the asbestos industry and asbestosis (33, 34). They investigated conditions in the asbestos industry by studying workers employed in the asbestos textile industry who would not be exposed to other potentially harmful or complicating dusts. Merewether and Price examined 369 workers of whom 95 (26%) had asbestosis and a further 21% had "precursive signs" of asbestosis. They noted that the incidence of asbestosis increased dramatically with the number of years employed in the asbestos industry. They also found that there were no definite cases of fibrosis until 5 or more years had elapsed from the start of employment, which suggested a "maturation period" during asbestos exposure prior to the onset of frank lung disease. They described early stages of the disease as follows:

> This disease, insidious in its onset, steadily advances with but faint warnings of its progress; inexorably it cripples the essential tissues of the lung, yet for a considerable period causes almost no inconvenience to the worker. As time goes on, however, the lungs find it more and more difficult in reaerating the blood, and breathing is quickened on slight exertions. Still the worker is able to remain at work, but is aware of his undue shortness of breath on extreme effort. Usually, however, he ascribes it to causes other than to the dust he is inhaling.

The report also describes symptoms, physical findings, and radiographic abnormalities in these workers. Although only a minority of the workers had chest roentgenograms, the role of chest roentgenograms in diagnosing the problem, however, was established. The report clearly delineates a latency or maturation period for the development of asbestosis and also notes that the severity and speed of onset of fibrosis were proportional to the intensity of asbestos exposure sustained by the worker. Clearly this is the first description of these two very important epidemiologic features of asbestosis. The Merewether and Price survey was a watershed article in the recognition of asbestosis. The information in the report was disseminated not only in Great Britain, but in medical journals in the United States as well. The report also resulted in the introduction in Great Britain of safety measures for asbestos factories and in the institution of medical supervision for asbestos workers.

After 1930, the medical literature on the harmful effects of asbestos grew rapidly in case reports and group studies from Europe and the United States. The first reports of cases of asbestosis in the United States were also published around 1930. In 1935, the United States asbestos industry produced a study of its workers by the Metropolitan Life Insurance Company (35). Chest roentgenograms of 126 persons who had worked for more than 3 years in the asbestos industry were studied. Fifty-three percent had asbestosis even by conservative radiographic interpretation and 31% had some radiographic signs of disease. Only 16% had no signs of asbestosis. Asbestos was clearly a severe problem in the United States as well as in Great Britain. As Selikoff and Lee noted, "asbestosis had now definitely arrived (1)."

F. RESULTS OF CONTAMINATION

Health risks for asbestos environmental exposure can be studied in terms of the incidence of altered structure and/or function of an organ and/or tissue or mortality. As has been previously discussed, the principle organ involved by the environmental air exposure is the lung. Early in this process of low-grade inflammation few, if any, symptoms are present and minimal fibrosis can be suspected by the auscultation of rales in the basilar lung fields. The more advanced state of fibrosis can be diagnosed as asbestosis when a history of asbestos exposure can be obtained and, in addition, if there is the presence of objective findings such as a restrictive ventilatory defect characterized by a forced vital capacity less than 80% of predicted, reduced single breath carbon monoxide diffusing capacity, and changes in the x-ray compatible with ILO-UC pneumoconiosis pattern. In the early 1970s, OSHA required that fewer than 5 asbestos fibers longer than 5 microns be present per cubic milliliter of air in industrial plants, and in 1974 the standards decreased the number of fibers that could be present per cubic millimeter of air to two (1). Because fibrosis (asbestosis) requires heavy exposure over a long period of time (usually 10 years or more of intermittent or continuous exposure) it is unlikely that asbestosis will develop among the many workers in asbestos manufacturing plants or users of asbestos products who began their exposure 15 years ago or less in the United States.

There are three benign changes that may occur in the pleural surfaces of the lung and chest secondary to asbestos exposure. Pleural effusion, which is usually a clear fluid with characteristics of an exudate (high protein content), is rarely detected because it may be minimal and transient. This condition was slow to be recognized and was first described by Eisenstadt (36, 37) and later studied more extensively by Gaensler (38). Rarely, pleural effusions related to asbestos exposure can be massive and bilateral. Few have required decortication for removing a thick pleural peal.

Pleural thickening, a more commonly recognized pleural reaction, was not generally recognized until a case report by Lynch and Smith in 1935 (39). It was subsequently recognized that some of the previously described radiographic abnormalities attributed to asbestosis were, in fact, due to the pleural thickening. The lack of early descriptions of pleural changes with asbestosis may have been a consequence of the fulminant nature of the parenchymal disease associated with very heavy exposure that produced death before the slower forming pleural plaques had developed. In a similar vein, it had only been the fulminant cases that had come to medical attention prior to that time. Gloyne emphasized that patients with asbestosis not infrequently had associated pleural fibrosis with dense adhesions (40, 41). In general, the more advanced the pulmonary fibrosis is, the more likely for pleural fibrosis to be present, and the pleural fibrosis is along the visceral surface (next to the lung) (42, 43).

The last asbestos-related pleural change worthy of note is parietal pleural plaques. They are regarded as a hallmark of asbestos exposure in both occupational and general environment (44, 45). These are shining white elevations with sharp borders that consist of fibro-hyaline connective tissue containing very few cells (46). The cells are usually seen in the periphery where a few inflammatory cells can be seen, indicating a low-grade inflammation. These plaques are best seen tangentially on roentgenograms. Consequently, they are best perceived in the flanks of the lung in a postero-anterior view or with oblique projections. Although the chest roentgenogram is the standard method of making the diagnosis of pleural plaques, this examination grossly underestimates the presence of plaques. Approximately 10% of pleural plaques that are present at necropsy can be seen on x-rays (46). Pleural plaques are occasionally found in connection with other occupational exposure such as silicosis or talcosis, but usually it indicates an exposure to asbestos (46). The pleural plaques themselves are harmless and usually produce no symptoms. Their presence may indicate a more ominous prognosis than generally thought, according to some authors (44, 47–49). One roentgenographic study on asbestos-exposed workers showed that people with such pleural abnormalities are more likely to develop progressive pulmonary fibrosis than those without (47). There may also be an increased risk of developing mesothelioma (48) and lung carcinoma (49).

The most serious health risk related to asbestos exposure is the occurrence of various cancers of the pleura, lung, larynx, and gastrointestinal tract. Mesotheliomas are malignant tumors of the pleura that may be signalled by dyspnea or chest pain, and a variety of other systemic symptoms such as weight loss and fever. Wagner focused attention on the association of diffuse pleural mesotheliomas and asbestos exposure (50). Surgery may be required for diagnosis as in the case of providing biopsy tissue, but it is never curative when used for treatment. The longer fibers are thought to be required for malignant transformation and, although most patients with this disease have had asbestos exposure, other minerals such as talc, mica, and, in Turkey, zeolite can also produce mesotheliomas (10, 51). Mesothelioma of the peritoneum may also occur. The amphiboles amosite and crocidolite appear to have greater carcinogenic properties for mesothelioma than chrysotile.

Carcinoma of the lung was first reported in a patient with asbestosis in 1935 by Lynch and Smith (52). Others who reported on autopsy findings in patients with asbestosis noted an increased incidence of lung cancer and this included women and some patients who were developing cancer at an earlier age (53). It is thought that the death rate was more common among workers who had been exposed for 2 years or more than those under 2 years of asbestos contact. Minimal exposure of less than a week increased the risk of lung cancer. The relationship of lung cancer to intensity of exposure, i.e., individuals with more severe exposure, was not as striking as it would be with pulmonary asbestosis. As one might expect, the time lapse since initial exposure is very important. Dr. Selikoff found that in the Mount Sinai cohort the death rate from lung cancer became apparent after 10 years from onset of exposure and peaked in the 25–34 years after first exposure (54). The cell type of lung cancers that are seen in asbestos-exposed individuals was reported to be the same as those that are seen in controls (presumably related to cigarette smoke) by Kannerstein (55). Whitwell, however, has reported that the histological cell type of lung cancer in workers suffering from asbestosis in the United Kingdom show a higher percentage (34%) of adenocarcinoma than would be expected in a group of cigarette smokers (56). Dr. Selikoff has also found that the addition of cigarette smoke to asbestos exposure appears to multiply the carcinogenic effect of asbestos exposure (1).

G. TYLER ASBESTOS WORKERS PROGRAM

The Tyler Asbestos Workers Program (TAWP) was a cancer control program established with funds from the National Cancer Institute in a group at high risk for developing lung cancer. A plant manufacturing asbestos insulation products operated in Tyler, Texas, from 1954 through February 1972 when it closed following violation citations from OSHA (57, 58). A predecessor installation in Paterson, New Jersey, operated from 1941 through 1954, using the same equipment and raw materials. The plant used only amosite asbestos and received the mineral in burlap sacks from Transvaal in South Africa. The sacks were removed from railroad boxcars and transferred to the plant for storage. Insulation was manufactured from amosite asbestos (approximately

90%) mixed with varying amounts (approximately 10%) of diatomaceous earth, sodium silicate, and mineral wool. The University of Texas Health Center at Tyler and the National Institute of Safety and Health (NIOSH) conducted mediical and laboratory studies in August 1971 on 62 workers. Seven of 16 workers with 10 or more years of employment were found to have asbestosis based on the epidemiologic criteria described by Murphy (59). There were present three or more of the following criteria: (1) significant dyspnea, (2) finger clubbing, (3) persistent rales, (4) restrictive pulmonary function, and (5) small roentgenographic opacities. All seven of these patients also had decreased single breath carbon monoxide diffusing capacity. Environmental surveys of plant operations conducted by the Department of Health, Education and Welfare from 1967 to 1971 revealed three to eighteen times as many fibers as allowed by OSHA standards (maximum of 5 fibers longer than 5 microns per milliliter of air) and deficient housekeeping practices. The Biometry Branch of NIOSH, using employment records, developed a computer master file of 878 workers. In addition, 65 individuals who were not on the NIOSH master file were identified as former employees of the plant plus 165 workers employed by Manpower, Incorporated, had had intermittent asbestos exposure unloading the amosite from railroad freight cars, and they were also considered part of the cohort, thus giving a total cohort of 1,108 workers.

The profile of the TAWP workers may be seen in Table 12-2.

Of the 1,108 workers who were employed at the plant, 866 workers were examined, which is 78% of the total. Of the 242 who were not seen, 71 were known dead and 91 had moved and could not be contacted. Therefore 946 were communicated with and 91.5% of these were examined. As one would expect, there was a gradual decrease of the number seen over time: 624 workers were seen three times, 398 were seen six times, 192 were seen nine times, and 6 were seen eleven times. Eighty-five percent, which is an unusually high number, of these workers were smokers. This included those who had once smoked but had stopped. Seventy-six percent of the workers were white and 23% were Black. The plant had been segregated until the mid 1960s and Black workers were not hired until then. The cohort was predominantly male comprising more than 99% of the total workforce. Nine females were all employed as clerical workers. The mean age at first exposure was 28 years, and the mean time from first exposure until present is 24 years. This large group of relatively young (at the age of first exposure) male smokers has had an increased death rate of cancer, particularly of the lung. Judging from Selikoff's data, their peak mortality could occur 10–15 years from now, 30–35 years post exposure (60, 61).

The mean duration of employment was 12.7 months. Of the 1,043 workers who had reliable records and who could give accurate work history, 144 worked one week or less, another 299 worked from one week to one month, 418 worked from one month to one year, and 182 worked from 1–20 years. The mean time from first exposure until first examination was 11.3 years.

In addition to the above mentioned workers, there was a group of 188 controls that included both smokers and non-smokers who were matched with the workers as far as age.

All individuals examined at TAWP were followed in the same manner. Some of the workers who had moved away from the area were followed in distant cities by both the TAWP staff and contract personnel. The quality of the x-rays in some of these former workers was substandard.

1. Each worker was given an appointment every 6 months by mail.
2. Workers were interviewed utilizing a health questionnaire of ten pages for the first visit and a two-page follow-up questionnaire for follow-up visits.

Table 2
Profile of TAWP Workers
From 1,108 Workers Employed

Workers examined	866
Smokers (including former smokers)	85%
Race	
White	73%
Black	27%
Sex	
Male	99%
Female	1%
Mean age at first exposure	28 years
Mean time from first exposure until present	24 years
Mean duration of employment	12.7 months
Mean time from first exposure until first examination	11.3 years
Mean time from first exposure until pleural calcification recorded	19.3 years

3. A physical examination was performed by a physician.

4. Chest roentgenograms were obtained and read independently by two board certified radiologists.

5. Pulmonary function tests were run on the Ohio 842 spirometer.

6. Sputum samples were collected by aerosol inhalation at the time of the visit and pooled every morning cough at home for 3 days.

7. Electrocardiogram was taken using an American Optical model 3200 instrument.

8. Hemoglobin and hematocrit tests were run.

9. Carcinoembryonic antigen (CEA) titers were measured by Hoffman–LaRoche Laboratory.

10. Urinalysis tests were performed.

11. Blood was drawn and processed for storage as frozen serum plasma for future studies.

H. PATIENT MANAGEMENT

As part of the TAWP contract stipulations, all patients with suspicious or definitive cytology findings were to be admitted to the hospital at the University of Texas Health Center for bronchoscopy and brush biopsy to localize the suspected carcinoma. All suspicious chest roentgenograms were also to be evaluated. Hospitalization was offered for medical and/or surgical management of bronchogenic carcinoma, mesothelioma, or asbestosis at no cost to the contract. Some patients were referred to their own private physicians if they chose to do so. For most workers, the University of Texas Health Center became the primary medical care facility for health problems, even those not related to asbestos exposure.

Three patients with positive sputum cytologies with negative roentgenograms were operated on for early cancers. Two of them had squamous cell carcinoma of the lung, one with cancer in situ with micro-invasion, and the third had squamous cell carcinoma of the larynx. One patient with an early coin lesion detected on chest roentgenogram had a right-upper lobectomy for squamous cell carcinoma. Several patients with positive cytologies and, in most cases, positive radiology developed rapidly spreading malignancies and have died. Two patients have had positive cytologies and refused localization and treatment. It is evident from this limited experience over a 5-year period that early diagnosis of cancer in an occupationally high-risk group can be accomplished by both sputum cytology with localization with fiberoptic bronchoscopy and with the use of serial chest x-rays. Whether or not this will affect long-term mortality in this group remains to be seen.

I. VENTILATORY STUDIES

The Ohio medical 842 dry rolling seal type spirometer was used. Expected normal values were obtained from the Ohio medical 120 normal value indicator, which uses regression equations with age and height as independent variables. The following spirometric measures were obtained: (1) forced vital capacity (FVC); (2) forced expiratory volume, at one second (FEV_1); (3) $\frac{FEV}{FVC}$%; (4) peak flow (PF); (5) forced expiratory flow, from 25% to 75% (FEF · 25–75%); (6) forced expiratory flow, from 0.2 to 1.2 liters (FEF · 0.2–1.2); (7) maximal voluntary ventilation (MVV). Both the observed and the expected values were recorded on all measurements. It was attempted to have three forced maneuvers performed at each examination. Initially, only the best test was recorded, chosen by the technician. After August 1977, however, all three trials were recorded.

Table 12-3 indicates the spirometry findings for the forced vital capacity (FVC) for the workers and controls as a percent of predicted. The values used for these calculations were the best values recorded for each participant. It is known that an individual could easily under-perform by putting less effort into the test but could never exceed his physiologic and mechanical capacity of the lung and airways. The difference shown between the workers and controls is statistically significant. It can be observed that approximately 23% of the workers had an (FVC) of less than 80% of predicted, whereas only 8% of the controls had values below the 80% predicted normal value. This was not a totally valid comparison because of the fact that the workers had a higher proportion of Blacks than the controls. Blacks have been shown in various studies to have a lower lung volume in flow rates than whites of the same age. The Department of Epidemiology and Biomathematics made a correction utilizing multiple linear regression with race considered as a dummy variable. A comparison of the FVC in workers and control groups after the removal of confounding factors still showed a greater reduction in the FVC between the worker groups. Other statistical analyses revealed that both the duration of employment and the time since first employment are significantly related to FVC as well as FEV_1. This may be seen in Table 12-4. Table 12-5 depicts the relationship of restrictive disease to duration of exposure. Of the individuals who were exposed less than one month, 19% demonstrated restrictive disease; whereas in workers exposed to greater than 36 months, 44.8% were demonstrating mild, moderate, or severe restrictive

Table 3
Spirometry Findings:
Forced Vital Capacity (% Of Expected)

FVC	Workers N	Workers %	Workers Cumulative %	Controls N	Controls %	Controls Cumulative %
50	8	.97	.97	0	0.00	0.00
50-60	16	1.93	2.90	1	.53	.53
60-70	43	5.19	8.09	4	2.13	2.66
70-80	123	14.86	22.95	10	5.32	7.98
80-90	211	25.48	48.43	29	15.43	23.40
90-100	174	21.01	69.44	42	22.34	45.74
100-110	142	17.15	86.59	58	30.85	76.60
110-120	82	9.90	96.50	33	17.55	94.15
120-130	21	2.54	99.03	10	5.32	99.47
130-140	7	.85	99.88	1	.53	100.00
140-150	1	.12	100.00	0	0.00	100.00
Total	828*	100.00	100.00	188	100.00	100.00

*Missing Values 26

disease. This confirms what many have shown in other studies. It is interesting from an evaluation of the smaller group of non-smokers that they do not show a decline relative to FVC with increasing exposures as do the smokers.

J. CHEST RADIOGRAPHY

The initial design of the chest radiography studies was to provide a complement to the sputum cytology as an early indicator of malignancies, particularly those in the periphery of the lung. Secondarily, a consideration was given to the documentation of interstitial and pleural changes in the lung. At each semi-annual visit, four films were taken: a PA inspiration and expiration and

Table 4
Pulmonary Function Tests And Asbestos Work History

Test	Duration Of Employment Significance	Time Since First Employment Significance
FVC	p = .001	p = .001
FEV_1	p = .022	p = .001
FEV_1 / FVC%	p = .07	p = .5

Table 5
Restrictive Disease And Duration of Employment

Duration	Normal	Restrictive*	Totals
<1 Month	167	40 (19.3%)	207
1-6 Months	171	44 (20.5%)	215
6-12 Months	47	25 (34.7%)	72
12-36 Months	59	23 (28%)	82
<36 Months	37	30 (44.8%)	67
	481	162 (25.2%)	643

two left lateral views utilizing 75–100-KV voltages. The fourth film was a high 350-KV inspiration PA view to assess the presence of both interstitial and pleural fibrosis and to evaluate its role in picking up early peripheral nodules. Two board certified radiologists read the films, one of whom later became certified as a pneumoconiosis-B reader. There were 49 patients who had chest roentgenograms that were suspicious of neoplastic disease. Of these, 12 have been histologically proven to be cancer and 11 have not been proven histologically but their diagnosis has been augmented by positive, suspect, or severely atypical cytopathology. In the final 26 the outcome remains to be seen. There were many cases confirmed to have asbestosis or pleural disease that were identified by chest radiographs. The radiographic findings for pneumoconiosis can be seen in Table 12-6. These findings were recorded on the last reading by the radiologist who was certified as a pneumoconiosis-B reader. There are statistically significant differences found between the workers and controls in regard to the irregular small opacities, pleural thickening, and ill-defined diaphragm and cardiac outlines. Table 12-7 depicts the radiographic findings of pleural changes and interstitial changes in workers vs. controls. It is not surprising that workers would have more pleural fibrosis if they also had more interstitial opacities. What was somewhat surprising was that the control group with no known occupational exposure history also had some pleural (5%) and interstitial (10%) changes. Table 12-8 demonstrates that the irregular small opacities are most common in the lower zone and least common in the upper zone of both right and left lungs. As one would suspect, both the interstitial radiographic findings of irregular small opacities and small rounded opacities increased with the duration of occupational asbestos exposure. Less than 10% of individuals with one month or less exposure had neither type of opacities, whereas between 30% and 40% of those with 5 years or more exposure and 60% to 70% of those with more than 10 years exposure had both small-irregular and small-rounded opacities. The same finding was present in regard to pleural radiographic findings and the duration of asbestos exposure. Only about 5% of workers with less than one month exposure had pleural fibrosis, whereas 60% of those with 10 years or more exposure had pleural fibrosis. Over the course of the 5-year surveillance, 22 workers with pleural plaques were noted to have calcification in the plaques. The workers with calcified pleural plaques were far more likely to have pleural thickening and irregular small opacities than those workers without calcified pleural plaques.

Table 6

Radiographic Findings: Pneumoconiosis

ILO-U/C Classification	Values	Workers n	Controls n	Significance Of Differences
Rounded small opacities	None	778	178	
	p (<1.5 mm)	72	10	$x^2 = 2.55$
	q (1.5-3 mm)	9	0	p = .28
	r (3-10 mm)	0	1	
Irregular small opacities	None	708	171	
	s (fine)	108	16	$x^2 = 9.03$
	t (medium)	42	2	p = 0.01
	u (coarse)	1	0	
Large Opacities	None	831	186	
	wd (well defined)	18	1	$x^2 = 2.16$
	id (ill-defined)	10	2	p = .34
Pleural Thickening: Costophrenic Angle	None	788	185	
	Right	23	2	$x^2 = 9.00$
	Left	24	1	p = 0.03
	Both	24	1	
Pleural Thickening: Chest Wall and diaphragm	None	701	179	
	Right	34	5	$x^2 = 21.5$
	Left	32	2	p = .001
	Both	92	3	
Ill-defined diaphragm	None	842	189	
	Right	7	0	$x^2 = 3.80$
	Left	6	0	p = 0.05
	Both	4	0	
Ill-defined cardiac outline	None	381	96	
	Grade 0	455	93	$x^2 = 7.34$
	Grade 1	18	0	p = 0.03
	Grade 2	3	0	
	Grade 3	2	0	
Pleural Calcification: Diaphragm	None	852	188	
	Right	2	0	$x^2 = .17$
	Left	3	1	p = .68
	Both	2	0	
Pleural Calcification: Chest Wall	None	850	188	
	Right	3	1	$x^2 = .44$
	Left	2	0	p = .51
	Both	4	0	
Pleural Calcification: Other	None	857	189	
	Right	0	0	$x^2 = .41$
	Left	1	0	p = .51
	Both	1	0	

K. SPUTUM CYTOPATHOLOGY

The clinical application of cytopathology to the diagnosis of epidermal cancer occurred in 1943 when Papanicolaou published his monograph on cervical cytology (62). Cytologic studies of bronchial secretions removed by rigid bronchoscope, and also sputum, revealed that bronchogenic carcinoma could be diagnosed by this

Table 7
Radiographic Findings

	Worker	Control
Pleural Changes	16%	5%
Interstitial Changes	21%	10%
Other Changes	26%	16%

means (63, 64). However, pulmonary cytology had limited practical use because of the anatomic characteristics of the trachea and bronchial tree and its relative inaccessibility as compared to the cervix. The development of the fiberoptic bronchoscope in Japan in the late 1960s and its subsequent application in the diagnosis of pulmonary lesions in this country made it possible for the clinician to localize some of the early lesions utilizing a brush to biopsy some of the segments beyond the reach of the fiberoptic bronchoscope (65, 66). The early detection of radiologic occult lung cancer by sputum and bronchial secretion cytopathology with subsequent localization with fiberoptic bronchoscopy was demonstrated in the early 1970s (67, 68).

Sputum specimens for cytopathological examination were col-

Table 8
Irregular Small Opacities By Zone
(Asbestos Workers Only)

	Right	Left
Upper	6%	10%
Middle	28%	31%
Lower	82%	67%

lected from each worker at the time of the semi-annual visit. An aerosol-induced specimen was obtained under the supervision of a technician. Each worker also received a container partially filled with fixative solution and was instructed to collect three consecutive early morning cough specimens and mail the container to the laboratory. In addition to the asbestos workers, two control groups comprised of smokers and non-smokers, with no known asbestos exposure, allowed validation of the technical quality of the study.

Until February 1976, the specimens were processed by the "pick and smear" technique (69). Four smears were stained by routine Papanicolaou method. Any specimen remaining was processed by a cell block and two slides were prepared. After February 1976, the specimens were prepared by the Saccomanno sputum concentration technique (70). The cytopathology results were reported in descriptive terms reflecting a progression from no atypia to the development of carcinoma.

- Unsatisfactory (no alveolar macrophages)
- No atypia
- Squamous metaplasia
- Mild atypia
- Moderate atypia
- Severe atypia
- Suspect carcinoma
- Positive for carcinoma

The designation of suspect carcinoma related to specimens that, in the opinion of the cytopathologist, contained cells consistent with carcinoma but not in sufficient quantity to justify a conclusive diagnosis of malignancy.

Ferruginous bodies were counted on up to four slides and each specimen was classified according to the number present as either few (1–14), moderate (15–29), or many (30 or more). The results of the cytopathology during the 5 years of the program may be seen in Table 12-9. They were classified in categories according to their highest (most severe) cytopathologic diagnosis. This same information is presented graphically in Fig. 12-1. Of the 858 workers, 176 (or 20.5%) showed no atypia, 11 (or 1.3%) showed severe atypia, 12 were suspect carcinoma, and 11 were positive carcinoma. The controls represent smokers and non-smokers who were matched for age with workers, and the others were non-asbestos pulmonary patients whose specimens were referred to the cytopathology laboratory.

Ferruginous bodies were identified in the sputum of 291 former workers (33.9%), 2 control patients (1.1%), and 4 other

Table 9

Cytopathology Diagnostic Classifications (May 31, 1979)

	Workers	Controls	Others
No specimens satisfactory for diagnosis	2 (.27%)	3 (1.6%)	0
No atypia	176 (20.5%)	42 (22.3%)	351 (57.3%)
Squamous metaplasia	388 (45.2%)	104 (55.3%)	167 (27.2%)
Mild atypia	163 (19.0%)	19 (10.1%)	64 (10.4%)
Moderate atypia	95 (11.1%)	17 (9%)	25 (4.1%)
Severe atypia	11 (1.3%)	1 (0.5%)	4 (0.7%)
Suspect carcinoma	12 (1.4%)	0 —	1 (0.2%)
Positive carcinoma	11 (1.3%)	2	1 (0.2%)
	858	188	613

patients (0.07%). These patients were classified according to the highest number of ferruginous bodies found on any one specimen. Of the workers, 201 had few ferruginous bodies, 26 had moderate, and 64 had many. Among the controls, 2 had few, and among the others 3 had few, and 1 had moderate. Figure 11-2 depicts the percentage of the 291 workers who had few (65.3%), moderate (8.9%), and many (22%) ferruginous in their sputum. This figure also compares the presence of ferruginous bodies with the method of sputum collection. It is interesting that more ferruginous bodies were detected by the aerosol collection method (28% vs. 6.2%) as compared with the 3-day spontaneous sputum collection method. Almost half (48.8%) were detected by both the aerosol and the spontaneous sputum method. Thus, it is more likely to find ferruginous bodies in an aerosol collected specimen than a 3-day spontaneous sputum collection method. However, more importantly, the correlation of the presence of ferruginous bodies, as well as atypia with other factors, was more consistent and yielded more significant correlations with the spontaneous sputum rather than the aerosol-induced specimens.

Tables 12-10 and 12-11 provide the correlation of both sputum cytopathology (in terms of cellular atypia and ferruginous bodies) with smoking, age at examination, duration of employment, and time since first employment. As one would expect, there is a strong correlation of abnormal sputum cytopathology with the

FIGURE 1

CYTOPATHOLOGY DIAGNOSIS 5/31/79

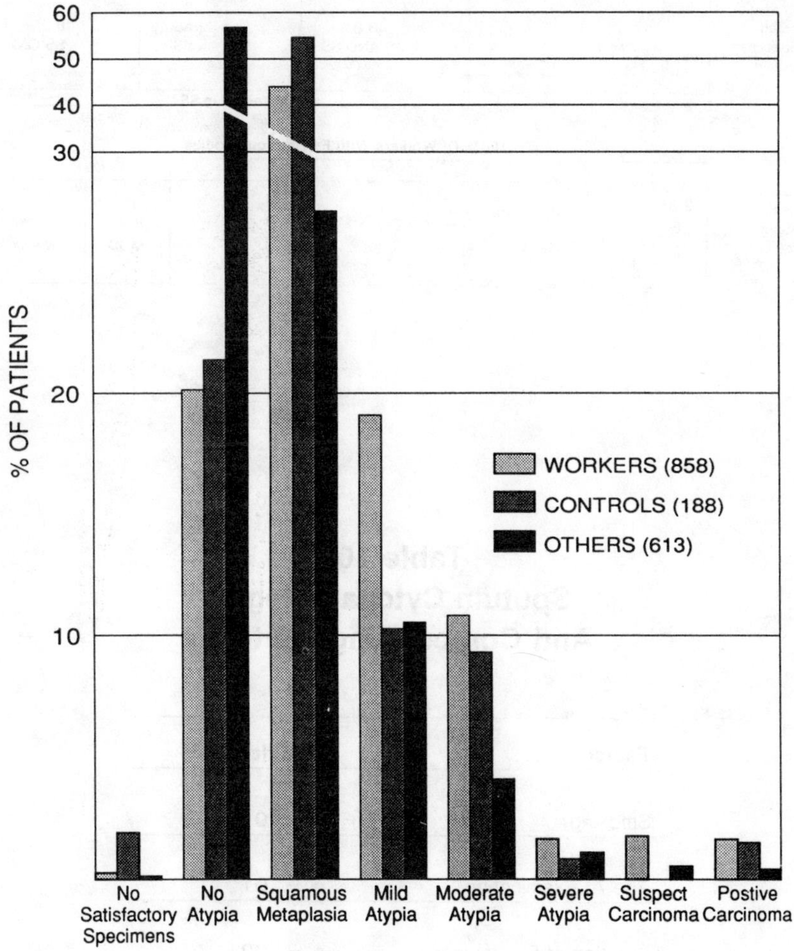

Figure 2
291 Workers With Ferruginous Bodies (33.9% Of 858)

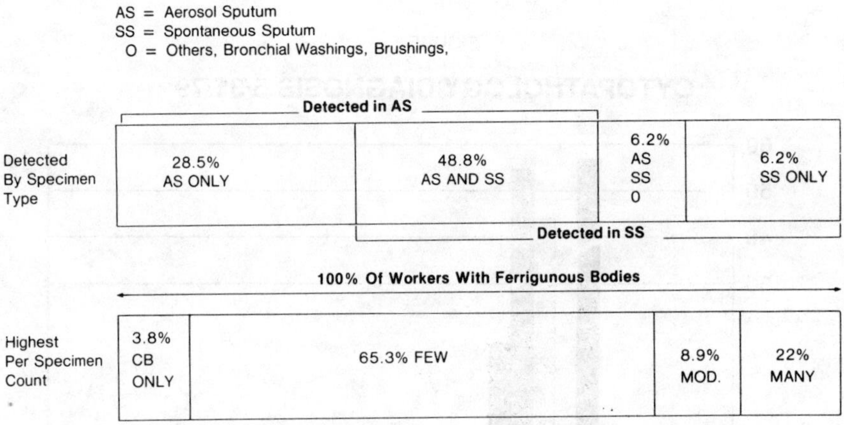

Table 10
Sputum Cytopathology And Confounding Factors

Factor	Significance*
Smoking	p = .01
Age At Examination	p = .01
Duration of Employment	p = .02
Time Since First Employment	p = .001

*Using multiple logistic regression and a dichotomous response variable (0 = normal through mild dysplasia 1 = moderate or worse dysplasia).

Table 11
Ferruginous Bodies and Confounding Factors

Factor	Significance
Smoking	p = .02*
Age At Examination	p = .001
Duration of Employment	p = .001
Time Since First Employment	p >.2

*For spontaneous specimens only.

presence or absence of smoking. This is particularly true in the spontaneous induced specimens. Approximately 85% of smokers have abnormal sputum cytopathology, whereas only 25% of nonsmokers have abnormal sputum cytopathology. A similar positive correlation exists with the age at examination with the younger patients having less abnormal cytopathology. The duration of employment, as well as time since first employment, are also positively correlated with the presence of abnormal cytopathology. Table 12-11 depicts the correlation of the presence of ferruginous bodies with various confounding factors. There was a correlation of the presence of ferruginous bodies and smoking in the spontaneous specimens only. A positive correlation also existed with age at examination and duration of employment. There was no correlation of the presence of ferruginous bodies with the time since first employment. Figure 12-3 demonstrates the correlation of the presence of ferruginous bodies with the presence of abnormal cytopathology. Approximately 15% of those with no atypia had ferruginous bodies, whereas greater than 90% of those who had positive carcinoma had ferruginous bodies. Figures 12-4 and 12-5 demonstrate that patients with no atypia are much less likely to have abnormal pleural changes as well as interstitial radiographic findings than those with moderate atypia or those with severe atypia through positive cytology for cancer.

The technical competence and expertise of the cytotech-

FIGURE 3

FERRUGINOUS BODIES AND CYTOPATOLOGY DIAGNOSIS+

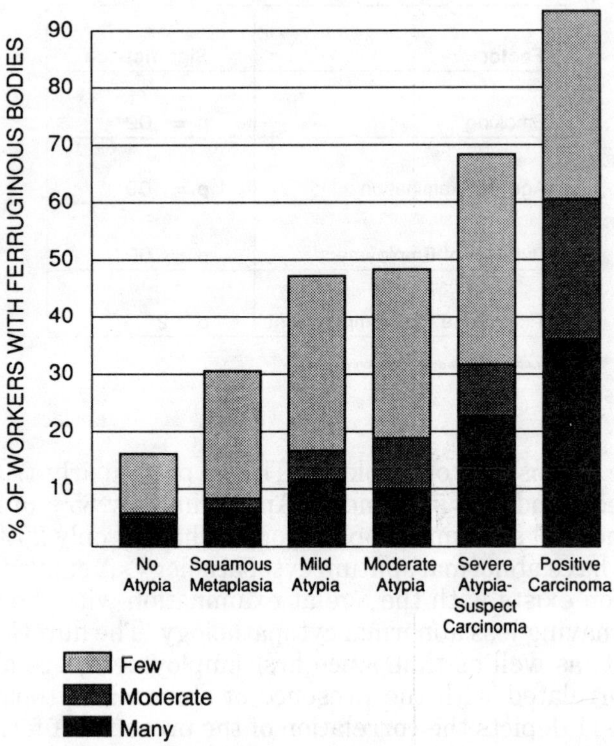

+Based on laboratory records

nologist and cytopathologist are major factors in the reliability of this clinical test. Quality control was performed by a review of 10% of the negative cases by the chief cytotechnologist. The cytotechnology results demonstrated that it is possible to detect lesions not visible radiographically in some cases and early localized and resectable lung cancer with a good potential for cure.

L. ASBESTOS BODIES AND UNCOATED FIBERS IN SPUTUM AND LUNG

The amphibole asbestos has several features that differ from chrysotile. The amosite fibers (Fig. 12-6) tend to break down into thin longer units that often conform to the dimensions consistent

FIGURE 4

PLEURAL RADIOGRAPHIC FINDINGS AND SPUTUM CELLULAR ATYPIA

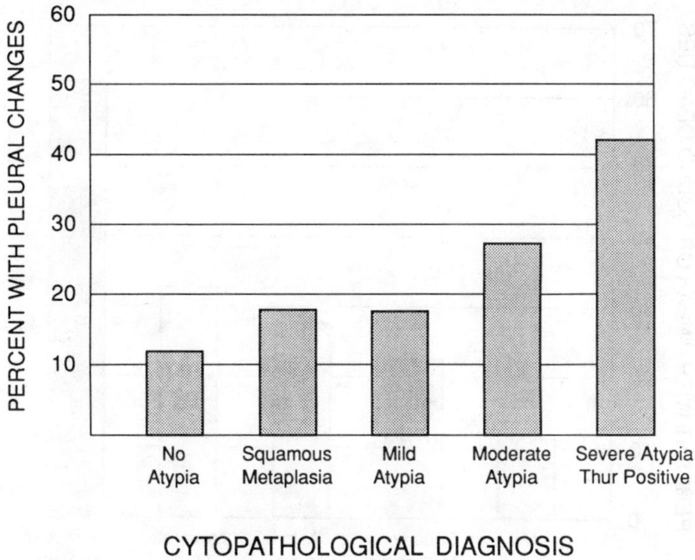

with a more carcinogenic potential (as per the Stanton hypothesis) (71, 72). These longer fibers, unlike the chrysotile form are more durable in tissue and less likely to be cleared. Furthermore, many of these fibers are within the range ($\geq 10\mu$) within which the formation of ferruginous coatings is possible. The ferruginous bodies found on such amphiboles are markers of past asbestos exposure and important diagnostically when tissue is evaluated by light microscopy. The more abundant uncoated fibers are generally below the detection limit of the microscope and thus may exist in large numbers and go undetected.

The use of combined light and electron microscopy in evaluating material from the TAWP has resulted in the following observations. While fiber length has long been recognized as an important determinant of which fibers become coated with ferruginous material, other factors also appear to be involved in the selection process. When ferruginous coatings were stripped from asbestos bodies collected from amosite-exposed individuals, it was commonly noted that other features such as etching of the surface, broken features both on ends and on the surface regions, as well as additional fraying and multifibrillar composition, were found

FIGURE 5

INTERSTITIAL RADIOGRAPHIC FINDINGS AND SPUTUM CELLULAR ATYPIA

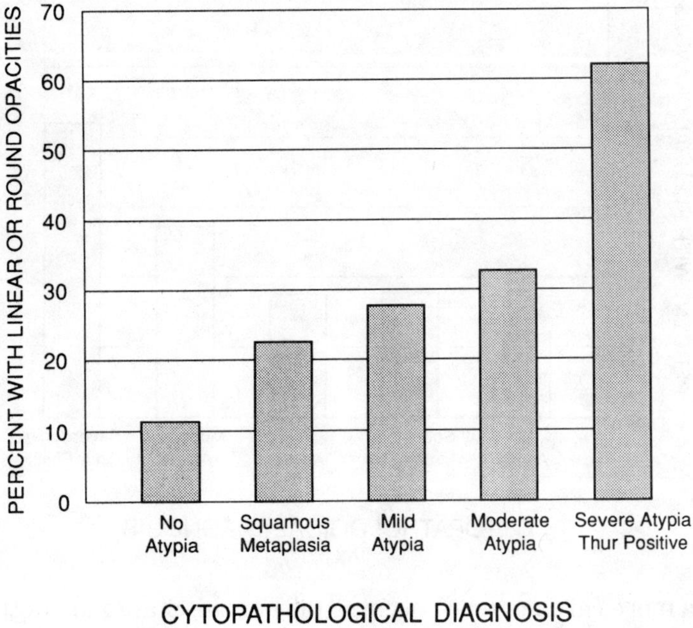

(Fig. 12-7). Many of the uncoated fibers within the samples were above the length, which is important in determining ferruginous body formation (≥10μ). However, these uncoated fibers had much smoother surfaces with very few irregularities (73).

Asbestos bodies (Fig. 12-8) have been noted in cytopathological screening of sputum from the TAWP cohort (74). However, further evaluation of sputum randomly selected from a data bank of samples was found to contain uncoated fibers of amosite asbestos indicating the continuing process of clearance resulted in removing the particulates from the lung years after last exposure (75, 76). These uncoated fibers are short (≤5) and are below the detectable limits of light microscopy.

Analysis of lung tissue from the cohort revealed the expected high concentrations of ferruginous bodies (77) and uncoated fibers (78) with two exceptions. Two workers in the study group were found to have fibrosis within the tissue samples, but no ferruginous bodies were found in either the section or on subsequent tissue digestion. This was in spite of multiple samples (to cover

Fig. 12-6 This scanning electron micrograph is a bulk sample—the commercial amosite as used in the Tyler facility. 400 magnification

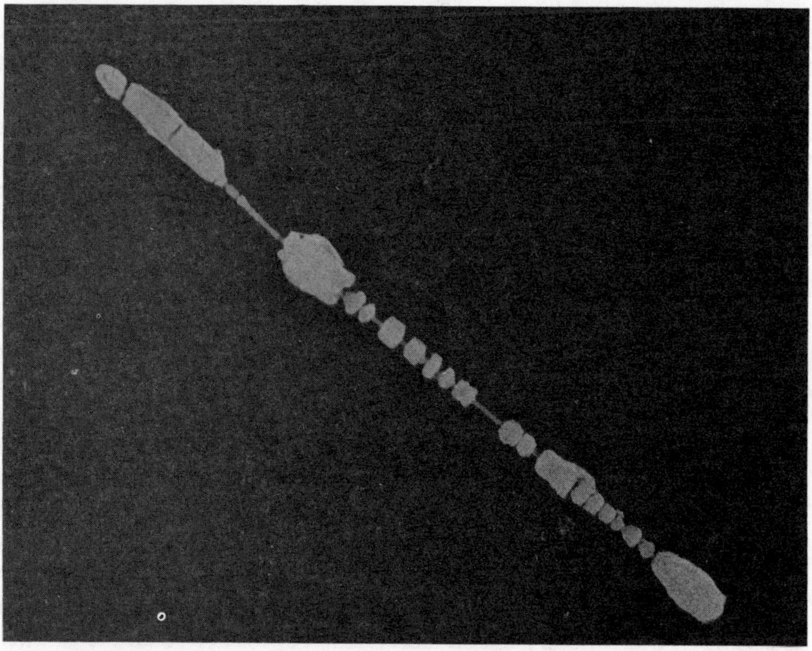

Fig. 12-7 This micrograph shows the core material from an asbestos body which has had its coat partially removed. 1300 magnification

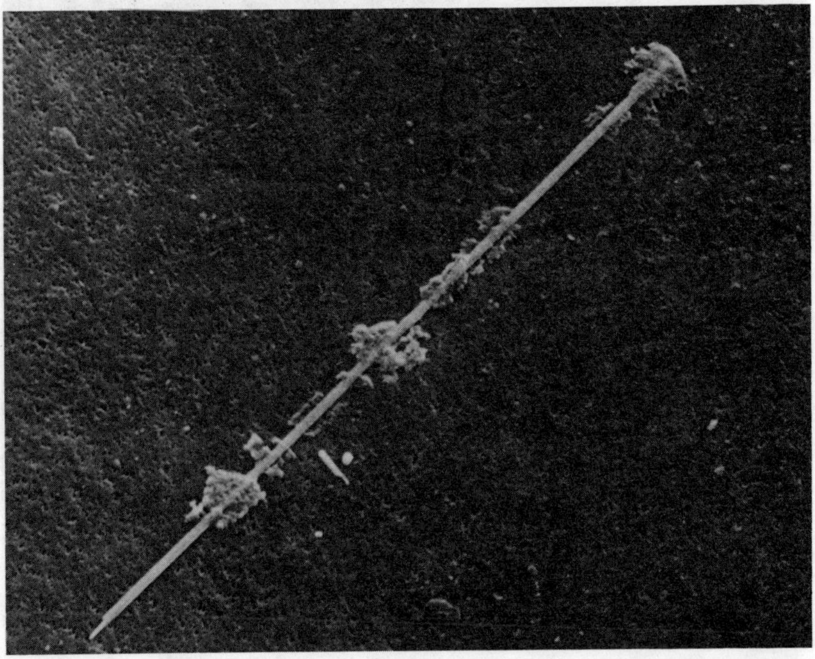

Fig. 12-8 Typical amosite cored ferruginous body, as collected from sputum, is shown in this field. 2800 magnification

random sampling error) and a relatively large total tissue area being sampled (≥5 gms.). Thus, if one were to use the definition set forth in the report of the pneumoconioses committee of the College of American Pathologists in the National Institute for Occupational Safety and Health in 1982 (79), the fibrosis as seen in the tissue could not have been attributed to the presence of asbestos since no ferruginous bodies were seen. The tissue digests, as analyzed by electron microscopy, revealed the presence of uncoated amosite (Fig. 12-9) of the appropriate length necessary for ferruginous body formation in numbers of 0.78 and 1.2×10^6 gm respectively (78). These findings raise serious questions as to the possibility of some individuals not being producers of ferruginous coatings and, furthermore, a concern for accepting a diagnosis contingent upon ferruginous bodies being seen in tissue sections. These findings could be viewed as "exceptions," however, one must recognize the number of such "exceptions" will never be appreciated unless adequate numbers of electron microscopy studies are carried out on tissue found lacking ferruginous bodies at the light microscopy level. Since this report, several other such cases have been referred to our Center including individuals with

Fig. 12-9 This uncoated amosite fiber is typical of those obtained from tissue of Tyler Asbestos Worker's Program. 7500 magnification

heavy tissue burden of short chrysotile fiber (which very rarely could be expected to form ferruginous bodies). This data stimulated other researchers to ask the same question concerning the necessity for ferruginous bodies to be present when linking asbestos as a cause of fibrosis. In fact, Dr. Warnock has recently reported that ≥500,000 uncoated amphibole fibers per gram should be considered adequate cause of fibrosis whether or not ferruginous bodies are seen (80).

The usefulness of small tissue samples is always of concern due to the potential for random sampling error. This concern is justifiable, particularly if a false negative is found. In an evaluation of the sensitivity of such small samples as might be obtained from transbronchial biopsy, a clear difference in the reliability of distinguishing amosite-exposed individuals was evident when varied techniques were used (81). The evaluation of tissue samples by light microscopy (or iron-stained sections) prove the least sensitive discriminator of which tissue had come from occupationally-exposed individuals vs. samples from non-occupationally exposed individuals. When the small samples were digested, ferruginous bodies were more readily found on the filter than had been noted in the tissue. The most sensitive mode of evaluation was found to be assessment of uncoated fibers via the transmission electron microscope. When the light microscopy screening of digested materials from the small samples was combined with the transmission electron microscopy analysis for uncoated fibers, a determination was achievable, which differentiated the amosite-exposed individuals from those samples from the general population (81). Analysis of tissue and body fluids referred to the services of the University of Texas Health Center at Tyler with a request for particulate analysis, whether from the TAWP or from other requests for consultation, have clearly indicated the importance of combining light and electron microscopy if one is to obtain the most accurate data regarding asbestos burden. Concerns are also raised when the final analysis of dust burden is carried out totally on information based on light microscopy.

In summary, the Tyler Asbestos Workers Program was a 5-year study, beginning in 1974, of sputum cytology, chest radiography, and pulmonary function studies of a large cohort of former insulation workers heavily exposed to amosite asbestos. Many of these workers have been followed more recently as a part of a chemoprevention cancer control trial. Much serial information has been obtained during the study period and correlation of the data is still in progress.

ACKNOWLEDGMENT

The authors are grateful for the valuable secretarial assistance provided by Maxine Clark.

REFERENCES

1. Selikoff IJ and Lee DHK. *Asbestos and Disease*, Academic Press, New York, 1978; pp 101–306.
2. Wyers H. Asbestosis. Postgrad Med J 1949; 25:63.
3. Anonymous. Benjamin Franklin and his asbestos purse. Asbestos, 1939; 21:2
4. Cirkel F."Asbestos—its occurence, exploitation and uses." Gout Printing Bur. Ottawa, 1905.
5. Bowles O. "The amosite industry." U.S. Dept Interior, BOM Bull. No 552, U.S. Govt Printing Office, Washington, D.C., 1955.
6. Anonymous. "People," brochure. Johns-Manville Corp., 1976.
7. Arai DT, Weill H. Clinical problems in asbestos-related diseases. in Preger L, et al. *Asbestos-Related Diseases*, Grune and Stratton, New York, 1978; pp 1–19.
8. Craighead JE, Moosman BT. The pathogenesis of asbestos-related diseases. N Eng J Med, 1982; 306:1446–1455.
9. Weill H, Waggenspock C, Bailey W, et al. Radiographic and physiologic patterns among workers engaged in manufacturing of asbestos cement products. J Occup Med, 1973; 15:248–252.
10. Becklake MR. Asbestos-related diseases of the lung and pleura: current clinical issues. Am Rev Respir Dis; August, 1982; 126:187–194.
11. Anderson HA, Lillis R, Daum SM, et al. Household contact asbestos neoplastic risk. Ann NY Acad of Sci, 1976; 271:311–323.
12. Churg A and Warnock ML. Asbestos fibers in the general population. Am Rev Respir Dis, 1980; 122:669–678.
13. Hughes JM and Weill H., Asbestos exposure quantitative assessment of risk. Am Rev Respir Dis, 1986; 133:5–13.
14. Netolizky A. Hygiene der textilindustries. Handbuch der hygiene. (Th Weyl, ed.) Vol. 8, Industrial Hygiene, Gustav Fischer Publ, JEWA, 1987; 1102–1103.
15. Annual report of the chief inspector of factories and workshops for the year 1898. London: H.M. Stationary Ofc., 1899; 171–172.
16. Annual report of the chief inspector of factories and workshops for the year 1899. London: H.M. Stationary Ofc., 1900; 264.

17. Annual report of the chief inspector of factories and workshops for the year 1906. London: H.M. Stationary Ofc., 1907; 219–220.
18. Murray HM. Departmental committee on compensation for industrial diseases minutes of evidence. Appendices and index. London: Wyman and Sons, 1907; 127–128.
19. Auribault M. Note sur l'hygiene et la securite des ouvriers dans la filatures et tissages d'amiante. Bull Insp Trav, Paris 1906; 120–132.
20. Scarpa L. Industria dell'amianto e tuberculosi. Proc Int Med Congr 18th, 1908; 358.
21. Collis EC. Dusty processes. Annual report of the chief inspector of factories and workshops for the year 1910. London: H.M. Stationary Ofc., 1911; 188.
22. Fahr T. Demonstrationen: Praparate und microphotogrammes von einen falle von pneumokoniose. Muenchener Med Woch. 1914; 11:625.
23. Pancoast HK, Miller TG, Landis HM. A roentgenologic study of the effects of dust inhalation upon the lungs. Trans Assoc Amer Phys, 1917; 32:97–108.
24. Hoffman FL. Mortality from respiratory diseases in the dusty trades (inorganic dusts). Washington, D.C.: U.S. Bur Labor Statistics Bull. No. 231, 1918:172–180.
25. Cooke WE. Fibrosis of the lungs due to the inhalation of asbestos dust. Brit Med J, 1924; 1:147.
26. Cooke WE. Pulmonary asbestosis. Brit Med J, 1927; 2:1024–1025.
27. McDonald S. Histology of pulmonary asbestosis. Brit Med J 1927; 2:1025–1026.
28. Seiler HE. A case of pneumoconiosis. Result of the inhalation of asbestos dust. Brit Med J., 1928; 2:982–983.
29. Haddow AC. Clinical aspects of pulmonary asbestosis. Brit Med J, 1929; 2:580–581.
30. Simson FW. Pulmonary asbestosis in South Africa. Brit Med J, 1928; 1:885–886.
31. Williams CL. Report of the medical officer of health for the year 1929. England: Barking Town Urban District Council, 1930; 62–64.
32. Davis GG, Salmonsen EM, Earywine JL. The pneumoconioses (silicosis) bibliography and laws—volume I. Chicago: Industrial Medicine Inc. 1934:153,166,182–183,208–210,213.
33. Merewether ERA, Price CW. Report on effects of asbestos dust on the lungs and dust suppression in the asbestos industry. HM Stationary Ofc, 1930.
34. Merewether ERA. The occurrence of pulmonary fibrosis and other pulmonary affections in asbestos workers. J Indust Hyg, 1930; 12:198–222,239–257.
35. Lanza AG, McConnell WG, Fehnel JW. Effects of the inhalation of asbestos dust on the lungs of asbestos workers. Publ Health Rep, 1935; 50:1–12.
36. Eisenstadt HB. Asbestos pleurisy. Dis Chest, 1964; 46:78–81.

37. Eisenstadt HB. Pleural effusion in asbestosis. N Eng J Med, 1974; 270:1025.
38. Gaensler EA, Kaplan AI. Asbestos pleural effusion. Ann of Int Med, 1971; 74:178–191.
39. Lynch KM, Smith WA. Asbestosis bodies in sputum and lung. Am Med Assoc J, 1930; 95:659.
40. Gloyne SR. The morbid anatomy and histology of asbestosis. Tubercle, 1933; 14:445–451.
41. Gardner LU. The pathology and roentgenographic manifestations of pneumoconiosis. JAMA, 1940; 114:535–545.
42. Beattie J, Knox JF. Studies of mineral content and particle distribution in the lungs of asbestos textile workers. *Inhalation, Particles and Vapours*, C. N. Davis, Oxford, New York, 1961; 419–433.
43. Stone MJ. Clinical studies in asbestosis. Amer Rev Respir Dis, 1940; 41:12–21.
44. Mollo F, Andrion A, Colombo A, Segnan N, Pira E. Pleural plaques and risk of cancer in Turin, Northwestern Italy. Cancer, 1984.
45. Churg A, DePooli L. Environmental pleural plaques in residents of a Quebec chrysotile mining town. Chest, July, 1988; 94:58–60.
46. Hillerdal G. Pleural plaques. *Acta Universitatis Upsaliensis*, 1980, Upsala, 1–126.
47. Sheers G. Asbestos-associated disease in employees of Devonport dockyard. Ann NY Acad Sci, 1977; 330:281–288.
48. Edge JR. Incidence of bronchial cancer in shipyard workers with pleural plaques. Ann NY Acad Sci, 1979; 330:289–294.
49. Fletcher DE. A mortality study of shipyard workers with pleural plaques. Br J Ind Med, 1972; 29:142–145.
50. Wagner JC, Sleggs CA, Marchand P. Diffuse pleural mesothelioma and asbestos exposure in the northwestern cape province. Br J Ind Med, 1960; 17:260.
51. Baris YI, Artovinti M, Sakin AA. Environmental mesothelioma in Turkey. Ann NY Acad Sci, 1979; 330:423–432.
52. Lynch KM and Smith WA. Pulmonary asbestosis, III, carcinoma of the lung in asbestosis-silicosis. Am J Cancer, 1935; 24–56.
53. Gloyne SR. Two cases of squamous carcinoma of the lung occurring in asbestosis. Tubercle, 1935; 17:5.
54. Selikoff IJ, Hammond EC and Seidman H. Cancer risk of insulation workers in the United States, environmental cancer research project, Lyon, France, International Agency for Research in Cancer, 1972.
55. Kannerstein M and Churg J. Pathology of carcinoma of the lung associated with asbestos exposure, Cancer, 1972; 30:14–21.
56. Whitwell F, Newhouse ML and Bennett DR. A study of the histological cell types of lung cancer in workers suffering from asbestosis in the United Kingdom. Br J Ind Med, 1974; 31:298–303.
57. Hurst GA, Spivey CG, Matlage WT, Miller JM, Faulk G, Hieger LR, McLarty JW, Greenberg SD. Tyler asbestos workers pro-

gram, part I: a medical surveillance model and method. Arc Environ Health, 1979; 34:432–439.

58. Johnson WM, Lemen RA, Hurst GA, Spiegel RM, Liu FHY. Respiratory morbidity among workers in an amosite insulation plant. J Occup Med, 1982; 24:994–999.
59. Murphy RLH, Ferris BG, Burgess WA, et al. Effects of low concentrations of asbestos: clinical, environmental, radiologic and epidemiological observations in shipyard pipecoverers and controls. N Eng J Med, 1971; 285:1271–1278.
60. Selikoff IJ, Hammond EC, Churg J. Carcinogenicity of amosite asbestos. Arch Environ Health, 1972; 25:183–186.
61. Selikoff IJ, Hammond EC and Seidman H. Cancer risk of insulation workers in the United States. International Agency for Research on Cancer; Lyon France, 1972.
62. Papanicolaou G and Traut H. Diagnosis of uterine cancer by vaginal smear. Commonwealth Fund, New York, 1943.
63. Herbut P and Clerf L. Bronchogenic carcinoma diagnosis by cytologic study of bronchoscopically removed secretions, JAMA, 1946; 130:1006–1012.
64. Woolner L and McDonald J. Carcinoma cells in sputum and bronchial secretions. A study of 150 consecutive cases in which results were positive. Surgery, Gynecology and Obstetrics, 1949; 88:273–290.
65. Zavala D, Richardson R, Murkerjee P, Bedell G. Use of the bronchofiberscope for bronchial brush biopsy-diagnostic results and comparison with other brushing techniques. Chest, 1973; 63:889–892.
66. Richardson R, Zavala D, Murkerjee P, Bedell G. The use of fiberoptic bronchoscopy and brush biospy in the diagnosis of suspected pulmonary malignancy, Amer Rev Respir Dis, 1974; 109:63–66.
67. Martini N, Beattie E, Cliffton E and Melamed M. Radiologically occult lung cancer: report of twenty-six cases. Surgical Clinic of North America, 1974; 54:811–823.
68. Fontana R, Sanderson D, Woolner L, Miller W, Bernatz P, Payne W and Taylor W. The Mayo lung project for early detection and localization of bronchogenic carcinoma: a status report. Chest, 1975; 67:511–522.
69. Greenberg S, Hurst G, Christianson S, Matlage W, Hurst I and Mabry L. Pulmonary cytopathology of former asbestos workers, report of the first year. Amer Rev Clin Path, 1977; 66:815–822.
70. Saccomanno G, Saunders R, Ellis H, Archer V, Bood B and Beckler P. Concentration of carcinoma of atypical cells in sputum. Acta Cytol, 1963; 7:305–309.
71. Stanton MF, Layard M, Tegeris A, Miller E, May M, Kent E. Carcinogenicity of fibrous glass: pleural response in the rat in relation to fiber dimension. J Natl Cancer Inst, 1977; 58:587–603.
72. Stanton MF, Layard M, Tegeris A, Miller E, May M, Morgan E, Smith A. Relation of particle dimension to carcinogenicity in am-

phibole asbestos and other fibrous materials. J Natl Cancer Inst, 1981; 67:965.

73. Dodson RF, O'Sullivan MF, Williams MG, Hurst GA. Analysis of cores of ferruginous bodies from former asbestos workers. Environ Res, 1982; 28:171–178.
74. McLarty JW, Greenberg SD, Hurst GA, Spivey CG, Seitzman LH, Hieger LR, Farley ML, Mabry LC. The clinical significance of ferruginous bodies in sputa. J Occup Med, 1980; 22:92–96.
75. Dodson RF, Williams MG, McLarty JW, Hurst GA. Asbestos bodies and particulate matter in sputum from former asbestos workers. Acta Cytol, 1983; 27:635–640.
76. Dodson RF, Williams MG, Corn CJ, Idell S, McLarty JW. Asbestos fibers in sputum—an indicator of past occupational exposure. Lab Invest, 1988; 58:144.
77. Dodson RF, Greenberg SD, Williams MG, Corn CJ, O'Sullivan MF, Hurst GA. Asbestos content in lungs of occupationally and nonoccupationally exposed individuals. JAMA, 1984; 252:68–71.
78. Dodson RF, Williams MG, O'Sullivan MF, Corn CJ, Greenberg SD, Hurst GA. A comparison of the ferruginous body and uncoated fiber content in the lungs of former asbestos workers. Am Rev Respir Dis, 1985; 132:143–147.
79. Craighead JE, Abraham JL, Churg A, Green FHY, Kleinerman J, Pratt PC, Seemayer TA, Vallyathan V, Weill H. The pathology of asbestos-associated diseases of the lungs and pleural cavities: diagnostic criteria and proposed grading schema. Arch Pathol Lab Med, 1982; 106:544–596.
80. Warnock ML, Wolery G. Asbestos bodies or fibers and the diagnosis of asbestosis. Environ Res, 1987; 44:29–44.
81. Dodson RF, Hurst GA, Williams MG, Corn CJ; Greenberg SD. Comparison of light and electron microscopy for defining occupational asbestos exposure in transbronchial lung biopsies. Chest, 1988, 94:366–370.

13

Asbestos Medical Research in Czechoslovakia

MIROSLAV NAVRÁTIL, M.D., Doc., C.Sc.

Institute of Hygiene and Epidemiology,
Praha, Czechoslovakia

Synopsis

H. EPIDEMIOLOGICAL STUDIES
1. Pleural Hyalinosis (Plaques)
2. Asbestos Neoplasia of the Lungs
3. Pleural (Peritoneal) Mesothelioma in Asbestos-Exposed Workers

I. CONCLUSION

BIOGRAPHY

Dr. Miroslav Navrátil is Associate Professor at Charles University in Prague, Czechoslovakia, and Leading Scientific Worker (Ph.D) at the Institute of Hygiene and Epidemiology, Prague. He is Head of the Laboratory of Lung Function Examination, Division of Occupational Diseases of the Respiratory System. He is interested in problems of pneumoconioses, namely asbestosis and asbestos-related diseases. He has published three monographs and more than 200 scientific articles, mainly in the Czechoslovak Medical Bibliography, but also in American, German, and other journals, on the topics related to biological effects of asbestos or other harmful dusts as well as to clinical physiology of respiration. Dr. Navrátil has been awarded several prizes of the Czechoslovak Medical Society J. E. Purkyně for his contribution to the progress in occupational and environmental health sciences. He was the first President of the Czechoslovak Society of Clinical Physiology of Respiration founded in 1967 and former National Delegate of the European Society of Clinical Physiology of Respiration (SEPCR). At present he is member of the Editorial Board of the Int. Arch. Occup. Environm. Health, Hamburg, FRG. His biography has been recorded in the Marquis Who's Who in the World, *7th Edition 1984/1985. Dr. Navrátil may be contacted at the Institute of Hygiene and Epidemiology, Center of Industrial Hygiene and Occupational Diseases, Šrobárova 48, 100 42 Praha 10, Czechoslovakia 293205.*

EDITORS' COMMENTARY

It is always of interest, in reviewing medical research, to learn what is happening in any one country—what is being done and why. Research involves procedures for approximating the truth, replication for assurance, and inferring further discovery possibilities. Thus, questions arise as to whether the same results, conclusions, and inferences are found in independent work in various countries where asbestos or dust exposure might be different, diagnosis and treatment might vary, or local conditions might have created unique problems. The following chapter presents a historical review of what has occurred in Czechoslovakia, under their unique health care system, with particular emphasis on long-term studies of exposed workers. The problems encountered were similar to those encountered in other countries and help to explain the gradual improvement in procedure and the variance found in early reported research data from various countries. The immunological and genotoxicological studies began early in Czechoslovakia (1960s). Pulmonary inflammatory processes with hyalinosis complicata has been identified as a disease entity. Special emphasis has now been placed on low-level exposure risks. It is also of interest that the health risks from asbestos were recognized in Czechoslovakia (the Bohemia area of Austria–Hungary) in 1897.

A. INTRODUCTION

In post-World War II Chezchoslovakia, in the face of a disorganized economy, industry devastated by war, and a 6-year occupation by Nazi Germany, all the responsibility for provision of national public health and medical care services throughout the

Accepted for publication 24 February 1989.

country was assumed by the government and its Ministry of Health. The organizational structure of the health system, including occupational health services, has undergone many changes during the past decades, consistent with the actual needs of the country and the availability of material and financial resources. The present-day pattern of health care provision for the industrial workforce population is based on the system represented by a network of in-plant physicians who hold the front-line position in providing preventive and curative care for the employees. The range of occupational health services they provide includes the hygienic supervision of the workplace, pre-employment, periodic and other health-control examinations, medical examinations for workmen's compensation purposes, assessment of the degree of loss of working capacity in case of occupational disease or invalidation, and many other activities. There is a close cooperation with specialists of various categories in the clinical departments of occupational diseases, such as pneumologists, cardiologists, allergologists, and many other specialists, depending on the health problem involved.

The in-plant physicians have very close links with the industrial hygiene divisions of the Hygiene Service centers as well as with the departments or clinics of occupational diseases responsible for in-patient and out-patient services in the region. The divisions of industrial hygiene provide the in-plant physician with some expert professional services, such as measurement of dust concentration level at the workplace and help in the prevention of the onset of occupational diseases through control of risks to worker's health. The help of the clinics or departments of occupational diseases lies in providing specialized laboratory services, radiological and functional examinations of the respiratory system, or in performing biochemical tests, all aimed at establishing the correct diagnosis of the disorder or disease. This combination of the industrial hygiene and occupational medical services is a good source of data that may serve as a starting point in conducting cross-sectional, long-term, or cohort follow-up studies among the industrial workforce population. Since the mid-1950s, Czechoslovakia has also two research institutes of the Ministries of Health in Prague and Bratislava, both oriented towards solution of the topical industrial hygiene and occupational health problems. Their research activities concerned with asbestos biological hazards have been performed as a rule as a team work headed by experienced research workers who were capable of coordinating the work of in-plant physicians; industrial hygienists; physicians at the clinics of occupational diseases; and the laboratory professionals specialized in immunological and cytogenotoxicological methods, oncological examination methods, and in the methods of the statistical evaluation of data. Emphasis has also been put on the experiences gained through contacts with the professionals abroad, e.g., in the United States, Canada, Great Britain, the U.S.S.R., France, both German states, Poland, Sweden, Finland, and other countries of the world.

Reports on asbestos medical research in Czechoslovakia are mostly published in the journal "Pracovní lékařství" (Occupational Health), an official journal of the Society of Occupational Health, in Czech or Slovak Language, with the summaries in English and Russian. The titles of citations referred to in the list of references are given in English translations. The only monograph on the biological effects of asbestos in man has been written by M. Navrátil[36] and was published in 1982.

B. ASBESTOS EXPOSURE RISKS IN THE CZECHOSLOVAK INDUSTRY

As an industrialized country, Czechoslovakia has many uses for asbestos and in many industrial branches, but the mining of the mineral is limited to a single asbestos deposit in Slovakia. This mine yields the so-called short-fiber, serpentine-type of asbestos (i.e., microasbestos), which is not well suited to usual commercial uses. This implies that almost all asbestos mineral required for common industrial purposes is imported from abroad, namely from Canada, the Soviet Union, South Africa, Zimbabwe, etc. The imported types of asbestos include mostly chrysotile, to a lesser extent also asbestiform amphiboles; one of these, crocidolite, should be completely excluded from import to Czechoslovakia in accordance with the ILO Convention no. 162.

Small deposits of fibrous serpentine-type minerals, namely clinochrysotile, orthochrysotile, or antigorite,[14] are available at some 25 locations throughout the country, but their industrial exploitation could be hardly expected to be cost-effective.

The risks of occupational exposure to asbestos are encountered among the workers engaged in the manufacture of asbestos cylinder head gaskets, brake and clutch linings, heat-resistant asbestos boards and insulating materials, or of asbestos-cement pipes and roofing sheets. The total number of workers at risk is relatively high, but the plants they work in are scattered through the whole country. Actually, there are only a few plants available where the number of workers is large enough to facilitate conclusive research work in this field. These are represented by two larger plants manufacturing asbestos textile, insulants, boards, and friction materials (plant A.Z., Central-Bohemian region—in operation since the 1920s; plant O.K., East-Bohemian region—in operation since the 1950s) and two larger plants manufacturing asbestos-cement products (plant E.B. in Bohemia and plant A.N. in Slovakia). The asbestos medical researches summarized in this chapter have been conducted in three of them (plants A.Z., O.K., and A.N.) and in the only asbestos mine and separating mill in Slovakia.

C. LEGAL ASPECTS OF ASBESTOSIS AND ASBESTOS-RELATED DISEASES

In Czechoslovakia, the occupational status of asbestos-induced fibrosis (asbestosis) was first legally recognized in 1947 by Law no. 47. According to this law, the criteria decisive for the recognition of this disease as occupational were as follows: the detailed specification of exposure conditions certified by the industrial hygienist; the presence of typical radiographic changes in the lungs; the presence of clinical functional disorders or the association with lung cancer. Since the first revision of this law in 1962 the presence of clinical functional disorders has no longer been necessary as a condition for the recognition of asbestosis as occupational in Czechoslovakia. This implies that radiographic changes in the lungs and a history of asbestos exposure are now sufficient evidence for notifying asbestosis or asbestosis with lung cancer as an occupational disease constituting the patient's right to financial compensation.

The subsequent revisions of the official list of recognized occupational diseases have focused on diseases other than asbestosis. The last revision was in 1988 (no. 149) leaving again unchanged the text concerning asbestosis. This legal document thus covers asbestosis and its association with lung cancer but not its association with pleural or peritoneal mesothelioma, a combination equally malignant to the patient. Nevertheless, notification of this combination is analogous as in asbestosis cases associated with lung cancer.

No other asbestos-related diseases are recognized as occupational by the Czechoslovak law. This implies that cases of pleural hyalinosis (plaques), for example, are recorded but do not have the status of an occupational disease. Such an approach is at least partly attributable to the fact that, according to law, every patient with a disease included in the official list of recognized occupational diseases has to be immediately removed from the original job and starts receiving partial or full compensation payment, depending on the extent of his or her work incapacity. This for instance contrasts the practice adopted in the German Democratic Republic where even the simple forms of pleural hyalinosis ("pleuraasbestose") are notified as occupational, but not all of them are eligible for financial cempensation; that comes only with a certain degree of disablement.[2b]

D. RESEARCH OF ASBESTOS BIOLOGICAL HAZARDS IN CZECHOSLOVAKIA

The first reference to the health risk run by workers spinning asbestos textile fibers to produce heat insulants was in 1897, i.e., at the time Czechoslovakia was part of the Austrian-Hungarian Monarchy, by Netolitzky,[39] the then secretary of the Ministry of the Interior in Vienna. In his "Handbuch der Hygiene" (Handbook of Hygiene), when describing breathing difficulties and coughing among workers in the asbestos textile industry in Tachov, western Bohemia, he could not possibly know the actual nature of the pulmonary process, but what he evidently did realize was the likelihood that the asbestos fibres released in the process of asbestos separation and spinning operations may, especially under bad dust conditions, penetrate into the mucous membranes of the respiratory tract.

Professional interest in the biological activity of asbestos was aroused in Czechoslovakia in the 1950s, in connection with a series of reports from abroad pointing to asbestos as a cause of lung fibrosis and its association with lung cancer. The first observations reported in 1950 were from Holomáň,[12] the chief medical representative of health insurance offices in Slovakia, who had surveyed all cases of notified occupational diseases. He examined 67 asbestos mine and mill workers and 49 workers from two asbestos-cement plants in Slovakia, but found no case of asbestosis at that time, in spite of a relatively long history of asbestos exposure in some of these workers (20–29 years).

A study conducted in the same plants some 6 years later by Nosál,[40] the head of the Clinic of Occupational Diseases in Bratislava, was carried out with a total of 88 asbestos workers. The result: 3 cases of asbestosis were diagnosed, notified, and compensated. It was then rightly assumed that the formation of fibrous tissue in the lungs of these patients was a result of exposure to long asbestos fibres, a conclusion consistent with the experimental results reported by Vorwald, Durkan, and Pratt in 1951.

Jindřichová,[16] the head of the Clinic of Occupational Diseases in Hradec Králové, related to plant O.K., did not do asbestos research of her own, but had greatly contributed to the spread of occupational health knowledge in this field by giving lectures to in-plant physicians attending the postgraduate training courses, with the aim of promoting interest in the health problems associated with work at risk of asbestos exposure. These lectures took place in 1955 and had a clear positive impact on the attitude of physicians towards this health hazard. This gave new impetus to formation of working groups concerned with a variety of asbestos-related problems, namely the relationship of asbestos to lung fibrosis, pleural hyalinosis, or neoplasia of the lung and pleura; immunological and genotoxicological impacts of asbestos exposure; methodology of radiographic and functional diagnosis of asbestosis; cohort studies of persons directly or indirectly exposed to asbestos dust.

E. OCCURRENCE OF ASBESTOSIS IN CONDITIONS OF THE CZECHOSLOVAK INDUSTRY

Two criteria now have to be met in Czechoslovakia prior to asbestosis notification as an occupational disease: (1) typical signs in radiographs and (2) a history of exposure to asbestos dust. Between 1954 and 1980, these notification conditions had been fulfilled in 114 asbestos workers employed in 5 asbestos plants known to be a source of most, if not all, cases of notified asbestosis in Czechoslovakia (Navrátil et al.[35]). The average number of new asbestosis cases reported annually was 4.2, and the situation in the years from 1981 to 1987 remained about the same, despite a slight downward trend in the overall incidence rate. The notification figures for individual years ranged from 0 to 10.

Notification of new cases of occupational diseases in Czechoslovakia is the responsibility of skilled and qualified physicians at the departments or clinics of occupational diseases, in order to ensure a uniform approach to assessment work. The responsibility for the postgraduate training studies of these physicians rests with the Chair of Occupational Diseases of the Postragraduate Medical Institutes in Prague and Bratislava and with the training places at the Clinics of Occupational Diseases in Prague and Bratislava.

The first pilot studies were initiated by the former Institute of Industrial Hygiene and Occupational Diseases in Prague (now the Institute of Hygiene and Epidemiology) and by the Clinic of Occupational Diseases in Prague. These studies involved a total of 129 workers from asbestos plant A.Z. manufacturing asbestos textile and friction materials. Signs of asbestosis were diagnosed in 7 workers: 1 worker had a combination of asbestosis with lung cancer, and there were recorded frequent symptoms of chronic bronchitis and lung emphysema among the people above 40 years of age (Rejsková[42]). These findings prompted Navrátil in 1956 and 1957[22,23] to intitiate a series of lung function examinations in these workers, with the aim to detect functional signs of lung emphysema. In these studies two groups of asbestos workers were evaluated: one of these included workers who had a long history of asbestos exposure but no signs of asbestosis; the other group consisted of those with clear signs of the disease. The control group was composed of individuals from a non-asbestos plant in the same area who worked under conditions relatively free of dust exposure risk. This lung ventilation study revealed that the functional changes typical for lung emphysema were primarily detectable in persons notified as cases of occupational asbestosis; this was taken as evidence that indicated that lung fibrosis was likely to combine with lung emphysema. In the 1950s, the spectrum of available lung function tests was rather limited so that the diagnosis had to be derived from spirogram values, outcomes of forced expiratory volume tests, and from the presence of radiographic and ausculation signs suggestive of lung emphysema. These observations were later (1982) confirmed by Dobiáš,[5] the head of the Second Institute of Pathologic Anatomy in Prague, in a special morphological study based on postmortem examinations of the deceased patients from plant A.Z. He observed that the interstitial fibrosis in the lungs of patients exposed to asbestos dust was frequently accompanied by the sites of tissue that could be characterized as "honeycomb lung." This clinical and pathologic research has resulted in a conclusion that the asbestosis located primarily in the lower lobes of the lungs leads to distinct signs of emphysema in the upper lung zones.

The radiographic appearances of the lungs of asbestosis patients from plant A.Z. are demonstrated in the figures that follow. The first of them (Fig. 13-1) is a case of asbestosis in a 60-year-old former female worker from the asbestos textile spinning mill, exposure time 25 years. The radiograph shows irregular opacities in the lower to central zones of the lung fields at concurrent heart hypertrophy. The second radiograph (Fig. 13-2) is from 1958 and

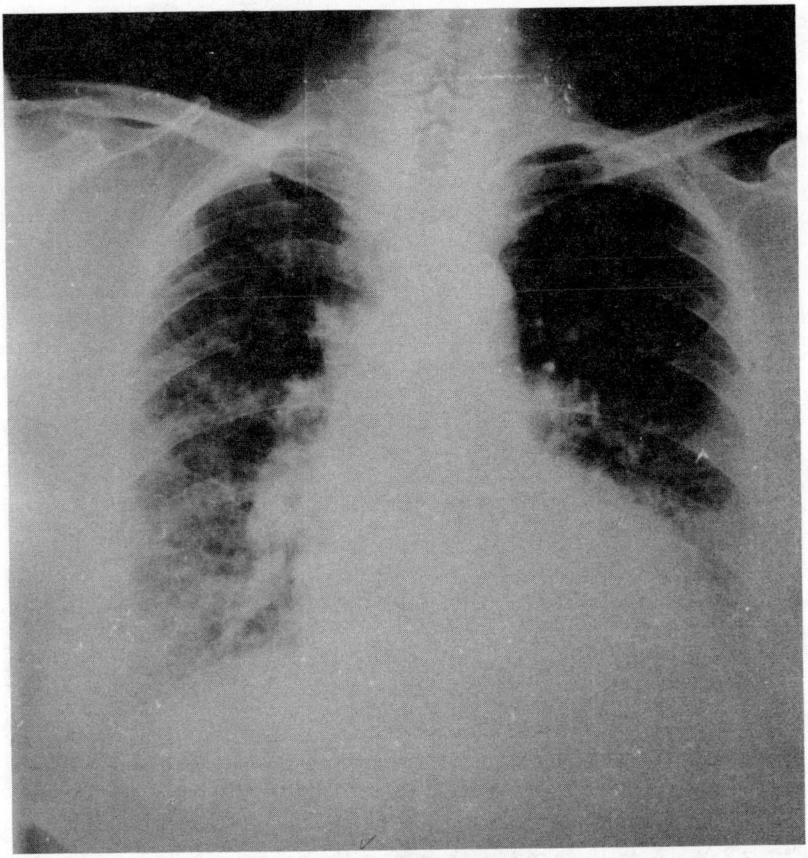

Fig. 13-1 A 60-year-old former female worker of the spinning department, 25 years of exposure. Asbestosis, arterial hypertension.

demonstrates a case of asbestosis in a 48-year-old male worker employed in the manufacture of asbestos boards 17 years after the first exposure to asbestos dust. During the subsequent 20 years the fibrotic process in the lungs accompanied with lung emphysema continued to deteriorate reaching in 1978 (Fig. 13-3) the advanced stage of asbestos characterized by coarse irregular opacities obscuring the normal vascular pattern of the lower and central zones of the lung field, together with signs of vesicular emphysema in the upper fields.

Asbestos plant O.K. has been the subject of research since the mid-1950s. During the 15-year period from 1955 to 1969 a total of 400 asbestos workers (147 males, 253 females) had been examined in this plant (Medek[21]). Asbestosis was diagnosed and noti-

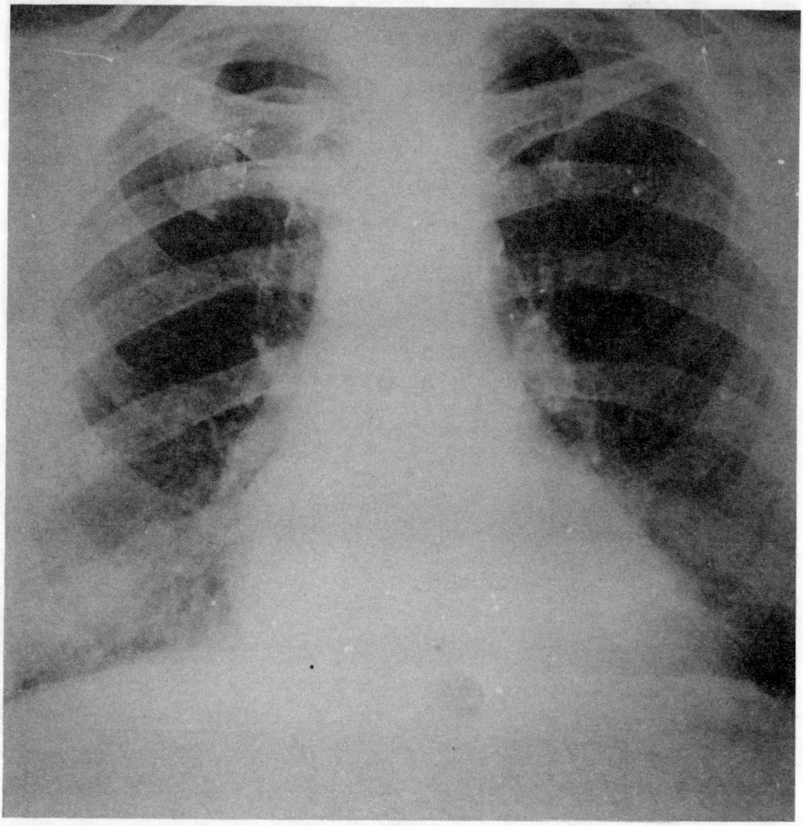

Fig. 13-2 A 48-year-old worker from the asbestos boards production, 17 years of exposure. Radiograph from 1958, the year of asbestosis notification.

fied in 15 of them, on the average within 9.9 years from the initial exposure to asbestos.[25] One of these patients had died of lung cancer. The dust conditions in plant O.K. had been far less favorable than those of plant A.Z. The dust concentration levels in plant O.K. in the 1950s ranged from 1.46 to 42.6 mg/m^3, in 1964 they dropped to 1.40–4.05 mg/m^3. All samples of dust were measured by the gravimetric method.

In the only chrysotile mine in Slovakia, 6 cases of asbestosis, 2 cases of lung cancer (Rovenský[44]), and no case of mesothelioma had been reported in the course of 30 years by the end of 1986. All asbestos victims were from the separating mill.

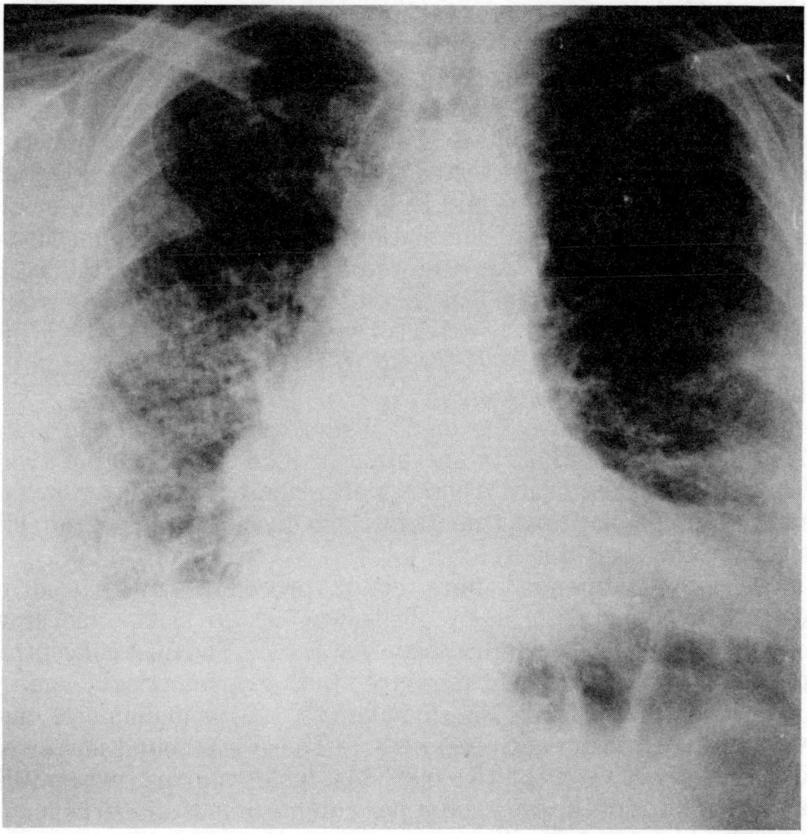

Fig. 13-3 The same worker as in Fig. 13-2 some 20 years later (1978). Progressive asbestosis in both lower lobes, pleural pericardial adhesions, emphysema in both upper fields.

F. ENVIRONMENTAL DUST MEASUREMENT IN ASBESTOS PLANTS

The research into the incidence of asbestosis and asbestos-related diseases proceeded hand-in-hand with researches of the working environment, with the aim to define the existing patterns of dose-response relationship. In Czechoslovakia, the industrial hygiene standard for dust required that all dust measurements be carried out gravimetrically. The original MAC limit for dust in asbestos plants (2 mg/m^3) was established in 1958. The more recent gravimetric limit standards differentiate between the dust containing less than 10% asbestos (4 mg/m^3) and that with more than 10% asbestos content (2 mg/m^3). Consistently with the worldwide trend towards fibre counting, the ILO dust standard (1 fibre/cm^3) has also been accepted in Czechoslovakia.

In 1967, three methods of gravimetric dust measurement employing membrane filters, filamentous filters, and an electrostatic precipitator were tested in plant A.Z. by Šimeček[45] from the Institute of Hygiene and Epidemiology in Prague. His study showed a high degree of correlation between the three methods, with $r = 0.974–0.997$. According to his measurements the average dust concentration was highest in asbestos mixing room (21.3 mg/m^3) followed by asbestos yarn production (7.85 mg/m^3) and spinning mill (1.08–1.15 mg/m^3). The mineral fraction in burnt samples of dust was 87%.

Table 13-1 shows the level of dust concentrations in plant A.Z. from the start of its operation in 1925 till the end of 1986. There is clear downward trend in workplace dust levels, a result of multimillion dollar investments into the dust control program initiated in the early 1960s.

The recommended fibre count procedure introduced in Czechoslovakia in the early 1980s was tested in the asbestos-cement plant A.N. near Bratislava by Juck.[17] The dust concentration at the workplace was measured both gravimetrically and by counting asbestos fibers >5 μm in length, <3 μm in diameter, and with a length-to-breadth ratio ≥3:1. There was found low or no correlation between the two methods, which implies that no reliable estimates of the fibre count per volume unit of air can be made from previous gravimetric measurements.

The present-day dust conditions in plant A.Z. as assessed by the fiber count technique appear to be relatively favorable and in line with the worldwide downward trend in the supply of asbestos fibres. This may perhaps justify the expectation that the asbestosis cases encountered in the productive age will be increasingly rare in the years to come.

Table 13-1 Environmental Conditions in Plant A.Z.*

Time Period	Dust Concentration, mg/m^3
1925 (start of production) until 1950	Uncertain values
1950–1964—irregular measurement	50 to 5
1965 until today—regular measurement	Under 10
1986—last results 12 sampling points	Mean 2.38

* The plant engaged in carding, spinning, and weaving to produce friction products and boards.

As shown in Table 13-1, gravimetric measurements in plant A.Z. in 1986 gave the 2.38 mg/m^3 dust concentration average from 12 measuring points. The dust concentration figures for 1987 were obtained by both gravimetry (mg/m^3) and the fibre count technique (f/cm^3). The values measured are presented in Table 13-2.

These data seem to provide evidence that shows that, as a result of gradual introductions of effective air-conditioning systems, present-day dust conditions in a great majority of workplaces tend to reach values close to the MAC limit.

G. DIAGNOSTICS OF HEALTH DAMAGE FROM ASBESTOS DUST EXPOSURE

The main research objectives in this field were radiologic techniques, lung function tests, and the examinations of biochemical, immunological and genotoxicological changes in asbestos-exposed persons.

1. Radiography of Lung Abnormalities

Morphologically, asbestosis is a form of lung disease marked by interstitial fibrosis affecting predominantly the basal areas of the lungs. The radiographic appearances of changes are now classified according to the ILO U/C scheme of International X-Ray Classification of Pneumoconioses, 1971 to 1980, extended to cover pneumoconioses with irregular opacities designated by the symbols "s, t, u" and profusion categories "1, 2, 3." As noted

Table 13-2 Dust Measurement in Plant A.Z., 1987

Sampling Point	1	2	3	4	Mean
Spinning					
a	8.54	5.73	2.04	1.81	4.53
b	2.46	3.37	1.56	0.69	2.00
Carding					
a	1.25	1.42	0.81	2.31	1.45
b	2.42	2.91	3.68	2.94	2.99
Asbestos metal products					
a	0.34	0.32	0.27	0.50	0.36
b	0.92	0.65	0.96	0.90	0.86

a = Gravimetric method: mg/m^3.
b = Fibre counting: f/cm^3.

by Navrátil,[29] who had studied thousands of radiographs from plant A.Z., this radiologic classification of asbestosis was in need of a radiological technique that would improve the appearance of lung interstitium. It became evident that neither the regular radiologic technique employing 50–80 kV nor the hard technique were suitable for this purpose. Moreover, the quality of foils and the developing technique, which all led to undesirable re-exposures due to repeated x-ray examinations. This gave rise to the so-called semi-hard technique using the voltage range 75–90 kV at 25–30 mAs, i.e., the kilovoltages that were above the upper limit for regular radiography but did not reach the level of hard technique voltages. The interfering effect of secondary radiation was limited by the use of Bucky grid 1:5, which helped greatly improve the quality of interstitial structure appearances.

The next two figures are a pair of radiograph sections targeted on the basal field of the right lung in a 43-year-old healthy female. The radiograph in Fig. 13-4 was obtained by the regular radiologic technique; that in Fig. 13-5 is a result of semi-hard technique. Figures 13-6 and 13-7 are the sections of the identical lung field in a 67-year-old former asbestos worker who had worked for 35 years in plant A.Z. It is evident that the radiographic details of the lung interstitial tissue examined by the semi-hard technique are in both cases far better defined than those obtained by regular technique. The semi-hard voltage technique with the Bucky grid is now routinely used with advantage at the Clinic of Occupational Diseases in Prague when examining the patients exposed to asbestos dust.

Semi-hard voltage methodology was first used by Navrátil[31] to classify irregular opacities and degrees of profusion in the radiographs of 85 plant A.Z. workers with an exposure history longer than 15 years (Table 13-3). This group of examinees comprised a subgroup of 34 workers whose asbestosis had been already notified and compensated and a subgroup of 51 individuals who had not met the asbestosis notification criteria preceding the International Classification system. This study revealed that the subgroup of asbestosis patients had a significant predominance of radiographic appearances belonging to profusion category "2" and opacity type "t" or "s." In contrast, the other subgroup exhibited rather type "s" opacity patterns and profusion categories "1" to "2." That was a clear confirmation of the usefulness of the ILO Classification system. As concerns additional symbols of the Classification, the subgroup of asbestosis patients had a clear predominance of "plc" symbol suggestive of the presence of pleural calcifications, in the subgroup of persons without asbestosis,

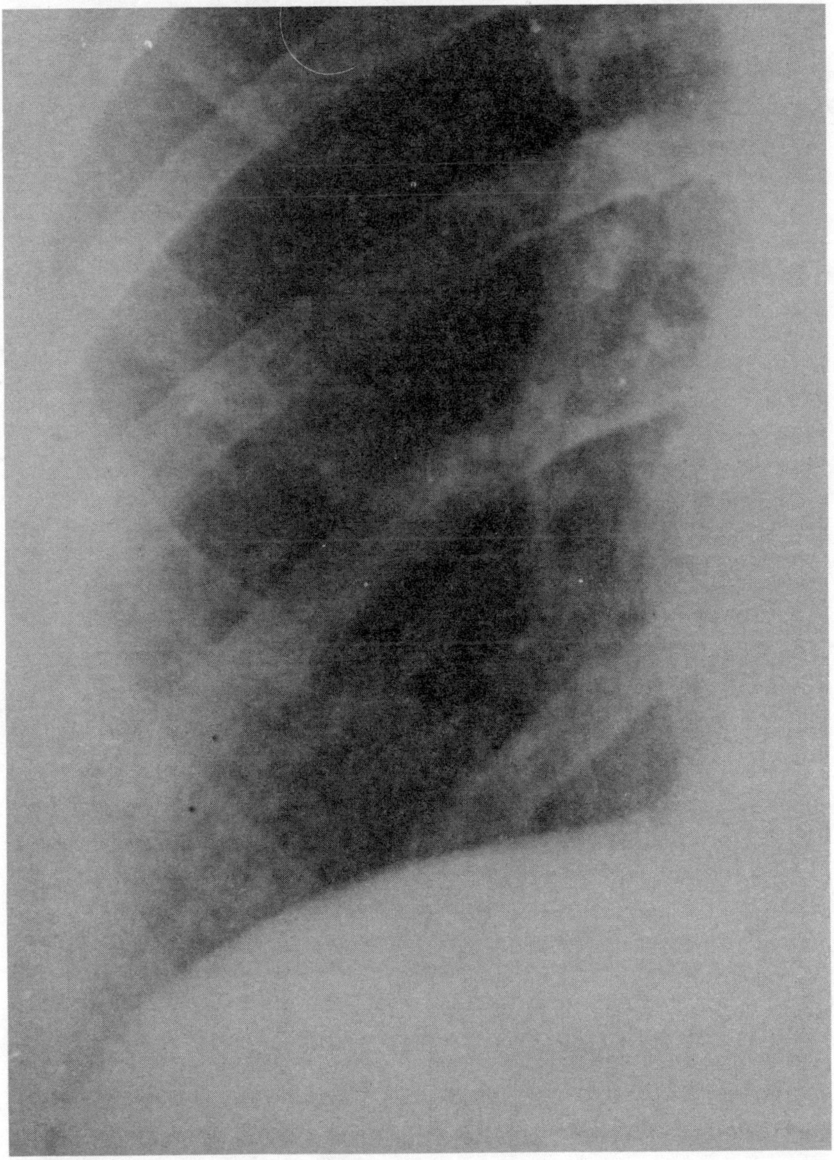

Fig. 13-4 Detail of the right-lower field with use of normal technique. A healthy woman 43 years of age.

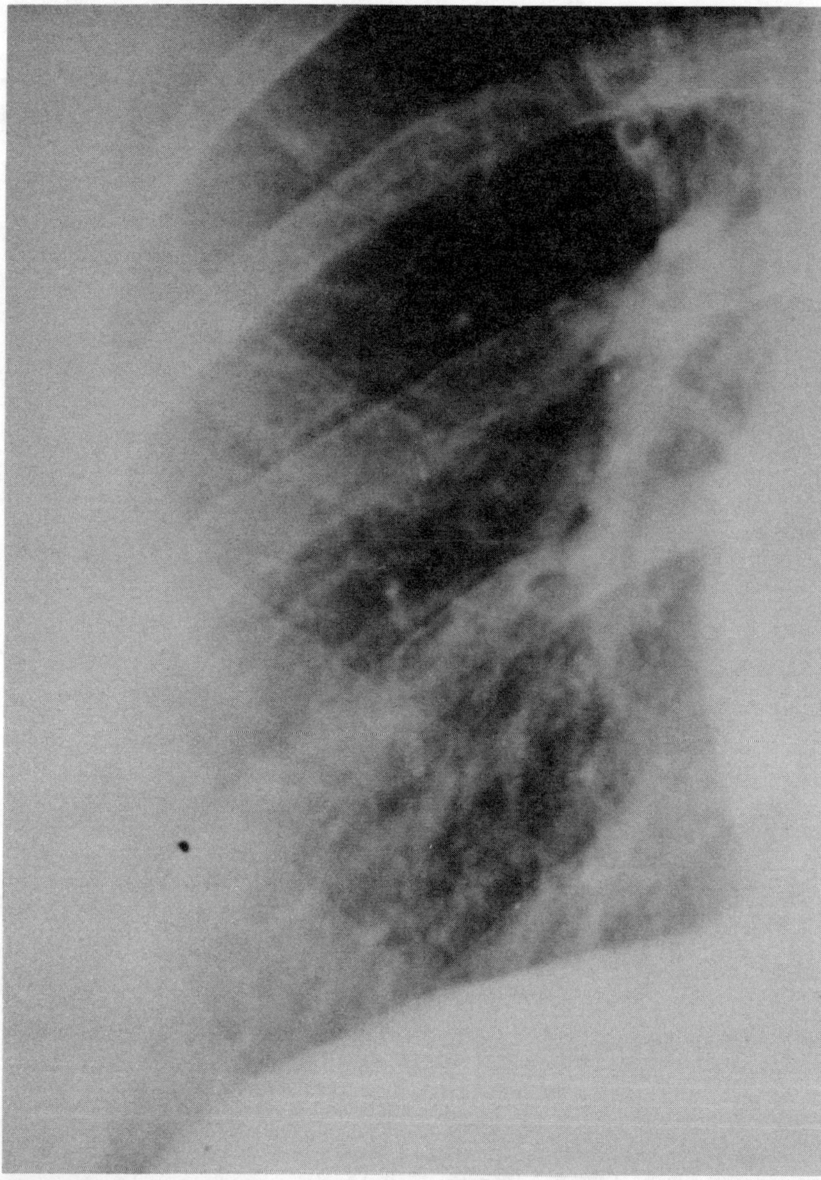

Fig. 13-5 The same woman as in Fig. 13-4 with use of semi-hard technique.

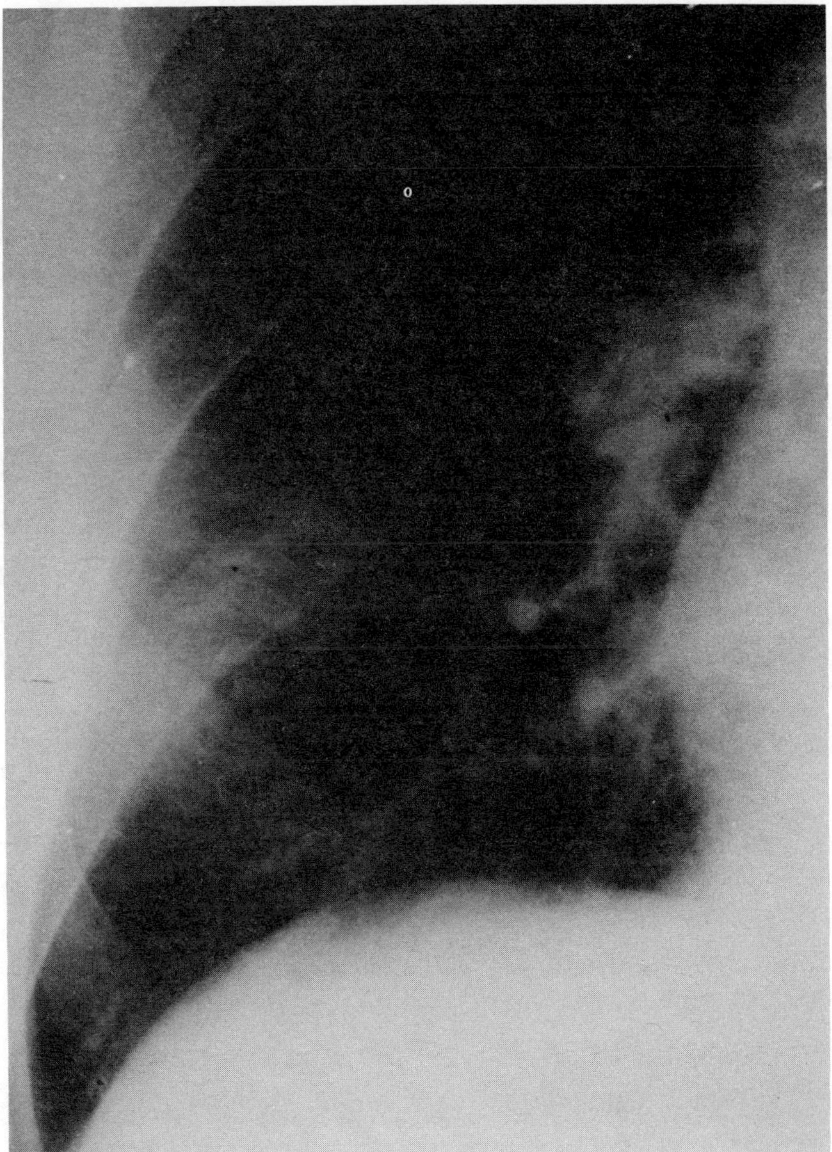

Fig. 13-6 Detail of the right-lower field with use of normal technique in a 67-year-old former asbestos textile worker, 35 years of exposure.

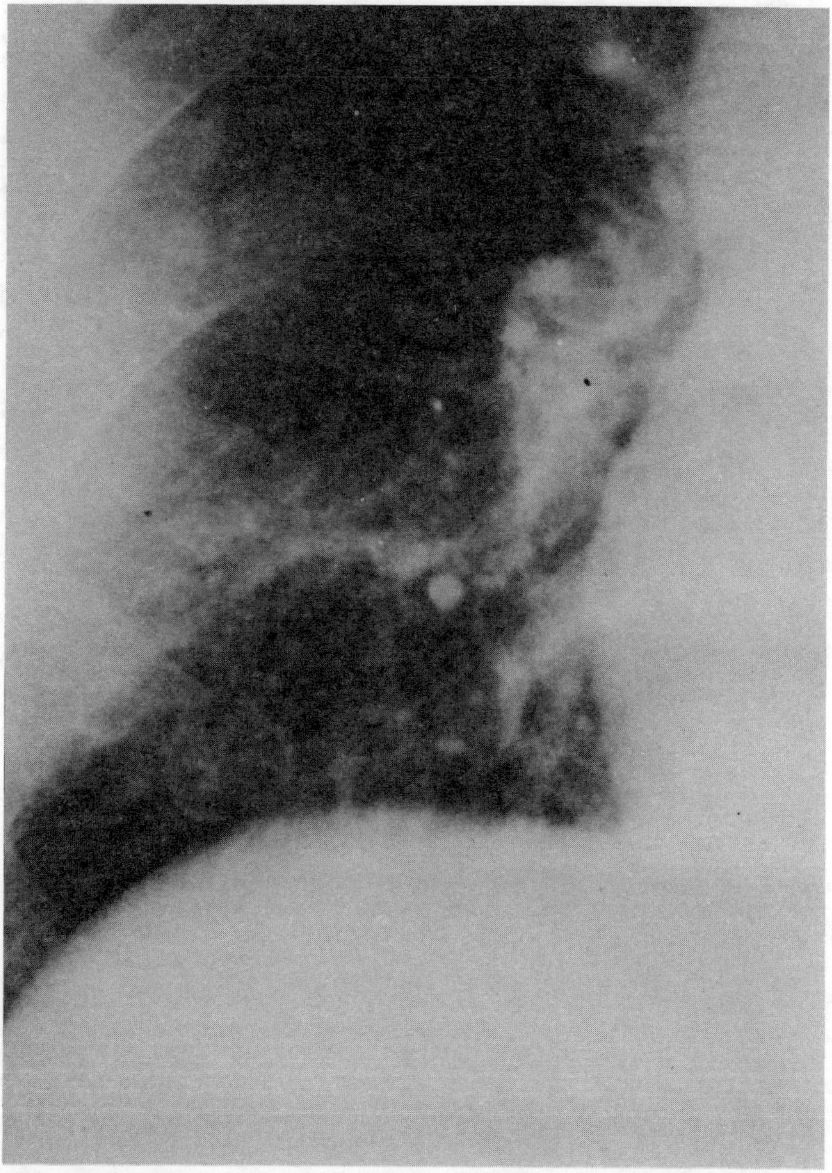

Fig. 13-7 The same man as in Fig. 13-6 with use of semi-hard technique.

Table 13-3 Radiological Signs—Type and Profusion—in 85 Persons with Exposure Exceeding 15 Years

Type/profusion	Asbestosis notified, number	Without asbestosis, number
	34	51
0	0	2
s/1	2	20*
s/2	9*	25*
s/3	4	1
t/1	2	2
t/2	13*	1
t/3	3	0
u/1	0	0
u/2	0	0
u/3	1	0
Additional symbols		
ca	1	0
co	4	2
pl	3	7*
plc	18*	13*
tb	1	2

* Figures are significantly higher, $p < 0.05$.

both "plc" and "pl" symbols for pleural abnormalities were recorded.

2. Functional Lung Disorders

The fibrotic changes in the lung interstitium are known to result in the restrictive pattern of functional lung disorders. On the other hand, simultaneous development of lung emphysema in the upper lobes of the lungs and its frequent combination with chronic bronchitis in the elderly, and particularly in smokers, oftentimes may give evidence of the presence of both restrictive and obstructive lung lesions.

In 1977, Navrátil[30] performed a series of lung function tests in the same group of 85 asbestos-exposed workers from plant A.Z. as in his previous study verifying the validity of x-ray signs of asbestosis. The following parameters were assessed: pulmonary ventilation (Fig. 13-8), intrapulmonary distribution, and transfer of CO (Fig. 13-9), blood gases and acid-base balance (Fig. 13-10).

FIG. 8.
VENTILATORY VALUES IN 85 PERSONS WITH EXPOSURE EXCEEDING 15 YEARS
M±s.D.

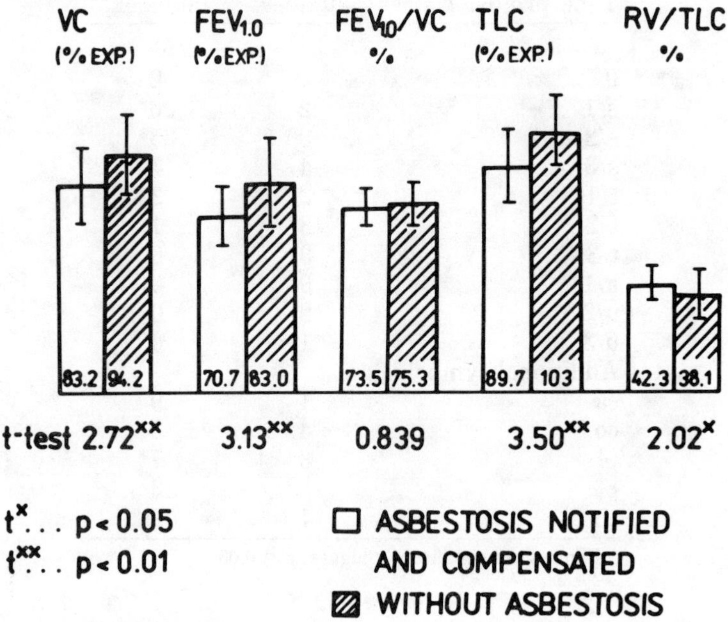

Generally, pulmonary ventilation parameters in persons with asbestosis were significantly worse than those of persons without the disease. The difference was most marked in the degree of restriction of total pulmonary capacity, followed by $FEV_{1.0}$ and vital capacity parameters. There was a slight increase in the residual volume to total pulmonary capacity ratio, the difference in the value of Tiffeneau index ($FEV_{1.0}/FVC$) was not significant as no obstructive bronchitis dominated the clinical picture of the ventilatory disorder. Asbestosis patients had impaired transfer of CO and a lowered alveolar to total pulmonary ventilation ratio; the intrapulmonary distribution in terms of nitrogen clearance values was again less favorable in the subgroup of asbestosis patients, but the difference did not reach the level of statistical significance.

Variations in the values of blood gases, acid-base balance, and the alveolar-arterial difference of O_2 were not statistically significant. The values of partial pressure of O_2 were in both subgroups somewhat lowered in comparison to age-specific national stan-

FIG. 9.

N_2 WASHOUT, ALVEOLAR VENTILATION AND TRANSFER CO IN THE SAME GROUPS. M± s.D.

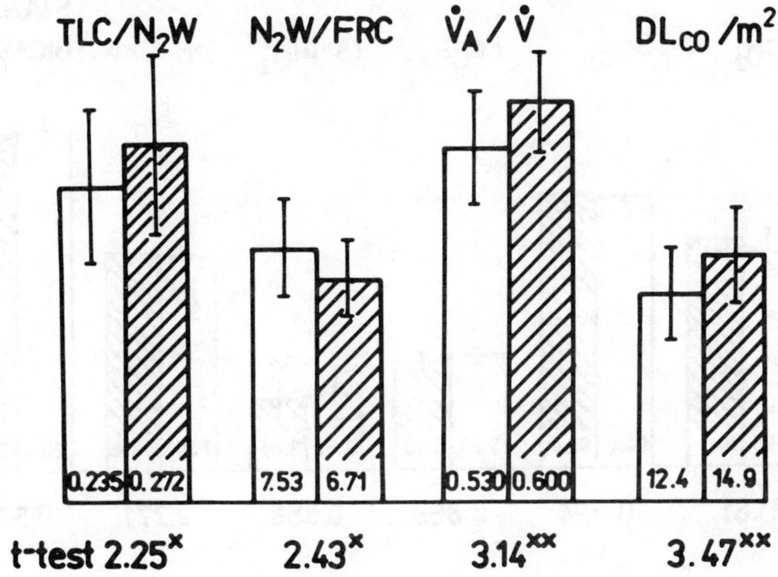

dards, and consistent with it was a slight increase in the value of the alveolar-arterial difference of O_2, but none of these variations reached the level of statistical significance. It was clearly evident that these partial disorders were well compensated and did not allow differentiation between the group of asbestosis patients and the individuals whose radiographic signs of asbestosis did not suggest occupational asbestosis.

Havel et al.[10] conducted studies in the working conditions of plant O.K. by examining a group of 59 male and 39 female asbestos workers, average age 50 years, average history of exposure longer than 20 years. The whole-shift energy output in these workers was 4.1 ± 1.0 MJ for males and 3.7 ± 1.2 MJ for females, their heart rate at the end of the shift reached the values of 99 ± 12/min in males and 105 ± 9/min in females. It became evident that these workers were well capable of performing medium-heavy work under unfavorable conditions of exposure to asbestos dust. In another study, the same author[9] compared the aerobic capacity during increasing work loads in three groups of workers with asbestosis, simple silicosis, and complicated stage of silicosis.

FIG. 10.
BLOOD GASES, pH AND STAND. BICARB.
IN THE SAME GROUPS
M ± s.D.

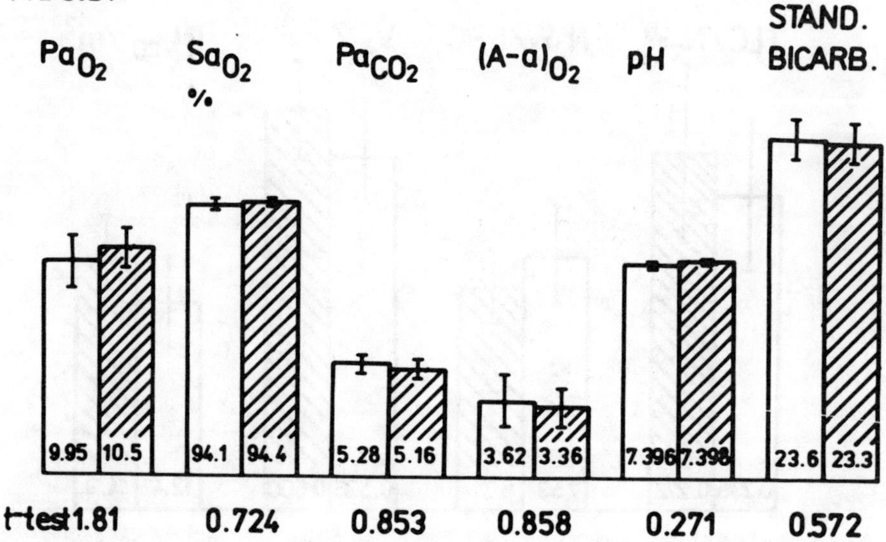

He measured the turn-over rate of air required for oxygen utilization (ventilatory equivalent) and found it to increase on the average by 10% in asbestosis patients, 25% in workers with simple silicosis, and 35% in complicated silicosis patients in comparison with the controls. This implies that asbestosis had a lesser impact on the lung ventilation function than the two types of silicotic process.

3. Immunological and Genotoxicological Research in Asbestos Workers

The immunological studies in persons occupationally exposed to asbestos dust were initiated in Czechoslovakia in the 1960s. This research was stimulated by the evidence that showed that the histological character of the interstitial connective tissue found in asbestosis cases was very similar to that of diffuse Hamman-Rich type fibroses exhibiting the immune responses investigated later by Turner-Warwick (1972).

In 1964, Medek and Rádl[20] studied the behavior of human plasma globulin fractions in the blood of employees occupationally exposed to asbestos in plant O.K. They examined a total of 30 patients (13 males and 17 females) notified as asbestosis cases, 14 persons with long-term exposures to asbestos but no radiographic signs of asbestosis, and a group of 100 healthy individuals serving as controls. The average levels of gamma globulins expressed in percent of the total serum protein content were as follows: asbestosis patients, 22.4 ± 4.86%; exposed persons with no signs of asbestosis, 16.2 ± 1.75%; controls, 16.0 ± 2.10%. The difference between asbestosis patients and control group turned out to be statistically significant.

Navrátil and Ježková[34] addressed this problem by using the immunological techniques developed later, namely demonstration of lung tissue autoantibodies on the basis of complement consumption. They examined 31 patients (15 males and 16 females) from plant A.Z. who had been notified as asbestosis cases and 47 persons (24 males, 23 females) from the same plant who had a history of long-term asbestos exposure but no radiographic signs of asbestosis. The ratio of autoantibody-positives and autoreactions, respectively, to autoantibody-negatives in the first group was 5 + 5 to 21, in the other group 7 + 5 to 35. In the control group of healthy blood donors, autoantibody-positive individuals accounted for less than 3% of the total number of controls. These immunological findings were somewhat less distinct than those reported by Turner-Warwick in 1972 in a group of patients with cryptogenic fibrotizing alveolitis, but the difference between the asbestosis group and the group of controls or the group of patients with non-specific respiratory diseases studied by Levinský and Ježková[18] in 1970 reached the level of high statistical significance.

The latest experimental studies concerning the immunologic activity of asbestos dust are from 1988. These studies performed by Hurbánková et al.[15] were carried out on rats intraperitoneally treated with chrysotile or rock wool dust. Within the first 48 hours posttreatment, both asbestos and rock wool dusts turned out to have a stimulating effect on the phagocytic activity of rat granulocytes and monocytic cells, but in the second phase (by the end of week 8) asbestos suppressed clearly the activity of cells and its inhibitory effect was significantly greater than that of rock wool dust.

Human genotoxicological studies in persons exposed to asbestos dust in plant O.K. were initiated by Srb et al.[48,49] They evaluated genetic damage in workers directly or indirectly exposed to asbestos, and in control group, by the frequency of chromosome aberrations detected in lymphocytes. The frequency of aberrant cells was highest in workers with direct exposure (2.62%–2.74%), lower in those without direct exposure (2.15%–2.61%), and lowest in the control group (1.55%). This is clearly indicative of the enhanced genotoxic activity in persons exposed to asbestos dust.

H. EPIDEMIOLOGICAL STUDIES

The primary attention of these studies has focused on the problem of asbestos-related diseases. These include: pleural hyalinosis (plaques) and neoplasia of the lungs and pleura, or the peritoneum (lung cancer, mesothelioma). Epidemiological research was largely done in asbestos plants A.Z. and O.K., both manufacturing asbestos textile, friction materials, and boards. Plant O.K. was founded in the 1950s as a sister plant of plant A.Z., which was put into operation in the 1920s. No wonder that most of these studies are linked with plant A.Z.

1. Pleural Hyalinosis (Plaques)

Pleural plaques, a disease of the pleura described also in Europe as pleural hyalinosis to reflect the hyaline nature of the connective tissue involved, was first reported in Czechoslovakia in 1962 by Hromek,[13] in a rural population not occupationally exposed to asbestos. The presence of pleural calcifications diagnosed in a total of 273 (2.77%) out of 9,871 radiographs of people living in that area was originally explained as a result of pleural tuberculosis, despite absence of case history data suggestive of a specific process in these people. In 1970, Rous and Studený[43] reported that, according to medical records, 9.7% of these people had pleural effusion in the past. At necropsy of the deceased they found calcified pearl-like formations in their pleura and associated them with residua of the past paratuberculous process originating in cattle. This conclusion was rejected as unsubstantiated by Dobiáš and Navrátil[3] in a pathological study of pleural hyalinosis in persons exposed to asbestos dust but also in individuals without history of asbestos exposure. They came to the conclusion that not only asbestos dust but also a variety of fibrous dusts other than asbestos may be responsible for the development of pleural plaques—e.g., fibres of erionite, sepiolite, etc., as we now know them from world epidemiological studies.

The observations of Hromek from 1962 were soon followed by a study of Marsová[19] (1969) who did research in the area closely related to the area that had been the focus of Hromek's interest. Marsová examined a total of 44,549 abreograms of the rural population in this area and found 241 (0.54%) of them to have typical appearances of pleural hyalinosis. All of the patients with positive abreograms had negative tuberculin reactions and the negativity of serological tests for parasites. It did not cause much surprise when the authoress found out that there had been a lime works in the area many years before, processing tremolite, a kind of amphibole mineral. That might have greatly contributed to the overall pollution of the environment.

Pleural hyalinosis and its relation to asbestos occupational exposure in plant A.Z. was the subject of a series of studies of Navrátil and his colleagues. Their observations can be summarized as follows: prevalence of pleural hyalinosis among workers exposed in plant A.Z. (a total of 800 employees and retired workers repeatedly examined by 1971[26]) was 5.2%; prevalence of the disease in a group of 133 persons who were not employed in plant A.Z. but had lived for more than 20 years in its close vicinity was 4.5%; prevalence of pleural hyalinosis in a group of 112 blood relatives of plant A.Z. workers with pleural hyalinosis was 3.7%; abreographic screenings of the population living within 15 km of plant A.Z. revealed that 1.7% out of 852 persons >40 years of age had this abnormality. The radiographic appearances of pleural hyalinosis and calcification processes in the above groups of examinees are demonstrated in Figs. 13-1 through 13-14.

Extended population studies among the rural population living in the vicinity of plant A.Z. were further conducted by Navrátil and Trippé.[27] They examined radiographs of 8,133 persons >40 years of age who had no history of occupational exposure to asbestos dust and found 28 (0.34%) of them to have pleural calcifications. This incidence rate of pleural hyalinosis was significantly lower than that of 800 asbestos workers from plant A.Z. who had a history of exposure longer than 10 years (42 cases, i.e., 5.3%). This low but still demonstrable existence of pleural calcification cases among the rural population in this area was obviously the result of previous environmental contamination with emissions from plant A.Z. taking place long before adoption of effective dust control programs.

Simultaneously with the above population study long-term dust concentration measurements in ambient air were conducted by Šimeček[46,47] in the locality adjacent to the area of plant A.Z. These measurements were conducted all year round by gravimetry from a measuring point located on the roof of one of the nearby village houses. The quantity of airborne dust was found to

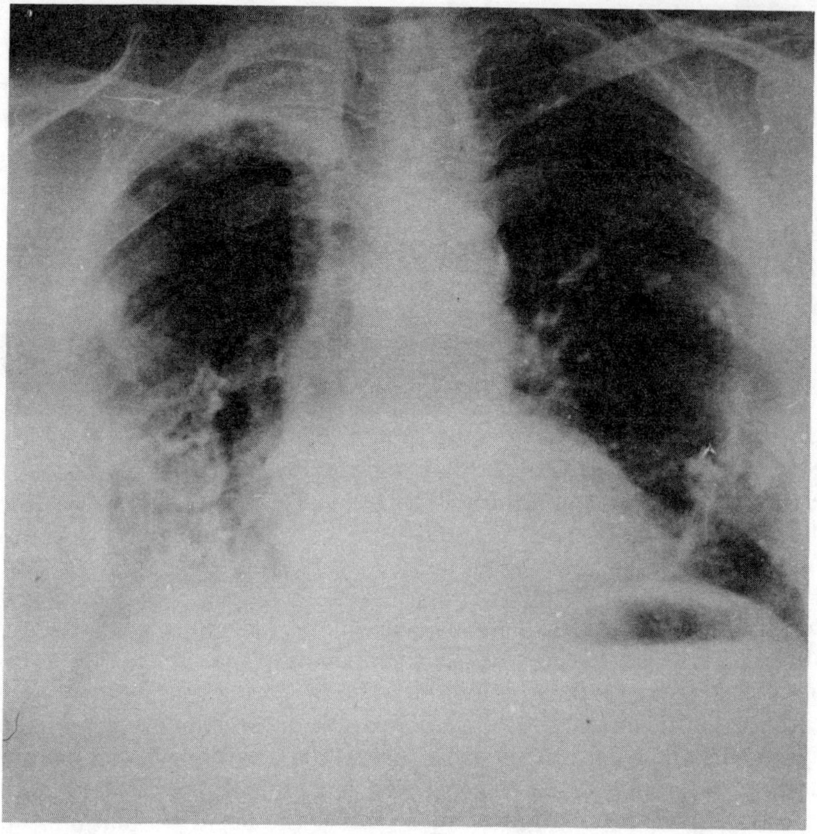

Fig. 13-11 A 56-year-old maintenance worker. Pleural calcifications on both sides.

exceed the Czechoslovak MAC limit of 0.15 mg/m^3 for dust in ambient air by 20% in summer months and by 50% in the winter. The samples of sedimented dust were found to contain dust fibers identified as chrysotile by the electron diffraction analysis.

A similar epidemiological study conducted by Pivec and Kropáček[41] is from 1979. They found 41 radiographic appearances typical for pleural hyalinosis in a set of radiographs from a village located in the direction of prevailing winds from an old asbestos-cement plant closed long before this study was initiated because of unfavorable hygienic conditions in this plant.

Long-term observation of pleural hyalinosis patients was the objective of a clinical and morphological study performed by Navrátil and Dobiáš.[28] This study involved a total of 50 active and retired asbestos workers from plant A.Z. who had been followed

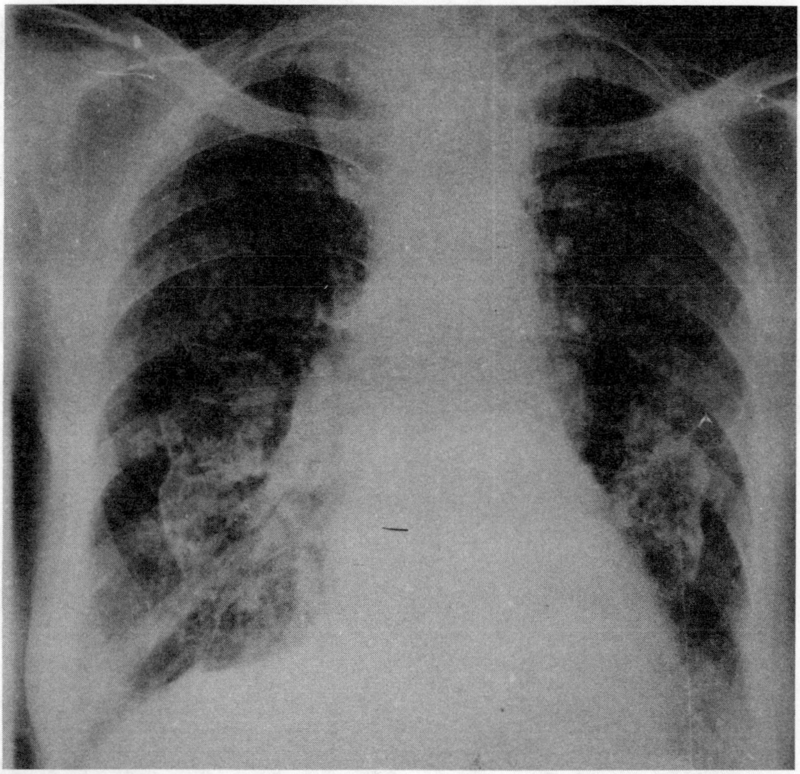

Fig. 13-12 A 72-year-old former carding room female worker. Large pleural calcification formations.

for a period of 7–19 years. All of those who had died during this period were autopsied. The clinical and radiological examination of these people was done by Navrátil and the physicians at the Clinic of Occupational Diseases in Prague; necropsy studies were performed by Dobiáš and the pathologists at the Second Institute of Pathologic Anatomy in Prague. The radiographic findings in 43 of these patients remained stationary during the whole period of observation, except for the increased intensity of opacities in some of them due to enhanced calcium deposits in the hyaline tissue. Twenty-five of these patients had been notified as cases of occupational asbestosis; in the remaining 25, no radiographic appearances meeting the criteria of asbestosis notification could be found.

Seven patients involved in this study experienced a sudden deterioration of the pathologic process resulting in formation of inflammatory exudate in the pleural cavity, in two cases bilat-

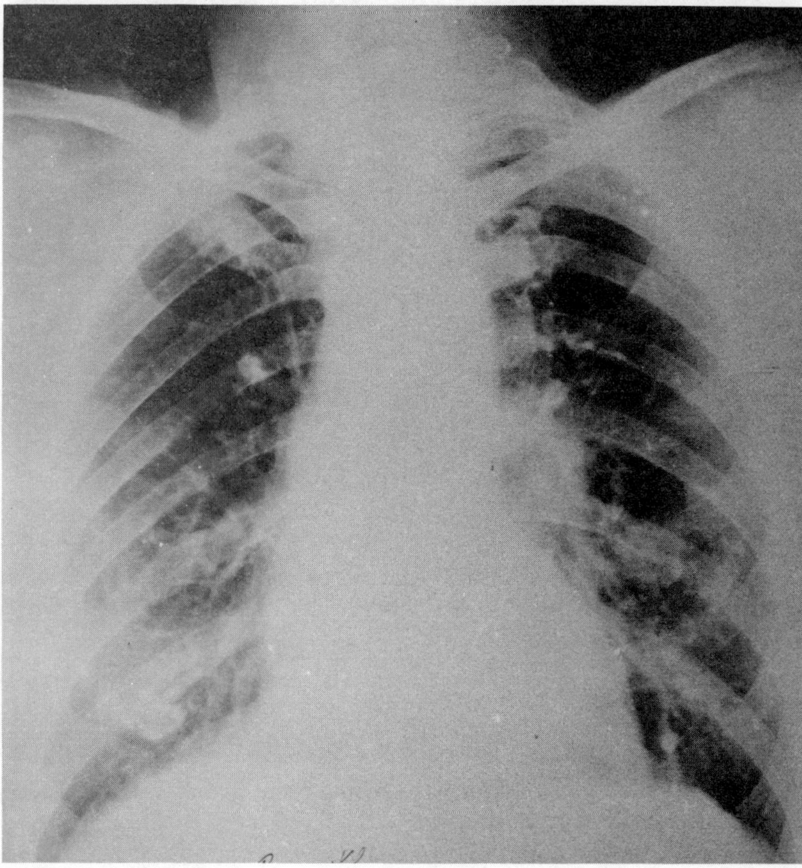

Fig. 13-13 A 68-year-old resident from the neighborhood of plant A.Z., former furniture plant worker. Pleural calcifications on both sides.

erally. Further progress of the disease was alarming and pointed to a possibility of malignancy. However, neither biopsy of the pleura nor cytology of effusion confirmed the presence of mesothelioma or cancer metastases. The tests for tuberculosis were negative. Four of these patients had died. At necropsy, a massive proliferation of the connective tissue into the pleural cavity was found. This malignant-like process must have caused a severe restriction during the patient's life judging by the degree of respiratory insufficiency and hypoxemia found in these patients prior to death. This unfavorable course of the pleural hyalinosis process was designated by Navrátil as hyalinosis complicata, in contradistinction to cases of common stationary hyalinosis that may be specified as hyalinosis simplex. The term hyalinosis complicata

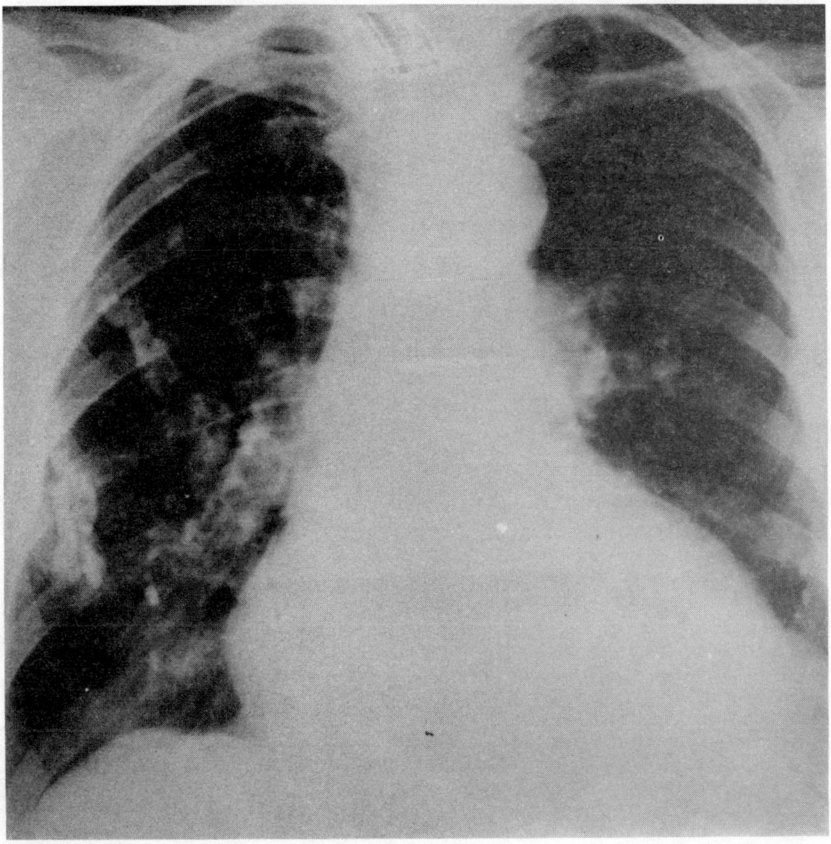

Fig. 13-14 A 65-year-old agricultural female worker from a village 10 km from plant A.Z. Large pleural calcifications on the right side, less marked changes on the left side.

has become common in the routine practice of occupational health services in Czechoslovakia and has also been accepted in the Federal Republic of Germany.[2a] Figures 13-15 through 13-17 demonstrate the stages of simple hyalinosis leading to the development of complicated hyalinosis.

Navrátil and his colleagues[32] had also taken interest in the fate of pleural hyalinosis persons who had had no history of asbestos exposure but lived in the neighborhood of plant A.Z. and were involved in the 1969–1970 population study. Of the 36 pleural hyalinosis patients 8 had died by the end of 1974. The cause of death in 4 of them was neoplasia (lung cancer, stomach cancer, leukemia, rotothel sarcoma), 4 died of vascular diseases common in the people of older age categories. None of those 36 pleural

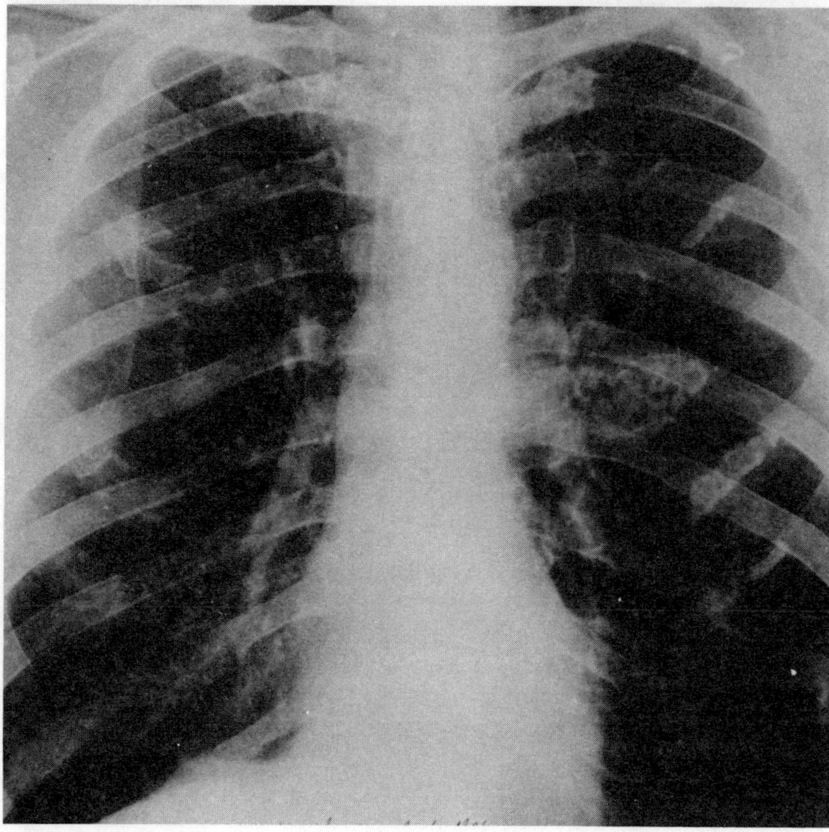

Fig. 13-15 A 58-year-old carding room worker in 1970. Bilateral simple pleural hyalinosis watched in the course of past 10 years.

hyalinosis patients was found to have the complicated form of the disease. The latest survey offering the data for a period after 1978 was published in 1988.[38] The available evidence seems to suggest that complicated hyalinosis is obviously a result of massive and long-term asbestos exposures under excessively bad dust conditions at the workplace, conditions no longer encountered in the present-day asbestos industry.

Regular radiologic examinations of workers with a history of exposure to asbestos need not necessarily detect all cases of pleural hyalinosis, especially when the content of calcium salts is not sufficient to give contrast plaques appearances. This prompted Hassmanová et al.[8] to examine a group of 57 workers from plant O.K., average age 49.7 years (41–61 years), average exposure 21.9 years (15–33 years), using a computer tomography (CT) tech-

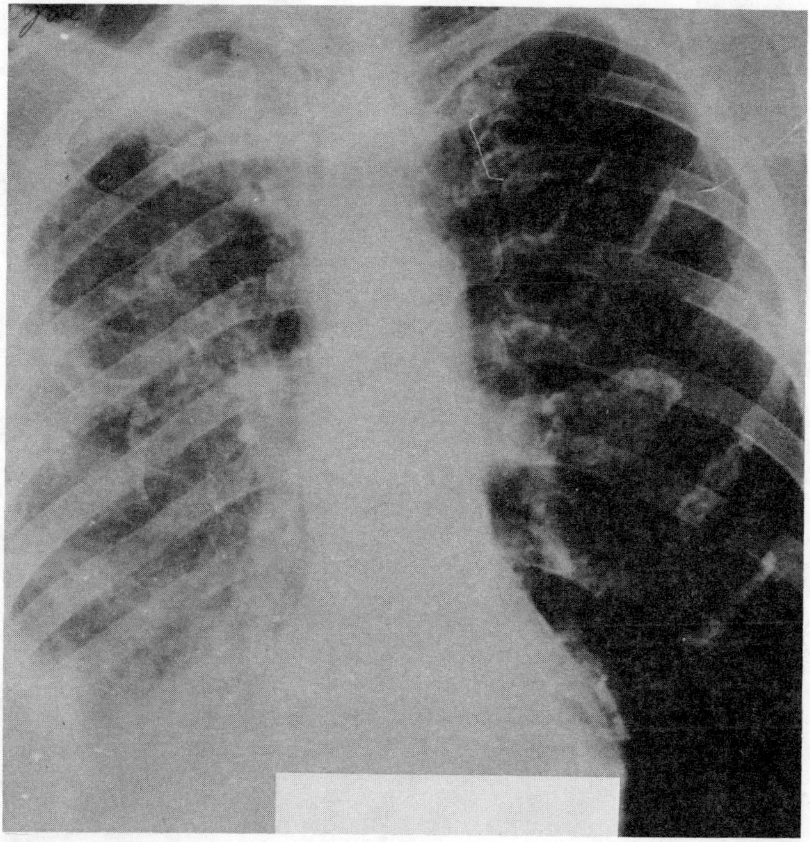

Fig. 13-16 The same patient as in Fig. 13-15 after 11 years (1981). Recent pleural inflammation and effusion on the right side.

nique. This technique yielded positive results in a total of 10 (27%) workers who had not been previously recognized by regular radiologic examination as having pleural plaques. However, the availability of CT remains rather limited in Czechoslovakia at present so that the technique hardly can be used for the purpose of regular periodic examinations of all workers running the risk of asbestos exposure.

2. Asbestos Neoplasia of the Lungs

The first observations of lung cancer in patients exposed to asbestos dust were reported by the pathologists. In 1961, Stejskal[50] described the presence of pulmonary carcinoma in 2 former asbestos workers from plant A.Z. who both had been

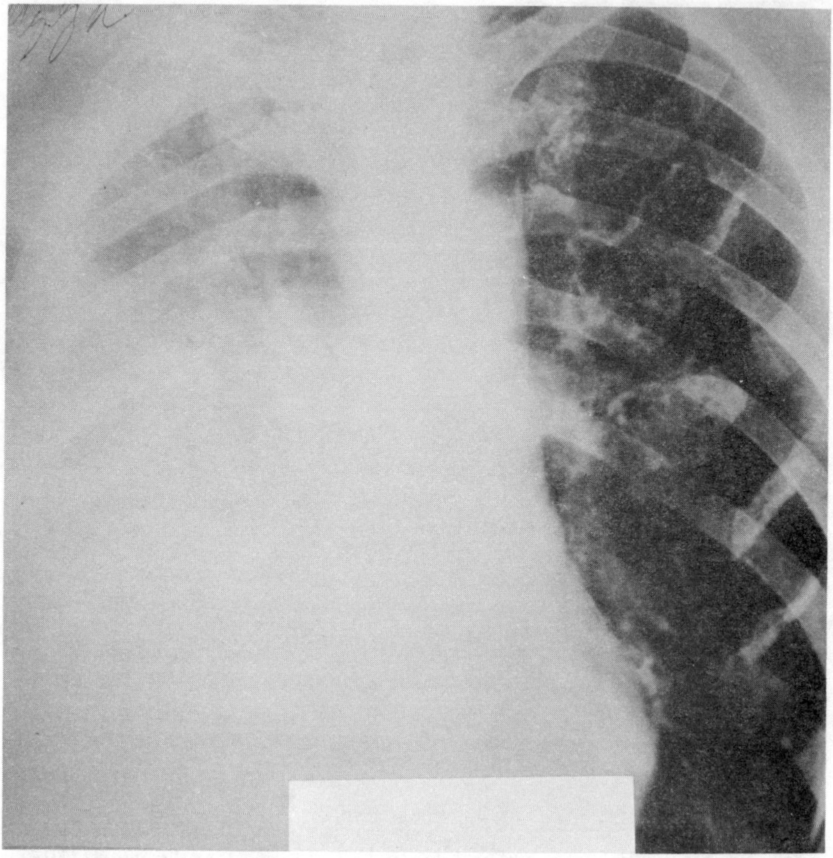

Fig. 13-17 The same patient as in Figs. 13-15 and 13-16 after 12 years from 1970 (1982). Increased pleural effusion accompanied by fibrous proliferation in the pleural cavity. Complicated hyalinosis. Necropsy confirmed the diagnosis, mesothelioma was not present.

regularly checked by Navrátil. Both asbestos victims had squamous cell cancer located in the basal lobes of the lung. A further case of lung cancer in association with asbestosis was described by Fingerland and Jindřichová[6] in 1962 in a worker of plant O.K. The cancer was again in the lower lobe of the lung.

First epidemiological data from plant A.Z. were reported by Navrátil et al.[24] in 1966. In the course of 13 years from 1954 to 1966 a total of 57 asbestosis cases were diagnosed and notified in this plant, and of these, 13% (5 males and 2 females) died of lung cancer. For the purpose of comparison, there was a 0.32% lung cancer death rate among the general population of a region of central Bohemia during the period 1956–1966 (320 cases of lung cancer per 100,000 deaths) and the frequency of lung cancer deaths among the deceased autopsied between 1959 and 1966 at the First Institute of Pathologic Anatomy in Prague was 4.63% (498 cases of lung cancer per 10,761 necropsis). All of the male lung cancer patients from plant A.Z. were smokers and had a history of asbestos exposure under bad dust conditions before, during, and shortly after the Second World War. The radiograph of one of these asbestos victims is demonstrated in Fig. 13-18; carcinogenic infiltration spreads from the hilus towards the right lower lobe, mild pleural calcifications can be seen on the left side.

In 1966, after completing this 13-year follow-up study of plant

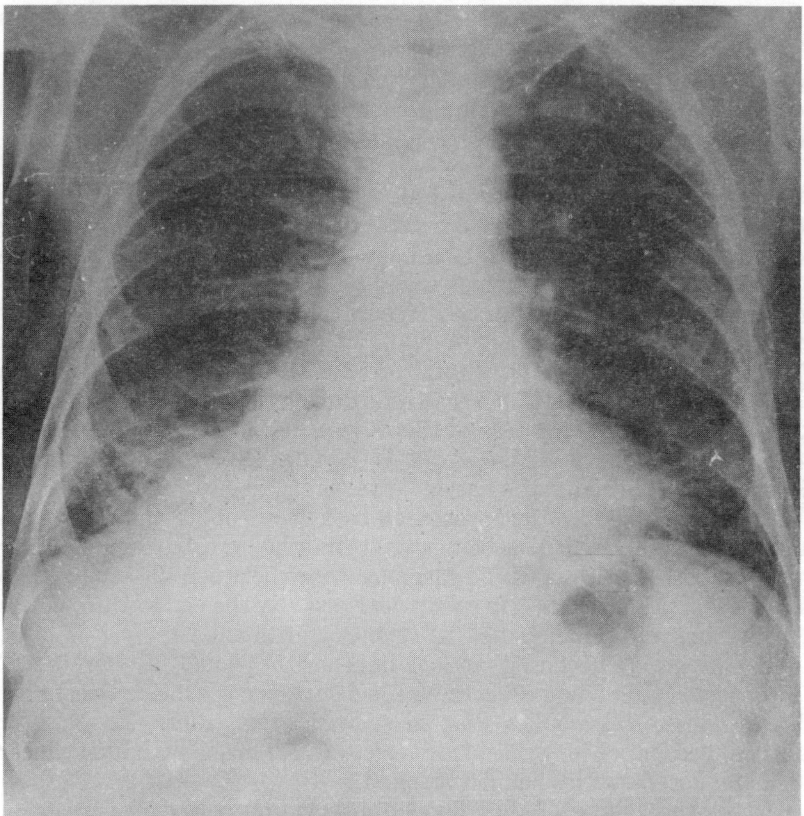

Fig. 13-18 A former asbestos textile worker, 68 years old, 18 years of exposure. Carcinogenic infiltration of the right-lower lobe. On the left side, mild pleural calcifications. Autopsy confirmed the presence of squamous cell cancer.

A.Z. workers, Navrátil and his colleagues had decided to initiate a new cohort study in this plant to be carried out for the next 20 years until 1987, with the aim at respiratory tract malignancies. Every examinee included in this study was screened every year by abreography, suspect cases were hospitalized and examined at the Clinic of Occupational Diseases in Prague. The first examination in 1966 was carried out in a cohort of 300 males and 220 females accounting for 81.1% of the total number of 641 workers employed in plant A.Z. at that time. The workers included in this cohort of 520 people had had a history of asbestos exposure longer than 5 years in 1966. Dust conditions in plant A.Z. tended to gradually improve during the period of observation (Table 13-1), and the pattern of 1985 neoplasia mortality figures for the cohort of plant A.Z. workers was distinctly different from that reported in the 1966 study.[24] The results of the cohort study completed in 1987[37] can be summarized as follows:

1. In 1985, 338 (65.0%) persons from the original number of cohort workers involved were still alive (181 males, 157 females); 171 (32.0%) persons were dead (112 males, 59 females); and 11 (2.1%) persons were missing. The age of those alive was 57.4 ± 11.8 years for males and 59.0 ± 10.7 years for females (mean ± S.D.). The age of the deceased at the time of death was 66.4 ± 10.8 years in males and 69.5 ± 10.8 years in females. The length of asbestos exposure in living males was 20.6 ± 8.5 years, in living females 20.4 ± 7.2 years. The length of exposure in the deceased was 18.0 ± 7.0 years for males and 14.4 ± 4.9 years for females.

2. From 1966 to 1985, a total of 52 cases of asbestosis had been notified and of these 35 (67.3%) had died during this period, 23 males and 12 females. The average age of these deceased persons at the time of death was 67.3 years for males and 75.2 years for females and did not significantly differ from the national average.

3. The controls were represented by a group of 303 railway wagon repairmen unexposed to asbestos dust or other noxious agents. This group comprised 260 males and 43 females born between 1905 and 1925 to match the age distribution in cohort workers. By the end of 1985, 65.7% (199 persons) of them had died, 181 males and 18 females.

4. Of the 171 deceased persons in cohort of plant A.Z. workers, 13 persons had died of lung cancer and 1 had survived the pneumonectomy. Nevertheless, this implies that those with lung cancer (12 males, 2 females) accounted for 8.1% of all deceased. All males with lung cancer were smokers, females had not smoked.

5. In the course of the 20-year observation period, 9 persons (7 males and 2 females) had died of pleural mesothelioma (one case was mesothelioma of the peritoneum), which accounts for 5.2% of 171 deceased. The time period elapsed from the start of asbestos exposure had exceeded more than 25 years in all of them.

6. In the group of controls 199 persons (181 males, 18 females) had died by the end of 1985. Lung cancer as a cause of death was diagnosed in 14 (7.7%) individuals, all of them male and smokers. The difference in the lung cancer prevalence rate between the cohort and control group of workers did not reach the level of statistical significance, a result far more favorable than that reported in the 1966 study.[24] This positive development had been evidently achieved through gradual improvements of dust conditions in plant A.Z., smoking habits of the workers were virtually unchanged during this period (70%–80% of workers were smokers).

7. One of the deceased in the group of controls had died of pleural mesothelioma. However, a detailed analysis of the whole-life personal history of this person revealed that this man had worked between 1925 and 1941 as a foundryman at an open-hearth furnace where he must have worn asbestos-protective clothing and gloves, which could not exclude the likelihood of previous asbestos exposures some 30 to 40 years before. Nevertheless, the incidence of mesotheliomas in the cohort of asbestos-exposed workers was significantly greater than that of control group ($X^2 = 6.17$; $p < 0.01$).

The incidences of the other asbestos-related types of malignancies (cancer of the gastrointestinal tract, larynx cancer) in the cohort of exposed workers and the control group were comparable.

3. Pleural (Peritoneal) Mesothelioma in Asbestos-Exposed Workers

Essentially, development of lung cancers in asbestos-exposed persons is a result of exposure to at least two environmental carcinogens, asbestos dust and the carcinogenic compounds from tobacco smoke in smokers. In contrast, the origin of pleural or peritoneal neoplasias is independent of tobacco carcinogens and is solely the result of asbestos dust action. The first report on the incidence of mesothelioma in Czechoslovakia was published by Audy and Žáček[1] in 1967, but the possible link with asbestos exposure remained unclear. Helbich and Římanová[11] reported pleural mesothelioma in 7 patients subject to pleural biopsy but also none of these patients had a clear history of exposure to asbestos or other fibrous minerals. Between 1964 and 1977, pathologist Zeman[51] had performed postmortem examinations of a total of 27 patients with pleural mesothelioma and found asbestos bodies in 5 samples from the pleural tissue or pleural fluid of the deceased persons who had had no positive history of asbestos exposure. He then concluded that these "ferruginous bodies" were bodies of fibrous minerals other than asbestos.

The epidemiology of mesotheliomas in persons exposed to asbestos in Czechoslovakia was the target of studies carried out by Navrátil and his team colleagues Dobiáš and Haškovcová from the Second Institute of Pathologic Anatomy at the Charles University in Prague. The first mesothelioma of the pleura was diagnosed clinically by Navrátil; the patient died in 1973 and was autopsied by Dobiáš.[4] At the time of death the patient, a former plant A.Z. employee with a 26-year history of exposure in the manufacture of asbestos boards, was 78 years old. When hospitalized in 1970 he had had 45 years from initial exposure to asbestos dust in 1925 (Figs. 13-19 and 13-20). His radiograph showed the presence of a large rounded opacity in the lower to central zones of the right

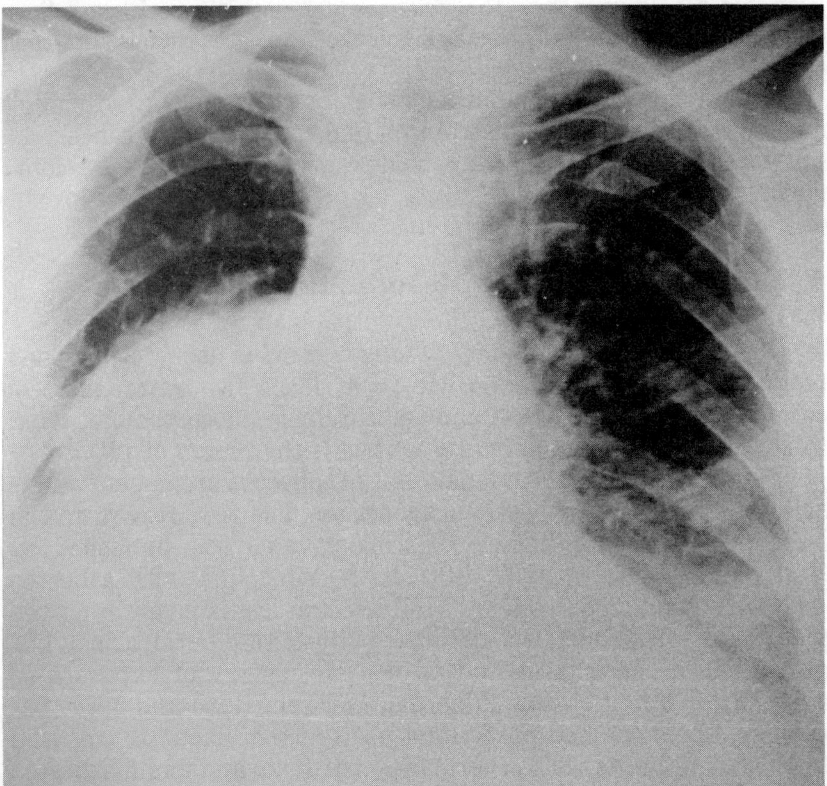

Fig. 13-19 A former asbestos boards manufacturing worker, 78 years old, 26 years of exposure, 45 years from the initial exposure. A large rounded opacity on the right side of the hemithorax. Pleural calcifications on the left side.

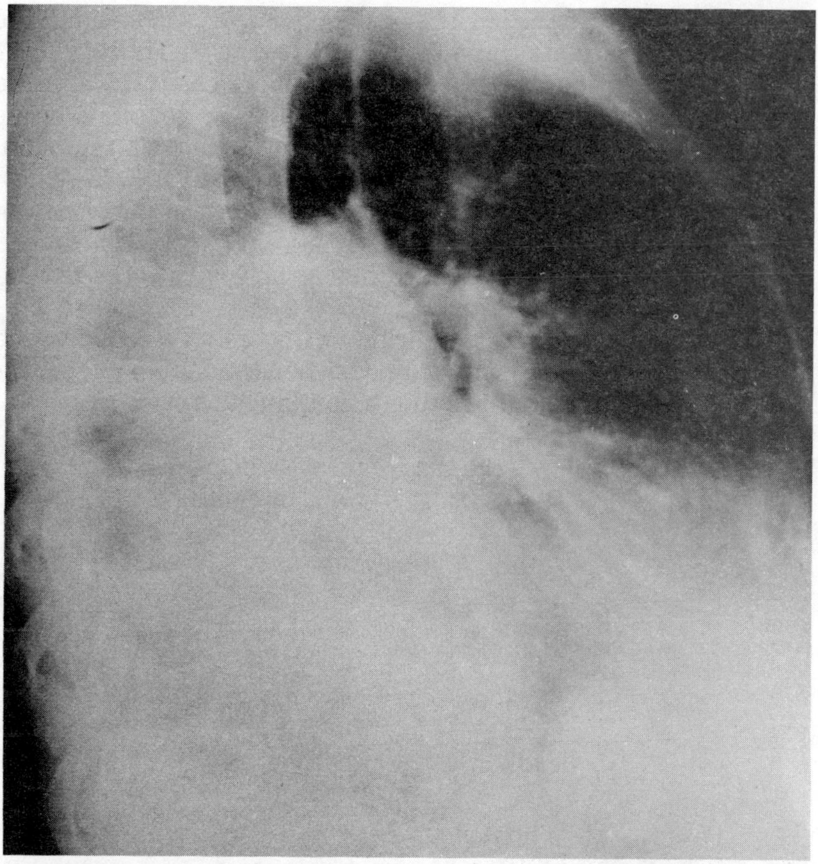

Fig. 13-20 The same patient as in Fig. 13-19. The right side oblique projection of the thorax showing a large rounded opacity located in the space of the posterior mediastinum above the diaphragm.

lung, the right-side oblique projection revealed that the tumor was located in the mediastinum posterius above the diaphragma.

At necropsy, a large rounded tumor and a massive tumorous infiltration spreading cranially towards the space between the pleura and the cervicobrachial plexus were found; that explained the agonizing pains in the right arm during life.

A survey of all mesothelioma cases from asbestos plants A.Z. and O.K. was prepared by Navrátil and Hassmanová and appeared in 1981.[33] Altogether, 7 cases of mesothelioma (6 males, 1 female) had been reported from these plants; of these, 6 were identified as pleural mesotheliomas, 1 case was peritoneal mesothelioma. All but one (described above) were diffuse mesotheliomas spreading over the surface of the pleura or peritoneum. The mesothelioma patients had died on the average within 1.43 years (1–3 years) from the clinical diagnosis of the disease. The average age at the time of death was 62.9 years (49–78 years), average exposure 23.7 years (15–34 years), and the time from the initial exposure to asbestos was on the average 27.7 years (21–45 years). The calendar year of the first exposure to asbestos dust was, on the average, the year 1942 (1925 to 1958), i.e., at the time of bad dust conditions at the workplace before and during the Second World War, or shortly after it.

Treatment with cytostatic drugs or Coparwax was ineffective in these patients. One patient underwent the surgery (decortication of the pleura), but the tumor continued to grow in spite of this radical intervention.

Figure 13-21 shows the case of mesothelioma in a 62-year-old

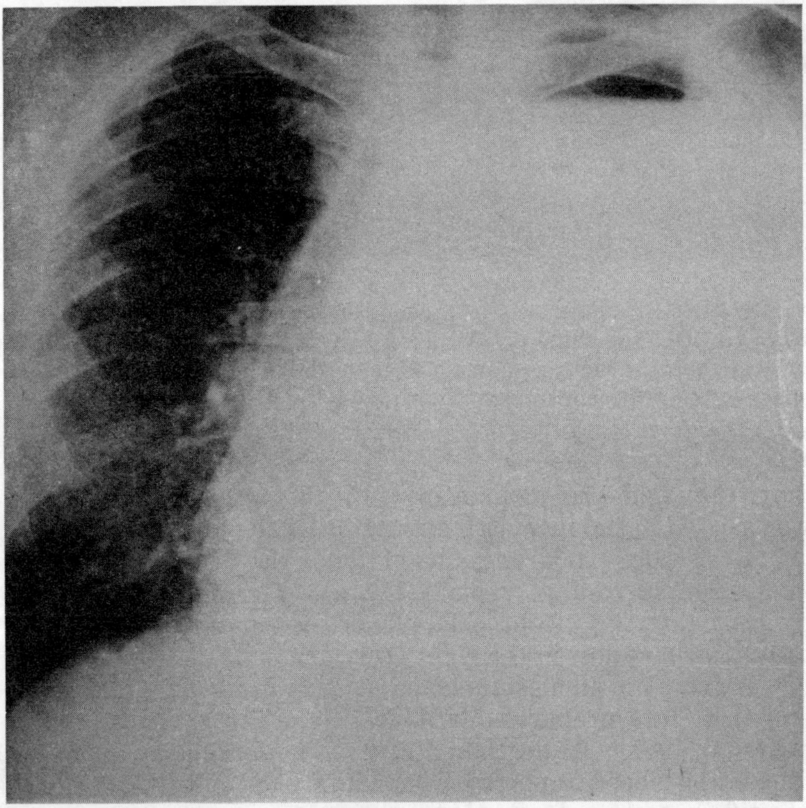

Fig. 13-21 A 62-year-old maintenance worker from plant A.Z. Total pleural effusion on the left side.

patient from plant A.Z. with a history of 16 years of exposure 35 years after the initial exposure to asbestos dust. The left-side pleural cavity is filled with effusion; its evacuation by puncture resulted in the collaps of the lung (Fig. 13-22); the pleural effusion tended to spontaneously gain in volume again.

Figure 13-23 is a case of mesothelioma in a 66-year-old patient from plant A.Z. after 20 years of exposure and 41 years after the first exposure to asbestos; the radiograph shows a large half-rounded opacity in the left lung and some more diffuse formation in the right hemithorax. At necropsy, diffuse mesothelioma involving the visceral and diaphragmatic pleura was found in the left lung of this patient (Fig. 13-24). The mesothelial tumors on the

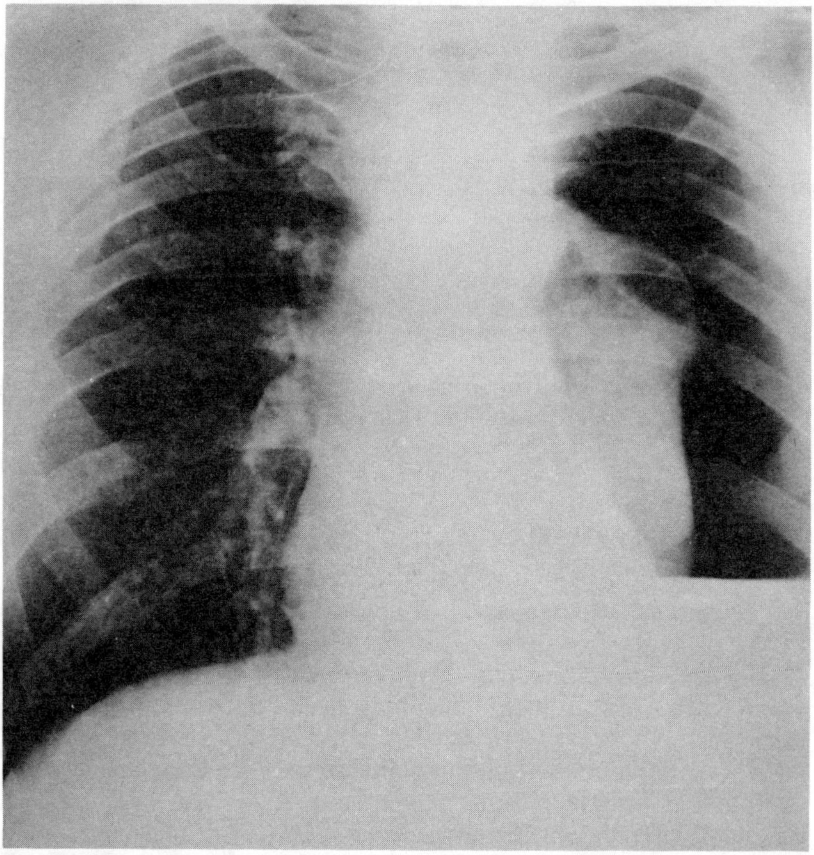

Fig. 13-22 The same patient as in Fig. 13-21. After the evacuating puncture of the pleural fluid (the collapse of the lung) fluid level rises again.

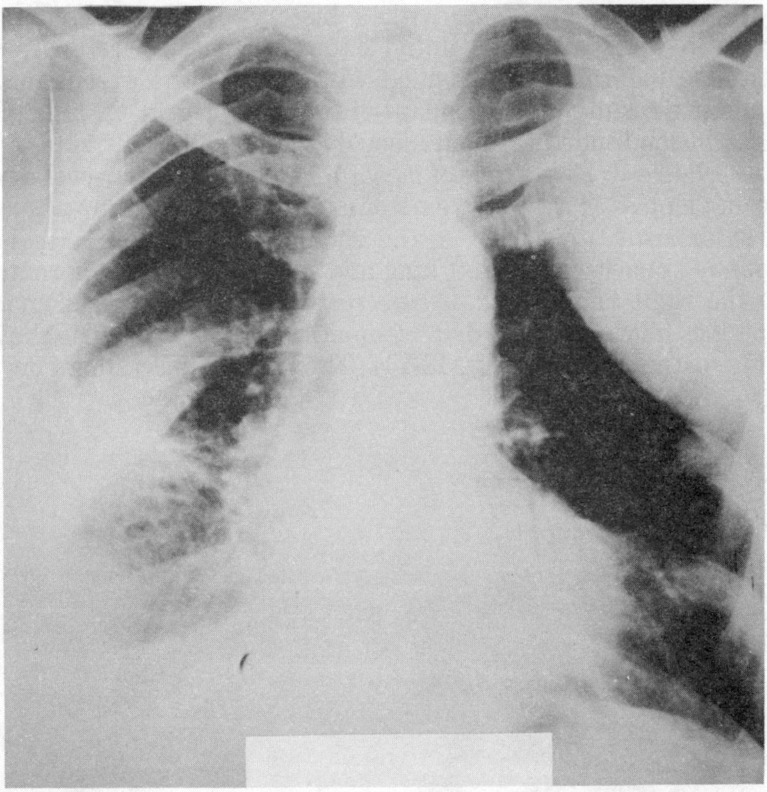

Fig. 13-23 A 66-year-old former asbestos boards worker, 20 years of exposure, 41 years from the initial exposure. Large half-rounded opacity on the left side, more diffuse formation in the right hemithorax.

right-side and left-side pleura were found to be histologically identical.

The morphological and histological features of mesotheliomas in the patients from plant A.Z. have been described by Dobiáš, Hašková, and Vodičková.[7] Most of these tumors were diffuse in form, with an epitheloid, fibromatous, or mixed-type histologic structure. No metastases were found; there was observed a single case of invasive mesothelioma penetration into the chest wall in a 62-year-old female patient from plant A.Z. that mimicked the diagnosis of primary breast cancer. However, histology of the subcutaneous infiltrations was clearly suggestive of primary diffuse malignant mesothelioma of the pleura.

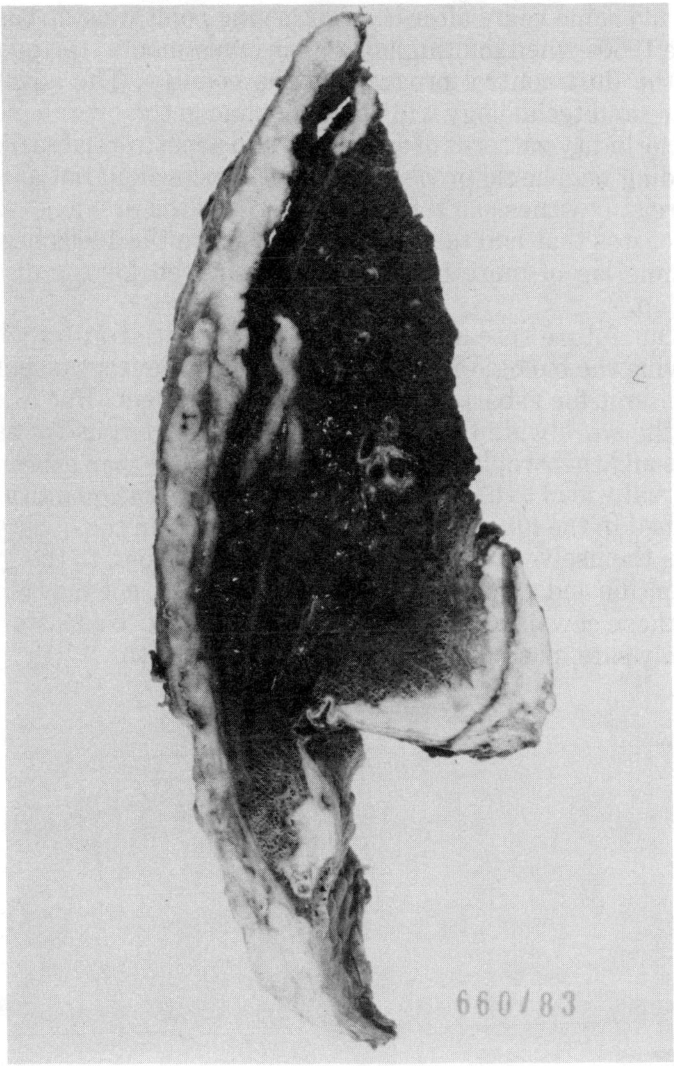

Fig. 13-24 The same patient as in Fig. 13-23. The pathological anatomy of the left lung showing the presence of diffuse tumorous pleural thickening on the walls of the lung and diaphragm.

I. CONCLUSION

The asbestos medical research in Czechoslovakia has provided evidence that shows the existence of extremely unfavorable dust conditions in asbestos plants in the years of the Second World

War and some years after it. The turning point was the beginning of the 1960s when multimillion dollar investments started to pour into the dust control program in the country. The advances in science and technology will no doubt change the overall mortality and morbidity patterns of asbestosis and asbesto-related diseases, including neoplastic processes, in Czechoslovakia, but at present we are still witnessing the consequences of the previous exposure to asbestos that had taken place well before the 1960s because of the time lag of more than 20 years required for the disease to develop.

Our future research programs will be faced with the task of studying the biologic activities of asbestos at levels well below the MAC limit for asbestos dust in the environment. But it is likely that the worldwide trend towards the restricted use of asbestos fibres and their replacement by minerals other than asbestos may eventually lead to a radical change not only in the quantity of dust retained in the lungs of the exposed, but also in the quality of the fibres themselves, which no longer should belong to the group of serpentine and amphibole mineral fibers. If so, one may only hope that these new fibres intended as an alternative to asbestos will be reliably safe, posing no hazards to human health.

REFERENCES

1. Audy, K., Žáček, V.: Malignant pleural mesotheliomas. /in Czech/. Vnitř.Lék. 13, No. 1, pp. 9–13, /1967/.

2.a. Berufskrankheiten Verordnung der Bundesrepublik Deutschland vom 22.3.1988.

2.b. Berufskrankheiten Gesetzliche Grundlagen, Veb Verlag Volk und Gesundheit, Berlin, pp. 66–70 /1987/.

3. Dobiáš, J., Navrátil, M.: Morphological features of pleural hyalinosis in persons with and/or without asbestosis. /in Czech/.Pracov. Lék. 25,No. 9, pp.369–372, /1973/.

4. Dobiáš, J., Navrátil, M.: Malignant pleural mesothelioma at asbestosis. /in Czech/. Pracov. Lék. 25, No. 10, pp. 434–437, /1973/.

5. Dobiáš, J.: Pathology of pulmonary asbestosis in asbestos exposed industrial workers in the Czech Socialist Republic. Acta Univ. Carol. Med. 38, No. 3/4, pp. 169–236, /1982/.

6. Fingerland, A., Jindřichová, J.: Asbestosis associated with lung cancer. /in Czech/. Pracov. Lék. 14, No. 10, pp. 468–471, /1962/.

7. Haškovcová, I., Dobiáš, J., Vodičková, S.: Morphological findings in pleural and peritoneal mesotheliomas induced by asbestos. /in Czech/. Stud.pneumol.phtiseol.Czechosl. 41, No. 6, pp. 397–403, /1981/.

8. Hassmanová, V., Hassman, P., Heger, L.: Pleural hyalinosis in asbestos exposed workers from the viewpoint of the computer tomography. /in Czech/. Acta Univ. Hradec Králové 27, No. 7/8, pp. 147–155, /1982/.

9. Havel, V., Hassmanová, V., Hassman, P.: Exploration of patients with asbestosis and silicosis by gradual exercise test. /in Czech/. Pracov. Lék. 29, No. 10, pp. 373–377, /1977/.

10. Havel, V., Havlová, L., Musil, M., Slezáčková, L., Treskoňová, G.: Health status and work load in employees of an asbestos products processing plant. /in Czech/. Pracov. Lék. 37, No. 8, pp. 281–286, /1985/.

11. Helbich, P., Římanová, V., Šnajdr, V., Kruml, J.: Contribution to the differential diagnostics of pleural fibromesothelioma. /in Czech /. Stud. pneumol. phtiseol. Czech. 32, No. 7/8, pp. 345–349. (1972).

12. Holomáň, K.: Problems of asbestosis in Slovakia. /in Slovak/. Pracov. Lék. 2, No. 2, pp. 69–72, /1950/.
13. Hromek, J.: Occurrence of characteristic pleural formations in the population of the region Jihlava. /in Czech/. Rozhl. Tuberk. 22, No. 6, pp. 405–414, /1962/.
14. Hrušková, J., Kouřimský, J.: Mineralogical identification of some Czechoslovak serpentine asbestos. Acta Mus. Nation. Pragae 24B, No. 1, pp. 61–71, /1968/.
15. Hurbánková, M., Ulrich, L., Barlogova, S.: Comparison of the phagocytosis activity of leukocytes after administration of asbestos and rock wool dust. /in Slovak/. Pracov. Lék., in print.
16. Jindřichová, J.: Remarks upon the asbestosis. /in Czech/. Prakt. Lék. 35, No. 17, pp. 397–398, /1955/.
17. Juck, A., Neumannová, E.: Influence of physical-metric properties of asbestos fibres on the measurement evaluation. /in Slovak/. Proceedings 2nd Int.Symp. Occup. Health Saf. Min. Tunnell., Prague, pp. 338–346, /1986/.
18. Levinský, L., Ježková, Z., Komárková, A., Felkelová, M.: Gli antigeni nella immunologia della fibrosa polmonare interstizziale diffusa tipo Hamman-Rich. Minerva pneumol. 9, pp. 113–115, /1970/.
19. Marsová, D.: Beitrag zur Atiologie der Pleuraverkalkungen. Z. Tuberk. 121, No. 5/6, pp. 329–334, /1964/.
20. Medek, V., Rádl, J.: Changes of blood serum proteins in subjects exposed to asbestos dust. /in Czech/. Pracov. Lék. 16, No. 8, pp. 349–352, /1964/.
21. Medek, V.: Der Einfluss des Asbeststaubes auf die Gesundheit der Arbeiter. Arbeitsmed., Soz.Med., Arbeitshyg. 4, No. 3, pp. 87–88, /1969/.
22. Navrátil, M.: Results of functional cardio pulmonary examination in workers with a long lasting asbestos exposure. /in Czech/. Pracov. Lék. 8, No. 5, pp. 329–333, /1956/.
23. Navrátil, M., Křeček, V., Cvachová, L.: To the problem of emphysema in asbestos products processing workers. /in Czech/. Pracov. Lék. 9, No. 2, pp. 111–116, /1957/.
24. Navrátil, M., Stejskal, J., Fingerland, A.: Occurence of lung cancer at asbestosis. /in Czech/. Pracov. Lék. 18, No. 6/7, pp. 256–260, /1966/.
25. Navrátil, M., Medek, V.: Klinischer und epidemiologischer Verlauf der Asbestose und ihrer Komplikationen in der Tschechoslowakei. Proceedings Congr. Biol. Wirk. Asb., Dresden, pp. 118–124, /1968/.
26. Navrátil, M.: Pleural calcifications due to asbestos exposure compared with the relevant findings in the non exposed population. Inhaled Particles III, Vol. 2, pp. 695–701, /1971/.
27. Navrátil, M., Trippé, F.: Prevalence of pleural calcification in persons exposed to asbestos dust and in the general population in the same district. Environm. Res. 5, No. 2, pp. 210–216, /1972/.

28. Navrátil, M., Dobiáš, J.: Development of pleural hyalinosis in long term studies of persons exposed to asbestos dust. Environm. Res. 6, No. 4, pp. 455–472, /1973/.
29. Navrátil, M.: Possibilities of the radiological diagnostics of asbestosis and its complications. /in Czech/. Pracov. Lék. 27, No. 9, pp. 312–313, /1975/.
30. Navrátil, M.: Contribution of the lung function examination to the x-ray diagnostics of asbestosis. /in Czech/. Pracov. Lék. 29, No. 3, pp. 91–95, /1977/.
31. Navrátil, M.: The advantages of the international x-ray classification ILO U/C 1971 for the diagnostics of asbestosis. /in Czech/. Pracov. Lék. 29, No. 6, pp. 214–217, /1977/.
32. Navrátil, M., Morávková, K., Trippé, F.: Follow-up study of pleural hyalinosis in individuals not exposed to asbestos dust. Environm. Res. 15, No. 1, pp. 108–118, /1978/.
33. Navrátil, M., Hassmanová, V.: Epidemiological and clinical picture of pleural and peritoneal mesotheliomas in asbestos exposed workers. /in Czech/. Stud. pneumol. phtiseol. Czech. 41, No. 6, pp. 404–410, /1981/.
34. Navrátil, M., Ježková, Z.: Lung tissue antibodies in persons with long lasting asbestos dust exposure. /in Czech/. Čas. Lék. Čes. 121, No. 52, pp. 1608–1611, /1982/.
35. Navrátil, M., Hassmanová, V., Nosál, M., Benický, L. Švandová, E.: Influence of long lasting asbestos exposure on health status and mortality of workers. Arch. Immunol. Ther. exper. /Wroclaw, Poland/ 30, No. 3/4, pp. 145–150, /1982/.
36. Navrátil, M.: Lung asbestosis and its complications,/in Czech/. Avicenum, Health Publ. Co., Prague /1982/.
37. Navrátil, M., Moráková, K., Gafronová, M., Hruška, F.: The twenty years cohort follow-up in an asbestos products processing plant. /in Czech/. Pracov. Lék. 39, No. 3, pp. 102–108, /1987/.
38. Navrátil, M., Morávková, K., Gafronová, M., Hruška, F.: The fate of people with pleural hyalinosis /plaques/: relationship to direct and indirect asbestos exposure. Czechoslovak Med. 11, pp. 146–156, /1988/.
39. Netolitzky, A.: Hygiene der Textilindustrie. Handbuch der Hygiene, G. Fischer Verlag, Jena, pp. 102–103, /1897/.
40. Nosál, M.: Asbestosis /in Slovak/. Pracov. Lék. 8, No. 3, pp. 198–200, /1956/.
41. Pivec, J., Kropáček, J.: Pleural hyalinosis /in Czech/. Stud. pneumol. phtiseol. Czechosl. 39, No. 9, pp. 601–609, /1979/.
42. Rejsková, M.: Results of the clinical examination in workers processing asbestos products. /in Czech/. Pracov. Lék. 8, No. 5, pp. 324–329, /1956/.
43. Rous, V., Studený, J.: Aetiology of pleural plaques.. Thorax 25, No. 3, pp. 270–284, /1970/.
44. Rovenský, E.: Lung and pleural diseases due to asbestos. /in

Slovak/. Stud. pneumol. phtiseol. Czech. 46, No. 4, pp. 247–254, /1986/.

45. Šimeček, J.: Beitrag zur Asbeststaubmessung. Staub-Reinhalt. Luft 27, No. 11, pp. 484–486, /1967/.
46. Šimeček, J.: Measurement of dust concentrations in the neighbourhood of the asbestos products processing plant. /in Czech/. Zdrav. techn. vzduchotechn. 14, No. 5, pp. 243–249, /1971/.
47. Šimeček, J.: Staubuntersuchungen in einem Beitrieb für Asbestverarbeitung und in seiner Umgebung. Staub-Reinhalt. Luft 31, No. 12, pp. 493–496, /1971/.
48. Srb, V., Kubzová, E., Musil, M.: Testing of the genotoxic activity in persons exposed to asbestos dust. I. /in Czech/. Pracov. Lék. 36, No. 5, pp. 175–178, /1984/.
49. Srb, V., Kubzová, E., Musil, M., Havel, V., Kubíková, K., Hartmann, H.: Testing of the genotoxic activity in persons exposed to asbestos dust. II. /in Czech/. Pracov. Lék. 37, No. 3, pp. 76–80, /1985/.
50. Stejskal, J.: Asbestosis and lung cancer. /in Czech/. Acta Univ. Carol. Med., Monograph. X, pp. 187–191, /1961/.
51. Zeman, V.: Asbestos bodies as a further criterium for the cytodiagnostics of mesothelioma? /in Czech/. Stud. pneumol. phtiseol. Czechosl. 39, No. 3/4, pp. 220–225, /1979/.

14

Asbestos and Asbestos-Induced Health Hazards in Bulgaria

T. BURILKOV, M.D., PH.D.
L. MIHAILOVA-DOCHEVA, PH.D.

Institute of Hygiene and Occupational Health
Medical Academy
Sofia, Bulgaria

Synopsis

BIOGRAPHY

Dr. Todor Burilkov is professor in occupational diseases at the Institute of Hygiene and Occupational Health (Dept. of Lung Diseases). He teaches courses for medical students and in postgraduate education on occupational health on both national and international levels. He has published five books and more than 150 scientific articles in English, German, Russian, and Bulgarian. His research interests include asbestosis and other pneumoconioses, occupational allergic and hypersensitivity diseases, work-related chronic nonspecific lung diseases, and occupational cancer. The author can be contacted at the Institute of Hygiene and Occupational Health, Clinic of Occupational Diseases, 15, Dimitar Nestorov str., 1431 Sofia, Bulgaria.

Lilia Milailova-Docheva is a geochemist-mineralogist and a scientific worker at the Institute of Hygiene and Occupational Health, Laboratory "Industrial Aerosols." She conducts mineralogic-chemical studies on dusts and minerals of occupational and ecological importance. On the basis of her studies on occupational asbestos dusts and asbestos as atmospheric pollutant in the birthplace, she defended a dissertation in 1976. She has more than 60 publications in English, German, Russian, and Bulgarian. Her research interests are asbestos minerals, biological activity of needlelike minerals as pollutants of the work and other environments; mineral raw materials (kizelgour, trass, bentonit); nonfibrogenic carbonate dusts, containing amorphous and semi-amorphous modifications of SiO_2; the role of free quartz surface, etc. The author can be contacted at the Institute of Hygiene and Occupational Health, Lab. "Industrial Aerosols," Medical Academy, 15, Dimitar Nestorov st., 1431 Sofia, Bulgaria.

EDITORS' COMMENTARY

In Bulgaria, special attention has been given to the fibrous nonasbestos and asbestos materials that occur in various geologic formations in the country. Various types of asbestos fibers have been specifically identified, exposure standards established, and controls implemented in various operations, such as mining, that may or may not be controlled in other countries. The following chapter begins with descriptive mineral characterizations of the type that is essential for scientific preciseness, careful delineation, and the replication of studies, which permit meaningful interpretation and application of results.

Where fiber counts of air samples are performed, the detection limit and mean error rate is given, the omission of which in the United States has created many management (false positive) and legal (false negative) problems. Descriptive precision of exposure also reduces interpretation errors, a problem of long standing in asbestos health matters, and this chapter provides some guidance in this regard. The authors attempt to relate differences in risk and onset of disease to exposure from different forms and morphology of asbestoform fibers. One of their conclusions is that coated fibers are not harmless but only have a longer latency period for a disease process to become manifest.

Hyaline and calcified pleural plaques have been experimentally produced by Burilkov and Kolev in rats, and Burilkov has previously reported non-occupational human calcified pleural plaques. Significant plaques, adhesions, and calcifications have been found in certain geographic regions of Bulgaria, with general adverse lung function and fibrotic changes. These regions have significant asbestos fibers present, originating from asbestos rock outcroppings in the cultivated soils, and significant exposure to asbestos can occur. The authors have found that hyaline plaques, which slowly increase in size and appear in additional lung locations, are gradually converted to calcified plaques. Asbestos fibers taken from human lungs were predominately less than 5 microns in length (when measured under electron microscopes) or 8 to 18 microns (under phase contrast microscopy).

The cause of pleural plaques was determined to be primarily anthophyllite fibers, rather than tremolite (another amphibole that was present). These fibers produced no unusual incidence of mesothelioma or bronchiogenic carcinoma. The lung cancer rate, among those with asbestosis, was three times that expected from the general population. The authors have postulated a minimal dose for initiation of pleural plaques and asbestosis, and a dose-response relationship. The maximum allowable concentration of airborne asbestos has been set in Bulgaria at a level significantly lower than in many other countries.

The authors propose maximum allowable concentrations of respirable airborne asbestos fibers that could, based on their research results, prevent either: (a) disabling diseases or (b) any adverse biological effect in either workplace or general environmental conditions. The nature and extent of the research reported in this chapter is of such a character that the results deserve special attention.

A. INTRODUCTION

The purpose of this chapter is to present the results of investigations, carried out with the active participation of the authors, of asbestos deposits in Bulgaria and of health hazards caused by them or by imported asbestos materials.

For the sake of conciseness, the scientific results discussed are principally those that reflect the specific features of the mineralogical, hygienic, epidemiological, or clinical aspects of the asbestos problem in Bulgaria or those aspects that may contribute to elucidating certain questions of general interest in other countries.

Accepted for publication 10 February 1989.

B. ASBESTIFORM MINERALS IN BULGARIA

1. Occurrence

a. Asbestos

Asbestos mineralizations in Bulgaria are concentrated in the Rhodope Mountains, but some occur in the Stara Planina Mountain and the Srednogorie Region as well (Fig. 14-1). They associate with ultrabasic bodies embedded in Precambrian metamorphic rocks. Asbestos mineralizations are the product of metasomatic processes caused by hydrothermal fluids penetrating the ultrabasic massifs. Alteration phenomena also include amphibolization, chloritization, talcization, carbonatization, etc. The specific chemical and thermodynamic environment of Bulgarian ultrabasic rocks have favoured the formation of anthophyllite-asbestos deposits, whereas tremolite- and picrolite-asbestos deposits are less common, and chrysotile-asbestos and sepiolite form rare lean mineralizations (1).

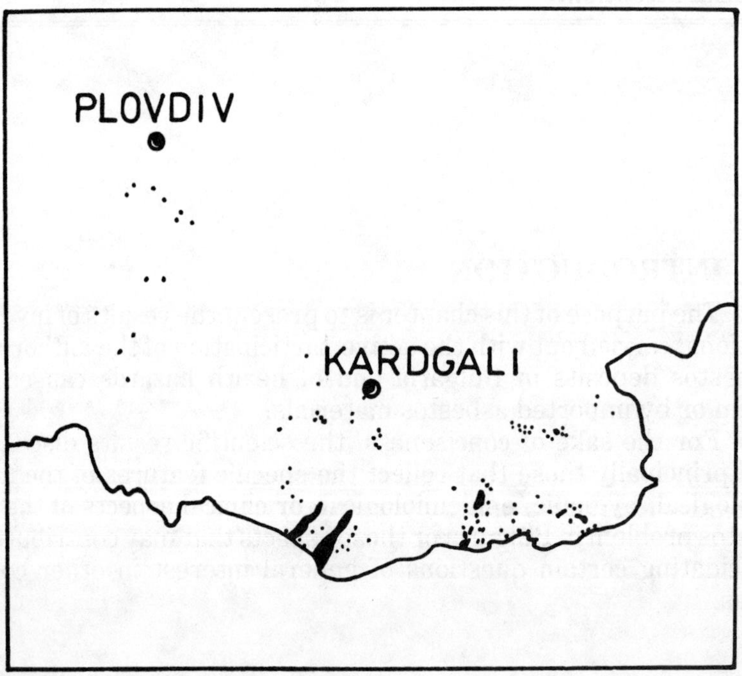

Fig. 14-1 Asbestos mineralization in ultrabasic rocks (southeast Bulgaria).

The amphibole types are typically of widely varied chemical composition, which reflects on the properties of crude asbestos: anthophyllite from some deposits has long fibers dispersing into fine fibrils, whereas tremolite is short-fibrous and brittle, which limits its practical value. Chrysotile-asbestos is not mined in Bulgaria. Picrolite is a promising material for future production (1). The numerous small sepiolite deposits found recently in this country are only of mineralogical and conceivably of ecological importance.

Talc is the main admixture in asbestos deposits. In addition, they contain small amounts of quartz (1%–2%) along with some chlorite, magnesite, dolomite, and vermiculite. About 1% of actinolite in the form of fine brittle fibers is present in asbestos from some deposits. Chrysotile-asbestos mineralizations are small and of no commercial value (2).

b. *Talc*

Monomineral talc formations are rarely found in nature. In Bulgaria there are several kinds of talc-bearing rocks of variable talc content: steatite (no commercial deposits in Bulgaria), talc schists (about 75% of talc), talc-magnesite, chlorite-talc, actinolite-talc, and tremolite-talc rocks. The main source of commercial talc in this country is a talc-magnesite deposit associated with ultrabasic rocks altered by processes of antigoritization, carbonatization, talcization, chloritization, and actinolitization (3). Technical rather than medicinal grades of talc are produced. Crude material contains talc (40%–60%) along with magnesite, spinelids, magnetite, amphibole minerals (anthophyllite, tremolite, and actinolite), and very little quartz (about 1%). Fiber content (1%–20%) depends on the grade of crude material. The latter has not been found to contain any sepiolite.

c. *Other Fibrous Minerals*

The considerable occurrence of ultrabasic rocks in Bulgaria as well as the wide use of amphibole-bearing rocks as building materials has made it necessary to do some preliminary research on the abundance of non-asbestos fibrous minerals for public health purposes (Table 14-1). Chain-structure silicates (actinolite, riebeckite, wollastonite, etc.) have been found to be fairly widespread (4). Layer-structure silicates may also form fibers, their needle-like morphology due to tubular coiling of structural sheets (sepiolite, palygorskite, etc.) as illustrated by sepiolite (Fig. 14-2) from a Bulgarian non-commercial deposit (5). Research has shown

Table 14-1 Fibrous Non-Asbestos Minerals in Some Bulgarian Commercial Raw Materials (4)

Fibrous Mineral Component	Chemical Composition (Kostov, 1964)	Commercial Raw Material
Wurtzite	ZnS	Pb-Zn ore
Ovichite	$5PbS \cdot Ag_2S \cdot 3Sb_2S_3$	Iron ore
Silimanite	$Al_2(O/SiO_4)$	Clay, chists
Actinolite	$Na_2Ca_4(Mg \cdot Fe)_{10}[(OH)_2O_2/Si_{14}O_{44}]$	Talc-magnesite
Ribecite	$Na_2Fe_5 \cdot Si_8O_{22}(OH)_2$	Basic quartz-sienite
Wolastonite	$Ca_3 \cdot [Si_3O_9]$	Marble, limestone
Chaluasite	$Al_4[(OH)_8/Si_4O_{10}](H_2O)_4$	
Antagorite	$Mg_6[(OH)_8/Si_4O_{10}]$	
Atapulgite } Paligorskite }	$Mg_5[Si_8O_{20}(OH)_2(H_2O)_4] \cdot 4H_2O$	Magnesite Copper ore
Sepiolite	$Mg_8Si_{12}O_{30}(OH)_{10} \cdot 6H_2O$	Talc-magnesite
Vivianite	$Fe_3[PO_4]_2 \cdot 8H_2O$	Pb-Zn ore
Apatite	$Ca_5[F(PO_4)_3]$	Pegmatite
Celestine	$Sr[SO_4]$	Limestone, mergel
Hydromagnesite	$Mg[OH/(CO_3)_2] \cdot 4H_2O$	Magnesite, Vermiculite, Serpentinite

that in addition to Bulgarian talc, fibrous mineral constituents are present in a considerable number of raw materials such as dolomite, magnesite, basalt, limestone, marble, etc. Such components are found in mine dust especially in skarn iron ore deposits affected by serpentinization. Microscopy of mine dust has shown the presence of about 1% of fibers 5–20 μm long and 1–2 μm in diameter.

2. Mineralogical Characteristics

Abestiform minerals in Bulgaria have been studied by a number of authors. The most comprehensive review is that of Bozhinov and Zheljazkova-Panayotova (1) from which we note the following characteristics of the five most common asbestiform varieties.

1. Anthophyllite asbestos is optically negative of positive elongation

Fig. 14-2 Morphological aspects of Bulgarian sepiolite (electrone scan, magn. 260 and 4800).

and parallel extinction. Ng′ = 1.615–1.628, Np′ = 1.597–1.608. DTA curves show a slight endothermal effect at 100°C and a well-defined endothermal effect having maxima in the range of 940°–1020°C. The strongest reflection in the x-ray diffractograms have d = 3.04–3.08 Å. Reflection intensities are affected by textural features. The highest absorption in IR spectra is found in the ranges 413–538 cm^{-1} and 900–1130 cm^{-1}. The 640–780 cm^{-1} interval is fairly instructive, anthophyllite spectra showing well-expressed differences as compared to tremolite spectra. The generalized crystallochemical formula of Bulgarian anthophyllite asbestos is:

$$(Mg_{5.1-6.4}Fe^{2+}_{0.4-1.0}A^{1}_{0.2-0.5}H_3O^{+}_{0-0.6})_{7.0}[(Si_{7.3-8.0}Al_{0-0.3}Fe^{3+}_{0-0.2})_{8.0}O_{21.6-22.0}(OH)_{0-0.4}](OH)_{1.4-2}O_{0-0.6},$$

where A^1 = Fe_{3+}, Al, Mn, Ca, Na, and K.

2. Tremolite asbestos is white, of silky lustre. Easily fiberized, it is of low elasticity. Microscopically it is colorless, of positive elongation, and oblique extinction $(Z \wedge c) = 14°–18°$, $Ng' = 1.623–1.627$, $Np' = 1.600–1.606$. DTA curves are characterized by a main endothermal effect with a maximum in the 970°–1000°C interval for the long-fibrous varieties and in the 1025°–1030°C interval for the radial-fibrous tremolite-asbestos. The strongest reflection in the diffractograms belongs to d = 3.106–3.134 Å. The highest absorption recorded by IR spectroscopy is in the intervals 420–550 cm^{-1} and 920–1110 cm^{-1}. Textural varieties show certain differences in the interval 690–760 cm^{-1}. The absorption at 3662 and 3678 cm^{-1} is also characteristic. The generalized crystallochemical formula of tremolite-asbestos is:

$$(Ca_{1.5-1.9}Na_{0-0.1}H_3O^{+}_{0-0.3})_{1.5-2.1}(Mg_{4.5-5.1}Fe^{2+}_{0.2-0.6}Mn_{0-0.4}Fe^{3+}_{0-0.1}Al_{0-0.2})_{4.8-5.5}[(Si_{7.7-8.0}Al_{0.02}Fe^{3+}_{0-0.2})_{7.9-8.0}O_{21.6-22.0}(OH)_{0-0.3}](OH)_{0.9-2.0}O_{0-2.1}.$$

There are no significant differences between tremolite and tremolite-asbestos.

3. Picrolite asbestos is grey green with cross or oblique fibres. It is brittle, not resistant to acids. Under the microscope it is colorless, of parallel extinction and positive elongation. $Ng' = 1.558–1.580$, $Np' = 1.551–1.572$. It is frequently resorbed by carbonates or talc. Its thermal pattern is rather complicated: an exothermal effect at 800°–842°C and two endothermal effects quite close to each other in the interval 700°–760°C. X-ray examinations show that picrolite-asbestos has antigorite structure. The series of strong reflections of d = 7.14–7.18, 3.59–3.61, and 2.521–2.536 Å is found to be invariably present. IR spectra are characterized by distinct absorption at 565–570 cm^{-1}, 965–1020 cm^{-1}, and 1075–1090 cm^{-1}. The generalized crystallochemical formula of picrolite-asbestos is:

$$Mg_{2.45-2.75}Fe^{2+}_{0.05-0.19}A^{1}_{0.14-0.37})_{2.84-3.0.2}[(Si_{1.95-2.08}Al_{0-0.05}Fe^{3+}_{0-0.01})_{2-2.1}O_5](OH)_{3.84-4.03}O_{0-0.15},$$

where A^1 = Fe^{3+}, Al, Mn, Ca, Na, K, and Ti.

4. Chrysotile asbestos is of grey-greenish color, silky lustre, and shows extraordinary bending, torsion, and grinding strength. Microscopically it is colorless, of parallel extinction, positive elongation, $Ng' = 1.549–1.552$, $Np' = 1.537–1.538$. DTA curves are characterized by two endothermal effects at 100°C and 690°–700°C and one exothermal

effect at 800°–820°C. Its diffraction pattern shows two strong reflections belonging to d = 7.37 Å and 3.67 Å. IR spectra are characterized by two well-defined peaks at 3650 cm^{-1} and 3690 cm^{-1}. There is well-expressed absorption in the 960–1080 cm^{-1} interval resolved in three peaks. The crystallochemical formula of chrysotile-asbestos from the Jakovica deposit is:

$Mg_{2.7}Fe^{2+}_{0.1}Fe^{3+}_{0.1}Si_{2.0}O_5(OH)_4$.

5. Asbestiform sepiolite forms veinlets of random or slip fibers. It is whitish to grey-greenish (weathered samples are rusty brown) and has low acid resistivity. It associates with calcite, talc, and pyrite. It shows parallel extinction, positive elongation, Ng′ = 1.542–1.549, Np′ = 1.530–1.538. DTA curves are characterized by three endothermal effects at 110°–150°C, 330°–380°C, and 800°–830°C and one exothermal effect in the interval 825°–852°C. The strongest reflection in fibrous sepiolite diffractograms belongs to d = 12.0–12.7 Å. IR spectra show all peaks characteristic of sepiolite. The crystallochemical formula of asbestiform sepiolite is:

$(Si_{11.60-11.65}Al_{0.07-0.26}Fe^{3+}_{0.1-0.28})_{12.0}(Mg_{7.40-7.78}Fe^{3+}_{0.12-0.35}$
$Fe^{2+}_{0-0.04}Ca_{0.13-0.20})_{7.88-8.14}O_{32.0}$.

C. "DUST" CONTROL

In Bulgaria, the main parameters to be determined for characterizing industrial asbestos-bearing aerosols are: total dust, respirable dust, content of asbestiform particles (gravimetric as well as counted, fibers/cm^3), and mineral species of the fibers (6). Permissible standards are included in the 1987 Bulgarian Tables of MAC-Values (7) for asbestos-bearing industrial dust (Table 14-2).

In our mineralogical studies, for the purposes of health protection, we have used a complex of chemical and physical methods for determining the mineral nature of asbestiform fibers, the content of asbestos relative to the other industrial dust constituents, the dimensional parameters of fibers and particle-size distribution of the other minerals, morphology, degree of agglomeration, content of soluble matter, etc. X-ray diffractometry and infra-red spectrometry were the most widely used methods. Asbestos contents (mass %) in dust samples of air from working environments, of raw and other materials, were determined through parallel analyses by IR-spectrophotometry using the KBr-disk technique and by x-ray diffractometry of dust samples on membrane filters (8). These analyses need samples of 3 mg, the detection limit being about 3% with mean relative error of 8% (for asbestos contents in the range between 10% and 100%).

Table 14-2 Some Maximum Allowable Concentrations (MAC) for Mineral Dusts in the Working Environment (MAC 16608–87, Bulgaria)

1. Asbestos dust, mixed, with asbestos content in the respirable dust under 10%:	
—asbestos-cement dust, total	4 mg/m^3
—asbestos-polymer dust, total	5 mg/m^3
—respirable dust	1 mg/m^3
2. Asbestos dust, mixed, with asbestos content in the respirable dust over 10% (Z), without other toxic or fibregenic components:	
—total dust	2 mg/m^3
—respirable dust (calculated from $\frac{0.1 \times 100}{Z(\%)}$	
6. Asbestos fibers with diameter under 3 μm and length over 5 μm:	
—respirable dust (gravimetric)	0.1 mg/m^3
—asbestos fibers (all kinds except crecidolite) (fibers/cm^3)	2 fibers/cm^3
—crecidolite fibers (fibers/cm^3)	1 fiber/cm^3
7. Talcum (medical and technical, talcum-magnesite) without asbestos and free crystaline silica	
—total dust	5 mg/m^3
—respirable dust	1 mg/m^3
8. Limestone without fibers and free crystaline silica under 2%—total dust	8 mg/m^3
9. Vermiculite without fibers and free crystaline silica under 2%—total dust	5 mg/m^3
10. Dolomite without fibers and free crystaline silica content under 2%—total dust	6 mg/m^3
11. Magnesite without fibers and free crystaline silica —total dust	6 mg/m^3

Petrographic microscopy in phase contrast is the main method for testing dust aerosols containing fibrous particles (9). Complementary methods are electron microscopy (TEM, SEM), microdiffraction, and energy dispersive analysis.

For identifying the mineral varieties of asbestos in mixed dust, raw, and other materials, dust control in Bulgaria uses also a combined optical-chemical method based on the differences between the refractive indices of asbestiform varieties (10) and their solubilities in certain chemical agents (11). The method permits distinguishing chrysotile from the amphibole types of asbestos, amphibole fibers from crocidolite, or amosite from anthophyllite (tremolite), if their content exceeds 2% and fiber diameters are not less than 0.5 μm.

Counting of asbestiform fibers was done in samples from membrane filters treated with acetone vapors and a drop of triacetyl. Counting followed international standards. The method is nonspecific in the presence of fibrous, flaky, or acicular particles other than asbestos (12).

For the identification of fibrous constituents in the human lung and pleura, dust samples collected in areas of endemic pleural plaques presents specific analytical difficulties. Asbestos in such samples has gone through "biological degradation" and the other constituents are also altered. Applicable methods in such cases are microdiffraction and energy dispersive analysis; but they permit only semiquantitative estimates of the mass content of fibrous particles.

The preliminary study of asbestos-bearing materials and asbestos-based productions provided data for preparing (13) a catalog to be used by government institutions in this country (1985).

In studying asbestos hazards in some larger-scale productions, we have found that determining *the dose of inhaled dust or asbestos* by workers at specified production sites is more relevant than determining the *average shift concentration* of respirable dust or asbestos. In calculating the dose of inhaled dust or asbestos, D, we used the formula

$$D = \frac{\Sigma C_1 \cdot V_1 \cdot T_1 + C_2 \cdot V_2 \cdot T_2 + \cdots + C_N \cdot V_N \cdot T_N}{1000} \text{ mg},$$

where C is the concentration of respirable dust or asbestos in mg/m^3, V is the lung ventilation in 1/min, and T is the time spent in the working environment during a shift or to perform an operation, respectively.

In professions (e.g., insulators in thermal power stations) involving variable periods of labor under varying strain (varying lung ventilation) in environments of varying dust content, chronometry of operations has been done during the working day or over longer cycles during the year. The dose of inhaled dust, respired asbestos, in such cases shows better correlation to the radiological signs of asbestosis than to the other widely used parameters such as the product of the mean dust concentration and the years of exposure (14, 15).

D. ASBESTOS IN THE WORKING ENVIRONMENT

The production of asbestos in Bulgaria is carried out in underground or in open mines. The concentration of respirable dust varies widely (from 1 to 5 MAC). Underground production creates the least amount of dust, while processing is still sometimes a source of considerable pollution. The asbestiform fibers consist barely of anthophyllite (the first enterprise) and tremolite (the second enterprise). An insignificant admixture of chrysotile is found in the aerosole in the underground production of anthophyllite and of actinolite in tremolite dust. Talc (42) shows the basic impurity of crude asbestos.

The quantity of anthophyllite in the mine air is about 11%, while during processing it rises sharply to 59%–66%, the presence of talc being from 5%–30%. The remaining mineral components are represented by carbonates, chlorite, or relics. Actinolite and chrysotile are found as single needles.

Anthophyllite disperses into much finer needles than tremolite: l/d ratio ~10 res. ~5.

Investigations of industrial dust in the production and processing of talc have established, as a basic component in all technological processes, talc (on an average 40%), magnesite (7%–30%), and asbestos (0.5%–17%). The remaining components (chlorite, hydromica, etc.) occur in quantities under 10%, quartz being at 1%–2%. Fiber length ranges between 2–40 μm, their thickness being 0.5–8 μm.

Soviet chrysotile asbestos of different qualities is used in the production of Bulgarian asbestos textiles. The quantity of chrysotile in the asbestos (50%–60%) depends on the type of the asbestos. The principal admixture is the scaly variety of chrysotile—serpentine antigorite. Almost all needles (15, 16) are respirable.

In shipbuilding, the shipworkers and the insulators are exposed, primarily, to imported chrysotile asbestos, whereas the ships carpenters are exposed to imported amosite-planes without their asbestos content being declared (17). Crocidolite has not been used.

In asbestos-cement production, the presence of two types of dust was established. There were free asbestos needles (7%–78%) in the warehouse and in the mixing section, while the quantity of needles diminishes significantly (2%–21%) in the processing of asbestos cement (turning of pipes). A considerable part of the needles, in the second aerosol, cannot be observed with a light microscope in phase contrast. When viewed with an electron microscope, it was established that the seemingly isometric particles are in fact a typical "hedgehog-like" agglomerate of cement and asbestos (Fig. 14-3). During our investigations, the greatest number of workers affected by asbestos were registered in the tooling section. When the dose of inhaled dust is compared with the asbestos-induced injuries, a complete correlation was established. Workers exposed to airborne asbestos needles get asbestosis after a minimal exposure of 13.8 ± 3.1 years, but when asbestos needles are agglomerated with cement, asbestosis sets in after 23.6 ± 2.9 years. This delayed effect must be connected with the slow liberation of asbestos from the deposed cement agglomerates. These results may clarify the contradictory data in the scientific literature regarding the risk incurred in processing asbestos-cement wares (18).

In repairing industrial furnaces and kilns as well as power stations, workers are exposed to a mixture of asbestos and quartz. Refractory bricks with a high content of free silica and asbestos (mainly anthophyllite, less commonly chrysotile) are used separately or in mixtures with perlite, water glass, and cement as protective coating and spraying (19, 20). There is an especially high risk in demolishing used masonry in furnaces and repairing old insulations and asbestos sprayings. The asbestos needles in the rubble removed during the repairs retain their morphology, but as a result of the higher temperatures their crystal lattice is changed (19).

The distribution of the asbestosis cases, according to the kind

Fig. 14-3 Dust from asbestos-pipe turning. TEM Multiple asbestos fibers.

of production and the clinical manifestations of the disease have been generalized in Table 14-3 (21).

From the list of the effected miners having worked or working with anthophyllite, 31 persons with calcified asbestos plaques are excluded. At the moment of diagnosis, their length of service and dust-free period amounted to less than 18 years, which is the minimal latency period for hyaline plaques to calcify. In the case of these miners, an endemic exposure is predominant.

Pulmonary asbestosis is most common with workers engaged in the production of asbestos textile, asbestos cement, and asbestos-plastic materials and insulation, in which chrysotile is used. On the other hand, the pleural and mixed variety (the parenchymal-pleural form of asbestosis) is most commonly found among workers engaged in the production and primary processing of anthophyllite and in furnace-repair work (Fig. 14-4. No pleural forms of asbestosis were found in enterprises producing asbestos-plastics or using technical talc in the production of rubber and paints.

Consecutive crushing and milling of asbestos and other minerals and the use of talc in rubber plants causes exposure to a mixed dust of asbestos, other silicates, or quartz. In some cases unusual mixed pneumoconioses, with basal diffuse asbestos fibro-

Table 14-3 Asbestosis Distribution Among Workers

Workers Exposed to Asbestosis	Form of Asbestosis, %				
	Lung Asbestosis	Plaques	Asbestosis and Plaques	Others	Total
Production	24.0	52.0	20.0	4.0	100
Primary processing	5.6	27.7	22.2	44.5	100
Asbestos textile	90.9	0.0	9.1	0.0	100
Asbestos cement	66.6	9.1	15.1	9.1	100
Asboplastic	66.6	0.0	22.2	11.2	100
Insulation	73.8	4.8	16.6	4.8	100
Thermal and power repair	53.8	30.8	7.7	7.7	100
Work with techn. talc	6.1	0.0	12.2	81.7	100
Total	47.6	15.1	15.5	21.8	100

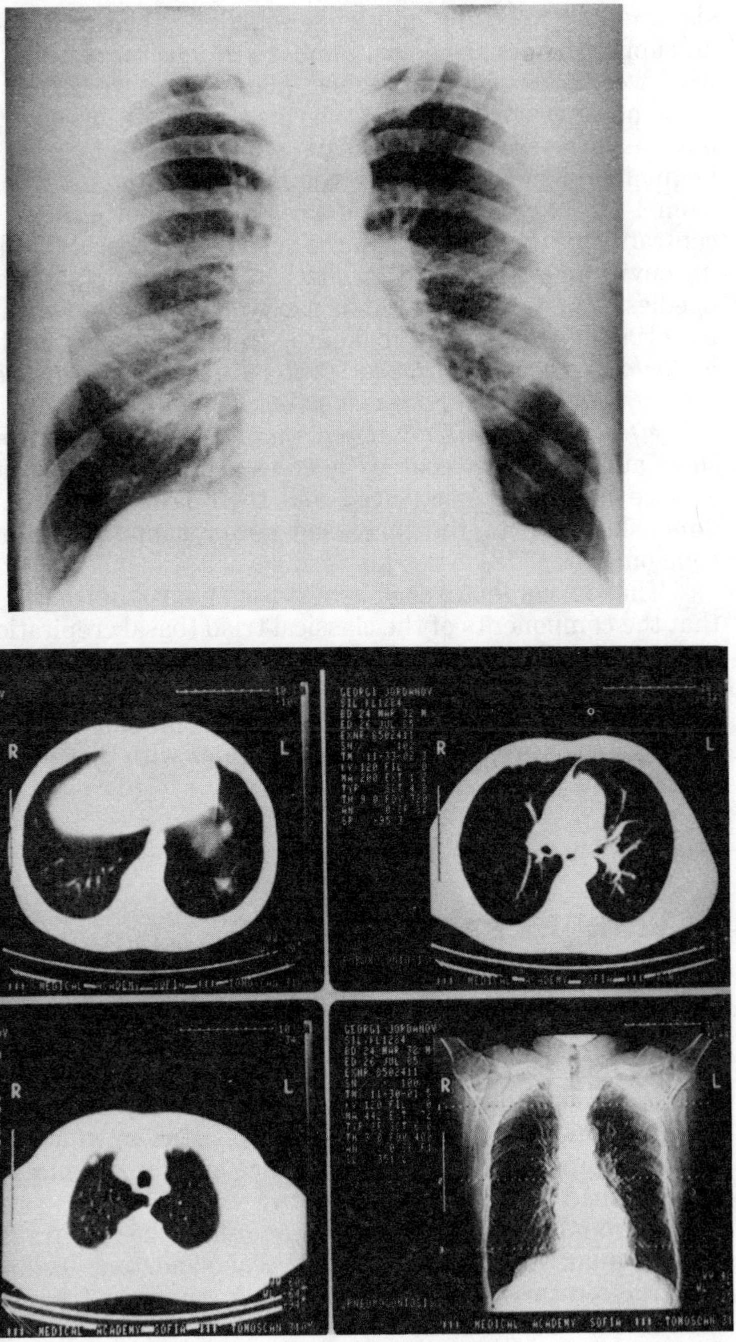

Fig. 14-4 Mixed silicoasbestosis in a kiln repair masson (upper). CT with hyaline pleural plaques (lower).

sis, are observed; and in others, rounded opacities in the middle and upper pulmonary fields. Similar x-ray pictures were observed in 45 workers with asbestos and quartz exposure (22).

The average length of service up to the discovery of the disease varies from 11 to 23 years, while the latent period from the beginning of the exposure to the moment of the diagnosis varies from 14 to 26 years. These indices depend not only on the concentration of the dust and on the respirable asbestos in the working environment, but also on whether the dust is in the form of free needles or of needles coated or partly agglomerated with another material—e.g., cement, bakelite, water glass, or rubber. *The biological reaction to these "coated" asbestos needles does not differ from that to free ones, in principle, but the disease begins to take effect after a considerably longer latent period.* The opinion of some authors, that "coated" needles are harmless because their surface has been inactivated and their respirable fraction has diminished due to the increased aerodynamic diameter of the conglomerates (18) is not justified.

The clinical features of asbestosis in our studies (21) indicate that the components of the classical triad (basal crepitations, cyanosis, and clubbing) are far from equally significant. A most frequent and constant feature is the crepitations (52.3%), which we found to be twice as frequent as cyanosis. Clubbing (3.3%) is a rare finding. In that respect, our data coincides with those of Bohlig et al (23).

E. FIBROUS PARTICLES IN CONSTRUCTION MATERIALS

An investigation was made of the dust during the production of basalt material, which was required by petrurgy (24). The basic mass of dust particles was made up of diopside, plagioclase, pyroxene, and small quantities of magnetite. There were also clusters, not quite fully formed, of fibrous particles, which according to the parameters of the crystal lattice and the chemical content, were defined as tremolite-actinolitic.

Fibrous components were discovered in the rock fragments of a stone quarry in North Bulgaria. The sandstone used for road construction proved to contain greatly changed tremolite (25). Fine-fibered sepiolite developed on the tremolite crystals (Fig. 14-5). This finding has aroused interest because of the increased death rate from lung cancer among silicosis patients from this

Fig. 14-5 Fibrous sepiolite-tremolite in sandstone rock of the Sokolovopit.

quarry (26) and because of similar observations (27) where carcinogenic activity was established experimentally.

The clinical significance of these findings is as yet unclear; they will become the object of further study.

F. PLEURAL PLAQUES

The pathogenesis of pleural plaques associated with asbestos exposure is obscure, and causes other than asbestos may be involved (28). Plaques occur more frequently after exposure to amphiboles than to chrysotile.

Hyaline and calcified pleural plaques have not been investigated experimentally, since they do not develop in animals for research purposes under usual conditions. Burilkov and Kolev (29) have worked out an *experimental model of hyaline and pleural plaques* in rats with the phenomenon of calciphylaxis described by Selye as a starting point. After an oral application of 1 ml 0.5% solution of dehydrotachysterol and intrapleural application of 50 mg of fibrous anthophyllite, macroscopic visible pleural plaques were obtained for the first time with calcification; the results were proved with the special staining by von Kossa as well as with IR-spectrophotometriy and x-ray diffraction of pleural tissue from laboratory rats.

G. ENDEMIC PLEURAL PLAQUES

In investigating the district of Avren (the Kurdjali region, the Eastern Rhodopas) in 1966, among the population not occupationally in contact with asbestos we discovered 138 cases with bilateral calcified pleural plaques (Fig. 14-6)—71.3% of the persons >30 years of age (30, 31). Plaques occur in persons of both sexes, their frequency increasing with age. A preliminary analysis tended to lead us towards the hypothesis that we had here an

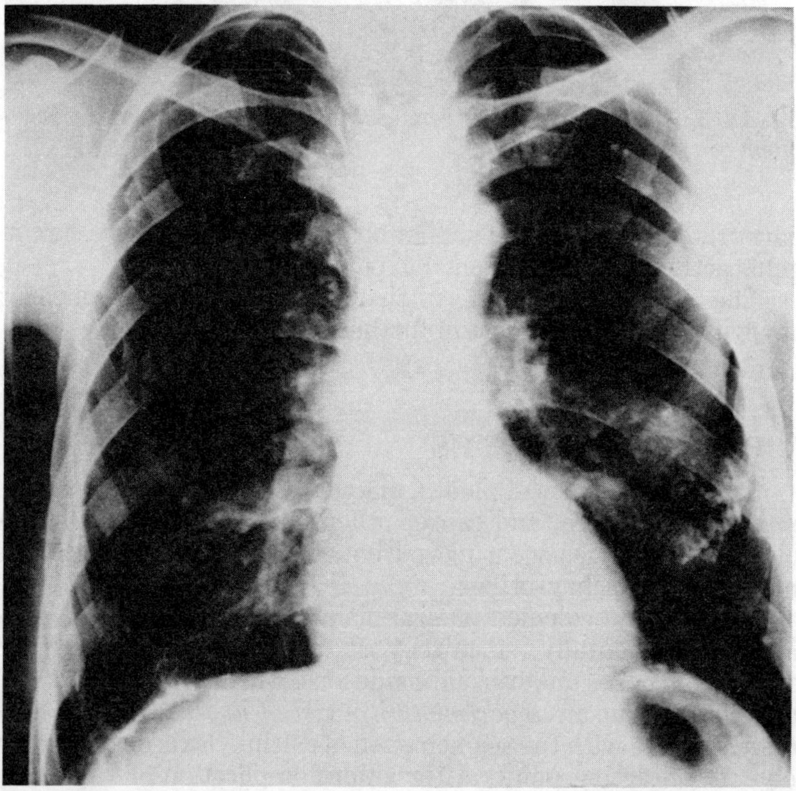

Fig. 14-6 Calcified pleural plaques: 58-year-old man from the endemic region without occupational asbestos exposure.

endemic form of pleural plaques, caused not only by air contamination from asbestos mines but also by the natural admixture of asbestos in the soil, which participates in the dust aerosol when the fields are ploughed and fibers get into the atmosphere.

So far, calcified pleural plaques were described in the literature about the population around an open anthophyllite mine (32) and in the vicinity of asbestos factories (33). The explanation was the pollution of the atmosphere with asbestos from industrial plants or factories. Czech authors (34) described an endemic region and connected the plaques with widespread tuberculosis of the cattle. To prove or reject our hypothesis, with the presence of asbestos mines in the region under investigation, we carried out a research project together with a team of clinicists, roentgenologists, pneumologists, experts in occupational health, mineralogists, and geochemists.

During the period 1967–1978 we carried out a fluorographic investigation of 101,935 persons >14 years of age in 57 towns or villages; among them we discovered 917 with indisputable calcified pleural plaques. The frequency of the findings in the separate districts was from 0 to 208 per 1,000. Of the plaques, 94.6% are attributable to the age group of persons >40. Their frequency increases with a correlation close to exponential in old people of both sexes, but the ratio between sexes is 2.3:1.0 in the men's favour (35, 36).

Beside pleural plaques among the population of the endemic region, we discovered pleural adhesions and calcifications with a different tuberculous-traumatic or undefined etiology. The pleural changes of all kinds occuring among the population of Avren are 9.8 times more frequent than among the control group of the peasant population (3,032 persons). Pleural accretions without calcification are 4 times more frequent in the region with endemic asbestosis.

Bilateral pleural plaques are found very rarely beyond the endemic regions. They were found in 2 people, 0.006% of a control group of 36,178 persons. After further questioning of one of the two (a woman of 52, a bibliographer) it was found that as a ballerina in her teens she used a lot of technical talc in putting on her tights (37).

The incidence of tuberculosis and the percentage of calcifications in the parenchyma are higher in the control group. The higher frequency of pleural changes in the endemic region cannot be explained with greater morbidity from tuberculosis. We did not establish any cases of active pulmonary tuberculosis among the persons with pleural plaques (37).

We further studied the question of endemic pleural plaques on a national scale, by examining the population of 131 towns or villages with geologically proved outcroppings of asbestos or ultrabasic rocks within their territory. In 71 of them, with a population of 65,985 persons, we found cases with pleural plaques.

Not all inhabitants of towns and villages in the vicinity of asbestos deposits are at risk. Negative results are to be found principally where the asbestos deposits are in uncultivated and unfrequented woodland and mountanous regions because the population does not inhale a dose sufficiently high for the formation of calcified plaques within the framework of normal life expectancy. In some mountain villages with a small number of inhabitants a negative result is possible because of statistical probability, but this does not exclude the possibility of cases with pleural plaques being found there (38, 39).

In the literature there is a widespread view that the calcified plaques do not impair lung function if they are not accompanied by pulmonary asbestosis. To clarify this question we examinded 632 persons from the districts of Avren and Golyamo Kamenyane, in the endemic region, and a control group of 734 inhabitants of a village with asbestos-free soil (40). As regards the population of the endemic region, a moderate but significant impairment of lung ventilation (VC) was established with unchanged dynamic indices. We made separate calculations for the values of 89 persons with calcified plaques in the same region. The mean values for VC are lower than those of the general population but the difference is statistically insignificant.

The explanation of these results we found in the fact that *hyaline plaques, unrecognized during life, are 6 to 7 times more frequent than the calcified ones*. That is why a considerable part of the popoulation over 35 in Avren and Golyamo Kamenyane have hyaline changes on the pleura. The persons with calcified plaques are a selected group with more massive hyalinosis of the pleura. We were the first to show that *pleural plaques are not meaningless* for lung function; they influence the mean value of VC in the whole population of the region. The investigations conducted by McDermott (41) and by Kree (42) confirmed the changes we found and their morphological correlate (lung fibrosis in the vicinity of plaques).

For a number of reasons, *a quick and cheap method for discovering hyaline plaques must be found*, as the use of expensive x-ray technology on a mass scale is not justified. That is why we have elaborated (43) a method for *echographic discovery* (linear scanning or “gray scale”) of hyaline pleural plaques, particularly of the typical diaphragmatic site (Fig. 14-7). The method is non-invasive, documentable, registers their thickness in mm, and detects plaques twice as often as roentgenography in oblique views.

We followed the *evolution of pleural plaques* over a period of 5 years in 100 persons. We copied the outline of the lungs and of the plauqes at the beginning and the end of the observation one over the other with the aid of the Heliocontrastor 70 Old Delft (Fig. 14-8). Thereafter we studied the evolution of the plaques semiquantitatively by means of the ILO classification and quantitatively by planimetry. Both methods showed that the plaques are not definitive formations, unlike the case by tbc and post-traumatic calcinosis, but are very dynamic in their localization and size. Hyaline plaques form a matrix for the deposition of calcium and their size is the maximal size calcified plaques can reach. Planimetry can give us more precise data but it is very labor consuming. The investigation conducted by Burilkov, Babadschov, and Dertliev (37) is unique of its kind. It proves the suitability of the ILO classification of pneumoconioses in providing a good semiquantitative evaluation of the evolution of pleural plaques, thereby fulfilling one of the tasks formulated by the International Committee of Experts.

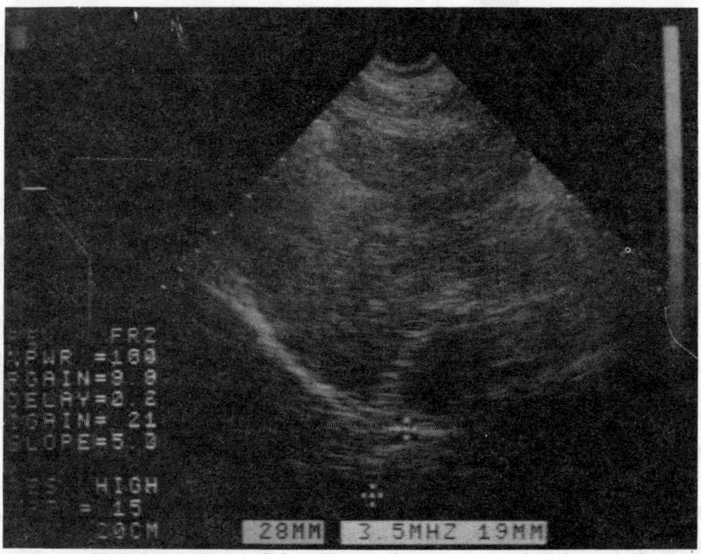

Fig. 14-7 Echography of hyaline plaques, invisible in Rö-graphy. Insulator with hyaline plaque on the anteroaxilar line with thickness 28 mm.

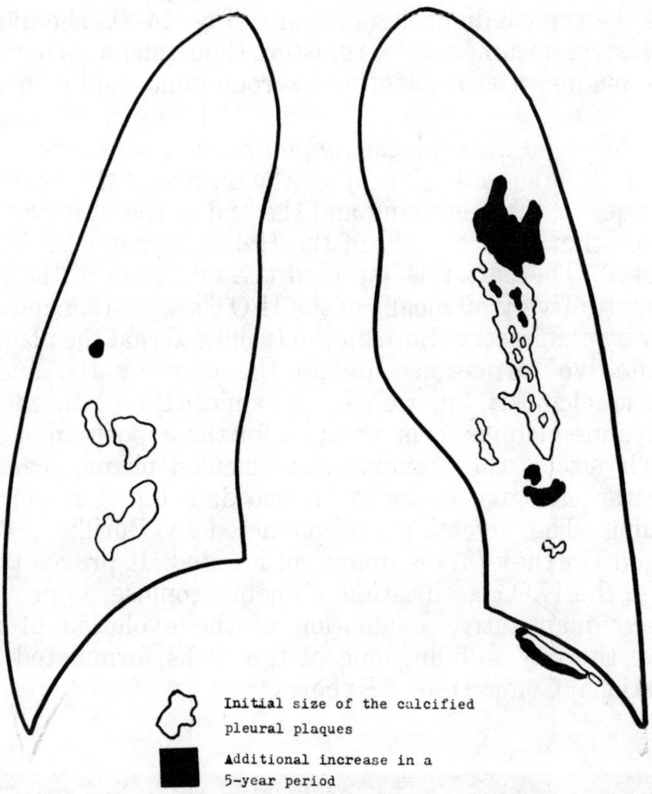

Fig. 14-8 Initial size of the calcified pleural plaques. Additional increase in a 5-year period.

1. Mineralogical Investigations

Asbestos mineralization exists in many places in southern Bulgaria, with outcropping rocks having no commercial value and unknown health significance. For our purposes, the mineralogical investigations (38, 44) were conducted along two lines:

1. Investigating the soil in villages, with and without pleural plaques detected among the population; special attention was paid to soil cultivated by families with pleural plaques (44).

2. Looking for pleural plaques among the population around known, but industrially unexploited, asbestos deposits.

It was established that:

- The presence of fibrous minerals in soil samples exceeded 2% in the fields of families with calcified pleural plaques.
- These fibrous particles originate from ultrabasic and serpentine rock outcroppings in the region of the affected villages.
- The needles belong to the amphiboles, anthophyllite (in some

regions), and tremolite (in others) (Fig. 14-9). The frequency of pleural plaques is many times higher in the presence of anthophyllite (6.2%) than in regions with only tremolite (0.2%).

- The chrysotile component weathers and disintegrates quickly, so there are practically no chrysotile fibers in the soil.

The absence of fibrous particles in some of the investigated fields does not exclude contact with asbestos, since we were unable to get soil samples from all fields under cultivation, and some were included in tracts of land belonging to cooperative farms. Asbestos fibers found in some women were only from the soil of the fields cultivated before their marriage.

The presence of sepiolite, a product of exogenic alteration of

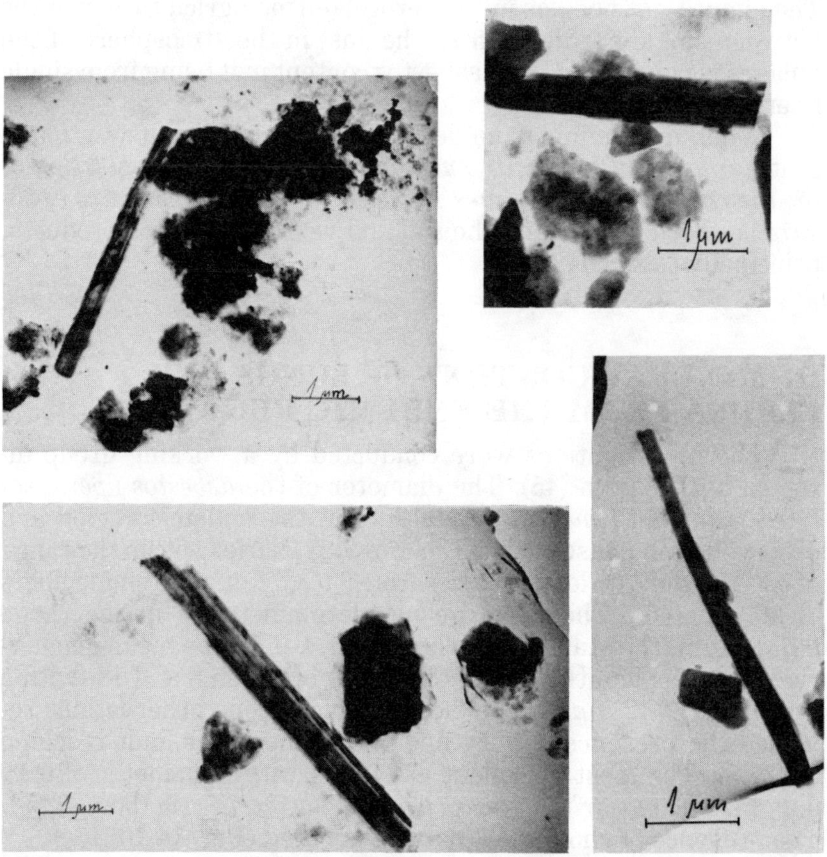

Fig. 14-9 Asbestos particles in the atmosphere of the endemic region. TEM: "Hitachi"—H (Cherneva, P., Mihailova-Docheva, L.; 1976).

serpentinized ultrabasic rocks (5), is of special interest. The "clay-like appearance" is typical of sepiolite; because of this, its fibrous morphology is established mainly by observing it with an electronic microscope.

The quantity of the fibrous component in the soil is within the range of 0.5%–8%. In size, the diameter varies within the range of 0.01–5 μm, and the length, from 5–150 μm. In our report (5) attention was drawn for the first time to the possible significance of sepiolite for occupational health and ecology.

2. Dust Control

The concentration of dust, in working soil, varies greatly depending on the climatic and seasonal conditions (5–100 mg/m^3). The quantity of needles in the aerosol during agricultural work is between single needles to 5%. The dust in the atmosphere of the villages is below MAC, the asbestos content in it being from single fibers to 1%.

When determining the dose of inhaled needles it was found that *living in villages with such a degree of asbestos pollution of the air cannot cause plaques unless a much more massive exposure is added* in working the soil and working with its products, principally tobacco (21).

H. MINERAL CONTENT OF LUNGS AND PLEURA FROM THE ENDEMIC REGION

The investigations were conducted by a working group directed by Dobreva (45). The diameter of the *asbestos fibers isolated from the lungs* of inhabitants of the endemic region and observed with phase contrast microscopy, varies within the range of 0.3–2.0 μm; the length varies from 3 to 60 μm, with single fibers of 80 μm (46). The mean geometric diameter is in the range 0.5–1.0 μm, the standard deviation is 1.4–1.7. The mean geometric values for length vary in the range between 8 and 18, with a maximum of 12.5 μm. The electron microscope observations revealed the presence of very fine fibers, the lower limit reaching 0.03 μm. The most prevalent are fibers with a diameter of 0.1–0.2 μm. *The majority of fibers are shorter than 5 μm* (50%–92%). The presence of short thick needles is noted (Fig. 14-10).

An investigation of *fibers from the pleura* was necessitated by unresolved pathogenetic questions and the high percentage of hyaline and calcified plaques without mesothelioma. The mineral

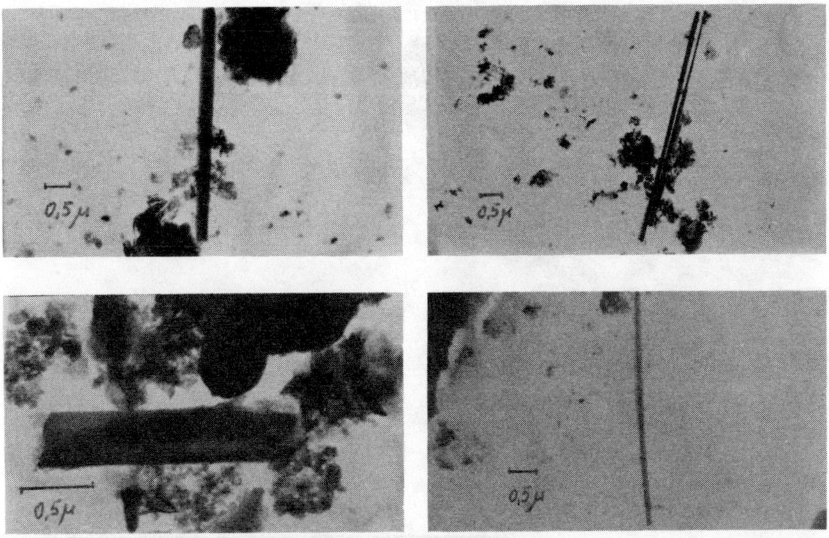

Fig. 14-10 Fibrous dust particles from lung tissue of endemic plaques carriers (by courtesy of Cherneva-Zhalova, 1988).

content of the pleura of 5 deceased inhabitants of an endemic region with asbestos-induced pleural plaques was investigated. X-ray diffraction established a mass of apatite where the differentiation of its varieties was difficult. After incineration of the dust, an insignificant quartz and talc content was found. The fibrous components established, when observed in phase contrast (1%–3%), have a varied morphology; their length varies from 0.5–42.6 μm, while the diameter varies from 0.02–1.4 μm. Some of the fibers have obvious marks of "corosion."

The mineral diagnostics of the fibers creates some analytical difficulties; wherever possible we made use of microdifraction and energy dispersive analysis. A considerable number of the fibers (80%) reveal a crystal structure and their diffraction a—long a prismatic section (113, 111, 212)—corresponds to asbestos of the amphibolic (anthophillite) type. A typical anthophyllite needle is shown (Fig. 14-11). Part of the fibers become amorphous; there is no diffractional pattern. In addition to silicon, they contain aluminum and iron; magnesium was not found.

These data confirm our hypothesis that *the cause of the endemic pleural plaques is mainly anthophyllite fibers* found in the dust from the pleura from the aerosols in the endemic region. Tremolite and chrysotile were not found in the dust from the pleura. *A typical feature of Bulgarian anthophyllite is their*

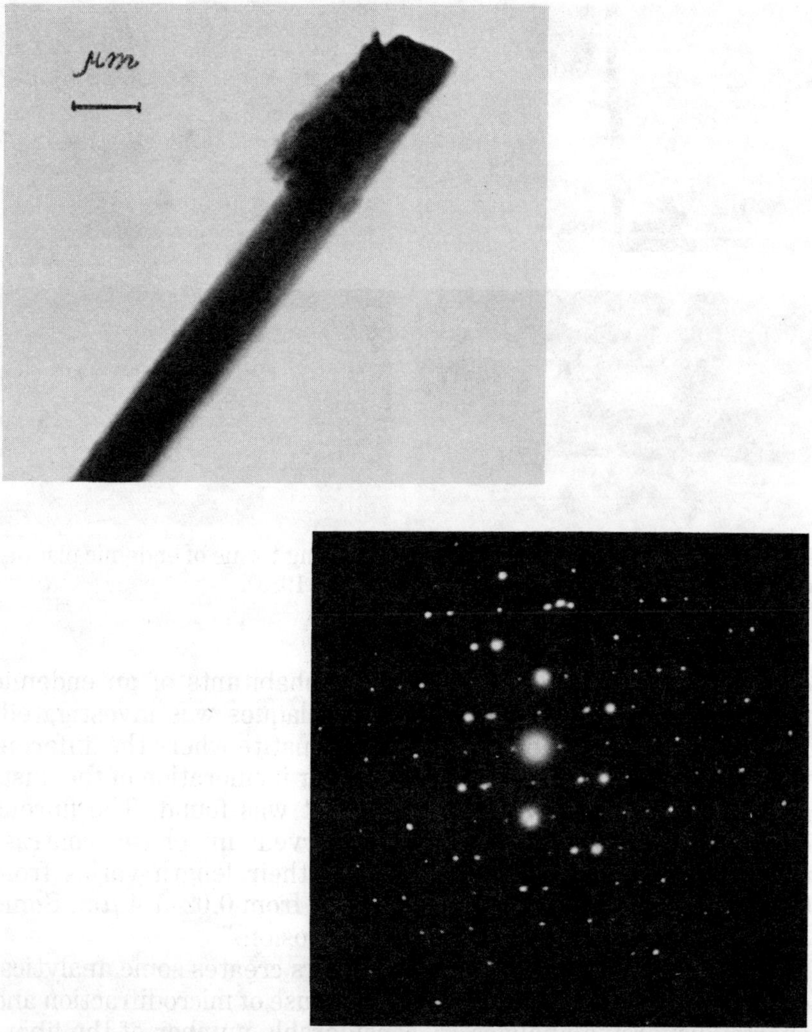

Fig. 14-11 Anthophyllite needles isolated from a pleural plaque. Inhabitant of an endemic region. EM: "Philips-420" microdifraction and energy dispersion analysis.

dispersal into considerably finer fibers compared with tremolite. The latter was found in the soils but not in the dust from the pleura.

The results of the investigations of the dust deposited in lung and pleura coincide with epidemiological observations of a 31-fold greater frequency of the pleural plaques in villages with anthophyllite in the soil compared with those where tremolite was found

(44). This corresponds to the absence of plaques among persons exposed to Bulgarian technical talc, the fibrous component of which contains mainly tremolite. In this connection, it is of interest to note the type of amphibolic admixtures to the chrysotile in the Canadian deposits, with different plaque frequency among the workers exposed. Moreover, our observation in the Dorkovo mine should be taken into account, where in the course of 20 years, a primarily tremolite bed turned into an anthophyllite one.

The endemic regions are a natural model for the study of the biological effect of asbestos and other fibrous minerals to be found there that have made their impact on the population for centuries. Here the long (sometimes more than 50 years) latency period, before the clinical manifestations of the asbestos-induced hazards, presents no problem.

I. ASBESTOS-INDUCED TUMORS IN BULGARIA

Observations over many years of areas in southern Bulgaria with endemic occurence of pleural plaques connected with the minerals anthophyllite, tremolite, and sepiolite in the soil, show no increase of mesothelioma, neither among the general population nor at the plaques carrier (21, 47). An increase of bronchial carcinoma can be proved only for persons with even minimal lung fibrosis.

When observing 206 cases with pulmonary asbestosis, 5 persons fell ill with lung cancer. After standardization according to sex, age, and length of period of observation, it was found that the attack rate for patients with asbestosis from bronchial carcinoma was 5.1 times greater than expected. Standardization as regards smoking was not possible. If we accept that smokers are twice as many among the asbestosis patients than in the control group, the attack rate remains 3-fold higher than what was expected (21).

The cases of diffuse malignant mesothelioma observed in Bulgaria (48) are evenly distributed in the country, having, with few exceptions, no known contact with asbestos and for the time being reflect the "natural level" of tumor conversion of mesothelial cells.

Having examined 116,217 persons in the endemic regions, we did not find cases of mesothelioma. In two persons from the endemic region, we found polycyclic formations at the chest wall, similar to the diffuse malignant mesothelioma. Observations in the course of 5 and 6 years respectively showed that these were forms of the so-called benign fibrous mesothelioma. Its connection with exposure to asbestos is disputed in the literature, but our observations favor the thesis that such benign tumors may be connected with irritation by asbestos fibers without carcinogenic potential (21).

Mesothelioma being such a rarity in Bulgaria does not demobilize us. It is not and will not be a problem for our endemic regions, but for industrial workers exposed to crocidolite and amosite, mesothelioma presents a real risk that may manifest itself clinically after a latency of 30–40 years. There is a considerable contingent of workers in Bulgaria who have been exposed to crocidolite since 1969 and to amosite since 1971.

An investigation by Kolev (49) with amorphous crocidolite questions the fibrous structure of asbestos as the predominant cause of induction of peritoneal mesothelioma. Similar results (50) were also achieved in working with milled Bulgarian and Russian anthophyllite. The fibrous type structure of some tumors and the long survival period of the respective test animals, give good grounds to think about the relatively benign character of these mesotheliomatas induced by anthophyllite.

Proceeding from intraperitoneal experiments with fibrous anthophyllite (21), Burilkov noted that the direct instillation of asbestos materials in the pleura or peritoneum eliminated the selective filter function of the ventilation process in the bronchial tree and the lungs, and the instilled quantity of asbestos material is many times greater than that found in the lungs of workers who died of asbestosis.

Pleural plaques and mesothelioma are not caused by a single agent with identical parameters. It can be produced from two separated groups of needles with different physical properties, inducing a plaque or mesothelioma. That is why we cannot speak of a causal connection between them, but only of a coincidence of two asbestos effects (47).

A simultaneous occurence of the two types of needles in the aerosol is to be expected from the crocidolite of some distinct deposits. Systematic x-ray controls for tumor detection are therefore only suggested for plaque carriers with exclusive or mixed crocidolite or amosite exposure, or with signs of even minimal lung fibrosis (47).

J. BIOLOGICAL RESPONSE TO ASBESTOS

We studied the *dependence between the quantity of inhaled asbestos and the biological response* of persons exposed in industrial production by proceeding from the data (45, 15, 19) on total dust, the respirable fraction, and the asbestos content in percentages. We calculated the cumulative dose following a method we worked out (15).

We determined the body response in occupational asbestos exposure in two ways:

1. As a risk of the appearance of initial radiological signs of asbestosis (percentage of persons with x-ray finding in the total number of people investigated with a definite cumulative dose).

2. In the form of length of service until the appearance of radiological signs of asbestosis among people having inhaled a different mean daily dose (in mg) of fine asbestos.

The results in both approaches with lung asbestosis favor the linear dependence with a threshold cumulative dose of 5 for aerosols with free needles and 10 for aerosols with agglomerated asbestos needles.

The asbestos content in the atmosphere of the endemic region (on average 0.0015 mg/m^3) is below MAC, but in the breathing zone of peasants at work in the fields (0.478 mg/m^3), it is twice as high. Merely by staying in the endemic region 8.7 mg of asbestos are inhaled on an average annually, but when engaged in active agricultural work in fields with asbestos outcroppings, it is 240.9 mg. The cumulative dose is determined mainly by the exposure during soil cultivation (21, 38).

Pleural plaques with calcifications appear when a minimal dose of about 2,500 mg of asbestos is inhaled. This minimal dose cannot be reached by merely living in the endemic region. The frequency of the calcified plaques increases sharply with a cumulative dose of about 6,000.

We do not share the opinion met with in the literature that the appearance and evolution of hyaline and calcified plaques are determined solely by the time factor, not by the dose. Our reasons for this being the following facts (21,38):

- A greater frequency of plaques with men whose cumulative dose is higher.
- A greater size and faster evolution of the plaques with persons having a double (endemic and professional) exposure, compared with persons having only an endemic exposure (additive effect of the additional dose).
- A higher asbestos content in pleural hyalinosis.

K. ASBESTOS EXPOSURE STANDARDS

The investigations on the relations between dose and response in man are directly connected with the *dust standards*. The results from the endemic region are significant as an original experiment on the biological effect of asbestos on man for life, mesothelioma excepted (21). They show that MAC for asbestos in the atmosphere suggested by Kogan (51) in the USSR in 1975 and the norm of 0.1 mg/m^3 introduced in the German Federal Republic and other countries will allow the inhalation of 10 to 40 times more asbestos over 60 years compared with the minimal dose for calcified plaques of 2,500 mg established by us.

We consider that MAC for asbestos in the atmosphere should amount to 0.006 mg/m^3, while in a working environment with 30 years as maximum length of service, it should amount to 0.012 mg/m^3 of respirable asbestos. These norms prevent the setting in of any kind of biological effect whatever.

If we limit ourselves to the clinically important and disabling forms (lung fibrosis and cancer), MAC for respirable asbestos in the environment may amount to 0.015 mg/m^3 and in the working environment to 0.03 mg/m^3.

L. RECOMMENDATIONS

Based on our extensive studies we are of the opinion that:

1. In workplace conditions both gravimetric methods and phase contrast counting are equally applicable. In spite of the differences in the methodological errors between these two methodologies, their results show a good correlation.
2. At low concentrations of asbestos needles in endemic regions and in environment in general, the analytical errors by direct gravimetric determination of asbestos fibers increase and therefore the method of counting asbestos needles in phase contrast becomes the leading one.
3. At low concentrations the counting determination in phase contrast serves for cleaning of the mass concentration with the help of appropriate factors; therefore, the priority at low concentrations pertains to the counting hygienic standards.
4. Standards should specify that only respirable fibers be counted. Electromicroscopic investigation gives additional information for the fine needles and their mineral kind; this is of a special importance for assessment of the carcinogenic risk and pathogenesis, but it could be neglected in the practice of gravimetric determination.
5. The minimum disability level at the workplace should be 0.06 fibers/cc or 0.03 mg/m^3, and as a general ambient air limit, 0.03 fibers/cc or 0.015 mg/m^3. The non-biological effect level at the workplace should be lower than 0.012 mg/m^3 or 0.024 fibers/cc at the workplace and 0.006 mg/m^3 or 0.012 fibers/cc in the ambient air. This represents a major reduction in permissible exposure levels and could constitute a major improvement in the reduction of adverse health effects from airborne asbestos of all types and forms. It represents a reasonable and appropriate application of present research knowledge to the field of occupational preventive medicine.

REFERENCES

1. Bozhinov, Kr., M. Zheljazkova-Panayotova. Asbestos and Asbestos Deposits in Bulgaria. Annuaire de l'Universite de Sofia "Kliment Ochridski" Faculté de Geologie et geographie. Livre 1, Geologie, Vol. 71, 73, 1979.
2. Mihailova-Docheva, L., D. Stefanov. Hygienische Bewertung der in Bulgarien angewandten Talkumarten. Z.f.die gesamte Hygiene und ihre Grenzgebiete, Hf.4, 1972, 233–235.
3. Kurchatov, V. Talc and talc deposits in Bulgaria - Dipl. 1978, University, Sofia, Bulgaria.
4. Mihailova-Docheva,L. Fibrous non-asbestos particles in some Bulgarian commercial minerals. Problemi na higienata, Vol.XIII, 1988, S151/155 (in Bulg.).
5. Burilkov, T., L.Mihailova-Docheva. Über den Sepiolitgehalt des Bodens in Gebieten mit endemischen Pleuraverkalkungen. Int. Arch.Arbeitsmed., 29, 95–101, 1972.
6. Burilkov, T.,M. Dobreva,St.Ivanova-Djubrilova. Mineral dusts in the work environment. Sofia, Medicina i Fizkultura, 1983.
7. BDC (Bulgarian State Standard) - 16608- 87.
8. Lukanova, R. Sravnitelnaja ocenka infrakrasnoy spektrometrii i nekatorih drugih kosvennih metodav kolichestvennovo opredelenija asbesta v promishlennoy pily, v "Izmerenie i normi-rovanie aerozolej fibrogennovo deistvija, izd. CEV, Postojannaja Komisija po sotrudnichestvo v oblasti zdravo-ohranenija, M., 1982, S 119–124.
9. Mihailova-Docheva, L., St. Ivanova-Dzhubrilova. Comparative evaluation on the microscopic and chemical method for determination of free crystal SiO_2. Works of NIHPZ, Sofia, 1969, pp 223–233.
10. Lukanova, R., S. Petrov, S. Nikolova. Methoden zur Identifizierung und Bestimmung des Asbestgehaltes in Industriestäuben, Gemeinschaftssymposium über Staubbekämpfung und Staublungenkrankheiten. 26–27 September 1981, Vidin, VRB, S. 10–14.
11. Nikolova St., (1986) Lichtmikroskopisches Verfahren zur Identifizierung von Asbest, Zeitschrift für die gesamte Hygiene und ihre Grenzgebiete,2, 93–95.

12. Dobreva, M., Dust control and measurement of asbestos in the working environment. Higiene i Zdraveopazvane, 1976, XIX, 3, 290–196.
13. Catalogue of asbestos-containing products in Bulgaria. Sofia, Ministry of Health, 1987 (Bulg. text).
14. Mihailova-Docheva, L. Mineralogische Studien in der Asbestindustrie in Bulgarien - Atemschutz - Informationen, 7, 1968, Hf.2, 32–34.
15. Burilkov T., M. Dobreva, L.Mihailova-Docheva. Über die Wechselbeziehungen Dosis-Antwort bei Asbestexpositon in Industriebetrieben und endemischen Gebieten. Gemeinschafts-Symposium über Staubbekämpfung und Staublungenkrankeiten. 26/27.IX.1981, Vidin, Bulgarien.
16. Dobreva,M., T.Burilov, V.Tocheva, L.Mihailova, R.Lukanova, V.Popova, P. Cherneva. Occupational risk in the asbestos-textile production. Problemi na higienata, Sofia, Vol.IV, 1979, 25–32 (Bulg. text).
17. Burilkov, T., L.Mihailova-Docheva, R. Lukanova, P.Cherneva, L.Babadjov, G. Kaprolov, St.Nikolova, N. Dragomirov, H. Jankova. Risk of asbestosis in shipyard workers. Higiene i Zdraveopazvane, 2, 1982, 129–134.
18. Burilkov, T., L. Mihailova-Docheva, R. Lukanova, M. Dobreva, V.Tocheva, V. Popova, P. Cherneva. Professional risk of Asbestos injuries in workers employed in asbestos-cement production. Coll. Problems of Hygiene Vol. V, 1980, pp. 125–13.
19. Barakova, V. Mineralogisch-chemische Untersuchung von asbesthaltigem Staub von Reparatur - und Isolierarbeiten in Kohlenkraftwerken. Symposium "Staublungenerkrankungen und ihre Prophylaxe" 14/16.12.1983, Bad Suderode, DDR.
20. Nazkov, L. Mixed pneumoconiosis in industrial kiln massons. Diss.,Sofia, 1986 (Bulg. text).
21. Burilkov, T. Investigations on the biological effects of asbestos minerals. Diss., Sofia, 1983 (Bulg. text).
22. Burilkov, T. Pneumokoniosediagnostik bei gemischter Asbest- und Quarzexposition. Int. Symp.Occup.Health and Safety in mining and tunneling, Prague, June 21–25, 1982.
23. Bohlig, H., Jakob, G., Müller H. Die Asbestose der Lungen, Stuttgart, Thieme, 1960.
24. Kostadinova, St. (unpublished, 1988)
25. Mihailova-Docheva, L. Nadelförmige Partikel (auss-chliesslich Asbest) in Bulgarischen Rohstoffen. Internationales Symp. über Staubbëkämpfung und Staublungenerkrankungen 30.V/1.VI.1986, Sliven,Bulgarien.
26. Petrov, Zh. Bronchialkrebs bei Steinbruchsilikose. Intern.Symposium Über Staubbekämpfung und Staublungenkrankheiten 26/27 Sept. 1981, Vidin, Bulgarien.
27. Spurny, K., Pott, F., Ruth, F., Weiss, G., H. Opiela. Identifizierung und krebserzeungende Wirkung von faserformigem Aktinolit aus einem Steinbruch. Staub, 39 (1979) 386–389.

28. Parkes, W.R. Occupational lung disorders, London, 1974, 289
29. Burilkov,T., K.Kolev. Contribution to an experimental model of pleural plaques. Hygiena i zdraveopazvane, 4, 1972, 348–352.
30. Burilkov,T. Occupational and endemic asbestos exposure. Ist National Congress of Social Medicine, Gabrovo, 1969 (Bulg.text).
31. Burilkov, T. Epidemiologie und Ätiologie der endemischen Pleura-Plaques in Bulgarien. ILO. - IV Int.Tagung über die Pneumokoniosen, Bukarest, 1971.
32. Kiviluoto, R. Pleural plaques and asbestos. In: Biological effects of asbestos. H.E. Whipple Ed. Ann. New York Ac.Sci. 132, 1965.
33. Anspach, M. Zur Ätiologie von Pleuraverkalkungen. Radiol. Diagn., 6, 1965, 341–347.
34. Rous, V., Studeny, J. Ketiology of pleural plaques. Thorax, 25, 1970, 270–284.
35. Burilkov, T., L.Mihailova, L. Badadjov. Endemic pleural asbestosis in Bulgaria. In: Ist Nat.Congress of Medical Geography, Plovdiv, 1970, 41–45 (Bulg.text).
36. Burilkov, T. Tuberulose- und Geschwulstmorbidität in einem Asbestose-Endemiegebiet. - Int.Conf. Biol.Effects Asbestos, 1968, 265–268.
37. Burilkov,T., L. Babadschov, P.Dertliev. Entwicklung und Verlauf von Pleuraverkalkungen bei Personen mit endemischer Asbestexposition. - Wissenschaft und Umwelt, *3*, 1980, 93–97.
38. Milhailova-Docheva, L. Chemical and mineralogical investigation of asbestos aerosols in industry and endemic pleural plaques regions. Diss.,Moscow, 1975 (in Russian)
39. Burilkov, T., L. Babadjov. Ein Beitrag zum endemischen Auftreten doppelseitiger Pleuraverkalkungen. - Prax. Pneumol., *24*, 1970, N 7, 433–438.
40. Burilkov, T., V.Popova. Lung function of the population in an endemic pleural plaques region. Problemi na pneumologiata i ftisiatriata (Sofia), IV vol., 1978 106–109 (in Bulg.).
41. McDermott, L. (Personal communication, 1980).
42. Kreel, G. CT in asbestosis. Arch. Immunol. Ther. Exp. (Pol.) 30, 1982, 150–155.
43. Burilkov, T., R.Krasteva. Ultrasound diagnostic of pleural plaques in asbestosis. Vatreshni bolesti, 5, 1983, 262–268 (in Bulg.).
44. Burilkov, T., L.Mihailova. Asbestos content of the soil and endemic pleural asbestosi. Environm.Res, 3, 443–451 (1970).
45. Dobreva, M. In: Asbestos health hazards and their prevention. Ed. M.Dobreva and T.Burilkova, Sofia, Profizdat, 1979 (in Bulg.).
46. Cherneva, P. Investivation of mineral dust from the lungs of anthophyllite-workers. Higiena i zdraveopaz-vane, Sofia, XXXI, 1, 22–28 (in Bulg.).
47. Burilkov, T. Über die Kausalitat von Pleura-Plaques und Asbest-induzierte Tumoren. Wissenschaft und Umwelt 2, 1985, 146–148.
48. Miltshev, M. Diseases of the pleura. Diss., Sofia, 1983 (in Bulg.).
49. Kolev, K. Experimentally induced mesothelioma in white rats in response to intraperitoneal administration of Amorphous crocido-

lite asbestos. Preliminary Report. Environmental Research, 29, 123–133 (1982).
50. Kolev,K., P. Usunov, W. Wlasow. Experimentelle asbestinduzierte Mesotheliome. Charakter und Besonder-heiten. Zschr. ges. Hygiene, 1986, 32, 2, 89–90.
51. Kogan,F.M. Asbestos-containing dusts and prevention of their harmful effects. Sverdlovsk (USSR), 1975, (in Russian).

15

Research and Prevention of Asbestos-Related Diseases in Israel

MARCUS WASSERMANN, M.D.
LEON NAIM, M.D., M.P.H.
CURT LEMESCH, M.D., M.P.H.

Hebrew University-Hadassah Medical School
Jerusalem, Israel

Synopsis

BIOGRAPHY

Dr. Marcus Wassermann is Professor Emeritus of Occupational Health at the Hebrew University-Hadassah Medical School Jerusalem. He is a member of the Panel of Experts in Occupational Health of the World Health Organization and 1976 Laureate of the Yant Memorial Award of the American Industrial Hygiene Association. He is also the author of publications in the field of Occupational Health, contributor of the ILO Encyclopaedia of Occupational Health and Safety and to other publications of the ILO and WHO. Dr. Wasserman may be contacted at the Department of Occupational Health, Hadassah Medical School, The Hebrew University, P.O. Box 1172, Jerusalem, 91010, Israel (telephone: 42-8111 or 02-42-1932).

Dr. Leon Naim has been the Regional Medical Inspector of the Ministry of Labour and Social Affairs for the Northern Region of Israel since 1963. Formerly, in the years 1960–1963, Dr. L. Naim worked as Occupational Health physician in the Dept. of Occupational Health of Kupat Holim in Haifa (Israel). Dr. L. Naim graduated as M.D. in 1955 from the School of Medicine of Paris (France) and M.P.H. from the School of Medicine of the Hebrew University of Jerusalem (Israel) in 1970. He has been a Member of the American Conference of Governmental Industrial Hygienists since 1967, and a Member of the International Commission on Occupational Health since 1966. Dr. Naim is the author of several educational publications in the field of Occupational Health.

Dr. Curt Lemesch has been the Chief Medical Labour Inspector of the Ministry of Labour and Social Affairs since 1977 and Occupational Health Physician at the Department of Occupational Health of Kupat Holim in Jerusalem since 1975.

Dr. Lemesch graduated as M.D. in 1965 from the School of Medicine of Santiago (Chile) and as M.P.H. from the School of Medicine of the Hebrew University of Jerusalem in 1973. He is a Member of the International Commission on Occupational Health and acts as the National Secretary in Israel for this organization. He is Coordinator of the Scientific Activity of the Israeli Society of Occupational Health Physicians and author of several publications in the field of Occupational Health.

EDITORS' COMMENTARY

The relatively recent development of asbestos regulations, investigatory procedures, and orientation of medical research in Israel is both interesting and provocative. The dust levels authorized, found, and remedied, in the context of available protective and preventive measures, is informative. There is an action level TLV-TWA of 0.125 fibers/cc of workplace air, but an undesignated zero-level goal for general or non-occupational ambient conditions. An Aggressiveness Index has been used for the assessment and categorization of asbestos cement pipes used for drinking water. In respect to mesothelioma in children, this chapter presents evidence and concepts relating to childhood exposure, short latency, transplacental transfer, and prenatal tumorigenesis. Recommendations are made for screening, surveillance, followup, cessation of smoking, and health education for those previously exposed to asbestos. Special emphasis has been placed on hazard communication (warnings) for asbestos production and product use situations, asbestos substitutes, and liaison with the worldwide interdisciplinary scientific community.

This report aims at reviewing the present knowledge concerning the health hazards associated with the use of asbestos fibers in Israel, as revealed by published data of governmental and institutional surveillance and investigations.

A. THE USE OF ASBESTOS IN ISRAEL

Since 1952, the main use of asbestos in Israel, is in manufacturing and processing of asbestos-cement products (sheets and pipes).

Accepted for publication 15 March 1989.

- In the only plant "ETANIT" in Nahariya (called ISASBEST until October 1985 and since then ETANIT), employing about 400 workers.
- In processing the products of the above-mentioned plant in about 50 workplaces, spread all over Israel, employing about 200 workers.

These asbestos products consist of cement reinforced with asbestos fibers; the average ratio is 90% cement to 10% asbestos.

Chrysotile and crocidolite asbestos are used in manufacturing these asbestos-cement products.[3] Crocidolite asbestos is imported mainly from South Africa. It contains silicon oxide 51%; magnesia 2%; iron compounds 36%; various alkalis 7%; and water 4%. Chrysotile asbestos is imported mainly from Canada, Zimbabwe, and the Soviet Union. It contains silicon oxide 39–43%; magnesia 35–42%; iron compounds up to 7%; various alkalis up to 3%, water 11.7–16.5%. In 1954, the first year of full production, 944 tons of asbestos were used in manufacturing. That amount of asbestos rose to about 10,000 tons in 1976. During that period chrysotile and cape crocidolite were used in the ratio of 10:1.[5]

The other uses of asbestos in Israel are as follows:

- About 70–1000 workplaces employ about 700 workers in the friction materials, mainly in removing and fixing brakes and clutches for vehicles, in many garages in israel. Since 1987 there is no more production of friction materials in Israel (that previously employed about 100 workers).
- About 400 workers are employed in removing old insulations containing asbestos in various plants in Israel. New insulation containing asbestos has been prohibited in Israel since 1978.
- About 100 workers are employed in preparing and using textile products containing asbestos (such as threads, protective fabrics, fireproof curtains) and gaskets.

A plant manufacturing textile products and brakelinings was founded in Tel-Aviv in the early 1950s. It later moved to Dimona, employing about 90 workers. It ceased its operations in 1986, after having been transferred again to Tel-Aviv.

Since their inception, the Israel Defence Forces have used asbestos in garages for brake shoe and clutch repair, in shipyards for engine insulation, in construction and in textile clothing.[24] Chrysolite is the main fiber used in these industries.

1. Permissible Exposure to Asbestos in the Working Environment in Israel

Since January 1987 (and by legislation, since July 14th 1988) the TLV-TWA (for 8 hours/working day) for all forms of asbestos is *0.5 fibers/cc air*. In the same time the Action-Level has been fixed to be *0.125 fibers/cc air* (i.e., 1/4 of the TWA!).

The history of permissible exposure (TWA) to asbestos in Israel is as follows:

- 2–25 years ago: 12 fibers/cc air; or 300 particles per cc (by koniometer).
- 1970–1975: 5 fibers/cc air.
- 1976–1979: 2 fibers/cc air.
- 1980–1986: 1 fiber/cc air (mentioned in the legislation of January 12, 1984).
- Since 1987: 0.5 fibers/cc air (as specified above).

2. Monitoring Asbestos in the Working Environment in Israel

In 1964 the Ministry of Labour published regulations concerning medical examinations of all the workers exposed to harmful dust, including asbesto, silica, and talc.[13]

Although these regulations did not define the standards of these 3 harmful dusts acceptable as TLV-TWA, the Environmental Laboratory of the Ministry of Labour carried out many environmental measurements. In that time the koniometer was used for measuring asbestos dust in "particles per cubic centimeter" (p/cc).

The TLV-TWA established at that time by the Environmental Laboratory was:

1. 300 p/cc for pure asbestos dust.
2. 1,200 p/cc for asbestos-cement dust and asbestos-resin dust.

Tables 15-1 and 15-2 present the average results of the monitoring carried out in the only two plants with exposure to asbestos dust in Israel in the years 1965–1970.[13]

Only since January 1984 (according to the legislation) has there been an obligation of periodic environmental monitoring of asbestos in the workplace at least once every three months by a laboratory examiner from one of the four authorized laboratories.

Nevertheless, environmental monitoring of asbestos, mainly in the ETANIT (ISASBEST) plant in Nahariya, has been carried out by the Laboratory of Occupational Hygiene of the Ministry of Labour and Social Affairs since 1975. The results showed a high exposure to asbestos until 1978 and were reflected in the medical findings. Since 1979, after having improved the environmental conditions of the above-mentioned ETANIT plant in Nahariya, most of the results of the environmental monitoring of asbestos in this plant have been below the permissible exposure level—a fact that gives us hope of not finding further asbestos-related diseases among the workers hired to work there since 1979.

Table 15-1 Asbestos-Cement Plant ISASBEST Nahariya

	Particles per cc	
	Found	Authorized Level
Opening and separating asbestos bags	1100–4000	300
Mixing asbestos and cement in mixers	1300–3000	1200
Production of asbestos-cement sheets	850–2000	1200
Sawing and turning asbestos-cement products (sheets, pipes, etc.)	1500–7000	1200
Polishing asbestos-cement products without suction	8500–10,000	1200
Crushing asbestos-cement products and filling bags	3100–8000	1200

There are four qualified laboratories for the dust assessment in the working and ambient environment:

1. The Laboratory for Occupational Hygiene of the Ministry of Labour.
2. Research Institute for Environmental Health, Ministry of Health, Tel-Aviv University.
3. The Institute for Occupational Health-Industrial Hygiene Unit, Tel-Aviv University, Sackler Faculty of Medicine.
4. The ETANIT Plant Laboratory of the Nahariya Asbestos-Cement Plant.

The creation of the ETANIT Plant Laboratory constitutes a significant achievement in the country's endeavors for the

Table 15-2 Production of Brakes and Clutches from Asbestos Resines Brake Band Tel-Aviv

	Particles per cc	
	Found	Authorized Level
Opening asbestos bags	2200–5650	300
Textile work of asbestos	500–6000	300
Mixing asbestos textile and resines and pressing	900–2000	1200
Polishing asbestos-resins products	7000–10,000	1200
Drilling in asbestos-resins products	3300	1200

implementation of the health protection programs for exposed workers. It is a stimulating example for other plants and industrial branches of Israel's economy, particularly for the chemical and metal industries.

In collaboration with and under the guidance of the Ministry of Labour, the ETANIT Plant had established a control system for dust concentration in the air at various work stations in the plant. The Ministry of Labour had authorized and required the ETANIT Plant Laboratory to inspect and carry out dust measurements in other factories where harmful dust may occur in the working and ambient environments. About 70–100 work stations established by the Ministry of Labour in other factories are under the supervision of the ETANIT Plant Laboratory. The Laboratory was until 1987 under the supervision of the Institute of Applied Fibrous Dust Research, Neuss, Germany, which supervised the reliability of the tests, trained testers, recommended equipment and methods and performed environmental tests around the Nahariya asbestos-cement plant. Since 1988, the supervision of the ETANIT Laboratory is carried out by the National Institute of Occupational Safety and Health, Cincinnati, Ohio, USA, the Asbestos International Association, London, England, and the Laboratory of the Ministry of Labour and Social Affairs, Tel-Aviv, Israel.

The full cooperation and strong support of concerned governmental institutions, physicians, workers, and management led to positive achievements in controlling the dust concentrations in the working environment of the ETANIT Plant.

The data in Table 15-3 displays the dust levels in 122 work stations (682 samples) as reported in 1984 in the Nahariya Plant.[23] Table 15-4 gives a summary of dust levels from 1977 to 1984. The frequency of measurements followed the recommendations of the new safety regulations for asbestos (Israel Governemnet Safety at Work Regulations, 1984).

3. Asbestos in the Ambient Environment

The wealth of environmental and epidemiological studies carried out in industrialized countries from the 1950s to the 1970s roused the concern that asbestos fibers may reach the general population by many different environmental pathways and may have biological effects on people not occupationally-exposed.[27, 20, 26, 21, 16A]

Episodic exposure to asbestos fibers in Israel reflected to a great extent the patterns reported in community surveys carried out in other industrialized countries:

Table 15-3 Summary of Dust Levels (1984) in 122 Work Stations (682 Samples)

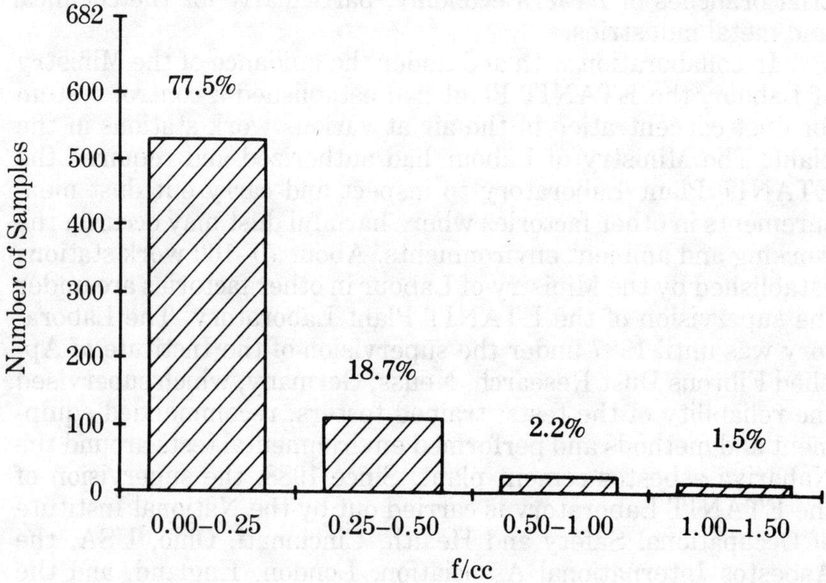

- Workers carrying out their jobs in the vicinity of asbestos contaminated workplaces.
- Neighborhood exposure occurring in the vicinity of asbestos factories, garages or construction sites where operations including asbestos exposure are carried out.
- Cutting asbestos boards in home repairs.
- Domestic exposure to asbestos contaminated clothing of asbestos workers.

Table 15-4 Summary of Dust Levels (1977-1984) in 122 Work Stations (682 Samples)

Year	No. of Stations Tested	No. of Tests	Yearly Average*
1977	45	106	1.29
1978	55	354	1.16
1979	134	276	0.44
1980	134	236	0.285
1981	115	798	0.23
1982	115	748	0.17
1983	121	905	0.21
1984	122	682	0.14

* Yearly average includes all ranges (f/ml).

- Re-use of bags, in which asbestos was packed, for packing agricultural products.
- Disposal of asbestos waste in unprotected sites.
- Occurrence of asbestos fibers in drinking water leaking out from asbestos-cement pipes.
- Practice of temporary second jobs in the construction industry.

Recognition of these harmful circumstances led to the elaboration of regulations that encompass a broad spectrum of preventive and protective measures aimed at controlling the risk of inhalation and ingestion of asbestos fibers by workers and the general public.

A governmental body was formed in 1983 to investigate these problems and recommend suitable measures: The National Medical Committee. It includes representatives from governmental and nongovernmental agencies.

A subsidiary of this body is The Israeli Technical Committee for Asbestos, dealing with the technical aspects associated with health hazards related to asbestos and other harmful dusts.[2] Its members include representatives of industry and delegates from the Ministries of Health and Labour, workers, and industry. Its main task is to advise the National Medical Committee with regard to policy recommendations for the use of the following substances: asbestos (amosite, chrysotile, crocidolite, anthopylite, tremolite, actinolite), talc, and crystalline silicon dioxide (quartz, cristobalite, tridynite).

The activities of the Technical Committee are not intended to replace any of the regular operations of other governmental agencies. In the first 4 years since its creation, it elaborated a number of requirements for occupational permissible levels and proper use of asbestos, talc, and crystalline silicon dioxide, which were included in the Joint Regulations of the Ministries of Health and Labour. It established the emission standard for asbestos and the new occupational standard of 0.5 f/cc. It also elaborated regulations concerning the methods of waste disposal, filtration, and the frequency of environmental inspections.

Due to the carcinogenic properties of asbestos, no standard was chosen for permissible concentration outside the boundaries of a plant because it should be practically 0 fibers/cc[3].

Whenever a problem concerning public health was suspected, its source was traced.

Measurements of asbestos concentrations in the general environment were performed using electron microscopy analysis (RTM-2). The analyses were carried out with the assistance of the Institute for Applied Fibrous Dust Research, Neuss, Germany. Several measurements of asbestos fiber concentration in the air were performed at different locations in Nahariya at various distances from the major asbestos-cement processing plant. So far the results do not indicate the presence of harmful concentrations; more analyses are needed before any definite conclusion can be reached. A comprehensive sampling program in rural and urban areas of the country is planned.

4. Asbestos-Cement Fibers in Drinking Water

After reviewing the available literature concerning this subject, the Israeli Technical Committee of the National Medical Committee, decided to use the Aggressiveness Index (A.I. = pH + log10 [Alk.] × [Ca^{++}]) as the criterion for the quality of the water source regarding asbestos-cement pipes. A study of the Ministry of Health–Department of Public Health on 740 sourcs revealed that 720 sources were "suitable waters"; 16 sources were classified as "should be under surveillance"; 4 sources were classified as aggressive (A.I. ≦ 10).

These findings led to the assessment that there is currently no evidence of human disease hazard in using asbesto-cement pipes for drinking water, provided that necessary precautions are taken in dealing with connecting pipes and dead points and provided that water velocity is kept below 6 m/s.

B. OCCUPATIONAL HYGIENE MEASURES

These measures have been specified very clearly in the new Safety at Work Regulations—Occupational Health and Hygiene of the Public and Workers in Asbestos, Talc and Crystalline Silica, 1984 (published January 12, 1984, and amended July 14, 1988, by the Ministry of Labour and Social Affairs and the Ministry of Health). We present the text of "Regulations Concerning Occupational Hygiene and Health of the Public and the Workers in Asbestos, Talc and Crystalline Silica—1984." Regulations 14–22 refer to the medical examination and the procedure to be followed according to the results of that examination.

The periodic medical examinations have revealed, so far, 60 cases of asbestos-related diseases, as reported to the Ministry of Labour and Social Affairs:

- 37 cases of asbestosis (including pleural plaques)
- 8 cases of lung cancer
- 15 cases of mesothelioma.

C. BIOLOGICAL EFFECTS ENGENDERED BY MAN'S EXPOSURE TO ASBESTOS

1. Asbestos Bodies

Respirable fibrous dust particles have been found to be ubiquitous in our environment. The presence of ferruginous bodies in the lungs of city dwellers suggest that at some time in their life, these people have been exposed either to asbestos dust or to similar fibrous dust particles. There is therefore a need for further investigation of ferruginous bodies in order to establish their characteristics.

New techniques developed by the Environmental Sciences Laboratory of the Mount Sinai School of Medicine enabled its investigators to report that in the New York City cases from the "general population" chrysotile fibers were found in the lung tissues of 76 (about 60%) of 126 cases.[7]

Asbestos bodies were found in 26 of 100 consecutive adult autopsies in Jerusalem.[18] The segmented golden-yellow bodies with their club-shaped ends were identified with the low power of the microscope (16 mm objective) and their properties confirmed by high power examination (4 mm objective). Only typical and complete asbestos bodies were counted. Pseudoasbestos bodies, easily recognized by their prominent central core of anthroacotic material, were ignored.

Asbestos bodies were present in 16 (29.1%) of the 55 males and in 10 (22.2%) of the 45 females. In both sexes asbestos bodies were found more frequently in the older age group. The maximum prevalence (34.5%) was in males more than 60 years of age (Table 15-5). The youngest patient in whom asbestos bodies were found was a man aged 38 years. Asbestos bodies, when present, were usually few in number (Table 15-6). In only two cases, both male,

Table 15-5 Prevalence of Asbestos Bodies in Basal Lung Smears

Age Group (Years)	Males		Females		Males and Females	
	Total	Positive	Total	Positive	Total	Positive
20 to 39	7	1			7	1
40 to 59	19	5	14	2	33	7
60+	29	10	31	8	60	18
TOTAL	55	16	45	10	100	26

Table 15-6 The Number of Asbestos Bodies per 300 Low Power Fields

No. of Asbestos Bodies per 300 lpf	Males	Females	Total
1 to 9	13	8	21
10 to 30	1	2	3
> 30	2	0	2
TOTAL	16	10	26

were more than 30 asbestos bodies found in 300 lpf, and in one of these cases histological sections revealed pulmonary fibrosis due to asbestosis.

Asbestos bodies were more frequently encountered in Ashkenazi than in non-Ashkenazi Jews. The authors of this survey support the prediction of Thomson and his associates[25] that increasing urban air contamination due to asbestos may prove to be accompanied by an increase in the frequency of pleural and peritoneal mesotheliomas.

In the period 1965–1970 periodic medical examinations were performed on 500 workers exposed to asbestos dust (mainly in the ISASBEST plant in Nahariya, Israel).

Of the 500 workers, 84 were repeatedly able to produce sputum specimens. In 21 of those cases (25%) asbestos bodies were found.

Exposure to asbestos dust in the asbstos-cement plant was discontinued in three cases with initial signs of asbestosis. Their followup for a period of 4 years after cessation of exposure revealed that asbestos bodies did not disappear completely from the sputum, although their number diminished considerably. No asbestos bodies were found in the sputum of people who had not been exposed to asbestos.[4]

2. Asbestos-Related Occupational Pathology

A study on the dynamics of work force and its health status in the ISASBEST asbestos-cement plant in Nahariya envisaged the period 1953–1970 and revealed the following data[3]:

In the 1953, the year of the establishment of the plant, there were about 1200 workers in ISASBEST, while in 1967 only 600 persons were employed. From 1953 until 1970, 3,240 workers had been employed in the asbestos-cement plant; 51% of them worked less than 1 year, and 67% of them worked 10 years or more. The decrease in the number of workers employed was due to technical and mechanical improvements in the manufacturing process. At the same time there was an increase in the use of asbestos in the plant, from 944 tons in 1953 to 7,207 tons in 1969.

Environmental monitoring had been carried out by the Ministry of Labour, with koniometers, and the standard was fixed at:

- 300 particles/cc for pure asbestos (all forms).
- 1,200 particles/cc for asbestos cement-dust.

The results showed a very high concentration of asbestos and asbestos-cement particles in most of the workplaces.

Since 1960, annual medical examinations have been carried out on some of the workers by the Department of Occupational Health of Kupat Holim, even before the promulgation of the legislation in 1964. The medical examination included: physical examination, x-ray of the lungs, ventilation test, sputum for asbestos bodies. The results showed:

- Until 1967, 3 cases of asbestosis were found, and these workers were removed from environments involving exposure to asbestos in their work.
- Only one case of mesothelioma was found in the Nahariya-Haifa region, without direct connection to asbestos work.
- The incidence of asbestos mortality in the plant until 1967, including the number of deaths of malignancies, was almost equal to its incidence in the general population in the same area for that time period.

A further study[5] on the working conditions and the health status of the workers in the ISASBEST plant in Nahariya during the period 1960–1978 reported the following data:

In 1954, the first full year of production, 944 tons of asbestos went into manufacturing, while in 1976 (at its peak) 10,000 tons of asbestos were used.

Since 1953, 3,608 workers had been employed at the ISASBEST plant; 750 were employed currently. In the peak period of employment, in 1967, there were 1,200 workers, but this number dropped to 600 due to the economic recession and improved technology. Of the entire workforce, 54.8% had been employed less than one year; 33% of the workers in 1977 had been employed 16 years, and 13% of that group had been with ISASBEST for 21–25 years.

Environmental monitoring in that plant began in 1960 (see Tables 15-7 and 15-8). It was carried out by the Laboratory of the Ministry of Labour and Social Affairs, with an impinger and later a koniometer. The early dust count indicated high pollution levels in the storage and handling stages of asbestos.

In 1972 the asbestos fiber count was introduced, and in 1979,

Table 15-7 Environmental Data in Stores

Year	Method	Hygiene Standard	Storage	Opening Bags	Filling Bags (Crocidolite)	Weighing Bags (Crocidolite)
1961	Impinger	175 particles (1–7 u/cc)	310		4300	1160
1962	Impinger	175 particles (1–7 u/cc)			1300	
1963	Impinger	175 particles (1–7 u/cc)		1200	4800	2100
1968	Koniometerey	300 particles (1–10 u/cc)	2	3600	Stations closed	
1969	Koniometerey	300 particles (1–10 u/cc)	200	1000	Stations closed	
1972	Fiber count	2 fibers/cc	6.5	3.0	Stations closed	
1975	Fiber count	2 fibers/cc	7	14	Stations closed	
			1	7.1	Stations closed	
1976	Fiber count	2 fibers/cc		3	Stations closed	
				4.5	Stations closed	
1977	Fiber count	2 fibers/cc	0.1	2.75	Stations closed	
				8.3		
1978	Fiber count	2 fibers/cc	1.8	1.9	Stations closed	
			0.95	1.5	Stations closed	

Table 15-8 Environmental Data at Processing and Molding

Year	Method	Hygiene Standard	Disc Saw	Voith Lathe	Polish and Grinding	Wet Molding
1961	Impinger	250 particles Mixed dust	1210	1078	840	
1962	Impinger	680 Mixed dust	370			
1963	Impinger	250 particles Mixed dust		960	1125	
1965	Koniometerey	1200 particles Mixed dust 1–10 u/cc	3250	1800		
1968	Koniometerey	1200 particles Mixed dust 1–10 u/cc			1600	800
1969	Koniometerey	1200 particles Mixed dust 1–10 u/cc	2250		1600	200
1972	Koniometerey	1200 particles Mixed dust 1–10 u/cc		50	125	60
1972	Fiber count	2 fibers per cc/	0.25	1.5	2.2	0.3
1975	Fiber count	2 fibers per cc	7	10–4.2	40	
1977	Fiber count	2 fibers per cc		4.0–0.32	1.5–0.36	1.11
1978	Fiber count	2 fibers per cc	0.4–1.8	1.9–1.85	1.6–2.1	0.5

70 work stations were monitored periodically using Casella Personnel Samples.

That study[5] reported 53 mortalities, divided into eleven groups according to the main cause of death: 6 groups belonged to the cateogry of malignant disease, and 5 groups included respiratory diseases—particularly chronic obstructive lung disease, diseases of the heart, blood vessels, cirrhosis, CNS disease, and 2 groups (3 cases) included diseases of unknown etiology (Tables 15-9–15-11).

The overall mortality rate due to malignant disease in the ISASBEST plant was 30%, while it was only 16.1% for the male population in Israel. Among the cancer cases in ISASBEST, there were 2 cases of bronchial carcinoma, one case of carcinoma of larynx, and one case of mesothelioma.

The figures of cancer of the respiratory system were low, only one single case of mesothelioma and the few cases of gastrointestinal neoplasms could not be statistically evaluated, yet there was a trend in the reduction of the mortality rate due to malignant diseases from 41% (in 1960–1966) to 30% in (1960–1978), owing to the important technological changes and the reduction of dust pollution at work sites.

3. Mesothelioma

The epidemiology of mesothelioma in the general population of Israel was studied for the period 1960–1982.[8,9] One hundred and fifteen mesothelioma cases were revealed during that period at the Israel Cancer Registry. In 18 cases the histologic diagnosis was not considered to be definite. The characteristics of the remaining 97 cases are presented in Tables 15-12–15-14.

Their distribution according to age at diagnosis and sex is presented in Table 15-12. There were 54 males (55.7%) and 43 females (44.3%). The highest frequency of cases (37.1%) was observed in the age group 45–59 years.

The highest frequency of mesothelioma according to the site of the tumor was found at the pleura level (55.8%) followed by peritoneal mesothelioma (41.9%) (Table 15-13).

Information on occupation and exposure to asbestos was obtained for only 64 cases (66.0%). In 6 cases there was a definite history of occupational exposure to asbestos fibers, 10 cases were occupied in trades where exposure to asbestos is highly probable, and 48 cases had occupations where asbestos exposure is not a common feature (Table 15-14).

These findings indicate that in addition to occupational ex-

Table 15-9 Main Causes of Death According to Age

Age at Death	All Causes	Malignant Diseases: Lung and Bronchi	Larynx	Stomach Colon	Mesothe-lioma	Leu-kemia	Other Neopl.	C.O.L.D. and Other Respiratory Diseases	C.V.D. C.V.A. P.V.D.	Other Causes	Acci-dents	Causes Unknown
17	1									1		
25–17	2										2	
31–35	4									2	2	
38–40	3				1	1			1			
41–45	9			2			1		2		4	
47–50	5	1					2			1	1	
51–55	7	1	1	1					4			
56–60	7			1				1	3	1		1
61–65	10						3		3	2		2
67–70	4								3	1		
83	1			1								
TOTAL	53	2	1	5	1	1	6	1	16	8	9	3

Table 15-10 Main Causes of Death According to Time of Exposure

Years of Exposure	All Causes	Malignant Diseases: Lung and Bronchi	Larynx	Stomach Colon	Mesothelioma	Leukemia	Other Neopl.	C.O.L.D. and Other Respiratory Diseases	C.V.D. C.V.A. P.V.D.	Other Causes	Accidents	Causes Unknown
Up to 1	2				1						1	
2	1									1		
4	2									1	1	
5	1										1	
6	5			1					1	1	2	
7	4						1				2	1
9	2						1				1	
10	3	1		1				1				
11	4			1					2	1		
12	3			1		1				1		
13	2									1		1
14	5	1							4			
15	2						1		1			
16	2								2			
17												
18	5		1				1		3			
19	3						1		1	1		
20	4								2		1	1
22	1			1								
23	2						1			1		
TOTAL	53	2	1	5	1	1	6	1	16	8	9	3

Table 15-11 Causes of Death—Chronologic Distribution

Year of Death	All Causes	Malignant Diseases: Lung and Bronchi	Larynx	Stomach Colon	Mesothe- lioma	Leu- kemia	Other Neopl.	C.O.L.D. and Other Respiratory Diseases	C.V.D. C.V.A. P.V.D.	Other Causes	Acci- dents	Causes Unknown
1960	1								1			
1961	1				1							
1962	2										1	1
1964	4			1			1		1		1	
1965	5			1						3	1	
1966	4	1		1		1						1
1967	5	1							1	1	2	
1968	1								1			
1969	2								2			
1970	2								2			
1971	10		1	1			3	1	2		2	
1972	1								1			
1973	3						1		1			1
1975	2			1						1		
1976	4						1		1	2		
1977	5								3		2	
1978	1									1		
TOTAL	53	2	1	5	1	1	6	1	16	8	9	3

Table 15-12 Mesothelioma in the General Population of Israel, 1960–1982: Percentage Distribution According to Age at Diagnosis and Sex

	Males		Females		Total	
Age Group	(No)	(%)	(No)	(%)	(No)	(%)
0–14	2	3.7	2	4.7	4	4.1
15–29	3	5.6	4	9.3	7	7.2
30–44	7	12.9	5	11.6	12	12.4
45–59	20	37.0	16	37.2	36	37.1
60–74	19	35.2	15	34.9	34	35.1
75–89	3	5.6	1	2.3	4	4.1
TOTAL	54	100.0	43	100.0	97	100.0

posure to asbestos, other factors, such as environmental exposure and household contacts may contribute to the incidence of mesothelioma in Israel.

Twenty-six cases of mesothelioma in children have been reported in the medical literature from 1964 to 1975. In the Israel Cancer Registry between 1960 and 1974, 4 cases were reported of mesothelioma in children.

The common denominator of these tumors was the high degree of malignancy. The majority of the patients died within a year of the onset of symptoms.

In adults it is clear that the majority of cases of mesothelioma occur in association with asbestos exposure. The case of a 3-year-old Pennsylvania girl, reported by Lieben and Pistawka (1967), the daughter of a ceramic engineer who worked in an insulation plant that used Canadian chrysotile and South African amosite, as well as other cases of mesothelioma in children included in large numbers of mesotheliomas in persons with known occupational

Table 15-13 Mesothelioma in the General Population of Israel, 1960–1982: Percentage Distribution According to Site of Tumor and Sex

	Males		Females		Total	
Site	(No)	(%)	(No)	(%)	(No)	(%)
Pleura	30	55.6	24	55.8	54	55.7
Peritoneum	24	44.4	18	41.9	42	43.3
Pericardium	—	—	1	2.3	1	1.0
TOTAL	54	100.0	43	100.0	97	100.0

Table 15-14 Mesothelioma in the General Population of Israel, 1960–1982: Percentage Distribution According to Asbestos Exposure History and Occupation

Asbestos Exposure	Occupation	Number	Percentage
Definite exposure	Asbestos-cement factory worker	6	6.2
Possible exposure	Building worker Electrician Metal worker Motor mechanic Welder, etc.	10	10.3
Probably no exposure	Accountant Dentist Housewife Musician Office clerk Rabbi Student, etc.	48	49.5
No information available		33	34.0
TOTAL		97	100.0

(Ratzer et al., 1967) or environmental (Barish, 1975) exposure to asbestos dust, raise the possibility of a relationship between exposure to asbestos fibers and mesothelioma in children (see Table 15-15).

The most conspicuous difference between the characteristics of mesothelioma in children and in adults is the duration of the latent period of this tumor (up to 14 years in children and from 20 to 55 years in adults). A number of mesotheliomas in adults in whom the exposure to asbestos fibers could be traced precisely to the early months of infancy or to the first years of childhood also had a latent period of 21 to 55 years (Table 15-16).

Apparently, asbestos exposure in these children took place in foetal life, as suggested by the relatively short latent period of mesothelioma in children, an experimental study showing the presence of asbestos fibers in foetuses after intravenous injection of asbestos dust into dams (Pontefract and Cunningham, 1973), and the cases of mesothelioma in adults in whom exposure to asbestos was traced to early childhood and infancy and in whom, nevertheless, the latent period of the tumor was similar to that occurring after occupational exposure to asbestos dust. (See the Appendix, "Literature Review," at the end of this chapter.)

Table 15-15 Mesothelioma in Children

Reference	Age (years)	Sex	Localization	Macroscopy	Microscopy
Kauffman & Stout (1964)	5	F	Peritoneal	Multiple	Papillary
	9	F	Pleural	Solitary	Fibrous
	12	M	Pleural	Solitary	Fibrous
	12	F	Pleural	Solitary	Fibrous
	14	M	Pleural	Diffuse	Fibrous
Hofmokl[a]	7	M	Pleural	Solitary	Mixed
Von Hibbler[a]	5	M	Pleural	Diffuse	Mixed
Jacobi & Balker[a]	6	M	Pleural	Solitary	Fibrous
Reals et al.[a]	2	M	Pleural	Diffuse mass	Fibrous
Bogardus et al.[a]	3	F	Pleural	Diffuse	Mixed
Reddy & Showramma[a]	12	F	Pleural	Diffuse	Mixed
Strutovskaia & Iudin[a]			Pericardial		
Turpin et al.[a]	2	F	Peritoneal	Multiple	Papillary
Lieben & Pistawka (1967)	3	F	Peritoneal		
Ratzer et al. (1967)	13		Pleural		Fibrous
	14	F	Pleural		Fibrous

McDonald et al. (1970)	<10	F	Peritoneal		
	>10	F	Pleural		
	>10	F	Pleural		
	>10	M	Pleural		Undifferentiated
Grundy & Miller (1972)	4	M	Pleural		Undifferentiated
	9	M	Pleural		Mixed
	11	M	Pleural		Undifferentiated-cystic
	12	M	Peritoneal		Mixed
	14	M	Pleural		Fibrous
Barish (1975)	12	F			
This study	1[b]	F	Pleural	Diffuse	Mixed
	3[b]	M	Peritoneal		Mixed
	11[b]	M	Peritoneal		Mixed
	12	F	Peritoneal		Mixed

[a] Cited in Kauffman & Stout (1964)
[b] Published previously (Lemesch et al., 1976)

Table 15-16 Exposure to Asbestos Dust During Childhood in Cases of Mesothelioma in Adults

Reference	Sex	Time of Exposure	Kind of Exposure	Age
Wagner (1965)		From 6 months until weaned	Environmental	21[a]
	F	From birth to the age of 5	Environmental	55[a]
Glage (1970)	F	From the age of 3 to 7	Parents occupationally exposed	47[a]
Smither (1974)	M	As a small boy	Environmental	40[a]
Anderson et al. (1976)	F	Early childhood	Father occupationally exposed	52[b]
Arul & Holt (1977)	F	From the age of 5 to 7	Environmental	43[a]

[a] At time of diagnosis
[b] At time of death

The initiation of tumorigenesis in the prenatal period of life may explain the rapid development of the tumoral process (due to lack of antagonism—e.g., immunological—generally encountered during youth and adult life).

As for the actual mechanism of penetration of asbestos fibers, experimental studies and observations in man suggest a direct migration in tissues and organs after inhalation, ingestion, or cutaneous exposure.

4. Studies on the Health Conditions of Ex-Asbestos Workers

The attempt to identify the health problems associated with the use of asbestos in Israel was difficult in view of the circumstances in which the industrialization process was taking place in the country[1]:

- A large number of workers with past exposure to asbestos and other pathogenic dusts were unaware of the potential harmful effects of those working conditions.
- Many small asbestos-consumer enterprises were not included in the routine labor and safety inspections.
- Lack of information among the general public and of the management and governmental authorities concerning the location of asbestos-waste disposal sites and correlated health risks.

- Excessive use of cigarettes among the Israeli public and working population.
- Insufficient data concerning the extent of industrial related lung diseases in Israel.

In 1984 a pilot screening program was conducted by the Israeli Ministry of Health-Acco Public Health Chest Clinic among former workers of the Nahariya asbestos-cement plant.[26] A total of 184 subjects were evaluated using medical and occupational questionnaires, clinical examinations, and pulmonary function tests (forced expiratory volume, forced vital capacity).

A total of 166 men and 18 women were evaluated in the screening program. Table 15-17 presents the data on 147 male production workers. All office workers of both sexes were excluded from the analysis as they were few in number and less exposed to asbestos dust. Individuals were grouped according to duration of employment (<1 year, 1–9 years, >10 years).

Of the production workers examined, 50.4% were current cigarette smokers; the lowest percentage of current smokers was observed in those individuals with 10 years of work exposure. The highest prevalence of breathlessness (able to walk normally on level ground but exhibiting breathlessness when walking quickly or climbing hills) was found in subjects exposed for 1–9 years ($p < 0.5$). Daily non-productive cough was less frequent in subjects exposed over the long term (>10 years); in this group rales (end-inspiratory crackles) were more prevalent ($p = 0.48$).

The results of the pulmonary function tests (FVC and FEV_1) and the percentage of predicted values (age and height adjusted) are presented in Table 15-18.

Significant decreases in both FVC and FEV_1 were observed in individuals with 10 or more years of work exposure to asbestos dust compared to groups with less exposure.

The authors of that study considered that with the findings reported by other investigators (Siracusa et al., 1984; Weil et al., 1975), the occurrence of rales and pulmonary function abnormalities may be the earliest demonstrable changes in the development of asbestosis. Accordingly, the findings of the Acco study may reflect a high prevalence of symptomatic asbestosis among long-term asbestos-exposed workers.

The Acco study also investigated the cancer deaths recorded in the period 1978–1984 among 2,800 ex-asbestos workers of the asbestos-cement plant of Nahariya. As summarized in Table 15-19, the study identified 8 cases of mesothelioma, 14 cases of lung cancer, 3 cases of colon/rectum cancer, and 1 case of oral cavity cancer.

The high level of asbestos-related cancer deaths and the morbidity patterns observed in the ex-asbestos workers of the Nahariya asbestos plant, the long and heavy exposure history of a sizeable portion of the workforce,[5] the long latency period of asbestos-induced diseases, as reported by Selikoff et al. (1980)[22] are all factors that led the Acco team of investigators to conclude that an increased morbidity and mortality may be expected in the years ahead among the ex-asbestos workers of the Nahariya plant.

These findings and the previous working conditions in asbestos occupational exposure, indicate the need for an active followup of Israeli ex-asbestos workers. The authors recommend a screening and surveillance program with emphasis on followup, health education, and smoking cessation.

Similar recommendations were the conclusion of a survey carried out on a group of 33 individuals from a cohort of 184 former workers in an asbestos-textile brake lining factory in Bnei Brak.[19] Those 33 ex-asbestos workers were interviewed to evaluate knowledge, attitudes and practices concerning smoking and asbestos (Table 15-20). About half of the ex-workers smoked and had knowledge, attitudes, and practices concerning smoking and asexposure to the asbestos–smoking interaction. Fewer knew that these risks persist in smokers after cessation of occupational exposure to asbestos dust and that smoking cessation can reduce these risks.

Twenty-three subjects in this group also underwent physical examination (Table 15-21). They were aged 60 years or over and complained of dyspnea, cough, and chest pain. Rales, decreased breath sounds, were found only in smokers and ex-smokers, but not in non-smokers. Ronchi and clubbing—one case each— were found in smokers and ex-smokers. Substantial depressions in observed–expected ratios for FVC and FEV_1 were found in smokers and ex-smokers but not in non-smokers. The findings of that survey emphasize the importance of programs on smoking alerts, smoking cessation clinics, and medical followup of former asbestos workers.

D. PREVENTION

The recognition of the adverse health effects associated with the use of asbestos as a major public health problem led to a series of positive steps taken by governmental and social bodies in Israel.

Table 15-17 Characteristics of Former Production Workers Examined in Screening Clinic (N=147)*

Length of Employment (Years)	No. of Patients	Age (Years)	Interval Since First Exposure (Years)	Percent Current Smokers	Pack Years[a]	No. and Percent		
						Breathlessness[b]	Cough	Rales[c]
≦1	30	44.2 ± 1.7	17.0 ± 1.2	67.7	17.7 ± 2.5	7(23.3)	21(70)	6(20)
1–9	52	49.6 ± 1.8	22.7 ± 0.1	61.5	22.7 ± 3.7	6(11.5)	13(25.0)	5(9.6)
≧10	65	65.6 ±1.1	28.0 ± 0.6	33.4	22.4 ± 3.3	1(1.5)	2(3.0)	8(12.3)

* Columns 3, 4, and 6 represent mean ± standard error.
[a] Pack years = no. of packs of cigarettes per day multiplied by no. of years of smoking.
[b] $X^2 = 6.358$; $p < 0.05$ for comparison of the three groups.
[c] $p = 0.048$, based on Fletcher's exact test of comparison between group with 10+ years of experience and two other groups.

Table 15-18 Pulmonary Function in Former Production Workers Examined in Screening Clinic (N = 147)*

Length of Employment (Years)	No. of Patients	FEV_1 (Liters)	Percent Predicted	FVC (Liters)	Percent Predicted
≦1	30	3.19 ± 0.08	85.7 ± 2.2	3.98 ± 0.15	83.3 ± 3.1
1–9	52	3.09 ± 0.12	85.8 ± 3.4	3.95 ± 0.13	84.8 ± 2.8
≧10	65	2.44 ± 0.31	71.0 ± 3.2	3.25 ± 0.91	72.3 ± 4.1

* Figures in columns 2–5 represent mean ± standard error.

1. Legislation

The 1984 Safety at Work Regulations concerning occupational hygiene and health of the public and the workers in asbestos, talc, and crystalline silica represent a positive, comprehensive, and very promising step in the approach of the asbestos use problem, an approach that may lead to a broad control of that problem.

These regulations are not directed to bringing a halt to the asbestos industry or use of asbestos products. They concentrate on preventive, reasonable, and feasible measures when dealing with asbestos or articles composed of asbestos and capable of giving rise to asbestos dust.

The regulations confer a legal obligation to maintain the concentration of asbestos fibers in the working environment within the limits established by the health authorities. They indicate also the limitations of the permissible exposure to harmful dust, the prohibition of employing youth, precautionary measures during the processing of asbestos materials, protective equipment and clothing, and personal hygiene and general hygiene measures.

2. Hazard Communication

High attention is given in the regulations to the importance of hazard communication. They bring the attention of people who may have been exposed, to the fact that asbestos, talc, and crystalline silica are harmful dusts.

High emphasis is placed on warning for both places where asbestos is processed as well as places where asbestos or asbestos-containing products are marketed. In the Hebrew booklet "Asbestos and Health"[14] written by one of us (L.N.), the following pictorial warnings carrying messages of hygiene and safety character

Table 15-19 Cancer Deaths Among Ex-Asbestos Workers (ISASBEST Ltd., Nahariya, 1978–1984)*

Disease	No. of Deaths[a] (O)	Mean Length of Exposure (Years)	Mean Interval from First Exposure (Years)	Mean Age at Death (Years)	No. of Expected Deaths[b] (E)	Standardized Mortality Ratio (O/E%)
Mesothelioma	8	11	24	56	0.07	11,429
Cancer of lung	14	20	23	61	6.6	212
Cancer of oral cavity	1	13	—	65	0.4	250
Cancer of colon/rectum	3	16	—	62	2.9	103
Total cancers	41	—	—	—	33.2	124

* Significance levels: Mesothelioma, $p < 0.001$; cancer of lung, $p < 0.01$; cancer of oral cavity and colon and total cancers, $p < 0.05$.

[a] Reported and confirmed from death certificates, hospital records, and pathological reports, whenever possible.

[b] Calculated from age-specific death rates for Jewish males in Israel for the period 1976–1978. The expected number for mesothelioma is derived from Lemesch 1976.

Table 15-20 Knowledge and Practices Concerning Asbestos-Smoking Hazards in 33 Ex-Asbestos Workers*

	Yes	No	No Answer
Knowledge[a]			
Asbestos exposure and smoking together increase risk for lung cancer	16	17	—
Smoking in ex-asbestos workers is dangerous	14	19	—
Smoking cessation in ex-asbestos workers reduces health risks	11	21	—
Asbestos-related diseases are compensible	12	20	1
Asbestos dust brought home is hazard for family	7	20	5
Practices			
Changed clothes before/after work	26	7	—
Showered before work	3	25	5
Showered after work	19	11	3
Separated clothes	19	12	2

* Status: 16 smokers, 7 ex-smokers, 8 non-smokers, 2 unknown.
[a] Source of knowledge: 4 from employer, 6 from friends, 4 from newspapers, 3 from television, 16 from present study.

to people exposed (see Figs. 15-1–14). Translation of the sub-titles to the figures are:

1. The use of compressed air for cleaning is forbidden; only use adequate vacuum cleaners.
2. In excessive dust concentration, use an adequate protective mask with suitable filter.
3. Use a vacuum cleaner to remove dust from work clothing.
4. If you smoke, take up a smoke-cessation program.
5. Drilling should be done with effective suction.
6. While cutting, use a vacuum cleaner to collect dust.
7. Only transport asbestos under suitable and secure conditions.
8. Only open asbestos bags using strong suction.
9. Take off and polish brake bands and clutches only with good, effective suction.
10. Beware! Contains asbestos! Working with this material may be harmful to your health. Use adequate equipment according to instructions.
11. Remove waste from insulation immediately. Don't leave dry asbestos waste!
12. Cleaning asbestos waste from the floor should be done with a broom. Use a wet cleaning system. Don't leave dry asbestos waste.

Table 15-21 Smoking Status in Relation to Age Distribution and Symptoms in 23 Ex-Asbestos Workers

Smoking Status	No. of Patients	Age (Range)	Length of Exposure (Years)	Symptoms			
				Dyspnea	Cough	Chest Pain	Any One Symptom
Smokers	7	52–79	5–12	2/7	3/7	1/7	3/7
Ex-smokers	8	49–72	5–13	5/8	4/8	3/8	7/8
Non-smokers	7	47–73	6–10	3/7	4/7	3/7	4/7
Unknown	1	55	—	1/5	1/1	1/1	1/1

13. Everything you always wanted to know about asbestos work and legislation!

14. "Warning—Harmful Dust! Avoid creating dust!
Inhalation of harmful dust may cause severe health impairment!
Smoking aggravates health!
Workers must wash up and change their work clothing before leaving the plant!
It is forbidden to take work clothing out of the plant! —Workers must be examined periodically by a qualified medical service!"

a. Environmental Monitoring and Protection

Regulation 24 indicates the employer's obligation to carry out measurements of harmful dust in the working environment and in the ambiental environment according to the instructions of the Israeli National Medical Committee. The measurements will be carried out by an authorized laboratory for monitoring harmful dust.

Regulation 25 refers to the suction and disposal of asbestos waste. Regulation 28 prohibits the use of asbestos for tiling, road paving, chiselling, or crushing, except for crushing in a plant holding proper authorization for such an activity.

b. Health Education

Several regulations in this 1984 legislation aim at directing the attention and participation in implementing measures aimed to prevent the occurrence of adverse health effects caused by the exposure to harmful dust in the working environment.

Regulation 10 stipulates the employer's duty to instruct the workers orally and in writing about safety hygiene and health hazards connected with work with this material. *The employer should ensure that every worker understands the subject in which he was instructed.* Regulation 8c requires the employer, in cooperation with the workers representatives and the Safety Committe in the plant, to organize suitable training for all workers, regarding health impairment caused by smoking when working with the material.

At such meetings, the workers' attention will be refreshed about the measures of personal hygiene, and general hygiene and warning signs, as stipulated in regulations 8–12.

On the assumption that such safety, hygiene, and education measures are suitably implemented in big enterprises, the question of small enterprises and one-man jobs or cottage-industry still remains to be pursued through community and trade union education programs, and involvement of health manpower—public health nurses, family physicians, and the medical community at large.

Fig. 1

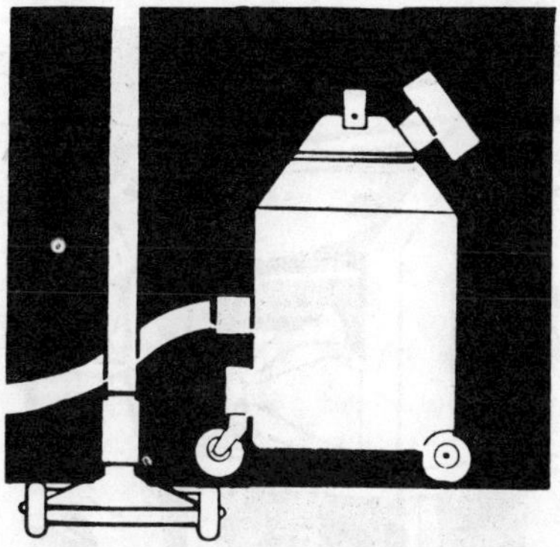

אסור לנקות בעזרת זרם אויר דחוס.
השתמש אך ורק בשואבי אבק מתאימים.

Fig. 2

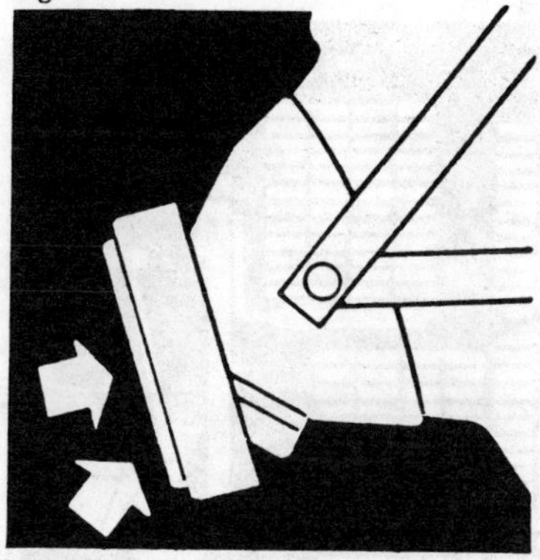

בריכוזי אבק חריגים השתמש במסכת מגן עם מסנן מתאים.

Fig. 3

בגדי עבודה אשר כוסו באבק, יש לנקות בשואב אבק קודם להסרתם.

Fig. 4

אם אתה מעשן הצטרף לקורס לגמילת עישון

Fig. 5

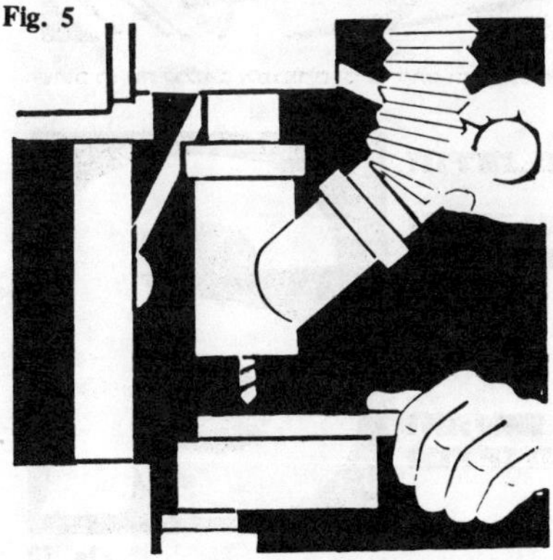

קדיחת חורים אך ורק עם מתקן תקין ליניקת האבק.

Fig. 6

בפעולות חיתוך יש להשתמש בשואבי אבק.

Fig. 7

טלטול והובלה של שקי אסבסט אך ורק בכלים מתאימים
ובאמצעים בטוחים.

Fig. 8

פתיחת שקי אסבסט והזנת החומו עם יניקה סמוך
להיוצרות האבק המזיק.

Fig. 9

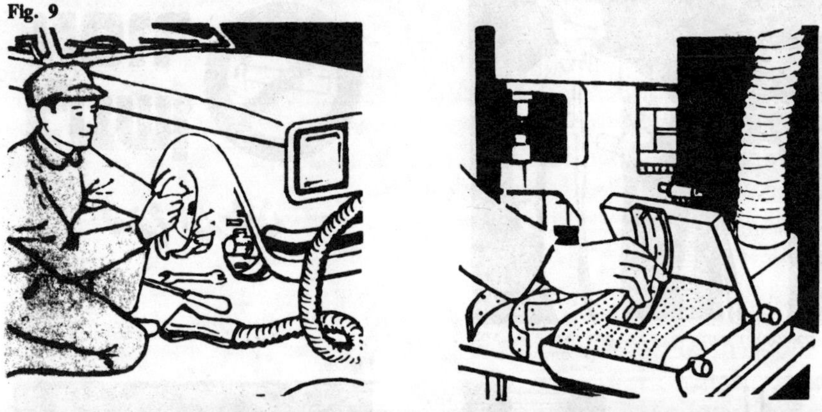

השחזת רפידות לבלמים ולמצמדים וכן פריקתם והרכבתם יש לבצע אך ורק עם יניקה טובה ויעילה.

Fig. 10

Fig. 11

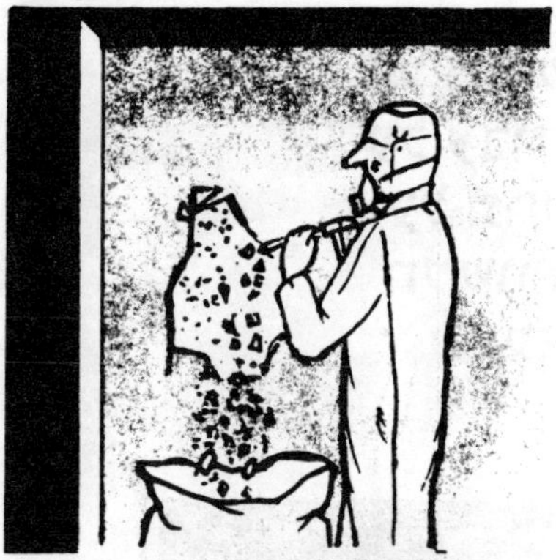

פסולת מהסרת בידוד המכיל אסבסט יש לאסוף מייד. אל תאפשר צבירת פסולת יבשה.

Fig. 12

ניקוי רצפה מסיבי אסבסט, שאריות וכו׳; אסור להשתמש במטאטא אלא במגב תוך כדי הרטבה. אל תאפשר צבירת פסולת יבשה.

3. The National Medical Committee

The 1984 Joint Regulations of the Ministries of Health and Labour concerning workers and public protection from the adverse health effects of harmful dust stipulated the formulation of a professional government-authorized body to deal with the problems contained in the Joint Regulations. The body is named the National Medical Committee.

In 1978 a committee was created under the auspices of the Ministry of Health in order to examine the health problems associated with the use of asbestos in Israel. The deliberations of that committee led to the elaboration of a report suggesting several modes of action.[1] Accordingly, the Ministry of Health, in collaboration with the Ministry of Labour, instituted in 1981 an interdisciplinary committee that included representatives of governmental agencies, the private sector, social organizations, the Histadrut and experts in clinical and environmental medicine. The deliberations of that interdisciplinary committee resulted in a document that comprised a series of regulations specifying worker health standards at the work site, follow-up examinations of workers, health education for workers with emphasis on smoking cessation, and the establishment of a permanent Pneumoconisos Panel endowed with both medical and technical input. The document was approved as law by the Knesset, the National Parliament of Israel, and was published in 1984 as: State of Israel, Safety at Work Regulations, Regulations Concerning Occupational Hygiene and Health of the Public and the Workers in Asbestos, Talc and Crystalline Silica—1984.

Fig. 13

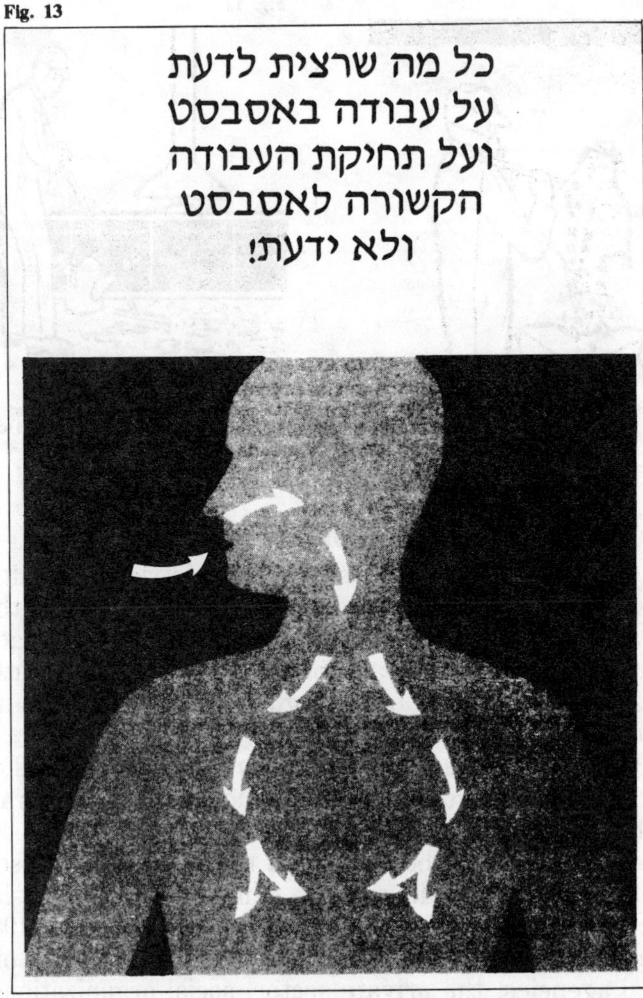

These regulations constitute a substantial and valuable step in the ensemble of activities aimed at bringing the health problems related to the use of asbestos in Israel under control. They represent a supply of new forces for activities that the Ministry of Labour and the Labour Sick Fund were already carrying out. The Ministry of Labour has been conducting regular examinations of industries using asbestos.[13] The Medical Branch of the Ministry of Labour endeavored to actively encourage periodic examinations of all workers at the industrial units of the Labour Sick Fund (Kupat Holim). The local circumstances of working conditions in a

Fig. 14

אזהרה
"זהירות — אבק מזיק!
המנע מיצירת אבק!
שאיפת אבק מזיק עלולה לגרום לנזק בריאות חמור!
עישון מחמיר את נזק הבריאות!
העובדים חייבים להתרחץ ולהחליף את בגדי העבודה לפני היציאה מהמפעל!
אסור להוציא בגדי עבודה מהמפעל!
העובדים חייבים לעבור בדיקה רפואית תקופתית אצל שירות רפואי מוסמך!".
אסור לעשן
ممنوع التدخين

country of immigrants undergoing industrialization in a framework of hard social conditions are an essential part of the explanation of the adverse health effects observed in work sites handling asbestos. Increasing the level of knowledge concerning the noxious potential of asbestos fiber, as was the situation until the 1970s all over the world, is another positive measure toward solving this problem.

4. The Pneumoconiosis Panel: Program and Achievements

Proposed activities:

- Identification of ex-asbestos workers and evaluation of their present health status, including x-ray examination and pulmonary function testing.
- Identification of small work sites processing asbestos.
- Improvement of laboratory facilities for assessment of the working and ambient environments.
- Provision of health education, especially smoking-cessation programs for workers exposed to asbestos, and ultimately, for the entire Israeli work force.
- Formation of panels of x-ray readers qualified to identify or exclude asbestos-related diseases.
- Investigation of alternative materials to be utilized in industry in order to reduce significantly the use of asbestos in the country at large.
- Identification of the sites of previous disposal of asbestos-containing waste.
- Maintenance of scientific contact with overseas institutions and researchers dealing with asbestos health risks.

Achievements:

- A panel of x-ray readers was formed.
- Provision of health education programs to asbestos and ex-asbestos workers.
- Improvement in the analytical measurements of the ambient environment.[1]

a. *The Functions of the National Medical Committee*

The National Medical Committee serves as a national expertise and information center to government offices and to public institutions regarding the work or use of harmful dust from technical, hygiene, and health points of view.

It centralizes all the information collected in the country with regard to the workers' and general publics' exposure to asbestos through occupational, domestic, or ambiental circumstances.

It recommends to the Minister of Health the nomination of Authorized Physicians and Qualified Readers.

It maintains evidence of the actual workers exposed to dust and of the ex-asbestos workers, and of data concerning their condition of health.

b. Substitutes for Asbestos

The Israeli Technical Committee for Asbestos, which serves as a subsidiary of the National Medical Committee, considered the possibility of the use of substitutes for asbestos in industry.[2]

The committee recommended banning two asbestos products that may release fibers into the air during use: drying fans containing asbestos insulation and asbestos-coated wire nets to produce uniform flames in gas burners. Alternatives to asbestos in automatic friction materials, such as brake, clutch, and transmission linings, have also been considered.

From a legal and medical point of view, this topic has generated vigorous debates on the availability and feasibility of substitutes for asbestos, since it has not been proven satisfactorily that most of the materials either meet the safety requirements in the final product and in addition they may have suspected side effects.[17]

Concern has been expressed[6] about the fact that the proposed substitutes for asbestos—the MMMF (*m*an-*m*ade *m*ineral *fi* bers)—such as glass wool and mineral wool (amorphous silica) once thought to be innocuous substitutes for asbestos, may be associated with increased risks of mortality from lung cancer, chronic pulmonary disease, roentgenografic modularity, and impairment of lung function.

In June 1987 the WHO-International Agency for Research on Cancer convened in Lyon a Working Group on the Evaluation of Carcinogenic Risks to Humans: Man-Made Mineral Fibers and Radon.[30]

In its deliberation the Working Group concluded with an Evaluation about the carcinogenity of man-made fibers:

- There is *sufficient evidence* for the carcinogenity of glass wool and of ceramic fibers in experimental animals.
- There is *limited evidence* for the carcinogenity of rock wool in experimental animals and for the carcinogenity of rock/slag wool in humans.
- There is *inadequate evidence* for the carcinogenity of glass wool and of glass filaments in humans.

Those findings emphasize once more the importance of the implementation of the legislation concerning work with harmful dusts, the promotion of hazard communication and health education both in the exposed working community as well as in the public at large.

c. Liaison with the Scientific Community Abroad

The present status of knowledge and approach to the asbestos health problems in Israel has greatly benefited from the liaison with members of the international community, who studied and dealt with this problem. Features of that liaison are:

• The Israel medical community benefits from a wealth of documentation provided by the libraries of medical schools and other institutions as well as by the individual endeavors to acquire at personal expense books and periodicals of interest.

• Participation of Israeli professionals in international conventions, visits to overseas institutions dealing with these problems, visits of foreign professionals to this country and their exchange of views with their Israeli counterparts.

Since this report deals with the history of the development of knowledge on asbestos problems in Israel it is noteworthy that Dr. Muriel L. Newhouse[15] and Mr. Jeremiah Lynch[12] were the first foreign scientists who came to Israel to discuss the medical and hygienic aspects of the asbestos problem with the medical and safety experts.

A remarkable contribution to the promotion of interest in and knowledge of the asbestos problem in Isreal was made in the last decade by the participation of Isreali professionals in symposiums abroad devoted to occupational and community risks related to asbestos exposure. Of high value were:

• The 1977 Johannesburg Asbestos Symposium organized by the South Africa Department of Mines—Medical Bureau for Occupational Diseases. [The proceedings of the Asbestos Symposium, edited by H. W. Glen, have been published by the National Institute of Metallurgy, Randburg, South Africa, 1978.]

• The 1978 New York Symposium on Health Hazards of Asbestos Exposure, organized by The New York Academy of Sciences and the Mount Sinai School of Medicine. [The proceedings of that symposium, edited by I. J. Kelikoff and E. C. Hammond, have been published by Annals of the New York Academy of Sciences, 330, 1979.]

In addition, further contributions were made by the 1985 Tel-Aviv Symposium:

• Advances in Asbestos Disease Research, organized by the Institute for Occupational Health of the Sacker Faculty of Medicine of the Tel-Aviv University, Kupat Holim Insurance Institute of the General Federation of Labour, Eretz Israel, in collaboration with the Environmental Sciences Laboratory of the Mount Sinai School of Medicine, the City University of New York, and the Department of Epidemiological Research—American Cancer Society, New York. [The Proceedings of that Symposium have been published by the American Journal of Industrial Medicine (1986, Vol. 10, 5/6.]

Scientists from the United States at that Symposium gave

two reports on the medical examination of a cohort of 1,117 asbestos insulation workers, members of the New York–New Jersey metropolitan area locals of the International Association of Heat and Frost Insulation and Asbestos Workers. One report, dealing with the clinical findings among that cohort of asbestos insulation workers, revealed that cigarette smoking had less influence on the prevalence of rales among asbestos workers; both smokers and non-smokers showed this finding when examined 30 or more years after the onset of asbestos exposure.[10]

That cohort of 1,117 asbestos insulation workers was established in 1963 and has been continously followed since then. A second report on the significance of cigarette smoking on those workers revealed that:

1. The presence of all radiographic abnormalities (pleural and pulmonary) increased with duration from onset of asbestos exposure.
2. A positive smoking history was associated with a significantly higher prevalence of small irregular opacities indicating interstitial pulmonary fibrosis. Such as association was not found for pleural fibrosis.[11]

E. CONCLUSION

The purpose of this report was to review the recorded circumstances and trends concerning the health protection of people exposed to asbestos in Israel. It encompasses the last three decades of Israel's industrial experience in which individuals, small enterprises, industrial plants, and people at large had been exposed to asbestos goods, asbestos fibers, and asbestos waste.

To a great extent this experience is similar to that portrayed by the history of occupational health and indutrialization in other countries.

A particularly optimistic feature of the asbestos issue in Israel today is the interdisciplinary approach; the endeavors to alert the working population to the problem of exposure to asbestos; the endeavor to encourage the exposed workers to play a role in their health protection and safety; the increased interest and improved resources for monitoring work and ambiental environments and the health status of exposed workers.

There is still room for promotion of further interest and suitable knowledge in the country's small enterprises, one-man outfits, and the general public. Man is the measure of all things, said Protagoras, about 2,500 years ago. In the 21st century, the followup of ex-asbestos and ex-MMMF workers, the maintenance of the health status of those exposed to asbestos or its substitutes will mirror the level of achievements in this domain of occupational health and safety in Israel.

ACKNOWLEDGMENT

The authors acknowledge the WHO-International Agency for Research on Cancer, the Annals of the New York Academy of Sciences and the American Journal of Industrial Medicine for the permission to reproduce a paper and some tables in this paper.

REFERENCES

1. Baum G.L. (1986): Public awareness of the problem of asbestos use in Israel. *Am. J. Ind. Med.*, 10:445–448.
2. Brenner S. & Anavi Z. (1986): Review of the Israeli Technical Committee for Asbestos. *Am. J. Ind. Med.*, 10:527–532.
3. Djerassi L., Iljon A. & Bar Nets (1970): Follow up of a population in an asbestos-cement plant. In: Wassermann M. & Sas H. (eds.), *Proceedings of the Second National Convention of the Israel Industrial Medical Society*, 54–58 (Hebrew).
4. Djerassi L. & Shmuelovsky L. (1972): Asbestos bodies. *The Family Physician*, Vol. 2, No. 3, 1–7 (Hebrew).
5. Djerassi L. Kaufman G. & Bar Nets (1979): Malignant disease and environmental control in an asbestos-cement plant. *Ann. NY Acad. Sci.*, 30:243–254.
6. Goldsmith J.R. (1986): Comparative epidemiology of men exposed to asbestos and man-made mineral fibers. *Am. J. Ind. Med.*, 10:543–552.
7. Langer A.M., Ashley R., Baden V., Berkeley C., Hammond E.C., Mackler A.D., Maggiore C.J., Nicholson W.J., Rohl A.N. Rubin I.B., Sastre A. & Selikoff I.J. (1973): Identification of Asbestos in Human Tissues. *J.O.M.*, Vol. 15, No. 3, p. 287.
8. Lemesch C., Steinitz R. & Wassermann M. (1976): Epidemiology of Mesothelioma in Israel. *Environ. Research*, 12:255–261.
9. Lemesch C., Katz L. & Steinitz R. (1986): Mesothelioma in Israel (1973–1982). *J. Royal Soc. Health*, 106:141–142.
10. Lerman Y., Selikoff I.J., Lilis R., Seidman H. & Gelb S.K. (1986): Clinical findings among asbestos workers in US: Influence of cigarette smoking. *Am. J. Ind. Med.*, 10:449–458.
11. Lilis R., Selikoff I.J., lerman Y., Seidman H. & Gelb S.K. (1986): Asbestosis: Interstitial pulmonary fibrosis and pleural fibrosis in a cohort of asbestos insulation workers: Influence of cigarette smoking. *Am. J. Ind. Med.*, 10:459–470.
12. Lynch J.R. (1972) Brake lining decomposition products. Seminar at the Hadassah Medical School Jerusalem—Dept. of Occupational Health.
13. Naim L. (1970): Dust problems in industrial plants in the country in

light of laboratory findings. In: Wassermann M. & Sas H. (eds.), *Proceedings of the Second National Convention of the Israel Industrial Medical Society*, 9–24 (Hebrew).
14. Naim L. (1988): Asbestos and Health. A Hebrew booklet, 28 pages, Haifa.
15. Newhouse M.C. (1970): The mortality of asbestos workers. In: Wassermann M. & Sas H. (eds.) *Proceedings Second National Convention of the Israel Industrial Medical Society*, 48–53.
16. Newhouse M. (1973): Asbestos in the work place and the community. *Am. Occup. Hyg.*, Vol. 16, 97–107.
17. Nicholson W.J. & Pundsack F.L. (1973): Asbestos in the environment. In: Bogovski P., Gilson J.C., Tumbrell V. & Wagner J.C. *Proceedings of the Conference on Biological Effects of Asbestos*, Lyon, pp. 126–130.
18. Peters G.A. & Peters B.J. (1988): *Sourcebook on Asbestos Diseases: Medical Legal and Engineering Aspects.* Vol. 3, pp. 87–88, New York.
19. Polliack A. & Sacks M.J. (1968): Prevalence of asbestos bodies in basal lung smears. *Isr. J. Med.*, Sci. 223–226.
20. Richter E.D., Tuck H., Sarel O., Shabbat Z & Weiler D. (1986): Smoking, morbidity and pulmonary function in a group of ex-asbestos workers: A pilot study. *Am. J. Ind. Med.*, 10:515–523.
21. Selikoff I.J., Churg J. & Hammond E.C. (1964): Asbestos exposure and neoplasia, *J.A.M.A.*, Vol. 188, 22–64.
22. Selikoff J., Bader R.A., Bader M.E., Churg E. & Hammond E.C. (1967): Asbestosis and neoplasia. *Am. J. Medicine*, Vol. 42, 4, 487–496.
23. Selikoff J., Hammond E.C. & Seidman H. (1980): Latency of asbestos disease among insulation workers in the United States and Canada. *Cancer*, 46:2736–2740.
24. Sharon A. (1986): Dust levels in an asbestos-cement factory: Problem solving. *Am. J. Ind. Med.*, 10:533–537.
25. Schlezinger Z. (1986): Use of asbestos in the Israel Defence Forces 10:539–541.
26. Thomson J.G., Kaschula R.O.C. & Macdonald R.R. (1963): Asbestos as a modern urban hazard. *S. Afr. Med. J.*, 37:77.
27. Tuck H., Tulchinsky T.H., Casper M. & Knaane H. (1986): Medical screening of former asbestos cement workers in Israel: a pilot program. *Am. J. Ind. Med.*, 10:471–478.
28. Wagner J.C., Sleggs C.A. & Marchand P. (1960): Diffuse pleural mesothelioma and asbestos exposure in the North Western Cape Province (1960). *Brit. J. Industr. Med.*, 17:260–271.
29. Wassermann M., Wassermann D., Steinitz R., Katz L. & Lemesch C. (1980): Mesothelioma in children. In: Wagner J.C. (ed. in chief): *Biological Effects of Mineral Fibers*, IARC 30:253–257.
30. WHO IARC (1988). Monographs on the Evaluation of Carcinogenic Risks to Humans: Man-Made Mineral Fibers and Radon. Vol 43, pp. 33–171.

APPENDIX

LITERATURE REVIEW

A literature review of mesothelioma in children is presented. The role of nonoccupational exposure to asbestos fibers in the etiology of mesothelioma, and the relatively short latent period of the disease in children are discussed. The transplacental transfer of the asbestos fibers and the physiology of the immunological system during intra-uterine life and infancy may explain some of the difference between mesothelioma in children and those in adults.

LITERATURE

Anderson, H.A., Lilis R., Daum S.M., Fishbein A.S. & Selikoff I.J. (1976). Household-contact asbestos neoplastic risk. *Ann. N.Y. Acad. Sci.*, 271:31–323.

Arul K.J. & Holt P.F. (1977). Mesothelioma possibly due to environmental exposure to asbestos in childhood. *Int. Arch. Occup. Environ. Health*, 40:141–143.

Barish Y.I. (1975). Pleural mesothelioma and asbestos pleurieies due to environmental asbestos exposure in Turkey: an analysis of 120 cases. *Hacettepe Bull. Med/Surg.*, 8:165–185.

Glage E. (1970) Malignes Pleura-Mesotheliom einer Erwachsenen nach Asbest-Exposition in Kindesalter. *Praxis Pneumologie*, 24:39–45.

Grundy G.W. & Miller R.W. (1972). Malignant mesothelioma in childhood. Report of 13 cases. *Cancer*, 30:1216–1218.

Kauffman S.L. & Stout A.P. (1964). Mesothelioma in children. *Cancer*, 17:539–544.

Lemesch C., Steinitz R. & Wassermann M. (1976). Epidemiology of mesothelioma in Israel. *Envrion. Res.*, 12:255–261.

Lieben J. & Pistawka H. (1967). Mesothelioma and asbestos exposure. *Arch. Envrion. Health*, 14:559–563.

McDonald A.D., Harper A., El Attar O.A. & McDonald J.C. (1970). Epidemiology of primary malignant mesothelial tumors in Canada. *Cancer*, 26:914–919.

Pontefract R.D. & Cunningham H.M. (1973). Penetration of asbestos through the digestive tract of rats. *Nature*, 243:352–353.

Ratzer E.R., Pool J.L. & Melamed M.R. (1967). Pleural mesotheliomas. Clinical experiences with thirty seven patients. *Am. J. Roentgenol.*, 99:863–880.

Smither W.J. (1974). Asbestos in the work place and community. *Environ. Health Prot.*, 9:327–329.

Wagner J.C. (1965). Epidemiology of diffuse mesothelial tumors: evidence of an association from studies in South Africa and the United Kingdom. *Ann. N.Y. Acad. Sci.*, 132:575–578.

16

Research on Asbestos Health Problems in the U.S.S.R.

FAVEL M. KOGAN, M.D.

Sverdlovsk Research Institute of Labor Hygiene and Occupational Diseases
Sverdlovsk, U.S.S.R.*

Synposis

* Director, S.G. Domnin, M.D.

BIOGRAPHY

Dr. Favel M. Kogan is Professor of Occupational Hygiene and the Head of the Laboratory of Hygiene of Labour in the Asbestos Industry of the Sverdlovsk Research Institute of Labour Hygiene and Occupational Diseases. He has published approximately 180 scientific publications dedicated to various problems in occupational medicine and one book about asbestos-containing dust and the prevention of its adverse health effects. He is a member of a scientific problem commission, which organizes the scientific activity in the field of Labour Medicine in the U.S.S.R. He is also a member of the Cancerogen Substances Committee, an advising organ of the Ministry of Public Health of the U.S.S.R. Doctor Kogan may be contacted at the Research Institute of Labour Hygiene and Occupational Diseases, 30, Popov Str., 620014, Sverdlovsk, Russian Republic, U.S.S.R.

EDITORS' COMMENTARY

The U.S.S.R. has been a major producer and user of asbestos for many years. Therefore, asbestos disease studies performed in that country are of special interest, particularly if those studies have a historical and corrective perspective. The lessons learned could be of valuable guidance to others. The following chapter presents evidence relating to a "no adverse health effect" level of exposure (in terms of asbestosis), in contrast with the risk-benefit and acceptable risk criteria often used in many other countries. Emphasis has been placed on what is technically achievable (technically feasible) in terms of the engineering control of harmful exposure, rather than heavy relative emphasis on cost or convenience criteria. The risk of stomach cancer is presented as a significant category of asbestos disease. The relative toxicity of chrysotile in inducing mesothelioma was determined to be equal to crocidolite. Selection of asbestos workers based on their susceptibility, sensitivity, or reaction to asbestos is described. Efforts to increase the asbestos workers' resistance to asbestos-related diseases, by use of chemicals, is an objective. The apparent exposure limits, while comparable to the levels of many countries, may not approximate the "no biological effect" level now being proposed in some countries. The medical research reported is a result of a long-term and continuing effort, which appears to have produced significant public health benefits.

A. INTRODUCTION

Although asbestos was found in Russia in the early 18th century, industrial mining and milling began in the Middle Urals only a century ago. During this period, the technology of asbestos

* Accepted for publication 4 June 1989.

production as well as the production of asbestos-containing materials, changed significantly. As a result of these changes, the output of asbestos increased; the U.S.S.R. is now the first producer of asbestos in the world and, undoubtedly, one of the main consumers.

The development of this production was not free from health consequences—chiefly the appearance of asbestos-induced diseases and their complications among the workers exposed to asbestos. The influence of asbestos-containing dust also was assessed based on the health status of the residents of adjacent cities.

In connection with this, in this country we began to conduct a vast program of scientific investigations in the field of labor conditions and their influence on the health of the workers, including the clinical features of asbestosis and its complications, and particularly oncological safety in the asbestos industry. Significant attention was given to the problem of non-occupational exposure and to the mechanisms of the biological action of asbestos. These studies were carried out by several institutes, but primarily in the Sverdlovsk Research Institute of Labour Hygiene and Occupational Diseases.

In asbestos mines, the serpentenite ore dust, containing less than 10% asbestos, contaminated the air of work sites where workers were engaged in drilling and excavation of the ore and rock and discharging the waste material into dumpcars and trucks. In the 1950s and 1960s, the level of dustiness exceeded MAC (maximum allowable concentration) only in mining of dry rock or in badly ventilated places (e.g., as in manual drilling of non-gabarit rock scraps). In the past 18 years, cases of asbestosis among the miners were detected only in those who carried out dusty manual operations for more than 15 years. In the following years, for the purpose of suppression of dust emissions, the drilling of non-gabarit scarps was mechanized, manual selection of crude asbestos eliminated, and the occupant cabins of mining machines (the operator's breathing area) were sealed and air conditioned. The mine shafts were systematically sprayed with special solutions that diminished surface friction.

Nevertheless, since the carriers were getting deeper (up to 300 m), the problem of dust and gas removal became more difficult. Numerous experiments showed that fixed powerful impellers (set motors) and mobile exhausters (self-propelled installations) were useful for local ventilation. The gas and dust problem could be reduced by the installation of neutralizers on truck exhaust tubes.

With the introduction of these and other measures, the mean concentration of the dust in the occupant cabins of mining machines decreased from 6.66 mg/m^3 in 1958 to 2.9 mg/m^3 in 1987. Taking into account the low (mean) 8% content of asbestos fibers in the dust and the relative low asbestosis morbidity, the MAC for this dust was established at the level of 4 mg/m^3.[12]

Judging by several publications[5,16], the technology of asbestos enrichment in the 1920s was very primitive; for example, sorting, drying, crushing, packing, hammering, and other work tasks were accomplished by very hard physical labor accompanied by high dust concentration. The enrichment was carried out on the basis of the old Ural method with open inclined separators. The rocks and bags filled with asbestos fibers were loaded manually on the trucks.

In the 1930s, new asbestos plants were built and their technology was based on the principle of pneumatic enrichment of asbestos fibers. The difficulty of most labor operations decreased as did the level of dustiness of the air in the working sites. (Even this lower level was too high as a result of the unsatisfactory state of the covers, ventilation, and cleaning of the dust emissions concomittent with the increase in the quantity of processed ore.) A similar situation was observed in the shops of the asbestos-textile plants.[33,50]

In the first years after World War II, wear and tear on equipment created unfavorable conditions of work, as was observed also during these years at Canadian asbestos mills.[39] In this period, the prevalence of occupational diseases increased just as the level of asbestos dust increased. In the 1950s and at the end of the 1960s, new mills were built with up-to-date equipment and with efficient systems for cleaning the dust emissions. As a result of fine cleaning in bag house filters with huge surface areas, the dust emissions were eliminated almost completely (from 16,500 t to 10 t per year) and the contamination of adjacent towns' atmospheres ceased. Almost complete mechanization and automation of the enrichment technology substantially reduced the number of persons exposed to dust. The work-site air was cleaned to 0.5 mg/m^3 after filtration and recycled to the shops; thus, the savings in one plant was 1 mln gigacalories.

The introduction of new technology and supplementary dust suppressing measures led to a significant decrease in the mean dustiness to 3–4 mg/m^3. Taking into account the average content of asbestos in the asbestos-rock dust mixture, one may assess the approximate concentration of asbestos fibers (0.3–0.5 mg/m^3). At an experimental mill, with hydro-technology for enrichment, the content of dust was lower than 1.7–1.9 mg/m^3. However, in industrial scale, the wetting enrichment method was carried out only in a small anthophyllite plant.

In addition to the asbestos mining industry, hygienic conditions and their influence on the health of the workers were studied in those who worked with asbestos textiles[23], asbestos insulation[44], friction materials,[52,14] and other branches of asbestos manufacture.

At the Ural's asbestos-textile plant, as well as in other regions, after the modernization of the technology, increased supervision of covering the equpment, and the implementation of a system of dust-suppressing control measures, the level of dustiness decreased to 1.5–4.5 mg/m^3, but remained twofold higher than the Soviet MAC in the spinning shop.

In the friction material industry, the dust factor in the preparation, mixing, and brake grinding shops was studied. The dust produced during the grinding of brakes (asbestos-rubber and asbestos-resin dust) was found to be much less fibrogenic than the chrysotile asbestos dust, despite the fact that the content of asbestos in the brakes exceeded 50%. Several foreign authors have indicated that during the use of the brakes, a continuous friction-high temperature is generated that leads to the thermal degradation of chrysotile and its transformation into forsterite (a much less harmful dust). We attempted to determine whether a degradation of asbestos within the friction material takes place due to the increase in temperature during machining, finishing, sawing, and other tasks. With the infrared spectroscopy technique, it was assessed that a maximum of 10% of the asbestos fibers were degraded. Therefore, it was not the degradation of the fibers but the almost complete covering of the fibers by resin or rubber that determines, perhaps, the lesser degree of fibrogenisity of asbestos-bakelite and asbestos-rubber dusts.

More than half of all the asbestos produced is used in the asbestos-cement industry (pipes, sheets, plates, etc.). The majority of asbestos-exposed workers are occupied in this branch of the asbestos industry. The hygienic studies carried out at many plants of this industry frequently determined that the content of asbestos was higher than the MAC (2 mg/m^3) in the preparation shops and in the finishing shops, where the concentration of asbestos-cement dust has a MAC of 6 mg/m^3.[3] Working conditions were studied in the production of synthetic and amphibole asbestos. Since there was only a pilot installation these data, of course, would not characterize the conditions at a real plant. It was observed that at the end of the industrial process (grinding and packing) there were some emissions.[47] In an experimental study, the fibrogenicity of three materials was assessed: the synthetic chrysotile asbestos, produced by a hydrothermal technique; Na Mn-hydroxyamphibole; and Mn-F-amphibole, by pyrogenic technique. Among these synthetic asbestos materials containing no metal or hydrocarbon impurities, the most fibrogenic was the synthetic chrysotile (more so even than its natural analogue). The synthetic asbestos dust produced a depressing action on the motion function of epithelium, hypersecretion of stomach, glandules, and dystrophical changes.[47]

B. ASBESTOSIS: CLINICAL AND OCCURRENCE DATA

The high levels of occupational exposure in the years preceeding World War II led to the appearance of many cases of asbestosis. Among the workers examined in asbestos mills in the late 1930s, asbestosis was diagnosed in 20% of the workers after an average of 8 years of work.[49] In various shops of an asbestos-textile plant, the number of workers presenting asbestosis reached 20 to 32%[30] and later about 43%.[50]

During this period, the most frequent complications of asbestosis were lung tuberculosis[49]. Among 470 subjects examined, 115 patients with asbestosis were detected with the TBC complication. In 1932, in the asbestos district, the tuberculosis morbidity was much higher (471/0000) than in the districts where metallurgical plants were located (165/0000) or where coal mines (144/0000) were situated. In fact, the morbidity due to tuberculosis in the "asbestos" shops of an asbestos-textile plant was about 1.6 times higher than in the "non-asbestos" shops.[29]

Beginning in 1948, at all asbestos manufacturing plants obligatory annual medical examinations were required. Among the workers of asbestos mills examined in 1947, there was 29.3% asbestosis diagnosed, including 3.4% of patients with asbestotuberculosis. The number of cases varied significantly depending on exposure, length of service, and age. Among the asbestotics, the morbidity rate from lung cancer and cancer of other sites proved to be much greater than in the standardized population of the adjacent towns.[21] At the same time, at autopsy, many cases of cancer were detected among the persons with asbestos exposure but *without* clinical and radiological signs of asbestosis at annual medical examinations. Therefore, it seems that fibrosis can be an influential co-carcinogenic factor but not the unique one[1].

The implementation of a vast program of dust-suppressing measures at the asbestos mills decreased the number of primary diagnosed cases of asbestosis from 30% in 1947 to 0.01% in 1986. In recent years, no cases of asbestosis have been diagnosed among some 9,000 examined persons.[24] At an asbestos-textile plant, the frequency of asbestosis was 0.5% of all examined. In the last few years, new cases have not occurred.

The study of the features of asbestosis and its complications began in this country in the pre-World War II period. Besides the classical symptoms of asbestosis (shortness of breath at work, dry cough and chest pains, interstitial diffuse fibrosis almost without nodules, ground glass appearance in the lower and middle lung lobes), a lowering of the mobility of the pleura with an obliteration of the costo-diaphragmal sinus was detected. Only in the second or third stage was asbestosis accompanied by an arterial hypoxemy. Nevertheless, no full correlation between hypoxemy and rates of respiratory function was observed. The decreasing VEC occurs mainly on account of minute volume (supplementary and reserve volumes). More than half of the asbestotics showed signs of myocardium distrophy, with a lowering of strike and minute volumes. Patients with asbestosis frequently developed dispeptic complaints,[30,50] albuminury and microhaematury, and a lowering of the antitoxic and anti-thrombin-creating functions of the liver. A series of changes in vegetative nervous system function was also detected: a depressed reaction of the UV erithema, a deceleration of resorption of water papule, and a distorted type of eye-heart reflex[30], which gave a minute discreption of the respiratory and circulatory function of the asbestotics. Sometimes the insufficiency of the outer respiration is found at the early stages of asbestosis. In addition, significant changes of blood circulation were detected, as well as decrease of the systolic and the minute volume of blood, a slower velocity of circulation, and a lowering of the myocardium contraction.

T. I. Andreeva, L. I. Matuzkova, and N. N. Frolova[1] carried out interesting clinico-radio-morphological comparisons in persons operated on in connection with asbesto-tuberculoma. They ascertained that the modification of the lung pattern in asbestosis is due to the involvement of small bronchi and bronchioli. It is interesting that coniotic alterations in lung tissue were present in the bioptic surgical preparates in patients in which asbestosis was not detected during numerous annual medical radiological examinations.

Studying the features of the anthophyllite asbestosis, Bunimovich[6] established, besides the signs similar to chrysotile asbestosis, a more frequently encountered noise (rubbing of pleura) and a weakened breath in more than half of those examined.

There is an upset of heart contraction (on ballistograms) and a lowered ballistographic index. These signs indicate a right ventricular insufficiency, which correlates with a decrease of systolic and minute volumes. Like chrysotile coniosis, anthophyllite asbestosis is frequently complicated by an interstitial pneumony but not by TBC or neoplasma.

Of great interest are the results of the clinical-functional investigations of people working under very low exposure (up to MAC) in asbestos-textile shops (group I) and people who have worked under comparatively low concentrations (but concentrations that are still 2- to 4-fold higher than the MAC (group II). It was established that the frequency of the respiratory complaints (cough, shortness of breath during exercise, chest pains) were observed almost twice more frequently in group II than in group I. The same relation was observed when the results of physical training were compared. The conventional parameters of the respiratory function (VEC, RVP, MVE, VEMS, Tiffneau index, SaO_2, $PaCO_2$) by the persons of group I were normal or slightly lowered; among the workers of group II, they were significantly lowered. The respiratory function was changing in a mixed manner (restrictive and obstructive), but with the prevalence of obstruction. Only in 6% of persons with length of service 10 to 19 years were found clinical signs characteristic of chronic bronchitis. Almost 45% of group I demonstrated pathological alterations of the mucosa of the upper respiratory tract (in group II it was 87%). The changes in bronchial permeability on the level of the middle and small bronchi, which are determined by the rates of the loop flux-volume ($\overline{V}50$, $\overline{V}70$), determined the development of a hypoxemy and impairment of the diffusion capacity.[42] By bronchiological investigation of persons who had been working at low concentrations, without serious complaints, there was a development of diffuse endobronchitis and tracheitis, with dystonia of the membranous wall of respiratory tracts. Therefore, groups working at low dust levels need the continuous attention of physicians.

Among the workers of the asbestos-cement industry, one detects rare cases of pneumoconiosis due to the influence of asbestos and cement dust mixtures[3]. At the same time, no cases of asbestosis were found among the workers involved in machining operations (turning, drilling, cutting, and so on). In experimental conditions, the significantly lower fibrogenicity of asbestos-cement dust was demonstrated in comparison with purer asbestos dust, but even lower fibrogenicity was demonstrated by the dust of the hydrated cement (without asbestos), which confirms the main role of asbestos fibers (in the process of fibrogenesis and the inhibitory role of fiber cover[26]).

Studying the problem of asbestosis, we are meeting some

supplementary problems. Particularly, it was ascertained that at a great number of asbestos mills, the repair and maintainance workers do not have continuous asbestos dust exposure, but intermittent short periods of intensive exposure (during the opening of engines and cleaning of premises) which are alternated with rather long periods of low exposure[22]). The total average dust exposure of the maintenance and repair workers is lower than that of the workers belonging to occupations in the main asbestos mills. The frequency of asbestosis was lower than among the workers of the main mill's occupations.

In rats inhaling asbestos dust with an intermittant regime (every other day at the dust concentrations twofold higher), the fibrogenic effect was lower than at every-day dusting at twofold lower concentrations.[7]

A. THE MECHANISM OF ASBESTOS BIOLOGICAL ACTION

In the past, Vorwald et al.,[53] Szimczikievicz and Wicek,[45] Kleosterkotter[17], and many other authors attributed the most important aspect of asbestos pathology to the length of the asbestos fiber. Meanwhile, studies carried out in this country demonstrated the fibrogenicity of many silicates with granular dusts (nepheline, olivine, and others).[31] The serpentinites—the asbestos containing ore—are also fibrogenic, although the percent of asbestos significantly influences the fibrogenesis[12].

We suppose that the high fibrogenicity of the chrysotile asbestos and of the other asbestos is due mainly to the surface properties: high specific surface, weakness of the intercrystallic bonds, determining the constitution of a great number of topochemical centers, and aging on the biosubstrate.[20] A more pronounced fibrogenicity of the long and thin fibers is determined, in our mind, by their better retention property. On the other hand, their active total surface area is greater. Obviously, the hardness of the fibers does *not* play a decisive role: carbon fibers, although harder than asbestos fibers, are less fibrogenic.[46] Velichkovsky et al.[48] studied the mechanism of phagocitosis of the fibrogenic dusts. As is known, phagocitosis is accompanied by active forms of oxygen and their derivatives: anion radicals, hydrogene peroxide, and single oxygen. The reactions with these oxidizing agents are followed by chemiluminiscence effect (CL). In contrast to other dusts, chrysotile asbestos (Tuva deposit) induced a CL reaction with a rapid achievement of the peak, rapid decrease, high amplitude, and quick decrease of the CL intensity. At the same time, dusts of weak fibrogenicity (chalk, talc, and so on) induce a weakly developing CL with small amplitude and long peak. CL developed slowly at small concentrations of dust (0.1 mg/ml), but by increasing the concentration from 0.25 to 0.5 mg/ml the CL achieved the maximum in 1 minute after the introduction of the dust. All these phenomena confirm the primordial importance of the surface features. In another series of experiments[15], the CL and the haemolytic potency of the chrysotile were studied. A suspension (0.5 mg/ml) induced the haemolysis of 35% of the erythrocytes at the Z-potential 39 mv. Therefore, the electric properties of the surface play a significant role. This role is demonstrated particularly clearly if one compares the specific surface, the Z-potential, and the fibrogenicity of 3 types of serpentinites with a different content of chrysotile. The chrysotile serpentinite (18% fibers) with larger specific surface (24 m^2/g) and Z-potential (29.6 kv), has a substantially stronger fibrogenic potential than antigorite (no fibers, specific surface 3.9 m^2/g, and Z-potential 13.6 kv). The content of the oxyproline in the lungs 9 months after the intratracheal instillation of the chrysotile serpentinite was equal to 4,129, and of antigorite −3,427 mkg (control series − 2,956 mkg). In our mind, there is the possibility of forecasting the fibrogenicity of a serpentinite-asbestos mixture (which is in almost all asbestos-containing dusts), taking into account these physical properties. At the same time we confirmed the non-inertness of serpentinite ore dust without fibers.[12]

D. ASBESTOS AND TUMOURS

During a long period (1947–1968), the mortality of lung, stomach, and uterus cancer patients among asbestos mine and mill workers was severalfold higher than among the general population of the adjacent town. In the following 15 years, the trend did not change in its basic features.[23]

The causes of this trend, in our opinion, are: the non-achievement of MAC values at several work places; the latent period of bronchogenic cancer, as well as of stomach cancer, which exceeds 20 years. (In our study, there were a number of people who worked for many years in conditions of high dustiness, but who died relatively recently.) We cannot exclude the role of the short-term episodic "splashes" of dust emissions, arising from intermittent exposure.

In many studies, the opinion is expressed that the increased mortality from mesothelioma of the pleura may be due only to amphiboles (mainly crocidolite) exposure.[8] Nevertheless, our attempt to prove this failed.

Among 50 districts of the Middle Ural region, the mortality rate from mesothelioma was the highest during a 10-year period (6-fold higher than in an average region) in the district where the chrysotile mines and mills were situated. The majority of the dead were ex-workers of these enterprsies or, what is of interest, ex-residents of the adjacent towns (near the old asbestos mills).[27]

Nevertheless, in well-accomplished inhalation experiments with animals[54], it was determined that chrysotile induced mesotheliomas in 2.9%, crocidolite in 2.8%, amosite in 0.7%. Therefore, the hypothesis about the "monopolyst" role of amphiboles is not confirmed.

At an asbestos-textile plant, the mortality rate from lung cancer for men was 3-fold and for women 3.5-fold higher than among the population of the adjacent district. The mortality rate from stomach cancer was 1.8- and 3.2-fold, respectively.[25] There was an indication of high dust levels in the 1940s and 1950s. But at an another plant of this type, where during 25 years the level of dustiness usually didn't exceed the MAC, the lung cancer mortality rate was 1.85-fold and 1.3-fold higher (for men and women, respectively) than among the general population of a big city where the above mentioned plant was situated.

At the same time, the total oncological mortality was lower than in the "control" city.[29] This fact led us to propose lowering of the MAC (2 mg/m^3) on the basis of an increased rate of lung cancer mortality. We suppose that MAC, for dust containing more than 30% fibers, must be lowered approximately to 0.5 mg/m^3 (0.15 mg of asbestos).

In the biggest asbestos-consuming industry (asbestos cement), the standardized mortality ratio (SMR) for lung and mainly stomach cancer was higher both in men and in women. At the same time SMR at these plants was lower than that for the asbestos industry.[3]

In an experiment, the intrapleural induction of asbestos mesothelioma of the pleura was 57%, with the induction of asbesto-cement dust at 40.7% and of portlant cement 2.3%. Thus, the oncogenicity of asbestos-cement dust was obviously lower than of asbestos dust[38], probably in connection with the shortness of the active surface of the asbestos due to a strong film of hydrated cement.

The majority of the epidemiological studies, in the various branches of the asbestos and asbestos-containing materials production industry, have indicated that as far as the lung cancer rate had increased, the stomach cancer mortality rate also increased. The stomach is indeed the main organ for the process of eliminating the cleared asbestos. One must confirm the action of asbestos on the mucosa of stomach by creating continuous contact conditions with the mucosa. The attempts to feed animals with asbestos-containing food failed to confirm the induction of tumours (obviously due to the relatively short time of residence in the stomach). We have used the small stomach model. In an artificially formed pocket of the rat stomach "a' démeure" polyethylene perforated capsule was implanted, into which a mixture of fat and chrysotile asbestos was placed. After two years persistence, in the glandular stomach, large numbers of benign and malignant tumours developed. In the control group (capsules filled with fat without asbestos), no tumours were detected.[28] Thus, the role of long contact of asbestos with the stomach tissue in the rise of the tumors was confirmed.

In connection with the increase of asbestos-containing materials and the development of new man-made mineral fibers (MMMF), the evaluation of their oncogenity became more expensive and difficult. In recent years, the applicability of short-term assays for these purposes was investigated for asbestos dust, various asbestos containing materials, and other fibers including MMMF. The most informative in comparison with the traditional methods are the following: micronucleus test and microbial test in host mediated system.[10]

Numerous intrapleural experiments (20 mg three times monthly)[37] studied pretumoral changes and tumours in the lungs and pleura of rats, hamsters, and monkeys. Milled commercial chrysotile induced mesotheliomas in 65.5%, its dust is 46.3%; milled synthetic chrysotile in 2.4%; antophyllite in 41.4%; and milled synthetic hydroxiamphibole in 54.5%. Intratracheal injections (10 mg twice monthly) of milled chrysotile into Syrian golden hamsters induced malignant tumours in 44.4%, synthetic chrysotile in 7.7%, magnesia-arphvedsonite (5 mg twice monthly) in 46.2%, and synthetic hydroxyamphibole in 19.2%. Benzo-(a)pyrene adsorbed or added to asbestos dust stimulated asbestos lung carcinogenesis, but did not influence the pleural carcinogenesis.[37] In intratracheal installation of Canadian chrysotile and N-nitrosodiaethylamine (per os and subcutaneously)[32], one observes a much higher mortality than in controls treated with asbestos or with polyglukine. In animals treated with asbestos, no lung tumours developed, but asbestos exerted a synergistic effect, increasing the incidence of lung tumours.

E. ASBESTOS SUBSTITUTES

Among the measures to be taken to decrease asbestos noxious effects in the recent years, an important place is occupied by the substitution of asbestos by MMMF. We have studied, in experimental conditions, the fibrogenic and carcinogenic properties of most used in the U.S.S.R. (MMMF basalt fibers). In intratracheal experiments, it was shown that basalt fibers with an average diameter of 0.3–3 mkm are less fibrogenic than chrysotile fibers, although one cannot consider them as biologically inert. The carbon fibers are also less fibrogenic than chrysotile. After intraperitoneal injection of 20 mg three times monthly, it was established that during 25–26 months the basalt fibers (BF) induced mesothelioma as did the chrysotile fibers, but the number of tumours was 3-fold less.[34] Therefore, BF can substitute for asbestos in some materials. But, the search for safer substitutes should be continued. The banning of asbestos must be preceded by the discovery of a safer fiber.

These results agreed with the conclusions of three main studies on MMMF carcinogenisity.[40,41,42]

The epidemiological data, based on the experience of European, Canadian, and American plants producing MMMF confirmed the increased lung, bladder, and skin cancer mortality among employees who had worked in mineral wool production for 20 or more years. Analogous results were achieved among Canadian glass wool workers, despite the fact that the exposure levels were rather low (0.1 to 0.2 f/ml) and that at these levels any increase in lung cancer is impossible.

We believe that in the near future, in attempting to improve the parameters of the MMMF, fibers would have smaller diameter for better insulation properties. Then, one may suppose that the MMMF parameters would aggravate their noxious action.

F. ASBESTOS AND THE GENERAL POPULATION

In our opinion, a matter of great interest was the fate of the town Asbest, situated on a great chrysotile asbestos deposit. During many years after World War II, the emissions of the asbestos mills represented a source of serious air contamination of the town's atmosphere. At a distance of 1–1.5 km from the mills the dust content of the outdoor air varied from 11 to 19 mg/m^3.[4] As a consequence, 17% of examined children at the age of 7 to 14 years, living in the area of intensive dust exposure, have had pneumonia, while in the other district situated more favorably from the mills, one finds only 9% of pneumonia in a similar group of children. In a group of older children, from the Asbest area, the respiratory disease incidence including pneumonia and TBC was substantially higher than in the control district.

In another study of our home scientist[11], among 26,000 people examined by means of fluorography, 488 cases with calcification of pleura were found; these cases were the result of long-term inhalation of dust that escaped by weathering of the asbestos-containing soils. We consider, nevertheless, that the author's conclusion about a "pleural form of a non-occupational asbestosis" is not exact: such serious statements should not be made on the basis only of findings of asbestos fibers in two of six samples of street dust.

Further, due to the construction of new up-to-date dust cleaning installations in the mills, demolition of the old enterprises, and other radical measures, the town atmosphere was substantially improved. In the later years (1975 to 1985), in 99% of long-term samples of air, the content of dust did not exceed the MAC for silica-containing dust in town atmosphere (0.3 mg/m^3). This value is, in our opinion, an appropriate (ad interim) level, in the absence of an official MAC for the asbestos, as in many other countries. At the same time, we do not consider resolved the problem of atmosphere cleaning because in many samples the concentrations exceeded the conditionally accepted average-day allowable concentration (which is equal to 0.1 mg/m^3) 2.8-fold. We cannot yet exclude the influence of a lot of small sources of dust emissions (the dryers, wastes, dusting construction sand bins, industrial explosions in mines, and so on).

G. DISCUSSION

Of course, the studies carried out in the U.S.S.R. on the "asbestos-health" problem are not exhausted. At the same time, several questions, perhaps, may be considered as having been determined. First, there is a serious reason to consider asbestosis mainly as an illness of the past, although the concentrations of asbestos in several shops did not achieve the MAC. At the same time, the increased lung and stomach cancer is maintained among the people working with asbestos even where the total oncological morbidity does not exceed the general indexes of mortality.

Although the main cause of this fact is the unachieved MAC level in several plants, among the workers of an asbestos-textile plant, where in the last 25 years the dustiness in the work place didn't exceed the MAC in force (2 mg/m^3), the risk of lung cancer was substantially higher than among the general population.

We believe that another co-carcinogenic factor should also be taken into account: the development of a diffuse interstitial fibrosis, which can create atypical conditions of vital cell activity. The disappearance of cases of asbestosis is a positive medical and social fact, but these cases belong, of course, to a clinically detectable illness and obviously don't relate to the thin net of fibrosis that develops latently and may serve as a propicious "soil" for oncological or non-oncological complications. We believe that technical anti-dust measures have not only technical but also certain economical limits. We suppose one must optimize the effectiveness of the medical examinations and the selection of the people who are not hypersensitive to asbestos dust.

The realization of this very important measure was considered up to now difficult, if not dubious, because we did not have the clear scientifically grounded criteria. Meantime, it was shown[35] that the degree of risk of developing asbestosis, besides the dust burden, depends on several factors: 1) social (comfortable residence, availability of garden or kitchen garden, smoking and alcohol habits); 2) preceding diseases (bronchitis, pneumonia, TBC, all forms of rheumatism); 3) biological (nationality, sex, age at onset of exposure). Thus, by equating these factors, a more precise observation of a control group was achieved in 88% of all cases[36]. Further, the role of genotype in the predisposition to asbestosis development was studied. Using a perfected dermatoglyphic method, the criterion for the evaluation of genotypic predisposition to this illness was received. It seems that a further development of these studies would be helpful in solving the problem of medical occupational selection of people for work with asbestos. For the multifactorial analysis, which is necessary for the conduct of such studies, the mathematical methods used are based on the pattern recognition theory.

To increase the individual resistance to asbestos exposure, among other medicines, there was successful treatment with glutaminic acid[2]: the content of oxyproline in the lungs of the treated rats after intratracheal installation of 50 mg/m^3 of asbestos was significantly lower than in the untreated animals. We would like to try to prove the preventive effect of this drug on a rather representative group of asbestos workers.

H. CONCLUSIONS

1. Mainly in the post-war period, a rather vast study of the "asbestos-health" problem, in many aspects, was carried out in the U.S.S.R.

2. Introduction of a large system of technical and medico-social measures at main asbestos production and manufacture enterprises permitted the decrease of the level of dustiness to values near to the MAC, and then to eliminate the appearance of new cases of asbestosis.

3. At the same time, even at exposures at MAC levels, during a 25-year followup, increased lung cancer mortality risk persisted.

4. At low levels of dustiness, the noxious effect of asbestos on the upper respiratory tracts and skin is not avoided.

5. The epidemiological studies showed an increased lung and stomach cancer risk in the asbestos-cement industry, in which the majority of people who suffered from asbestos exposure worked. The experimental studies confirmed the oncogenicity, not only of "pure" asbestos dust, but also of the complex asbestos-hydrated cement dust (although it was lower than pure asbestos).

6. Stomach cancer is the logical effect of continuous elimination of the asbestos fibers from the lung. Epidemiological evidence showing increased mortality from this cancer was confirmed by an experimental study (with a small stomach model) with a substantial yield of malignant and benign tumours. We consider stomach cancer in asbestos workers an occupational disease similar to lung cancer.

7. MMMF cannot be considered as biologically inert dusts and the antidust measures (against their biological action) must be strengthened. At the same time, it was ascertained that both the fibrogenicity and the oncogenicity of basalt, carbon, and glass fibers, are certainly lower than that of asbestos. The search for safe asbestos substitutes should be continued.

8. A sharp lowering of the atmospheric concentration in areas of asbestos mills and other plants permitted the decrease in risk of general and oncological diseases among the population without asbestos occupational exposure. It is necessary to determine a MAC for asbestos dust in town atmospheres, despite the methological difficulties.

9. To a certain degree, engineers and scientists working with the dust suppressing measures have exhausted their resources: even negligible lowering of dust levels has become very expensive. Greater significance, under these conditions, may be in the optimization of medical and occupational selection of people not as susceptible to asbestos dust. The basis for this selection is proposed: a system of 16 criteria of different kinds, which permits prognostication of illness (asbestosis).

10. Despite the difficulties, it's appropriate to identify and test medicines for the inhibition of fibrosis development (which may be, indirectly, also a cancer preventive remedy).

11. A system of dust emission suppression decreased the atmo-

spheric contamination. Among the residents of a certain town, having no occupational exposure, the lung cancer SMR was not higher than the average regional rate.

12. Taking into account the increasing use of fiber mixtures (asbestos and MMMF) in various branches of industry, the examination of this highly adaptable and economically viable dust is now in our opinion rather important.

REFERENCES

1. Andreeva T.D., Matuzkova L.I., Frolova N.N., Proc. Biol. wirkung des Asbestos. 1968, Intern. Konfer. Dresden, 204–206.
2. Aronova G.V. et al., Gigiena truda i prof. zabol., 1980, N 1, 12–13.
3. Balashov V.A. et al., Gigiena truda i prof. zabolevania, 1983, 9, 8–12.
4. Bobyleva A.T., et al., Gigiena i sanitaria, 1958, N 11.
5. Bogoslovsky S.M., Systema professionalnoi klassifikatsii. Report on X Pirogov's Congress of Physicians in 1907, M. 1913.
6. Bunimovich G.I., Proc: Biol. wirkung des Asbestes, 1968, 2 Intern. confer. Dresden, 200–202.
7. Deminov A.G., Kogan F.M., Proc. "Prof. bolesni pylevoi etiologii", 1984, 54–59.
8. Dunnigan J., Am. J. Ind. Med., 1988, 13, Commentary.
9. Enterline P.E., Marsh G.M. in "Biol. effects of man-made mineral fibres", 1984, v.1, 311–339.
10. Frash V.N., Vanchugova N.N., Experimentalnaia onkologia, 1987, 2, 8–14.
11. Ginsburg E.A. et al., Klinicheskaia meditsina, 1970, 12, 55–60.
12. Gurvich V.B., Kogan F.M., Gigiena truda i prof. zabol., 1982, 7, 28–31.
13. Gurvich V.B. et al., Gigiena truda i prof. zabol., 1983, 5, 1–5.
14. Iatsenko A.S. et al., Proc. "Professionalnye bolezni pylevoi etiologii", M. 1988, v.2, 58–63.
15. Iahiiaev A.V. et al., Gigiena i sanitaria, 1986, 6, 34–38.
16. Izrael M.L., Gigiena truda i tehnika bezopasnosti, 1923, 4.
17. Klosterkotter W., Dresden Second Intern. Konf. "Biol. action of asbestos", 1968, 47–52.
18. Kogan F.M., Proc. "Professionalnye bolezni pylevoi atiologii", Sverdlovsk, 1963, 35–49.
19. Kogan F. M., Troitskii S. Yu., Proc. "Professionalnye bolezni pylevoi etiologii", 1963, 153–163.
20. Kogan F.M. "Pathogenesis of pneumoconioses". Proc of All-Union Symposium 18-20 nov. 1968. Sverdlovsk, 1970, 16–34.
21. Kogan F.M. et al., Gigiena truda i profzabolevaia, 1971, N 4, 43–46.

22. Kogan FM., Deminov A.G. et al., Proc.: Professionalnye bolezni pylevoi etiologii, 1977, M., 127–133.
23. Kogan F.M., Guselnikova N.A., Proc.: "Occupational cancer", v.2, 1981, M., 24–29.
24. Kogan F.M., Deminov A.G., Guselnikova N.A., Gurvich V.B., Arch. immun. et therapiae experim., 1982, 30, 277–283.
25. Kogan F.M., Guselnikova N.A., Proc. "Professionalnye bolezni pylevoi etiologii, 1983,M.
26. Kogan F.M., Balashov V.A., Elnichnych L.N., Gigiena truda i prof. zabolevania, 1986, N 4, 45–49.
27. Kogan F. M., Serzin S.A., Gigiena truda i profzabolevania, 1986, N 9, 9–12.
28. Kogan, F.M., Vanchugova M.N., Frash V.N., Brit. Journ. of Ind. Med., 1987, 44: 682–686.
29. Kogan F.M. et al., Gigiena truda i prof. zabolevania, 1987, N 3, 37–40.
30. Kovnatsky M.A., Proc. "Kliniko-gigienicheskie materialy po ozdorovleniu asbestovoi promyshlennosti", Leningrad, 1940.
31. Kovantsky M.A., "Silikatozy", Edit. "Meidtsina", Leningrad, 1957.
32. Küng-Vösemae Vinkmann F., "Biol. effects of mineral fibres", V.I. 1980. Lyon, 305–311.
33. Levins E.M. "Kliniko-gigienicheskie materialy po ozdorovleniu asbestovoi promyshlennosti", Leningrad, 1940.
34. Nikitina O.V. et al. Proc. "Prof. bolezni pylevoi etiologii", 1988, v.I, 14–18.
35. Polzik E.V. et al., Gigiena i sanitaria, 1988, N 3, 27–29.
36. Polzik M.V. et al., Med. Del Iavoro, 1989, in press.
37. Pylev L.N., Biol. effects of mineral fibres, 1980, v.I, 343–355.
38. Pylev L.N. et al., Gig. truda i prof. zabol., 1988, N 7, 55–57.
39. Rutherford, Johnstone. Occupational diseases, Philadelphia, 1942.
40. Saracci R., Simonato L., Acheson E.D. et al. Brit. Journ. of Industr. Med., 1984, v.41, 425–436.
41. Shannon H.S., Hayes M.V. et al. Biol. effects of man-made mineral fibres, 1984, v.I, 133–177.
42. Sogomonian G.V. Gigiena truda i prof. zabolevania, 1985, N 7, 20–22.
43. Stolbun B.M., Bachireva I.D. Proc. "Biol. wirkung des Asbestos", 1968, Intern. Konf. Dresden, 202–205.
44. Svirskiy E.L. Dust factor in asbestoscontaining heat insulation materials industry and their use. Diss., Sverdlovsk, 1968.
45. Szymczykiewicz K., Wiecek E., Med. pracy, 1962, 2, 85–97.
46. Troitskaia N.A. et al. Gig. i Sanit., 1984, N 6, 18–20.
47. Valagov A.G. Hygienic characteristic of syntetic asbestos. Diss., 1970, Sverdlovsk.
48. Velichkovsky B.T., Vladimirov Yu. A., Korkina L.G., Suslova T.B. Vestnik Akademii meditsinskih nauk, 1982, N 10, 45–51.

49. Vilenskiy M.M. Asbestosis and tuberculosis. Diss. doct., Sverdlovsk, 1940.
50. Taits S.A. Asbestosis—as an occup. disease. Diss., M., 1949.
51. Tiushniakova N.V. et al. Proc. "Professionalnye bolesni pylevoi etiologii", 1988, v.2, 63.
52. Troitskiy S.Iu. Dustiness in the industry of friction materials with asbestos as filler. Diss. Sverdlovsk, 1970.
53. Vorwald A.J. et al. Arch. Ind. Hyg. 3, I, 43, 1951.
54. Wagner J.C., Berry G., Skidmore J.W., Timbrell V., 1974, Brit. J. Cancer, 29, 252–269.
55. Wieschows S.R. Rock Products, N 8, 1947.

17

Malignant Tumor Mortality Rates in Asbestos Textile Workers

NELLY A. GUSELNIKOVA, M.D.
Ural State University
Sverdlovsk, U.S.S.R.

Synposis

BIOGRAPHY

Dr. Nelly Guselnikova, after completing her studies at Sverdlovsk Medical Institute, was for many years an assistant in the Department of Hygiene of Labour. In 1975, she received the grade of Candidate of Medical Sciences. Her dissertation was dedicated to the study of influence of work conditions, in the asbestos industry, on the epidemiology of asbestos-induced diseases. Further studies have been carried out on other asbestos manufacturing processes in the asbestos-textile and asbestos-cement industries. During her post-graduate work, the interests of senior scientist N. Guselnikova have been concentrated on the occupational cancer problem. She may be contacted at The Ural State Univesrity, Lenin av., 51, 620051 Sverdlovsk, USSR.

EDITORS' COMMENTARY

There have been many informative medical research studies conducted in the USSR and Dr. Guselnikova's report on her extensive epidemiological studies of asbestos textile workers is no exception. She indicates that occupational exposure to long chrysotile asbestos fibers (>5 microns) does produce a significant risk of lung, bronchial tube, and stomach cancer (even for what some observers might believe is fairly low fiber concentration levels). No increase in risk was found from smoking. In terms of asbestosis, a dose-response was found and higher levels of airborne asbestos fibers produced a substantial increase in the frequency of asbestosis, the disease was manifested earlier, and there were other concommitant disease complications.

In regard to what is *technically achievable* in terms of engineering controls to *minimize* worker exposure to airborne asbestos fibers, Dr. Guselnikova has proposed certain exposure limits. Eliminating all but the fibers normally counted (by PLM), this would be about 0.1 to 0.2 mg/m^3, and would be considered a practical technical goal to minimize adverse health effects. This compares to a general standard for asbestos containing dust of 2 mg/m^3 in the USSR. It is in agreement with the recommendations of Kogan (USSR) and the criteria in some other countries. It pertains to the prevention of asbestosis and certain forms of cancer, not to the elimination of all asbestos induced disease processes. It does not imply a safe limit of exposure nor even the elimination of lung cancer. Where asbestos is to be used, such practical guidance criteria are highly desirable as objectives and limits.

A. INTRODUCTION

The history of asbestos textile production is nearly a hundred years old. Asbestos containing textile products have been used for heat insulation, anti-fire protection, as a filtering material, and for many other uses. In the majority of products, the asbestos has the function of a reinforcing material or as a filler in plastics, rubber, cements, bitumen, and other substances. For some textile products, the asbestos dust that is created is often a "free state" (together with a little cotton).

One of the primary occupational hazards in this industry is the presence of asbestos containing dust at all stages of the manufacturing process. Prolonged inhalation of asbestos containing dust, having fibrogeneous properties, may lead to the develpment of a serious occupational disease (including but not limited to asbestosis). In some situations, it has been observed that, among these workers, there is an excess number of malignant diseases of the lungs, stomach, and other organs.

It is noteworthy that the first cases of asbestosis that were diagnosed, as early as 1907, concerned workers in an asbestos textile factory. During the following years, there were studies covering the same textile production that made it possible to determine some of the peculiarities of asbestosis and the frequency of occurrence of malignant tumors (2–7). British investigators established an increased mortality rate due to cancer among the workers of asbestos textile factories. But, in the Soviet Union, the prevalence of oncological diseases among the workers engaged in asbestos textile production shops is, as yet, in need of a comprehensive study. The number of such shops is quite considerable. Therefore, we studied the mortality rate from cancer in asbestos textile production, focusing on two asbestos textile manufacturing plants in different localities and characterized by different conditions of labor.

The asbestos textile production involves a number of separate process steps, namely: preparation of the mix, roving production, spinning, twisting, manufacture of cloth, and packing. The preparation of the mix consists of loosening the asbestos and cotton, then mixing the components in the loosening machine, a pressing-mixing unit, or a loosening spreading machine (scutcher). Then, with the use of pneumatic transport, the mixture is fed into the feed bunkers of mixers or onto metering trays sprinkled with a water emulsion. This prepared mixture is fed to a

* Accepted for publication on 27 March 1989.

carding machine for the loosening and separation of fibers and cleaning to remove foreign matter, resulting in the formation of thin (ca 4 mm) slivers. The steps of spinning, twisting, and weaving, as well as the preparation of asbestos packing, are quite similar at any of the asbestos textile production shops. The majority of those process steps are accompanied by the emanation of hazardous dust.

The present study included a complex investigation of the state of health of workers exposed over a considerable period of time to the asbestos containing dust hazard in concentrations considerably exceeding the exposure limit (e.g., AT Plant no. 1). This was compared to the workers at production sites where the concentration of asbestos-containing dust was close to, or not exceeding, the exposure limit (2 mg/m^3) (e.g., AT Plant no. 2). We also studied the sanitary and hygienic conditions of work, the disperse-morphological composition of the dust, the prevalence of asbestos-caused diseases, the mortality rate due to cancer and have made an evaluation of exposure limits from the perspective of oncological safety.

B. RESULTS

At the beginning of the 1960s, the average dust content in the air at the AT Plant no. 1 was as follows: the mixture preparation area was within 25 mg/m^3, the carding machine area was 16 mg/m^3, and the removal of roving product area was 9 mg/m^3. In the spinning shop, the dust varied from 7 to 15.0 mg/m^3; in the twisting shop it was from 6.0 to 7.0 mg/m^3; in the asbestos packing shop it was 3.0 to 5.0 mg/m^3; and in the weaving shop it was from 2.0 to 6.0 mg/m^3. In 1970, a new asbestos textile production building was erected. The process flow, ventilation systems, and the cleaning of dust-laden exhaust air were fully modernized. Hence, the average dust content in the shops, according to the data in our recent studies, decreased in the preparation and the carding shops (down to 1.6–3.0 mg/m^3), at the spinning and twisting operation (down to 3.8–4.5 mg/m^3), and in the weaving and packing sections (down to 1.0 mg/m^3). Despite a substantially increased amount of asbestos being processed, the dust content level was only slightly higher than the MAC (2 mg/m^3), while the weaving and packing shows were even lower.

On the other hand, considering the prolonged latency period for the manifestation of cancer development, in comparing the level of dust content in the air with the data on the oncological mortality rate, attention should be given to the dust concentrations and the characteristics of the 1950s and 1960s. Quite a number of persons, reported dead during the period covered by our epidemiological study, started working much earlier (during the period, according to some available data, when the level of dust content was much higher).

The basic raw material used in asbestos textile production is asbestos of higher grades, but slightly contaminated with serpentine rock dust. However, in the airborne *dust* the quantity of *fibers* was found to be only 20% in the preparation shop and up to 30% in the spinning shop (as counted under 15 × 90 magnification). The prevailing dust was granular rock particles.

An epidemiological analysis of mortality, due to malignant tumors, was carried out according to the methods of the Ministry of Health of the USSR (1).

As shown in Table 17-1, the risk index (RI) of death from lung and stomach cancer is higher among asbestos-exposed males as compared with referenced male patients (but it is not statistically significant). However, the increase is statistically significant for total oncological mortality. Among the female workers formerly employed at the plant, the risk is significantly increased for stomach and all localizations mortality.

We assume that it was the work in the preparation and carding shops that contributed to the development of the asbestos-induced cancer among both male and female workers. The female workers were employed, in general, in the weaving, packing, and rewinding-and-twisting operations and some other shops. Despite the apparent great difference in the average mortality rates, they were statistically nonsignificant. This may be due to the small number of persons in the workers group.

Investigations on the mortality rate due to cancer, for large contingents of asbestos workers, both in our country (8,9) and

Table 17-1 Observed and Expected Mortality Rates Due to Malignant Tumors (Workers of AT Plant No. 1 Compared to Reference Patients)

	Males		Females	
Localization of Tumor	Ratio	P	Ratio	P
Lungs and bronchial tubes	3.0 ± 1.5	>0.05	3.5 ± 2.1	>0.5
Stomach	1.8 ± 0.9	>0.05	3.2 ± 1.1	<0.5
Other	2.1 ± 0.7	<0.05	2.0 ± 0.7	<0.5
All localizations	2.8 ± 0.8	<0.05	2.3 ± 0.5	<0.5

abroad (10), have shown that the death rate from malignant tumors is reliably higher, as compared with the other populations, when such groups were subjected to prolonged exposure of dust in high concentrations. In workers with a comparatively small length of dust exposure hazard (less than 15 to 20 years) and not exposed to the effect of high concentrations of asbestos containing dust, such differences are either non-existent or the data are unreliable. The most important factors in the medical evaluation of the likelihood of cancer are the dust concentrations, the exposure time, and, more important, the period from the *onset* of work with asbestos. Among the male workers who have died from cancer of the lung, the elapsed time averaged 27 years, and for cancer of the stomach it was 23 years. Among female workers occupied in the principal occupations (carding, weaving, cording, packing, and weaving), the average latent period of those who died from cancer of the lungs was 26 years and for cancer of the stomach it was 21 years. The actual dust exposure time was considerably less than the latency period, as has also been shown by other authors (5,6).

Table 17-2 shows the risk of mortality from oncological diseases among the workers engaged in mining and dressing asbestos ore operations compared with those working at the AT plants (ATPs). The risk among both the male and female workers at the ATP no. 1 is slightly lower than that among the workers occupied in mining and dressing (during the same 32-year period and living in one and the same region). As compared with the mines and mills operation (chrysotile asbestos), the dust content in the working zone of the ATP no. 1 is, without doubt, substantially lower. During the same period of years in the mining and (especially) the milling operations, the dust content even in averaged figures remained very high, i.e., hundreds of mg/m^3. The fiber content in

Table 17-2 Observed and Expected Mortality Rates from Malignant Tumors (Workers of Different Asbestos Plants Compared to a Reference Population)

Localization of Tumor	Males			Females		
	Mining	Milling	ATP	Mining	Milling	ATP
Lungs	3.3*	5.5*	3.0*	5.1*	4.4	3.5
Stomach	2.7*	3.0*	1.8*	3.5*	5.6*	3.2*

* Statistically significant differences.

the dust in the mining process was close to 9%, while in the milling process it was 10%–12%. Thus, while in asbestos textile production the proportion of fibers in the dust was 2 to 3 times higher, the total amount of fibers inhaled in the process of milling was actually higher.

The results of our investigations confirm the conclusions of several authors on the carcinogenic risk of workers occupied in the asbestos textile production under the conditions of high dust levels in the ambient air.

Of considerable interest, in our opinion, is a perspective study of mortality rate due to cancer among the workers of the asbestos textile plants. Such a study was carried out at ATP no. 2, located in a different region from the ATP no. 1. For this purpose, we retrospectively selected a team of workers engaged at ATP no. 2, where the concentrations of asbestos containing dust over a period of more than 20 years did not exceed the MAC (or exceeded it very slightly). At the same time, dust levels exceeding the exposure limit 2- to 4-fold were observed, some of the years, at a number of working places in the spinning and twisting shops.

The average dust content in the ambient air of the working zone, from 1960 to 1981, was as follows: in the quality control department it was 1.0 mg/m^3, in the instrumentation and apparatus section it was 1.1 mg/m^3, in the twisting shop it was 1.6 mg/m^3, while in the weaving shop it was 1.1 mg/m^3, and in the spinning shop it was 2.3 mg/m^3.

A study of the disperse-morphological composition of the airborne dust (with optical microscope 15 $\times$ 90) has shown that the dust consisted of 85% to 95% particles sized less than 5 μm, i.e., the dust was of a finely dispersed class. The grain particles over 5 μm in size were more frequently encountered in the spinning and twisting shops. The content of fibrous particles in the samples, taken from different sections, was within 5.5% to 7.8%.

In accordance with the international criteria, the fibers we took into account were those having a ratio, between the length and diameter, which was substantially higher than 3 : 1, *the length not less than 5 μm and the diameter not more than 3 μm.*

The *biological aggressiveness* of asbestos containing dust, as is kown, is determined not only by the concentration of dust in the air, but also by its diverse morphological properties, i.e., the fibrous character of dust, diameter of particles, and the ratio of parameters (length to diameter).

In an earlier period (1975) (11), at ATP no. 1 it was found that, in the preparation shop, the content of fibers was only 19.9%, in the spinning and rewinding shops it was 30%, in the packing shop it was 23.4%, and in the weaving shop it was 16.7%. The E-potential of chrysotile asbestos dust was +27.2 mV. Judging by its physico-chemical characteristics, there are sufficient grounds to classify the asbestos-containing airborne dust in the asbestos textile industry as biologically more aggressive than the dust in mining and milling or other numerous enterprises using asbestos.

In the 1960s, the prevalence of *asbestosis* at ATP no. 1 was nearly *6.5 times higher* than in a comparative exposure group of workers of asbestos mills located in the same town. Twofold higher was the number of first detected cases of asbestosis (per 100 patients). Moreover, *signs of asbestosis developed earlier and 2.5-fold more often was complicated* by tuberculosis of the lungs. On the other hand, the data on the level of dust content in the air at both plants differed only slightly. Hence, the difference in the manifestation of occupational diseases can be explained, mainly, due to higher concentration of fibers in the ambient air of the asbestos textile production work area.

At the same time, among the workers engaged in the ATP no. 2, during a more than 20-year period under conditions of dustiness not exceeding the MAC (2 mg/m^3), no cases of asbestosis have been diagnosed. This fact tends to prove that the accepted (in the Soviet Union) exposure limit of 2 mg/m^3 should be considered as justifiable in regard to the fibrogenesity of asbestos containing dust.

We attempted to assess the degree of cancer risk mortality for workers exposed to the MAC level of dust over a long period of working life. The epidemiological study of malignant tumors, among the workers occupied at ATP no. 2, was carried out based on the prospective method with a retrospectively selected cohort. This method, in our opinion, has certain advantages over the retrospective method, since it provides for a relevant response when performing studies of relatively small groups and when analyzing the dose-response relationship.

The prospective method of study was based on a followup (over a period of 10 to 20 or more years) of the health of persons exposed to the hazard of the factor being studied. The selected cohort consisted of workers engaged at ATP no. 2 and working from 1960 with their health record traced and covered over a 24-year period. The number of worker-years in the observation was 12,900. The estimate of cancer risk is based on the rates of mortality among the population of a large size town, by sex and age.

The results of this study give ample grounds to believe that the relative risk (RR) of the death from oncological disease of all localizations is lower than unity, both among the males and females (Table 17-3).

At the same time, the relative risk of death from cancer of the lungs among the male workers was 1.85 and among the female workers it was 1.31 higher than the reference population. The average duration of exposure of the male workers at the plant, who died from cancer of the lungs, was 11.9 years. The average concentration of asbestos containing dust during this period varied between 0.4 to 2.6 mg/m^3. The latent period (time from the beginning of exposure until the appearance of the disease) was 16.0 years. The duration of exposure in the shop was 7 years, while the average concentration of dust during this period was within 0.7 to 3.2 mg/m^3. Among the female workers, one cleaner in the card shop died from cancer of the lungs. The latent period in that case was 11 years.

C. DISCUSSION

The mortality rates from cancer of all localizations among the workers of ATP no. 2 does not exceed that of the reference city population. In our opinion, this situation can be explained by the low dust content in the working zone of the shops at ATP no. 2.

A study of the smoking hazard among the observed group failed to reveal any difference as compared with the reference population group (73.0% and 75.7%, respectively). The small number of cases of lung cancer among the workers in the selected cohort permits making some assumptions only. The duration of exposure to the dust hazard and the latent period among all who died from the disease are relatively short. Perhaps this is associated with the fact that they started working at the asbestos textile production plant at a medium or older age. Meanwhile, the *cancer*

Table 17-3 Relative Risk (RR) of Death from Oncological Diseases Among the Workers at ATP No. 2

Localization of Tumor	RR Male	RR Female
All localizations	0.51	0.46
Lung cancer	1.85	1.31

risk increased proportionally to the age at which they began their work with asbestos (12). It is important to consider that even with an average exposure below the MAC, we cannot exclude episodical peaks of dustiness.

Some investigators (13) are of the opinion that the dose-response relationship (frequently of lung cancer compared to exposure to the asbestos hazard) has a linear character. Thus, even for cumulative exposures the RR can be higher. But other authors (14) have indicated that any correlation of exposure dose and cancer mortality rate is valid only for groups with prolonged exposure (more than 20 years).

D. CONCLUSION

An asbestos containing dust concentration of 2 mg/m^3 cannot be considered safe in regard to lung cancer, particularly when there is a high content of asbestos in the dust mixture. The increased mortality rate, due to cancer of the lungs, among the workers of ATP no. 2, tends to confirm this conclusion.

A certain causal role may be attributed to the fact that some workers afflicted by cancer may have started their asbestos exposure at an older age and have been subject to dust hazard exposure in concentrations higher than the set exposure limit. In our opinion, this has resulted in curtailing the duration of the latent period. It is difficult to state, specifically, what level of asbestos could be considered safe from the oncological point of view. There is no generally accepted threshold of carcinogenicity, particularly for asbestos.

Some authors (15) deny the possibility of establishing the oncologically safe concentrations of asbestos dust. Especially in far lower concentrations of dust, any dose-response or threshold extrapolation is speculative and uncertain. However, for practical reasons, the establishment of such an exposure limit is necessary.

We propose, in terms of an averaged value, the following exposure limits for asbestos textile shops: where the content of asbestos in the dust is within 20%–30%, 0.5 mg/m^3; where the content is 10%–20%, 1 mg/m^3; for less than 10%, 2 mg/m^3. We believe that from the technical point of view such values are achievable and medically desirable.

REFERENCES

1. Methodical Instructions. Restropective Study of Mortality Rate Due to Malignant Tumors with Regard to Possible Effect of Productional Factors. Science and Research Institute of Hygiene and Occupational Diseases, Sverdlovsk, 1980.
2. Kovnatski, M.A. Silicosis. *"Medgiz" Pub. H.*, 1957.
3. Grodzenchik, N.A. Clinics of Initial Forms of Asbestosis, as Based on Dynamic Observation Data. Dissertation of Candidate for Science Degree, L., 1955.
4. Doll, R. *Brit. J. Ind. Med.*, 1955, 12, 2, p. 81–87.
5. Peto J. et al. *Brit. J. Ind. Med.*, 1977, 34, p. 169–174.
6. Newhouse, M.K. *LARC Scient. Pub. N.*, v. 8, Lyon, France, 1973, p. 203–208.
7. Enterlne, P.E. *Ann. N.Y. Acad. Sci.*, 1965, 132, p. 156–165.
8. Kogan, F. M., Guselnikova, N.A., and Gulevskaya, M.R. *Gigiena i Sanit.*, 1972, No. 7, P. 29–32.
9. Guselnikova, N.A., Kogan, F.M. PROC, U, 1983, p. 109–111.
10. MacDonald, J.C., et al. *Arch. Environm. Health*, 1971, v. 22, p. 677–686.
11. Kogan, F.M. Asbestos-Containing Dusts and Safety Measures for Precluing their Hazardous Effect on the Workers' Health, Sverdlovsk, 1975.
12. Ebbessen P. *Mech. Ageing and Developm.*, 1984, v. 25, No. 3.
13. Dement, J.M., Harris, R.L., Symons, M.Y. et al. *Ann. Occup. Hyg.*, 1982, v. 26, pp. 869–887.
14. MacDonald, J.C., Liddell, F.D.K., Gibbs, G.W. et al. *Brit. J. Ind. Med.*, 1980, v. 37, p. 11–24.
15. Grawfood, A. *Health and Safety at Work*, 1983, v. 6, No. 13, p. 37–38.

18

Medical Surveillance After Asbestos Exposure

JEFFREY L. LEVIN, M.D., M.S.P.H.
RICHARD S. KRONENBERG, M.D.

University of Texas Health Center
Tyler, Texas, U.S.A.

Synopsis

BIOGRAPHY

Dr. Jeffrey L. Levin is an Assistant Professor of Medicine at the University of Texas Health Center at Tyler. He is a graduate of the University of Texas Medical School at San Antonio and is a diplomate of the American Board of Internal Medicine. He completed postgraduate training in occupational medicine at the University of Kentucky and has a special interest in occupational lung disease. Dr. Levin is also a member of both the American College of Physicians and the American College of Occupational Medicine.

Dr. Richard S. Kornenberg is Professor and Chairman of the Department of Medicine and Head of Occupational Medicine Services at the University of Texas Health Center at Tyler. He is a graduate of Northwestern University Medical School and holds board certifications in Internal Medicine and Pulmonary Disease. Dr. Kronenberg has a special interest in asbestos-related diseases. He is a member of the National Asbestos Council Safety and Health Committee and lectures extensively on the health hazards of asbestos for Texas A & M University as well as several other environmental training organizations.

EDITORS' COMMENTARY

At several conferences on asbestos abatement, a physician was scheduled to discuss medical surveillance after asbestos exposure. One simply said that there was nothing to talk about because there was so little that could be done for those already exposed or manifesting an asbestos disease process. Others indicated that medical monitoring was required by government regulation or employment contracts and that they would do what was prescribed despite some personal frustration as to the purpose for doing it. The reasons it is required include early detection for treatment, feedback on the adequacy of asbestos control measures, for epidemiology, and for medical research. It is also perceived as a threat to employers: if workers are harmfully exposed, they will be subsequently identified and the employer's fault determined. The following Chapter describes who performs the required medical surveillance, how and when it is performed, and why it should be accomplished.

A. INTRODUCTION

The concept of medical surveillance following exposure to hazardous materials in the workplace is not new. The dangers to health from occupational exposure to asbestos have also been recognzied for many years, dating as far back as Roman civilization. (1) However, it was not until the turn of this century that anecdotal reports of scarring of the lung associated with asbestos crept into the scientific literature, and not until the 1930s that the first clinical and epidemiologic studies were performed to describe this phenomenon. (2) Scattered case reports of lung cancer and mesothelioma came even later, and a certain link between asbes-

Accepted for publication 21 December 1988.

tos and these diseases did not appear until the studies by Doll (1955) and Wagner (1960). (3,4)

In 1964, Selikoff, Churg, and Hammond published results concerning asbestos and cancer in a group of insulation workers. (5) The significance of their finding lies in the discovery of an increased mortality from cancer in a group involved in the use, rather than in the mining, milling, or manufacturing of asbestos. (2) The number of people at risk from employment in these latter trades had remained relatively small. By 1964, however, asbestos was used widely in industry and had found its way into many consumer products. The number of people exposed as users of the fibrous material continues to grow as has the body of data showing the relationship with lung cancer as well as with cancers of the gastrointestinal tract, larynx, and kidney. (6).

As a consequence of these findings, control of asbestos exposure is now strictly regulated. These regulations also mandate medical surveillance among individuals with ongoing exposure. The nature of surveillance outside of this limited regulatory realm has been less certain. What should the approach be for household contacts of individuals who have worked with asbestos in the past without proper protection? How should school and public building exposure as well as other urban exposures be evaluated?

This chapter will focus on general principles concerning prevention, the rationale for medical monitoring, and the nature of appropriate surveillance. Current regulatory standards which outline medical surveillance requirements for asbestos are discussed. Finally, an attempt will be made to clarify the significance of "low level" asbestos exposure and a reasonable approach to medical monitoring proposed.

B. PREVENTION AND THE SENTINEL HEALTH EVENT

The principle of the sentinel health event (SHE) was first introduced by Rutstein et al. in 1976. (7) In short, the sentinel health event is defined as "a preventable disease, disability, or untimely death where occurrence serves as a warning signal that the quality of preventive and/or therapeutic medical care may need to be improved." (8) This concept grew out of the use of maternal and infant mortality rates as markers of health care. (9) The list of SHEs compiled by Rutstein and colleagues has been updated and a table directed specifically at occupational diseases developed. (8, 10) As such, the sentinel health event (occupational) or SHE(O) heralds the need for medical surveillance and motivates change in the occupational setting to protect workers. (8,9) Table 18-1 provides examples of the SHE(O).

The notion of prevention is implicit in this context and deserves further mention. Ideally, the preferred level of intervention in the disease process is at the stage of exposure, susceptibility or risk modification, more commonly referred to as primary prevention. (11) For example, exercise would constitute a single element in a multifactorial approach to the primary prevention of coronary artery disease. Not uncommonly, however, the term prevention is applied to the detection of already existent disease in an early stage where the progression of the process can be slowed or arrested. Thus, secondary prevention is a term suitably applied to the initial diagnosis of an asymptomatic hypertensive patient. Finally, the term tertiary prevention applies to those more unfortunate circumstances where a disease is advanced and medical intervention is aimed at rehabilitation and improved function. The heart attack victim would be a candidate for such a course of prevention. For any given disease process, there may be considerable overlap of these three levels of prevention. This point is illustrated in Fig. 18-1 with heart attack used as an example.

As applied to asbestos-related diseases, prevention and the sentinel health event play key roles. The primary approach to prevention lies in an attempt to minimize asbestos exposure. Although asbestos-related diseases are ultimately incurable and less amenable to tertiary prevention, their early detection can lead to a decrease in premature morbidity and mortality. This is true whether it occurs through treatment of an early cancer or vacination for pneumonia. Furthermore, the development of these

Table 18-1 Example Sentinel Health Events-Occupational [SHE(O)S] and the Industry or Occupation to which They Are Linked (see text)

SHE(O)	Industry or Occupation
Hemangiosarcoma of the liver	Vinyl chloride polymerization
Mesothelioma	Asbestos production and utilization
Bladder cancer	Rubber and dye industry (beta naphthylamine)
Coalworkers' pneumoconiosis	Coal mining
Byssinosis	Cotton industry
Aplastic anemia	Exposure to benezene, explosive manufacturing, radiologist, etc.

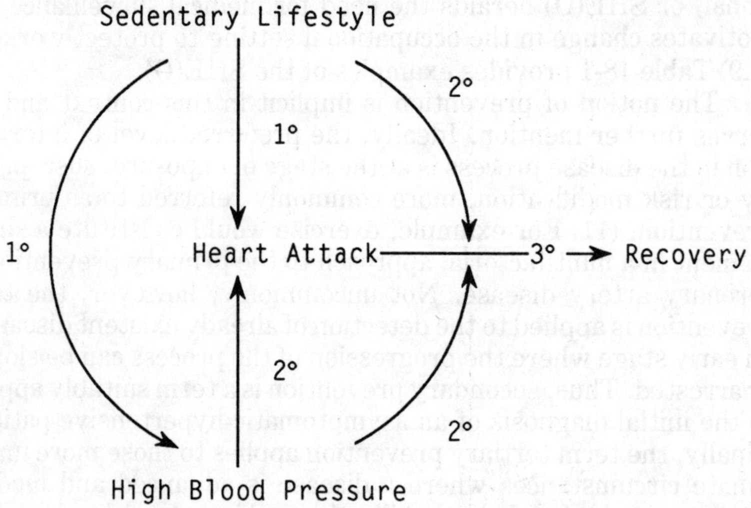

Fig. 18-1 The levels of prevention and their overlap. Heart attack is used as an example. 1° = primary prevention; 2° = secondary prevention; 3° = tertiary prevention.

diseases should continue to signal the need to evaluate individuals who have been subject to related exposures in the past (Fig. 18-2).

C. GENERAL PRINCIPLES OF MEDICAL MONITORING

An in-depth review of the definition of screening and factors affecting the yield of a screening test can be found elsewhere and are beyond the scope of this chapter. (11) A few details are, however, germane to this discussion.

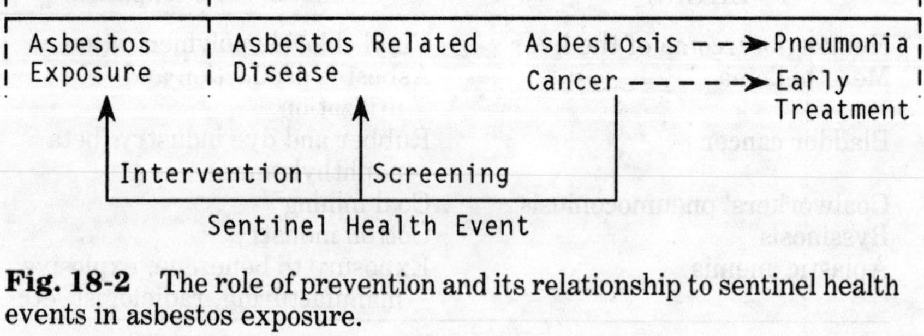

Fig. 18-2 The role of prevention and its relationship to sentinel health events in asbestos exposure.

To screen or monitor a population for a given disease represents an attempt to separate those most likely to have it from those most likely to be unaffected. (11) Inherent in this definition is the fact that these individuals are generally asymptomatic or possess limited symptoms. Factors which affect the yield of any given test include its sensitivity for detecting the illness or problem, the degree to which it is specific for that illness or problem, the reproductibility of results (precision), and the extent to which the disease is prevalent in the population. Certainly, the yield of a program directed at detecting asbestos-related disease will be far superior among a group of insulators versus a group of farmers.

Those items which must be considered in screening individuals for any disease process are listed in Table 18-2. (11,12) Most are self-explanatory, but a few points deserve mention. Firstly, tests used for screening must, of necessity, be acceptable to both patient and examiner. Clearly, few individuals who are symptomatic will submit to a study which is distasteful or causes pain. Secondly, it has become increasingly apparent in the current economic atmosphere that the screening tests themselves, as well as diagnosis and treatment, must be cost effective. This is especially true among the asbestos-related diseases where the exposed population at risk is substantial. Finally, there must be some understanding of the natural history of the disease process in order to make discovery meaningful for intervention and follow-up.

Before proceeding to a rationale for surveillance specifically

Table 18-2 Factors To Be Considered in Screening for a Given Disease

1. The disease sought should be an important health problem.
2. There should be an accepted treatment for individuals with disease (even if just for prevention of complications).
3. Diagnostic and treatment facilities should be available.
4. A latent period or early symptomatic stage should be detectable.
5. An approach to diagnosis should exist.
6. Screening tests should be acceptable to both the population and the examiner.
7. Some understanding of the natural history of the disease should exist.
8. An approach to treatment should be agreed upon.
9. The cost of screening for the disease as well as further diagnostic studies and treatment should be considered in the overall scheme of health care costs.
10. Case-finding should represent an ongoing process.

aimed at asbestos-related diseases, it would serve well to mention a couple of examples of high risk groups where medical surveillance has been effective. Workers in the cotton textile industry undergoing monitoring with lung function tests stand to benefit by the early identification of decrements in lung function due to byssinosis and consequent removal from high dust areas. (13) Nearer to the topic at hand, ongoing screening programs of former asbestos workers have played a role in the early detection of cancer. (14).

D. RATIONALE FOR SURVEILLANCE AND WHOM TO MONITOR

Following a discussion of the sentinel health event and prevention, the need to monitor individuals with history of asbestos exposure should be increasingly apparent. These diseases do in fact constitute an important health problem, especially in view of the extent of the population exposed.

A strong association exists between long-term, heavy exposure to asbestos and cancer, especially among smokers. (4,5,15) Asbestosis, a disease characterized by scarring (fibrosis) of the lung tissue (parenchyma), also occurs among those with such exposure. *In fact, short-term, heavy exposure of just a few months has been shown to increase the risk of developing both cancer and asbestosis.* (16) Although a higher incidence of cancers of the gastrointestinal tract, larynx, and kidney has been observed among heavily exposed persons, lung cancer as well as pleural and peitoneal mesothelioma are more common. (6)

Other findings commonly associated with this level of exposure include diffuse and circumscribed scarring of the lung surface (pleural fibrosis) as well as non-malignant accumulations of fluid in the chest cavity (benign asbestos effusions). (17–19) These findings are significant as markers of exposure, although in some instances they can be related to functional disability. (18)

These disease processes and their associated radiographic and functional abnormalities will be discussed in greater detail in later chapters of the *Sourcebook on Asbestos Diseases*. The reason for mentioning them here is to raise the issue of need for medical monitoring. Perhaps the more challenging question does not address the rationale for surveillance but rather whom to monitor.

Few would argue the obvious need to screen for disease among heavily exposed occupational groups such as insulators and asbestos manufacturing personnel. It is, however, the risk of exposure to low levels of asbestos which is surrounded by the greatest controversy. Consequently, surveillance of these exposure groups and the appropriate approach to monitoring are equally controversial.

What does low-level signify? Low-level asbestos exposure refers to those situations in which contact with the substance occurs in other than the "usual asbestos trades." Asbestosis is an uncommon finding in this setting, making the risk of cancer the most significant concern. (20) Two key factors have made the study of this cancer risk difficult. Firstly, asbestos-realated diseases are characterized by a latent period of at least 20 and up to 30 or 40 years from the time of first expousre. (6,20) Secondly, actual exposure data has been limited in the past, making quantitative definition of dose-response relationships difficult. A linear dose-response relationshp has been shown to exist between heavier exposure levels and cancer. (16) However, the nature of the dose-response relationship has only been theoretically defined for low levels of contact and the existence of a "threshold" remains under debate. (21–25) The significance of the presence of asbetos in lungs of non-occupationally exposed urban dwellers makes this debate an important one. (26–28) The National Research Council has attempted to develop cancer risk estimates for such levels of non-occupational exposure. (29–31)

A thorough review of the literature concerning low-level asbestos exposure is beyond the scope of this discussion. It should be pointed out, however, that in addition to the anecdotal reports of increased cancer risk (32–34) more recent studies have been performed to help quantify this risk. Table 18-3 directs the reader to a few of the areas of concern as well as to studies which have been performed to address those areas. The existence of several studies supporting cancer risk points out the need for surveillance among these individuals as a prudent and useful measure. By educating individuals concerning the increased risks of smoking, more favorable outcomes can be achieved. Early recognition of nonmalignant disease can result in preventive and rapid treatment

Table 18-3 Sample Categories of Low Level Asbestos Exposure and Selected Studies Addressing Cancer Link for Each Area

Exposure Category	Supporting References	Refuting References
Urban dwellers/environmental exposure	35	36–38
Household contacts	41, 42	
School children	23	
Brake repairs	43	
Asbestos-insulated buildings		44
Textile workers (reprocessed textiles)	45–47	

measures for pulmonary infections. Finally, early detection of cancer can improve prognosis and short-term morbidity.

E. CURRENT REGULATORY REQUIREMENTS FOR MEDICAL MONITORING

Now that general principles concerning prevention and medical monitoring have been reviewed and a rationale for asbestos surveillance established, requirements concerning medical monitoring for asbestos-related diseases can be examined. Three federal standards currently exist which outline medical surveillance requirements for workers exposed to asbestos. (48–50) For the most part, the frequency and components of the monitoring differ very little among the three. Rather, the major differences lie with the individuals covered by each standard. Table 18-4 summarizes the frequency and nature of the monitoring as well as the workers affected by each ruling.

The standards specify that special attention should be given to the pulmonary, cardiovascular, and gastrointestinal systems in performance of the history and physical examination. In addition, a specified respiratory questionnaire is provided for the initial evaluation as well as for periodic assessments (interim history). This constitutes a reasonable approach considering the fact that these are the systems most likely to be affected by asbestos.

The medical evaluation must be performed by or under the direction of a licensed physician. (49) Chest roentgenograms must be interpreted in accordance with International Labor Office criteria by a B-reader, a board certified/eligible radiologist, or by an experienced physician with known expertise in pneumoconioses. (4,51) Posterior-anterior chest films only are required. In all instances, evaluations are only required annually, and an employee need not undergo pre-assignment, preplacement, or termination evaluations if performed within the past year.

An important comment should be directed at the frequency of the chest roentgenogram. This frequency is to be determined by the examining physician except in the case of 29 CFR 1910.1001. In this case, the frequency of the chest x-ray is specified at every five years except in the case where more than ten years have elapsed since first exposure. Under these circumstances, the chest film is obtained in accordance with age: 1) 15 to 35, every 5 years; 2) 35+ to 45, every 2 years; 3) 45+, every year. The rationale for such a regimen will be described later.

Table 18-4 Regulations Concerning Medical Surveillance for Asbestos Exposure (CFR = Code of Federal Regulations, f = Fiber, cc = Cubic Centimeter, FVC = Forced Vital Capacity, FEV_1 = Forced Expiratory Volume at One Second)

Standard	Employees Covered by Standard	Frequency	Surveillance Components
40 CFR 763 (Environmental Protection Agency)	State and local government employees involved in asbestos abatement projects.	1) Pre-assignment for negative-pressure respirator use. 2) At or above 0.1f/cc averaged over 8 hours for 30 or more days per year (within 10 working days following day 30 of exposure). 3) Annually thereafter. 4) Physician specified if more frequent than annually.	1) Medical and work history. 2) Standardized questionnaires. 3) Physical exam. 4) Chest x-ray at physician discretion. 5) FVC and FEV_1. 6) Other exams/tests at physician discretion.
29 CFR 1926.58	Exposures in construction industry as defined by 29 CFR 1910.12.	Same as 40 CFR 763.	Same as 40 CFR 763.
29 CFR 1910.1001 (Occupational Safety and Health Administration)	Exposures in all industries covered by the Occupational Safety and Health Act except as provided elsewhere.	If exposure is at or above 0.1 f/cc averaged over 8 hours, the following exams are to be performed: –pre-placement –annual –termination	Same as in 40 CFR 763 except for x-ray (See text).

F. DIAGNOSTIC TOOLS AVAILABLE FOR EVALUATION OF ASBESTOS-RELATED DISEASES

Mutliple diagnostic tools exist for use in the evaluation of asbestos-related diseases. Open lung biopsy serves as the gold standard for the actual tissue diagnosis of disease, but carries a level of morbidity too high for use in routine medical surveillance. Although biopsy of the lung lining and removal of fluid through a needle from the chest cavity (thoracentesis) or abdominal cavity (paracentesis) can be useful adjuncts in the diagnosis of malignant and benign asbestos-effusions, these too have very specific indications and do not constitute tools for routine monitoring. Furthermore, the incidence of benign asbestos effusions among asbestos-exposed workers is approximately 3.1 percent, suggesting that thoracentesis would not be a study performed as a matter of routine. (52)

Until more recently, the medical/occupational history and physical examination, chest radiograph, and pulmonary function studies have served as the mainstays of diagnosis and medical surveillance. (53) Pleural scars (plaques) are the msot common radiographic finding on the chest film and typical plaques are quite specific for asbestos exposure. (54) There is a limited percentage of cases of disease where pulmonary function changes predate x-ray findings. (18) Consequently, all three components mentioned above should be obtained in order to detect disease as early as possible in the greatest number of exposed individuals.

The value of the lateral and oblique chest radiographs is somewhat controversial. In a study by Hillerdel, 18.8 percent of all individuals having plaque disease on chest radiograph were discovered only when the lateral view was added to the posterior-anterior x-ray. (55) Although others have reported on the usefulness of oblique films, a recent study by Sherman, et al. has suggested otherwise. (54,56) The conclusion at this point is that the posterior-anterior and lateral chest films should be obtained to screenfor asbestos disease.

Pulmonary function testing (spirometry) has proved to be a useful tool for industrial medical surveillance. Determination of special aspects of pulmonary function such as lung volumes and diffusion capacity has also been shown to be of value in the detection of restrictive changes and gas exchange impairment which can accompany asbestos-related disease. (53) However, these special lung function tests are more difficult to perform and require special equipment, factors which limit their usefulness as screening tests.

Microscopic analysis of sputum is well recognized as a useful technique for the detection of malignancy in the lung. (57) However, the absence of sputum findings does not preclude the existence of malignancy. The hallmark finding which suggests an increased burden of asbestos in the lung is the fiber which has been coated by cells in the lung (asbestos body). The limitation of this technique lies in the substantial burden of asbestos which must be present (coated and uncoated fibers) in order to detect a single asbestos body in sputum. Such asbestos loads may not exist among low level exposures.

Bronchoalveolar lavage has similarly gained popularity as a tool to document or confirm asbestos exposure. This is a technique in which a small amount of fluid is instilled and retrieved from the lung utilizing a flexible, fiberoptic scope passed into the lung via the nose and throat. In addition to providing direct visualization of the larger airways, the fluid can be analyzed by special methods for cell content and the presence of asbestos bodies. There is increasing evidence to suggest a correlation between exposure extent, tissue burden, and number of asbestos bodies in lavage fluid. (58–61) In addition, an increase in inflammatory cells in the lung has been shown in lavage fluid as well as by gallium 67 pulmonary uptake as an early manifestation of the scarring process which occurs due to inorganic dust inhalation. (62,63) The latter procedure is a nuclear medicine study which can detect areas of inflammation in the body due to the uptake of gallium by inflammatory cells.

More recent reports have shown that high resolution computerized tomography (CT scan) is an extremely sensitive x-ray technique for detection and characterization of both pleural and parenchymal abnormalities associated with asbestos exposure. (54) Finally, cardiopulmonary exercise testing may demonstrate a fall in the oxygen saturation of the blood during exercise, which may suggest otherwise undetectable interstitial disease in cases of asbestos exposure.

G. PROPOSED MEDICAL SURVEILLANCE AFTER ASBESTOS EXPOSURE

The existence of multiple modalities for the diagnosis of asbestos-related diseases does not make all of them appropriate tools for medical surveillance. Asbestos bodies in sputum and bronchoalveolar lavage fluid may serve as measures of asbestos burden in lung tissue, but do not confirm the presence or absence of disease. (Thorough history taking alone is the best way to characterize the degree of exposure.) Furthermore, bronchoscopy and lavage with technical fluid analysis is costly and carries with it a certain level of morbidity and discomfort for patients. These factors preclude its use as a screening device. Gallium studies and pulmonary exercise testing may identify inflammatory or interstitial processes, but lack specificity for asbestos-related disease. Due to their costs and labor intensive efforts, they too are less likely to be useful tools in medical monitoring. Computerized tomography, although highly sensitive, is neither cost-effective nor time-effective as a screening study.

Based upon these comments, it should be clear that medical/occupational history and examination, two-view chest x-ray, and spirometry should remain the primary constituents of medical surveillance for asbestos. In addition, the occupational medicine specialist, the pulmonologist with experience in occupational diseases of the lung, and the radiologist with experience in reading chest films for pneumoconiosis constitute the physician team best qualified to survey for and diagnose asbestos-related disease.

The final issue which remains to be addressed deals with the frequency and content of screening evaluations. Certainly a baseline consisting of the above three components should be established, regardless of the anture of exposure. Subsequent evaluation must be individualized to the circumstances of findings on baseline evaluation, degree of exposure, age of the individual, and period since onset of exposure. Certainly those individuals with already existent asbestos-related disease or histories of very heavy exposure merit more intensive follow-up. Age is an important factor because the latent period for the development of disease is shorter among older individuals. (16).

The regimen as outlined in 29 CFR 1910.1001 (see Table 18-4) serves as a reasonble approach to ongoing monitoring. (49) Recall that chest x-rays of younger individuals are not performed as frequently nor of those whose initial exposure occurred less than ten years previously. However, as individuals get older or the latent period legnthens, the benefits of early disease detection outweigh the risk of x-ray exposure and the cost of annual radiography. (16).

H. CONCLUSIONS AND FUTURE DIRECTIONS

The rationale for surveillance following exposure to asbestos is relatively straightforward. Secondary prevention in asbestos-related diseases plays a key role in reducing morbidity and mortality and may help convince exposed individuals to stop smoking.

Equally important is the recognition of mesothelioma as a sentinel health event and as a harbinger of the need to alter an exposure or search for other individuals potentially affected.

The physician encounter, the chest x-ray, and pulmonary function testing offer a sound and cost-effective evaluation for the monitoring of disease, mandated or otherwise. Other diagnostic tools mentioned in this chapter carry specific indications and serve as valuable adjuncts to the conclusive diagnosis of suspect disease.

Ongoing research of cohorts with low level exposure to asbestos is critical to the understanding of the role played by this type exposure. Better quantification of dose will play an important role. Prospective study will also be necessary to outline the future role of such procedures as bronchoalveolar lavage or sputum cytology as well as staining for asbestos in the diagnosis and surveillance of disease. Perhaps as new therapeutic or primary preventive modalities are introduced, the issue of surveillance will no longer be a consideration.

ACKNOWLEDGMENT

We would like to thank Brigitte Stoglin for her diligence in the clerical preparation of this manuscript.

REFERENCES

1. Casteleman BI. *Asbestos: Medical and Legal Aspects,* 2nd ed. Clifton, N.J.: Law & Business, Inc., 1986, pp. 1–37.
2. Last JM, ed. *Maxey-Rosenau Public Health and Preventive Medicine,* 12th ed. Norwalk: Appleton-Century-Crofts, 1986, pp. 523–45.
3. Doll R. Mortality from lung cancer in asbestos workers. Brit J Industr Med 1955; 12:81–6.
4. Wagner JC, Sleggs CA, Marchand P. Diffuse pleural mesothelioma and asbestos exposure in the North Western Cape Province. Brit J Industr Med 1960; 17:260–71.
5. Selikoff IJ, Churg J, Hammond EC. Asbestos exposure and neoplasia. J Am Med Assoc 1964; 188:22–6.
6. Selikoff IJ, Hammond EC, Seidman H. Mortality experience of insulation workers in the United States and Canada, 1943–1976. Ann NY Acad Sci 1979; 330:91–116.
7. Rutstein DD, Berenberg W, Chalmers TC, Child CG, Fishman AP, Pervin EB. Measuring the quality of medical care: a clinical method. N Eng J Med 1976; 294(11):582–8.
8. Rutstein DD, Mullan RJ, Frazier TM, Halperin WE, Melius JM, Sestito JP. Sentinel health events (occupational): a basis for physician recognition and public health surveillance. Am J Public Health 1983; 73:1054–62.
9. Rutstein DD. The principle of the sentinel health event and its application to the occupational diseases. Arch Environ Health 1984; 39(3):158–68.
10. Rutstein DD, Berenberg W, Chalmers TC, Fishman AP, Perrin EB, Zuidema GD. Measuring the quality of medical care: second revision of tables of indexes. N Engl J Med 1980; 302:1146.
11. Mausner JS, Kramer S. *Epidemiology: An Introductory Text,* 2nd ed. Philadelphia: W.B. Saunders Company, 1985, pp. 1–21, 214–38, 323–5.
12. Wilson JMG, Jungner F. Principles and practice of screening for disease. Public Health Papers No. 34. Geneva: WHO, 1968.
13. *Code of Federal Regulations,* Title 29, Part 1910, Section 1043. Washington: U.S. Government Printing Office, 1987.

14. Greenberg SD, Hurst GA, Matlage WT, Miller JM, Hurst IJ, Mabry LC. Tyler asbestos workers program. Ann NY Acad Sci 1976; 271:353–64.
15. Hammond EC, Selikoff IJ, Seidmen H. Asbestos exposure, cigarette smoking and death rates. Ann NY Acad Sci 1979; 330:473–90.
16. Seidman H, Selikoff IJ, Hammond EC. Short-term asbestos work exposure and long-term observation. Ann NY Acad Sci 1979; 330:61–89.
17. Rosenstock L, Hudson LD. Nonmalignant asbestos-induced pleural disease. Semin Respir Med 1986; 7(3):197–202.
18. Jones RN, McLoud T, Rockoff SD. The radiographic pleural abnormalities in asbestos exposure: relationship to physiologic abnormalities. J Thorac Imag 1988; 3(4):57–66.
19. Benign asbestos pleural effusions (editorial). Lancet 1988; 1(8595):1145–6.
20. Churg J, et al. *Biological Effects of Asbestos*. Bethesda: National Institutes of Health, 1973.
21. Peto J. Dose-response relationships for asbestos-related disease: implications for hygiene standards—Part II. Mortality. Ann NY Acad Sci 1979; 330:195–203.
22. Brown, K. A threshold for asbestos related lung cancer. Br J Ind Med 1986; 43(3):556–8.
23. Hughes JM, Weill H. Asbestos exposure—quantitative assessment of risk. Am Rev Respir Dis 1986; 133(1):5–13.
24. Finkelstein MM. A study of dose-response relationships for asbestos associated disease. Br J ind Med 1985; 42(5):319–25.
25. Levin JL, Garcia JGN. Cancer risk of low level asbestos exposure. JNAC 1989; in press.
26. Churg A, Warnock ML. Asbestos fibers in the general population. Am Rev Respir Dis 1980; 122:669–78.
27. Dodson RF, Greenberg SD, Williams MG, Corn CJ, O'Sullivan MF, Hurst GA. Asbestos content in lungs of occupationally and nonoccupationally exposed individuals. J Am Med Assoc 1984; 252(1):68–71.
28. Case BW, Sebastien P. Environmental and occupational exposures to chrysotile asbestos: a comparative microanalytic study. Arch Environ Health 1987; 42(4):185–91.
29. National Research Council. *Asbestiform Fibers: Nonoccupational Health Risks*. Washington: National Academy Pres, 1984, pp. 13–5.
30. Aroesty J, Wolf K. Risk from exposure to asbestos. Science 1986; 234:923.
31. Breslow L, Brown S, Van Ryzin J. Risk from exposure to asbestos: response. science 1986; 234–923.
32. Ferguson GC, Watson H. Mesothelioma due to domestic exposure to asbestos. Br Med J 1984; 288:1654.
33. Booth SJ, Weaver EJM. Malignant pleural mesothelioma five years

after domestic exposure to blue asbestos (letter). Lancet 1986; 1(8478):435.
34. Scansetti G. Pleural mesothelioma after a short interval from first exposure in the wine filter industry. Am J Ind Med 1984; 5(4): 335–9.
35. Leclerc A, Goldberg M. Goldberg P, Deloumeaux J, Fuhrer R. Geographical distribution of respiratory cancer in New Caledonia. Arch Environ Health 1987; 42(5):315–20.
36. Churg AM, Warnock ML. Numbers of asbestos bodies in urban patients with lung cancer and gastrointestinal cancer and in matched controls. Chest 1979; 76(2):143–9.
37. Neuberger M, Kundi M, Friedl HP. Environmental asbestos exposure and cancer mortality. Arch Environ Health 1984; 39(4):261–5.
38. McDonald JC. Health implications of environmental exposure to asbestos. Environ Health Perspect 1985; 62:319–28.
39. Hammond EC, Garfinkel L, Selikoff IJ, Nicholson WJ. Mortality experience of residents in the neighborhood of an asbestos factory. Ann NY Acad Sci 1979; 330:417–22.
40. Marsh GM. Critical review of epidemiologic studies related to ingested asbestos. Environ Health Perspect 1983; 53:49–56.
41. Anderson HA, Lilis R, Daum SM, Selikoff IJ. Asbestosis among household contacts of asbestos factory workers. Ann NY Acad Sci 1979; 330:387–99.
42. Vianna NJ, Polan AK. Non-occupational exposure to asbestos and malignant mesothelioma in females. Lancet 1978; 1:1061–3.
43. Rodelsperger K. Asbestos dust exposure during brake repair. Am J Ind Med 1986; 10(1):63–72.
44. Cordier S, Lazar P, Brochard P, Bignon J, Ameille J, Proteau J. Epidemiologic investigation of respiratory effects related to environmental exposure to asbestos inside insulated buildings. Arch Environ Health 1987; 42(5):303–9.
45. Quinn MM, Kriebel D, Buiatte E, Paci E, Sini S, Vannucchi G, Zappa M. An asbestos hazard in the reprocessed textile industry. Am J. Ind Med 1987; 11:255–66.
46. Paci E, Dini S, Buiatti E, Seniori Costantini A, Lenzi S, Zappa M. Malignant mesothelioma in non-asbestos textile workers in Florence. Am J. Ind Med 1987; 11:249–54.
47. Paci E, Buiatti E, Geddes M. A case-referent study of lung tumors in non-asbestos textile workers. Am J Ind Med 1987; 11:267–73.
48. *Code of Federal Regulations*, Title 40, Part 763, Section 121. Washington: U.S. Government Printing Office, 1987.
49. *Code of Federal Regulations*, Title 29, Part 1910, Section 1001. Washington: U.S. Government Printing Office, 1987.
50. *Code of Federal Regulations*, Title 29, Part 1926, Section 58. Washington: U.S. Government Printing Office, 1987.
51. International Labour Office. *Guidelines for the Use of ILO International Classification of Radiographs of Pneumoconioses*. Geneva: International Labour Office, 1980.

52. Epler GR, McLoud TC, Gaensler EA. Prevalence and incidence of benign asbestos pleural effusion in a working population. J Am Med Assoc 1982; 247(5):617–22.
53. Dement JM, Merchant JA, Green FHY. Asbestosis. *Occupational Respiratory Diseases*, DHHS (NIOSH) Publication No. 86-102. Washington: U.S. Government Printing Office, 1981, pp. 287–327.
54. Gefter WB, Conant EF. Issues and controversies in the plain-film diagnosis of asbestos-related disorders in the chest. J Thorac Image 1988; 3(4):11–28.
55. Hillerdal G. Short report: value of the lateral view in diagnosing pleural plaques. Arch Environ Health 1986; 41(6):391–2.
56. Sherman CB, Barnhart S, Rosenstock L. Use of oblique chest roentgenograms in detecting plaural disease in asbestos-exposed workers. JOM 1988; 30(9):681–3.
57. Greenberg SD. Recent advances in pulmonary cytopathology. Hum Pathol 1983; 14(10):901–12.
58. De Vuyst P, Jedwab J. Dumortier P, Vandermoten G, Vande Weyer R, Yernault JC. Asbestos bodies in bronchoalveolar lavage. Am Rev Respir Dis 1982; 126:972–6.
59. De Vuyst P, Dumortier P, Moulin E, Yourassowsky N, Yernault JC. Diagnostic value of asbestos bodies in bronchoalveolar lavage fluid. Am Rev Respir Dis 1987; 136:1219–24.
60. De Vuyst P, Dumortier P, Moulin E, Yourassowsky N, Roomans P, de Francquen P, Yernault JC. Asbestos bodies in bronchoalveolar lavage reflect lung asbestos body concentration. Submitted for publication.
61. Gellert AR, Kitajewska JY, Uthayakumar S, Kirkham JB, Rudd RM. Asbestos fibres in bronchoalveolar lavage fluid from asbestos workers: examination by electron microscopy. Br J Ind Med 1986; 43:170–6.
62. Begin R, Masse S, Cantin A, Bisson G, Bergeron D. Imaging the pneumoconioses: a multidïsciplinary approach. J Thorac Imag 1988; 3(4):37–50.
63. Rebuck AS, Braude AC. Bronchoalveolar lavage in asbestosis. Arch Intern Med 1983; 143:950–2.

19

Guidelines for the Use of ILO International Classification of Radiographs of Pneumoconioses: Revised 1980 Edition

Synopsis

EDITORS' COMMENTARY

GUIDELINES

EDITORS' COMMENTARY

The following ILO guidelines provide the worldwide uniform system for interpreting and coding of radiological patterns for all the pneumoconioeses. The 1971 version appeared as an Appendix to Volume I of the *Sourcebook on Asbestos Diseases*, and the 1980 version, which is being used in 1989, is printed in its entirety below. These guidelines are widely used or consulted not only by radiologists, but by allied health specialists, lawyers, and others. The ILO notations are found in the medical records of those given x-rays to determine the presence of an asbestos-related disease. It is a uniform procedure for determining and interpreting the presence, location, degree of severity, character, and coding of all the pneumoconioses.

This standard system for interpeting chest x-rays or radiographs was initiated 73 years ago and was upgraded or modified in 1930, 1958, 1968, 1971, and 1980. The ILO classification system has been specified for use by various government entities thoughout the world, is utilized for quick communication purposes in the medical research literature, and is applied in most diagnoses of pneumoconiosis. It is found in medical reports and in diagnostic evidence introduced in contested personal injury claims and lawsuits. The written "guidelines" for interpreting radiographs is supplemented by a set of "standard films" or standard reference radiographs to help assure uniformity in "reading" or interpreting the x-ray film. Greater consistency was needed in classifying the pneumoconioses so a certification program was undertaken by NIOSH (U.S. National Institute of Occupational Safety and Health) and lists have been published of those physicians who have been approved or certified by NIOSH as "B-Readers" (see Chapter 20 in this volume).

22
(Rev. 80)

OCCUPATIONAL SAFETY
AND HEALTH SERIES

GUIDELINES FOR THE USE OF ILO INTERNATIONAL CLASSIFICATION OF RADIOGRAPHS OF PNEUMOCONIOSES

REVISED EDITION 1980

INTERNATIONAL LABOUR OFFICE GENEVA

The International Programme for the Improvement of Working Conditions and Environment (PIACT) was launched by the International Labour Organisation in 1976 at the request of the International Labour Conference and after extensive consultations with member States. PIACT is designed to promote or support action by member States to set and attain definite objectives aiming at "making work more human". The Programme is thus concerned with improving the quality of working life in all its aspects: for example, the prevention of occupational accidents and diseases, a wider application of the principles of ergonomics, the arrangement of working time, the improvement of the content and organisation of work and of conditions of work in general, a greater concern for the human element in the transfer of technology. To achieve these aims, PIACT makes use of and co-ordinates the traditional means of ILO action, including:

- the preparation and revision of international labour standards;
- operational activities, including the dispatch of multidisciplinary teams to assist member States on request;
- tripartite meetings between representatives of governments, employers and workers, including industrial committees to study the problems facing major industries, regional meetings and meetings of experts;
- action-oriented studies and research; and
- clearing-house activities, especially through the International Occupational Safety and Health Information Centre (CIS) and the Clearing-house for the Dissemination of Information on Conditions of Work.

The Clearing-house for the Dissemination of Information on Conditions of Work aims to set up a network of institutions which will forward information about their research projects, meetings, publications and training activities on a regular basis. Its computerised data base will provide quick access to this information, which will be disseminated to institutions in various forms, including replies to ad hoc requests.

This publication is the outcome of a PIACT project.

Guidelines for the use of ILO International Classification of Radiographs of Pneumoconioses

Revised edition 1980

OCCUPATIONAL SAFETY
AND HEALTH SERIES
No. 22 (Rev.)

GUIDELINES FOR THE USE OF ILO INTERNATIONAL CLASSIFICATION OF RADIOGRAPHS OF PNEUMOCONIOSES

REVISED EDITION 1980

INTERNATIONAL LABOUR OFFICE GENEVA

ISBN 92-2-102463-6
ISSN 0078-3129

This edition first published 1980
Fifth impression 1987

The designations employed in ILO publications, which are in conformity with United Nations practice, and the presentation of material therein do not imply the expression of any opinion whatsoever on the part of the International Labour Office concerning the legal status of any country, area or territory or of its authorities, or concerning the delimitation of its frontiers. The responsibility for opinions expressed in signed articles, studies and other contributions rests solely with their authors, and publication does not constitute an endorsement by the International Labour Office of the opinions expressed in them.
Reference to names of firms and commercial products and processes does not imply their endorsement by the International Labour Office, and any failure to mention a particular firm, commercial product or process is not a sign of disapproval.

ILO publications can be obtained through major booksellers or ILO local offices in many countries, or direct from ILO Publications, International Labour Office, CH-1211 Geneva 22, Switzerland. A catalogue or list of new publications will be sent free of charge from the above address.

Printed by the International Labour Office, Geneva, Switzerland

FOREWORD

During the past 50 years the International Labour Office has promoted discussion and published a series of guidelines on ways of classifying chest radiographs of persons with pneumoconiosis. The aim has been to standardise classification methods and facilitate international comparisons of pneumoconiosis statistics and research reports. The ILO 1980 INTERNATIONAL CLASSIFICATION OF RADIOGRAPHS OF PNEUMOCONIOSES is a further development towards this objective. It retains the same basic principles embodied in former editions of ILO classifications (i.e. those of 1950, 1958, 1968 and 1971 editions); it clarifies some ambiguities in the earlier texts; it consolidates advances made previously; and it introduces a few modifications which permit more detailed documentation of radiographic features characteristic of pneumoconiosis. The present classification covers the radiological appearances seen in all types of pneumoconiosis.

These improvements have been based on a careful review of international experience in the use of earlier classifications. The review involved active contributions of numerous experts, organisations and institutions at various national and international meetings. Particular recognition should be given to the work accomplished by the International Workshop on the ILO/UC 1971 Classification System, sponsored by the Task Force on Pneumoconioses of the American College of Radiology with the support of the National Institute of Occupational Safety and Health, U.S. Department of Health, Education and Welfare and with the co-operation of the ILO (Washington, D.C., September, 1978). A valuable contribution has been provided by the detailed technical discussions organised by the Working Group on Radiodiagnosis under the auspices of the Commission of European Communities in Luxembourg, London and Hasselt. At the Fifth International Pneumoconioses Conference, convened by the ILO in Caracas (Venezuela) from 29 October to 3 November 1978, a Working Group on Radiological Classification examined the final recommendations on the text of the revised classification and the selection of standard radiographs illustrating it.

The ILO 1980 Classification is accompanied by a new set of standard radiographs illustrating, and in some cases defining, the features described. The standard radiographs were selected following several controlled trials which involved more than 40 experts from different countries. The films include some that were distributed by the ILO in 1971, and others have been added. There has been no change in the level of profusion of small opacities depicted by the standards which now define the four main categories of profusion; but, with the assistance of the American College of Radiology, a greatly improved photocopying technique has been used to produce the films. The standard radiographs are now available from the ILO.

The intensive international activity which preceded publication of these guidelines has involved so many notable experts, institutions and organisations that it would be invidious to single out particular names, with one exception. Professor George Jacobson* died on 18 March 1979, a few days after making the last of his many vigorous contributions to the preparatory work on the classfication. The publication of this booklet is an appropriate occasion to record his devotion to the aims of the ILO Classification and to radiology of pneumoconioses.

The ILO extends its warm thanks to all concerned for their valuable assistance. The aim has always been to improve the understanding of pneumoconioses problems. The advances represented by the 1980 Classification are expected to further assist the continuing struggle to protect the health of workers occupationally exposed to airborne dusts.

---

*Dr. George Jacobson, Professor Emeritus, Department of Radiology, School of Medicine, University of Southern California, Los Angeles, USA; Chairman of the ILO Working Groups on Radiological Classification, Geneva, 1968, Bucharest, 1971 and Caracas, 1978.

CONTENTS

C O N T E N T S

ILO 1980 INTERNATIONAL CLASSIFICATION OF RADIOGRAPHS OF THE PNEUMOCONIOSES

INTRODUCTION

Scope of the Classification

This Classification provides a means for recording systematically the radiographic abnormalities in the chest provoked by the inhalation of dusts. The scheme is designed for classifying the appearances of postero-anterior chest radiographs (Note 1).

Object of the Classification

The object of the Classification is to codify the radiographic abnormalities of pneumoconiosis in a simple reproducible manner. The Classification does not define pathological entities, nor take into account working capacity. The Classification does not imply legal definitions of pneumoconiosis for compensation purposes, nor set nor imply a level at which compensation is payable.

Complete and Short Classification

There are Complete and Short Classifications which are complementary and compatible.

Uses of the Classification

The Complete Classification has been found to have wider uses than anticipated in 1971. It is now extensively used internationally for epidemiological research, for the surveillance of those in dusty occupations and for clinical purposes. Use of the scheme may lead to better international comparability of pneumoconiosis statistics. It is also used for recording in a systematic way part of the information needed for assessing compensation.

The Short Classification is intended for clinical and other uses to which the 1950, 1958, 1968 and 1971 (short) ILO Classifications have been put.

The Complete and Short Classifications are arranged so that it is possible to use any combination of them to suit particular needs. For example, in coal workers' pneumoconiosis where pleural changes are relatively uncommon but a full classification of rounded opacities may be needed, it is possible to use the Complete Classification for the small opacities and the Short Classification for the pleural change.

In the interest of international comparability and to assist in the interpretation of publications on pneumoconiosis where this Classification is used, it is desirable to specify whether the Complete or Short Classification was employed; and also which set of standard radiographs was used. (Note 2).

Standard radiographs and written definitions

The Classification is based on a set of standard radiographs, a written text and a set of notes. In some parts of the scheme the standard radiographs take precedence over the text for the definitions; the text makes it clear when this is so. (Note 3).

GENERAL INSTRUCTIONS FOR THE USE OF THE CLASSIFICATION

There are no features to be seen in a chest radiograph which are pathognomonic of dust exposure. But the following recommendations are made for the classification of a postero-anterior radiograph:

1. if any of the appearances of the pleura or the parenchyma are consistent with pneumoconiosis, proceed with the Classification. Do not classify any appearances which are definitely not pneumoconiosis, but record these using Symbols and Comments (Note 4);

2. if it is probable that all the appearances seen are the result of some other aetiology, do not classify, but record opinion using appropriate Symbols and Comments (Note 4);

3. if the appearances might be due to pneumoconiosis, record the observations according to the Classification, but note also what other aetiology was considered.

COMPLETE CLASSIFICATION

Recording technical quality

Four grades of technical quality are used:-

1. Good.

2. Acceptable, with no technical defect likely to impair classification of the radiograph for pneumoconiosis.

3. Poor, with some technical defect but still acceptable for classification purposes.

4. Unacceptable.

If technical quality is not Grade 1, a comment should be made about the technical defects (Note 5).

Parenchymal abnormalities

Small Opacities

Profusion

The category of profusion is based on assessment of the concentration of opacities (Note 6) by comparison with the standard radiographs. For profusion the written definitions are a guide, but the standard radiographs take precedence (Note 7).

Category 0	-	small opacities absent or less profuse than the lower limit of category 1.
Categories 1, 2 and 3	-	represent increasing profusion of small opacities as defined by the corresponding standard radiographs.

By using the 12-point scale of profusion, the Classification recognises the existence of a continuity of change from no small opacities to the most advanced category. While still retaining the four major categories, 0, 1, 2 and 3, as defined by the standard radiographs, this scale readily permits subdivision into more categories and provides extra information. The instructions for using this 12-point scale are:- The radiograph is classified in the usual way into one of the four major categories by comparison with the standard radiographs. If during the process the major category above or below is seriously considered as an alternative, this is recorded. Thus, category 2/1 is profusion of major category 2, but with category 1 having been seriously considered as an alternative. Profusion which is without serious doubt category 2, that is, near the middle of the major category, should be classified 2/2.

In radiographs within category 0, a subdivision is also possible. Thus category 0/1 is profusion of category 0, but category 1 was seriously considered. Category 0/0 is a radiograph in which there are no small opacities, or if a few are thought to be present they are not sufficiently definite or numerous for category 1 to be considered. If the absence of small opacities is particularly obvious, the profusion should be recorded as 0/-. Within category 3 a radiograph showing markedly higher profusion than would be classified as 3/3 should be recorded as 3/+. Thus, the short four-point scale becomes the complete twelve-point scale: 0/-, 0/0, 0/1; 1/0, 1/1, 1/2; 2/1, 2/2, 2/3; 3/2, 3/3, 3/+. (Note 8). It must be emphasised that other abnormalities may be present regardless of the category of profusion of small opacities.

Extent

The zones in which the opacities are seen are recorded. The lungs are divided into six zones - upper, middle, and lower, right and left - by horizontal lines drawn at one-third and two-thirds of the vertical distance between the lung apices and the domes of the diaphragm.

The category of profusion of small opacities is determined by considering the profusion as a whole over the affected zones of the lung, and by comparing this with the standard radiographs. Where there is a marked (three minor categories or more) difference in profusion in different zones of the lung, then the zone or zones showing this marked lesser degree of profusion are ignored for the purpose of classifying the profusion (Note 9).

Shape and size

The shape and size (Note 10) of small opacities are recorded. Two kinds of shape are recognised: rounded and irregular. In each case, three sizes are differentiated. They are illustrated by standard radiographs which take precedence over the following written definitions. The letters p, q, r denote the presence of small rounded opacities, where

p = diameter up to about 1.5 mm;

q = diameter exceeding about 1.5 mm and up to about 3 mm;

r = diameter exceeding about 3 mm and up to about 10 mm.

The letters s, t, u denote the presence of small irregular opacities, where

s = width up to about 1.5 mm;

t = width exceeding 1.5 mm and up to about 3 mm;

u = width exceeding 3 mm and up to about 10 mm.

To record shape and size, two letters must be used. Thus if the reader considers that all or virtually all opacities seen are of one shape and size, then this should be noted by recording the symbol twice, separated by an oblique stroke (for example, q/q). If, however, another shape (or size) is seen, then this should be recorded as the second letter (for example, q/t). 'q/t' would mean that the predominant small opacity is round and of size q, but that there are significant numbers of small irregular opacities present of size t. In this way any combination of small opacities may be recorded (Note 11).

Standard radiographs illustrating both rounded and irregular shapes should be used for comparisons when the shape of opacity is in doubt or when both shapes are present.

Large Opacities

The examples of large opacities in the standard radiographs show abnormal opacities greater than 10 mm in diameter. The categories are defined in terms of dimensions of the opacities:

Category A - an opacity having a greatest diameter exceeding about 10 mm and up to and including about 50 mm, or several opacities each greater than about 10 mm the sum of whose greatest diameters does not exceed about 50 mm.

Category B - one or more opacities larger or more numerous than those in category A whose combined area does not exceed the equivalent of the right upper zone.

Category C - one or more opacities whose combined area exceeds the equivalent of the right upper zone.

Pleural abnormalities

Pleural Thickening

Site (chest wall, diaphragm, costophrenic angle), width and extent of pleural thickening are recorded separately and defined in the text below (Note 12).

Chest Wall

Types: Circumscribed (plaques), and/or diffuse (Note 12).

Site: Pleural thickening of the chest wall is recorded separately for the right and left chest walls.

Width: For pleural thickening seen along the lateral chest wall the measurement of the maximum width of the shadow is made from the inner line of the chest wall to the inner margin of the shadow seen most sharply at the parenchymal-pleural boundary. The maximum width usually occurs at the inner margin of the rib shadow at its outermost point.

a = maximum width up to about 5 mm.
b = maximum width over about 5 mm and up to about 10 mm.
c = maximum width over about 10 mm.

For pleural thickening seen face on (en face), the presence is recorded, even if it can also be seen in profile. If pleural thickening is seen face on only, width usually can not be measured.

Extent: Extent is defined in terms of the maximum length of pleural involvement, or as the sum of maximum lengths, whether seen in profile or face on.

1 = total length equivalent to up to one quarter of the projection of the lateral chest wall.

2 = total length exceeding one quarter but not one half of the projection of the lateral chest wall.

3 = total length exceeding one half of the projection of the lateral chest wall.

Diaphragm

A plaque involving the diaphragmatic pleura is recorded separately as present or absent, right or left. This is illustrated by an example in the standard radiographs (Note 13).

Costophrenic angle obliteration

The lower limit for this obliteration is defined by the standard radiograph showing profusion category 1/1 t/t. Such thickening is recorded separately from thickening over other areas (Note 14). If the thickening extends further up the chest wall, the radiograph should be classified as costophrenic angle obliteration and pleural thickening on the chest wall, if the latter is extent 1 or greater. Costophrenic angle obliteration is recorded as absent or present. The site, right or left, is specified.

Pleural Calcification

Site and extent are recorded for the two lungs separately. The following numerical definitions of extent take precedence over the examples in the standard radiographs (Note 15).

Site: Chest wall, diaphragm, and other. The latter includes calcification of the mediastinal and pericardial pleura.

Extent: 1 = an area of calcified pleura with greatest diameter up to about 20 mm, or a number of such areas the sum of whose greatest diameters does not exceed about 20 mm.

Extent: 2 = an area of calcified pleura with greatest diameter exceeding about 20 mm and up to about 100 mm, or a number of such areas the sum of whose greatest diameters exceeds about 20 mm but does not exceed about 100 mm.

3 = an area of calcified pleura with greatest diameter exceeding about 100 mm, or a number of such areas whose sum of greatest diameters exceeds about 100 mm.

Symbols

Symbols to record radiographic features of importance are listed below. Their use is obligatory. Examples are included in the standard radiographs and in the diagrams (Note 16).

It is to be taken that the definition of each of the Symbols is preceded by an appropriate word or phrase, such as "suspect", "changes suggestive of", "opacities suggestive of", etc.

The Symbols are:

ax - coalescence of small pneumoconiotic opacities (Note 16)

bu - bulla(e)

ca - cancer of lung or pleura

cn - calcification in small pneumoconiotic opacities

co - abnormality of cardiac size or shape

cp - cor pulmonale

cv - cavity

di - marked distortion of the intrathoracic organs

ef - effusion

em - definite emphysema

es - eggshell calcification of hilar or mediastinal lymph nodes

fr - fractured rib(s)

hi - enlargement of hilar or mediastinal lymph nodes

ho - honeycomb lung

id - ill defined diaphragm (Note 16)

ih - ill defined heart outline (Note 16)

kl - septal (Kerley) lines

od - other significant abnormality

pi - pleural thickening in the interlobar fissure or mediastinum

px - pneumothorax

rp - rheumatoid pneumoconiosis

tb - tuberculosis

The calcified primary complex of tuberculosis or other granulomatous processes, such as coccidioidomycosis or histoplasmosis should not be coded under tb. Such appearances should be noted under Comments.

Comments

Comments should be recorded pertaining to the classification of the radiograph, particularly if some other cause is thought to be responsible for a shadow which could be thought by others to have been due to pneumoconiosis; also to identify radiographs for which the technical quality may have affected the reading materially.

SHORT CLASSIFICATION

The detailed rules of how the Short Classification is to be used are as in the Complete Classification but with simplification. The details recorded are as follows:

Technical Quality

Technical quality is recorded 1, 2, 3 or 4 as for the Complete Classification (page 4).

Small Opacities

Profusion by comparison with standard radiographs into the four principal categories: 0, 1, 2 and 3 (page 4).

Shape and size by comparison of the predominant opacity pattern with standard radiographs.

If rounded, p, q or r.

If irregular, s, t or u as for Complete Classification (page 6).

Large Opacities

Category A, B or C as for Complete Classification (page 6).

Pleural Changes

Pleural thickening is recorded as symbol pt.
Pleural calcification is recorded as symbol pc.

Symbols

As for Complete Classification, together with pt and pc. All are obligatory (page 9).

Comments

Comments should be recorded as for Complete Classification (page 10

EXPLANATORY NOTES

These notes are to assist in the understanding of the principles and use of the Classification. They do not take precedence over the written text but are intended to reduce ambiguities and differences in its use. They are based on experience with the previous Classifications.

Note 1 Scope

The Classification now covers all types of pneumoconiosis. It is designed for use with postero-anterior chest radiographs. This is not to say that other views should not be considered in the full clinical assessment of any individual.

Note 2 Standard Radiographs

The 1980 Classification is accompanied by a new set of standard radiographs which were selected after international trials. The trials were designed to obtain better illustrations of features described in the Classification.

Note 3 Definitions

In the past it has not been quite clear whether the standard radiographs or the text takes precedence in terms of definition. This is now clarified throughout.

Note 4 General Instructions

Comments must be recorded about appearances which are definitely or probably not pneumoconiosis. This may permit the resolution of apparent major discrepancies between readers.

Note 5 Technical Quality

It has been suggested that for epidemiological studies (when it may not be possible to replace a technically poor radiograph by a better one) more detail should be recorded about technical defects. In particular, if the parenchyma is visible and the pleura not, or vice versa, only part of a complete reading may be usefully available for statistical analysis. However, no specific recommendation about such recording is made at this time.

Note 6 Small opacities - order of recording

Profusion relates better than size to indices of exposure within any one occupational group. Since 1971 profusion has been recorded first.

Note 7 Standard radiographs for profusion of small opacities

Current research on the use of the Classification includes trials designed to test the validity and utility of additional standard radiographs for profusion. These are expected to illustrate (a) the boundary points on the continuum of profusion between the four major categories, and (b) the profusion characteristic of mid-categories, using only sections of the lung. The text describing the Classification has been prepared so that it may be used unchanged if trials are completed successfully and additional standard radiographs become available. (See also Appendix C).

In the Classifications from 1950 to 1971 the definitions in the text of the categories of profusion of small opacities included reference to the degree of obscuration of the normal vascular pattern of the lung - no obscuration in Category 1, sometimes and partially in Category 2, and usually, partly or totally in Category 3. In the 1980 Classification this information is omitted in the text but will be apparent from inspection of the standard films. The degree of obscuration may be of assistance in deciding the category of small opacities.

Note 8 Twelve-point scale for profusion of small opacities

The twelve categories of the complete Classification represent divisions on a continuous scale of profusion of small opacities. In practice it is no more difficult to use than the four categories of the short Classification. On the contrary, most readers find that the 12-point scale is helpful because it enables them to codify the appearances of radiographs that are not obviously similar to the standards. For instance, categories 0/1 and 1/0 may be used to represent "suspect" pneumoconiosis.

The twelve categories range from an exceptionally "normal" radiograph at one end of the scale (0/-) to an advanced Category 3 at the other (3/+). The intermediate ten categories are arbitrary divisions of increasing profusion between these two extremes. The concept of a continuum of radiological abnormality is consistent with results from extensive epidemiological research on relationships between radiological classifications and (a) cumulative dust exposures, and (b) the dust content of post-mortem lungs; it is supported also by studies of the variability between different readers' classifications of the same radiographs.

Note 9 Determining profusion over different zones

Classification of a radiograph for profusion of small opacities requires a mental process of integrating profusion over the affected zones. Earlier Classifications referred to this process as "averaging". This might be confused with arithmetical averaging of the numbers which symbolise the categories. Therefore the word "averaging" is not used in the 1980 Classification.

Note 10 Shape and size of small opacities

The 1980 Classification distinguishes between the concepts Shape and Size of small opacities. The symbols used are the same as those defined in previous Classifications under the general heading Type.

For small opacities shape and size are both known to be important. For example, in coalworkers' pneumoconiosis, profusion of p and q opacities relates better to dust content of the lung than the profusion of size r opacities. Also men with small p opacities tend to have lower values of gas transfer of carbon monoxide. Asbestos workers with a "u" pattern have worse prognosis.

Note 11 Mixtures of shapes and sizes

The 1980 Classification permits recordings of mixtures of shapes and sizes of small opacities on the same radiograph. When, as usually occurs, only one shape (and size) is seen, the symbol denoting that shape and size must be recorded twice on the reading sheet (for example, record p/p when only small rounded opacities of size p are seen). This rule avoids ambiguities on the written records and emphasises that not all radiographs with small opacities show mixtures of shapes.

Note 12 Pleural Thickening

Shadows are produced by thickening of the visceral and parietal layers of the pleura. Confident identification of which surface is thickened may not always be possible using the postero-anterior radiograph. But separation may be useful because there may be differing aetiologies, natural histories and relations to disability.

Pleural thickening occurs in two principal forms, the different appearances of which are illustrated in the standard radiographs. Both types may occur together. Separation of the two types is usually, but not always possible. In some cases small peripheral shadows of indeterminate type occur.

(a) Circumscribed shadows (non-calcified hyaline plaques)

The standard radiographs include an example of the characteristic appearance of these shadows. They are normally the result of thickening of the parietal pleura, and are the precursors of calcified plaques.

The extent of these shadows in relation to the length of the lateral chest wall provides a rough measure of their size. But a postero-anterior radiograph may reveal only a small proportion of their full extent. The width of the shadow measured between the inner edge and the chest wall is highly influenced by the precise position of the plaque on the chest wall, so that this measurement may not be an indication of severity.

(b) Diffuse shadows

The standard radiographs include examples of the appearances of these shadows. This is the well recognised type of pleural thickening seen also in many non-pneumoconiotic conditions. It is probably the result of thickening of the visceral pleura. It is less specific to asbestos and other fibrous mineral dust exposure, but it is a feature in some cases of severe asbestosis. The word 'diffuse' refers to the tendency to produce a general veiling of lung parenchymal detail. In some cases the shadow produces a sharply defined line along the chest wall due to it being seen in profile (edge on). When this appearance is well developed the maximum width of the shadow is recordable. The extent is recorded as for circumscribed shadows. These two measurements may provide the best index of the severity of visceral pleural involvement.

Note 13 Diaphragm

Circumscribed thickening (plaque) of the diaphragmatic pleura is considered by some as highly specific to exposure to asbestos and other fibrous dusts. The shadows are identifiable most easily when shaped like a crater. Diffuse thickening is less specific to past dust exposure and accompanies costophrenic angle obliteration. If it is extensive, it should be recorded using the symbol id (see Note 16).

Note 14 Costophrenic angle obliteration

This is recorded separately from other pleural thickening because it frequently occurs, at least unilaterally, in those not exposed to asbestos or other dust. Costophrenic angle obliteration is, however, of special relevance in asbestos exposed people. "Leafing" of the diaphragm should not be recorded as filling of the angle even though it leads to obscuration of the costophrenic angle.

Note 15 Pleural calcification

Pleural calcification may be due to trauma, old infections, or exposure to asbestos, talc and some other minerals. The mineral dusts tend to produce bilateral changes. The calcification varies from just detectable spicules a few millimetres long to large areas covering nearly the whole lung. The large plaques have "rolled" edges and have been likened in appearance to holly leaves or candlewax.

Note 16 Symbols

It is highly desirable that the reading sheet should contain the full list of Symbols, as it is only by doing this that a check can be made of the completeness of recording. Failure to use all the Symbols and Comments in statistical analyses is likely to lead to unnecessary unexplained differences between observers.

Attention is drawn to the following points.

The Symbol ax (coalescence of small opacities) may be recorded in the presence of large opacities.

The Symbol id (ill-defined diaphragm) should only be recorded if more than one-third of one hemidiaphragm is affected.

The Symbol ih (ill-defined heart outline) should only be recorded if the length of border affected is more than one-third on the left cardiac border.

USING THE CLASSIFICATION

Efficient use of the Classification requires good viewing and recording conditions. It is assumed that readers have good vision (with the aid of spectacles if necessary). The following recommendations are particularly important for epidemiological studies.

Viewing

The viewing boxes on which the radiograph to be classified and the standards are to be displayed need to be near enough for the observer to see shadows only 1 mm in diameter, that is about 250 mm distance, but it must also be possible to view the whole radiograph from about twice this distance. The observer should be seated and not have to lean uncomfortably far forward to view the radiograph closely. (In some departments of radiology the viewing boxes are too far from the edge of the table to provide satisfactory conditions.)

The minimum number of viewing spaces on a viewing box is two and the optimum probably five. It is recommended that the radiograph to be classified is placed in the middle, and the more commonly used standard radiographs on either side. Whatever the arrangement, it is important to make it easy to select and put up the standard radiographs for comparison. Failure to do this discourages readers from regular use of standards, and this is thought to be one of the causes of inter-observer variability.

The viewing boxes must be clean. The intensity of illumination should be uniform over the whole surface and visually identical over the areas where the comparisons are being made. A pair of well matched single viewing boxes is adequate but a longer box, about 1600 mm x 400 mm is preferable.

(A box with two standard sized 1500 mm colour matched 80w fluorescent tubes mounted 100 mm behind an opal plastic screen 3 mm thick will give a very uniform and well illuminated screen of 1600 x 400 mm to hold four 400 x 400 mm radiographs.)

The general illumination in the room should be low without direct daylight. The room should be quiet, comfortable and free from distractions.

Epidemiological reading protocols

When classifying radiographs for epidemiological purposes it is essential that the reader does not consider any information about the individuals concerned, other than the radiographs themselves. Awareness of supplementary details specific to individuals can introduce bias into results. If the epidemiological objective is to make comparisons between two or more groups, then the radiographs from all groups should be mixed, and presented to the reader in random order. Failure to observe these principles may invalidate conclusions from the study.

Recording

Recording of results should be standardised and systematic. If the results are to be analysed with the help of a computer then the proforma should be designed accordingly. In all cases, it is important to make provision for recording definitely the absence of any feature not seen, and whether or not any Comments are being made on the radiograph concerned. This avoids ambiguity in the interpretation of blanks on the pro-forma. Clerical help for recording results is valuable when classifying large numbers of radiographs. The assistant should then be asked to remind the reader of failure to report the presence or absence of any feature included on the pro-forma.

Reading rates

The number of radiographs classifiable per unit time can vary greatly. Factors influencing reading rates include the prevalence of abnormalities on the radiographs, their technical quality, the experience of the reader, the purpose of the reading exercise, and the length of the reading session. Some readers can work comfortably for two or two-and-a-half hours with no break. With clerical help they may classify several hundred radiographs in that time if the abnormality rate is low. Others prefer to arrange their work as a series of shorter sessions (perhaps one or one-and-a-quarter hours each), with intervals for rest.

Number of readers

It is recognised that there is considerable variation in repeated readings of the same radiograph, not only from reader to reader, but also between readings by the same reader. It is strongly recommended that at least two, and preferably three independent readings are made for each radiograph.

When many radiographs are being read, intra-observer variation (that is, variation in repeated readings by the same reader) should also be assessed.

APPENDICES

These have been prepared by various experts to assist understanding of the principles and development of the Classification. Some of the views expressed may be controversial. The Appendices are not a part of the text of the ILO 1980 INTERNATIONAL CLASSIFICATION OF RADIOGRAPHS OF THE PNEUMOCONIOSES.

APPENDIX A

EQUIPMENT AND TECHNOLOGY : GUIDANCE NOTES*

It has long been recognised that the exposures received by radiographs of the chest have a marked influence on the radiographic appearance of lesions of pneumoconiosis. Consequently, readers of radiographs which demonstrate evidence of pneumoconiosis will find difficulty in applying the ILO 1980 Classification for reporting the characteristics of this disease unless the exposures used in making the radiographs are maintained within an optimum range. Application of the system will only be as satisfactory as radiographic technical quality is good.

The importance of image density and radiation exposure to technical excellence in chest radiography is difficult to over-emphasise. It is known that by far the greatest causes of poor technical quality in chest radiographs (well over ninety percent) are over-exposure and under-exposure, unsatisfactory gross image contrast, poor screen-film contact and fog. Medical training should include the fundamentals of radiographic technique so that physicians are able to determine the causes of poor technical quality when encountered. Some technologists work without adequate supervision by knowledgeable physicians, and, until recently, convenient densitometric instruments have not been available with which the quality of each radiograph can be measured at the time it is made.

What is clearly needed are (1) improved training programmes in radiographic technology for both physicians and technologists; (2) closer liaison between physicians and technologists in

---

* Prepared by H. Bohlig, Y. Hosoda, G. Jacobson (deceased) and R. Morgan.

day-to-day practice, and (3) widespread use of the recently available pocket densitometers to determine the technical quality of each chest radiograph when it is made.

Using subjective criteria, the most desirable chest radiograph for the detection of abnormalities of the pneumoconioses is one in which the pulmonary parenchymal markings are shown in greatest detail, the costopleural junctions are clearly seen, and the major pulmonary vessels are visible through the cardiac shadow. While it is important to visualise the details of the mediastinal structure as well, this is usually not possible on a radiograph made for assessment of pneumoconiosis.

On physical grounds, a radiograph of satisfactory technical quality may be defined as one in which the exposure has been such that the optical densities of the images of interest fall between 0.3 and 1.7 and in which the difference in optical density between the darkest image of interest and the lightest is 1.0 or more. The inherent contrast (i.e. the density vs log exposure gradient) of radiographs falls off rapidly as optical densities descend below 0.3 and hence, image quality becomes increasingly unsatisfactory as this occurs. Above an optical density of 1.7, the inherent contrast of radiographs remains good but extraneous light entering the observer's eyes from light sources other than the x-ray viewing boxes tends to impair the contrast of the radiographic image when projected on the retinae. Hence, technical quality deteriorates for images having optical densities much above 1.7 density units. (See also Appendix C, paragraph 8).

Equipment

The installation and maintenance of the radiographic equipment is of the greatest importance. The electric power source should be independent of other users. It must be of adequate capacity, for example, having a resistance of not more than 0.1 Ω and should be subject to no more than 5 per cent fluctuation. The voltage drop between the main supply and the x-ray unit when the unit is at its maximum output should not exceed 10 per cent. The radiographic unit must be carefully calibrated at the time of installation and should be recalibrated periodically. Preventive maintenance at regular intervals is strongly recommended.

The generator should have a minimum capacity of 300 mA at 125 kV. The generator must be full-wave rectified. It should be equipped with an accurate timer ($\pm$ 1 per cent) capable of minimum exposure of no more than 10 ms. Ideally, three-phase generators should be used for both fixed and mobile units. However, in the case of mobile units, when it may not be feasible to use three-phase generators, condensor-discharge units may be the apparatus of choice.

A rotating anode tube is essential. It should have as small a focal spot as feasible for the anticipated load, but in no instance should this exceed 2 mm in diameter.

The total filtration, added and inherent, of the primary x-ray beam should be the equivalent of 2 mm of aluminium.

The radiation should be confined by means of a collimator to the portion of the subject to be examined. This will not only decrease radiation hazard, but also will improve detail by reducing scattered radiation. The collimator should have adjustable diaphragms, a light beam for centring, and be designed so that the projected field cannot exceed the size of the film. Evidence of collimation should be visible at the edges of the film as "cone cuts".

Medium speed (par speed) intensifying screens should be used. They provide the best compromise between sharp definition and short exposure. The cassettes in use should contain screens of the same speed. Both films and screens should be tested and matched for speed, and cassettes should be checked periodically for screen cleanliness, contact and defects.

The x-ray film should be of a general purpose type and of medium sensitivity. High speed film is not recommended. To improve collimation, the film should be no larger than needed to cover both lungs, including the costophrenic angles.

When using kilovoltages of 80 and above, reduction of secondary radiation by a grid or other means is essential. A 10:1, 100-line per inch fixed grid or an air-gap of 200 mm with a 2.5 m focal spot-film distance may be used.

Automatic processing should be employed whenever possible. If only manual processing is available, a constant time-temperature technique must be followed meticulously. An improper exposure cannot be corrected by improper processing.

Technique

Correct centring of the x-ray tube and careful positioning of the subject are of great importance for the proper visualisation of anatomic structures and comparison of serial examinations. For the PA projection, the x-ray tube should be centred to the centre of the film and the x-ray beam directed horizontally. The shoulders should be positioned so that the scapulae are outside the lung fields. The exposure should be made at full inspiration and immediately after this has been reached, to avoid the Valsalva effect. It is desirable, but not essential, that all the clothes above the waist be removed.

The focal spot-film distance should be fixed at 1.8 m (6 feet) and should not be less than 1.5 m (5 feet).

For reasons given above, a variable high kilovoltage, constant milliampere-second technique is recommended. Exposure factors employed may vary somewhat with each generator and tube. The highest range of kilovoltage and shortest range of milliamperes-seconds obtainable should be used. For the average subject, with an AP chest diameter between 210 and 230 mm, the usual exposure factors will be 5 mAs at approximately 125 kV. The recommended exposure time is 1/60 (0.017) s; not exceeding 1/30 (0.03) s. (Based on 60 Hz current. For 50 Hz current, exposure times are 1/50 (0.02) and 1/25 (0.04) s respectively.)

With larger diameters of the chest, additional exposure is obtained by increasing the kilovoltage. The milliampere-second product is increased only when the kilovoltage required to give a proper exposure exceeds the capability of the generator or x-ray tube. With focal spot-film distances of less than 1.8 m (6 feet) the technique should be adjusted by decreasing the milliampere-second product.

When using a lower kilovoltage technique, the exposure factors for an average subject will be approximately 300 mA, 0.05 s (15 mAs) at 75 kV. For larger subjects, greater amounts of radiation are obtained by increasing either the milliampere-second product or the kilovoltage.

It is recognised however that the question of optimal radiographic technique remains a controversial matter among experts internationally.

Physical criteria for excellence of technical quality in chest radiographs

A. Optical density

1. Hilar regions should exhibit a minimum of 0.2 units of optical density above fog.

2. Parenchymal regions should exhibit a maximum of 1.8 units of optical density above fog.

B. Gross image contrast* should fall within the range of 1.0 and 1.4 units of optical density.

C. X-rays tube potentials and use of grids

1. Potentials of 70 to 100 kVp: use grids for all subjects whose posteroanterior dimension exceeds 220 mm.

2. Potentials over 100 kVp: use grid for all subjects.

D. Exposure time

Not greater than 0.1 s, and preferably 0.05 s or less.

E. Film-screen combination

Use medium-speed films and screens to assure adequate image detail. Good screen-film contact is essential with periodic testing mandatory.

F. Processing

Maintain strength and temperature of processing chemicals within limits recommended by manufacturer.

G. Assumptions

1. Cleanliness of films and screens and of processing fluids and equipment is maintained.

2. Care in subject positioning is taken.

3. Subject movement is prevented.

---

* The difference in optical density between the darkest segment of the lung parenchyma and the lightest portions of the hilar regions.

APPENDIX B

CHANGES FROM THE ILO U/C 1971 CLASSIFICATION*

Title and Scope

U/C is omitted from the title. This stood for UICC/Cincinnati and was included in the 1971 title to draw attention to its incorporation of the UICC/Cincinnati 1970 Classification devised to cover asbestosis which was not covered in the ILO 1968 scheme. The Classification now covers all types of pneumoconiosis so reference to specific types is no longer necessary.

Object and Uses of the Classification

These have been separated and slightly modified.

General Instructions

The wording has been clarified and a reminder is added to record other conditions not thought to be due to pneumoconiosis. This additional information in the Symbols and Comments can assist in resolving some discrepancies between observers.

Recording Radiographic Quality

This is now formally part of the Classification. This permits comparisons of the general quality of radiographs in different surveys. It also allows exclusion from analysis of data referring to radiographs of quality too poor to permit satisfactory classification.

Use of Standard Radiographs

In earlier versions of the Classification it was not always clear whether the appearances to be classified were defined primarily by the standard radiographs or by the text which describes the system. The 1980 Classification states specifically, for each feature, which method of definition has precedence and which should be regarded as providing supplementary information.

---

* Prepared by J.C. Gilson and C.E. Rossiter.

Profusion of small opacities

The degree of obscuration of the normal vascular pattern is no longer included as part of the definition of small opacities as profusion is now defined by comparison with the standard radiographs. However, it is included in Note 7.

Profusion and Type (Shape)

Experience using the 1971 scheme has shown that while some radiographs are classified consistently by all readers as 'rounded' and others as 'irregular', there are many radiographs for which some readers record 'rounded' and others 'irregular'. There are also radiographs where both types are recorded. This has caused serious difficulties in interpretation and analysis.

The 1980 Classification provides a means of reducing these difficulties and obtaining more information without loss of continuity with the 1971 scheme and without the introduction of new standards or definitions of the types of opacities.

Profusion

In the 1971 scheme recording of combined profusion was optional. In the 1980 scheme a single measure of profusion is recorded first using the appropriate standard radiographs. This places emphasis on the usually more important index, because the profusion of small opacities relates much better to intensity of past dust exposure than does the type of opacity.

The twelve-point scale for measuring profusion is retained unaltered except that the symbol 3/+ replaces the earlier symbol 3/4. (There is no category 4.)

The wording of the method used for deciding on the category of profusion has been amended to remove any suggestion that arithmetical averaging of profusion in different zones is required.

Type (Shape and Size)

In the 1971 Classification the <u>Type</u> referred to a complex of <u>shape</u> (roundness or irregularity) of the opacity and its <u>size</u>. Type and size were defined by standard radiographs and for rounded opacities (p, q, r) by an approximate measurement of the diameter (up to 1.5 mm; 1.5 - 3 mm; up to 10 mm). Dimensions for the irregular opacities were not provided but it was intended in the UICC/Cincinnati 1970 Classification that s, t, u irregular opacities should approximately 'match' the p, q, r rounded opacities for size.

In the 1980 scheme shape and size are defined by the standard radiographs using the same letters p, q and r for rounded opacities and s, t and u for irregular opacities. However, in the text s, t and u are given approximate sizes, in terms of width of opacity, to formalise the match of the rounded opacities:

s = width up to about 1.5 mm.

t = width exceeding 1.5 mm and up to about 3 mm.

u = width exceeding 3 mm and up to about 10 mm.

It is required to use two of the letters describing shape and size, thus providing a means for recording systematically the shape and size of small opacities which are a mixture of rounded and irregular. As two letters have to be used, a repetition of the same letter affirms positively that the opacities are all or predominantly of one shape and one size.

Rounded and irregular opacities clearly have different significance in relation to the type of mineral dust to which exposure has occurred. For example, coal produces mainly rounded opacities and asbestos mainly irregular. Future research will show whether the degree of roundness - irregularity relates to prognosis in minerals producing a mixed pattern.

In summary: the 1980 scheme provides for recording a single measure of profusion on a 12-point scale and for recording opacities of different shapes and/or sizes, while retaining a high measure of comparability with the 1971 scheme.

Large Opacities

No changes are made in the definition of A, B and C, but the qualifying words well defined (wd) and ill defined (id) are no longer used.

Pleural abnormalities

These are now recorded separately right (R) and left (L). This was recommended because in practice each is assessed separately and the recording of the two independently provides more information for no extra effort.

Thickening; Chest Wall

Type

Pleural thickening is divided into two types, circumscribed (plaques) and diffuse, and their appearances are exemplified in the standard radiographs.

Width

The definitions have been slightly altered to bring them in accord with other dimensions in the classification. The word 'grade' is omitted. It is also made clear that the width is measured from the inner line of the chest wall to the inner margin of the shadow seen most sharply at the parenchymal-pleural boundary (the cross-sectional width) and not its less well defined edge extending over the surface of the lung. The classification also requires the presence of pleural thickening seen face on to be recorded even if the width can not be measured.

Extent

An extra subdivision of extent has been included to provide more information about lesser changes. The word 'grade' has been omitted. Pleural thickening seen face on is included in the assessment of extent:

1. total length equivalent to up to one quarter of the projection of the lateral chest wall;

2. total length exceeding one quarter but not one half of the projection of the lateral chest wall;

3. total length exceeding one half of the projection of the lateral chest wall.

In the 1971 scheme it was not clear whether pleural thickening on the diaphragm - pleural plaques - should be added to that on the chest wall in assessing extent. In the 1980 scheme they are specifically excluded from the assessment of extent, but their presence is recorded.

Ill-defined Diaphragm and Cardiac Outline

These are no longer recorded in the main Classification but their presence noted without grades or lower limit standards in the Symbols, but using as lower limits the definitions in the 1971 Classification.

They were omitted from the main Classification because of their relatively low prevalence and great rarity as the sole evidence of exposure to dusts.

Symbols

The use of all Symbols is now obligatory. All are now two letters only to facilitate recording and computing. The additions and modifications are:

fr = fractured rib(s)

id = ill defined diaphragm

ih = ill defined heart outline

kl = septal (Kerley) lines - previously k

pi = thickening of interlobar fissure

rp = rheumatoid pneumoconiosis - previously rl

tb = tuberculosis (excluding primary focus). This replaces tba and tbu.

Comments

Comments were optional in previous Classifications. They should now always be added; for example, when there are technical faults making it difficult or impossible to classify the films adequately; also when there are features which might be included or excluded in the Classification by other observers. Thus, causes of big observer variation might become identifiable.

APPENDIX C

RECOMMENDATIONS FOR FUTURE RESEARCH*

Discussions at the meetings of experts which advised the ILO on the preparation of the 1980 Classification were based on wide experience in the use of earlier versions of the Classification. The experts identified several areas where additional information would be expected to lead to further improvements. Recommendations for continuing research on the classification of radiographic appearances of the pneumoconioses included the following.

1. Assessment of the 1980 Classification

Changes in the present (1980) Classification, as compared with the ILO U/C 1971 Classification, have been summarised in Appendix B. Quantitative studies aimed at describing the effects of changes in the procedures will assist interpretation of future pneumoconiosis statistics and research reports. Whenever possible, designs for such studies should be specific to particular changes that have been adopted.

2. Standard "boundary" radiographs

The 1980 standard radiographs show patterns of profusion of small opacities which are typical of appearances classifiable as near the middle of the four main categories defined by the scheme (so-called "mid-category standards"). It is possible that classification might be easier, and that precision would be increased, if there were available standard radiographs which define the three boundaries between the four main categories. The existence of such "boundary standards" would constitute an improvement in the definitions of categories of profusion, and would be particularly useful in helping to distinguish between categories 0/1 and 1/0. Some experts feel that, in the first place, research on the usefulness of boundary radiographs should be concentrated on this region of the continuum of abnormality.

International trials which preceded the selection of the 1980 set of "mid-category standards" identified several radiographs which might be regarded as "boundary standards": expert opinion was divided fairly evenly on whether they

---

*Prepared by J.C. Gilson and M. Jacobsen

should be classified into one or the other sub-category adjacent to a boundary between two main categories. It is desirable to continue research on boundary standards to get better knowledge on how they are to be used. Each experimental set will be accompanied by suggestions on how they may be used and tested.

3. Sectional and composite standard radiographs

Some readers find that the present standard radiographs are inconvenient in practice because of their size and number. There have been experiments with small copies of sections of standard radiographs, and with composite reproductions of these copies. It is recommended that this work should continue. Tests are required to determine the optimal area for a section and to assess the effects of using such standards rather than the present set.

4. Profusion of small opacities

The 1980 Classification requires that the profusion of small opacities should be determined by comparison with the standard and by integrating the profusion seen over the affected zones of the lung. It includes provision for indicating which of (six) zones are affected. It may be easier, and more reproducible, to record profusion separately for each of the four quadrants of the lung. Composite standard radiographs incorporating images of the four quadrants might assist such a change in procedure. It is recommended that the suggested change in the method for recording profusion might be tested in parallel with research on the production of composite standard radiographs.

5. Large opacities

Several reports indicate surprisingly poor between-reader agreement in recording the presence of large opacities. Identification and systematic documentation of the reasons for such inconsistency would be valuable.

6. Pleural thickening

It is difficult to distinguish clearly between abnormal thickening of the parietal and visceral layers of the pleura, and there are problems of nomenclature. Yet the distinction may be important pathologically, and it is thought by some to have aeteological significance. Further consideration needs to be given to how to improve the method for recording radiological evidence of pleural abnormalities. (See also Note 12.)

7. Shape and size of small opacities

The 1980 Classification clarifies the difference between the concepts shape and size of small rounded opacities. There is provision also for recording the presence of mixtures of shapes (and sizes). This opens the way for further research on the prognostic and aetiologic significance of different combinations of shapes. The new convention will also facilitate studies of whether different sizes of small irregular opacities represent real pathological distinctions or whether they are merely radiological reflections of different degrees of profusion of the smallest lesions recognisable as irregular opacities.

8. Technical quality of radiographs

The present system for recording technical quality does not include a standardized notation to indicate the nature or suspected cause of the inadequacies observed. Yet it is known that readers differ in their assessments of quality, and that their assessments affect their classifications. More studies are required to determine the way in which different imperfections influence readers' use of various parts of the Classification, and on how their judgement of quality can be recorded in a standard way. Use of quantitative measurements of film density may provide an objective index to assist quality assessments. This could lead to raising radiographic standards and to a better understanding of factors influencing subjective assessments of radiographic quality.

9. Non-pneumoconiotic shadows

The General Instructions for the use of the 1980 Classification (page 3) preserves the principle from earlier Classifications that radiographic appearances regarded as "definitely not pneumoconiosis" are not to be classified; but the use of Symbols and Comments are now obligatory in such cases. Differences between readers in what they regard as "definitely not pneumoconiosis" and "probably the result of some other aetiology" should be studied.

Some experts believe that application of the Classification for epidemiological purposes would be more objective if the descriptive notation defined by the Classification were used in all cases where the shadows seen are consistent with the appearances of the standard radiographs and the definitions in the text (pp. 4 to 10), irrespective of whether the appearances are thought to be due to pneumoconiosis. Obligatory use of Symbols and Comments would ensure that a reader's opinion that the shadows classified are not due to dust exposure would be recorded and available for statistical analysis. It is recommended that research should continue on this matter.

APPENDIX D

READING SHEET

The section on USING THE CLASSIFICATION (pp 18 to 20) gives guidance on the conditions and procedures which are particularly important for epidemiological studies involving the radiology of the pneumoconioses. An example of a reading sheet which may be used to record systematically all the information required by the Complete Classification is provided as a further aid. The word example is emphasised. Alternative designs may often be appropriate for particular applications.

The sheet illustrated can be used easily to transfer data into a form suitable for machine processing. If this intended then it will be helpful to use capital letters (rather than lower-case letters) to record all features and Symbols. Permissible symbols are indicated in brackets ( ), using lower-case letters consistent with the text describing the Classification.

The letters Y and N are used on the sheet to represent the words "Yes" and "No". Alternative symbols may be desirable if reading sheets are prepared in languages other than English.

Note that there may be no blanks to the right of the dashed line. This provides a useful visual aid to verify that a radiograph has been classified properly before it is removed from the viewing box.

* Prepared by M. Jacobsen and C.E. Rossiter.

READING SHEET • suitable for use with the ILO 1980 INTERNATIONAL CLASSIFICATION OF RADIOGRAPHS OF THE PNEUMOCONIOSES	IDENTIFICATION DATA FILM READER READING DATE
FILM QUALITY	Grade (1, 2, 3, 4)
	Comment made (Y, N)
SMALL OPACITIES	Profusion (12-point scale)
	Extent (R L)
	(✓ appropriate zones)
	Shape and size (2 of p,q,r,s,t,u; or repeated symbol)
LARGE OPACITIES	Presence (Y, N)
	Size (A, B, C)
PLEURAL THICKENING CHEST WALL - CIRCUMSCRIBED [PLAQUES]	Presence (Y, N)
	Face on (Y, N) (R L)
	Width (a, b, c)
	Extent (1, 2, 3)
- DIFFUSE	Presence (Y, N)
	Face on (Y, N)
	Width (a, b, c)
	Extent (1, 2, 3)
DIAPHRAGM	Presence (Y, N)
	Site (✓ site)
COSTOPHRENIC ANGLE OBLITERATION	Presence (Y, N)
	Site (✓ site)
PLEURAL CALCIFICATION	Presence (Y, N)
CHEST WALL	Site (✓ site) (R L)
DIAPHRAGM	Site (✓ site)
OTHER	Site (✓ site)
	Extent (1, 2, 3)
SYMBOLS	Used ? (Y, N)
up to 6† from	ax bu ca cn co cp cv di ef em es fr hi ho id ih kl od pi px rp tb
(† Record further symbols in COMMENTS section)	
COMMENTS (Write comments)	Made ? (Y, N)

• NO BLANKS ARE PERMISSIBLE TO THE RIGHT OF THE DASHED LINE

APPENDIX E

DESCRIPTIONS OF STANDARD RADIOGRAPHS*
(1980 Revision)

The standard radiographs accompanying the ILO 1980 International Classification of Radiographs of the Pneumoconioses consist of 22 films.

Two radiographs illustrate the appearance classifiable as category 0/0 for profusion of small opacities.

Eighteen radiographs depict appearances classifiable as categories 1/1 through 3/3 for profusion and p/p through t/t for shape and size of small opacities and as categories A through C for size of large opacities. Descriptions of these radiographs are given in the accompanying tables, with notation defined in the Classification and with additional Comments as appropriate. The site of small opacities is shown by a tick in the boxes symbolizing the zones of the lungs as follows:

	Right	Left
Upper		
Middle		
Lower		

The two remaining radiographs are composite reproductions of sections. One depicts the increasing profusion of irregular small opacities of size "u". The other illustrates various types of pleural abnormality.

Note that the Technical Quality of eight of these radiographs has been judged as meriting grade 2 only. This is because the international trials which preceded the selection of the 1980 set of standards did not yield any better quality examples of the features concerned.

---

* Prepared by C. Amoudru, H. Bohlig, J.A. Dick, J.C. Gilson, A. Minette and R. Morgan

DESCRIPTIONS OF STANDARD RADIOGRAPHS

1980 STANDARD RADIOGRAPHS SHOWING	TECHNICAL QUALITY	SMALL OPACITIES			LARGE OPACITIES	PLEURAL THICKENING				PLEURAL CALCIFICATION	SYMBOLS	COMMENTS
		PROFUSION	SHAPE-SIZE	EXTENT		CHEST WALL: CIRCUM-SCRIBED (PLAQUES)	CHEST WALL: DIFFUSE	DIAPHRAGM	COSTOPHRENIC ANGLE OBLITERATION			
0/0 (example 1)	1	0/0	-	-	No	No	No	No	No	No	None	Vascular pattern is well illustrated.
0/0 (example 2)	1	0/0	-	-	No	No	No	No	No	No	None	Also shows vascular pattern, but not as clearly as example 1.
1/1; p/p	1	1/1	p/p	R L: ✓✓ / ✓✓ / ✓✓	A	No	No	No	No	No	rp.	Rheumatoid pneumoconiosis in left lower zone. Small opacities are present in all zones, but the profusion in the right-upper zone is typical of (some would say a little more profuse than) that classifiable as category 1/1.
2/2; p/p	2	2/2	p/p	R L: ✓✓ / ✓✓ / ✓✓	No	No	No	No	No	No	pi; tb.	Quality defect: radiograph is too light.
3/3; p/p	1	3/3	p/p	R L: ✓✓ / ✓✓ / ✓✓	No	No	No	No	Yes R L: ✓ –	No	ax.	None
1/1; q/q	1	1/1	q/q	R L: ✓✓ / ✓✓ / – –	No	No	No	No	No	No	None	Illustrates profusion 1/1 better than shape or size.
2/2; q/q	1	2/2	q/q	R L: ✓✓ / ✓✓ / ✓✓	No	No	Yes R L: ✓✓; Width: a a; Extent: 1 1	No	Yes R L: ✓✓	No	None	None

DESCRIPTIONS OF STANDARD RADIOGRAPHS (continued)

1980 STANDARD RADIOGRAPHS SHOWING	TECHNICAL QUALITY	SMALL OPACITIES			LARGE OPACITIES	PLEURAL THICKENING				PLEURAL CALCIFICATION	SYMBOLS	COMMENTS
						CHEST WALL						
		PROFUSION	SHAPE-SIZE	EXTENT		CIRCUM-SCRIBED (PLAQUES)	DIFFUSE	DIAPHRAGM	COSTOPHRENIC ANGLE OBLITERATION			
3/3; q/q	2	3/3	q/q	R L ✓ ✓ ✓ ✓ ✓ ✓	No	No	No	No	No	No	pi.	Quality defects: poor definition of pleura and cut basal angles.
1/1; r/r	2	1/1	r/r	R L ✓ ✓ ✓ ✓ 	No	No	No	No	Yes R L ✓	No	None	Quality defect: subject movement. Profusion of small opacities is more marked in right lung.
2/2; r/r	2	2/2	r/r	R L ✓ ✓ ✓ ✓ ✓ ✓	No	No	No	No	No	No	None	Quality defects: radiograph too light and contrast too high. The heart shadow is slightly displaced to the left.
3/3; r/r	1	3/3	r/r	R L ✓ ✓ ✓ ✓ ✓ ✓	No	No	No	No	No	No	ax; ih.	None
1/1; s/t	2	1/1	s/t	R L ✓ ✓ ✓ ✓ ✓	No	No	No	No	No	No	kl.	Quality defect: cut bases. Kerley lines in lower right zone.
2/2; s/s	2	2/2	s/s	R L ✓ ✓ ✓ ✓	No	No	No	No	No	No	em.	Quality defect: distortion of bases due to shrinking. Emphysema in upper zones.

DESCRIPTIONS OF STANDARD RADIOGRAPHS (continued)

1980 STANDARD RADIOGRAPHS SHOWING	TECHNICAL QUALITY	SMALL OPACITIES: PROFUSION	SMALL OPACITIES: SHAPE-SIZE	SMALL OPACITIES: EXTENT	LARGE OPACITIES	PLEURAL THICKENING: CHEST WALL: CIRCUM-SCRIBED (PLAQUES)	PLEURAL THICKENING: CHEST WALL: DIFFUSE	PLEURAL THICKENING: DIAPHRAGM	PLEURAL THICKENING: COSTOPHRENIC ANGLE OBLITERATION	PLEURAL CALCIFICATION	SYMBOLS	COMMENTS
3/3; s/s	2	3/3	s/s	R L ✓ ✓ ✓ ✓ ✓ ✓	No	No	Yes R L ✓ ✓ Width: a a Extent: 3 3	No	No	No	ho; ih; pi.	Quality defect: radiograph is too light. Honeycomb lung appearance is not marked.
1/1; t/t Costophrenic angle obliteration	1	1/1	t/t	R L ✓ ✓ ✓ ✓	No	No	Yes R L ✓ ✓ Width: a a Extent: 2 2	No	Yes R L ✓	Yes R L ✓ Extent: 2	None	This radiograph defines the lower limit for costophrenic angle obliteration. Note shrinkage in lower lung fields.
2/2; t/t	1	2/2	t/t	R L ✓ ✓ ✓ ✓ ✓ ✓	No	No	Yes R L ✓ ✓ Width: a a Extent: 1 1	No	No	No	ih.	Pleural thickening is present in the apices of the lung.
3/3; t/t	1	3/3	t/t	R L ✓ ✓ ✓ ✓ ✓ ✓	No	No	No	No	No	No	hi; ho; id; ih; tb.	None
1/1; u/u 2/2; u/u 3/3; u/u	-	-	-	-	-	-	-	-	-	-	-	This composite radiograph illustrates the mid-categories of profusion of small opacities classifiable for shape and size as u/u.
A	2	2/2	p/q	R L ✓ ✓ ✓ ✓ ✓ ✓	A	No	No	No	No	No	None	Quality defects: radiograph is too light and pleural definition is poor.

DESCRIPTIONS OF STANDARD RADIOGRAPHS (continued)

1980 STANDARD RADIOGRAPHS SHOWING	TECHNICAL QUALITY	SMALL OPACITIES			LARGE OPACITIES	PLEURAL THICKENING				PLEURAL CALCIFICATION	SYMBOLS	COMMENTS
		PROFUSION	SHAPE-SIZE	EXTENT		CHEST WALL: CIRCUM-SCRIBED (PLAQUES)	CHEST WALL: DIFFUSE	DIAPHRAGM	COSTOPHRENIC ANGLE OBLITERATION			
B	1	1/2	p/q	R L ✓ ✓ ✓ ✓ ✓ ✓	B	No	No	No	No	No	ax; co.	Definition of pleura is slightly imperfect.
C	1	2/1	q/t	R L ✓ ✓ ✓ ✓ ✓ ✓	C	No	No	No	No	No	bu; di; em; es; hi; ih.	The small opacities are difficult to classify because of the presence of the large opacities. Note the left costophrenic angle obliteration. This is not classifiable because it does not reach the lower limit defined by the standard radiograph 1/1; t/t.
Pleural thickening (circum-scribed)	-	-	-	-	-	Yes	No	No	No	No	-	The pleural thickening present face on, is of indeterminate width, and extent 2.
Pleural thickening (diffuse)	-	-	-	-	-	No	Yes	No	No	Yes	-	The pleural thickening present in profile, is of width a, and extent 2. Not associated small calcifications.
Pleural thickening (calcifi-cation) diaphragm	-	-	-	-	-	No	No	Yes	No	Yes	-	Circumscribed, calcified pleural thickening of extent 2.
Pleural thickening (calcifi-cation) chest wall	-	-	-	-	-	Yes	No	No	No	Yes	-	Calcified and uncalcified pleural thickening present face on, is of indeterminate width, and extent 2.

APPENDIX F

DIAGRAMS*

The diagrams on the following pages are intended only to provide a pictorial aide memoire to the definitions of the Complete Classification and they do not subsitute for the standard radiographs or the written text.

The diagrams representing the symbols provide simple reminders of the symbols to be used, particularly for those whose main language is not English. It is recognised that these diagrams can not possibly illustrate all the manifestations of many of the symbols, for example ca, cp, cd.

* Prepared by H. Bohlig and R. Kiviluoto.

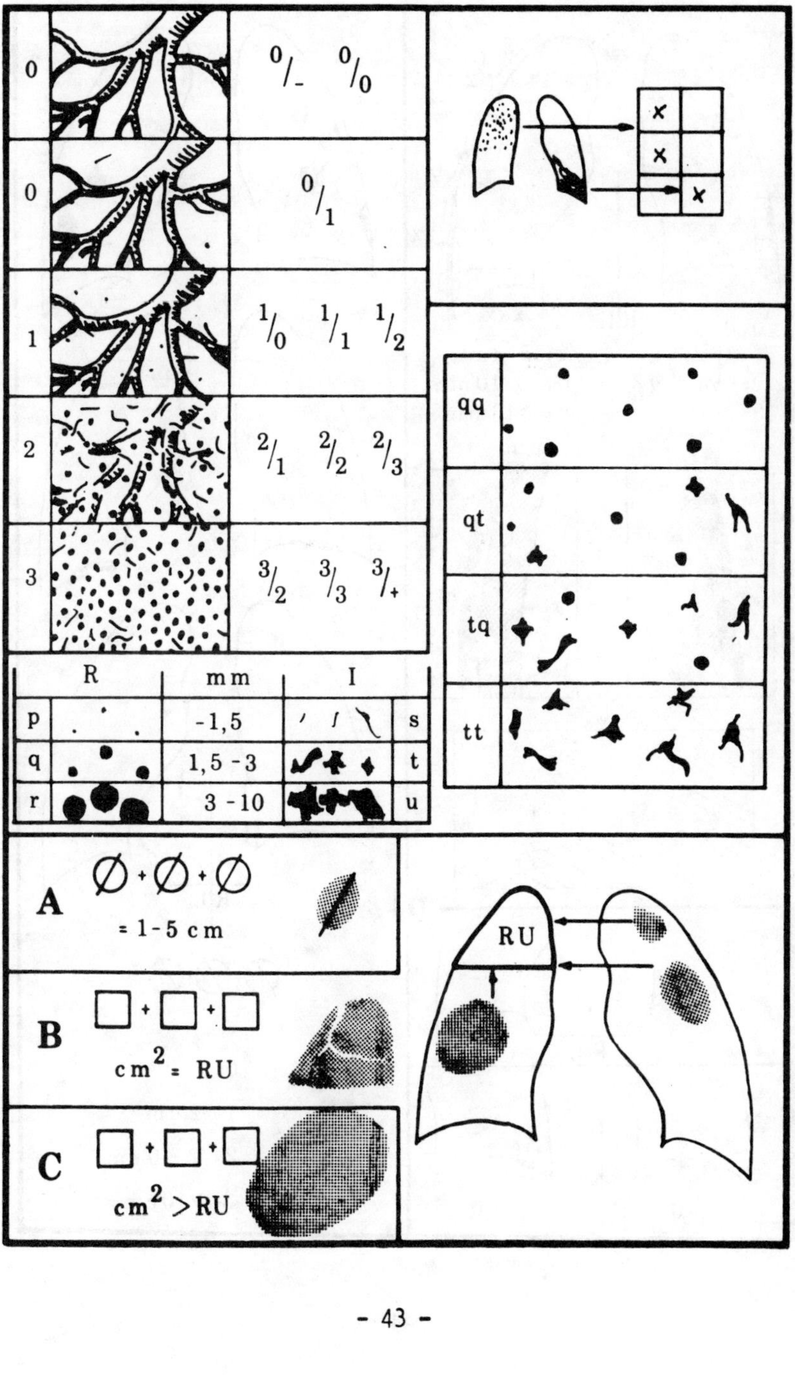
0
0/- 0/0
0
0/1
1
1/0 1/1 1/2
2
2/1 2/2 2/3
3
3/2 3/3 3/+
R
mm
I
p
-1,5
s
q
1,5 - 3
t
r
3 - 10
u
qq
qt
tq
tt
A
Ø + Ø + Ø
= 1 - 5 cm
B
□ + □ + □
cm² = RU
C
□ + □ + □
cm² > RU
RU

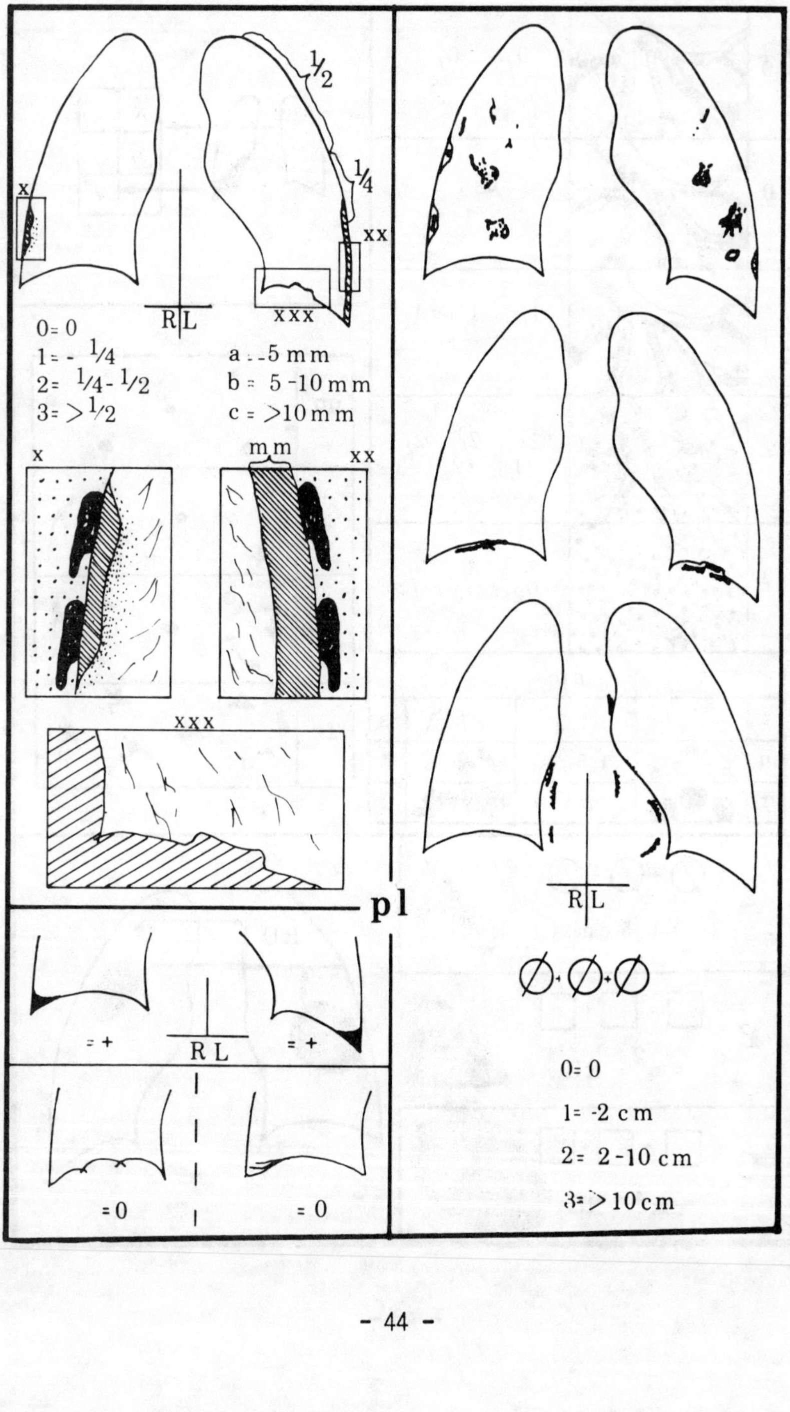
1/2
1/4
x
xx
xxx
R L
0= 0
1= - 1/4
2= 1/4 - 1/2
3= > 1/2
a : -5 mm
b = 5 -10 mm
c = >10 mm
x
mm
xx
xxx
pl
= +
R L
= +
= 0
= 0
R L
Ø+Ø+Ø
0= 0
1= -2 cm
2= 2 -10 cm
3= > 10 cm

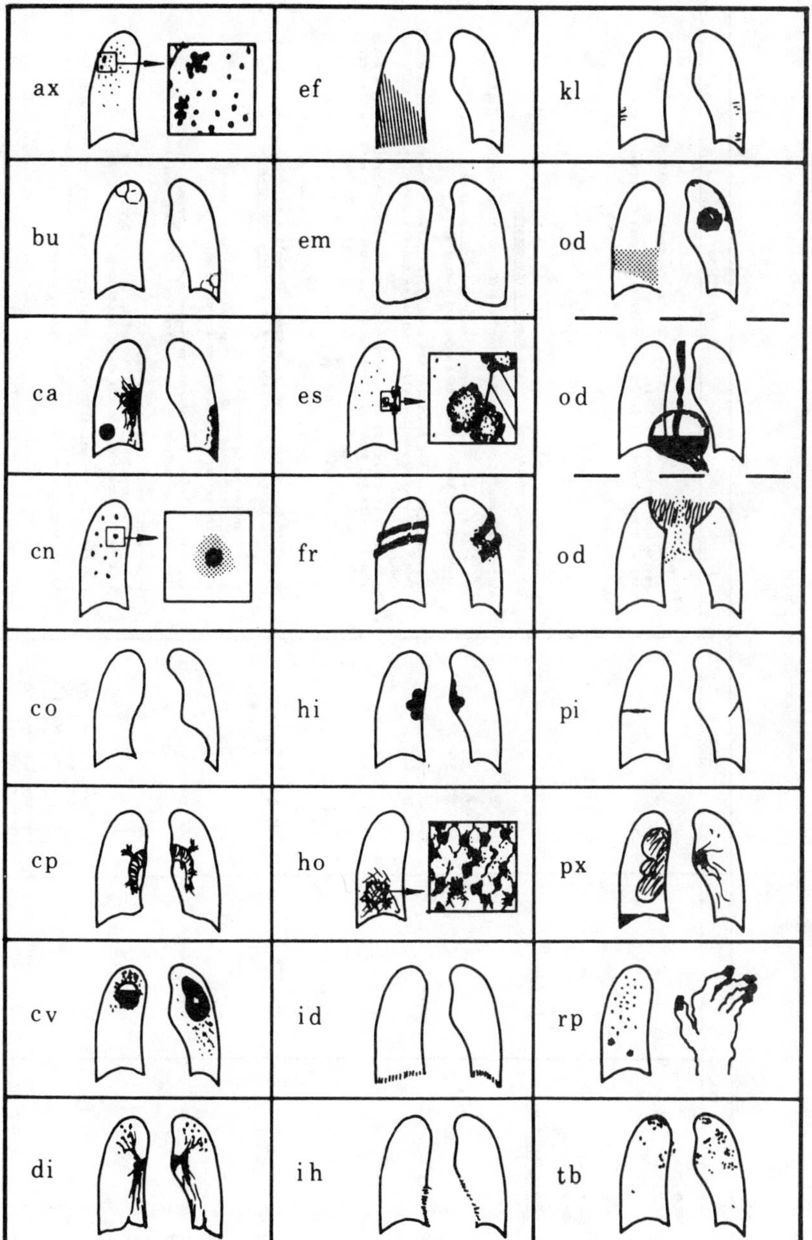
ax
ef
kl
bu
em
od
ca
es
od
cn
fr
od
co
hi
pi
cp
ho
px
cv
id
rp
di
ih
tb

APPENDIX G

ILO 1980 INTERNATIONAL CLASSIFICATION OF RADIOGRAPHS OF THE PNEUMOCONIOSES

SUMMARY OF DETAILS OF CLASSIFICATION

FEATURES		CODES	DEFINITIONS
TECHNICAL QUALITY		1. 2 3 4	Good. Acceptable, with no technical defect likely to impair classification of the radiograph for pneumoconiosis. Poor, with some technical defect but still acceptable for classification purposes. Unacceptable.
PARENCHYMAL ABNORMALITIES			
Small opacities	Profusion		The category of profusion is based on assessment of the concentration of opacities by comparison with the standard radiographs.
		0/- 0/0 0/1 1/0 1/1 1/2 2/1 2/2 2/3 3/2 3/3 3/+	Category 0 - small opacities absent or less profuse than the lower limit of category 1. Categories 1, 2 and 3 - represent increasing profusion of small opacities as defined by the corresponding standard radiographs.
	Extent	RU RM RL LU LM LL	The zones in which the opacities are seen are recorded. The right (R) and left (L) thorax are both divided into three zones - upper (U), middle (M) and lower (L). The category of profusion is determined by considering the profusion as a whole over the affected zones of the lung and by comparing this with the standard radiographs.
	Shape and Size		
	rounded	p/p q/q r/r	The letters p, q and r denote the presence of small rounded opacities. Three sizes are defined by the appearances on standard radiographs. p = diameter up to about 1.5mm. q = diameter exceeding about 1.5mm and up to about 3mm. r = diameter exceeding about 3mm and up to about 10mm.
	irregular	s/s t/t u/u	The letters s, t and u denote the presence of small irregular opacities. Three sizes are defined by the appearances on standard radiographs. s = width up to about to 1.5mm. t = width exceeding about 1.5mm and up to about 3mm. u = width exceeding 3mm and up to about 10mm.
	mixed	p/s p/t p/u p/q p/r q/s q/t q/u q/p q/r r/s r/t r/u r/p r/q s/p s/q s/r s/t s/u t/p t/q t/r t/s t/u u/p u/q u/r u/s u/t	For mixed shapes (or sizes) of small opacities the predominant shape and size is recorded first. The presence of a significant number of another shape and size is recorded after the oblique stroke.

FEATURES		CODES	DEFINITIONS
Large opacities		A B C	The categories are defined in terms of the dimensions of the opacities. Category A - an opacity having a greatest diameter exceeding about 10mm and up to and including 50mm, or several opacities each greater than about 10mm, the sum of whose greatest diameters does not exceed about 50mm. Category B - one or more opacities larger or more numerous than those in category A whose combined area does not exceed the equivalent of the right upper zone. Category C - one or more opacities whose combined area exceeds the equivalent of the right upper zone.
PLEURAL ABNORMALITIES			
Pleural Thickening			
Chest wall	Type		Two types of pleural thickening of the chest wall are recognised: circumscribed (plaques) and diffuse. Both types may occur together.
	Site	R L	Pleural thickening of the chest wall is recorded separately for the right (R) and left (L) thorax.
	Width	a b c	For pleural thickening seen along the lateral chest wall the measurement of maximum width is made from the inner line of the chest wall to the inner margin of the shadow seen most sharply at the parenchymal-pleural boundary. The maximum width usually occurs at the inner margin of the rib shadow at its outermost point. a = maximum width up to about 5mm. b = maximum width over about 5mm and up to about 10mm. c = maximum width over about 10mm.
	Face on	Y N	The presence of pleural thickening seen face-on is recorded even if it can be seen also in profile. If pleural thickening is seen face-on only, width can not usually be measured.
	Extent	1 2 3	Extent of pleural thickening is defined in terms of the maximum length of pleural involvement, or as the sum of maximum lengths, whether seen in profile or face-on. 1 = total length equivalent up to one quarter of the projection of the lateral chest wall. 2 = total length exceeding one quarter but not one half of the projection of the lateral chest wall. 3 = total length exceeding one half of the projection of the lateral chest wall.
Diaphragm	Presence	Y N	A plaque involving the diaphragmatic pleura is recorded as present (Y) or absent (N), separately for the right (R) and left (L) thorax.
	Site	R L	

FEATURES		CODES	DEFINITIONS
<u>Costophrenic angle obliteration</u>	Presence	Y N	The presence (Y) or absence (N) of costophrenic angle obliteration is recorded separately from thickening over other areas, for the right (R) and left (L). <u>thorax</u>. The lower limit for this obliteration is defined by a <u>standard radiograph</u>.
	Site	R L	If the thickening extends up the chest wall then both costophrenic angle obliteration and pleural thickening should be recorded.
<u>Pleural calcification</u>			The site and extent of pleural calcification are recorded separately for the two lungs, and the extent defined in terms of <u>dimensions</u>.
	Site		
	chest wall	R L	
	diaphragm	R L	
	other	R L	"other" includes calcification of the mediastinal and pericardial pleura.
	Extent	1 2 3	1 = an area of calcified pleura with greatest diameter up to about 20mm, or a number of such areas the sum of whose greatest diameters does not exceed about 20mm. 2 = an area of calcified pleura with greatest diameter exceeding about 20mm and up to about 100mm, or a number of such areas the sum of whose greatest diameters exceeds about 20mm but does not exceed about 100mm. 3 = an area of calcified pleura with greatest diameter exceeding about 100mm, or a number of such areas whose sum of greatest diameters exceeds about 100mm.
SYMBOLS			It is to be taken that the definition of each of the Symbols is preceded by an appropriate word or phrase such as "suspect", "changes suggestive of", or "opacities suggestive of", etc.
		ax	- coalescence of small pneumoconiotic opacities
		bu	- bulla(e)
		ca	- cancer of lung or pleura
		cn	- calcification in small pneumoconiotic opacities
		co	- abnormality of cardiac size or shape
		cp	- cor pulmonale
		cv	- cavity
		di	- marked distortion of the intrathoracic organs
		ef	- effusion
		em	- definite emphysema
		es	- eggshell calcification of hilar or mediastinal lymph nodes
		fr	- fractured rib(s)
		hi	- enlargement of hilar or mediastinal lymph nodes
		ho	- honeycomb lung
		id	- ill-defined diaphragm
		ih	- ill-defined heart outline
		kl	- septal (Kerley) lines
		od	- other significant abnormality
		pi	- pleural thickening in the interlobar fissure or mediastinum
		px	- pneumothorax
		rp	- rheumatoid pneumoconiosis
		tb	- tuberculosis
COMMENTS	Presence	Y N	Comments should be recorded pertaining to the classification of the radiograph, particularly if some other cause is thought to be responsible for a shadow which could be thought by others to have been due to pneumoconiosis; also to identify radiographs for which the technical quality may have affected the reading materially.

OCCUPATIONAL SAFETY AND HEALTH SERIES

Organisation of occupational health services in developing countries (No. 7) (12.50 Swiss francs)

Dust sampling in mines (No. 9) (8 Swiss francs)

Occupational health problems of young workers (No. 26) (10 Swiss francs)

Safety and health in shipbuilding and ship repairing (No. 27) (12.50 Swiss francs)

Safe construction and installation of escalators (No. 28) (6 Swiss francs)

Médecine du travail, protection de la maternité et santé de la famille (No. 29) (9 Swiss francs)

Organisation of family planning in occupational health services (No. 31) (9 Swiss francs)

Radiation protection in mining and milling of uranium and thorium (No. 32) (35 Swiss francs)

Noise and vibration in the working environment (No. 33) (17.50 Swiss francs)

Migrant workers - Occupational safety and health (No. 34) (12.50 Swiss francs)

Safe use of pesticides (No. 38) (12.50 Swiss francs)

5th International report on the prevention and suppression of dust in mining, tunnelling and quarrying (No. 40) (15 Swiss francs)

Safety and health of migrant workers. International Symposium (No. 41) (30 Swiss francs)

Building work. A compendium of occupational safety and health practice (No. 42) (25 Swiss francs)

Optimisation of the working environment (No. 43) (35 Swiss francs)

Civil engineering work. A compendium of occupational safety practice (No. 45) (20 Swiss francs)

Prevention of occupational cancer. International Symposium (No. 46) (47.50 Swiss francs)

Education and training policies in occupational safety and health and ergonomics. International Symposium (No. 47) (35 Swiss francs)

6th International report on the prevention and suppression of dust in mining, tunnelling and quarrying (No. 48) (17.50 Swiss francs)

Dermatoses et professions (No. 49) (15 Swiss francs)

Human stress, work and job satisfaction. A critical approach (No. 50) (15 Swiss francs)

Stress in industry. Causes, effects and prevention (No. 51) (12.50 Swiss francs)

Success with occupational safety programmes (No. 52) (17.50 Swiss francs)

Occupational hazards from ionising electromagnetic radiation (No. 53) (17.50 Swiss francs)

The cost of occupational accidents and diseases (No. 54) (17.50 Swiss francs)

The provisions of the Basic Safety Standards for Radiation Protection relevant to the protection of workers against ionising radiation (No. 55) (6 Swiss francs)

Psycho-social factors at work: Recognition and control (No. 56) (15 Swiss francs)

Protection of workers against radio-frequency and microwave radiation: A technical review (No. 57) (17.50 Swiss francs)

Price: 7.50 Swiss francs

(Price for the set of radiographs provided on request)

ISBN 92-2-102463-6

20

List of NIOSH Certified Roentgenographic Interpreting Physicians: B-Readers by State and Alphabetical Order

U.S. DEPARTMENT OF HEALTH AND HUMAN SERVICES
PUBLIC HEALTH SERVICE
CENTERS FOR DISEASE CONTROL
NATIONAL INSTITUTE FOR OCCUPATIONAL SAFETY AND HEALTH
DIVISION OF RESPIRATORY DISEASE STUDIES

Federal Coal Mine Health and Safety Act of 1969 (Title II, Section 203(a)) and Title 42, Code of Federal Regulations, Part 37, Specifications for Medical Examinations for Underground Coal Miners. January 1, 1989.

EDITORS' COMMENTARY

The following list of 1989 NIOSH approved B-readers provides access to those who have some minimally certified capability to interpret x-rays in accord with generally accepted standard criteria. This is necessary for legal actions, so reliance can be placed on known "experts." It is also necessary for medical research, so that greater credence can be given diagnostic signs and conclusions. It is a means of assuring consistent and comparable radiographic interpretations. Similar indicia of qualification are often desirable or reasonably necessary for other disciplines or subject matter specialists in all phases of asbestos health, legal, and technical endeavors. For example, is the industrial hygienist board certified (C.I.H.) or the engineer state licensed (P.E.)? Are the asbestos abatement technicians properly trained, tested, and certified? There are good reasons, based on recent past experience, for having specialists demonstrate that they do have the unique knowledge necessary to deal intelligently and effectively with the problems implicit in this recalcitrant public health arena.

LIST OF APPROVED B-READERS FEDERAL COAL MINE HEALTH AND SAFETY ACT OF 1969

STATE-AL

Dr. Oliver Charles Baker
924 So 18th St
Birmingham AL 35256
Phone: 205-933-8936

Dr. James W. Ballard
3932 Knollwood Drive
Birmingham AL 35243
Phone: 205-967-1689

LIST OF APPROVED B-READERS FEDERAL COAL MINE HEALTH AND SAFETY ACT OF 1969

STATE-AL

Dr. Michael B Brady
273 Park Terrace
Mobile AL 36604
Phone: 205-478-3741

Dr. R Clifford Game
1528 N 26th St
Birmingham AL 35234
Phone: 205-226-6138

Dr. Allan Robert Goldstein
860 Montclaire Rd S-862
Birmingham AL 35213
Phone: 205-591-2545

Dr. Cynthia Oliver Lorino
3972 Japonica Lane
Mobile AL 36609
Phone: 205-460-7042

Dr. Henry P Thode
7300 Augustine Drive
Anchorage AL 99504
Phone: 907-552-3097

Dr. Ben V Branscomb
1717 Sixth Ave South
Birmingham AL 35243
Phone: 205-934-4125

Dr. Robert White Gillmann
401 Bay St.
Gadsden AL 35901
Phone: 205-543-3200

Dr. Nancy Jo Jennings
2009 7th St NW
Birmingham AL 35215
Phone: 205-854-4220

Dr. A David Russakoff
801 Princeton S W STE 615
Birmingham AL 35211
Phone: 205-780-1963

Dr. James Clinton Walker Jr
3603 Cliff RD S
Birmingham AL 35205
Phone: 205-783-3700

STATE-AR

Dr. Joseph D Calhoun
31 Shannon Dr
Little Rock AR 72207
Phone: 501-663-3944

Dr. Robert William Laakman
14 St Andrews
Little Rock AR 72212
Phone: 501-223-3471

STATE-AZ

Dr. John Robert Muhm
9885 E Cochise Dr
Scottsdale AZ 85258
Phone: 602-860-0330

LIST OF APPROVED B-READERS FEDERAL COAL MINE HEALTH AND SAFETY ACT OF 1969

STATE-CA

Dr. Martin Lawrence Barman
145 Valeria
Fresno CA 93701
Phone: 209-268-8722

Dr. Leroy T. Barnes
3696 Aureola Blvd
Los Angeles CA 90018
Phone: 213-295-2097

Dr. Poonam Batra
912 Teakwood Rd
Los Angeles CA 90049
Phone: 213-472-6910

Dr. James Louis Caplan
1125 S Beverly Dr #400
Los Angeles CA 90035
Phone: 213-477-6779

Dr. Robert John Cassling
16942 Bollinger Dr
PAC Palisades CA 90272
Phone: 213-459-8223

Dr. Jagdish Chazra
28751 Jaeger Dr
Laguna Niguel CA 92677
Phone: 714-831-9430

Dr. Raymond Thomas Cummins
160 Westgate Drive
San Francisco Ca 94127
Phone: 415-666-7811

Dr. L Evan Custer
Alta Bates Hospital
Berkeley CA 94705
Phone: 415-540-1566

Dr. Edward Drasin
76 Silverwood Drive
Lafayette CA 94549
Phone: 415-420-6088

Dr. Jacob Alan Epstein
161 Hillcrest Rd
Berkeley CA 94705
Phone: 415-547-0821

Dr. Myra Lee Feffer
6227 Lindenhurst Av
Los Angeles CA 90048
Phone: 213-854-6440

Dr. David S Feigin
8256 Caminito Lacayo
La Jolla CA 92037
Phone: 619-455-6545

Dr. Ethel J Finck
2436 N Common Wealth Ave
Los Angeles CA 90027
Phone: 213-226-7245

Dr. Jonathan Harold Fish
2814 Derby St
Berkeley CA 94705
Phone: 415-548-9197

Dr. Gordon Gamsu
Box 0628 Radlgy UC Med Ct
San Francisco CA 94143
Phone: 415-476-1451

Dr. Clara V Gelbard
2080 Century Park E #608
Los Angeles CA 90067
Phone: 213-203-0377

LIST OF APPROVED B-READERS FEDERAL COAL MINE HEALTH AND SAFETY ACT OF 1969

STATE-CA

Dr. Philip Cary Goodman
15 Mesa Ave
San Francisco CA 94116
Phone: 415-821-8024

Dr. Susan A M Gootnick
329 Goodhill Rd
Kentfield CA 94904
Phone: 415-461-4006

Dr. Jay S Gordonson
1200 North State St
Los Angeles CA 90033
Phone: 213-226-7261

Dr. Arthur Tobias Gronner
24 Caberret Ct
Lafayette CA 94549
Phone: 415-284-1396

Dr. Frank Burnette Hamlett
319 Laurel St
San Diego CA 92101
Phone: 619-672-0061

Dr. Philip Harber
CHS 37-131 UCLA
Los Angeles CA 90024
Phone: 213-825-4837

Dr. Howard William Higholt
4 Possum Ridge Rd
Rolling Hills CA 90274
Phone: 213-541-8855

Dr. Horton Corwin Hinshaw Jr
450 Sutter St
San Francisco CA 94108
Phone: 415-982-7168

Dr. Bernard Kordan
P O Box 9519
Bakersfield CA 93389
Phone: 901-528-6111

Dr. Maurice M Lapp
1250 Upper Happy Vly Road
Lafayette CA 94549
Phone: 415-284-1375

Dr. Charles Dudley Lee
120 Elm Street
San Diego CA 92101
Phone: 619-487-1700

Dr. Robert Martin Lincoln
1523 Kingsford Drive
Carmichael CA 95608
Phone: 916-972-8481

Dr. John Peter Livoni
79 Scripps Dr #100
Sacramento CA 95825
Phone: 916-921-1300

Dr. Kenneth E Lynch
16732 Intrepid Lane
Huntington Bch CA 92649
Phone: 213-592-3435

Dr. Patricia J McEveney
2001 Dwight Way
Berkeley CA 94704
Phone: 415-540-4460

Dr. William Peter Meseroll
121 Sotoyome St
Santa Rosa CA 95404
Phone: 707-546-4062

LIST OF APPROVED B-READERS FEDERAL COAL MINE HEALTH AND SAFETY ACT OF 1969

STATE-CA

Dr. Gerald L Meyers
3001 Colby St
Berkeley CA 94705
Phone: 415-845-7968

Dr. Blaine Lewis Montgomery
6833 Abottswood Dr
Rnch Palos Verd CA 90274
Phone: 213-325-1221

Dr. David Leonard Moody
P O Box 2503
Santa Cruz CA 95063
Phone: 408-475-7829

Dr. Michael Peter Norton
1441 Kingsford Drive
Carmichael CA 95608
Phone: 916-488-8152

Dr. Jacob J Parker
331 Locust Ave
San Rafael CA 94901
Phone: 415-456-5543

Dr. William Frank Pfisterer
2555 E Chapman #500
Fullerton CA 92631
Phone: 714-526-2241

Dr. Daniel Powers
623 Las Casas Avenue
Pac Palisades CA 90272
Phone: 213-973-6269

Dr. Leslie Preger
166 Merced Ave
San Francisco CA 94127
Phone: 415-534-8055

Dr. Joy Mei Price
2001 Dwight Way
Berkeley CA 94704
Phone: 415-540-4460

Dr. Bolar Rama Rao
100 Trinidad Bend
Coronado CA 92118
Phone: 619-424-8524

Dr. Marvin A Rawitch
1401 Avocado Ave
Newport Bch CA 92660
Phone: 714-640-1221

Dr. Carolyn Sue Ray
1850 Pennsylvania Ave
Fairfield CA 94533
Phone: 707-429-2495

Dr. John W Renner
16822 Coral Cay Lane
Huntington Bch CA 92649
Phone: 213-592-1575

Dr. William Maxwell Russell
3193 Benedict Cyn Dr
Beverly Hills CA 90210
Phone: 213-276-3449

Dr. Hisaji Q Sakai
1844 San Miguel Dr 302
Walnut Creek CA 94596
Phone: 415-947-0560

Dr. E Nicholas Sargent
1200 North State St
Los Angeles CA 90033
Phone: 213-226-4950

LIST OF APPROVED B-READERS FEDERAL COAL MINE HEALTH AND SAFETY ACT OF 1969

STATE-CA

Dr. Kanagal Satyanarayana
3912 E Rolling Green Lane
Orange CA 92667
Phone: 714-637-1625

Dr. Marc B Schenker
626 Coolidge St
Davis CA 95616
Phone: 916-752-3317

Dr. Gary Shrago
112 Wildwood Gardens
Piedmont CA 94611
Phone: 415-547-0293

Dr. Mark Geoffrey Stein
27 Silver Crescent
Irvine CA 92715
Phone: 714-854-5427

Dr. Irwin Steinberg
2711 Angelo Drive
Los Angeles CA 90077
Phone: 213-276-8069

Dr. Keith Edwin Mosun Tao
41 Magnolia Place
Danville CA 94526
Phone: 415-947-0560

Dr. David A Tenenberg
P O Box 70
Danville CA 94526
Phone: 415-676-0140

Dr. Daniel L Torrance
31423 Marne Dr
R Palos Verdes CA 90274
Phone: 213-377-4313

STATE-CO

Dr. Lawrence Leroy Emmons
7290 S Andes Ct
Aurora CO 80016
Phone: 303-680-9927

Dr. William Louis Jobe
2465 So Downing
Denver CO 80210
Phone: 303-777-7585

Dr. Kathleen Kreiss
1400 Jackson St
Denver CO 80206
Phone: 303-398-1525

Dr. John Terry Leever
1060 Orchard
Grand Junction CO 81501
Phone: 303-243-4528

Dr. James E MacLean
2492 Sage Run Ct
Grand Junction CO 81505
Phone: 303-241-0744

Dr. Lawrence Harvey Repsher
8300 W 38th Ave
Wheat Ridge CO 80033
Phone: 303-425-8579

LIST OF APPROVED B-READERS FEDERAL COAL MINE HEALTH AND SAFETY ACT OF 1969

STATE-CT

Dr. Mark Richard Cullen
333 Cedar Street
New Haven CT 06510
Phone: 203-436-2846

Dr. Philip Anthony Dimenno
212 Natchaig Dr
Meriden CT 06450
Phone: 203-237-9653

Dr. Raymond G Haddad
267 Grant St
Bridgeport CT 06602
Phone: 203-384-3794

Dr. Donald H Hulnick
137 Chestnut Hill Rd
Ridgefield CT 06877
Phone: 203-431-9376

Dr. David A Lund
100 Grand St
New Britain CT 06052
Phone: 203-224-5556

Dr. William Austin Lynch
85 Jefferson St STE 706
Hartford CT 06106
Phone: 203-246-5403

Dr. Harold Moskowitz
14 Arlen Way
W Hartford CT 06117
Phone: 203-233-7220

Dr. Coralie Shaw
55 Chimney Corner Circle
Guilford CT 06437
Phone: 203-453-3500

Dr. Michael Barry Teiger
1000 Asylum Avenue
Hartford CT 06105
Phone: 203-278-3812

Dr. Donald S Weinstein
9 Farmstead Lane
Waterford CT 06385
Phone: 203-447-2069

STATE-DC

Dr. David Richard Buck
110 Irving St
Washington DC 20010
Phone: 202-541-6456

STATE-DE

Dr. Clifton Howard Hunt
6 Halsey Drive
Wilmington DE 19807
Phone: 302-655-6830

Dr. Joseph Ronald Peacock
1601 Milltown Rd Suite 11
Wilmington DE 19808
Phone: 215-793-1102

LIST OF APPROVED B-READERS FEDERAL COAL MINE HEALTH AND SAFETY ACT OF 1969

STATE-DE

Dr. Herman Joseph Stein
515 Andover Rd
Wilmington DE 19803
Phone: 302-478-0120

STATE-FL

Dr. Arthur Raymond Brooker
13550 N 31st Suite 140
Tampa FL 33613
Phone: 813-971-2056

Dr. Stuart M Brooks
5030 Paloma Dr
Tampa FL 33624
Phone: 813-960-1669

Dr. William S Cole
821 Sunnybrook Lane
Melbourne FL 32935
Phone: 305-254-4908

Dr. Susan Linda Curry
615 E Princeton St
Orlando FL 32803
Phone: 305-894-7185

Dr. Garth Richard Drewry
6 C Columbia Drive
Tampa FL 33606
Phone: 813-253-2721

Dr. Ilan Allan Feingold
12900 SW 70th Ave
Miami FL 33156
Phone: 305-253-6026

Dr. James Edward Hannah
315 Virginia Drive
Winter Park FL 32789
Phone: 407-647-4011

Dr. Allan E Katz
6449 38th Ave N
St Petersburg FL 33710
Phone: 813-381-0275

Dr. James Philip Krainson
6131 SW 104 St
Miami FL 33156
Phone: 305-666-0211

Dr. Aaron M Longacre
13550 N 31st St
Tampa FL 33612
Phone: 813-971-0694

Dr. Robert Joseph Mezey
6740 SW 99th Terrace
Miami FL 33156
Phone: 305-666-1858

Dr. Robert I Miller
2371 S Ponte Vedra Blvd
Ponte Vedra Bch FL 32082
Phone: 904-829-3554

Dr. Sandra Alice Ann Oldham
8740 SW 85 Terrace
Miami FL 33173
Phone: 305-549-6894

Dr. Katherine Reed
13550 N 31st St Suite 140
Tampa FL 33613
Phone: 813-971-2056

LIST OF APPROVED B-READERS FEDERAL COAL MINE HEALTH AND SAFETY ACT OF 1969

STATE-FLA

Dr. Martin Larry Silbiger
11720 Lipsey Rd
Tampa FL 33618
Phone: 813-961-0789

Dr. William Campbell Walker
300 Riverside Dr E
Bradenton FL 34208
Phone: 813-745-7571

STATE-GA

Dr. Anthony Michael Costrin
#18 Chatuachee Crossing
Savannah GA 31406
Phone: 912-598-0685

Dr. Richard A Elmer
6500 Vernon Woods Dr NE
Atlanta GA 30328
Phone: 404-252-3430

Dr. Abulkalam W Haque
6090 Heards Creek Dr
Atlanta GA 30328
Phone: 404-255-1416

Dr. Asher Marks
P O Box 263
Rabon Gap GA 30568
Phone: 305-446-3811

Dr. Frank Maynard Thames Jr
417 4th Ave P O Box 1924
Albany GA 31703
Phone: 912-883-1220

Dr. Walter S Dunbar
2062 Imperial Drive NE
Atlanta GA 30345
Phone: 404-636-2788

Dr. David Jay Frolich
4668 Savage Creek Dr
Macon GA 31210
Phone: 912-744-1238

Dr. Donald Hubert Manning
3 Fendig Rd
St Simons Isl GA 31522
Phone: 912-267-7415

Dr. Richard Sanford Simmons
1550 Doctors Dr Suite 301
Lagrange GA 30240
Phone: 404-884-2641

STATE-HI

Dr. John Louis Cieply
1893 Kihi St
Honolulu HI 96821
Phone: 808-373-9248

Dr. Carl Phillip Hallenborg
930 Kaheka St Ph B5
Honolulu HI 96814
Phone: 808-943-0262

LIST OF APPROVED B-READERS FEDERAL COAL MINE HEALTH AND SAFETY ACT OF 1969

STATE-HI

Dr. Philip J W Lee
1507 S King St Suite 101
Honolulu HI 96826
Phone: 808-949-5938

Dr. Norman Odell Polk
45 176 Kokokahi Pl
Kancohe HI 96744
Phone: 808-234-2163

Dr. David Hidefumi Sakuda
321 N Kuakini St
Honolulu HI 96817
Phone: 808-547-9545

STATE-IA

Dr. Robert Walter Hartung
2322 E Kimberly Road
Davnport IA 52807
Phone: 319-359-3931

Dr. Gregory Alan Hicklin
3012 Patricia Dr
Des Moines IA 50322
Phone: 515-278-5553

Dr. Stuart Kent Lehr
1212 Pleasant LL9
Des Moines IA 50309
Phone: 515-283-6171

Dr. Dwight Keith Rafferty
2996 133rd Way NW
West Des Moines IA 50265
Phone: 515-276-1243

STATE-IL

Dr. Jeffrey H Agee
536 Shorline Dr
Decator IL 62521
Phone: 217-423-3385

Dr. Richard Marcus Bauer
104 Oakmont Road
Highland Park IL 60035
Phone: 312-432-3828

Dr. Dharmashi Vishanji Bhat
Rt 3 Box 11A
Carterville IL 62918
Phone: 618-985-4000

Dr. R Barton Bridges
301 W Lincoln
Belleville IL 62220
Phone: 618-235-0955

Dr. David W Cugell
1419 Judson Ave
Evanston IL 60201
Phone: 312-328-1828

Dr. John J Fennessy
5841 So Maryland Ave
Chicago IL 60637
Phone: 312-702-6162

LIST OF APPROVED B-READERS FEDERAL COAL MINE HEALTH AND SAFETY ACT OF 1969

STATE-IL

Dr. John J Fitzpatrick
5300 Stony Creek Dr
Oaklawn IL 60453
Phone: 312-636-7081

Dr. William Joseph Heiser
3604 Spanish Trace
Springfield IL 62702
Phone: 217-546-8012

Dr. Stephen M Hessl
3528 N Janssen
Chicago IL 60657
Phone: 312-633-5310

Dr. Paul A Holdener
301 West Lincoln
Belleville IL 62221
Phone: 618-235-0955

Dr. James Philip Kase
1840 Cambridge
Flossmoor IL 60422
Phone: 312-798-8611

Dr. Stephen Edward Lehnert
301 W Lincoln
Belleville IL 62222
Phone: 618-235-0955

Dr. David Morton Main
602 W University
Urbana IL 61801
Phone: 217-337-3190

Dr. Boyd Eastham Nelson
105 Oak Ridge Ct
Decatur IL 32521
Phone: 217-428-3672

Dr. Sanford Eugene Rabushka
2100 Lincoln Pk W
Chicago IL 60614
Phone: 312-878-8700

Dr. Ami Hai Eliezer Rubin
Northwestern Mem Hospital
Chicago IL 60611
Phone: 312-908-8163

Dr. Lee Sider
710 N Fairbanks Ct
Chicago IL 60611
Phone: 312-908-5133

Dr. Terrence A Tyrrell
66 Signal Hill Bld
Belleville IL 62223
Phone: 618-397-7688

Dr. Charles G Wieland
53 Hemlock St
Belleville IL 62221
Phone: 618-235-6435

Dr. Lawrence P Zarian
930 Taylor Drive
Gurnee IL 60031
Phone: 312-367-6036

STATE-IN

Dr. Benny S Ko
R R 32 Box 320
Terre Haute IN 47803
Phone: 812-232-0021

Dr. Alfred P Lessure
412 S E Sixth St
Evansville IN 47713
Phone: 812-426-8329

LIST OF APPROVED B-READERS FEDERAL COAL MINE HEALTH AND SAFETY ACT OF 1969

STATE-IN

Dr. William Elmer McGraw
9117 Sand Key Ln
Indianapolis IN 46256
Phone: 317-842-0655

Dr. Gordon C McLaughlin III
8440 Coral Reef Court
Indianapolis IN 46256
Phone: 317-842-2465

Dr. James B Moffett
8154 Durgin Terrace
Crown Point IN 46307
Phone: 219-769-0629

Dr. Leon Nazarian
7001 W Cheyenne
Muncie IN 47304
Phone: 216-933-2873

Dr. Jeff W Selby
421 Chestnut St
Evansville IN 47713
Phone: 821-426-9537

Dr. Aram Semerdjian
8319 Linden Ave
Munster IN 46321
Phone: 219-972-1030

Dr. Robert D Tarver
RR 1 Box SW 223
New Palestine IN 46163
Phone: 317-861-5563

Dr. Anthony V Zancanaro
1701 N Senate Blvd
Indianapolis IN 46202
Phone: 317-929-8876

STATE-KS

Dr. William R Allen
9201 Parallel Pkwy
Kansas City KS 66112
Phone: 913-334-4110

Dr. William R Allen Jr
9201 Parallel Parkway
Kansas City KS 66112
Phone: 913-651-7085

Dr. Timothy E Allen
823 Mulvane St
Topeka KS 66606
Phone: 913-334-4110

Dr. William Thomas Braun III
3243 E Murdock
Wichita KS 67208
Phone: 316-685-2711

Dr. Kelly Zack Hart
2213 W 49th Terrace
Westood Hills KS 66205
Phone: 913-371-4343

Dr. James Wilson Owen
823 Mulvane
Topeka KS 66606
Phone: 913-234-3451

LIST OF APPROVED B-READERS FEDERAL COAL MINE HEALTH AND SAFETY ACT OF 1969

STATE-KY

Dr. Glen Ray Baker
126 Scenic View Heights
Corbin KY 40701
Phone: 606-528-4644

Dr. Jeffrey S Bisker
1400 Willow Ave
Louisville KY 40204
Phone: 502-451-3426

Dr. Bruce Charles Broudy
1221 South Broadway
Lexington KY 40504
Phone: 606-255-6841

Dr. Abdulkader Dahhan
2615 Village Center
Harlan KY 40831
Phone: 606-573-1085

Dr. John Francis Dineen
3417 Fleetwood Drive
Lexington KY 40502
Phone: 606-266-9615

Dr. Karen W Fitzgerald
P O Box 427
Cynthiana KY 41031
Phone: 606-234-3092

Dr. Dennis Herman Halbert
141 Cedar Cr Rd
Pikeville KY 41501
Phone: 606-437-9824

Dr. John Morris Harrison
328 Whitfield Dr
Lexington KY 40503
Phone: 606-273-3492

Dr. Mary Louise Harty
9021 Bingham Dr
Louisville KY 40222
Phone: 502-426-1676

Dr. Abul Hashem
P O Box 2107
Whitesburg KY 41858
Phone: 606-633-7975

Dr. Thomas M Jarboe
100 N Eagle Creek Drive
Lexington KY 40509
Phone: 606-255-6841

Dr. Kil Bong Kim
Pikeville Medical Bldg
Pikeville KY 41501
Phone: 606-432-1357

Dr. Jerome L Krumpelman
P O Box 698
Richmond KY 40475
Phone: 606-624-2695

Dr. Emery E Lane
323 E Chestnut St
Louisville KY 40202
Phone: 502-588-5814

Dr. Arthur Lieber
Albert B Chandler Med Ctr
Lexington KY 40536
Phone: 606-233-52222

Dr. Thomas R Marshall
3004 Taylorsville Rd
Louisville KY 40205
Phone: 502-456-6145

LIST OF APPROVED B-READERS FEDERAL COAL MINE HEALTH AND SAFETY ACT OF 1969

STATE-KY

Dr. William Martin Obryan
1102 Triplett St Ste 1300
Owensboro KY 42301
Phone: 502-926-8810

Dr. Ashok R Patel
100 Gorman Ridge
Hazard KY 41701
Phone: 606-439-5057

Dr. Rayudu B Polisetty
730 Sun Valley Terrace
Hazard KY 41701
Phone: 606-439-1331

Dr. Robert Neil Pope
PO Box 1875 1102 Triplett
Owensboro KY 42302
Phone: 502-926-8810

Dr. Alex Poulos
P O Box 2648
Pikeville KY 41501
Phone: 606-432-1357

Dr. Robert W Powell
224 E Broadway
Louisville KY 40202
Phone: 502-587-0915

Dr. Truman D Simmons
Harlan Arh
Harlan KY 40831
Phone: 606-573-4213

Dr. Gregory P Stark
2233 Montgomery Ave S B
Ashland KY 41101
Phone: 606-329-1185

Dr. Carol B Stelling
1424 Essex Park
Lexington KY 40502
Phone: 606-233-5581

Dr. Sam H Traughber
1910 So Va St
Hopkinsville KY 42240
Phone: 502-886-0251

Dr. Paul O Wells
Ivy Hill Box 113
Harlan KY 40831
Phone: 606-573-3396

Dr. John Howell Woodring
162 N Arcadia Park
Lexington KY 40503
Phone: 606-277-5927

STATE-LA

Dr. Robert Neal Brown
618 S Ryan
Lake Charles LA 70601
Phone: 318-436-7571

Dr. Dean W Geheber
3888 Government St
Baton Rouge LA 70806
Phone: 504-344-3753

Dr. Richard C Hebert
3772 North Blvd
Baton Rouge LA 70806
Phone: 504-343-6602

Dr. Daniel A Herpin
Suite 105 2770 2nd Ave
Lake Charles LA 70601
Phone: 318-477-0775

LIST OF APPROVED B-READERS FEDERAL COAL MINE HEALTH AND SAFETY ACT OF 1969

STATE-LA

Dr. David Rex Hunter
3601 Red Oak Ct
New Orleans LA 70114
Phone: 504-392-3434

Dr. Charles Claiborne Matth
1514 Jefferson Hwy
New Orleans LA 70121
Phone: 504-838-3495

Dr. Clay A Waggenspack Jr
3772 N Blvd
Baton Rouge LA 70806
Phone: 504-343-6602

Dr. Robert Norwood Jones
1700 Perdido St
New Orleans LA 70112
Phone: 504-588-5265

Dr. Randel Andrew Patty
888 Dubois Drive
Baton Rouge LA 70808
Phone: 504-766-0781

STATE-MA

Dr. Elisha Hornblower Atkin
48 Banks St
Somerville MA 02144
Phone: 617-625-1267

Dr. Edward A Gaensler
80 E Concord St
Boston MA 02118
Phone: 617-247-6253

Dr. Reginald Greene
Mass Gen Hosp Fruit St
Boston MA 02114
Phone: 617-726-8391

Dr. Stuart J Masters
34 Brookside Drive
Pittsfield MA 01201
Phone: 413-443-4386

Dr. Elizabeth H Moore
16 Marlborough
Boston MA 02116
Phone: 617-726-8399

Dr. Peter J Barrett
10 Martins Lane
Hingham MA 02043
Phone: 617-749-5876

Dr. M Elon Gale
175 Brookline St
Newton MA 02167
Phone: 617-244-3344

Dr. Peter John Jederlinic
38 Draper Ave
Westwood MA 02090
Phone: 617-762-5615

Dr. Theresa C Mcloud
Mass Gen Hosp
Boston MA 02114
Phone: 617-726-8307

Dr. L Christine Oliver
Mass Gen Hosp Fruit St
Boston MA 02114
Phone: 617-232-8247

LIST OF APPROVED B-READERS FEDERAL COAL MINE HEALTH AND SAFETY ACT OF 1969

STATE-MA

Dr. John David Poutasse
593 Holmes Rd
Pittsfield MA 01201
Phone: 413-442-8371

Dr. Alan Marshall Schwartz
33 Nichols Rd
Cohasset MA 02025
Phone: 617-383-0941

Dr. Joanne O Shepard
Mass General Hosp
Boston MA 02114
Phone: 617-726-8773

Dr. Richard H Taus
20 Webster St #213
Brookline MA 02146
Phone: 617-731-9316

Dr. Cynthia Umalitorres
79 Newton Ave No
Worcester MA 01602
Phone: 617-856-2160

Dr. Robert G Wilkinson
20 Stanford Drive
Hingham MA 02043
Phone: 617-749-2914

STATE-MD

Dr. Morteza Seyed Ahmadian
801 Toll House Ave
Frederick MD 21701
Phone: 301-663-5185

Dr. Joseph Francis Branda
9811 Mallard Dr
Laurel MD 20708
Phone: 301-776-4777

Dr. Orn Eliasson
9584 Woodblock Row
Columbia MD 21045
Phone: 301-992-1899

Dr. Robert E Ensor
549 Broadwater Rd
Arnold MD 21012
Phone: 301-647-9441

Dr. Bob W Gayler
601 N Broadway
Baltimore MD 21205
Phone: 301-955-5525

Dr. Frank Anthony Giargiana Jr
4935 Pale Orchid Court
Columbia MD 21044
Phone: 301-730-0961

Dr. Lee Allan Goodman
5748 Cross Country Blvd
Baltimore MD 21209
Phone: 301-367-8282

Dr. Harold Melton Hagen
12301 Piney Glen Lane
Potomac MD 20854
Phone: 301-299-3374

Dr. Christopher M Harvey
21 Scottsdale Ct
Lutherville MD 21093
Phone: 301-296-0872

Dr. Thomas E Hobbins
915 Poplar Hill Rd
Baltimore MD 21210
Phone: 301-323-8588

LIST OF APPROVED B-READERS FEDERAL COAL MINE HEALTH AND SAFETY ACT OF 1969

STATE-MD

Dr. Irving Bernard Joffe
7 Pomona S Apt 2
Pikesville MD 21208
Phone: 301-653-0609

Dr. Gordon Craig Johnson
8004 Carita Ct
Bethesda MD 20817
Phone: 301-427-7034

Dr. Nagi Fouad Khouri
2411 Still Forest Road
Baltimore MD 21208
Phone: 301-955-8438

Dr. Young Choo Kim
13407 Bladon Rd
Phoenix MD 21131
Phone: 301-666-9420

Dr. Myung Sup Kim
418 Washington St
Cumberland MD 21502
Phone: 301-759-5142

Dr. Rodolfo Espaldon Lim
27 Teaberry Ln
Frostburg MD 21532
Phone: 301-689-1384

Dr. Samuel Veirs Mace
6006 Lakehurst Dr
Baltimore MD 21210
Phone: 301-377-6039

Dr. Robert Francis Miller
600 Memorial Ave
Cumberland MD 21502
Phone: 301-777-5751

Dr. Louis Dominic Napoli
5 Stapleford Hall Ct
Potomac MD 20854
Phone: 301-299-7448

Dr. Jack E Nissim
2435 W Belvedere Ave
Baltimore MD 21215
Phone: 301-466-0653

Dr. Behram Pastakia
8715 Irvington Ave
Bethesda MD 20817
Phone: 301-496-7700

Dr. Lawrence J Pazdurek
1 Lamont Place
Glen Arm MD 21057
Phone: 301-592-7310

Dr. Arnold Raizon
5437 Grove Ridge Way
Rockville MD 20852
Phone: 301-897-5406

Dr. George Peter Saba
3921 Foxhill Dr
Ellicott City MD 21043
Phone: 301-461-1738

Dr. William W Scott
218 Goodale Road
Baltimore MD 21212
Phone: 301-435-7850

Dr. Penelope Pate Scott
218 Goodale Rd
Baltimore MD 21212
Phone: 301-578-5713

LIST OF APPROVED B-READERS FEDERAL COAL MINE HEALTH AND SAFETY ACT OF 1969

STATE-MD

Dr. Henry J Silverman
166 W Montgomery St
Baltimore MD 21237
Phone: 301-528-1326

Dr. Allan Wayne Skrenta
10143 Pasture Gate Lane
Columbia MD 21044
Phone: 301-730-6371

Dr. Ronald Jeffrey Stanfiel
9457 Pursuit Ct
Columbia MD 21045
Phone: 301-730-4466

Dr. Philip Anthony Templeto
1711 S Charles St
Baltimore MD 21230
Phone: 301-685-1455

Dr. Clifford James Turner
9001 Shad Lane
Potomac MD 20854
Phone: 301-299-2594

Dr. William Dean Wehunt
5616 Lake Christopher Dr
Rockville MD 20855
Phone: 301-977-7537

Dr. Paul Saurel Wheeler
302 Somerset Rd
Baltimore MD 21210
Phone: 301-955-5423

Dr. Philip Whittlesey
600 Northern Pkwy W
Baltimore MD 21210
Phone: 301-323-4411

STATE-ME

Dr. Robert Patterson Andrew
297 Center St
Bamgor ME 04401
Phone: 207-234-2500

Dr. Robert J Isler
Maine Medical Center
Portland ME 04102
Phone: 207-871-2571

Dr. Jon Perley Pitman
45 Golden St
Lewiston ME 04240
Phone: 207-768-2901

Dr. Robin Mark Wood
RFD#3 Box 390
Augusta ME 04330
Phone: 207-547-3563

STATE-MI

Dr. Gordon Herman Beute
6411 Wardell Ct
W Bloomfield MI 48033
Phone: 313-876-1331

Dr. Frederick Ross Birkhill
31 Shady Hollow Dr
Dearborn MI 48124
Phone: 313-278-9224

LIST OF APPROVED B-READERS FEDERAL COAL MINE HEALTH AND SAFETY ACT OF 1969

STATE-MI

Dr. Kenneth Robert Casey
2799 West Grand Blvd
Detroit MI 48202
Phone: 801-363-3343

Dr. Marco John Dibiase
8381 N Hillcrest Dr
Berrien Springs MI 49103
Phone: 616-473-3195

Dr. John Kevin Drumm
1010 Lone Pine Road
Bloomfield Hill MI 48013
Phone: 313-258-6803

Dr. Michael S Eichenhorn
2799 W Grand Blvd
Detroit MI 48202
Phone: 313-876-2436

Dr. John Charles Hall
1401 Creyts Rd
Lansing MI 48917
Phone: 517-322-4000

Dr. Lawrence Robert Irish
2765 Flushing Road
Flint MI 48504
Phone: 313-232-1197

Dr. Rehana N Kapadia
5864 Nanevact
W Bloomfield MI 48322
Phone: 313-851-5220

Dr. Raymond S Kurtzman
6919 Woodbank
Birmingham MI 48010
Phone: 313-626-7763

Dr. Paul Arthur Kvale
676 Middlesex
Grosse Point Pk MI 48230
Phone: 313-331-4676

Dr. Carol June Maywood
7381 Radcliff Dr
West Bloomfield MI 48322
Phone: 313-855-3561

Dr. Kathleen Ann McCarroll
4871 Malibu Drive
Bloomfield Hill MI 48013
Phone: 313-626-2773

Dr. Jay L Pearlberg
28090 Tavistock Trail
Southfield MI 48034
Phone: 313-876-1331

Dr. Kenneth D Rosenman
MI St Univ Rm 8338 Cl Ctr
Lansing MI 48824
Phone: 517-353-1864

Dr. Abdul Razzak Sadik
23760 Woodward
Pleasant Ridge MI 48069
Phone: 313-545-1330

Dr. Allen J Solomon
501 Canterbury
Saginaw MI 48603
Phone: 517-792-2746

Dr. Joseph Tablot
1311 N Michigan
Saginaw MI 48602
Phone: 517-753-7501

LIST OF APPROVED B-READERS FEDERAL COAL MINE HEALTH AND SAFETY ACT OF 1969

STATE-MN

Dr. Gregory Lee Aughenbaugh
200 2nd St SW
Rochester MN 55905
Phone: 507-284-2271

Dr. John Edward Bjorgen
5714 Woodstock Ave
Golden Valley MN 55422
Phone: 612-544-9399

Dr. Larry R Brown
Mayo Clinic East 2
Rochester MN 55901
Phone: 507-285-0850

Dr. Anthony Michael Cook
1544 S Mississippi R Blvd
St Paul MN 55116
Phone: 612-690-3105

Dr. James Richard Flink
255 N Smith Ave #201
St Paul MN 55102
Phone: 612-224-5895

Dr. Gerald A Gretsch
6 Buffalo Road
North Oaks MN 55110
Phone: 612-484-8621

Dr. Douglas B Ketcham
901 Lowry Medical Arts
St Paul MN 55102
Phone: 612-298-8256

Dr. Joseph Harry Tashjian
1172 Aquarius Lane
Eagan MN 55123
Phone: 612-454-7372

STATE-MO

Dr. Joseph Vincent Cusumano
6319 Alexander Dr
St Louis MO 63105
Phone: 314-726-5860

Dr. John Joseph Lang
507 Fairways Cir
St Louis MO 63141
Phone: 314-567-1293

Dr. Robert Gordon Levitt
13134 Thornhill Drive
St Louis MO 63131
Phone: 314-822-1703

Dr. Alfred Dows Shaplin
12668 Westport Dr
St Louis MO 63146
Phone: 314-576-6348

Dr. Jerry Michael Speckman
6537 Valley Rd
Kansas City MO 64113
Phone: 816-276-4141

Dr. Lee M Steinberg
5155 Raytown Rd
Kansas City MO 64133
Phone: 816-358-2040

Dr. Murali Sundaram
11636 Larkridge Lane
St Louis MO 63126
Phone: 314-577-8025

Dr. Theodore Martin Vollmar
7244 Forsyth 1E
St Louis MO 63105
Phone: 314-721-4363

LIST OF APPROVED B-READERS FEDERAL COAL MINE HEALTH AND SAFETY ACT OF 1969

STATE-MO

Dr. Mark Steven Wald
11133 Dunn Rd Suite B 208
St Louis MO 63136
Phone: 314-355-2300

STATE-MS

Dr. Daniel Michael Doyle
725 North St
Pittsfield MS 01201
Phone: 413-499-4161

Dr. Robert Brent Harrison
5519 Ridgewood Rd
Jackson MS 39211
Phone: 601-956-8060

STATE-NC

Dr. Brian Arthur Boehlecke
625 Tinkerbell Road
Chapel Hill NC 27514
Phone: 919-942-7909

Dr. Ray Joseph Bouzigard
2000 Greenbriar Rd
Kinston NC 28501
Phone: 919-527-7077

Dr. Robert H Choplin
300 S Hawthorne Rd
Winston Salem NC 27103
Phone: 919-748-4316

Dr. Bruce E Fee
1350 So Kings Dr
Charlotte NC 28207
Phone: 704-372-8750

Dr. Boyd Bennett Gasque Jr
1708 N Elm Street
Lumberton NC 28358
Phone: 919-739-3669

Dr. Joseph John Gerdes
130 Lake Concord Rd
Concord NC 28025
Phone: 704-786-0214

Dr. Warren Lamar Harrell Jr
1237 Brookwood Dr
Shelby NC 28150
Phone: 704-482-5176

Dr. Carl White Hoffman
P O Box 1527
Lumberton NC 28358
Phone: 919-738-8222

Dr. Edward William Kouri
2408 Cross Country Rd
Matthews NC 28105
Phone: 704-847-3956

Dr. John Daughtry Marriott
134 Oakleaf Drive
Morehead City NC 28557
Phone: 919-726-7444

LIST OF APPROVED B-READERS FEDERAL COAL MINE HEALTH AND SAFETY ACT OF 1969

STATE-NC

Dr. Edwin Newman
3734 Columbine Cir
Charlotte NC 28211
Phone: 704-364-0568

Dr. Kenneth Howe Winter
3307 Waldron Drive
Greensboro NC 27408
Phone: 919-288-2988

Dr. Michael David Weaver
#9 Doctors Park
Greenville NC 27834
Phone: 919-752-5000

STATE-NE

Dr. Charles A Dobry
747 No 89th Ave
Omaha NE 68114
Phone: 402-559-6983

STATE-NH

Dr. Eugene Schwartz
816 Alton Woods Dr
Concord NH 03301
Phone: 603-271-4477

STATE-NJ

Dr. Judith Korek Amorosa
60 Prospect St
Somersville NJ 08876
Phone: 201-722-9695

Dr. Roger Alan Berg
21 Watchung Road
Short Hills NJ 07078
Phone: 201-467-1180

Dr. Stephanie Flicker
7 Larsen Park Drive
Marlton NJ 08053
Phone: 609-983-9690

Dr. Donald Auerbach
12 Wicklow Ct
Cherry Hill NJ 08003
Phone: 609-424-0327

Dr. Susan M Daum
130 Kinderkanack Rd
River Edge NJ 07661
Phone: 201-487-7337

Dr. Howard Matthew Kipen
RD 2 Box 210 C
Basking Ridge NJ 07920
Phone: 201-463-4773

LIST OF APPROVED B-READERS FEDERAL COAL MINE HEALTH AND SAFETY ACT OF 1969

STATE-NJ

Dr. Neil Robert Kramer
624 Kingscroft
Cherry Hill NJ 08034
Phone: 609-667-9632

Dr. G Tom Morea
55 E Rt 70
Marlton NJ 08053
Phone: 609-956-7577

Dr. Alan William Osborne
222 Kimball Ave
Westfield NJ 07090
Phone: 201-233-2564

Dr. Elaine B Panitz
34 Cleveland Lane
Princeton NJ 08540
Phone: 609-448-3737

Dr. Alan Raymond Pope
209 E Maple Ave
Moorestown NJ 08057
Phone: 609-234-4917

Dr. Phalimar S Prabhu
810 Abbott Blvd
Fort Lee NJ 07024
Phone: 201-224-0333

Dr. Burton Schaffer
Kings Hwy & Princeton Ave
Woodbury NJ 08096
Phone: 609-848-4998

Dr. Theresa Ann Smith
23 Hawthorn Dr
Westfield NJ 07090
Phone: 201-233-9044

Dr. Julie K Timins
20 Footes Lane
Morristown NJ 07960
Phone: 201-267-7847

STATE-NM

Dr. William I Christensen
P O Box 6231
Albuquerque NM 87197
Phone: 505-262-7600

STATE-NY

Dr. John McCulloch Austin
622 West 168 Street
New York NY 10032
Phone: 212-694-2981

Dr. Donald W Bidwell
28 Fall St
Seneca Falls NY 13148
Phone: 315-568-8957

LIST OF APPROVED B-READERS FEDERAL COAL MINE HEALTH AND SAFETY ACT OF 1969

STATE-NY

Dr. Gerald A Black
5132 Muirfield Drive
Fayetteville NY 13066
Phone: 315-637-5471

Dr. Brian Block
167 Brandywine Dr
Williamsville NY 14221
Phone: 716-688-5725

Dr. Jack S Deitch
5 The Dell
Woodbury NY 11797
Phone: 516-367-4902

Dr. John Carroll Democker
564 Ridge Rd E
Rochester NY 14621
Phone: 716-544-1750

Dr. Rodney Ivan Ehrlich
412 W 110th St Apt 41
New York NY 10025
Phone: 212-241-4790

Dr. Azimi Farhad
301 Prospect Ave
Syracuse NY 43203
Phone: 315-424-5274

Dr. Alfred Franzblau
Mt Sinai Hosp Box 1057
New York NY 10029
Phone: 212-241-6173

Dr. Guy G Freeman
146 Manetto Hill Road
Plainview NY 11803
Phone: 516-931-2120

Dr. Louis Mark Germaine
174 Tewkesbury Road
Scarsdale NY 10583
Phone: 914-725-5258

Dr. Steven George Herbert
2035 Rte 65 Rd 2
Holcomb NY 14469
Phone: 716-624-2790

Dr. John David Kennedy
2273 Clinton Av So
Rochester NY 14618
Phone: 716-442-9171

Dr. Arfa Khan
95 Karol Place
Jericho NY 11753
Phone: 516-932-7170

Dr. Donald A Killam
340 Presidential Way
Guilderland NY 12084
Phone: 518-869-3249

Dr. Everett Marc Lautin
245 East 93rd St Apt 27G
New York NY 10128
Phone: 212-831-3745

Dr. Robert Frederic Lautin
429 East 52nd Street
New York NY 10022
Phone: 212-752-4684

Dr. Ruth Lilis
420 East 51st St
New York NY 10022
Phone: 212-650-8806

LIST OF APPROVED B-READERS FEDERAL COAL MINE HEALTH AND SAFETY ACT OF 1969

STATE-NY

Dr. David Eric Magarik
2508 Bayberry Lane
Vestal NY 13850
Phone: 607-797-8555

Dr. Albert Miller
179 West Shore Rd
Great Neck NY 11024
Phone: 516-829-5665

Dr. Harry J Pinsky
257 Pelham Road
Rochester NY 14610
Phone: 716-244-4904

Dr. Joseph Rosenstein
93 Ampersand Ave Box 647
Saranac Lake NY 12983
Phone: 518-891-4141

Dr. John Clayton Sanborn
7014 Highfield Rd
Fayetteville NY 13066
Phone: 315-446-9045

Dr. Thomas Francis Stephens
324 Avalon Drive
Rochester NY 14618
Phone: 716-244-1475

Dr. John W Vance
1275 Delaware Ave
Buffalo NY 14209
Phone: 716-886-5650

Dr. Paul Mark Velt
185 Edgemoor Road
Rochester NY 14618
Phone: 716-442-6066

Dr. Andrew Arthor Wallman
650 Shore Rd 5G
Long Beach NY 11561
Phone: 516-889-6204

Dr. John C Wandtke
Univ of Rochester Med Ctr
Rochester NY 14642
Phone: 716-275-3509

Dr. Donald Richard Woloszyn
401 Main St
Oneota NY 13820
Phone: 607-432-7611

Dr. Robert E Woods
397 Dansworth
Youngstown NY 14174
Phone: 716-745-7529

Dr. Ralph D Zehr
642 10 Walker Hill Road
Waverly NY 14892
Phone: 607-565-4838

Dr. Theodore Fiske Van Andt
79 Stayvesant Rd
Pittsford NY 14534
Phone: 716-338-3580

STATE-OH

Dr. Wynn Wygal Adam
321 Shady Crest Dr
Kettering OH 45429
Phone: 513-299-2998

Dr. Ronald A Bailey
2398 Brian Dr
Beachwood OH 44122
Phone: 216-464-2398

LIST OF APPROVED B-READERS FEDERAL COAL MINE HEALTH AND SAFETY ACT OF 1969

STATE-OH

Dr. Jeffrey Scott Benseler
500 Queensgate Rd
Springboro OH 45066
Phone: 513-748-2588

Dr. Thomas William Church
1554 Pro Dr
Lima OH 45805
Phone: 419-999-2940

Dr. Robert Alan Clark
234 Goodman St
Cincinnati OH 45267
Phone: 513-872-7226

Dr. Alan Marshall Cohen
2935 Fontenay
Shaker Heights OH 44120
Phone: 216-921-2552

Dr. Jeffrey Robert Crass
3395 Scranton Road
Cleveland OH 44109
Phone: 216-459-3484

Dr. James P Farner
1094 Tote Rd
Austinburg OH 44010
Phone: 216-466-1321

Dr. Thomas Thurman Fox
3780 Rushmore Drive
Columbus OH 43220
Phone: 614-451-4116

Dr. Gerald J Gelford
8936 Slagle
Centerville OH 45459
Phone: 513-433-6898

Dr. Leopold Gonzalez
Cleveland Cl 9500 Euclid
Cleveland OH 44123
Phone: 216-444-6637

Dr. Steven Edward Gordon
4228 Nantucket Dr
Toledo OH 43623
Phone: 419-885-3242

Dr. George L Grauel
22320 Needlewood Circle
Strongsville OH 44136
Phone: 216-238-3286

Dr. Steven Douglas Haas
6644 Worthington Galena
Worthington OH 43085
Phone: 614-431-5115

Dr. George David Jacobs
2730 Navarre Ave
Oregon OH 43616
Phone: 419-693-0506

Dr. Kenneth R Kattan
6741 Meadowridge Lane
Cincinnati OH 45237
Phone: 513-731-2197

Dr. Mary Anne King
15431 Edgewater Drive
Lakewood OH 44107
Phone: 216-226-8663

Dr. George Ogden Kress
144 Campus View Blvd
Worthington OH 43085
Phone: 614-885-0845

LIST OF APPROVED B-READERS FEDERAL COAL MINE HEALTH AND SAFETY ACT OF 1969

STATE-OH

Dr. Richard Henry Laib
5382 Manortree Ln
Cincinnati OH 45238
Phone: 513-451-7191

Dr. Richard Kenneth Lenhart
32298 Orchard Park Dr
Avon Lake OH 44012
Phone: 216-933-6865

Dr. Sutek Lie
989 Hillcreek Lane
Gates Mills OH 44040
Phone: 216-844-7170

Dr. Stanley J Lucas
2905 Burnet Ave
Cincinnati OH 45219
Phone: 513-221-1436

Dr. Gregory A MacNealy
1249 Laurelwood Rd
Dayton OH 45409
Phone: 513-222-5841

Dr. John Arthur Mitchell
241 Riverdale Dr
Defiance Oh 43512
Phone: 419-784-5943

Dr. Richard David Patterson
400 Wabash Ave
Akron OH 44307
Phone: 216-384-6450

Dr. Carlos F Pena
3207 E Erie Ave
Lorain OH 44052
Phone: 216-288-1342

Dr. David Ellis Radebaugh
3060 Woodsmill
Bath OH 44210
Phone: 216-659-3777

Dr. Yagnesh R Raval
2952 Shawnee Trail
Piqua OH 45356
Phone: 513-778-4788

Dr. Peter W Reed
1521 Fairway Drive
Lima OH 45805
Phone: 419-991-7541

Dr. Nancy Sue Reinhardt
5900 Munger Rd
Centerville OH 45459
Phone: 513-433-6437

Dr. Ralph Taylor Shipley
234 Goodman St M/L 742
Cincinnati OH 45267
Phone: 513-558-6016

Dr. Harold B Spitz
6331 Grand Vista
Cincinnati OH 45213
Phone: 513-631-1589

Dr. Jay Sheldon Thompson
3609 Park E Dr Suite 404N
Beachwood OH 44122
Phone: 216-292-2755

Dr. Lawrence G Thorley
476 Kar A Bru St
Amherst OH 44001
Phone: 216-988-2254

LIST OF APPROVED B-READERS FEDERAL COAL MINE HEALTH AND SAFETY ACT OF 1969

STATE-OH

Dr. Stephan M Ticich
5319 Rosecliff Dr
Lorain OH 44053
Phone: 216-282-5613

Dr. Jerome F Wiot
234 Goodman St
Cincinnati OH 45229
Phone: 513-872-4396

STATE-OK

Dr. Charles E Eckman
816 N W 138th St
Edmond OK 73013
Phone: 405-751-5360

Dr. Thomas Harold Johnson
3141 Stonybrook Rd
Oklahoma City OK 73120
Phone: 405-751-6263

STATE-PA

Dr. Stanley L Altschuler
8040 Roosevelt Blvd
Philadelphia PA 19152
Phone: 215-331-3700

Dr. Claus Ludwig Anderson
4815 Liberty Ave
Pittsburgh PA 15224
Phone: 412-687-5573

Dr. Judith Marsha Aronchick
407 S 23 St
Philadelphia PA 19146
Phone: 215-735-2025

Dr. Vallabhaneni S Babu
154 Lindenvale Drive
McMurray PA 15317
Phone: 412-941-4963

Dr. Joseph Marc Becker
548 Winding Way
Merion Station PA 19066
Phone: 215-667-2180

Dr. Joseph Michael Behun
419 Maple Lane Edgeworth
Sewickley PA 15143
Phone: 412-741-8094

Dr. Eddy Armin Bresnitz
166 N Latchs Lane
Bala Cynwyd PA 19004
Phone: 215-664-6208

Dr. Richard Henry Crain
307 Meadow Lane Edgeworth
Sewickley PA 15143
Phone: 412-741-7888

Dr. Michael Terrence Czuba
1150 Seventh St
Waynesburg PA 15370
Phone: 412-627-5358

Dr. Nilima Dash
131 Wescott Drive
Pittsburgh PA 15237
Phone: 412-367-4307

LIST OF APPROVED B-READERS FEDERAL COAL MINE HEALTH AND SAFETY ACT OF 1969

STATE-PA

Dr. M Epstein David
1514 Knox Rd
Wynnewood PA 19096
Phone: 215-896-7312

Dr. Edgar Lee Dessen
20 North Laurel Street
Hazelton PA 18201
Phone: 717-455-3608

Dr. Paul E Epstein
126 Righters Mill Road
Gladwyne PA 19035
Phone: 215-896-5441

Dr. Jonathan Lynn Evans
608 N Mckean Street
Butler PA 16001
Phone: 412-282-4401

Dr. Mervyn Feierstein
21 Sandringham Drive
Bala Cynwyd PA 19004
Phone: 215-664-0995

Dr. Paul C Fiehler
109 Alleyne Dr
Pittsburgh PA 15215
Phone: (Not available.)

Dr. Stanley Bruce Fiel
1208 Drayton Ln
Philadelphia PA 19151
Phone: 215-642-3905

Dr. Stephen Neal Fisher
1252 Malvern Street
Pittsburgh PA 15217
Phone: 412-682-3004

Dr. Allan Perry Freedman
51 N 39th Street
Philadelphia PA 19104
Phone: 215-662-8060

Dr. Maija Guna Freimanis
5543 Wilkins Av
Pittsburgh PA 15217
Phone: 412-521-6533

Dr. Arnold C Friedman
524 Hoffman Drive
Bryn Mawr PA 19010
Phone: 215-527-8016

Dr. Carl Robert Fuhrman
431 Edgewood Road
Pittsburgh PA 15221
Phone: 412-243-5354

Dr. John P Galgon
1162 Belair Dr
Allentown PA 18103
Phone: 215-432-2906

Dr. Morris Zachary Gardner
Ct Med PV 1200 Center Ave
Pittsburgh PA 15219
Phone: 412-562-3106

Dr. Robert Edward Gates
815 White Oak Cr
Pittsburgh PA 15228
Phone: 412-561-0224

Dr. Warren Bruce Gefter
243 Wiltshire Road
Philadelphia PA 19151
Phone: 215-649-4449

LIST OF APPROVED B-READERS FEDERAL COAL MINE HEALTH AND SAFETY ACT OF 1969

STATE-PA

Dr. George Benjamin Goodman
2527 Club House Drive
Wexford PA 15090
Phone: 412-935-8505

Dr. Hugh Holman Hoke Jr
2445 Butter Road
Lancaster PA 17601
Phone: 717-393-6872

Dr. Joseph Abraham Horton
4255 Parkman Ave
Pittsburgh PA 15213
Phone: 412-683-3475

Dr. Reese Joseph James
20 Houston Road
Yardley PA 19067
Phone: 215-321-3411

Dr. Claude Rembert Johnson
2301 N 50th St
Philadelphia PA 19131
Phone: 215-473-8574

Dr. Lawrence M Kaplan
620 Wyomissing Blvd
Wyomissins PA 19610
Phone: 215-372-3949

Dr. Robin Lloyd Kaplan
36 N 11th Street
Reading PA 19601
Phone: 215-372-4591

Dr. Peter Donald Kaplan
856 Foxland Drive
Pittsburgh PA 15243
Phone: 412-531-9899

Dr. John A Kibelstis
3775 Fox Run Dr
Allentown PA 18103
Phone: 215-434-3652

Dr. Phillip Eugene King
1000 Drexel Ave
Johnstown PA 15905
Phone: 814-536-6671

Dr. Karen F Kuhns
USS Irwin Works Box 878
Dravosburg PA 15034
Phone: 412-675-7411

Dr. Paul David Laman Jr
109 Hillcrest Rd
Pittsburgh PA 15238
Phone: 412-681-0122

Dr. Marc S Lapayowker
2301 Cherry St 9D
Philadelphia PA 19103
Phone: 215-569-4182

Dr. Stanley Philip Laucks Jr
20 North Laurel Street
Hazelton PA 18201
Phone: 717-455-3608

Dr. Richard Barry Levine
304 Dogwood Lane
Elins Park PA 19117
Phone: 215-884-1523

Dr. Jeffrey A Levy
901 Goucher St
Johnstown PA 15905
Phone: 814-536-7226

LIST OF APPROVED B-READERS FEDERAL COAL MINE HEALTH AND SAFETY ACT OF 1969

STATE-PA

Dr. Anthony John Limberakis
636 Crosswicks Rd
Rydal PA 19046
Phone: 215-576-0887

Dr. Michael Lippman
525 Winding Way
Merion PA 19066
Phone: 215-667-4832

Dr. Burton Marks
542 S 12th St
Reading PA 19602
Phone: 213-374-0766

Dr. Kailash Nath Mathur
73 Sherwood Road
Pottsville PA 17901
Phone: 717-622-4030

Dr. Joseph M Mazzei
1142 Nevada St
Pittsburgh PA 15218
Phone: 412-281-6540

Dr. Todd William McCune
Nvl Shpyrd Bldg 657
Philadelphia PA 19112
Phone: 215-465-9109

Dr. William J McMahon
74 Stonehenge Dr
Washington PA 15301
Phone: 412-225-9450

Dr. Gregory C Mieckowski
220 Primrose Drive
Sarver PA 16055
Phone: 412-828-0456

Dr. Wallace T Miller
3400 Spruce St
Philadelphia PA 19104
Phone: 215-662-3035

Dr. David M Murphy
506 Anthwyn Rd
Merion PA 19066
Phone: 304-293-4095

Dr. Ingrid E Naugle
26 Newgate Rd
Pittsburgh PA 15202
Phone: 412-761-7680

Dr. Gregory Randolph Owens
916 Wade W
Oakmont PA 15139
Phone: 412-624-1929

Dr. William E Palmer
320 Main St
Johnstown PA 15901
Phone: 814-533-0587

Dr. Joseph R Patterson
1086 Franklin St
Johnstown PA 15905
Phone: 814-536-7226

Dr. Ernest J Pick
1106 Beech Rd
Rosemont PA 19010
Phone: 215-527-0867

Dr. Robert G Pickerill
524 Grove Avenue
Johnstown PA 15902
Phone: 814-535-6925

LIST OF APPROVED B-READERS FEDERAL COAL MINE HEALTH AND SAFETY ACT OF 1969

STATE-PA

Dr. Ramesh S Pradhan
1310 University Drive
Yardley PA 19067
Phone: 215-493-1314

Dr. David Samuel Prince
441 Levering Mill Rd
Bala Cynwyd PA 19004
Phone: 215-667-2596

Dr. Paul Dennis Radecki
724 Winding Rd
Jenkintown PA 19046
Phone: 215-884-9328

Dr. Usho S Rishi
66 Holland Road
Pittsburgh PA 15235
Phone: 412-241-2192

Dr. William F Rosner
290 Ames Circle
Huntingdon Vly PA 19006
Phone: 215-947-4777

Dr. John H Scott
147 Woodshire Dr
Pittsburgh PA 15215
Phone: 412-782-5455

Dr. Paul Robert Sherban
212 Old Trinity Place
Lancaster Pa 17602
Phone: 717-393-1064

Dr. John G Shively
26 Priscilla Lane
Carnegie PA 15106
Phone: 412-359-3038

Dr. Frank John Simone
Indiana Hosp Dept of Rad
Indiana PA 15701
Phone: 412-357-7125

Dr. Henry K Smith
145 Northgate Dr
Camphill PA 17011
Phone: 717-657-7200

Dr. John Joseph Solic
3901 South Atherton St
State College PA 16801
Phone: 814-466-7911

Dr. Alan Stankiewicz
623 Lang Ave
Patton PA 16668
Phone: 814-764-8508

Dr. Robert M Steiner
129 Gypsy Lane
Wynnewood PA 19096
Phone: 215-649-0569

Dr. James Lang Sundheim
700 Quincy Ave
Scranton PA 18500
Phone: 717-969-4030

Dr. Theodore A Tristan
353 N 28th St
Camp Hill PA 17011
Phone: 717-761-2958

Dr. Stephen Wartella Jr
25 James St
Kingston PA 18704
Phone: 717-288-3744

LIST OF APPROVED B-READERS FEDERAL COAL MINE HEALTH AND SAFETY ACT OF 1969

STATE-PA

Dr. Patrick W Wolfe
713 Viewmont Ave
Johnstown PA 15905
Phone: 814-255-1069

Dr. Ho Joon Yoo
1510 Wintergreen Ln
Fairview PA 16415
Phone: 814-474-5100

Dr. Frank A Yarussi
110 Fort Cauch Rd
Pittsburgh PA 15241
Phone: 412-831-8550

STATE-RI

Dr. William Michael Colaiac
127 Power St
Providence RI 02906
Phone: 401-456-2206

Dr. David Grant Kern
18 Wilcox Ave
Pawtucket RI 02860
Phone: 401-723-6616

STATE-SC

Dr. Charles Frederick Greer
945 White Point Court
Charleston SC 29412
Phone: 803-795-4709

Dr. Daniel Ravenel
0 Gibbes St
Charleston SC 29401
Phone: 803-577-6666

Dr. Jennings Gillen Pressly
1210 W Faris Rd
Greenville SC 29605
Phone: 803-232-9351

Dr. Stephen Irwin Schabel
669 Shortwood Street
Charleston SC 29412
Phone: 803-795-7969

STATE-SD

Dr. Glenn S Roush
34 Jackson St
Deadwood SD 57732
Phone: 605-578-2727

LIST OF APPROVED B-READERS FEDERAL COAL MINE HEALTH AND SAFETY ACT OF 1969

STATE-TN

Dr. Herbert Blumen
1000 So Yates Rd
Memphis TN 38119
Phone: 901-683-7088

Dr. John Paul Limbacher II
935 E 6th Street
Cookeville TN 38501
Phone: 615-528-5609

Dr. Henry P Pendergrass
6207 Hillsboro Rd
Nashville TN 37215
Phone: 615-322-3450

Dr. William Kirk Swann
406 Blount Prof Building
Knoxville TN 37920
Phone: 615-524-5403

Dr. Muram Helen T Winer
2043 Hickory Crest
Memphis TN 38119
Phone: 901-755-5490

Dr. Thomas R Duncan
2405 Hidden Lake
Columbia TN 38401
Phone: 615-381-4267

Dr. Sanford Hewitt Morrow III
1423 E Brow Rd
Signal Mountain TN 37377
Phone: 615-778-7375

Dr. Jeffery Dale Sargent
28 Midway
Briston TN 37620
Phone: 615-968-2311

Dr. Larry Haynes Westerfiel
Holston Valley Comm Hosp
Kingsport TN 37662
Phone: 615-245-2251

STATE-TX

Dr. Jerome Harrison Arndt
206 Steeplechase Dr
Irving TX 75062
Phone: 214-717-4427

Dr. William W Bryant
2122 Treemont Ln
Orange TX 77630
Phone: 883-405-6409

Dr. Harold D Cain
801 West 34 Street
Austin TX 78705
Phone: 512-459-1111

Dr. Bernard L Bradley
2202 Southgate
Houston TX 77030
Phone: 713-941-0088

Dr. Samuel H Cade
3600 Gaston Ave
Dallas TX 75246
Phone: 214-820-3219

Dr. Mark Colin Clark
200 Ashworth
Austin TX 78746
Phone: 512-459-1111

LIST OF APPROVED B-READERS FEDERAL COAL MINE HEALTH AND SAFETY ACT OF 1969

STATE-TX

Dr. Patrick M Conley
6624 Fannin Street
Houston TX 77030
Phone: 713-797-1551

Dr. Andrew M Dale
1417 S Wall
Tyler TX 75701
Phone: (Not available.)

Dr. George Luis Delclos
6565 Fannin M S F 907
Houston TX 77030
Phone: 713-790-2076

Dr. Luis Alonso Desantos
7826 Candle Lane
Houston TX 77071
Phone: 713-774-2993

Dr. Thomas Wayne Ertzner
8725 Mountain Top
San Antonio TX 78255
Phone: 512-670-5289

Dr. Martha E Glenn
7627 Fair Oaks Parkway
Boerne TX 78006
Phone: 512-755-8805

Dr. Michael S Green
Rt 4 Box 1025
Tyler TX 75703
Phone: 214-839-3521

Dr. John Michael Holbert
7575 Cambridge #502
Houston TX 77054
Phone: 713-799-1058

Dr. Brenda Lee Lefkoff Holb
7575 Cambridge St #502
Houston TX 77054
Phone: 713-799-1058

Dr. Linda Oconnell Judge
3517 Pinehurst Cr
Dallas TX 75234
Phone: 214-620-9767

Dr. Ann Ratliff Mootz
9519 Robin Meadow Drive
Dallas TX 75243
Phone: 214-688-3711

Dr. Mary Ann Mullican
2518 Del Monte Dr
Houston TX 77019
Phone: 713-523-8670

Dr. Dale B Riepe
1201 Garden Dr
Mt Pleasant TX 75455
Phone: 214-572-9247

Dr. Hugh C Sheffield Jr
1419 31st Street
Nederland TX 77627
Phone: 409-722-4984

Dr. James Robert Shepherd
Rt 5 Box 549
Lindale TX 75771
Phone: 214-877-3451

Dr. Robert Keith Wilson
6535 Fannin Street
Houston TX 77030
Phone: 713-790-2076

LIST OF APPROVED B-READERS FEDERAL COAL MINE HEALTH AND SAFETY ACT OF 1969

STATE-UT

Dr. Jack J Davis
333 South 900 East St
Salt Lake City UT 84102
Phone: 801-535-8249

Dr. Andrew Jonathan Ghio
714 E Nibley View Court
Salt Lake City UT 84106
Phone: 304-599-9359

Dr. William James Morrison
Lds Hospital 325 8th Ave
Salt Lake City UT 84143
Phone: 801-321-1791

Dr. Attilio David Renzetti Jr
1801 London Plane Rd
Salt Lake City UT 84124
Phone: 801-278-0823

Dr. William L Ellingson
1175 Bloomington Drive S
St George UT 84770
Phone: 702-877-1592

Dr. Howard Mann
4075 E Powers Circle
Salt Lake City UT 84124
Phone: 801-277-8621

Dr. Rodney C Peterson
1350 So 1000 E
Mapleton UT 84663
Phone: 801-489-8534

STATE-VA

Dr. James Porter Baker
213 61st Street
Virginia Beach VA 23451
Phone: 804-422-5742

Dr. Dorothy R Brodie
1547 Bruton Court
Mclean VA 22101
Phone: 703-356-7423

Dr. Alfred Philip Coccaro
7742 Carreigh Parkway
Springfield VA 22152
Phone: 703-569-9026

Dr. James Karnes Davis
1409 Riversedge Rd
Newport News VA 23606
Phone: 804-595-7980

Dr. Brent D Brandon
Rt 1 Box 262
Natural Bridge VA 24578
Phone: 703-291-2731

Dr. James R Castle
1111 S Jefferson St
Roanoke VA 24016
Phone: 703-342-6701

Dr. Charles Hunter Cockrell
510 S Sycamore St #H
Petersburg VA 23803
Phone: 804-861-3917

Dr. Kathleen Ann Deponte
P O Box 408
Norton VA 24273
Phone: 703-679-1151

LIST OF APPROVED B-READERS FEDERAL COAL MINE HEALTH AND SAFETY ACT OF 1969

STATE-VA

Dr. E H Derring Jr
3905 Old Shell Rd
VA Beach VA 23452
Phone: 804-625-5800

Dr. C J Donlan Jr
250 W Brambleton Ave #201
Norfolk VA 23510
Phone: 804-625-5800

Dr. William M Fogel
101 Gunby Dr
Richmond VA 23229
Phone: 804-285-9729

Dr. David R Foreman
533 W Riverview Dr
Suffolk VA 23434
Phone: 804-539-5180

Dr. Allen A Frey
1318 Swift Creek Lane
Manakin Sabot VA 23101
Phone: 804-784-3084

Dr. Glenn Matthew Giessel
7103 C Jahnke Rd
Richmond VA 23225
Phone: 804-320-4243

Dr. John Bruce Hauser
2037 Crystal Spring
Roanoke VA 24014
Phone: 703-981-7122

Dr. Daniel Anthony Henry
MCV Box 615
Richmond VA 23298
Phone: 804-786-6831

Dr. Kirk Edward Hippensteel
1111 S Jefferson St
Roanoke VA 24016
Phone: 703-342-6701

Dr. Howard Jolles
13730 Elmstead Rd
Midlothian VA 23113
Phone: 804-794-3572

Dr. Robert M. Kesler
7606 Maory Arch
Norfolk VA 23505
Phone: 804-423-4409

Dr. Shiv Navani
15 Oakwood Circle
Big Stone Gap VA 24219
Phone: 703-523-3668

Dr. Subramaniam K Parantham
1731 Holton Ave
Big Stone Gap VA 24219
Phone: 703-523-4920

Dr. Bharat Raojibhai Patel
Rt 2 Box 546
Radford VA 24141
Phone: 703-731-2720

Dr. Anthony Vincent Proto
3023 River Hills Lane
Midlothian VA 23113
Phone: 804-379-1353

Dr. Cullen B Rivers
11 Roslyn Hills Dr
Richmond VA 23229
Phone: 804-288-5965

LIST OF APPROVED B-READERS FEDERAL COAL MINE HEALTH AND SAFETY ACT OF 1969

STATE-VA

Dr. Emory H Robinette
Rt 7 Foxfile Estates
Abingdon VA 24210
Phone: 703-628-1106

Dr. Paul J Rubis
4110 Nine Mile
Richmond VA 23223
Phone: 804-222-1716

Dr. George Andrew Solack
8308 Weller Ave
Mclean VA 22102
Phone: 703-893-9386

Dr. Frederick P Stitik
Depaul Hosp 150 Kingsley
Norfolk VA 23505
Phone: 804-955-5394

Dr. Cecile Stephanie Rose
Box 267 Med Coll of VA
Richmond VA 23298
Phone: 804-786-9357

Dr. James Oneil Shaw
534 Kerry Lake Dr
Newport Naus VA 23602
Phone: 804-599-2732

Dr. Bruce Neal Stewart
1111 S Jefferson St
Roanoke VA 24016
Phone: 703-342-6701

Dr. Joseph Marion Straughan
Box 856
Wise VA 24293
Phone: 703-328-6625

STATE-VT

Dr. William G B Graham
Lake Road
Charlotte VT 05445
Phone: 802-425-3124

STATE-WA

Dr. Richard C Auerbach
3664 NW Lakeness Rd
Poulsbo WA 98370
Phone: 206-697-1604

Dr. Jeffrey Michael Cary
4600 92nd Ave SE
Mercer Island WA 98040
Phone: 206-232-3689

Dr. Timothy Edward Bruya
S 3249 High Drive
Spokane WA 99203
Phone: 509-455-8466

Dr. David Parker Christie
601 Belmont E #A 3
Seattle WA 98102
Phone: 206-322-0898

LIST OF APPROVED B-READERS FEDERAL COAL MINE HEALTH AND SAFETY ACT OF 1969

STATE-WA

Dr. J David Godwin
8501 SE 80th St
Mercer Island WA 98040
Phone: 206-232-5702

Dr. Beverly Emiko Hashimoto
1100 Ninth Ave
Seattle WA 98111
Phone: 206-223-6851

Dr. Marie Emily Lee
2055 Interlaken Pe
Seattle WA 98112
Phone: 206-223-6951

Dr. Jonathan H Ostrow
3500 E Huron St
Seattle WA 98100
Phone: 206-325-8841

Dr. Robert H Rosenberg
8670 NE 17th
Bellevue WA 98004
Phone: 206-454-6954

Dr. Dorsett David Smith
4310 Colby Ave
Everett WA 98203
Phone: 206-259-5496

Dr. Julie Emiko Takasugi
1660 S Columbian Way
Seattle WA 98108
Phone: (Not available.)

Dr. Alan Coombs Whitehouse
104 W Fifth
Spokane WA 99204
Phone: 509-458-3960

STATE-WI

Dr. Philip Richard Albert
708 11th Street
Wausau WI 54401
Phone: 715-842-4058

Dr. Henry A Anderson
200 Lakewood Blvd
Madison WI 53704
Phone: 608-266-1253

Dr. Joseph Michael Collins
303 W Coventry Ct #119
Glendale WI 53217
Phone: 414-352-5679

Dr. Lawrence R Goodman
8700 W Wisconsin Ave
Milwaukee WI 53226
Phone: 414-351-6051

Dr. Mack Alan Karnes
5900 S Lake
Cudahy WI 53110
Phone: 414-769-4062

Dr. Larry A Lindesmith
W 4965 Woodhaven Drive
La Crosse WI 54601
Phone: 606-788-2274

Dr. William T Luckey
1545 W Spruce Ct
River Hills WI 53217
Phone: 414-351-4034

Dr. Uri Vaisman
1069 E Bay Point Rd
Bayside WI 53217
Phone: 414-352-3215

LIST OF APPROVED B-READERS FEDERAL COAL MINE HEALTH AND SAFETY ACT OF 1969

STATE-WV

Dr. Fonad H Abdalla
Rt 1 Box 330 C
Elkins WV 26241
Phone: 304-636-1925

Dr. Roger A Abrahams
360 B Bakers Ridge Rd
Morgantown WV 26505
Phone: 304-599-2504

Dr. David Abramowitz
1212 Williamsburg Way
Charleston WV 25314
Phone: 304-346-7747

Dr. Edward Doy Aycoth
No 9 Princeton Med Art Cl
Princeton WV 24740
Phone: 403-487-1474

Dr. Maurice A Bassali
P O Box 2062
Beckley WV 25802
Phone: 304-255-3306

Dr. John Anthony Bellotte
136 Carriage Court
Bridgeport WV 26330
Phone: 304-842-5935

Dr. Carl Brooks Binns
401 Division St
So Charleston WV 25309
Phone: 304-766-7141

Dr. Enrico John Cappiello
Sr Box 216A
Spanishburg WV 25922
Phone: 304-425-6314

Dr. W Alva Deardorff
4620 Maccorkle Ave S W
S Charleston WV 25309
Phone: 304-343-4625

Dr. Rafael K Deramos
Rt 1 Box 183 B
Bluefield WV 24701
Phone: 304-425-6581

Dr. Rocco Joseph Digioacchi
P O Box 111
Richwood WV 26261
Phone: 304-846-2972

Dr. Carl Ronald Duncan
6 Wild Acre Rd
Charleston WV 25314
Phone: 304-344-5951

Dr. Paul Francke
1414 Connell Rd
Charleston WV 25314
Phone: 304-346-0270

Dr. Dominic J Gaziano
3100 Maccorkle Ave #402
Charleston WV 25304
Phone: 304-346-1811

Dr. Ravindra Kumar Gogineni
1608 Kirklee Road
Charleston WV 25314
Phone: 304-766-7141

Dr. Ali A Goodardi
103 Partridge Lane
Beckley WV 25801
Phone: 304-252-8039

LIST OF APPROVED B-READERS FEDERAL COAL MINE HEALTH AND SAFETY ACT OF 1969

STATE-WV

Dr. Ray A Harron
P O Box 400
Bridgeport WV 26330
Phone: 304-622-3900

Dr. Thomas Knight Hodous
765 Northwest Dr
Morgantown WV 26505
Phone: 304-599-8859

Dr. Michael Thomas Hogan
1378 Braewick Drive
Morgantown WV 26505
Phone: 304-599-9374

Dr. Janis Leigh Hurst
609 Farms Dr
Fairmont WV 26554
Phone: 304-366-5906

Dr. John W Kennard
5 Orchard Rd
Wheeling WV 26003
Phone: 304-232-1595

Dr. V S Kullman
6 Lakeview Dr
Wheeling WV 26003
Phone: 304-277-5591

Dr. N Leroy Lapp
1285 Fairfield St
Morgantown WV 26505
Phone: 304-599-2361

Dr. Johnsey Lee Leef Jr
1440 Alexandria Place
Charleston WV 25314
Phone: 304-348-6044

Dr. Kerry W McCluney
St Lukes Hosp
Bluefield Hosp WV 24701
Phone: 304-325-3733

Dr. I Ranavaya Mohammed
123 Rice Street
Beckley WV 25802
Phone: 304-255-2500

Dr. Edwin James Morgan
Rt 7 Box 518
Morgantown WV 26505
Phone: 304-292-4160

Dr. Alan Richard Nichols
301 Med Arts Bldg
Charleston WV 25301
Phone: 304-343-4625

Dr. Mahendra M Patel
6 Hunter Point Rd
Charleston WV 25314
Phone: 304-345-0403

Dr. Joseph J Renn III
118 Diamond Ct
Morgantown WV 26505
Phone: 304-599-4497

Dr. James T Smith
1420 Connell Rd
Charleston WV 25314
Phone: 304-342-4984

Dr. Lois M Speiden
109 Eastview Lane
Beckley WV 25801
Phone: 304-252-9442

LIST OF APPROVED B-READERS FEDERAL COAL MINE HEALTH AND SAFETY ACT OF 1969

STATE-WV

Dr. Gregory R Wagner
2630 Putnam Ave
Hurricane WV 25526
Phone: 304-526-0630

Dr. James Michael Wills
211 Fairview Ave
Beckley WV 25801
Phone: 304-252-5599

Dr. Martin Stuart Wershba
416 Division St
So Charleston WV 25301
Phone: 304-766-7141

Dr. George Luis Leon Zaldiv
16 Norwood Road
Charleston WV 25314
Phone: 304-346-1811

OTHER LOCATIONS

Dr. Edurdo Algranti
Al Lorena 320 Ap 22
01424 Sao Paulo Brazil
Phone: 011-885-4907

Dr. William Douglas Bennett
59 Rose Park Drive
Toronto Canada
Phone: 416-489-5380

Dr. Jean Louis Boucher
3 Place Baribeau
Levis Canada
Phone: 418-833-2828

Dr. Patrick Brochard
40 Avenue De Verdun
Creteil France

Dr. David Bruce Coultas
Address Unknown
Phone: 505-292-0752

Dr. Marc J Desmeules
2725 Ch Ste Foy
Quebec City Canada
Phone: 418-656-4747

Dr. Gregory Neil Bender
Address Unknown
Phone: 808-637-9097

Dr. Arne Borgersen
Pilveien 2
0855 Oslo 8 Norway
Phone: 000-323-3007

Dr. Michel Bovo
1207 Bld Mt Royal
Outremont
Phone: 516-272-3284

Dr. Neil Cass Colman
47 Arlington
Westmount Canada
Phone: 514-934-0502

Dr. Curtis E Cummings
Address Unknown
Phone: 609-921-0745

Dr. Donald Arthur Enarson
Dept of Med Pulmonary Med
WC Mackenziehsc
Phone: 604-875-4122

LIST OF APPROVED B-READERS FEDERAL COAL MINE HEALTH AND SAFETY ACT OF 1969

OTHER LOCATIONS

Dr. E Wayne Gilley
Address Unknown

Dr. Kurt Georg Hering
Rosenowstr 7
4600 Dort Mund Germany
Phone: 023-141-7002

Dr. William Keith C Morgan
Windmere Rd Univ Hospital
London Ontario Canada
Phone: 519-663-3606

Dr. John Doty Newell
Address Unknown
Phone: 602-299-2730

Dr. Mettupalayam M Rajendra
Address Unknown
Phone: 304-242-8519

Dr. Gordon H Twedt
Address Unknown
Phone: 817-236-7988

Dr. Sverre Vedal
2775 Heather St
Vancouver, Canada
Phone: 604-875-4122

Dr. Hans Woitowitz
Aulweg 129
Giessen

Dr. Anders Johan Zitting
Inst of Occupational Hlth
Helsinki Finland
Phone: 358-042-4233

Dr. Andrew W Goodwin
Address Unknown

Dr. Michel Lafortune
10890 Waverly
Montreal Canada
Phone: 514-332-1112

Dr. Nestor Luiz Muller
1537 West 58th Ave
Vancouver Canada
Phone: 604-261-5428

Dr. Gaston L Ostiguy
122 Jasper Ville Mont Roy
Mon Quebec Canada
Phone: 514-731-0895

Dr. Jacques Sansoucy
265 Dufferin
Valleyfield Canada
Phone: 514-373-5195

Dr. Claude Arthur Vallee
227 Kindersley Montreal
Quebec Canada
Phone: 514-731-4734

Dr. Theresa Marie Vogel
Address Unknown
Phone: 301-484-5359

Dr. Dansereau Yves
821 Gaboury St S
St Bruno Canada
Phone: 514-653-7310

ALPHABETICAL LISTING OF B-READERS

Adapted from the State-by-State List of NIOSH Certified Roentgenographic Interpreting Physicians (1989)

Dr. Fonad H Abdalla
RT 1 Box 330 C
Elkins WV 26241
Phone: 304-636-1925

Dr. Roger A. Abrahams
360 B Bakers Ridge Rd
Morgantown WV 26505
Phone: 304-599-2504

Dr. David Abramowitz
1212 Williamsburg Way
Charleston WV 25314
Phone: 304-346-7747

Dr. Wynn Wygal Adam
321 Shady Crest Dr
Kettering OH 45429
Phone: 513-299-2998

Dr. Jeffrey H Agee
536 Shoreline Dr
Decator IL 62521
Phone: 217-423-3385

Dr. Morteza Seyed Ahmadian
801 Toll House Ave
Frederick MD 21701
Phone: 301-663-5185

Dr. Edurdo Algranti
Al Lorena 320 AP 22
01424 Sao Paulo Brazil
Phone: 011-885-4907

Dr. Philip Richard Albert
708 11th Street
Wausau WI 54401
Phone: 715-842-4058

Dr. Timothy E Allen
823 Mulvane St
Topeka KS 66606
Phone: 913-334-4110

Dr. William R Allen
9201 Parallel Pkwy
Kansas City KS 66112
Phone: 913-334-4110
or 913-651-7085

Dr. Stanley L Altschuler
8040 Roosevelt Blvd
Philadelphia PA 19152
Phone: 215-331-3700

Dr. Judith Korek Amorosa
60 Prospect St
Somersville NJ 08876
Phone: 201-722-9695

Dr. Claus Ludwig Anderson
4815 Liberty Ave
Pittsburgh PA 15224
Phone: 412-687-5573

Dr. Henry A Anderson
200 Lakewood Blvd
Madison WI 53704
Phone: 608-266-1253

Dr. Robert Patterson Andrew
297 Center St
Bamgor ME 04401
Phone: 207-234-2500

Dr. Jerome Harrison Arndt
206 Steeplechase Dr
Irving TX 75062
Phone: 214-717-4427

Dr. Judith Marsha Aronchick
407 S 23 St
Philadelphia PA 19146
Phone: 215-735-2025

Dr. Elisha Hornblower Atkin
48 Banks St
Somerville MA 02144
Phone: 617-625-1267

Dr. Donald Auerbach
12 Wicklow Ct
Cherry Hill NJ 08003
Phone: 609-424-0327

Dr. Richard D Auerbach
3664 NW Lakeness Rd
Poulsbo WA 98370
Phone: 206-697-1604

Dr. Gregory Lee Augenbaugh
200 2nd St SW
Rochester MN 55905
Phone: 507-284-2271

Dr. John McCulloch Austin
622 West 168 Street
New York NY 10032
Phone: 212-694-2981

Dr. Edward Doy Aycoth
No 9 Princeton Med Art Cl
Princeton WV 24740
Phone: 304-487-1474

Dr. Vallabhaneni S Babu
154 Lindenvale Drive
McMurray PA 15317
Phone: 412-941-4963

Dr. Ronald A Bailey
2398 Brian Dr
Beachwood OH 44122
Phone: 216-464-2398

Dr. Glen Ray Baker
126 Scenic View Heights
Corbin KY 40701
Phone: 606-528-4644

Dr. James Porter Baker
213 61st Street
Virginia Beach VA 23451
Phone: 804-422-5742

Dr. Oliver Charles Baker
924 So 18th St
Birmingham AL 35256
Phone: 205-933-8936

Dr. James W Ballard
3932 Knollwood Drive
Birmingham AL 35243
Phone: 205-967-1689

Dr. Martin Lawrence Barman
145 Valeria
Fresno CA 93701
Phone: 209-268-8722

Dr. Leroy T Barnes
3696 Aureola Blvd
Los Angeles CA 90008
Phone: 213-295-2097

Dr. Peter J Barrett
10 Martins Lane
Hingham MA 02043
Phone: 617-749-5876

Dr. Maurice A Bassali
PO Box 2062
Beckley WV 25802
Phone: 304-255-3306

Dr. Poonam Batra
912 Teakwood Rd
Los Angeles CA 90049
Phone: 213-472-6910

Dr. Richard Marcus Bauer
104 Oakmont Road
Highland Park IL 60035
Phone: 312-432-3828

Dr. Joseph Marc Becker
548 Winding Way
Merion Station PA 19066
Phone: 215-667-2180

Dr. Joseph Michael Behun
419 Maple Lane Edgeworth
Sewickley PA 15143
Phone: 412-741-8094

Dr. John Anthony Bellotte
136 Carriage Court
Bridgeport WV 26330
Phone: 304-842-5935

Dr. Gregory Neil Bender
Address Unknown
Phone: 808-637-9097

Dr. William Douglas Bennett
59 Rose Park Drive
Toronto, Ont, Canada
Phone: 416-489-5380

Dr. Jeffrey Scott Benseler
500 Queensgate Rd
Springboro OH 45066
Phone: 513-748-2588

Dr. Roger Alan Berg
21 Watchung Road
Short Hills NJ 07078
Phone: 201-467-1180

Dr. Gordon Herman Beute
6411 Wardell Ct
W Bloomfield MI 48033
Phone: 313-876-1331

Dr. Dharmashi Vishanji Bhat
RT 3 Box 11A
Carterville IL 62918
Phone: 618-985-4000

Dr. Donald W Bidwell
28 Fall St
Seneca Falls NY 13148
Phone: 315-568-8957

Dr. Carl Brooks Binns
401 Division St
So Charleston WV 25309
Phone: 304-766-7141

Dr. Frederick Ross Birkhill
31 Shady Hollow Dr
Dearborn MI 48124
Phone: 313-278-9224

Dr. Jeffrey S Bisker
1400 Willow Ave
Louisville KY 40204
Phone: 502-451-3426

Dr. John Edward Bjorgen
5714 Woodstock Ave
Golden Valley MN 55422
Phone: 612-544-9399

Dr. Gerald A Black
5132 Muirfield Drive
Fayetteville NY 13066
Phone: 315-637-5471

Dr. Brian Block
167 Brandywine Dr
Williamsville NY 14221
Phone: 716-688-5725

Dr. Herbert Blumen
1000 So Yates Rd
Memphis TN 38119
Phone: 901-683-7088

Dr. Brian Arthur Boehlecke
625 Tinkerbell Road
Chapel Hill NC 27514
Phone: 919-942-7909

Dr. Arne Borgersen
Pilveien 2
0855 Oslo 8 Norway
Phone: 323-3007

Dr. Jean Louis Boucher
3 Place Baribeau
Levis Quebec Canada
Phone: 418-833-2828

Dr. Ray Joseph Bouzigard
2000 Greenbriar Rd
Kinston NC 28501
Phone: 919-527-7077

Dr. Michel Bovo
1207 Bld Mt Royal
Outremont New York
Phone: 516-272-3284

Dr. Bernard L Bradley
2202 Southgate
Houston TX 77030
Phone: 713-941-0088

Dr. Michael B Brady
273 Park Terrace
Mobile AL 36604
Phone: 205-478-3741

Dr. Joseph Francis Branda
9811 Mallard Dr
Laurel MD 20708
Phone: 301-776-4777

Dr. Brent D Brandon
Rt 1 Box 262
Natural Bridge VA 24578
Phone: 703-291-2731

Dr. Ben V Branscomb
1717 Sixth Ave South
Birmingham AL 35243
Phone: 205-934-4125

Dr. William Thomas Braun III
3243 E Murdock
Wichita KS 67208
Phone: 316-685-2711

Dr. Eddy Armin Bresnitz
166 N Latchs Lane
Bala Cynwyd PA 19004
Phone: 215-664-6208

Dr. R Barton Bridges
301 W Lincoln
Belleville IL 62220
Phone: 618-235-0955

Dr. Patrick Brochard
40 Avenue De Verdun
Creteil France

Dr. Dorothy R Brodie
1547 Bruton Court
McLean VA 22101
Phone: 703-356-7423

Dr. Arthur Raymond Brooker
13550 N 31st Suite 140
Tampa FL 33613
Phone: 813-971-2056

Dr. Stuart M Brooks
5030 Paloma Dr
Tampa FL 33624
Phone: 813-960-1669

Dr. Bruce Charles Broudy
1221 South Broadway
Lexington KY 40504
Phone: 606-255-6841

Dr. Larry R Brown
Mayo Clinic East 2
Rochester MN 55901
Phone: 507-285-0850

Dr. Robert Neal Brown
618 S Ryan
Lake Charles LA 70601
Phone: 318-436-7571

Dr. Timothy Edward Bruya
S 3249 High Drive
Spokane WA 99203
Phone: 509-455-8466

Dr. William W Bryant
2122 Treemont Ln
Orange TX 77630
Phone: 883-405-6409

Dr. David Richard Buck
110 Irving St
Washington DC 20010
Phone: 202-541-6456

Dr. Samuel H Cade
3600 Gaston Ave
Dallas TX 75246
Phone: 214-820-3219

Dr. Harold D Cain
801 West 34 Street
Austin TX 78705
Phone: 512-459-1111

Dr. Joseph D Calhoun
31 Shannon Dr
Little Rock AR 72207
Phone: 501-663-3944

Dr. James Louis Caplan
1125 S Beverly Dr #400
Los Angeles CA 90035
Phone: 213-477-6779

Dr. Enrico John Cappiello
Sr Box 216A
Spanishburg WV 25922
Phone: 304-425-6314

Dr. Jeffrey Michael Cary
4600 92nd Ave SE
Mercer Island WA 98040
Phone: 206-232-3689

Dr. Kenneth Robert Casey
2799 West Grand Blvd
Detroit MI 48202
Phone: 801-363-3343

Dr. Robert John Cassling
16942 Bollinger Dr
Pac Palisades CA 90272
Phone: 213-459-8223

Dr. James R Castle
1111 S Jefferson St
Roanoke VA 24016
Phone: 703-342-6701

Dr. Jagdish Chazra
28751 Jaeger Dr
Laguna Niguel CA 92677
Phone: 714-831-9430

Dr. William I Christensen
PO Box 6231
Albuquerque NM 87197
Phone: 505-262-7600

Dr. David Parker Christie
601 Belmont E #A 3
Seattle WA 98102
Phone: 206-322-0898

Dr. Robert H Choplin
300 S Hawthorne Rd
Winston Salem NC 27103
Phone: 919-748-4316

Dr. Thomas William Church
1554 Pro Dr
Lima OH 45805
Phone: 419-999-2940

Dr. John Louis Cieply
1893 Kihi St
Honolulu HI 96821
Phone: 808-373-9248

Dr. Mark Colin Clark
200 Ashworth
Austin TX 78746
Phone: 512-459-1111

Dr. Robert Alan Clark
234 Goodman St
Cincinnati OH 45267
Phone: 513-872-7226

Dr. Alfred Philip Coccaro
7742 Carrieigh Parkway
Springfield VA 22152
Phone: 703-569-9026

Dr. Charles Hunter Cockrell
510 S Sycamore St #H
Petersburg VA 23803
Phone: 804-861-3917

Dr. Alan Marshall Cohen
2935 Fontenay
Shaker Heights OH 44120
Phone: 216-921-2552

Dr. William Michael Colaiac
127 Power St
Providence RI 02906
Phone: 401-456-2206

Dr. William S Cole
821 Sunnybrook Lane
Melbourne FL 32935
Phone: 305-254-4908

Dr. Joseph Michael Collins
303 W Coventry Ct #119
Glendale WI 53217
Phone: 414-352-5679

Dr. Neil Cass Colman
47 Arlington
Westmount Canada
Phone: 514-934-0502

Dr. Patrick M Conley
6624 Fannin Street
Houston TX 77030
Phone: 713-797-1551

Dr. Anthony Michael Cook
1544 S Mississippi R Blvd
St Paul MN 55116
Phone: 612-690-3105

Dr. Anthony Michael Costrin
#18 Chatuachee Crossing
Savannah GA 31406
Phone: 912-598-0685

Dr. David Bruce Coultas
Address Unknown
New Mexico
Phone: 505-292-0752

Dr. Richard Henry Crain
307 Meadow Lane Edgeworth
Sewickley PA 15143
Phone: 412-741-7888

Dr. Jeffrey Robert Crass
3395 Scranton Road
Cleveland OH 44109
Phone: 216-459-3484

Dr. David W Cugell
1419 Judson Ave
Evanston IL 60201
Phone: 312-328-1828

Dr. Mark Richard Cullen
333 Cedar Street
New Haven CT 06510
Phone: 203-436-2846

Dr. Curtis E Cummings
Address Unknown
New Jersey
Phone: 609-921-0745

Dr. Raymond Thomas Cummins
160 Westgate Drive
San Francisco CA 94127
Phone: 415-666-7811

Dr. Susan Linda Curry
615 E Princeton St
Orlando FL 32803
Phone: 305-894-7185

Dr. L Evan Custer
Alta Bates Hospital
Berkeley CA 94705
Phone: 415-540-1566

Dr. Joseph Vincent Cusumano
6319 Alexander Dr
St Louis MO 63105
Phone: 314-726-5860

Dr. Michael Terrence Czuba
1150 Seventh St
Waynesburg PA 15370
Phone: 412-627-5358

Dr. Abdulkader Dahhan
2615 Village Center
Harlan KY 40831
Phone: 606-573-1085

Dr. Andrew M Dale
1417 S Wall
Tyler TX 75701
Phone: (Not available)

Dr. Nilima Dash
131 Wescott Drive
Pittsburgh PA 15237
Phone: 412-367-4307

Dr. Susan M Daum
130 Kinderkanack Rd
River Edge NJ 07661
Phone: 201-487-7337

Dr. M Epstein David
1514 Knox Rd
Wynnewood PA 19096
Phone: 215-896-7312

Dr. Jack J Davis
333 South 900 East St
Salt Lake City UT 84102
Phone: 801-535-8249

Dr. James Karnes Davis
1409 Riversedge Rd
Newport News VA 23606
Phone: 804-595-7980

Dr. W Alva Deardorff
4620 MacCorkle Ave SW
S Charleston WV 25309
Phone: 304-343-4625

Dr. Jack S Deitch
5 The Dell
Woodbury NY 11797
Phone: 516-367-4902

Dr. George Luis Delclos
6565 Fannin M S F 907
Houston TX 77030
Phone: 713-790-2076

Dr. John Carroll Democker
564 Ridge Rd E
Rochester NY 14621
Phone: 716-544-1750

Dr. Kathleen Ann Deponte
PO Box 408
Norton VA 24273
Phone: 703-679-1151

Dr. Rafael K Deramos
Rt 1 Box 183 B
Bluefield WV 24701
Phone: 304-425-6581

Dr. E H Derring Jr
3905 Old Shell Rd
Virginia Beach VA 23452
Phone: 804-625-5800

Dr. Luis Alonso Desantos
7826 Candle Lane
Houston TX 77071
Phone: 713-774-2993

Dr. Marc J Desmeules
2725 Ch Ste Foy
Quebec City Canada
Phone: 418-656-4747

Dr. Edgar Lee Dessen
20 North Laurel Street
Hazelton PA 18201
Phone: 717-455-3608

Dr. Marco John Dibiase
8381 N Hillcrest Dr
Berrien Springs MI 49103
Phone: 616-473-3195

Dr. Rocco Joseph Digioacchi
PO Box 111
Richwood WV 26261
Phone: 304-846-2972

Dr. Philip Anthony Dimenno
212 Natchaig Dr
Meriden CT 06450
Phone: 203-237-9653

Dr. John Francis Dineen
3417 Fleetwood Drive
Lexington KY 40502
Phone: 606-266-9615

Dr. Charles A Dobry
747 No 89th Ave
Omaha NE 68114
Phone: 402-559-6983

Dr. C J Donlan Jr
250 W Brambleton Ave #201
Norfolk VA 23510
Phone: 804-625-5800

Dr. Daniel Michael Doyle
725 North St
Pittsfield MS 01201
Phone: 413-499-4161

Dr. Edward Drasin
76 Silverwood Drive
Lafayette CA 94549
Phone: 415-420-6088

Dr. Garth Richard Drewry
6 C Columbia Drive
Tampa FL 33606
Phone: 813-253-2721

Dr. John Kevin Drumm
1010 Lone Pine Road
Bloomfield Hill MI 48013
Phone: 313-258-6803

Dr. Walter S Dunbar
2062 Imperial Drive NE
Atlanta GA 30345
Phone: 404-636-2788

Dr. Carl Ronald Duncan
6 Wild Acre Rd
Charleston WV 25314
Phone: 304-344-5951

Dr. Thomas R Duncan
2405 Hidden Lake
Columbia TN 38401
Phone: 615-381-4267

Dr. Charles E Eckman
816 NW 138th St
Edmond OK 73013
Phone: 405-751-5360

Dr. Rodney Ivan Ehrlich
412 W 110th St Apt 41
New York NY 10025
Phone: 212-241-4790

Dr. Michael S Eichenhorn
2799 W Grand Blvd
Detroit MI 48202
Phone: 313-876-2436

Dr. Orn Eliasson
9584 Woodblock Row
Columbia MD 21045
Phone: 301-992-1899

Dr. William L Ellingson
1175 Bloomington Drive S
St George UT 84770
Phone: 702-877-1592

Dr. Richard A Elmer
6500 Vernon Woods Dr NE
Atlanta GA 30328
Phone: 404-252-3430

Dr. Lawrence Leroy Emmons
7290 S Andes Ct
Aurora CO 80016
Phone: 303-680-9927

Dr. Donald Arthur Enarson
Dept of Med Pulmonary Med
WC Mackenziehsc B.C. Canada
Phone: 604-875-4122

Dr. Robert E Ensor
549 Broadwater Rd
Arnold MD 21012
Phone: 301-647-9441

Dr. Jacob Alan Epstein
161 Hillcrest Rd
Berkeley CA 94705
Phone: 415-547-0821

Dr. Paul E Epstein
126 Righters Mill Road
Gladwyne PA 19035
Phone: 215-896-5441

Dr. Thomas Wayne Ertzner
8725 Mountain Top
San Antonio TX 78255
Phone: 512-670-5289

Dr. Jonathan Lynn Evans
608 N McKean Street
Butler PA 16001
Phone: 412-282-4401

Dr. Azimi Farhad
301 Prospect Ave
Syracuse NY 43203
Phone: 315-424-5274

Dr. James P Farner
1094 Tote Road
Austinburg OH 44010
Phone: 216-466-1321

Dr. Bruce E Fee
1350 So Kings Dr
Charolotte NC 28207
Phone: 704-372-8750

Dr. Myra Lee Feffer
6227 Lindenhurst Ave
Los Angeles CA 90048
Phone: (Not available)

Dr. Mervyn Feierstein
21 Sandringham Drive
Bala Cynwyd PA 19004
Phone: 215-664-0995

Dr. David S Feigin
8256 Caminito Lacayo
La Jolla CA 92037
Phone: 619-455-6545

Dr. Ilan Allan Feingold
12900 SW 70th Ave
Miami FL 33156
Phone: 305-253-6026

Dr. John J Fennessy
5841 So Maryland Ave
Chicago IL 60637
Phone: 312-702-6162

Dr. Paul C Fiehler
109 Alleyne Dr
Pittsburgh PA 15215
Phone: (Not available)

Dr. Stanley Bruce Fiel
1208 Drayton Ln
Philadelphia PA 19151
Phone: 215-642-3905

Dr. Ethel J Finck
2436 N Common Wealth Ave
Los Angeles CA 90027
Phone: 213-226-7245

Dr. Jonathan Harold Fish
2814 Derby St
Berkeley CA 94705
Phone: 415-548-9197

Dr. Stephen Neal Fisher
1252 Malvern Street
Pittsburgh PA 15217
Phone: 412-682-3004

Dr. Karen W Fitzgerald
PO Box 427
Cynthiana KY 41031
Phone: 606-234-3092

Dr. John J Fitzpatrick
5300 Stony Creek Dr
Oaklawn IL 60453
Phone: 312-636-7081

Dr. Stephanie Flicker
7 Larsen Park Drive
Marlton NJ 08053
Phone: 609-983-9690

Dr. James Richard Flink
255 N Smith Ave #201
St Paul MN 55102
Phone: 612-224-5895

Dr. William M Fogel
101 Gunby Dr
Richmond VA 23229
Phone: 804-285-9729

Dr. David R Foreman
533 W Riverview Dr
Suffolk VA 23434
Phone: 804-539-5180

Dr. Thomas Thurman Fox
3780 Rushmore Drive
Columbus OH 43220
Phone: 614-451-4116

Dr. Paul Francke
1414 Connell Rd
Charleston WV 25314
Phone: 304-346-0270

Dr. Alfred Franzblau
Mt Sinai Hosp Box 1057
New York NY 10029
Phone: 212-241-6173

Dr. Allan Perry Freedman
51 N 39th Street
Philadelphia PA 19104
Phone: 215-662-8060

Dr. Guy G Freeman
146 Manetto Hill Road
Plainview NY 11803
Phone: 516-931-2120

Dr. Maija Guna Freimanis
5543 Wilkins Ave
Pittsburgh PA 15217
Phone: 412-521-6533

Dr. Allen A Frey
1318 Swift Creek Lane
Manakin Sabot VA 23101
Phone: 804-784-3084

Dr. Arnold C Friedman
524 Hoffman Drive
Bryn Mawr PA 19010
Phone: 215-527-8016

Dr. David Jay Frolich
4668 Savage Creek Dr
Macon GA 31210
Phone: 912-744-1238

Dr. Carl Robert Fuhrman
431 Edgewood Road
Pittsburgh PA 15221
Phone: 412-243-5354

Dr. Edward A Gaensler
80 E Concord St
Boston MA 02118
Phone: 617-247-6253

Dr. M Elon Gale
175 Brookline St
Newton MA 02167
Phone: 617-244-3344

Dr. John P Galgon
1162 Belair Dr
Allentown PA 18103
Phone: 215-432-2906

Dr. R Clifford Game
1528 N 26th St
Birmingham AL 35234
Phone: 205-226-6138

Dr. Gordon Gamsu
Box 0628 Radlgy UC Med Ct
San Francisco CA 94143
Phone: 415-476-1451

Dr. Morris Zachary Gardner
Ct Med Pv 1200 Center Ave
Pittsburgh PA 15219
Phone: 412-562-3106

Dr. Boyd Bennett Gasque Jr
1708 N Elm Street
Lumberton NC 28358
Phone: 919-739-3669

Dr. Robert Edward Gates
815 White Oak Cr
Pittsburgh PA 15228
Phone: 412-561-0224

Dr. Bob W Gayler
601 N Broadway
Baltimore MD 21205
Phone: 301-955-5525

Dr. Dominic J Gaziano
3100 MacCorkle Ave #402
Charleston WV 25304
Phone: 304-346-1811

Dr. Warren Bruce Gefter
243 Wiltshire Road
Philadelphia PA 19151
Phone: 215-649-4449

Dr. Dean W Geheber
3888 Government St
Baton Rouge LA 70806
Phone: 504-344-3753

Dr. Clara V Gelbard
2080 Century Park E #608
Los Angeles CA 90067
Phone: 213-203-0377

Dr. Gerald J Gelford
8936 Slagle
Centerville OH 45459
Phone: 513-433-6898

Dr. Joseph John Gerdes
130 Lake Concord Rd
Concord NC 28025
Phone: 704-786-0214

Dr. Louis Mark Germaine
174 Tewkesbury Road
Scarsdale NY 10583
Phone: 914-725-5258

Dr. Andrew Jonathan Ghio
714 E Nibley View Court
Salt Lake City UT 84106
Phone: 304-599-9359

Dr. Frank Anthony Giargianajr
4935 Pale Orchis Court
Columbia MD 21044
Phone: 301-730-0961

Dr. Glenn Matthew Giessel
7103 C Jahnke Rd
Richmond VA 23225
Phone: 804-320-4243

Dr. E Wayne Gilley
Address Unknown
Phone: Unknown

Dr. Robert White Gillmann
401 Bay St
Gadsden AL 35901
Phone: 205-543-3200

Dr. Martha E Glenn
7627 Fair Oaks Parkway
Boerne TX 78006
Phone: 512-755-8805

Dr. J David Godwin
8501 SE 80th St
Mercer Island WA 98040
Phone: 206-232-5702

Dr. Ravindra Kumar Gogineni
1608 Kirklee Road
Charleston WV 25314
Phone: 304-766-7141

Dr. Allan Robert Goldstein
860 Montclaire Rd S- 862
Birmingham AL 35213
Phone: 205-591-2545

Dr. Leopold Gonzalez
Cleveland Cl 9500 Euclid
Cleveland OH 44123
Phone: 216-444-6637

Dr. Ali A Goodardi
103 Partridge Lane
Beckley WV 25801
Phone: 304-252-8039

Dr. George Benjamin Goodman
2527 Club House Drive
Wexford PA 15090
Phone: 412-935-8505

Dr. Lawrence R Goodman
8700 W Wisconsin Ave
Milwaukee WI 53226
Phone: 414-351-6051

Dr. Lee Allan Goodman
5748 Cross Country Blvd
Baltimore MD 21209
Phone: 301-367-8282

Dr. Philip Cary Goodman
15 Mesa Ave
San Francisco CA 94116
Phone: 415-821-8024

Dr. Andrew W Goodwin
Address Unknown
Phone: Unknown

Dr. Susan A M Gootnick
329 Goodhill Rd
Kentfield CA 94904
Phone: 415-461-4006

Dr. Steven Edward Gordon
4228 Nantucket Dr
Toledo OH 43623
Phone: 419-885-3242

Dr. Jay S Gordonson
1200 North State St
Los Angeles CA 90033
Phone: 213-226-7261

Dr. William G B Graham
Lake Road
Charlotte VT 05445
Phone: 802-425-3124

Dr. George L Grauel
22320 Needlewood Circle
Strongsville OH 44136
Phone: 216-238-3286

Dr. Michael S Green
Rt 4 Box 1025
Tyler TX 75703
Phone: 214-839-3521

Dr. Reginald Greene
Mass Gen Hosp Fruit St
Boston MA 02114
Phone: 617-726-8391

Dr. Charles Frederick Greer
945 White Point Court
Charleston SC 29412
Phone: 803-795-4709

Dr. Gerald A Gretsch
7 Buffalo Road
North Oaks MN 55110
Phone: 612-484-8621

Dr. Arthur Tobias Gronner
24 Caberret Ct
Lafayette CA 94549
Phone: 415-284-1396

Dr. Steven Douglas Haas
6644 Worthington Galena
Worthington OH 43085
Phone: 614-431-5115

Dr. Raymond G Haddad
267 Grant St
Bridgeport CT 06602
Phone: 203-384-3794

Dr. Harold Melton Hagen
12301 Piney Glen Lane
Potomac MD 20854
Phone: 301-299-3374

Dr. Dennis Herman Halbert
141 Cedar Cr Rd
Pikeville KY 41501
Phone: 606-437-9824

Dr. John Charles Hall
1401 Creyts Rd
Lansing MI 48917
Phone: 517-322-4000

Dr. Carl Phillip Hallenborg
930 Kaheka St Ph B5
Honolulu HI 96814
Phone: 808-943-0262

Dr. Frank Burnette Hamlett
319 Laurel St
San Diego CA 92101
Phone: 619-672-0061

Dr. James Edward Hannah
315 Virginia Drive
Winter Park FL 32789
Phone: 407-647-4011

Dr. Abulkalam W Haque
6090 Heards Creek Dr
Atlanta GA 30328
Phone: 404-255-1416

Dr. Philip Harber
CHS 37-131 UCLA
Los Angeles CA 90024
Phone: 213-825-4837

Dr. Warren Lamar Harrell Jr
1237 Brookwood Dr
Shelby NC 28150
Phone: 704-482-5176

Dr. John Morris Harrison
328 Whitfield Dr
Lexington KY 40503
Phone: 606-273-3492

Dr. Robert Brent Harrison
5519 Ridgewood Rd
Jackson MS 39211
Phone: 601-956-8060

Dr. Ray A Harron
P O Box 400
Bridgeport WV 26330
Phone: 304-622-3900

Dr. Kelly Zack Hart
2213 W 49th Terrace
Westwood Hills KS 66205
Phone: 913-371-4343

Dr. Robert Walter Hartung
2322 E Kimberly Road
Davenport IA 52807
Phone: 319-359-3931

Dr. Mary Louise Harty
9021 Bingham Dr
Louisville KY 40222
Phone: 502-426-1676

Dr. Christopher M Harvey
21 Scottsdale Ct
Lutherville MD 21093
Phone: 301-296-0872

Dr. Abul Hashem
P O Box 2107
Whitesburg KY 41858
Phone: 606-633-7975

Dr. Beverly Emiko Hashimoto
1100 Ninth Ave
Seattle WA 98111
Phone: 206-223-6851

Dr. John Bruce Hauser
2037 Crystal Spring
Roanoke VA 24014
Phone: 703-981-7122

Dr. William Joseph Heiser
3604 Spanish Trace
Springfield IL 62702
Phone: 217-546-8012

Dr. Daniel Anthony Henry
MCV Box 615
Richmond VA 23298
Phone: 804-786-6831

Dr. Steven George Herbert
2035 Rte 65 Rd 2
Holcomb NY 14469
Phone: 716-624-2790

Dr. Richard C Hebert
3772 North Blvd
Baton Rouge LA 70806
Phone: 504-343-6602

Dr. Kurt Georg Hering
Rosenowstr 7
4600 Dortmund Germany
Phone: 023-141-7002

Dr. Daniel A Herpin
Suite 105 2770 2nd Ave
Lake Charles LA 70601
Phone: 318-477-0775

Dr. Stephen M Hessl
3528 N Janssen
Chicago IL 60657
Phone: 312-633-5310

Dr. Gregory Alan Hicklin
3012 Patricia Dr
Des Moines IA 50322
Phone: 515-278-5553

Dr. Howard William Higholt
4 Possum Ridge Rd
Rolling Hills CA 90274
Phone: 213-541-8855

Dr. Horton Corwin Hinshaw Jr
450 Sutter St
San Francisco CA 94108
Phone: 415-982-7168

Dr. Kirk Edward Hippensteel
1111 S Jefferson St
Roanoke VA 24016
Phone: 703-342-6701

Dr. Thomas E Hobbins
915 Poplar Hill Rd
Baltimore MD 21210
Phone: 301-323-8588

Dr. Thomas Knight Hodous
765 Northwest Dr
Morgantown WV 26505
Phone: 304-599-8859

Dr. Carl White Hoffman
P O Box 1527
Lumberton NC 28358
Phone: 919-738-8222

Dr. Michael Thomas Hogan
1378 Braewick Drive
Morgantown WV 26505
Phone: 304-599-9374

Dr. Hugh Holman Hoke Jr
2445 Butter Road
Lancaster PA 17601
Phone: 717-393-6872

Dr. Brenda Lee Lefkoff Holbert
7575 Cambridge St #502
Houston TX 77054
Phone: 713-799-1058

Dr. John Michael Holbert
7575 Cambridge #502
Houston TX 77054
Phone: 713-799-1058

Dr. Paul A Holdener
301 West Lincoln
Belleville IL 62221
Phone: 618-235-0955

Dr. Joseph Abraham Horton
4255 Parkman Ave
Pittsburgh PA 15213
Phone: 412-683-3475

Dr. Donald H Hulnick
137 Chestnut Hill Rd
Ridgefield CT 06877
Phone: 203-431-9376

Dr. Clifton Howard Hunt
6 Halsey Drive
Wilmington DE 19807
Phone: 302-655-6830

Dr. David Rex Hunter
3601 Red Oak Ct
New Orleans LA 70114
Phone: 504-392-3434

Dr. Janis Leigh Hurst
609 Farms Dr
Fairmont WV 26554
Phone: 304-366-5906

Dr. Lawrence Robert Irish
2765 Flushing Road
Flint MI 48504
Phone: 313-232-1197

Dr. Robert J Isler
Maine Medical Center
Portland ME 04102
Phone: 207-871-2571

Dr. George David Jacobs
2730 Navarre Ave
Oregon OH 43616
Phone: 419-693-0506

Dr. Reese Joseph James
20 Houston Road
Yardley PA 19067
Phone: 215-321-3411

Dr. Thomas M Jarboe
100 N Eagle Creek Drive
Lexington KY 40509
Phone: 606-255-6841

Dr. Peter John Jederlinic
38 Draper Ave
Westwood MA 02090
Phone: 617-762-5615

Dr. Nancy Jo Jennings
2009 7th St NW
Birmingham AL 35215
Phone: 205-854-4220

Dr. William Louis Jobe
2465 So Downing
Denver CO 80210
Phone: 303-777-7585

Dr. Irving Bernard Joffe
7 Pomona S Apt 2
Pikesville MD 21208
Phone: 301-653-0609

Dr. Claude Rembert Johnson
2301 N 50th St
Philadelphia PA 19131
Phone: 215-473-8574

Dr. Gordon Craig Johnson
8004 Carita Ct
Bethesda MD 20817
Phone: 301-427-7034

Dr. Thomas Harold Johnson
3141 Stonybrook Rd
Oklahoma City OK 73120
Phone: 405-751-6263

Dr. Howard Jolles
13730 Elmstead Rd
Midlothian VA 23113
Phone: 804-794-3572

Dr. Robert Norwood Jones
1700 Perdido St
New Orleans LA 70112
Phone: 504-588-5265

Dr. Linda OConnell Judge
3517 Pinehurst Cr
Dallas TX 75234
Phone: 214-620-9767

Dr. Rehana N Kapadia
5864 Nanevact
W Bloomfield MI 48322
Phone: 313-851-5220

Dr. Lawrence M. Kaplan
620 Wyomissing Blvd
Wyomissins PA 19610
Phone: 215-372-7949

Dr. Peter Donald Kaplan
856 Foxland Drive
Pittsburgh PA 15243
Phone: 412-531-9899

Dr. Robin Lloyd Kaplan
36 N 11th Street
Reading PA 19601
Phone: 215-372-4591

Dr. Mack Alan Karnes
5900 S Lake
Cudahy WI 53110
Phone: 414-769-4062

Dr. James Philip Kase
1840 Cambridge
Flossmoor IL 60422
Phone: 312-798-8611

Dr. Kenneth R Kattan
6741 Meadowridge Lane
Cincinnati OH 45237
Phone: 513-731-2197

Dr. Allan E Katz
6449 38th Ave N
St. Petersburg FL 33710
Phone: 813-381-0275

Dr. John W Kennard
5 Orchard Rd
Wheeling WV 26003
Phone: 304-232-1595

Dr. John David Kennedy
2273 Clinton Av So
Rochester NY 14618
Phone: 716-442-9171

Dr. David Grant Kern
18 Wilcox Ave
Pawtucket RI 02860
Phone: 401-723-6616

Dr. Robert M Kesler
7606 Maory Arch
Norfolk VA 23505
Phone: 804-423-4409

Dr. Douglas B Ketcham
901 Lowry Medical Arts
St Paul MN 55102
Phone: 612-298-8256

Dr. Arfa Khan
95 Karol Place
Jericho NY 11753
Phone: 516-932-7170

Dr. Nagi Fouad Khouri
2411 Still Forest Road
Baltimore MD 21208
Phone: 301-955-8438

Dr. John A Kibelstis
3775 Fox Run Dr
Allentown PA 18103
Phone: 215-434-3652

Dr. Donald A Killam
340 Presidential Way
Guilderland NY 12084
Phone: 518-869-3249

Dr. Kil Bong Kim
Pikeville Medical Bldg
Pikeville KY 41501
Phone: 606-432-1357

Dr. Myung Sup Kim
418 Washington St
Cumberland MD 21502
Phone: 301-759-5142

Dr. Young Choo Kim
13407 Bladon Rd
Phoenix MD 21131
Phone: 301-666-9420

Dr. Mary Anne King
15431 Edgewater Drive
Lakewood OH 44107
Phone: 216-226-8663

Dr. Phillip Eugene King
1000 Drexel Ave
Johnstown PA 15905
Phone: 814-536-6671

Dr. Howard Matthew Kipen
Rd 2 Box 210 C
Basking Ridge NJ 07920
Phone: 201-463-4773

Dr. Benny S Ko
R R 32 Box 320
Terre Haute IN 47803
Phone: 812-232-0021

Dr. Bernard Kordan
P O Box 9519
Bakersfield CA 93389
Phone: 901-528-6111

Dr. Edward William Kouri
2408 Cross Country Rd
Matthews NC 28105
Phone: 704-847-3956

Dr. James Philip Krainson
6131 SW 104 St
Miami FL 33156
Phone: 305-666-0211

Dr. Neil Robert Kramer
624 Kingscroft
Cherry Hill NJ 08034
Phone: 609-667-9632

Dr. George Ogden Kress
144 Campus View Blvd
Worthington OH 43085
Phone: 614-885-0845

Dr. Kathleen Kreiss
1400 Jackson St
Denver CO 80206
Phone: 303-398-1525

Dr. Jerome L Krumpelman
P O Box 698
Richmond KY 40475
Phone: 606-624-2695

Dr. Karen F Kuhns
USS Irwin Works Box 878
Dravosburg PA 15034
Phone: 412-675-7411

Dr. V S Kullman
6 Lakeview Dr
Wheeling WV 26003
Phone: 304-277-5591

Dr. Raymond S Kurtzman
6919 Woodbank
Birmingham MI 48010
Phone: 313-626-7763

Dr. Paul Arthur Kvale
676 Middlesex
Grosse Point PKMI 48230
Phone: 313-331-4676

Dr. Robert William Laakman
14 St Andrews
Little Rock AR 72212
Phone: 501-223-3471

Dr. Michel LaFortune
10980 Waverly
Montreal, Q., Canada
Phone: 514-332-1112

Dr. Richard Henry Laib
5382 Manortree Ln
Cincinnati OH 45238
Phone: 513-451-7191

Dr. Paul David Laman Jr
109 Hillcrest Rd
Pittsburgh PA 15238
Phone: 412-681-0122

Dr. Emery E Lane
323 E Chestnut St
Louisville KY 40202
Phone: 502-588-5814

Dr. John Joseph Lang
507 Fairways Cir
St Louis MO 63141
Phone: 314-567-1293

Dr. Marc S Lapayowker
2301 Cherry St 9D
Philadelphia PA 19103
Phone: 215-569-4182

Dr. N Leroy Lapp
1285 Fairfield St
Morgantown WV 26505
Phone: 304-599-2361

Dr. Maurice M Lapp
1250 Upper Happy Vly Road
Lafayette CA 94549
Phone: 415-284-1375

Dr. Stanley Philip Laucks Jr
20 North Laurel Street
Hazelton PA 18201
Phone: 717-455-3608

Dr. Everett Marc Lautin
245 East 93rd St Apt 27G
New York NY 10128
Phone: 212-831-3745

Dr. Robert Frederic Lautin
429 East 52nd Street
New York NY 10022
Phone: 212-752-4684

Dr. Charles Dudley Lee
120 Elm Street
San Diego CA 92101
Phone: 619-487-1700

Dr. Marie Emily Lee
2055 Interlaken PE
Seattle WA 98112
Phone: 206-223-6951

Dr. Philip J W Lee
1507 S King St Suite 101
Honolulu HI 96826
Phone: 808-949-5938

Dr. Johnsey Lee Leef Jr
1440 Alexandria Place
Charleston WV 25314
Phone: 304-348-6044

Dr. John Terry Leever
1060 Orchard
Grand Juction CO 81501
Phone: 303-243-4528

Dr. Stephen Edward Lehnert
301 W Lincoln
Belleville IL 62222
Phone: 618-235-0955

Dr. Stuart Kent Lehr
1212 Pleasant LL9
Des Moines IA 50309
Phone: 515-283-6171

Dr. Richard Kenneth Lenhart
32298 Orchard Park Dr
Avon Lane OH 44012
Phone: 216-933-6865

Dr. Alfred P Lessure
412 S E Sixth St
Evansville IN 47713
Phone: 812-426-8329

Dr. Richard Barry Levine
304 Dogwood Lane
Elkins Park PA 19117
Phone: 215-884-1523

Dr. Robert Gordon Levitt
13134 Thornhill Drive
St Louis MO 63131
Phone: 314-822-1703

Dr. Jeffrey A Levy
901 Goucher St
Johnstown PA 15905
Phone: 814-536-7226

Dr. Sutek Lie
989 Hillcreek Lane
Gates Mills OH 44040
Phone: 216-844-7170

Dr. Arthur Lieber
Albert B Chandler Med Ctr
Lexington KY 40536
Phone: 606-233-5222

Dr. Ruth Lilis
420 East 51st St
New York NY 10022
Phone: 212-650-8806

Dr. Rodolfo Espaldon Lim
27 Teaberry Ln
Frostburg MD 21532
Phone: 301-689-1384

Dr. John Paul Limbacher II
935 E 6th Street
Cookeville TN 38501
Phone: 615-528-5609

Dr. Anthony John Limberakis
636 Crosswicks Rd
Rydal PA 19046
Phone: 215-576-0887

Dr. Michael Lippman
525 Winding Way
Merion PA 19066
Phone: 215-667-4832

Dr. Robert Martin Lincoln
1523 Kingsford Drive
Carmichael CA 95608
Phone: 916-972-8481

Dr. Larry A Lindesmith
W 4965 Woodhaven Drive
La Crosse WI 54601
Phone: 606-788-2274

Dr. John Peter Livoni
79 Scripps Dr #100
Sacramento CA 95825
Phone: 916-921-1300

Dr. Aaron M Longacre
13550 N 31st St
Tampa FL 33612
Phone: 813-971-0694

Dr. Cynthia Oliver Lorino
3972 Japonica Lane
Mobile AL 36609
Phone: 205-460-7042

Dr. Stanley J Lucas
2905 Burnet Ave
Cincinnati OH 45219
Phone: 513-221-1436

Dr. William T Luckey
1545 W Spruce Ct
River Hills WI 53217
Phone: 414-351-4034

Dr. David A Lund
100 Grand St
New Britain CT 06052
Phone: 203-224-5556

Dr. Kenneth E Lynch
16732 Intrepid Lane
Huntington Bch CA 92649
Phone: 213-592-3435

Dr. William Austin Lynch
85 Jefferson St Ste 706
Hartford CT 06106
Phone: 203-246-5403

Dr. Samuel Veirs Mace
6006 Lakehurst Dr
Baltimore MD 21210
Phone: 301-377-6039

Dr. James E MacLean
2492 Sage Run Ct
Grand Junction CO 81505
Phone: 303-241-0774

Dr. William J McMahon
74 Stonehenge Dr
Washington PA 15301
Phone: 412-225-9450

Dr. Gregory A MacNealy
1249 Laurelwood Rd
Dayton OH 45409
Phone: 513-222-5841

Dr. David Eric Magarik
2508 Bayberry Lane
Vestal NY 13850
Phone: 607-797-8555

Dr. David Morton Main
602 W University
Urbana IL 61801
Phone: 217-337-3190

Dr. Howard Mann
4075 E Powers Circle
Salt Lake City UT 84124
Phone: 801-277-8621

Dr. Donald Hubert Manning
3 Fendig Rd
St Simons Isl GA 31522
Phone: 912-267-7415

Dr. Asher Marks
P O Box 263
Rabon Gap GA 30568
Phone: 305-446-3811

Dr. Burton Marks
542 S 12th St
Reading PA 19602
Phone: 215-374-0766

Dr. John Daughtry Marriott
134 Oakleaf Drive
Morehead City NC 28557
Phone: 919-726-7444

Dr. Thomas R Marshall
3004 Taylorsville Rd
Louisville KY 40205
Phone: 502-456-6145

Dr. Charles Claiborne Matth
1514 Jefferson Hwy
New Orleans LA 70121
Phone: 504-838-3495

Dr. Stuart J Masters
34 Brookside Drive
Pittsfield MA 01201
Phone: 413-443-4386

Dr. Kailash Nath Mathur
73 Sherwood Road
Pottsville PA 17901
Phone: 717-622-4030

Dr. Carol June Maywood
7381 Radcliff Dr
West Bloomfield MI 48322
Phone: 313-855-3561

Dr. Joseph M Mazzei
1142 Nevada St
Pittsburgh PA 15218
Phone: 412-281-6540

Dr. Kathleen Ann McCarroll
4871 Malibu Drive
Bloomfield Hill MI 48013
Phone: 313-626-2773

Dr. Kerry W McCluney
St Lukes Hosp
Bluefield Hosp WV 24701
Phone: 304-325-3733

Dr. Todd William McCune
Nvl Shpyrd Bldg 657
Philadelphia PA 19112
Phone: 215-465-9109

Dr. Patricia J McEveney
2001 Dwight Way
Berkeley CA 94704
Phone: 415-540-4460

Dr. William Elmer McGraw
9117 Sand Key Ln
Indianapolis IN 46256
Phone: 317-842-0655

Dr. Gordon C McLaughlin III
8440 Coral Reef Court
Indianapolis IN 46256
Phone: 317-842-2465

Dr. Theresa C McLoud
Mass Gen Hosp
Boston MA 02114
Phone: 617-726-8307

Dr. William Peter Meseroll
121 Sotoyome St
Santa Rosa CA 95404
Phone: 707-546-4062

Dr. Gerald L Meyers
3001 Colby St
Berkeley CA 94705
Phone: 415-845-7968

Dr. Robert Joseph Mezey
6740 SW 99th Terrace
Miami FL 33156
Phone: 305-666-1858

Dr. Gregory C Mieckowski
220 Primrose Drive
Sarver PA 16055
Phone: 412-828-0456

Dr. Albert Miller
179 West Shore Rd
Great Neck NY 11024
Phone: 516-829-5665

Dr. Robert Francis Miller
600 Memorial Ave
Cumberland MD 21502
Phone: 301-777-5751

Dr. Robert I Miller
2371 S Ponte Vedra Blvd
Ponte Vedra Bch FL 32082
Phone: 904-829-3554

Dr. Wallace T Miller
3400 Spruce St
Philadelphia PA 19104
Phone: 215-662-3035

Dr. John Arthur Mitchell
241 Riverdale Dr
Defiance OH 43512
Phone: 419-784-5943

Dr. James B Moffett
8154 Durgin Terrace
Crown Point IN 46307
Phone: 219-769-0629

Dr. I Ranavaya Mohammed
123 Rice Street
Beckley WV 25802
Phone: 304-255-2500

Dr. Blaine Lewis Montgomery
6833 Abottswood Dr
Rnch Palos Verd CA 90274
Phone: 213-325-1221

Dr. David Leonard Moody
P O Box 2503
Santa Cruz CA 95063
Phone: 408-475-7829

Dr. Elizabeth H Moore
16 Marlborough
Boston MA 02116
Phone: 617-726-8399

Dr. Ann Ratliff Mootz
9519 Robin Meadow Drive
Dallas TX 75243
Phone: 214-688-3711

Dr. G Tom Morea
55 E Rt 70
Marlton NJ 08053
Phone: 609-956-7577

Dr. Edwin James Morgan
Rt 7 Box 518
Morgantown WV 26505
Phone: 304-292-4160

Dr. William Keith C Morgan
Windmere Rd Univ Hospital
London Ontario Canada
Phone: 519-663-3606

Dr. William James Morrison
LDS Hospital 325 8th Ave
Salt Lake City UT 84143
Phone: 801-321-1791

Dr. Sanford Hewitt Morrow III
1423 E Brow Rd
Signal Mountain TN 37377
Phone: 615-778-7375

Dr. Harold Moskowitz
14 Arlen Way
W Hartford CT 06117
Phone: 203-233-7220

Dr. John Robert Muhm
9885 E Cochise Dr
Scottsdale AZ 85258
Phone: 602-860-0330

Dr. David M Murphy
506 Anthwyn Rd
Merion PA 19066
Phone: 304-293-4095

Dr. Nestor Luiz Muller
1537 West 58th Ave
Vancouver, B.C. Canada
Phone: 604-261-5428

Dr. Mary Ann Mullican
2518 Del Monte Dr
Houston TX 77019
Phone: 713-523-8670

Dr. Louis Dominic Napoli
5 Stapleford Hall Ct
Potomac MD 20854
Phone: 301-299-7448

Dr. Ingrid E Naugle
26 Newgate Rd
Pittsburgh PA 15202
Phone: 412-761-7680

Dr. Shiv Navani
15 Oakwood Circle
Big Stone Gap VA 24219
Phone: 703-523-3668

Dr. Leon Nazarian
7001 W Cheyenne
Muncie IN 47304
Phone: 216-933-2873

Dr. Boyd Eastham Nelson
105 Oak Ridge Ct
Decatur IL 32521
Phone: 217-428-3672

Dr. John Doty Newell
Address Unknown
Arizona
Phone: 602-299-2730

Dr. Edwin Newman
3734 Columbine Cir
Charlotte NC 28211
Phone: 704-364-0568

Dr. Alan Richard Nichols
301 Med Arts Bldg
Charleston WV 25301
Phone: 304-343-4625

Dr. Jack E Nissim
2435 W Belvedere Ave
Baltimore MD 21215
Phone: 301-466-0653

Dr. Michael Peter Norton
1441 Kingsford Drive
Carmichael CA 95608
Phone: 916-488-8152

Dr. William Martin OBryan
1102 Triplett St Ste 1300
Owensboro KY 42301
Phone: 502-926-8810

Dr. Sandra Alice Ann Oldham
8740 SW 85 Terrace
Miami FL 33173
Phone: 305-549-6894

Dr. L. Christine Oliver
Mass Gen Hosp Fruit St
Boston MA 02114
Phone: 617-232-8247

Dr. Alan William Osborne
222 Kimball Ave
Westfield NJ 07090
Phone: 201-233-2564

Dr. Gaston L Ostiguy
122 Jasper Ville Mont Roy
Montreal Quebec Canada
Phone: 514-731-0895

Dr. Jonathan H Ostrow
3500 E Huron St
Seattle WA 98100
Phone: 206-325-8841

Dr. James Wilson Owen
823 Mulvane
Topeka KS 66606
Phone: 913-234-3451

Dr. Gregory Randolph Owens
916 Wade W
Oakmont PA 15139
Phone: 412-624-1929

Dr. William E Palmer
320 Main St
Johnstown PA 15901
Phone: 814-533-0587

Dr. Elaine B Panitz
34 Cleveland Lane
Princeton NJ 08540
Phone: 609-448-3737

Dr. Subramaniam K Parantham
1731 Holton Ave
Big Stone Gap VA 24219
Phone: 703-523-4920

Dr. Jacob J Parker
333 Locust Ave
San Rafael CA 94901
Phone: 415-456-5543

Dr. Behram Pastakia
8715 Irvington Ave
Bethesda MD 20817
Phone: 301-496-7700

Dr. Ashok R Patel
100 Gorman Ridge
Hazard KY 41701
Phone: 606-439-5057

Dr. Bharat Raojibhai Patel
Rt 2 Box 546
Radford VA 24141
Phone: 703-731-2720

Dr. Mahendra M Patel
6 Hunter Point Rd
Charleston WV 25314
Phone: 304-345-0403

Dr. Joseph R Patterson
1086 Franklin St
Johnstown PA 15905
Phone: 814-536-7226

Dr. Richard David Patterson
400 Wabash Ave
Akron OH 44307
Phone: 216-384-6450

Dr. Randel Andrew Patty
888 Dubois Drive
Baton Rouge LA 70808
Phone: 504-766-0781

Dr. Lawrence J Pazdurek
1 Lamont Place
Glen Arm MD 21057
Phone: 301-592-7310

Dr. Joseph Ronald Peacock
1601 Milltown Rd Suite 11
Wilmington DE 19808
Phone: 215-793-1102

Dr. Jay L Pearlberg
28090 Tavistock Trail
Southfield MI 48034
Phone: 313-876-1331

Dr. Carlos F Pena
3207 E Erie Ave
Lorain OH 44052
Phone: 216-288-1342

Dr. Henry P Pendergrass
6207 Hillsboro Rd
Nashville TN 37215
Phone: 615-322-3450

Dr. Rodney C Peterson
1350 So 1000 E
Mapleton UT 84663
Phone: 801-489-8534

Dr. William Frank Pfisterer
2555 E Chapman #500
Fullerton CA 92631
Phone: 714-526-2241

Dr. Ernest J Pick
1106 Beech Rd
Rosemont PA 19010
Phone: 215-527-0867

Dr. Robert G Pickerill
524 Grove Avenue
Johnstown PA 15902
Phone: 814-535-6925

Dr. Harry J Pinsky
257 Pelham Road
Rochester NY 14610
Phone: 716-244-4904

Dr. Jon Perley Pitman
45 Golden St
Lewiston ME 04240
Phone: 207-768-2901

Dr. Rayudu B Polisetty
730 Sun Valley Terrace
Hazard KY 41701
Phone: 606-439-1331

Dr. Norman Odell Polk
45 176 Kokokahi Pl
Kancohe HI 96744
Phone: 808-235-2163

Dr. Alan Raymond Pope
209 E Maple Ave
Moorestown NJ 08057
Phone: 609-234-4917

Dr. Robert Neil Pope
P O Box 1875 1102 Triplett
Owensboro KY 42302
Phone: 502-926-8810

Dr. Alex Poulos
P O Box 2648
Pikeville KY 41501
Phone: 606-432-1357

Dr. John David Poutasse
593 Holmes Rd
Pittsfield MA 01201
Phone: 413-442-8371

Dr. Robert W Powell
224 E Broadway
Louisville KY 40202
Phone: 502-587-0915

Dr. Daniel Powers
623 Las Casas Avenue
Pac Palisades CA 90272
Phone: 213-973-6269

Dr. Phalimar S Prabhu
810 Abbott Blvd
Fort Lee NJ 07024
Phone: 201-224-0333

Dr. Ramesh S Pradhan
1310 University Drive
Yardley PA 19067
Phone: 215-493-1314

Dr. Leslie Preger
166 Merced Ave
San Francisco CA 94127
Phone: 415-534-8055

Dr. Jennings Gillen Pressly
1210 W Faris Rd
Greenville SC 29605
Phone: 803-232-9351

Dr. Joy Mei Price
2001 Dwight Way
Berkeley CA 94704
Phone: 415-540-4460

Dr. David Samuel Prince
441 Levering Mill Rd
Bala Cynwyd PA 19004
Phone: 215-667-2596

Dr. Anthony Vincent Proto
3023 River Hills Lane
Midlothian VA 23113
Phone: 804-379-1353

Dr. Sanford Eugene Rabushka
2100 Lincoln Pk W
Chicago IL 60614
Phone: 312-878-8700

Dr. David Ellis Radebaugh
3060 Woodsmill
Bath OH 44210
Phone: 216-659-3777

Dr. Paul Dennis Radecki
724 Winding Rd
Jenkintown PA 19046
Phone: 215-884-9328

Dr. Dwight Keith Rafferty
2996 133rd Way NW
West Des Moinesia 50265
Phone: 515-276-1243

Dr. Arnold Raizon
5437 Grove Ridge Way
Rockville MD 20852
Phone: 301-897-5406

Dr. Mettupalayam M Rajendra
Address Unknown
West Virginia
Phone: 304-242-8519

Dr. Bolar Rama Rao
100 Trinidad Bend
Coronado CA 92118
Phone: 619-424-8524

Dr. Yagnesh R Raval
2952 Shawnee Trail
Piqua OH 45356
Phone: 513-778-4788

Dr. Daniel Ravenel
O Gibbes St
Charleston SC 29401
Phone: 803-577-6666

Dr. Marvin A Rawitch
1401 Avocado Ave
Newport Bch CA 92660
Phone: 714-640-1221

Dr. Carolyn Sue Ray
1850 Pennsylvania Ave
Fairfield CA 94533
Phone: 707-429-2495

Dr. Katherine Reed
13550 N 31st St Suite 140
Tampa FL 33613
Phone: 813-971-2056

Dr. Peter W Reed
1521 Fairway Drive
Lima OH 45805
Phone: 419-991-7541

Dr. Nancy Sue Reinhardt
5900 Munger Rd
Centerville OH 45459
Phone: 513-433-6437

Dr. Joseph J Renn III
118 Diamond Ct
Morgantown WV 26505
Phone: 304-599-4497

Dr. John W Renner
16822 Coral Cay Lane
Huntington Bch CA 92649
Phone: 213-592-1575

Dr. Attilio David Renzetti Jr
1801 London Plane Rd
Salt Lake City UT 84124
Phone: 801-278-0823

Dr. Lawrence Harvey Repsher
8300 W 38th Ave
Wheat Ridge CO 80033
Phone: 303-425-8579

Dr. Dale B Riepe
1201 Garden Dr
Mt Pleasant TX 75455
Phone: 214-572-9247

Dr. Usho S Rishi
66 Holland Road
Pittsburgh PA 15235
Phone: 412-241-2192

Dr. Cullen B Rivers
11 Roslyn Hills Dr
Richmond VA 23229
Phone: 804-288-5965

Dr. Emory H Robinette
Rt 7 Foxfire Estates
Abingdon VA 24210
Phone: 703-628-1106

Dr. Cecile Stephanie Rose
Box 267 Med Coll of VA
Richmond VA 23298
Phone: 804-786-9357

Dr. Robert H Rosenberg
8670 NE 17th
Bellevue WA 98004
Phone: 206-454-6954

Dr. Kenneth D Rosenman
Mi St Univ Rm 8338 Cl Ctr
Lansing MI 48824
Phone: 517-353-1864

Dr. William F Rosner
290 Ames Circle
Huntingdon Vly PA 19006
Phone: 215-947-4777

Dr. Joseph Rosenstein
93 Ampersand Ave Box 647
Saranac Lake NY 12983
Phone: 518-891-4141

Dr. Glenn S Roush
34 Jackson St
Deadwood SD 57732
Phone: 605-578-2727

Dr. Ami Hai Eliezer Rubin
Northwestern Mem Hospital
Chicago IL 60611
Phone: 312-908-8163

Dr. Paul J Rubis
4110 Nine Mile
Richmond VA 23223
Phone: 804-222-1716

Dr. A David Russakoff
801 Princeton SW Ste 615
Birmingham AL 35211
Phone: 205-780-1963

Dr. William Maxwell Russell
3193 Benedict Cyn Dr
Beverly Hills CA 90210
Phone: 213-276-3449

Dr. George Peter Saba
3921 Foxhill Dr
Ellicott City MD 21043
Phone: 301-461-1738

Dr. Abdul Razzak Sadik
23760 Woodward
Pleasant Ridge MI 48069
Phone: 313-545-1330

Dr. Hisaji Q Sakai
1844 San Miguel Dr 302
Walnut Creek CA 94596
Phone: 415-947-0560

Dr. David Hidefumi Sakuda
321 N Kuakini St
Honolulu HI 96817
Phone: 808-547-9545

Dr. John Clayton Sanborn
7014 Highfield Rd
Fayetteville NY 13066
Phone: 315-446-9045

Dr. Jacques Sansoucy
265 Dufferin
Valleyfield Quebec Canada
Phone: 514-373-5195

Dr. Jeffery Dale Sargent
28 Midway
Bristol TN 37620
Phone: 615-968-2311

Dr. E Nicholas Sargent
1200 North State St
Los Angeles CA 90033
Phone: 213-226-4950

Dr. Kanagal Satyanarayana
3912 E Rolling Green Lane
Orange CA 92667
Phone: 714-637-1625

Dr. Stephen Irwin Schabel
669 Shortwood Street
Charleston SC 29412
Phone: 803-795-7969

Dr. Burton Schaffer
Kings Hwy & Princeton Ave
Woodbury NJ 08096
Phone: 609-848-4998

Dr. Marc B Schenker
626 Coolidge St
Davis CA 95616
Phone: 916-752-3317

Dr. Eugene Schwartz
816 Alton Woods Dr
Concord NH 03301
Phone: 603-271-4477

Dr. Alan Marshall Schwartz
33 Nichols Rd
Cohasset MA 02025
Phone: 617-383-0941

Dr. John H Scott
147 Woodshire Dr
Pittsburgh PA 15215
Phone: 412-782-5455

Dr. Penelope Pate Scott
218 Goodale Rd
Baltimore MD 21212
Phone: 301-578-5713

Dr. William W Scott Jr
218 Goodale Road
Baltimore MD 21212
Phone: 301-435-7850

Dr. Jeff W Selby
421 Chestnut St
Evansville IN 47713
Phone: 812-426-9537

Dr. Aram Semerdjian
8319 Linden Ave
Munster IN 46321
Phone: 219-972-1030

Dr. Coralie Shaw
55 Chimney Corner Circle
Guilford CT 06437
Phone: 203-453-3500

Dr. James ONeil Shaw
534 Kerry Lake Dr
Newport Naus VA 23602
Phone: 804-599-2732

Dr. Alfred Dows Shaplin
12668 Westport Dr
St Louis MO 63146
Phone: 314-576-6348

Dr. Hugh C Sheffield Jr
1419 31st Street
Nederland TX 77627
Phone: 409-722-4984

Dr. Joanne O Shepard
Mass General Hosp
Boston MA 02114
Phone: 617-726-8773

Dr. James Robert Shepherd
Rt 5 Box 549
Lindale TX 75771
Phone: 214-877-3451

Dr. Paul Robert Sherban
212 Old Trinity Place
Lancaster PA 17602
Phone: 717-393-1064

Dr. Ralph Taylor Shipley
234 Goodman St M/L 742
Cincinnati OH 45267
Phone: 513-558-6016

Dr. John G Shively
26 Priscilla Lane
Carnegie PA 15106
Phone: 412-359-3038

Dr. Gary Shrago
112 Wildwood Gardens
Piedmont CA 94611
Phone: 415-547-0293

Dr. Lee Sider
710 N Fairbanks Ct
Chicago IL 60611
Phone: 312-908-5133

Dr. Martin Larry Silbiger
11720 Lipsey Rd
Tampa FL 33618
Phone: 813-961-0789

Dr. Henry J Silverman
116 W Montgomery St
Baltimore MD 21237
Phone: 301-528-1326

Dr. Richard Sanford Simmons
1550 Doctors Dr Suite 301
Lagrange GA 30240
Phone: 404-884-2641

Dr. Truman D Simmons
Harlan Arh
Harlan KY 40831
Phone: 606-573-4213

Dr. Frank John Simone
Indiana Hosp Dept of Rad
Indiana PA 15701
Phone: 412-357-7125

Dr. Allan Wayne Skrenta
10143 Pasture Gate Lane
Columbia MD 21044
Phone: 301-730-6371

Dr. Dorsett David Smith
4310 Colby Ave
Everett WA 98203
Phone: 206-259-5496

Dr. Henry K Smith
145 Northgate Dr
Camphill PA 17011
Phone: 717-657-7200

Dr. James T Smith
1420 Connell Rd
Charleston WV 25314
Phone: 304-342-4984

Dr. Theresa Ann Smith
23 Hawthorn Dr
Westfield NJ 07090
Phone: 201-233-9044

Dr. George Andrew Solack
8308 Weller Ave
McLean VA 22102
Phone: 703-893-9386

Dr. John Joseph Solic
3901 South Atherton St
State College PA 16801
Phone: 814-466-7911

Dr. Allen J Solomon
501 Canterbury
Saginaw MI 48603
Phone: 517-792-2746

Dr. Irwin Steinberg
2711 Angelo Drive
Los Angeles CA 90077
Phone: 213-276-8069

Dr. Lee M Steinberg
5155 Raytown Rd
Kansas City MO 64133
Phone: 816-358-2040

Dr. Robert M Steiner
129 Gypsy Lane
Wynnewood PA 19096
Phone: 215-649-0569

Dr. Carol B Stelling
1424 Essex Park
Lexington KY 40502
Phone: 606-233-5581

Dr. Bruce Neal Stewart
1111 S Jefferson St
Roanoke VA 24016
Phone: 703-342-6701

Dr. Frederick P Stitik
DePaul Hosp 150 Kingsley
Norfolk VA 23505
Phone: 301-955-5394

Dr. Joseph Marion Straughan
Box 856
Wise VA 24293
Phone: 703-328-6625

Dr. Murali Sundaram
11636 Larkridge Lane
St Louis MO 63126
Phone: 314-577-8025

Dr. James Lang Sundheim
700 Quincy Ave
Scranton PA 18500
Phone: 717-969-4030

Dr. William Kirk Swann
406 Blount Prof Building
Knoxville TN 37920
Phone: 615-524-5403

Dr. Jerry Michael Speckman
6537 Valley Rd
Kansas City MO 64113
Phone: 816-276-4141

Dr. Lois M Speiden
109 Eastview Lane
Beckley WV 25801
Phone: 304-252-9442

Dr. Harold B Spitz
6331 Grand Vista
Cincinnati OH 45213
Phone: 513-631-1589

Dr. Ronald Jeffrey Stanfiel
9457 Pursuit Ct
Columbia MD 21045
Phone: 301-730-4466

Dr. Alan Stankiewicz
623 Lang Ave
Patton PA 16668
Phone: 814-764-8508

Dr. Gregory P Stark
2233 Montgomery Ave S B
Ashland KY 41101
Phone: 606-329-1185

Dr. Thomas Francis Stephens
324 Avalon Drive
Rochester NY 14618
Phone: 716-244-1475

Dr. Mark Geoffery Stein
27 Silver Crescent
Irvine CA 92715
Phone: 714-854-5427

Dr. Herman Joseph Stein
515 Andover Rd
Wilmington DE 19803
Phone: 302-478-0120

Dr. Julie Emiko Takasugi
1660 S Columbian Way
Seattle WA 98108
Phone: (Not available)

Dr. Joseph Talbot
1311 N Michigan
Saginaw MI 48602
Phone: 517-753-7501

Dr. Keith Edwin Mosun Tao
41 Magnolia Place
Danville CA 94526
Phone: 415-947-0560

Dr. Robert D Tarver
RR 1 Box SW 223
New Palestine IN 46163
Phone: 317-861-5563

Dr. Joseph Harry Tashjian
1172 Aquarius Lane
Eagan MN 55123
Phone: 612-454-7372

Dr. Richard H Taus
20 Webster St #213
Brookline MA 02146
Phone: 617-731-9316

Dr. Michael Barry Teiger
1000 Asylum Avenue
Hartford CT 06105
Phone: 203-278-3812

Dr. Philip Anthony Templeto
1711 S Charles St
Baltimore MD 21230
Phone: 301-685-1455

Dr. David A Tenenberg
P O Box 70
Danville CA 94526
Phone: 415-676-0140

Dr. Stephan M Ticich
5319 Rosecliff Dr
Lorain OH 44053
Phone: 216-282-5613

Dr. Henry P Thode III
7300 Augustine Drive
Anchorage AL 99504
Phone: 907-552-3097

Dr. Jay Sheldon Thompson
3609 Park E Dr Suite 404N
Beachwood OH 44122
Phone: 216-292-2755

Dr. Lawrence G Thorley
476 Kar A Bru St
Amherst OH 44001
Phone: 216-988-2254

Dr. Julie K Timins
20 Footes Lane
Morristown NJ 07960
Phone: 201-267-7847

Dr. Daniel L Torrance
31423 Marne Dr
R Palos Verdes CA 90274
Phone: 213-377-4313

Dr. Sam H Traughber
1910 So Va St
Hopkinsville KY 42240
Phone: 502-886-0251

Dr. Theodore A Tristan
353 N 28th St
Camp Hill PA 17011
Phone: 717-761-2958

Dr. Clifford James Turner
9001 Shad Lane
Potomac MD 20854
Phone: 301-299-2594

Dr. Gordon H Twedt
Address Unknown
Texas
Phone: 817-236-7988

Dr. Terrence A Tyrrell
66 Signal Hill Blvd
Belleville IL 62223
Phone: 618-397-7688

Dr. Cynthia Umalitorres
79 Newton Ave No
Worcester MA 01602
Phone: 617-856-2160

Dr. Uri Vaisman
1069 E Bay Point Rd
Bayside WI 53217
Phone: 414-352-3215

Dr. Claude Arthur Vallee
227 Kindersley, Montreal
Quebec Canada
Phone: 514-731-4734

Dr. Theodore Fiske Van Andt
79 Stayvesant Rd
Pittsford NY 14534
Phone: 716-338-3580

Dr. John W Vance
1275 Delaware Ave
Buffalo NY 14209
Phone: 716-886-5650

Dr. Sverre Vedal
2775 Heather St
Vancouver B.C. Canada
Phone: 604-875-4122

Dr. Paul Mark Velt
185 Edgemoor Road
Rochester NY 14618
Phone: 716-442-6066

Dr. Theresa Marie Vogel
Address Unknown
Maryland
Phone: 301-484-5359

Dr. Theodore Martin Vollmar
7244 Forsyth 1E
St Louis MO 63105
Phone: 314-721-4363

Dr. Clay A Waggenspack Jr
3772 N Blvd
Baton Rouge LA 70806
Phone: 504-343-6602

Dr. Gregory R Wagner
2630 Putnam Ave
Hurricane WV 25526
Phone: 304-526-0630

Dr. James Clinton Walker Jr
3603 Cliff Rd S
Birmingham AL 35205
Phone: 205-783-3700

Dr. William Campbell Walker
300 Riverside Dr E
Bradenton FL 34208
Phone: 813-745-7571

Dr. Mark Steven Wald
11133 Dunn Rd Suite B 208
St Louis MO 63136
Phone: 314-355-2300

Dr. Andrew Arthor Wallman
650 Shore Rd 5G
Long Beach NY 11561
Phone: 516-889-6204

Dr. John C Wandtke
Univ of Rochester Med Ctr
Rochester NY 14642
Phone: 716-275-3509

Dr. Stephen Wartella Jr
25 James St
Kingston PA 18704
Phone: 717-288-3744

Dr. Michael David Weaver
#9 Doctors Park
Greenville NC 27834
Phone: 919-752-5000

Dr. William Dean Wehunt
5616 Lake Christopher Dr
Rockville MD 20855
Phone: 301-977-7537

Dr. Donald S Weinstein
9 Farmstead Lane
Waterford CT 06385
Phone: 203-447-2069

Dr. Paul O Wells
Ivy Hill Box 113
Harlan KY 40831
Phone: 606-573-3396

Dr. Martin Stuart Wershba
416 Division St
So Charleston WV 25301
Phone: 304-766-7141

Dr. Larry Haynes Westerfiel
Holston Valley Comm Hosp
Kingsport TN 37662
Phone: 615-245-2251

Dr. Paul Saurel Wheeler
302 Somerset Rd
Baltimore MD 21210
Phone: 301-955-5423

Dr. Alan Coombs Whitehouse
104 W Fifth
Spokane WA 99204
Phone: 509-458-3960

Dr. Philip Whittlesey
600 Northern Pkwy W
Baltimore MD 21210
Phone: 301-323-4411

Dr. Charles G Wieland
53 Hemlock St
Belleville IL 62221
Phone: 618-235-6435

Dr. Robert G Wilkinson
20 Stanford Drive
Hingham MA 02043
Phone: 617-749-2914

Dr. James Michael Wills
211 Fairview Ave
Beckley WV 25801
Phone: 304-252-5599

Dr. Robert Keith Wilson
6535 Fannin Street
Houston TX 77030
Phone: 713-790-2076

Dr. Muram Helen T Winer
2043 Hickory Crest
Memphis TN 38119
Phone: 901-755-5490

Dr. Kenneth Howe Winter
3307 Waldron Drive
Greensboro NC 27408
Phone: 919-288-2988

Dr. Jerome F Wiot
234 Goodman St
Cincinnati OH 45229
Phone: 513-872-4396

Dr. Hans Woitowitz
Aulweg 129

Dr. Patrick W Wolfe
713 Viewmont Ave
Johnstown PA 15905
Phone: 814-255-1069

Dr. Donald Richard Woloszyn
401 Main St
Oneota NY 13820
Phone: 607-432-7611

Dr. Robin Mark Wood
RFD #3 Box 390
Augusta ME 04330
Phone: 207-547-3563

Dr. John Howell Woodring
162 N Arcadia Park
Lexington KY 40503
Phone: 606-277-5927

Dr. Robert E Woods
397 Dansworth
Youngstown NY 14174
Phone: 716-745-7529

Dr. Frank A Yarussi
110 Fort Cauch Rd
Pittsburgh PA 15241
Phone: 412-831-8550

Dr. Ho Joon Yoo
1510 Wintergreen Ln
Fairview PA 16415
Phone: 814-474-5100

Dr. Dansereau Yves
821 Gaboury St S
St Bruno, Quebec, Canada
Phone: 514-653-7310

Dr. George Luis Leon Zaldiv
16 Norwood Road
Charleston WV 25314
Phone: 304-346-1811

Dr. Anthony V Zancanaro
1701 N Senate Blvd
Indianapolis IN 46202
Phone: 317-929-8876

Dr. Lawrence P Zarian
930 Taylor Drive
Gurnee IL 60031
Phone: 312-367-6036

Dr. Ralph D Zehr
642 10 Walker Hill Road
Waverly NY 14892
Phone: 607-565-4838

Dr. Anders Johan Zitting
Inst of Occupational Hlth
Helsinki Finland
Phone: 358-042-4233